Children's Hearings and the Sheriff Court

Children's Hearings and the Sheriff Court

Brian Kearney, MA, LLB, Solicitor
Sheriff of Glasgow and Strathkelvin

Edinburgh
Butterworths
2000

United Kingdom	Butterworths, a Division of Reed Elsevier (UK) Ltd, 4 Hill Street, EDINBURGH EH2 3JZ and Halsbury House, 35 Chancery Lane, LONDON WC2A 1EL
Australia	Butterworths, a Division of Reed International Books Australia Pty Ltd, CHATSWOOD, New South Wales
Canada	Butterworths Canada Ltd, MARKHAM, Ontario
Hong Kong	Butterworths Hong Kong, a division of Reed Elsevier (Greater China) Ltd, HONG KONG
India	Butterworths India, NEW DELHI
Ireland	Butterworth (Ireland) Ltd, DUBLIN
Malaysia	Malayan Law Journal Sdn Bhd, KUALA LUMPUR
New Zealand	Butterworths of New Zealand Ltd, WELLINGTON
Singapore	Butterworths Asia, SINGAPORE
South Africa	Butterworths Publishers (Pty) Ltd, DURBAN
USA	Lexis Law Publishing, CHARLOTTESVILLE, Virginia

A CIP Catalogue record for this book is available from the British Library.

First published in 1987.

ISBN 0 406 89080 3

Typeset by Phoenix Photosetting, Chatham, Kent
Printed and bound by Bookcraft (Bath), Midsomer Norton

Visit us at our website: www.butterworthsscotland.com

Foreword

When the first edition of this book appeared in 1987, I was happy to congratulate Sheriff Kearney on producing a helpful textbook which would appeal to a wide variety of readers interested in the children's hearing system. I have no doubt that the first edition fully achieved its purpose of providing a systematic exposition of the legal principles and procedures relating to children's hearings.

However, regular updating and reform of the law have been features of the last quarter of the twentieth century. Since 1987, the law relating to child protection has been amended in a variety of respects by the Children (Scotland) Act 1995. That Act made changes in terminology, and gave some new powers to children's hearings. Also, and very importantly, the Act gave the courts a number of additional powers in the form of new orders which the courts can make in regard to children in need of supervision or protection.

In view of these changes in the law, the new edition of this work is very timely. The new chapters dealing with Child Assessment Orders, Child Protection Orders and Exclusion Orders will be particularly helpful. Reading these chapters, and indeed the whole book, should greatly assist all who have to deal with this difficult and sensitive area of the law.

Of course, apart from new matter necessitated by legal changes, a great deal of material from the first edition has been repeated in amended and updated form. The Model Applications and the advice on filling in forms will be particularly helpful to those who have to prepare and present such documents.

Once again Sheriff Kearney, whose knowledge of the law in this field is unrivalled, deserves congratulations for expanding and bringing up to date the first edition of his work. Like its predecessor, this edition should prove to be a valuable *vade mecum* for lawyers, reporters, social workers and others who become involved in the children's hearing system. They all owe a considerable debt of gratitude to Sheriff Kearney.

Donald M Ross
The Right Hon. Lord Ross, formerly the Lord Justice Clerk

To
Elizabeth, Marie and Pauline

Preface

Well before the publication of the first edition of this book in 1987 the integrity of the children's hearing system had been recognised both in the courts and by the general public. Notable amongst the judicial decisions was the analysis by Lord President Emslie in *McGregor v D*[1] which in effect defined the essence of the system and gave direction to the further development of the law. Since 1987 there have been further important judicial pronouncements recognising the special nature of the system. In *Sloan v B*[2] Lord President Hope, amongst many other matters, identified the special value of separation of trial from disposal and in *Harris v F*[3] Lord Justice Clerk Ross explained the justification for the civil standard of proof in cases wherein child abuse is alleged in terms of the public policy of protecting children. In *Constanza v M*[4] Lord President Rodger emphasised the importance of safeguarding the rights of the referred child by refusing to allow any dilution of the principle that where offences are alleged against a child the criminal standard of proof must be attained. There have also been a number of reports of inquiries and other reports wherein the practices and administration of the system were considered and it was largely as a result of these that the Children (Scotland) Act 1995 was enacted. This Act, although introducing a number of important changes did not change the basis of the system and the Scottish Executive has indicated its continuing support for the system, even indicating that it favoured investigation of an extension of the system to include more children in the system.[5] The case of *McMichael v United Kingdom*[6] brought the European Convention on Human Rights and Fundamental Freedoms to bear on the hearings system and it remains to be seen what will be the effect of incorporation of the Convention into Scots domestic law by the Human Rights Act 1998.

This book aims to up-date the first edition. As in the first edition I have tried to explain the workings of the children's hearings system and its relationship with the sheriff court in a way which I hope will be accessible to the wide range of people, not just the lawyers, who work within the system. I have tried to state the law as at 1 October 2000, just before the Human Rights Act came into force. I have at certain places given some indication of how the arrival of that Act might affect the working of the system in certain particular aspects but thought it premature to try to supply an exhaustive survey. I have also been able to incorporate some references to case law handed down after that date.

---

1 1977 SC 330, 1977 SLT 182.
2 1991 SLT 530.
3 1991 SLT 242, 1991 SCLR 124.
4 1997 SC 217, 1997 SLT 1396, 1997 SCLR 510.
5 *The Scottish Executive Response*, dated 9 June 2000 to the *Report on the Advisory Group on Youth Crime – It's a Criminal Waste*, Edinburgh 2000.
6 (1995) 20 EHRR 205.

There are many people whom I have to thank. I am honoured that Lord Ross has taken the time to read the work in proof and write the Foreword. Very special thanks are due to Mr Brian Lister, the Reporter Manager for the Central West area of the Scottish Children's Reporter Administration. Mr Lister patiently read through the work in draft, gave me great help in relation to present practice, made innumerable suggestions for improvements and also saved me from many errors. As if that were not enough he was then kind enough to give up hours of his time to reading the entire work in proof. Without Mr Lister's skill and knowledge the merchantable quality of this book would be seriously diminished. I also obtained valuable help from Mrs Margaret Burt, Chair of the Scottish Safeguarders' Association, Ms Alison Cleland, Solicitor, of Napier University, Mr Alisdair Gordon, Solicitor, Ms Evelyn Grant, Reporter Manager for the North, Mr Gerald McHugh of the Scottish Executive, Ms Romy Langeland, Depute Director, Social Work Services Department, Glasgow City Council, Mrs Marion Pagani, Chair of the Glasgow Children's Panel, Mrs Janys Scott, Advocate, Mrs Margaret Small, Authority Reporter for East Dunbartonshire, Mr David Stewart of the Scottish Executive and Professor Fred Stone. I am indebted to the Convention of Scottish Local Authorities and the Principal Reporter, Mr Alan Miller, for enabling me to reproduce respectively the COSLA note of safeguarders' fees and SCRA Form F. I must also express my gratitude to Professor Kenneth McK Norrie of Strathclyde University for the many discussions we have had which have helped to focus my views on various matters. It is one of the benefits of sitting as a sheriff in Glasgow that one is able constantly to exchange views with the other sheriffs here and these exchanges have been very valuable. In particular I would mention the useful discussions which have taken place between Sheriff J Kenneth Mitchell and myself. I should also like to thank the members of the Sheriff Clerk's staff here for advice on matters of practice. I am aware that I have received many helpful suggestions from others over the years and I thank them also. I am also most grateful to the staff of Butterworths for their patient and skilful help. I should also like to mention with gratitude the encouragement given to me by Miss Margaret Cherry in 1998 when the task of embarking on writing a second edition sometimes seemed too daunting to contemplate. In spite of all the help I have received I of course take responsibility for the text and for any errors which remain.

Preparing this edition has kept me away from many family responsibilities. I am very conscious that my wife Elizabeth and her sisters Marie and Pauline have over the last two and a half years gone out of their way to give me the time and space to work on this book and I dedicate it to them.

Brian Kearney
Glasgow
October 2000

Contents

PART VII: APPEALS FROM THE SHERIFF 549

Appendices

Bibliography

Cleland, A and Sutherland, E E, *Children's Rights in Scotland*, Edinburgh 1996

Dickson W G, *A Treatise on the Law of Evidence in Scotland* (3rd edn by PJ Hamilton Grierson, 1887) Edinburgh (*'Dickson on Evidence'*)

Field, D and Rait, F E, *The Law of Evidence in Scotland*, Edinburgh 1996 (*'Field and Rait on Evidence'*)

Gordon, Sir Gerald H (ed), *Renton and Brown's Criminal Procedure* (6th edn, up-dated every six months) Edinburgh (*'Renton and Brown'*)

The Criminal Law of Scotland (2nd edn, 1978) and First Supplement (1984) Edinburgh (*'Gordon on Criminal Law'*)

Hallet, C et al, *The Evaluation of Children's Hearings in Scotland*, Four Volumes, 1998–2000, The Scottish Office and The Scottish Executive

Lockyer, A and Stone, F, *Juvenile Justice in Scotland – Twenty-five Years of the Welfare Approach*, Edinburgh 1998

Macphail, I D, *Evidence – A Revised Version of a Research Paper on the Law of Evidence in Scotland* (1987) Edinburgh (*'Macphail on Evidence'*)

Sheriff Court Practice, (2nd edn, ed GCB Nicholson and AL Stewart), Edinburgh 1998

Macphail, I D, and Ruxton, L, *Evidence*, in *The Laws of Scotland – Stair Memorial Encyclopaedia*, volume 10 (1990) Edinburgh (*'Macphail and Ruxton on Evidence'*)

Martin, F M and Murray, K (eds), *Children's Hearings* (1976) Edinburgh

The Scottish Juvenile Justice System (1982) Edinburgh

Martin, F M, Fox S, and Murray K, *Children out of Court* (1981) Edinburgh

Meek, R I M, and Ors (eds), *In the Child's Best Interests*, Scottish Child and Family Alliance, Edinburgh 1991 (distributed by HMSO)[*]

Nichols, D (General Ed), *Butterworths Scottish Family Law Service*, Edinburgh (up-dated every six months)

Norrie, K McK, *Children's Hearings in Scotland*, Edinburgh 1997

Children (Scotland) Act 1995, revised edn Edinburgh 1998

Report of the Committee on Children and Young Persons, Scotland (1964), Cmnd 3065, HMSO (The Kilbrandon Report)

Sutherland, E E, *Child and Family Law*, Edinburgh 1999

Wadham, J and Mountfield, H, *Blackstone's Guide to the Human Rights Act 1998*, London 1999

Walker, A G, and Walker, N M L, *The Law of Evidence in Scotland* (1964) Edinburgh and Glasgow (*'Walker and Walker on Evidence'*)

Wilkinson, A B, *The Scottish Law of Evidence*, (1986) London/Edinburgh

Wilkinson, A B and Norrie, K McK, *Parent and Child* (2nd edn, ed K McK Norrie), Edinburgh 1999 (*'Wilkinson and Norrie on Parent and Child, second edn'*)

---

[*] Difficult to obtain and a little out of date, but still a valuable insight into the task of the children's reporter – edited inter alia by Russell Meek, one of the first reporters and one of the inspirers and advisers in relation to the first edition of this book.

Glossary of Scottish Legal Terms and Expressions

It is now the fashion to try to avoid technical words and Latin expressions. Since, however, anyone reading the literature and cases relevant to the children's hearings system will encounter such expressions many of them have been included in this book. This glossary attempts to explain them in plain words. Also included are some common abbreviations.

Act of Sedurunt: Act or set of rules regulating procedure enacted by the Court of Session.

Actus reus: The external conduct constituting a crime or offence (cf mens rea).

Aliunde: Otherwise; elsewhere.

Amotio: Literally, 'removal'; that part of the crime of theft comprising the physical moving of the object.

Art and part: Good Scottish expression meaning as an accomplice or accessory.

Avizandum: Literally, 'to be considered'; used when a judge does not issue an immediate decision but reserves judgment for the time being in order to deliver a considered opinion later.

Competent: Lawful; within the rules; that which it is within the power (usually of a court) lawfully to do.

Corpus: Short for 'corpus delicti': literally the body or substance of the offence, the facts which make up the crime.

Crave: that part of a petition or application to the court which contains the formal request to the court or tribunal for the order which is being requested.

Curator ad litem: Person appointed by a court to look after the interests of a person in relation to a particular litigation who for some reason lacks full legal capacity.

De fidele administratione: literally, 'in relation to faithful administration'; the oath (or affirmation) 'de fidele administratione' is administered by the judge or sheriff to a person, such as an interpreter or occasionally a shorthand writer, on his/her taking office in the course of a court case.

Debate: Legal argument before a sheriff or other judge aimed at achieving a definite order of court.

Diligence: The process of putting a decree or order of court into effect, such as enforcing the attendance of witnesses, procuring the production of documents, and enforcing payment of money.

Eiusdem generis: Of the same kind: the rule of interpretation of statutes and other documents whereby where a list of particular things in a class of things is followed by an expression such as 'or otherwise', the contents of 'otherwise' will be interpreted as referring only to further members of that class.

Ex parte: on behalf of one side only.

Ex proprio motu: on its own motion; said where a court or tribunal makes an order or raises a question on its own initiative and not on the motion of one of the parties.

Expenses: The legal costs of a court case in Scotland.

Expressio unius, exclusio alterius: The express mentioning of one particular member of class of things implies exclusion of all other members of that class.

Extract: Formal document issued by the clerk of court containing the essential elements of the order of court.

Functus officio: literally, having performed his/her office; said where it is contended that a court or officer of court has completed the duties imposed and has no further standing in the proceedings.

Furth of: Beyond.

Haver: Holder of a document or other piece of material evidence.

In foro contentioso: literally, in a contentious forum; in a setting wherein each side is present and able to advance in full its side of the case.

In hoc statu: literally 'in this state'; said, generally in giving the decision of the court where the judge wishes to indicate that the decision has been taken against the background of the particular circumstances prevailing at the time and that the court is not tying itself to that decision and may change it in changed circumstances.

Incompetent: unlawful; not within the rules; that which it is beyond the powers (usually of a court or tribunal) lawfully to do.

Indictment: The final full form of the charge served on an accused person in solemn procedure (qv).

Interlocutor: The decision or order pronounced by the court and written in the minutes of proceedings.

Instance: Part of the heading of a court writ containing the names and addresses of the parties.

Joint Minute: Formal document signed by the agents of parties to a court case agreeing a set of facts or mode of procedure.

Leading question: a question asked of a witness which leads the witness excessively firmly in the direction which the questioner wants to go, i.e. which suggests the answer to the witness.

Letters of Second Diligence: Order of court compelling the attendance of a witness at a specific diet of the court.

Mens rea: literally, the guilty mind; criminal intent – the mental element of evil intention which is a necessary element in nearly all common law crimes but which may be absent in many statutory offences.

Mutatis mutandis: literally, those things which require to be changed having been changed; generally used where there is said to be substantial similarity between two situations but there are some things which will require to be changed.

Nobile Officium: The equitable jurisdiction of the Court of Session and High Court of Justiciary to make legal provision for circumstances not provided for in the existing law when the interests of justice so demand.

Obiter: Literally, 'by the way': an observation by a judge on the law which is not strictly necessary for the determination of the case and which is therefore not fully authoritative.

Ordain: Formally order or require – used to signify that the order of the court has the full authority of the court and that wilful disregard of it may lead to a finding of contempt of court.

Pannel, panel: Formal (becoming obsolescent) term for the accused person, mainly in relation to solemn procedure (qv).

Precognosce, precognition: To interview a potential witness with a view to finding out what the witness's evidence in court is likely to be; the resulting 'precognition' will contain the precognoscer's record of the interview but may not be an exact quotation of the words of the witness.

Pro bono publico: for the public good; a solicitor or advocate who acts for a client without fee my be described as acting 'pro bono'.

Pro veritate: (Taken) as true.

Prima facie case: Loosely, a case the evidence of which on its face entitles a party to some legal remedy; more precisely used to refer to the stage in a particular case in which evidence has been led and that evidence, if believed, would be sufficient in law to entitle the party relying upon it to draw the conclusion in law which he or she seeks to draw.

Process: the proceedings in a court case; *or* the bundle of documents comprising the court papers in the case – documents added to this bundle are said to be 'lodged in process' and will generally be included in the 'inventory of process'.

Procurator Fiscal: The public prosecutor in Scotland.

Proof: That which establishes the existence or non-existence of a fact; *or* the particular sitting of a court, usually a civil court, at which evidence is led.

Quantum valeat: For what it may be worth.

Quoad ultra: As regards the rest.

Res gestae: The whole thing done: when it has been averred that something has happened it is permissible to lead evidence as to the whole event – evidence which appears to go beyond this may be inadmissible because 'it is not part of the res gestae'.

Res judicata: Literally, the matter has been judged upon already; used where it is being argued that it is not competent for the court the consider an allegation or make a ruling because there has already been a decision on the matter and, in the case of an allegation against a person, that it would be wrong to subject the person accused to a second trial on the same subject matter.

Solemn procedure: The highly formal criminal procedure for prosecution of more serious crimes in the High Court and Sheriff Court. The procedure starts by way of Petition and later on an Indictment (qv) may be served and the case will be tried by a High Court judge, or a Sheriff, with a jury of fifteen.

Sui generis: Of its own particular kind; in a class by itself.

Summary procedure: The less elaborate criminal procedure for the prosecution of crime in the Sheriff Court and the District Court. The proceedings start by summary complaint and are tried, without a jury, by the Sheriff, Stipendiary Magistrate or Justices of the District Court.

Timeous, timeously: In due time; within the time limit prescribed by a rule of law.

Ultra vires: Beyond the powers (of); said when a legislative body, court, tribunal or official has exceeded the powers conferred upon it or him/her.

Abbreviations

CAO: Child Assessment Order.

CPAC: Children's Panel Advisory Committee.

CPO: Child Protection Order,

CSWO: Chief Social Work Officer.

JPA: Justice of Peace Authorisation (for protection of child under s 61 of the Act).

SWD: Social Work Department.

EO: Exclusion Order

Table of statutes

Table of statutory instruments

Table of cases

Part I
The hearings and the children's reporter

CHAPTER 1

The general jurisdiction of the children's hearing

THE CHILDREN'S PANEL AND THE CHILDREN'S HEARINGS

The children's panel

1.01 Under the Children (Scotland) Act 1995, s 39(1) a children's panel has to be set up for every local government area, which nowadays means the 32 councils set up under the Local Government etc (Scotland) Act 1994, s 2. The local authority is required to arrange for the publication of the names and addresses of the panel members by having them available for public inspection at its principal offices and at any place where the voters' roll is exhibited.[1]

1 Children (Scotland) Act 1995, Sch 1, para 12.

The appointment of panel members

1.02 The statutory framework for the appointment of panel members is set out in the Children (Scotland) Act 1995, Sch 1, as read with the Scotland Act 1998, s 53(2)(c). The power to appoint panel members lies ultimately with the Scottish Ministers. Each local authority is bound to form a Children's Panel Advisory Committee (CPAC) with the task of submitting suitable names to Scottish Ministers and advising them on the suitability of these names and also on any other matter relating to the general administration of panels which Scottish Ministers may refer. Schedule 1, para 8 allows for two or more local authorities, who have obtained the written consent of the Scottish Ministers, to appoint, instead of individual CPACs, a 'joint advisory committee' which is to have the powers of, and is to be regarded as, a CPAC.

CHILDREN'S PANEL ADVISORY COMMITTEE

Composition and functions of CPAC

1.03 A CPAC must comprise at least five members, of whom two are to be nominated by the local authority and three, including the chairman, by the Scottish Ministers. Scottish Ministers may, at the request of a local authority, provide for additional members of the CPAC, to a maximum of five. The chairman of the CPAC must live within the relevant local authority area. The local authority must make such arrangements as it considers appropriate to enable the CPAC to obtain suitable names for submission to Scottish Ministers who may, in addition to appointing panel members, also appoint a chairman and deputy chairman from amongst the panel members. Scottish Ministers may take measures to train panel members. The Children (Scotland) Act 1995, Sch 1, para 11 is headed 'Expenses of Panel Members' and provides that the local authority may pay to panel members, potential panel members, CPAC members and members of any sub-committee appointed by a CPAC 'such allowances as may be determined by the Secretary of State [now Scottish Ministers]'. There is no provision for payment of any salary or fee to panel members or CPAC members, but they are recompensed for loss of wages and out-of-pocket expenses and this outlay constitutes a considerable part of the cost of running the hearings system. Panel members are generally appointed for a specific period, commonly five years, and they may be re-appointed on the recommendation of the CPAC. It is unusual, although by no means unknown, for a panel member to continue as such for more than ten years. The average is about five years.[1] Schedule 1, para 2 provides that a panel member 'may be removed from office by the Secretary of State [now Scottish Ministers] at any time' but such removal must have the consent of the Lord President of the Court of Session.[2]

1 Andrew Lockyer *Citizen's Service and Children's Panel Membership* Scottish Office (1992), para 7.2.6.
2 Tribunals and Inquiries Act 1992, s 7(1)(e) and Sch 1, para 8.

Attributes and training of panel members

1.04   The Children (Scotland) Act 1995, like the Social Work (Scotland) Act 1968, does not prescribe any qualification for panel membership, but government circulars have desiderated the inclusion of persons who have 'shown themselves capable of taking reasonable unbiased attitudes towards children in trouble' and for the exclusion of 'persons with a clear pre-disposition towards taking a "hard" or "soft" line'.[1] Persons professionally involved in advising hearings or carrying through their decisions are also in practice not appointed as panel members in the local authority areas wherein they are so employed.[2] Panel members are ineligible for jury service[3] *and are statutorily entitled to time off work to enable them to carry out their duties.*[4] Panel members are trained in legal and child care matters before appointment and are also provided with in-service training. Several of the Scottish universities now each have a department in which there is a member or members of staff specialising in the training of panel members.

1 Social Work Services Group circular SW7/1969, Appendix A, para 1.
2 For an analysis of the characteristics of panel members, see Martin and Murray (eds) *Children's Hearings* (1976) ch 6.
3 Law Reform (Miscellaneous Provisions) (Scotland) Act 1980, s 1 and Sch 1.
4 Employment Protection (Consolidation) Act 1978, s 29(1)(c).

1.05 Each children's panel has a chairman or chairwoman and a deputy.[1] Such chairpersons have extensive administrative responsibilities including the arrangements for convening panel members to hearings. The chairpersons meet from time to time as the Scottish Children's Panel Chairmen's Group. Hearings are subject to the supervision of the Scottish Council on Tribunals and a member of the Council, or of the Scottish Committee of the Council, has the right to attend a hearing.[2] The offices of chairperson and deputy chairperson of the children's panel of a local authority are onerous, although unsalaried. The chairperson, whom failing the deputy, has inter alia the responsibility of selecting chairmen and members of individual hearings, either directly or by way of the operation of standing arrangements effected after consultation with the principal reporter and panel members.[3]

1 Children (Scotland) Act 1995, Sch 1, para 1.
2 C(S)A 1995, s 43(3)(a).
3 Children's Hearings (Scotland) Rules 1996, SI 1996/3261, r 10(1).

Degree of immunity of hearing members: wrongful detention and defamation

Immunity of High Court and Court of Session judges and sheriffs

1.06 Hearing members, like judges of the Court of Session and the High Court of Justiciary and sheriffs, make decisions affecting the liberty and good name of those appearing before them[1] and have to issue statements, in the form of reasons for decisions,[2] containing matter which may on the face of it be highly defamatory of third parties. Court of Session and High Court judges and sheriffs, being 'the King's judges directly',[3] are, as the law stands at present, absolutely immune from any form of process or claim arising out of any acting or statement done or said in their judicial capacity.[4]

1 Cf 25.21 ff below.
2 23.32 ff below.
3 *M'Creadie v Thomson* 1907 SC 1176 at 1182.
4 *Harvey v Dyce* (1876) 4 R 265; *Russell v Dickson* 1998 SLT 96; *Renton and Brown's Criminal Procedure* (6th edn, ed Sir Gerald H Gordon QC) paras 27-01 and 27-02; cf *McMichael v UK* [1995] 20 EHRR 205 at para 47: but see the reservations as to the contemporary applicability of the older cases expressed in the opinion of Temporary Judge T G Coutts QC in *Russell v Dickson* 1998 SLT 96 at 101H.

Degree of immunity of judges of the lower courts

1.07 The justices of the district court enjoy qualified privilege, that is to say they cannot be successfully sued for wrongful imprisonment unless the pursuer can aver and prove malice and want of probable cause.[1] This qualified privilege does not attach if the justice acts beyond his powers, but an honest mistake in applying the law may not render a justice liable, even if wrongful detention has resulted.[2]

1 Criminal Procedure (Scotland) Act 1995, s 170.
2 *McPhee v Macfarlane's Exor* 1933 SC 163; see *Renton and Brown* para 27-05.

Degree of immunity of panel members –claim for defamation

1.08   The position of hearing members is not set out in the Children (Scotland) Act 1995 or any other statute. The tribunal constituting the hearing is a judicial, or at least a quasi-judicial, body. The question of whether or not a hearing is an 'independent' tribunal was raised but not decided in *McMichael v United Kingdom*[1] but it is submitted that the provision that the removal of panel members from office by the Scottish Ministers can now only be effected with the consent of the Lord President of the Court of Session goes a long way to supporting the proposition that they are an independent and judicial body. In any event, since panel members are statutorily appointed persons fulfilling a public function in the public interest they are privileged in respect of any claim for wrongful detention unless malice and want of probable cause can be specifically averred and proved.[2] Malice may be inferred from actings.[3] In relation to any claim for defamation, it is submitted that a children's hearing is a judicial, or at least a quasi-judicial, body and that therefore hearing members enjoy absolute privilege.[4]

1 [1995] 20 EHRR 205.
2 *Macaulay v School Board of North Uist* (1887) 15 R 99 per Lord Craighill at 102 and per LJ-C Macdonald at 103.
3 Cf *Fraser v Mirza* 1993 SLT 527. See the illuminating discussion of the relationship between the concepts of malice and want of probable cause (in the context of wrongful apprehension) in D M Walker *The Law of Delict* (2nd edn, 1981) p 689 ff.
4 See D M Walker *The Law of Delict* (2nd edn, 1981) at 803 and the cases therein cited.

The Human Rights Act 1998 – the European Convention for the Protection of Human Rights and Fundamental Freedoms

1.09   On 2 October 2000 the Human Rights Act 1998 ['the 1998 Act'] comes into force. The 19ℇ 3 Act enacts that many of the provisions of the European Convention ℈r the Protection of Human Rights and Fundamental Freedoms [the European Convention'], which are to be known as 'Convention rights',[1] are to have effect in our law.[2] Amongst these Convention rights are those conveyed by the European Convention, art 5(5) which provides: 'Everyone who has been the victim of arrest or detention in contravention of the provision of this article shall have an enforceable right to compensation.' Children's hearings and courts are public authorities[3] and as such must not act in a way which is incompatible with a Convention right.[4] With one exception, damages may not be awarded in any proceedings brought under the 1998 Act in respect of a judicial act, which includes, it is thought, acts of hearing members as well as of sheriffs and judges, provided that such acts are in good faith and in the exercise of their jurisdictions.[5] The exception is any act in contravention of article 5(5)[6] and a person whose rights under this article have been violated may recover damages against the Crown and the minister responsible must be joined as a party.[7]

1 Human Rights Act 1998, s 1(1).
2 HRA 1998, s 1(2).
3 HRA 1998, s 6(3)(a).
4 HRA 1998, s 6(1).
5 HRA 1998, s 9(3) and (5).
6 HRA 1998, s 9(3).
7 HRA 1998, s 9(4).

Children *prima facie* eligible to jurisdiction of a hearing

The Act's definition of 'child'

1.10   It is a precondition of eligibility to the jurisdiction of a hearing that the candidate be a 'child' for the purposes of the Children (Scotland) Act 1995, Pt II, Chs 2 and 3. Section 93(2) of the Act defines a 'child' for these purposes as: a child who has not reached 16 years of age; a child who has not reached 18 and in respect of whom a supervision requirement of a children's hearing is in force; and a child whose case has been referred to a hearing under s 33 of the Act (that is, a child who has been subject to an order made in England, Wales or Northern Ireland corresponding to a Scottish supervision requirement). Section 93(2) also provides that the provisions of Pt II, Chs 2 and 3 shall apply to a person who has failed to attend school regularly without reasonable cause and who is over 16 but is not over school age, which is construed[1] in accordance with the Education (Scotland) Act 1980, s 31.[2]

1 Children (Scotland) Act 1995, s 93(1).
2 For a discussion of when, in law, one reaches a given age, see D B Smith 'Computation of Age' 1962 SLT (News) 161.

Person between 16 and 17 and a half

1.11   A person between 16 and 17 and a half, not subject to a supervision requirement, may be dealt with by a hearing if he or she has been found guilty of or pleaded guilty to an offence charged summarily (in the sheriff court or the district court) and the sheriff or justice has called for the advice of a hearing under the Criminal Procedure (Scotland) Act 1995, s 49(6) and (7), provided that the hearing has advised in favour of a remit to the hearing for disposal and the sheriff or justice has accepted such advice.

Age of criminal responsibility only applicable in s 52(2)(i) cases

1.12   Where the grounds of referral to a hearing[1] comprise any ground other than an offence by the child, there is no downward limitation of age. Where the ground of referral is an alleged offence by a child, however, that child must have reached, as at the date of the alleged offence, the age of criminal responsibility, namely eight, before he or she can be held to have 'committed an offence'.[2]

1 1.18 below.
2 Criminal Procedure (Scotland) Act 1995, s 41; *Merrin v S* 1987 SLT 193; cf *Constanda v M* 1997 SCLR 510.

Ascertainment of age of referred child

1.13   The Children (Scotland) Act 1995, s 47, substantially echoing provisions contained in several of its predecessors,[1] provides that the hearing shall, at the outset of proceedings, make inquiry as to the age of the child and proceed with the hearing only if the child declares that he or she is a child or it so determines – and a fresh declaration or determination may be made at any time before the conclusion of the proceedings.[2] The age so declared or determined shall then be deemed to be the age of the child for the purposes of Pt II of the Act and no

varrant or requirement made by a hearing shall be
subsequent proof that the age was different.[3] A child
e age of 16 after a hearing has started to consider his or
before the case has been decided, remains subject to the
jurisdiction in relation to the pending case.[4]

al Work (Scotland) Act 1968, s 55; the Children Act 1908, s 123(1); and the
d Young Persons (Scotland) Act 1937, s 103(1).
Scotland) Act 1995, s 47(1).
/5, s 47 (2) and (3).
4 C(S). /95, s 93(3).

Obtaining extract of birth certificate

1.14 An extract certificate of a Scottish birth may be obtained from the Registrar of Births, Deaths and Marriages at the office where the birth was registered or from: The Registrar General for Scotland, General Register Office for Scotland, New Register House, Edinburgh EH1 3YT. The date and place of birth of the child should be provided and the parents' names if known, including the maiden name of the mother. At the time of writing the fee is £13.

Jurisdiction of hearings: territorial

Jurisdiction tends to follow the child

1.15 A children's hearing may only deal with a case once it has been referred to it by the children's reporter.[1] Although there is no specific territorial limitation in the Children (Scotland) Act 1995, the decisions of hearings can only be implemented in the first instance by the local authority within whose area they operate[2] and therefore the reporter of the child's residence will in practice deal with the case – in short, jurisdiction will tend to follow the child.[3] In practice the location of the event giving rise to the referral and the place where the child lives will often coincide and the notifying agency[4] will inform the local reporter who will consider referring the child to a locally convened hearing. The lack of rigid regulation of territorial jurisdiction may have the advantage of flexibility: for example when a child is outside the local authority area within which he resides, the reporter nearest to the facts of the case would be able to cause the case to be dealt with by a hearing in the local authority area of the child's residence. A hearing may at any time request the principal reporter to arrange for a case to be transferred to a hearing in another local authority area if satisfied that the case could be better considered by such hearing.[5] The possibility of a hearing exercising jurisdiction over a child who did not reside in its area in respect of facts which did not arise in its area was mentioned but not discussed or decided in one of the Orkney cases.[6] The operative time is when the reporter refers the case of the child to a children's hearing, stating the grounds of referral.[7] Thus, where a reporter had received information regarding a child's case and, after investigation under s 65 of the Act, had intimated that he intended to refer the child's case to a children's hearing but, before the referral could be effected, the child was removed from Scotland, it was held that there was no jurisdiction and that therefore, when the matter came to the sheriff for proof, the sheriff was correct to dismiss the case and discharge the referral on the ground of no jurisdiction.[8]

1 Children (Scotland) Act 1995, s 65. See ch 2 below for discussion of the role and function of the reporter, the terms 'principal reporter' and 'children's reporter', and the Scottish Children's Reporter Administration.
2 C(S)A 1995, ss 71(1) and 93(1); cf *L v McGregor* 1980 SLT 17; *Mitchell v S* 2000 SLT 524 at 526J–527A.
3 Cf the position in relation to the granting of a child protection order by the sheriff, discussed at 5.02 below: the observation per Sheriff Principal Robert Hay CBE WS: 'the view which some other sheriffs principal and I take at this stage is that jurisdiction follows the child'.
4 E g the police, under C(S)A 1995, ss 61(5) and 53(3), a local authority under s 53(1), or 'any person' under s 53(2).
5 C(S)A 1995, s 48.
6 *Sloan, Petr* 1991 SLT 527 at 529C.
7 *Mitchell v S* 2000 SLT 524 at 527H–528D.
8 *Mitchell v S* 2000 SLT 524 at 528 E, F.

Transfer of case to another children's hearing

1.16 A hearing which considers that a case it is hearing could be better considered by a hearing in another local government area may request the reporter to effect a transfer and where this is done any grounds accepted or established do not require to be accepted or established again.[1]

1 Children (Scotland) Act 1995, s 48.

Statutory grounds of a hearing's jurisdiction

The conditions of referral

1.17 The Children (Scotland) Act 1995, s 52(1) provides that the question of whether compulsory measures of supervision are necessary for a child 'arises' if at least one of the conditions set out in subsection (2) of the section is satisfied with respect to him or her. By saying that the issue of compulsory measures of supervision 'arises' in these circumstances the Act makes clear that satisfaction of one or more of the conditions is a necessary but not sufficient condition of compulsory measures of supervision being required. Before the judgement may be made that measures are necessary the conditions in s 16 have to be met.[1] Subsections (2)[2] and (3) are in these terms:

'(2) The conditions referred to in subsection (1) above are that the child—
(a) is beyond the control of any relevant person;
(b) is falling into bad associations or is exposed to moral danger;
(c) is likely—
   (i) to suffer unnecessarily; or
   (ii) be impaired seriously in his health or development;
due to a lack of parental care;
(d) is a child in respect of whom any of the offences mentioned in Schedule 1 to the Criminal Procedure (Scotland) Act 1995 (offences against children to which special provisions apply) has been committed;

(e) is, or is likely to become, a member of the same household as a child in respect of whom any of the offences referred to in paragraph (d) above has been committed;

(f) is, or is likely to become, a member of the same household as a person who has committed any of the offences referred to in paragraph (d) above;

(g) is, or is likely to become, a member of the same household as a person in respect of whom an offence under sections 1 to 3 of the Criminal Law (Consolidation) (Scotland) Act 1995 (incest and intercourse with a child by step-parent or person in position of trust) has been committed by a member of that household;

(h) has failed to attend school regularly without reasonable excuse;

(i) has committed an offence;

(j) has misused alcohol or any drug, whether or not a controlled drug within the meaning of the Misuse of Drugs Act 1971;

(k) has misused a volatile substance by deliberately inhaling its vapour, other than for medicinal purposes;

(l) is being provided with accommodation by a local authority under section 25, or is the subject of a parental responsibilities order obtained under section 86, of this Act and, in either case, his behaviour is such that special measures are necessary for his adequate supervision in his interest or the interest of others.

(3) In this Part of this Act, "supervision" in relation to compulsory measures of supervision may include measures taken for the protection, guidance, treatment or control of the child.'

The meanings of the conditions of referral are discussed in ch 46 of this book.

1 For further discussion of the s 16 principles in this regard see, in relation to the reporter, 2.16 ff below, and in relation to the hearing, ch 25.
2 As amended by the Criminal Procedure (Consequential Provisions) (Scotland) Act 1995, s 3 and Sch 4, para 97(4).

1.18   Of the conditions in the Children (Scotland) Act 1995, s 52(2) only condition (i) refers explicitly to the commission of an offence by a child. It is central to the philosophy of the system to regard the commission of an offence by the child as simply one amongst the various conditions listed in s 52(2) as prima facie evidence that the child requires compulsory measures of supervision.[1] A child subject to a supervision requirement, whether residential or not, becomes a 'looked after' child.[2] The issue of how far a supervision requirement carries the right to medical examination and treatment is discussed later.[3] 'Supervision' does not, however carry the whole 'rights' and responsibilities of the parent.[4] It may, however, involve an order being made whereby the child is liable, with the agreement of the Chief Social Work Officer and the person in charge of the relevant establishment, to be required to reside in secure accommodation.[5]

1 Cf Children and Young Persons: Scotland (1964) Cmnd 2306 (hereafter referred to as 'the Kilbrandon Report') para 138.
2 Children (Scotland) Act 1995, s 17(6)(b).
3 25.24 below.
4 Contrast Children and Young Persons (Scotland) Act 1937, s 79(4).
5 C(S)A 1995, s 70(9).

Terminology

'Care and protection' and 'offence by a child' cases

1.19 The phrases 'care or protection cases' (or, more idiomatically 'care and protection' cases) and 'offence cases' which are used widely in relation to the hearings system have no statutory authority or definition. 'Offence cases' is generally used to refer to cases under the Children (Scotland) Act 1995, s 52(2)(i), but since paras (d), (e), (f) and (g) of s 52(2) also make reference to 'offences' (in these instances offences against the child) the wordier but more accurate expressions 'offence by a child cases' or 's 52(2)(i) cases' may be thought to be preferable. The term 'care and protection cases' may be used as a shorthand way of referring to all cases not based on an offence by the child or on failure to attend school regularly without reasonable excuse. The latter may be termed 'education cases'. The opposition between 'care and protection' cases and others implied in the foregoing terminology may be objected to on the ground that all cases before hearings are truly cases concerning the care or protection of the child.[1] Of course this objection is in principle well founded but as the terminology is well embedded in ordinary practice it is convenient to use it, provided that one remembers that it is only used for convenience.

1 Cf the discussion of the parallel section of the Social Work (Scotland) Act 1968 by Lord Dunpark in his dissenting opinion in *Merrin v S* 1987 SLT 193 at 197 ff.

'Relevant person'

1.20 *Definition.* The provisions of the Social Work (Scotland) Act 1968, s 30 defining 'parent' as including 'guardian',[1] with 'guardian' very broadly defined,[2] have been swept away in favour of 'relevant person', a newly minted concept intended to embrace all persons lawfully having parental responsibilities or rights in respect of the child. 'Relevant person' means:

> '(a) any parent enjoying parental responsibilities or parental rights under Part I of this Act;
> (b) any person in whom parental responsibilities or rights are vested by, under or by virtue of this Act; and
> (c) any person who appears to be a person who ordinarily (and other than by reason only of his employment) has charge of, or control over, the child'.[3]

1 Social Work (Scotland) Act 1968, s 30(2).
2 SW(S)A 1968, s 94(1).
3 Children (Scotland) Act 1995, s 93(2)(b).

1.21 *Parent enjoying parental responsibilities or parental rights under Part I of the Act.* This category includes:

- a child's mother, whether or not she is or has been married to the father;[1]
- the child's father if married to the child's mother at the time of conception or subsequently (the father being regarded as married even if the purported marriage was (a) voidable or (b) void but wrongly believed

(whether by error of law or of fact) in good faith to be valid by the mother and father);[2]

- any person, including an unmarried father, in whom is vested parental rights or responsibilities under the Children (Scotland) Act 1995, s 11(2)(b) or s 11(2)(h) or of the Law Reform (Parent and Child) (Scotland) Act 1986 ('the 1986 Act'), s 3(1) (which is a provision analogous to s 11 of the 1995 Act but repealed by that Act) or any other order, disposal or resolution affecting parental responsibilities or rights;[3]
- the child's (unmarried, presumably) father who has entered a formal agreement in appropriate form and registered in the Books of Council and Session with the mother whereby he becomes vested in parental responsibilities as at the date of such registration;[4] and
- an unmarried father, who has been validly appointed as guardian of the child under a testamentary disposition in terms of s 7 of the Act.

1 Children (Scotland) Act 1995, s 3(1)(a).
2 C(S)A 1995, s 3(1)(b) and (2).
3 C(S)A 1995, s 3(3).
4 C(S)A 1995, s 3(1)(b) and 4.

1.22 *Any person in whom parental responsibilities or rights are vested by, under or by virtue of this Act.*   This category includes a natural person[1] (not necessarily a parent) who has been vested with parental rights and responsibilities under the Children (Scotland) Act 1995, s 11(2)(b) or appointed as guardian under s 11(2)(h). It also includes any person, not necessarily a natural person, vested with parental responsibilities under s 86 of the Act.[2]

1 Children (Scotland) Act 1995, s 15(4).
2 Interpretation Act 1978, s 5 and Sch 1, definition of 'person'.

1.23 *Can foster parents be relevant persons?*   The definition of relevant person includes '(c) any person who appears to be a person who ordinarily (and other than by reason only of his employment) has charge of, or control over, the child'.[1] Professor Norrie has expressed the view: 'Foster carers who ordinarily have charge of or control over the child will also be "relevant persons" for the purposes of proceedings before children's hearings.'[2] In the case of children placed with foster carers by private arrangement it is difficult to resist the conclusion that the issue of charge and control be regarded as entirely a matter of fact. It is submitted that the position of a child in foster care as a result of a decision of a hearing may be different. Such a child is a 'looked after child'[3] for whom the local authority has the responsibilities set out in the Children (Scotland) Act 1995, s 17(1). The Arrangements to Look After Children (Scotland) Regulations 1996 reg 6[4] provides as follows in relation to the care plan which the local authority has to prepare for such a child:

'(4) The care plan shall, so far as is reasonably practicable, be agreed by the local authority with–
(a) a parent of the child, or
(b) if there is no such person, the person ordinarily with charge of or control over the child,
before the child is looked after.'

This provision itself is not without ambiguity but it seems to imply that the 'person ordinarily with charge or control' with whom the local authority should consult is intended to mean the de facto carer before the local authority acquired the responsibilities under s 17(1). It may therefore be, as discussed and ultimately dismissed by Norrie,[5] that a child residing with foster carers at the behest of a hearing, and therefore liable to be removed from them by a hearing, cannot be regarded as being 'ordinarily' having the charge or control of such child. The writer understands that in practice reporters do not, in relation to notifying hearings, cite foster carers with whom a child is residing under a supervision requirement. In a case decided in April 2000 grounds of referral had been stated, alleging that foster carers nominated by a children's hearing had assaulted one of their charges. A safeguarder was appointed and she adopted the stance of the foster carers, who denied the allegation. She appointed a solicitor, who acted as effective contradictor at the s 68 proof. The sheriff (the writer) found the grounds not established and observed:

> 'Yet in a case such as this persons in the [foster carers'] situation have an interest in the proceedings not only as potential adopters but as persons able to give the hearing and the court information as to the interests of the child. The child also has an interest that his or her recent carers should be able to do this. In the present case, no doubt by good judgment rather than good luck, but by no means automatically, the hearing and thereafter the Sheriff appointed a safeguarder who, as it happened, adopted substantially the stance of the [foster parents] and thereby provided a contradictor without whose services the outcome of this proof could well have been very different. It is not however satisfactory that the representation of foster carers such as the [naming them] should be dependent on such fortuitous circumstances. Apart from anything else [the solicitor for the safeguarder] was throughout representing the safeguarder who was safeguarding the interests of the children. It was only because the safeguarder "supported" the [foster carers] that their voice was heard. This situation will not necessarily obtain in other cases. The matter will become more urgent when, on 2nd October of this year, the Human Rights Act 1998 incorporates into our domestic law the European Convention on Human Rights. The decisions of hearings and sheriffs in cases such as this may determine the civil rights of the foster carers and, as is now well known, Article 6(1) of the Convention entitles everyone to a hearing on such a determination by a fair and impartial tribunal. In my view Scottish Ministers should examine the issue of the representation of foster carers in children's hearings cases as a matter of urgency.'[6]

1 Children (Scotland) Act 1995, s 93(2)(b).
2 Wilkinson and Norrie *Parent and Child* (2nd edn, 1999) para 18.04; cf Norrie *Children's Hearings in Scotland* (1997) pp 12, 13.
3 C(S)A 1995, s 17 (6)(b)
4 SI 1996/3262.
5 *Children's Hearings in Scotland* (1997) pp 12, 13.
6 *Cunninghame v JD and SD* 2000 Fam LB 46–5.

Reservation to Lord Advocate of right to prosecute children

1.24 The Kilbrandon Report recommended that the Crown should retain an overriding discretion to prosecute children in appropriate cases, envisaging that the exercise of such power would arise 'only exceptionally and on the gravest crimes, in which major issues of public interest must necessarily arise, and in which, equally as a safeguard for the interests of the accused, trial under criminal procedure is essential'.[1] The Criminal Procedure (Scotland) Act 1995, s 42(1) reflects this recommendation by providing that no child under 16 shall be prosecuted for any offence 'except on the instructions of the Lord Advocate'. The section also provides that children under 16 may only be prosecuted in the High Court or the sheriff court (i e not in the district court nor, presumably, the Lyon Court); but that children over 16, even if under supervision of a children's hearing, may be prosecuted in the district court.

1 Kilbrandon Report, paras 124 and 125.

THE LORD ADVOCATE'S DIRECTIONS AS TO THE PROSECUTION OF CHILDREN

1.25   The general rule for prosecutors is that criminal proceedings should not be taken against a child under 16 years of age unless there are compelling reasons in the public interest for so doing. The presumption is in favour of such cases being dealt with by the reporter in terms of the Children (Scotland) Act 1995, Pt I, Chs 2 and 3. However, as provided by the Criminal Procedure (Scotland) Act 1995, s 42(1), already noticed, there remain cases which prosecutors are enjoined to regard as the exceptions, in which prosecution is considered to be the most appropriate response. From the outset the Lord Advocate has regarded this type of provision as entitling him to issue general rules as to the categories of offences which should be considered for prosecution in the ordinary criminal courts. The propriety of this course was sustained in *M v Dean*[1] which also held that the fact of the concurrence of the Lord Advocate in the prosecution of a child under summary procedure did not require to be narrated on the face of the complaint. These categories, while unchanged in principle, have required modification from time to time.

1 1974 SLT 229.

1.26   A revised set of categories of offences which are to be reported to procurators fiscal with a view to possible prosecution, with accompanying 'Explanatory Notes', was issued to Chief Constables on the authority of the Lord Advocate of the day with effect from 3 August 1987. The following is a slightly amended version dated March 1996.

REPORTING TO PROCURATORS FISCAL OF OFFENCES ALLEGED TO HAVE BEEN COMMITTED BY CHILDREN

Revised categories of offences

Category 1
Offences which require by law to be prosecuted on indictment or which are so serious as normally to give rise to solemn proceedings on the instructions of the Lord Advocate in the public interest.

Category 2
Offences alleged to have been committed by children aged 15 years or over which in the event of conviction oblige or permit a court to order disqualification from driving.

Category 3
Offences alleged to have been committed by children as described in s 30(1)(b) of the Social Work (Scotland) Act 1968.[1]

Explanatory notes

1. *Category 1*

i.   Offences which require by law to be prosecuted on indictment fall under two heads – (1) common law offences which are within the exclusive jurisdiction of the High Court of Justiciary namely treason, murder and rape; and (2) statutory offences for which the statute only makes provision for prosecution on indictment or for a penalty on conviction on indictment – for example, contraventions of the Firearms Act 1968, s 16, 17(1) and (2), and 18(1), the Road Traffic Act 1988, s 1, and the Criminal Law (Consolidation) (Scotland) Act 1995, s 5(1).

ii. Offences of culpable homicide, attempted murder, assault to the danger of life, sodomy, assault and robbery involving the use of firearms, attempted rape, incest and related offences (contrary to the Criminal Law (Consolidation) (Scotland) Act 1995, ss 1–3) are offences which are normally indicted in the High Court of Justiciary.

iii. Other offences which may fall into this category as being normally prosecuted on indictment are assault to severe injury or permanent disfigurement, assault with intent to rape, serious assault and robbery (in particular involving the use of weapons other than firearms), assault with intent to rob involving the use of firearms, fireraising and malicious mischief causing or likely to cause great damage to property or danger to life, all Misuse of Drugs Act offences involving possession of Class A drugs and possession with intent to supply and supply of any controlled drugs.

It should be emphasised that only offences which are normally prosecuted on indictment are to be reported.

2. *Category 2*
This category applies exclusively to children aged 15 years and over. Children will be prosecuted for this type of offence only if the procurator fiscal considers that it would be in the public interest to obtain a disqualification which would still be in force when the child becomes 16 and that in the event of conviction it is likely that the court would impose such a disqualification. Minor Road Traffic Act offences carrying a liability to discretionary disqualification should not normally be reported.

3. *Category 3*
There is no restriction on the forum for the prosecution of children over 16 years of age who can be proceeded against in the District Court.

4. When reporting to procurators fiscal cases against adults in which it is alleged that a child also committed the offence (not being an offence specified in categories 1 to 3) along with the adult, the report should state that a copy of the report has been sent to the reporter for action in respect of the child.

5. The annexed direction does not preclude you from reporting to procurators fiscal any other offences, alleged to have been committed by children, where you are of the opinion that, for special reasons (which must be stated in the report), prosecution might be considered.

1 Now the Children (Scotland) Act 1995, s 93(2)(b)(ii).

Government guidance

1.27   In March 1999, the *Blueprint for the Processing of Children's Hearings Cases* was published.[1] This document, although non-statutory, contains valuable practical information and guidance.

1 *Blueprint for the Processing of Children's Hearings Cases – Inter-agency Code of Practice and National Standards* (Scottish Office Social Work Services Group, March 1999) was developed by a working group set up by Scottish Office Minister Sam Galbraith and chaired by Mrs Sally Kuenssberg CBE, the Chairman of the Scottish Children's Reporter Administration.

Legal Aid

1.28   In general, legal aid is available to children and relevant persons in respect of proceedings before the sheriff, the sheriff principal on appeal, and the Court of Session on appeal.[1] Application is made to the sheriff who will deal with the matter in chambers. The sheriff may grant an application without hearing parties, but should fix a hearing if considering refusing. Legal aid is not available for the instruction of legal representation before sessions of children's hearings, although advice under the Legal Advice and Assistance scheme may be available. As will be noticed at the appropriate places, some solicitors are prepared to represent clients without charge at hearings. Detailed consideration of certain aspects of legal aid is given later.[2]

1 Legal Aid (Scotland) Act 1986, s 29 as substituted by the Children (Scotland) Act 1995, s 92.
2 E g 39.10ff below.

CHAPTER 2

The children's reporter

THE PRINCIPAL REPORTER AND HIS LOCAL OFFICERS

2.01 The sole channel of cases to a children's hearing is the reporter.[1] The Kilbrandon Report,[2] noting that competency to assess legal issues would be one of the essential characteristics of a reporter, indicated a preference for the reporter to have a legal qualification as well as administrative experience relating to the child welfare and educational services. In the event, however, the powers[3] to prescribe minimum qualifications for reporters have not been exercised. After the court had ruled[4] that only legally qualified persons could appear before the sheriff in proceedings under the Social Work (Scotland) Act 1968, the government of the day enacted that reporters without legal qualification were entitled to appear, provided they had at least one year's experience[5] and these provisions have been re-enacted by statutory instruments of 1997.[6] It has been doubted if the foregoing provisions allow a non-legally qualified reporter to appear before a sheriff principal on appeal.[7] The writer has some doubts about this doubt – discussed later.[8] A reporter who is an advocate or a solicitor holding a practising certificate may, of course, conduct proceedings before the sheriff and the sheriff principal without having acquired one year's experience as a reporter. A solicitor who is entitled to appear before the sheriff by virtue of the 1997 statutory instruments does not require to hold a practising certificate in terms of the Solicitors (Scotland) Act 1980, s 14.[9]

1 The criminal and civil courts can, of course, in certain defined circumstances, refer a child or remit a child for disposal under the Criminal Procedure (Scotland) Act 1995, ss 48 and 49 and under the Children (Scotland) Act 1995, s 54, but even then the case is referred through the reporter: see 3.16 ff below.
2 At para 98.
3 Now in the Children (Scotland) Act 1995, s 40(1).
4 In *Kennedy v O* 1975 SC 308.
5 Children Act 1975, s 82; Reporters (Conduct of Proceedings before the Sheriff) (Scotland) Regulations 1975, SI 1975/2251.
6 Reporters (Conduct of Proceedings before the Sheriff) (Scotland) Regulations 1997, SI 1997/714; cf Reporters (Conduct of Proceedings before the Sheriff) (Scotland) (Amendment) Regulations 1997, SI 1997/1084.
7 *Templeton v E* 1998 SCLR 672; *N v Children's Hearing Reporter* (5 November 1998, unreported), Fort William Sheriff Court, Sheriff Principal D J Risk QC.
8 At 54.23 below.
9 *Miller v Council of the Law Society of Scotland* 2000 SLT 513.

2.02 The reporter occupies a central position in the functioning of the legal machinery of the hearings system and, although warnings are repeatedly sounded[1] against making facile analogies with criminal law and practice, the position and function of the reporter has some affinities with those of the procurator fiscal and Crown Office.

1 E g in *McGregor v T and P* 1975 SC 14 at 20; cf *McGregor v D* 1977 SLT 182 and *W v Kennedy* 1988 SLT 583.

THE PRINCIPAL REPORTER AND THE SCOTTISH CHILDREN'S REPORTER ADMINISTRATION

SCRA, the Principal Reporter and reporters

2.03   The Local Government etc (Scotland) Act 1994 ('the 1994 Act'), Pt III set up a centralised structure for reporters who had hitherto been appointed and organised by local authorities. The Scottish Children's Reporter Administration ('SCRA' or 'the Administration') is enacted as the body responsible for the appointment of the Principal Reporter[1] except for the appointment of the first ever Principal Reporter, whose appointment was the responsibility of the Secretary of State.[2] The status, constitution and proceedings of SCRA are governed by the 1994 Act, Sch 12. The Board of SCRA at present comprises a chairman, deputy chairman, the Principal Reporter and five ordinary members. The Principal Reporter is its chief officer[3] and the general function of the Administration is to facilitate the Principal Reporter in the performance of his functions under the Children (Scotland) Act 1995 and the Criminal Procedure (Scotland) Act 1995.[4] The consent of the Scottish Ministers to the appointment of a Principal Reporter is necessary.[5] The Administration may, with the consent of the Scottish Ministers, appoint 'officers' to assist the Principal Reporter in his duties[6] and it is responsible for their management and deployment throughout Scotland.[7] It is expressly provided that the Administration is to play no part in directing or guiding the Principal Reporter in the exercise of his statutory duties under the Act and the Criminal Procedure (Scotland) Act 1995.[8] A reporter may not, without the consent of SCRA, be employed by a local authority.[9] The Principal Reporter is entitled to delegate his functions, other than his obligation under s 130 of the 1994 Act to make an Annual Report to the Administration, to other officers of the Administration.[10]

1 Local Government etc (Scotland) Act 1994, s 128(4).
2 LG(S)A 1994, s 127(2).
3 LG(S)A 1994, s 128(2).
4 LG(S)A 1994, s 128(3).
5 LG(S)A 1994, s 128(4); Scotland Act 1998, s 53(2)(c).
6 LG(S)A 1994, s 128(5); SA 1998, s 53(2)(c).
7 LG(S)A 1994, s 128(7).
8 LG(S)A 1994, s 128(8).
9 LG(S)A 1994, s 40(2).
10 LG(S)A 1994, s 131.

Independence of reporters

2.04 The independence of the Principal Reporter and the other reporters is fortified by the provisions in the Local Government etc (Scotland) Act 1994, s 129[1] entitling them to appeal to the Scottish Ministers against dismissal by the Administration. Other officers engaged by the Administration may be prescribed by the Scottish Ministers for similar protection.[2]

1 Read with the Scotland Act 1998, s 53(2)(c).
2 Local Government etc (Scotland) Act 1994, s 129(2); SA 1998, s 53(2)(c).

The administrative structure

2.05 SCRA has its headquarters in Ochil House, Springkerse Business Park, Stirling, FK7 7XE (tel: (01786) 459500; fax: (01786) 459533). The Principal Reporter has delegated his functions[1] to an 'Assistant Principal Reporter', 'Reporter Managers', 'Authority Reporters' and reporters. The Administration has divided Scotland's 32 local authority areas into four groups which may be called 'SCRA Regions'. They are: Central West, based in Hamilton; East, based in Edinburgh; West, based in Glasgow; and North, based in Inverness.[2] Each of these Regions comprises several local authority areas and is headed by a Reporter Manager. Each Reporter Manager leads a number of Authority Reporters each of whom leads a number of reporters. The officers to whom the Principal Reporter has thus delegated his functions are entitled to carry out the functions of the Principal Reporter under the Children (Scotland) Act 1995 or any other enactment.[3] They must comply with any guidance or instructions issued by the Principal Reporter.[4] In practice persons wishing to notify or deal with the reporters' service in relation to the duties and functions conferred by the Act and subordinate legislation on 'The Principal Reporter' will generally deal with one or more of the officers at local level to whom the Principal Reporter has delegated his powers. SCRA has the responsibility for providing the premises within which children's hearings take place.

1 Local Government etc (Scotland) Act 1994, s 130.
2 For the detailed list see *The Scottish Law Directory 2000* (T & T Clark) pp A37, 38.
3 Children (Scotland) Act 1995, ss 40(5) and 93(1).
4 LG(S)A 1994, s 131(2).

Terminology

2.06 In this book the term 'reporter' or 'children's reporter' is used as the generic term for reporters and the term 'Principal Reporter' is reserved for the holder of that office. The procedure in relation to an application to the sheriff following non-acceptance (under the Children (Scotland) Act 1995, s 65(7)) or non-understanding (under s 65(9)) of grounds of referral is governed by the provisions of s 68 of the Act and is referred to as a 's 68 application'.

THE POWERS AND IMMUNITIES OF THE REPORTER – IN GENERAL

2.07   The specific duties of the reporter will be discussed in later chapters. It is the purpose of the rest of this chapter to set out the features common to these responsibilities.

Extent of immunity of reporter – wrongful detention and defamation

2.08   SCRA does not enjoy any immunity or privilege of the Crown[1] but it may be assumed that reporters, acting in the course of their duties, enjoy the degree of immunity accorded to any public official acting within the scope of his or her office, namely qualified privilege, i e immunity from any action of damages except upon averment of malice and want of probable cause.[2] This immunity is not absolute and malice may be inferred from circumstances such as want of probable cause.[3] In 1865 the use of an illegal warrant which had been wrongly granted by a sheriff was held to be sufficient to found an action of damages against the procurators fiscal who had operated it.[4] In this case Lord Justice-Clerk Inglis stated: 'There can be no probable cause for the execution of an illegal warrant.' The modern law affecting the immunity of public officials is discussed in *Hester v MacDonald*[5] and *Russell v Dickson*.[6]

1 Local Government etc (Scotland) Act 1994, Sch 12, para 2(b).
2 Cf *Fraser v Mirza* 1993 SLT 527, noticed at 1.08 above.
3 See 1.06 ff above for discussion of these concepts in the context of the similar position of hearing members.
4 *Bell v Black and Morrison* (1865) 3 M 1026.
5 1961 SC 370.
6 1998 SLT 96, noticed at 1.06 above; see the reservations expressed by the judge at 1998 SLT 101H as to the contemporary applicability of the older cases.

Privilege of oral and written submissions and reports

2.09   A pleader in court is accorded absolute privilege in relation to both oral and written pleadings.[1] It has been submitted already[2] that a hearing is a judicial, or at least a quasi-judicial, body. It is accordingly submitted that the grounds of referral and the reports and other papers which the reporter requires to lay before courts and hearings and the oral submissions which the reporter makes to hearings and courts are absolutely privileged.

1 *Williamson v Umphray and Robertson* (1890) 17 R 905; for discussion of privilege as a defence to an action of defamation see above Walker *The Law of Delict* (2nd edn) p 798 ff.
2 At 1.08 above.

The Human Rights Act 1998 – The European Convention for the Protection of Human Rights and Fundamental Freedoms

2.10   One of the consequences of the incorporation into our law, with effect from 2 October 2000, of the Convention has been noticed already in the context of actings of panel members, judges and sheriffs.[1] SCRA, the Principal Reporter and reporters are public authorities[2] and as such may not act in a way which is incompatible with Convention rights. Actings of reporters are not, per se, judicial acts for the purpose of the Human Rights Act 1998, s 9 and accordingly SCRA and reporters are generally liable to proceedings under s 7(1) in respect of alleged violation of *any* of the 'Convention rights' as specified in the 1998 Act, s 1(1) and set out in Sch 1. It is thought, however, that actings of reporters in obedience to directions by children's hearings or courts are acts 'done on the instructions, or on behalf, of a judge'[3] and as that therefore, in relation to such acts the liability of the reporter to proceedings under s 7(1) would, like the acts of panel members, judges and sheriffs, be limited to alleged violations of Article 5(5). It may be that such actings would be regarded as actings of the children's hearing or court which gave the instruction and that proceedings would be competent against the Crown.[4]

1 At 1.09 above.
2 Human Rights Act 1998, s 6(3)(b).
3 'Judge' includes tribunal member – HRA 1998, s 9(5).
4 HRA 1998, s 9(4).

Powers and duties of reporter in relation to referrals

General

2.11   The functions of the reporter in relation to referrals are administrative, involving the recording and transmission of information; investigative, involving checking and amplifying available information; deliberative, involving a discretion as to what action to take (and indeed whether it is appropriate to take any action at all); and executive in the sense of causing a certain significant event to take place, notably in connection with the detention or otherwise of children who have been brought to his or her notice, setting in motion procedures before hearings, and, to an extent, supervising the carrying through of decisions of hearings. The reporter's duties and powers may be found, along with much other material, in the Children (Scotland) Act 1995, Pt II, Chs 2 and 3, in the Children's Hearings (Scotland) Rules 1996,[1] and in Ch 3 of the Act of Sederunt (Child Care and Maintenance Rules) 1997,[2] in the Children's Hearings (Transmission of Information etc) (Scotland) Regulations 1996[3] and in the Secure Accommodation (Scotland) Regulations 1996[4]. During the course of a hearing the reporter effectively acts as legal adviser to the hearing members. This is nowhere stated explicitly in the Act or the Rules but it is implied throughout – for example by the provision in the Act relating to appeals against decisions of the sheriff whereby the reporter is accorded a right of appeal 'on behalf of the children's hearing'.[5] In *Miller v Council of the Law Society of Scotland*[6] the Principal Reporter, in pleadings which appear to be carefully worded, averred: 'a reporter's duties involve attendance at children's hearings at which the reporter requires to carry out the statutory duties and functions of the pursuer [the Principal Reporter] ... At such hearings, all reporters, whether legally qualified or not, offer their views to members of the children's hearing on any legal issues that arise'.

1 SI 1996/3261.

2 SI 1997/291.
3 SI 1996/3260.
4 SI 1996/3255.
5 Children (Scotland) Act 1995, s 51(12)(b).
6 2000 SLT 513 at 516L.

Initial recording and investigative function; the further investigation of referrals

2.12   The reporter's first duty, chronologically, is to note the particulars of the case, including, when known, the name and address of the informant.[1] Thereafter the reporter must make such initial investigation as he thinks necessary.[2] The extent of these investigations is a matter for the reporter to decide. In some cases, for example if the reporter is not minded to take any further action, little or even no investigation may be required. Where the reporter decides that some initial investigation is required he may ask for a report from the local authority on such matters as he considers relevant, and the local authority must supply such a report.[3] The reporter may extend his inquiries beyond the matters in the local authority's social inquiry report. He or she may request information from police or from a voluntary body such as Children First (the RSSPCC). The reporter's own staff may be employed.[4] The reporter may also wish to obtain medical reports but has no automatic access to the medical records of hospitals or general practitioners. If and when an application has been made to the sheriff under the Children (Scotland) Act 1995, s 68 or when an application to hear fresh evidence has been made under s 85 the reporter may request that the procurator fiscal supply information.[5] In 'offence by a child' cases the reporter will frequently rely on the police report forwarded to him or her; if further investigation seems to be required the reporter may request full statements from the police, ask the police to investigate further, or arrange for precognitions by him or herself. The reporter (and other parties) may also in certain circumstances use the ordinary procedures of the court for the recovery of documents or other material.[6]

1 Children's Hearings (Scotland) Rules 1996, r 3(1).
2 Children (Scotland) Act 1995, s 56(1).
3 C(S)A 1995, s 56(2).
4 Cf Local Government etc (Scotland) Act 1994, s 128(5).
5 C(S)A 1995, s 53(4).
6 The Administration of Justice (Scotland) Act 1972, s 1(1) – discussed at 30.41 ff below.

Consideration of referrals: emergence of other grounds

2.13   The abiding concern of the reporter is whether or not the child whose case has been notified is, on the facts available, in need of compulsory measures of supervision. The reporter is bound to have regard to the whole facts and is not confined to considering the facts relative to the ground of referral which may have been in the mind of the reporting agency. For example, on considering an 'offence by a child' case the reporter may discover facts or circumstances making it advisable to proceed on one or more of the other conditions of referral in addition to or instead of the 'offence by a child' ground: for example there may be facts suggesting that the child is likely to suffer unnecessarily because of lack of parental care,[1] or that the child is falling into bad associations or is exposed to moral danger[2]

1 Children (Scotland) Act 1995, s 52(2)(c).
2 C(S)A 1995, s 52(2)(b); cf *Constanda v M* 1997 SCLR 510, 1997 SLT 1396, discussed at 46.05 below.

DISCRETION OF THE REPORTER – THE SECTION 16 PRINCIPLES

General

2.14 The decision as to whether the child does appear to require compulsory measures of supervision is within the reporter's discretion. In the first edition of this book it was said,[1] under reference to sundry sections of the Social Work (Scotland) Act 1968: 'The principle on which this discretion is to be exercised, although not set out explicitly in a single provision, emerges clearly from a consideration of Part III of the Act as a whole: the reporter's fundamental concern is with the best interests of the child'. Similarly the Children (Scotland) Act 1995 does not expressly guide the reporter but the provision in s 16(1) of the Act that where a children's hearing decides, or a court determines, any matter with respect to a child then the welfare of the child throughout childhood shall be the paramount consideration ('the paramountcy principle') in effect must govern the approach of the reporter whose task it may be to bring a child before a hearing or a sheriff. The other principles set out in s 16, which may be referred to for short as the 'consulting the child principle'[2] and the 'no non-beneficial order principle'[3] apply to certain decisions of hearings and sheriffs and must be taken into account by a reporter who may, where the respective principles apply, require to justify a course of action or proposed action by reference to them.[4]

1 At p 24.
2 Children (Scotland) Act 1995, s 16(2).
3 C(S)A 1995, s 16(3).
4 These principles have been referred to (e g in Norrie (*Children's Hearings in Scotland* (1997)) at 45 and *passim*) as 'the three overarching principles' and this engaging phrase has to an extent passed into common usage. It is, however, not adopted in this book because it may seem to carry a connotation of universality which may be misleading. Not even the paramountcy principle is universal and the application of the other two is strictly delimited by C(S)A 1995, s 16(2) and (3) when read with s 16(4).

The paramountcy principle

2.15 The Children (Scotland) Act 1995, s 16(1) provides that where a hearing decides or a court determines *any* [emphasis supplied] matter with respect to a child then the 'welfare of that child *throughout his childhood* [emphasis supplied] shall be their or its paramount consideration'.

Derogation from the paramountcy principle – s 16(5)

2.16   The Children (Scotland) Act 1995, s 16(5) enacts a derogation from the principle of the paramountcy of the interests of the child by providing that this principle may be set aside if a hearing in making a decision or a court in making a determination should consider that it is necessary so to do 'for the purpose of protecting members of the public from *serious* [emphasis supplied] harm (whether or not physical harm)'. The detailed applications of the foregoing principles to various specific decisions of hearings and determinations of courts will be discussed later at their appropriate places.

Derogation from the paramountcy principle – exercise of judgment on matters of fact or law

2.17   It is submitted that it is clear that where a reporter, hearing or court has to exercise judgment on a matter of fact or law – that is, to decide something not within the realms of discretion – then the paramountcy principle has no application. For example, if the sheriff, on considering the evidence in proof, thinks, as a matter of fact or law, that no stateable case exists it would be improper for him or her to decide to sustain the grounds of referral merely because he or she believed that to do so would be in the interests of the child. Similarly, if, in the course of a proof, the reporter comes to think that there is no case in fact or in law, should not, in the belief that it is in the interests of the child to keep the matter before a hearing, insist upon proceeding with the application.[1] Other examples of decisions and determinations in relation to which the paramountcy principle has no application will be noticed at the appropriate places.

1 Cf *Constanda v M* 1997 SCLR 510 at 512E per Lord President Rodger, rejecting the possibility of holding that uncorroborated evidence as to offences by a child could, without other evidence, be employed to constitute a ground of referral based on the Social Work (Scotland) Act 1968, s 32(2)(b) ('moral danger'): 'To hold otherwise would be to deprive the child of the safeguard which Parliament provided in section 42(6) [of the Social Work (Scotland) Act 1968]. That cannot be allowed, even although the reporter may have acted with the best of intentions and may consider that in seeking to avoid the difficulties posed by section 42(6) she is trying to help the child.'

Consulting the child

2.18   The Children (Scotland) Act 1995, s 16(2) provides that in the circumstances set out in s 16(4) the hearing or sheriff, taking into account the age and maturity of the child, shall so far as practicable (a) give to the child an opportunity to indicate if he wishes to express his views, (b) if he does so wish, to give him an opportunity to express them and, (c) to have regard to such views as may be expressed. Section 16(4) specifies the circumstances in which this principle applies, and includes most of the operative and advisory decisions of hearings and certain specified determinations of sheriffs on child protection matters and determinations of sheriffs where disposing of appeals against decisions of children's hearings.

No non-beneficial order

The statutory provision

2.19   The Children (Scotland) Act 1995, s 16(3) provides, in relation to the various operative decisions of hearings and sheriffs listed in s 16(4)(a)(i) and (ii) and (b), that 'no requirement or order so mentioned shall be made with respect to the child concerned unless the children's hearing consider, or as the case may be the sheriff considers, that it would be better for the child that the requirement or order be made than that none should be made at all'. It should be noted that the wording of this provision excludes from the no non-beneficial order principle: advice by a hearing to a sheriff considering an application under s 60(7) of the Act to set aside or vary a CPO;[1] the drawing up by the hearing under s 73(13) of the Act of a report to court providing advice under s 73(13) of the Act;[2] and decisions of sheriffs upholding an appeal from a decision of a children's hearing other than by substitution for the disposal by the children's hearing of the sheriff's own disposal.[3]

1 Children (Scotland) Act 1995, s 60(10).
2 Reports anent a proposed application for a parental responsibilities order under C(S)A 1995, s 86, and reports anent applications under the Adoption (Scotland) Act 1978, ss 12 and 18.
3 C(S)A 1995, s 51(5)(c)(iii).

Terminology

2.20   This principle has been called 'the minimum intervention principle'.[1] It is submitted that this is not ideal terminology. All the statute provides is that a requirement or order should only be made where 'it would be better for the child that the requirement or order be made than that none should be made at all'.[2] This only means that the tribunal should not intervene unless satisfied that some form of intervention is preferable to none at all: beyond that, the subsection gives no direction. Of course unnecessarily intrusive intervention is undesirable, and indeed this is almost a tautology, but the term 'the minimum intervention principle' carries the overtone 'the less intervention, the better' and this can lead to misunderstandings. The term 'no order principle' is also in current use. This expression is also, it is submitted, not ideal, seeming as it does to carry the overtone, to adapt George Orwell, 'Orders bad: no order good'. It is submitted that 'no non-beneficial order' is the least misleading and most informative way of summarising the principle imported by the Children (Scotland) Act 1995, s 16(3). This matter is more fully discussed later.[3]

1 Norrie *Children (Scotland) Act 1995* (1998) p 48; Norrie *Children's Hearings in Scotland* (1997) p 103.
2 Children (Scotland) Act 1995, s 16(3).
3 At 25.11ff below.

DISCRETION OF THE REPORTER – THE PRACTICALITIES

2.21   Of course the foregoing principles have to be observed by courts and hearings and are not directly incumbent on reporters, but the consideration that these principles will be binding on courts and hearings must be a factor controlling the exercise of the reporter's discretion in considering appropriate courses of action. Having regard to the wide range of offences by the child and of 'care and protection' situations ranging from the most trivial and marginal to the most serious, the exercise of the reporter's discretion is one of the most significant and important within the reporter's province. The careful reporter will carry through his or her inquiries with care and tact, being aware that the knowledge of the mere fact that a child is being investigated may itself affect the situation.

2.22   There may sometimes be pressures (e g from neighbours and/or the media) to bring a child to a hearing even if the grounds are doubtful: but the reporter must be positively satisfied (a) that there is evidence sufficient to support one or more of the conditions of referral and (b) that compulsory measures of supervision are necessary for the individual child under consideration. A reporter should not frame grounds of referral on a speculative basis, perhaps hoping that the grounds will be accepted but having no good reason to believe that they will be able to be proved if not accepted.[1] The reporter's decision to proceed or not is not challengeable in court under the Act, but the decision of the reporter not to take action, even if intimated to the relevant person, does not bar the Crown from prosecuting.[2]

1 Cf the position of the procurator fiscal – *M'Arthur v Stewart* 1955 JC 71, 1955 SLT 434.
2 *Mackinnon v Dempsey* (9 November 1984, unreported) High Court of Justiciary.

Child already subject to supervision requirement

2.23   Where a child is already subject to a supervision requirement and other apparent grounds are drawn to the reporter's attention the reporter must consider whether to state fresh grounds of referral. In some cases it may be thought appropriate to continue to rely on the stated grounds and it has been accepted by the First Division[1] that a hearing may take into account information not contained in the grounds of referral, even where the new information would of itself constitute a fresh ground of referral. In many cases, however, it will be preferable and in accordance with good practice, where a significantly new ground of referral appears to exist, to bring the child to a hearing in relation to the new matter – where this is not done the hearing and continued hearings will require to have the existence of the new 'ground' explained separately and this may lead to a skewing of the discussion of the child's case.[2] Where fresh grounds of referral are stated in respect of a child already under supervision the hearing, before disposing of the case on the basis of the new grounds, must review the earlier requirement in accordance with the Children (Scotland) Act 1995, s 73(9)–(12).[3]

1 In *O v Rae* 1992 SCLR 318, 1993 SLT 570.
2 Cf the discussion of the importance of 'comprehensiveness' in stating grounds of referral, at 16.06ff below.
3 Children (Scotland) Act 1995, s 65(3).

DISCRETION OF REPORTER – THE OPTIONS

2.24 After considering the facts of the case the reporter may take one of four courses: no referral to a hearing; an informal discussion or warning; a reference to the local authority so that it may provide support for the child and the family; and referral to a hearing.

No referral to a hearing

2.25 The reporter may decide that 'a children's hearing does not require to be arranged'.[1] In this event he or she must keep a record of the decision[2] and convey his or her decision to: the child; any relevant person; and the person who has brought the case to his or her notice 'or any of those persons'.[3] The last phrase seems to indicate a discretion as to whether all of the persons listed need to be informed. In practice the reporter will inform all the persons mentioned unless, exceptionally, there should be a special reason making it inappropriate so to do. If the information was received from a local authority or from the police then the local authority and the relevant chief constable must be told.[4]

1 Children (Scotland) Act 1995, s 56(4).
2 Children's Hearings (Scotland) Rules 1996, SI 1996/3261, r 3(2)(a).
3 C(S)A 1995, s 56(4).
4 1996 Rules, r 3(2)(b).

Informal discussion or warning

2.26 Reporters have long regarded it as permissible in appropriate circumstances to meet the child and family to advise and/or warn. There is no provision in the Children (Scotland) Act 1995 or the Children's Hearings (Scotland) Rules 1996 in relation to such procedure but it seems sensible.[1] The practice of making a 'deferred decision' has been criticised.[2] The reporter may also ask the police to warn the child. Disposing of the case by informal discussion or warning is a version of 'No referral to a hearing' and the provisions mentioned at 2.25 above as to recording and notification of persons apply.

1 *Report of the Inquiry into Child Care Policies in Fife* (HC Paper 191 (1992–93)) ('The Fife Report') p 446.
2 The Fife Report p 598.

Reference to local authority

2.27 The reporter, if not minded to refer the child to a hearing, may refer the case to a local authority so that that authority may make arrangements 'for the advice guidance and assistance' of the child and the family under the Children (Scotland) Act 1995, Pt II, Ch 1 (ss 16–38 – 'Support for Children and Their Families').[1] Disposal in this way also attracts the recording and notification provisions mentioned at 2.25 above.

1 Children (Scotland) Act 1995, s 56(4)(b).

Referral to a hearing

2.28   In the event of the reporter's deciding that compulsory measures of supervision are necessary, then a hearing must be arranged.[1] The procedures for initiating a hearing are discussed in subsequent chapters.

1 Children (Scotland) Act 1995, s 56(6).

Consequence of not referring to a hearing

2.29   Where the reporter adopts any course other than referral of the child to a hearing, he or she may not at any other time bring the child to a hearing on the *sole* basis of the information obtained during the initial investigation under the Children (Scotland) Act 1995, s 56.[1] It is thought that the decision of the reporter becomes absolute on intimation to the child or relevant person.[2] It is clear, both from the wording of s 56(5) and from the case law,[3] that if new facts emerge later the reporter will be able to rely on the facts on which no action was taken as part of a new, wider, general pattern.[4] This consideration lends force to the obligation on the reporter to note the decision 'that no further action is required as mentioned in subsection (4) of section 56 of the Act'.[5] It may also be thought to reflect the special character of these proceedings ('civil proceedings *sui generis*'[6]).

1 Children (Scotland) Act 1995, s 56(5).
2 Cf *Thom v HM Advocate* 1976 JC 76.
3 E g *McGregor v D* 1981 SLT (Notes) 97.
4 *Kennedy v S* 1986 SLT 679 at 681J.
5 Children's Hearings (Scotland) Rules 1996, SI 1996/3261, r 3(2)(a).
6 Per Lord President Emslie in *McGregor v D* 1977 SLT 182 at 185.

Referral to reporter of a looked after child placed in secure accommodation

2.30   A local authority may make, in respect of a child looked after by it, an interim placement in secure accommodation.[1] Within 24 hours of doing so the local authority must advise the reporter of the details of the placement.[2] On receipt of such notification the reporter must, within 72 hours, consider which of the foregoing options to choose.[3]

1 Secure Accommodation (Scotland) Regulations 1996, SI 1996/3255, reg 7.
2 SI 1996/3255, reg 7(2)(b).
3 SI 1996/3255, reg 8(1) and (2).

Part II
Entering the system

Introduction of the child into the system: cases not arising under the Child Protection procedures

Notification by 'any person'

3.01 The Children (Scotland) Act 1995, s 53(2)(b) allows any person who has reasonable cause to believe that compulsory measures of supervision *may* be necessary to give to the reporter such information as he has been able to discover. 'Any person' includes a neighbour or relative; it also includes a judge or sheriff.

Referrals arising from police action

3.02 The Children (Scotland) Act 1995, s 53(2)(a) requires a police constable who has reasonable cause to believe that compulsory measures of supervision *may* be necessary to give to the reporter such information as he has been able to discover.

3.03 Under the Police (Scotland) Act 1967, s 17(1) the following duty, amongst others, is placed upon the police:

'(b) Where an offence has been committed (whether within or outwith the police area for which the police force is maintained) to take all lawful measures, and make reports to the appropriate prosecutor, as may be necessary for the purpose of bringing the offender with all due speed to justice.'

The Children (Scotland) Act 1995, s 53(3) obliges a constable who requires to report to the prosecutor under this provision to report also to the reporter. In practice the police, when reporting to the procurator fiscal cases which appear to fall within the Lord Advocate's categories of cases which will generally be prosecuted in the ordinary courts, normally will also send a copy to the reporter. In cases not falling within the Lord Advocate's categories[1] only the reporter is informed.

1 Reproduced at 1.26 above.

3.04 The Criminal Procedure (Scotland) Act 1995, s 43(1) and (2), as amended by the Crime and Punishment (Scotland) Act 1997, s 55, provides that where a person who is apparently a child is apprehended with or without warrant and cannot be brought forthwith before a sheriff then the police may release him on an undertaking to attend at the hearing of the charge on a written and signed undertaking being entered into by him or his parent or guardian.[1] Section 43(3) specifies the circumstances in which such liberation shall not be allowed (ie where the charge is one of homicide or other grave crime, where it is necessary in the interest of the child to remove him from association with a reputed criminal or prostitute, or where the officer has reason to believe that his liberation would defeat the ends of justice). Section 43(4) of the same Act provides for the detention of such a child in a place of safety other than a police station until he can be brought before a sheriff, unless the officer certifies that it is impracticable to do so, that the child is of so unruly a character that he cannot safely be so detained, or that by reason of the child's state of health or of his mental or bodily condition, it is inadvisable so to detain him.

1 The Criminal Procedure (Scotland) Act 1995 has not caught up with the concept of the 'relevant person'.

3.05 The Criminal Procedure (Scotland) Act 1995, s 43(5) provides that where a child has not been liberated the constable shall so inform the reporter. On receiving such notification the reporter proceeds under s 63(1) of the Act which requires him, unless he considers that compulsory measures of supervision are not required, to arrange a hearing which shall begin not later than the third day after the receipt of the notification.[1] If the reporter decides that compulsory measures of supervision are not necessary, then he directs that the child should be released;[2] otherwise the child may be kept at the place of safety until the hearing[3] and it will then be for the hearing to decide whether or not to keep the child in a place of safety under s 66 of the Act.[4] Such a hearing may also, anomalously, direct the reporter to arrange a hearing for the purposes of s 65(1) of the Act.[5]

1 Children (Scotland) Act 1995, s 63(2).
2 C(S)A 1995, s 63(3)
3 C(S)A 1995, s 63(4).
4 C(S)A 1995, s 63(5)(a); for discussion of the powers of a hearing in relation to the detention of a child see ch 21 below.
5 C(S)A 1995, s 63(5)(b).

Notification by local authority

General obligation to investigate and notify

3.06 A local authority which receives information which suggests that a child *may* require compulsory measures of supervision *shall*, after making such further inquiries if any which it may think necessary, convey the information to the reporter.[1] Local authorities, mainly through their social work services and education departments, have an abundance of information in relation to children which, depending on the interpretation placed on such information, could or could not lead to the conclusion that compulsory measures of supervision may be necessary. Social work departments should try to approach the question in a way which gives appropriate weight to the statute's use of the terms 'may' and 'shall'. It has been said, in relation to the parallel provisions of the Social Work (Scotland) Act 1968:

'We think the proper question to ask is whether a good reasoned case could be made for compulsory measures of care and that therefore the position can well arise when a [social] worker may be personally unconvinced that compulsory measures are appropriate but still be under obligation to send the information to the Reporter, together of course, with his views on the matter, but leaving the decision to the Reporter as to whether or not to place the matter before a hearing'.[2]

1 Children (Scotland) Act 1995, s 53(1).
2 Fife Report (1992) p 459.

Education cases

3.07　The Children (Scotland) Act 1995, s 52(2)(h) enacts 'has failed to attend school regularly without reasonable excuse'[1] as a condition which, if satisfied, may justify the inference that compulsory measures of supervision are necessary. The meaning of this ground of referral is considered later.[2]

1 Discussed more fully at 46.19 below.
2 At 46.19 and 46.20 below.

Other sources

3.08　Children apparently in need of compulsory measures of supervision but who have not been made the subject of the statutory Child Protection procedures[1] may come to the notice of the reporter by report from a variety of sources such as the area health board, the doctor, the police, voluntary bodies, concerned relatives and neighbours, and the like.

1 Discussed in ch 4 below.

Children accommodated by local authority or for whom local authority is responsible

3.09　A local authority is bound to provide accommodation for any child within its area who appears to require such accommodation by reason of there being no one who has parental responsibility for the child, that he or she is lost or abandoned or that the carer of the child has for the time being ceased to provide such accommodation or care.[1] A local authority may also have parental responsibility for a child by having been granted this by order of the sheriff on an application by it.[2] Such a child is not, of course, per se in need of compulsory measures of supervision. If, however, it appears to the local authority that the child's behaviour is such that special measures are necessary for his adequate supervision in his interest or the interest of others, then the local authority may report the child's case to the reporter for consideration under the Children (Scotland) Act 1995, s 52(2)(l).[3]

1 Children (Scotland) Act 1995, s 25.
2 C(S)A 1995, s 86.
3 Discussed at 46.24 ff below.

3.10　As already noticed,[1] a local authority may make, in respect of a child looked after by it, an interim placement in secure accommodation.[2]

Within 24 hours of doing so the local authority must advise the reporter of the details of the placement.[3] On receipt of such notification the reporter must, within 72 hours, consider which course of action to adopt.[4]

1 At 2.30 above.
2 Secure Accommodation (Scotland) Regulations 1996, SI 1996/3255, reg 7.
3 SI 1996/3255, reg 7(2)(b).
4 SI 1996/3255, reg 8(1) and (2).

Ultimate decision as to referral is for reporter

3.11   Reports from local authorities are a substantial source of referrals to reporters. Even where satisfied that there is evidence of a condition of referral the reporter, of course, retains discretion as to whether or not to refer the child to a hearing.

Referral by a criminal court in respect of offences against children

3.12   The Criminal Procedure (Scotland) Act 1995, s 48 provides that a court before whom a person is convicted of certain specified offences may refer a child against whom specified offences have been committed to the reporter and may certify that the offence shall be a ground established for the purposes of the Children (Scotland) Act 1995, Pt II, Ch 3. The Criminal Procedure (Scotland) Act 1995, s 48 also provides that the court may refer to the reporter any child who is, or is likely to become, a member of the same household as the person who has committed certain specified offences. The section also provides for the referral to the reporter of a child who is or is likely to become a member of the same household as the child who was the victim of the offence concerned.

3.13   The offences for this purpose are: offences under The Children and Young Persons (Scotland) Act 1937, s 21 [being a person who 'habitually wanders from place to place' and takes with him any child of school age and does not attend to the child's education properly] and offences mentioned in the Criminal Procedure (Scotland) Act 1995, Sch 1 [a wide range of offences including sexual offences and assault]. The offences specified for the latter purpose are offences mentioned in the said Sch 1 and 'any offence in respect of a person aged 17 years or over which constitutes the crime of incest'.

No prescribed procedure

3.14   No procedure has been enacted whereby the court may be formally moved to make a reference to the reporter in terms of the said Criminal Procedure (Scotland) Act 1995, s 48 and the matter is often left for the judge or sheriff to decide on his or her own initiative. There is no reason why the reporter should not, as is sometimes done, write to the procurator fiscal, suggesting that the court might be asked to consider the possibility of a remit.

3.15 On such a referral to the reporter being made by a court, the reporter still retains a discretion to refer or not to refer the child to a hearing. If the reporter does so decide it would seem clear that the child or relevant person could not dispute the ground of referral on its facts, but presumably a challenge could be made on the basis that the remit had not been made or the certificate not granted or that the child referred to the hearing by the reporter was not the child named in the certificate.

Referral (principally by civil court) in respect of apparent grounds of referral

3.16 The Children (Scotland) Act 1995, s 54 deals mainly with referrals by civil courts and introduces a parallel power in the civil courts to the power, discussed above, which the criminal courts have enjoyed from the beginning. Where it appears to a court in the course of the 'relevant proceedings' that any condition of referral other than under the Children (Scotland) Act 1995, s 52(2)(i) (the commission of an offence by the child) is satisfied in respect of 'a child' the said court *may* refer the matter to the reporter, specifying the condition.[1] The 'relevant proceedings' are:

'(a) an action for divorce or judicial separation or for declarator of marriage, nullity of marriage, parentage or non-parentage;
(b) proceedings relating to parental responsibilities or parental rights within the meaning of Part I of this Act;
(c) proceedings for an adoption order under the Adoption (Scotland) Act 1978 or for an order under section 18 of that Act declaring a child free for adoption; and
(d) proceedings for an offence against section 35 (failure by parent to secure regular attendance by his child at a public school, 41 (failure to comply with an attendance order) or 42(3) (failure to permit examination of child) of the Education (Scotland) Act 1980.'[2]

1 Children (Scotland) Act 1995, s 54(1).
2 C(S)A 1995, s 54(2).

3.17 On receiving such a referral the reporter shall make such investigations as he or she thinks appropriate[1] and then, if the reporter considers that compulsory measures of supervision *are* necessary, he or she must arrange a hearing to consider the case under the Children (Scotland) Act 1995, s 69 at which hearing the condition specified by the court will count as a ground established at a proof before the sheriff under s 68 of the Act.[2]

1 Children (Scotland) Act 1995, s 54(3)(a).
2 C(S)A 1995, s 54(3)(b).

Factors affecting the court's decision on whether to remit with certification

3.18 The decision of the court to refer a child under this section is one to which the welfare principle applies, but not the no non-beneficial order principle or the principle of consulting the views of the child. The child referred may be any child about whom the court has heard evidence, and not only the child principally concerned in the relevant proceedings. The court should remember that a child may become subject to a condition of referral where he or she is or is likely to become a member of the same household as a Schedule 1 offender or of a victim of a Schedule 1 offender or a victim of certain sex offences.[1]

1 Children (Scotland) Act 1995, s 52(2)(e), (f) and (g).

Desirability of caution by court considering remit

3.19   In view of the consideration that the principal issue before the court in the relevant proceedings will generally be matters other than matters directly relevant to proving or not the existence of one of the relevant conditions under the Children (Scotland) Act 1995, s 52(2) it is submitted that judges and sheriffs should be very cautious indeed in referring children under this section. Moreover: a child would not generally be separately represented in the course of the relevant proceedings (although such a child might have a curator *ad litem* or safeguarder to safeguard his or her interests) and it may therefore be doubted whether the child's case dealt with in this way would be regarded as having been decided by an independent tribunal before which the child had been represented, thus involving potential conflict with the European Convention, art 6 and the UN Convention on the Rights of the Child, art 9(2). As noted already[1] it is competent for a judge or sheriff, as a 'person' under s 53(2)(b) of the Act, to refer a child to the reporter for investigation, and it is submitted that this will frequently be the preferable course.

1 At 3.01 above.

Remit by criminal court to a hearing for disposal

Child subject to a supervision requirement

3.20   Where a child already subject to a supervision requirement pleads guilty to or is found guilty of a criminal offence other than an offence for which the sentence is fixed by law the High Court *may* and the sheriff or district court *shall*, before disposing of the case, request that the reporter arrange a children's hearing for the purpose of obtaining their advice as to the treatment of the child.[1] The reporter is then bound to arrange a hearing to consider the case and give advice to the court. On receiving the hearing's advice the court may then dispose of the case or remit it to the reporter to fix a hearing to dispose of the case.[2] It is for the court, at its own hand if necessary, to take note that an accused person appears to be a child and to make 'due enquiry' as to his age, although any order or judgment of the court shall not be invalidated by any subsequent proof that the age was incorrectly stated.[3] It is prudent for the court, when considering the disposal of a person who may be a child for this purpose, ie a person under 16 or[4] a person under 18 and subject to a supervision requirement, to ask whether or not a supervision requirement is in force in respect of that person.

1 Criminal Procedure (Scotland) Act 1995, s 49(3) as amended by the Crime and Disorder Act 1998, Sch 8, para 118.
2 CP(S)A 1995, s 49(3).
3 CP(S)A 1995, s 46(1) and (5).
4 In terms of the Children (Scotland) Act 1995, s 93(2)(b).

Position if court omits to make 'due enquiry'

3.21 It would appear clear that if the court, on making its 'due enquiry', is not given the correct information, then the sentence stands.[1] It is, however, less clear what the position would be in the event of the sheriff proceeding to sentence a child under supervision without a hearing's advice because he or she had either omitted to carry out the inquisitorial duty under the Criminal Procedure (Scotland) Act 1995, s 46(1) or had, through oversight or otherwise, omitted to call for the hearing's advice. It is thought that such an irregularity would be treated by the Justiciary Appeal Court as an irregularity entitling the Appeal Court to direct that the advice of the children's hearing be obtained but would not be regarded as constituting a fundamental nullity.[2]

1 Criminal Procedure (Scotland) Act 1995, s 46(5).
2 Cf *Auld v Herron* 1969 JC 4.

Position if advice not provided

3.22 It happens from time to time that, for one reason or another, the advice sought by the court is not forthcoming even although that advice may have been called for by the court in obedience to the statutory duty incumbent upon it under the Criminal Procedure (Scotland) Act 1995, s 49(3). It may be, for example, that a child has not attended the hearing arranged under the Children's Hearings (Scotland) Rules 1996, rule 22(1) and that the hearing has not seen fit to deal with the matter in the absence of the child under rule 22(2). Since the court is enjoined not merely to request but also to give 'consideration' to the advice, and since there is no provision for dispensing with such advice because of impracticability of obtaining it, there would seem to be no alternative but for the court to renew its request for the advice of the hearing and, if necessary, to use its powers to commit the child to a 'place of safety chosen by the local authority' or, if the child is over 14 and if the court 'certifies that he is of so unruly a character that he cannot safely be so committed or that he is so depraved a character that he is not a fit person to be so detained', to commit him to a remand centre or, if no remand centre is available, to prison.[1] In the latter event the child would be brought to the hearing under escort.

1 Criminal Procedure (Scotland) Act 1995, s 51(1)(b) and s 51(1)(aa) – inserted by the Crime and Punishment (Scotland) Act 1997, s 56(2).

Child not subject to a supervision requirement

3.23 Where a child[1] who is not subject to a supervision requirement pleads guilty to or is found guilty of an offence other than an offence for which the sentence is fixed by law[2] the court may, instead of making an order, remit the child directly to the reporter to arrange a hearing for the disposal of the case.[3] Alternatively the court may request that the reporter fix an advice hearing and, on considering the advice, either dispose of the case or remit to a hearing for disposal.[4]

1 Criminal Procedure (Scotland) Act 1995, s 307(1) and Children (Scotland) Act 1995, s 93(2)(b).
2 For further discussion see 3.25 below.

3 CP(S)A 1995, s 49(1)(a).
4 CP(S)A 1995, s 49(1)(b) and (2).

Child aged 16 to 17 and a half not subject to a supervision requirement

3.24   Where a person between 16 and 17 and a half who is not subject to a supervision requirement pleads guilty to or is found guilty of an offence under summary jurisdiction procedure, the court may direct the reporter to arrange an advice hearing and, on considering the advice, either dispose of the case or, *if the hearing have so advised*, remit to the hearing for disposal.[1]

1 Criminal Procedure (Scotland) Act 1995, s 49(6) and (7).

'Sentence which is fixed by law'

3.25   None of the provisions permitting a remit to a hearing for disposal affect an offence 'the sentence of which is fixed by law'.[1] Many road traffic offences in which children become involved attract minimum statutory sentences unless special reasons can be shown – for example, contravention of the Road Traffic Act 1988, s 2 carries a minimum period of disqualification for one year, and thereafter till the driving test has been successfully attempted. Children aged 15 and over who are alleged to have committed an offence punishable by disqualification from driving are, in terms of the Lord Advocate's Directions as to the Prosecution of Children, to be reported to the procurator fiscal with a view to prosecution and such prosecutions are reasonably common. While children who are so prosecuted will frequently be sentenced by the sheriff, it is tentatively submitted that the said provisions of the Road Traffic Act do not constitute sentences fixed by law and that it is competent for the sheriff to remit such a child who has committed such an offence to a hearing for disposal. This has been done on some occasions without appeal by the Crown.

1 Criminal Procedure (Scotland) Act 1995, s 49(5).

Jurisdiction of hearing following remit

3.26   Once remitted to the hearing for disposal, the jurisdiction of the court ceases and the child's case stands referred to a hearing.[1]

1 Criminal Procedure (Scotland) Act 1995, s 49(4).

Appearances before hearings as part of child's 'record'

3.27   A person found guilty of an offence in any criminal court may expect a list of his previous criminal convictions to be laid before the court. Such a history constitutes one of the sources of essential information for a sensible disposal of the case. Appearances before children's hearings, even when the offences committed have been grave and the disposal by the hearing radical, are not 'convictions' (although an accepted or proved ground of referral under the Children (Scotland) Act 1995, s 52(2)(i) acquires a rehabilitation period under the Rehabilitation of Offenders Act 1974, s 5(5)(f)) and therefore should not appear on any notice of convictions.[1] If, of course, the court calls for a social inquiry report the child's history will be covered, usually in some detail. The difficulty is that in the absence of knowledge of such appearances the court may not think to call for a social inquiry report and, short of calling for such reports in all cases involving persons under 18 (a course of action which would place further strains on already fully stretched social work departments), the court may resort to the unsatisfactory expedient of simply asking if there have been any appearances before hearings.

1 Although the writer has seen some notices of previous convictions listing disposals by hearings.

CHAPTER 4

Introduction of the child into the system by emergency orders

Introductory

Emergency orders and who may apply for them

4.01 The Children (Scotland) Act 1995, largely as a consequence of recommendations of Lord Clyde in the Orkney Report, introduced measures, principally Child Protection Orders (CPOs), Child Assessment Orders (CAOs) and Exclusion Orders (EOs), including Interim EOs – all of which only sheriffs are empowered to make – aimed at securing the protection of children in situations of emergency in such a way as to cause the least practicable disturbance to the children's lives and due regard for their rights so far as consistent with their best interests. The competence to apply for such orders is not conferred specifically on the children's reporter although, as we shall see, as 'any person' the reporter is entitled so to apply. Reporters are of course aware of their powers in this regard but are circumspect in using these powers. The local authority is the public agency specifically vested with the right to apply for such orders and in practice nearly all the orders applied for have been applied for at the instance of the local authority either as local authority or as 'any person'. The local authority is well placed to apply for emergency orders by virtue of its access to resources such as children's homes and foster homes. On at least one occasion a curator *ad litem* has applied for a CPO. The statutory forms of application for Child Protection Orders, Child Assessment Orders and Exclusion Orders require intimation on the reporter who may, on receiving intimation, enter into the case by the appropriate statutory procedures. An Emergency Protection Order (EPO) may be granted by a justice of the peace under s 61 of the Act on the application of any person or a local authority where it is not practicable for an application to be made to the sheriff or not practicable for the sheriff to consider the application.

Who may grant the CPO, EO and CAO

4.02 'Sheriff' is not defined in the Children (Scotland) Act 1995 and accordingly has the meaning ascribed by the general legislation governing the sheriff court, ie a resident sheriff acting within any part of the sheriffdom for which he or she is appointed;[1] and an honorary sheriff.[2] In practice an honorary sheriff should not be employed to consider such applications unless he or she is also a full-time or retired sheriff or judge or possibly, in an emergency, where he or she, although not a full-time or retired sheriff or judge, is a solicitor or an advocate. 'Floating' sheriffs have full jurisdiction in such courts as they are entitled to sit by virtue of their commissions and as directed by the Scottish Ministers acting through the Justice Department of the Scottish Executive when a resident sheriff is ill or otherwise unable to perform his or her duties, or where a vacancy occurs or when for any reason it appears expedient to do so.[3] Part-time sheriffs enjoy a similar jurisdiction.[4] In general, sheriffs principal do not exercise jurisdiction to grant emergency orders under the Act but since there is no possibility of an appeal in relation to a decision of a sheriff in relation to the granting of a CPO[5] there would seem to be no reason in principle why a sheriff principal should not be entitled to consider an application for a CPO.

1 Sheriff Courts (Scotland) Act 1971, s 7.
2 SC(S)A 1971, s 17.
3 SC(S)A 1971, s 10(2), Scotland Act 1998, s 53(2)(c).
4 Bail, Judicial Appointments etc (Scotland) Act 2000, ss 5 and 6.
5 Children (Scotland) Act 1995, s 51(15)(a).

Procedure generally – 'civil' character of these proceedings

4.03 The Act of Sederunt (Child Care and Maintenance Rules) 1997, Pt II sets out inter alia the procedural rules governing the application for and processing of applications for the foregoing emergency orders. Many of the rules apply to all three orders but some do not apply at certain stages of certain orders. The general rules will be given here, with the exceptions indicated. The application of these rules to individual processes will be noted and incorporated by reference at the appropriate places. Such applications are not, of course, proceedings under the Children (Scotland) Act 1995, s 68 and therefore the ruling by Lord President Emslie in *McGregor v D*,[1] to the effect that proceedings under the Social Work (Scotland) Act 1968, s 42 (the parallel section to s 68 of the 1995 Act) are 'civil proceedings *sui generis*', has no direct application. It is submitted, however, that the reasoning of Lord President Emslie[2] may be applied with equal validity to the child protection code constituted by the provisions for the various emergency protection measures in the 1995 Act and that therefore the sheriff court proceedings relative to these measures should also be regarded as civil. It will be submitted[3] that in these proceedings the civil standard of proof applies where evidence is led, even when an offence by a person against a child is in issue.

1 1977 SC 330, 1977 SLT 182 at 185.
2 'Looking first at the provisions of the Act which are intended to secure the well-being of children in need of care'.
3 At 42.10 below.

The appointment of a safeguarder or curator ad litem

Summary of provisions affecting safeguarders

4.04 The statutory provisions governing the appointment and function of safeguarders are discussed later,[1] but a summary may be helpful here. When considering any proceedings under the Children (Scotland)

Act 1995, Pt II, Chs 2 or 3 (ss 39–93 inclusive), except an application for a Child Protection Order,[2] the sheriff is bound to consider if a safeguarder should be appointed.[3] It has long been competent for *courts* to appoint curators *ad litem* to represent the interests of children who are parties to cases. In the practice of hearings law the court has frequently exercised its right to appoint curators *ad litem* for children and this practice has now received recognition in the rules.[4] Safeguarders are entitled to a comparatively small fee and their expenses are borne by the local authority.[5] Sheriffs sometimes appoint solicitors as curators *ad litem* in preference to appointing safeguarders because of the limited remuneration payable to solicitor-safeguarders, who are not regarded as eligible for legal aid, as opposed to solicitor-curators, who are so regarded.[6] A sheriff may, in an exceptional case, wish to appoint a particular person as safeguarder or curator, subject to availability and practicality. The sheriff clerk may be able to advise on availability and practicability and may also try to achieve an approximate even-handedness in the distribution of work amongst practitioners so interested. The provisions and practices anent safeguarders in the context of the children's hearing itself, and in the proceedings before the sheriff under ss 68 and 51 of the Act, will be examined at their appropriate places.[7] A safeguarder may appear personally in the proceedings or instruct a lawyer.[8] Where the safeguarder is an advocate or solicitor he or she shall not act as advocate or solicitor for the child – who may have instructed his or her own legal representation. The safeguarder represents the interests of the child, whereas the legal representative of the child acts on the child's instructions.[9] A safeguarder who intimates that he or she does not intend to become a party to the proceedings shall report to the sheriff on the extent of his or her inquiries and as to his or her conclusions as to the interests of the child in the proceedings.[10] Such a safeguarder is entitled to notification of subsequent interlocutors and may seek leave to become a party to the proceedings later on.[11]

1 At 17.02 ff below.
2 Children (Scotland) Act 1995, s 41(2).
3 C(S)A 1995, s 41(1).
4 SI 1997/291 r 3.5(2)(c).
5 C(S)A 1995, s 41(4) – see further discussion at 17.06 and 17.07 below.
6 Cf the Legal Aid (Scotland) Act 1986, s 29(1), as substituted by Children (Scotland) Act 1995, s 92.
7 Ch 17 below (hearing procedures), ch 34 below (s 68 procedures) and ch 51 below (appeal procedures).
8 SI 1997/291, r 3.9.
9 For further discussion of representation of children see 22.14 and ch 31 below.
10 SI 1997/291, r 3.10(1).
11 SI 1997/291, r 3.10(2) and (3).

Appointment of curator ad litem

4.05 Where a sheriff has appointed a curator *ad litem* the formal terms of the 1997 rules, r 3.8 clearly do not attach but in practice the person so appointed will generally be given the appropriate papers by the reporter and will operate in the same way as the safeguarder would.

The views of the child

Orders in relation to which the child should be consulted

4.06   The sheriff must have regard to the principle of *consulting the child* when considering whether to make, vary or discharge a CAO or an EO, and when considering whether to vary or discharge a CPO.[1] This requirement does not obtain when an application to *make* a CPO[2] is being considered. In order to give effect to this requirement where it applies provision is made for service of the relevant application or first order on the child and the child may give his or her views by attending the hearing or otherwise.[3] The procedures for the child to convey his or her views are noted later.[4]

1 Children (Scotland) Act 1995, s 16(2) and (4).
2 Or an EPO under C(S)A 1995, s 61(1) or (2).
3 SI 1997/291, r 3.4(a), (b) and (c).
4 At 4.10 below.

Dispensing with service on child

4.07   Where the sheriff is satisfied, taking account of the age and maturity of the child, that it would be inappropriate to order service on the child, the sheriff may dispense with service on the child; and when thus satisfied that it would be inappropriate for the child to attend, the sheriff may dispense with the attendance of the child at the hearing of the application.[1] *The sheriff may, on the motion of the applicant or of his or her own motion order that a specified part of the application is not served on the child.* If the applicant wishes the sheriff so to dispense he or she should indicate accordingly at the appropriate part of the relevant application form and state reasons. If the sheriff does not so dispense then the child will receive one of Forms 26–29 inclusive, depending on which application is being sought. A child aged 12 years or more shall be presumed to be of sufficient age and maturity to express a view.[2] This in practice means that very good reason will have to be shown for dispensing with service on a child aged 12 or over. It does not mean that there is a presumption that children aged 11 or less are not of sufficient maturity: the sheriff must judge the matter on its merits on the information available and may request the applicant to address him or her on the matter.

1 SI 1997/291, r 3.3.
2 Children (Scotland) Act 1995, s 16(2).

Forms 26–29

4.08   These forms, in so far as they seek the views of the child, are substantially identical. Each gives the child the choice of writing to the court with his or her views or coming to court, with or without an adviser, who may be a lawyer, and telling the sheriff his or her views directly. Once the child has 'indicated' his wish to express his views the sheriff 'may order such steps to be taken as he considers appropriate to ascertain the views of the child'.[1] It is thought that such indication may be by any mode. If, for example, a social worker making an application has obtained an indication from the child that the child wishes to express a view and reported this to the sheriff then the child must be given an opportunity of expressing it. In the event that the child has told the social worker the content of his or her views it is submitted that the sheriff should be slow to regard this as constituting an opportunity to express them: it is thought that in such a situation the sending to the child of the appropriate form would not be dispensed with.

1 SI 1997/291, r 3.5(1)(a).

The first order

4.09   In an application for a CAO,[1] an application to vary or set aside a CPO,[2] an application for an Exclusion Order,[3] and an application to vary or recall an EO,[4] the sheriff clerk must immediately fix a hearing of the application and issue a *first order* in the style of Form 32.[5] In the case of an application for a CPO the sheriff, on receiving the application, proceeds immediately to hear and consider it and if it is granted the applicant has to effect service on the persons named in the application, including the child, unless service on the child has been dispensed with in terms of the Rules 1997, r 3.3. The 'first order' in relation to a CPO is accordingly this order for service.[6] For further discussion see 5.09 below. In the case of an application for an Interim EO[7] the hearing before the sheriff is immediate and if granted the application is served on the child or not, as the sheriff thinks fit.[8] It is competent to apply to the sheriff for authorisation to serve orally.[9] Where such an application has been granted the first order will include this authorisation.

1 Children (Scotland) Act 1995, s 55.
2 C(S)A 1995, s 60.
3 C(S)A 1995, s 76.
4 C(S)A 1995, s 79.
5 Reproduced in Appendix 5.
6 C(S)A 1995, s 57(5); SI 1997/291, r 3.30 and Forms 47 and 48.
7 C(S)A 1995, s 76(4).
8 SI 1997/291, rr 3.37(c), 3.36 and 3.12(c).
9 See 7.11 ff below.

Obtaining the child's views

Modes of obtaining the views of the child

4.10   Where the child has indicated a wish to express views the sheriff may order such steps as he or she considers appropriate to obtain the child's views.[1] The sheriff has a wide discretion as to how to take the views of the child.[2] The rules specify, without prejudice to this discretion, four possible methods:[3]

> '(a) by the child orally or in writing;
> (b) by an advocate or solicitor acting on behalf of the child;
> (c) by any safeguarder or curator ad litem appointed by the court; or
> (d) by any person (either orally or in writing), provided the sheriff is satis-fied that that person is a suitable representative and is duly authorised to represent the child.'

1 SI 1997/291, r 3.5(1)(a).
2 SI 1997/291, r 3.5(2).
3 SI 1997/291, r 3.5(2)(a)–(d).

Sheriffs hearing from children directly

4.11   There are and have long been differing views amongst judges and sheriffs as to how ready judges and sheriffs should be to see and speak to children in person.[1] In *Macdonald v Macdonald*[2] the Lord Ordinary decided a case relating to the 'custody' of a child on the basis of his interview with the child, in substitution for proof, and was reversed and criticised in the Inner House. Thereafter, between 1985 and the coming into force of Children (Scotland) Act 1995, in 1997, judges and sheriffs have been particularly cautious. The 1995 Act may be thought to point the sheriff towards listening to children directly. The consideration that the sheriff and the sheriff alone is statutorily entitled, if he or she chooses to do so, to keep the child's views secret,[3] may support this view. But receiving and recording confidences from a child may pose formidable problems.[4] Sheriffs and judges are well aware of the limitations of 'interviews' with children and are conscious of the possibility of the child having been prompted and also of the constraints inseparable from the artificial atmosphere of an interview 'in chambers', however child-friendly the sheriff may try to make his or her room. It is suggested that the sheriff should take such advice as he or she can – for example from social workers or psychologists who have knowledge of the child – as to the advisability of seeing the child. If a safeguarder or curator *ad litem* has been appointed and is available it is suggested that it will often be advantageous for him or her to be present. In all cases it is suggested that the sheriff clerk be present. When seeing a girl, the writer always tries to have a female sheriff clerk present.

1 See the authorities cited in Wilkinson and Norrie, *Parent and Child* (1993) p 255, n 46.
2 1985 SLT 245.
3 SI 1997/291, r 3.5(4).
4 See 4.13 below.

The record of the views of the child

'Confidential' views of the child

4.12   Where the child has given his or her views orally to the sheriff the sheriff shall record those views in writing.[1] The sheriff *may* direct that *any* written views given by a child *or any written record* of the child's views shall be kept in a separate confidential envelope and available to the sheriff only.[2] Accordingly, if the views of the child have come to the notice of the sheriff by way of a report from a safeguarder[3] then these provisions apply. There is no obligation on the sheriff to reveal that confidential views have been given.

1 SI 1997/291, r 3.5(3).
2 SI 1997/291, r 3.5(4).
3 See 34.17 below.

Problems for the law of evidence

4.13 The exercise of the foregoing power must create serious problems for the law of evidence: if such views were to form a material part of the sheriff's decision then, in a question with a person who had not had notice of them, it could be argued that this was a breach of the 'fair notice' aspect of the principles of natural justice[1] and of the European Convention art 6(1).[2] An awareness of these difficulties may cause sheriffs to be cautious in the exercise of this power. *Quaere*, however, if the discretion thus vested in the sheriff by statutory instrument may not place the sheriff under some obligation to advise a child of the existence of such discretion and to ask the child if there is anything important the child wishes to impart which is not to be passed on. The UN Convention on the Rights of the Child, art 12 provides:

> '1. States Parties shall assure to the child who is capable of forming his or her own view the right to express those views *freely* [emphasis supplied] in all matters affecting the child, the views of the child being given due weight in accordance with the age and maturity of the child.
> 2. For this purpose, the child shall in particular be provided the opportunity to be heard in any judicial and administrative proceedings affecting the child, either directly, or through a representative or an appropriate body, in a manner consistent with the procedural rules of national law.'

How, it may be asked, can a child express his or her views *freely* if he or she knows that these views will in ten minutes be passed on to an abusing carer?

1 But see *Kennedy v A* 1986 SLT 358 per L J-Clerk Ross: 'The principles of natural justice must yield to the interests of the child', quoted with approval by Lord President Hope in *O v Rae* 1992 SCLR 318, 1993 SLT 570.
2 Cf *McMichael v UK* (1995) 20 EHRR 205.

Practical problems

4.14 In practice the keeping of information completely confidential may be easier said than done. If the sheriff is in his or her decision visibly influenced by what the child has told him or her in secret it may not be too difficult for a third party to work out what the child has told the sheriff. It is suggested that the sheriff, if telling the child of the power to hear 'confidential' views, should consider advising the child of this difficulty (which may well come as no surprise to the child). Formidable practical difficulties may also be presented to the sheriff, for example in the event of the child telling the sheriff in confidence that a person has a transmissible disease.

Interpretation of the confidentiality provisions

4.15 There has as yet been no reported decision of the Court of Session interpreting these provisions. However, the issue has arisen in two cases, in the sheriff court. In *Dosoo v Dosoo*[1] Sheriff Daphne Robertson had to consider an action of divorce in which interim contact with the three children of the marriage had been reduced to nil. A report had been commissioned and one of the parties applied to the court to allow the contents of the report to be disclosed in terms of the relevant rule of court, which gives the sheriff a discretion to authorise such disclosure. The solicitor instructed by the children opposed the motion, saying that they had both 'specifically asked that their views be held as confidential as they feared repercussions should these be disclosed to the defender'. The court reporter had noted the children as expressing 'palpable fear'. The cases of *In re D*[2] and *McMichael v United Kingdom*[3] were cited to the sheriff who distinguished them and observed that both had been decided before the enactment of the Children (Scotland) Act 1995 and that she had regard to the UN Convention on the Rights of the Child, art 12, as embodied in the new rules.[4] She accordingly decided not to follow *In re D* or *McMichael* and refused the application, stating: 'I agree that for a child to be able to express his views "freely" he must be able to feel confident in privacy if he so wishes and the Court should respect that privacy except in very compelling circumstances.'

1 1999 SCLR (Notes) 905.
2 [1996] AC 593.
3 1995 (29) EHRR 205.
4 Ordinary Cause Rules, r 33.20.

4.16   In *McGrath v McGrath*[1] Sheriff Principal Edward F Bowen QC, Sheriff Principal of Glasgow and Strathkelvin, had to deal with an appeal from a sheriff who had had to consider a motion to vary the amount of contact to be enjoyed by a parent after a divorce action. The child had told her curator *ad litem* that 'she was scared about her parents finding out what she said, and that both parents had told her that whatever she said would remain a secret'. The curator *ad litem* had reported this to the sheriff who, on the basis of what the child had said, refused the motion to vary contact. The sheriff stated: 'Although I have jurisprudential reservations about a system which permits the non-disclosure of information which is material, I decided to take into account what I was told, but not to reveal it. The present system is meant to focus on children's rights. The child had a right not to be treated like a ping-pong ball, and to have her confidences respected.' The parent who had applied for the variation of contact appealed to the sheriff principal.

1 1999 SCLR (Notes) 1121.

4.17   In the appeal, the cases of *In re D*, *McMichael* and *Dosoo* were cited to the Sheriff Principal, and his attention was directed to the terms of the Ordinary Cause Rules, r 33.20. The sheriff principal allowed the appeal, recalled the interlocutor of the sheriff, and remitted the case for reconsideration. The sheriff principal stated, in essence, two reasons. In the first place he noted that the provisions of r 33.20 had not been observed, in that the views had not been given to the sheriff directly but through the agency of the curator *ad litem*, and, perhaps more significantly, had not been recorded, as r 33.20 required. The sheriff principal commented: 'The situation is that the views of the child remain a secret shared only amongst the Sheriff, the curator and the child. An appeal court is deprived of any opportunity of considering whether the discretion to withhold disclosure of the views was exercised properly.' In the second place the sheriff principal took the view that the Children (Scotland) Act 1995 did not itself introduce any concept of a right to confidentiality but he acknowledged that the requirement to allow the child to give his or her views 'freely' might have this implication. On this point the sheriff principal stated:

'The Sheriff in [*Dosoo*] and the Sheriff in the present case were in my view correct when they recognised that views can often be expressed "freely" only where confidentiality can be assured. The practicalities involved in reconciling the right to a fair hearing and a child's right to express his views are thus of immense difficulty. They can best be resolved in my view by having regard to the principles set out by Lord Mustill [in *In re D*] which involved taking the fundamental principle that a party is entitled to disclosure of all materials as a starting point and next considering whether disclosure of the material would involve a real possibility of significant harm to the child.'

In his commentary on this decision Sheriff Kelbie states:[1]

'I have reluctantly come to the view, perhaps more strongly than the Sheriff Principal in the present case, that it is not possible to give any assurance of confidentiality to a child who wishes to express a view, since it is destructive of the basic requirements of a fair hearing to base one's decision on material which is unknown to the parties and to which they have no opportunity to respond and which they have no opportunity to challenge. To that extent, the requirements of the European Convention must prevail over those of the U.N. Convention. But I look forward to being persuaded that there is some other solution to this conundrum.'

In an attempt to persuade Sheriff Kelbie, the writer would suggest that no one principle is absolute and that where a judge or sheriff is satisfied that there is a 'real possibility' of 'significant harm' to the child by revealing his or her views to a potentially abusing carer, then the law should not compel such a revelation. It has been said that the safety of the people is the supreme law. It is said that the state is '*parens patriae*'. Should not the state look after the safety of its children?

1 1999 SCLR 1126.

4.18   The difference of approach between the sheriff in *Dosoo v Dosoo* and the sheriff principal in *McGrath v McGrath*[1] would appear to be that Sheriff Robertson decided in effect that there should not be disclosure 'except in very compelling circumstances', whereas Sheriff Principal Bowen decided in effect that the presumption was in favour of disclosure except where disclosure 'would involve a real possibility of significant harm to the child'. It is tentatively submitted that the more cautious approach adopted by Sheriff Principal Bowen may be more consistent both with our responsibilities under the European Convention and with the principles of natural justice. It is, however, perhaps worth remarking that Sheriff Robertson – standing the court reporter's reference to 'palpable fear' on the part of the children – might well, even if she had adopted the test proposed by Sheriff Bowen, have concluded that there should be non-disclosure. In practice it may turn out that there will be few instances of sheriffs and judges deciding to reveal the views of the child where there is, in the opinion of the judge or sheriff concerned, a real possibility of significant harm to the child. It seems likely that sooner or later the matter will be tested under reference to the European Convention on Human Rights.

1 See 4.16.

CHAPTER 5

The Application for a Child Protection Order – Children (Scotland) Act 1995, s 57

Persons who may apply for a Child Protection Order ('CPO')

5.01   The sheriff 'may' make a CPO on the application of 'any person'[1] or 'a local authority',[2] provided that the sheriff is satisfied as to the relevant statutory criteria. In the case of an application at the instance of any person the sheriff has to be satisfied as follows (emphases supplied):

> '(a) that there are reasonable grounds to *believe* that a child—
>> (i) is being so treated (or neglected) that he is suffering *significant harm*; or
>> (ii) will suffer such harm if he is not removed to and kept in a place of safety, or if he does not remain in the place where he is then being accommodated (whether or not he is resident there); and
> (b) that an order under this section is *necessary* to protect that child from such harm (or such other harm)'.[3]

In the case of an application at the instance of a local authority the sheriff 'may' make a CPO if satisfied as follows (emphases supplied):

> '(a) that they have reasonable grounds to *suspect* that a child is being or will be so treated (or neglected) that he is suffering or will suffer *significant harm*;
> (b) that they are making or causing to be made enquiries to allow them to decide whether they should take any action to safeguard the welfare of the child; *and*
> (c) that those enquiries are being frustrated by access to the child being unreasonably denied, the authority having reasonable cause to believe that such access is *required as a matter of urgency*.'[4]

The latter provision is enacted as being 'without prejudice' to the previous provision, making it clear, if such clarification were necessary, that the powers conferred upon the local authority are not to be taken as diminishing the powers conferred upon any person. Accordingly a local authority may be 'any person'. (The definition for the purposes of the Children (Scotland) Act 1995, Pt I of 'person' as a natural person[5] has no application to Pt II.) There is no reason to suppose that the reporter may not be 'any person' but in practice reporters do not apply for CPOs, although it might in an exceptional situation be appropriate for a reporter to do so. The application forms for a CPO are found in the Act of Sederunt (Child Care and Maintenance Rules) 1997, Form 47 (Application by a local authority) and Form 48 (Application by any person (other than a local authority)).

---

1 Children (Scotland) Act 1995, s 57(1).
2 C(S)A 1995, s 57(2).

3 C(S)A 1995, s 57(1).
4 C(S)A 1995, s 57(2).
5 C(S)A 1995, s 15(4).

Territorial jurisdiction

5.02   In 1998 a case arose where a CPO was sought in relation to a child born in a maternity hospital within the jurisdiction of one sheriffdom to parents whose normal residence was in another sheriffdom. There was some unclarity as to which sheriff had jurisdiction and on 29 June 1998 Sheriff Principal Robert Hay CBE WS issued an informal practice note including the following: 'The 1995 Act is silent on jurisdiction in relation to such orders, but the view which some other sheriffs principal and I take at this stage is that jurisdiction follows the child'. It may be thought that some support for this view may be drawn from the discussion of territorial jurisdiction in *Mitchell v S*.[1]

1 2000 SLT 524 at 526J–527A.

Significant harm

5.03   The essential concept is 'significant harm'. Such harm may be physical or emotional and may be the consequence of neglect as well as of positive action. 'Significant' means more than transient. It may be thought that one way of assessing whether harm was significant is by comparison of the 'harm' under consideration with the potential harm of detaching the child from the home setting. The cases on lack of parental care[1] may be consulted. Where the harm appears to be the result of neglect rather than positive action it may in some cases be more appropriate to apply for a Child Assessment Order under the Children (Scotland) Act 1995, s 55.[2]

1 Cited at 46.06 below.
2 See discussion at 13.03 and 14.29 below.

Terms and conditions of a CPO

The basic provision – 'place of safety'

5.04   A CPO may, subject to such terms and conditions as the sheriff considers appropriate, effect any one or more of the following:

> '(a) require any person in a position to do so to produce the child to the applicant;
> (b) authorise the removal of the child by the applicant to a place of safety,[1] and the keeping of the child at that place;
> (c) authorise the prevention of the removal of the child from any place where he is being accommodated;
> (d) provide that the location of any place of safety in which the child is being kept should not be disclosed to any person or class of person specified in the order.'[2]

The Children (Scotland) Act 1995, s 93(1) provides:

> '"place of safety", in relation to a child means—
> (a) a residential or other establishment provided by a local authority;
> (b) a community home within the meaning of section 53 of the Children Act 1989;
> (c) a police station; or
> (d) a hospital, surgery or other suitable place, the occupier of which is willing temporarily to receive the child.'

It has been questioned if this definition includes the home of a member of the child's extended family or even the home of an approved foster carer. The application of the *eiusdem generis* rule to paragraph '(d)' may suggest that 'other suitable place' should be read as referring to a place of the same type as 'hospital' or 'surgery', namely a medical establishment. It is submitted that the application of the *eiusdem generis* rule may be inappropriate here. It has no pre-eminence as a canon of statutory interpretation. In *Quazi v Quazi*[3] Lord Scarman described it as 'at best, a very secondary guide to the meaning of the statute. The all-important matter is to consider the meaning of the statute'. It only applies where the contrary intention does not appear. The statute should be read as a whole.[4] It is submitted that to read a statute such as the 1995 Act, whose manifest purpose[5] is to secure the welfare of children in the way which is best suited to the individual child, in such a way as to exclude as a possible place of safety what will in many cases be the most appropriate and 'child-friendly' setting is paradoxical and unnecessary.

1 For discussion of 'place of safety', see 5.24 below.
2 Children (Scotland) Act 1995, s 57(4).
3 [1980] AC 744 at 823 and 824.
4 *A-G v Prince Ernest Augustus of Hanover* [1957] AC 436 at 463.
5 C(S)A 1995, s 16(1).

Ancillary directions

5.05   When making a CPO the sheriff is bound, *whether asked to do so by the applicant or not*, to consider whether it is necessary to give directions as to contact with parents and others.[1] Inter alia such directions may prohibit contact with any such persons or make such contact subject to such conditions as the sheriff considers appropriate in order to safeguard and promote the welfare of the child.[2] Different directions may be made in respect of different persons or classes of persons. In practice directions as to contact frequently prohibit contact with named persons reasonably believed to have been neglecting or abusing the child or at least limit such contact to situations wherein contact can be supervised, for example by the local authority (per the Social Work Department) or by a relative who can be trusted to have regard to the welfare of the child. When applying for a CPO the applicant may at the same time apply for a direction in relation to the carrying out by the applicant of such parental responsibilities or parental rights in relation to the child as the applicant considers 'necessary to safeguard or promote the welfare of the child'. Without prejudice to the generality of the foregoing provision, the statute lists the following directions as being competent:

'(a) any examination as to the physical or mental state of the child;
(b) any other assessment or interview of the child; or
(c) any treatment of the child arising out of such an examination or assessment,
which is to be carried out by any person.'[3]

Unlike the directions in relation to contact, the sheriff is not under obligation to consider these matters *ex proprio motu*, but, having regard to the sheriff's radical responsibility to apply the welfare principle[4] there would seem to be nothing to prevent the sheriff from asking the applicant if he or she wishes to ask for one or more of these directions.

1 Children (Scotland) Act 1995, s 58(1).
2 C(S)A 1995, s 58(2).
3 C(S)A 1995, s 58(5).
4 C(S)A 1995, s 16(1).

5.06 Before making such a direction the sheriff must consider that making the direction is necessary to safeguard or promote the welfare of the child and the sheriff may make the direction subject to such condition(s) as he or she considers appropriate, having regard in particular to the duration of the CPO.[1] The duration of a CPO is governed by the statutory provisions[2] and is contingent on a variety of factors: for example an initial hearing, arranged by the reporter under the Children (Scotland) Act 1995, s 59(2), may, on the second working day[3] after the implementation of the CPO, decide that the order should not be continued, thus terminating it.[4] The longest period for which a CPO can endure is until the beginning of a children's hearing arranged by the reporter under s 65(1) on the eighth working day[5] after implementation. Accordingly the sheriff should not make a direction affecting a longer period. A direction ceases to have effect if the sheriff grants an application to cancel it or where the CPO to which it is attached expires.[6]

1 Children (Scotland) Act 1995, s 58(6).
2 C(S)A 1995, s 60 – discussed in ch 8 below.
3 C(S)A 1995, s 59(3).
4 C(S)A 1995, s 60(6)(a).
5 C(S)A 1995, s 65(2).
6 C(S)A 1995, s 58(7).

Scope of ancillary directions

Subsection (5) of s 58 in general

5.07 This subsection is in essence a listing of possible directions which may be made under subsection (4). The introductory phrase 'Without prejudice to the generality of subsection (4) above' makes it clear that directions other than those specifically listed may be made. For the meaning and scope of the directions to be properly understood it is necessary to consider them in the wider context of the basic provisions of the Children (Scotland) Act 1995. Section 1 of the Act sets out the parental responsibilities and specifies that these responsibilities supersede 'any analogous duties imposed on a parent at common law'. Section 2(1) of the Act sets out parental rights but links them to the enabling of a parent 'to fulfil his parental responsibilities in relation to his child'. Parental rights must moreover be exercised having regard to the views of the child (if he or she wishes to express them), taking account of the child's age and maturity, with a child of 12 being presumed to be of sufficient age and maturity to form a view. It follows that any direction made under s 58(5) must be regarded as the transferring to the local authority of a right which was originally vested in the parent in order to enable that parent to fulfil his or her parental responsibilities and subject to the same obligation of consulting the views of the child as attached to the parent in the first place.

Directions in terms of subsection (5) of s 58 – the views of the child – the consent of the child

5.08   Although the sheriff, when considering whether or not to grant a CPO, is not statutorily obliged to seek the views of the child,[1] it would appear to follow from the foregoing considerations that a local authority which has obtained parental responsibilities by virtue of a direction under the Children (Scotland) Act 1995, s 58(5) must, as the parent would have had to, have regard to the views of the child if the child wishes to express them. The necessity of obtaining the consent of the child who is able to express a view is also enacted by s 90 of the Act. Professor Norrie[2] states that 'any direction given will not be directed towards the applicant (as is the case with a direction as to contact), but towards the person whose exercise or fulfilment of parental responsibilities or rights is to be regu- lated'. In the event of a CPO being granted on the application of a local authority it would appear that the child becomes 'looked after' by that authority.[3] A local authority is obliged, in relation to a child so 'looked after' to 'safeguard and promote his welfare'.[4] It is accordingly submitted, *pace* Norrie, that a local authority may be granted a CPO with a condition that there is granted to the local authority the parental responsibilities as to a medical examination of the child which the parents or relevant persons would have had. That is, the local authority would receive the same power to consent to such examination (subject to having regard to the views of the child, where appropriate, and having regard to the child's age and maturity), as would the parent or relevant person. Further: having regard to the existence of the direction within the CPO the local authority, it is submitted, would not be entitled to withhold that consent. Norrie states:[5] 'It follows that a direction as to medical examination, assessment or treatment would be competent only when the child is too young to consent to that examination or treatment himself or herself, for only then does the question of exercise of parental responsibilities or parental rights arise.' While accepting the underlying logic of Norrie's position, it is submitted that the situation is better expressed by saying that it is competent for the local authority to apply for and obtain a CPO with a direction for medical examination in respect of a child, and that if such is granted the local authority becomes the equivalent of the parent for that purpose, except that it must, subject only to the consent of the child where the child is of sufficient age and maturity, arrange for the medical examination etc to be held.

1   Children (Scotland) Act 1995, s 16(2) and (4)(b).
2   *Children's Hearings in Scotland* (1997) p 202.

3 C(S)A 1995, s 17(6).
4 C(S)A 1995, s 17(1)(a).
5 *Children's Hearings in Scotland* (1997) p 203.

Other orders sought

5.09   Part 1 of the application for a CPO provides space for the name and address and phone and fax numbers of the applicant and for information, when the applicant is 'any person', as to the 'capacity in which application made'. It also provides for the identification particulars to be given of 'OTHER PERSONS WHO [sic] THE APPLICANT BELIEVES SHOULD RECEIVE NOTICE OF THE APPLICATION' and lists these persons as: Child [subject to possibility of non-disclosure of whereabouts of the child being considered desirable, see 5.10 and 5.22 below]; Relevant persons(s); Safeguarder;[1] Local Authority [where the applicant is 'any person']; The Principal Reporter; and 'Any other person who should receive notice of the application'. The form glosses in relation to the latter category: 'For example, any person who is caring for the child at the time of the application being made: insert name, address and telephone number of person and provide details of their interest in the application and/or child.'

1 The requirement to notify a safeguarder may seem on the face of it anomalous but see 5.11 below.

Non-disclosure of address of child; dispensing with service on child

5.10   In addition to considering which of the 'Terms and Conditions' and 'Ancillary Orders' should be applied for, the applicant must consider if any other orders may be desirable. In particular the applicant may wish that the address or whereabouts of the child not be disclosed or that service on the child of all or part of the application should be dispensed with.[1] The applicant who wishes to exclude the child from receiving all or any part of the application should be ready amply to justify this request since involvement of the child, except where it would be detrimental to him or her, is fundamental to the philosophy of the system. As will be noticed in the following paragraph, it will be rare for there to be a safeguarder in post who can be notified, but where there is such notification then it will be easier to allow dispensation with service on the child.

1 Act of Sederunt (Child Care and Maintenance Rules) 1997, SI 1997/291, r 3.3(a).

Notification of safeguarder[1]

5.11   The Children (Scotland) Act 1995, s 41(2) makes it explicitly clear that the provisions of the rest of that section as to safeguarders shall not apply to proceedings under s 57 of the Act. There can therefore be no question of a safeguarder being in post in relation to the s 57 application at the times of the preparation or presentation to the sheriff of Forms 47 or 48. A safeguarder's office probably only endures until the disposal of pending proceedings.[2] The possibility of a safeguarder being in post would therefore only appear to exist in the event of the child's being the subject of other pending proceedings at the time of the application for the CPO.

1 Form 47, Part 1 and Form 48, Part 1.
2 *Catto v Pearson* 1990 SCLR 267, 1990 SLT (Sh Ct) 41.

Order for service of first order orally

5.12 The reporter is bound, where a CPO has been implemented and the reporter has not exercised his or her powers to discharge the child from the place of safety[1] and has not received an application under the Children (Scotland) Act 1995, s 60(9) to set aside or vary the CPO, to arrange a hearing 'on the second working day after that order [the CPO] is implemented'.[2] It is accordingly sensible, in order to give the other parties as much notice as possible, to make use of the provision entitling oral service.[3] With these considerations in mind local authorities generally ask sheriffs to grant an order allowing oral service of the first order. In order to effect this a paragraph in approximately the following style may be added as part of 'ANY OTHER ORDER' in Part 3 of the form:

> 'and, (c) owing to the urgency of the situation, to make an order authorising the Applicant's representative(s) AB [and CD], being (an) officer(s) of the Local Authority, to serve the Order and appropriate Notice(s) by way of personal service and/or oral service, all in terms of Rules 3.13(2), 3.15(3) and 3.16(1)(c) of the Act of Sederunt (Child Care and Maintenance Rules) 1997.'

1 Children (Scotland) Act 1995, s 60(3).
2 C(S)A 1995, s 59(3) – for discussion of these procedures see ch 8 below.
3 Act of Sederunt (Child Care and Maintenance Rules) 1997, SI 1997/291, r 3.15(3).

Applying for a CPO – translating the rules into practice

Preliminary moves

5.13 By far the most applications for CPOs originate with the local authority. At the time of writing only a few CPOs have been applied for which did not originate from the local authority. Typically, application for a CPO will be contemplated when the social work department has obtained information that a child – frequently a child already known to the department – is in imminent danger because of a development over which the department has no control. For example a parent who is the sole or sole remaining carer for the child may be engaging in a prolonged drinking bout; or the department may have information that a Schedule 1 offender is about to come and stay in the household of which the child is a member, against a background of the child's carer within the household being reasonably thought likely to be unable or unwilling adequately to protect the child. If time permits a Child Protection case conference[1] will be held at which the decision to ask for a CPO is taken. On the decision to apply for a CPO being taken one or more social workers will prepare an application in the style of Form 47 or Form 48. The law and practice as to who may represent the local authority before the sheriff are discussed later.[2] Only a person entitled to represent the local authority should sign the application.

1 An interdisciplinary meeting of child care professionals, often chaired by a social work
  manager or senior social worker.
2 ch 6 below.

Section 57(1) or section 57(2)?

5.14   As noticed already,[1] the basis of an application under the Children
(Scotland) Act 1995, s 57(1) is the applicant's having reasonable grounds
to *believe* that the child is suffering or will suffer *significant harm* if not
removed from a place or if he or she does not remain in a place and that an
order is *necessary* to protect the child. The basis of a s 57(2) application is:
the applicant's having reasonable grounds to *suspect* significant harm etc;
and *the making of inquiries by the applicant* which, by reason of a *denial of
access to the child*, is being frustrated in circumstances where the authority
has reasonable cause to *believe* that such access is required as a *matter of
urgency*. Accordingly the social workers must come to a clear decision as
to which set of highlighted concepts more appropriately applies to the
child's situation and be ready to justify their stance to the sheriff.

1 At 5.01 above.

**Filling up the application form – Form 47 and Form 48 of the Act of
Sederunt (Child Care and Maintenance Rules) 1997**

Which form?

5.15   Form 47, which is framed so as to reflect the provisions of the
Children (Scotland) Act 1995, s 57(2) is headed 'APPLICATION FOR A
CHILD PROTECTION ORDER BY LOCAL AUTHORITY'. Form 48,
which is framed so as to reflect s 57(1), is headed 'APPLICATION FOR A
CHILD PROTECTION ORDER BY ANY PERSON (OTHER THAN A
LOCAL AUTHORITY)'. As noticed already,[1] a local authority may be 'any
person'. The important thing for social workers is to decide which subsection they are relying on. The rule would seem to require the local
authority to employ Form 47. In that event care must be taken to adapt it
appropriately. It may be that where s 57(1) is being relied upon the social
workers should employ Form 48 and adapt its heading. It is submitted
that a sheriff should not reject an application on account of any concern as
to which of the two forms has been used, provided that the application is
substantially valid. In practice the sheriff may allow amendment of the
application form in order to cure any informality. Forms 47 and 48 are
included in Appendix 12.

1 At 5.01 above.

Part 1 of Form 47

5.16   'DETAILS OF APPLICANT AND OTHER PERSONS WHO[1] THE
APPLICANT BELIEVES SHOULD RECEIVE NOTICE OF THE APPLI-
CATION' The *applicant* will almost always be the local authority.[2]
Accordingly its designation should be given here, for example 'Glasgow
City Council'. Sometimes the social worker principally involved will add
his or her name, for example 'Mary White, Senior Social Worker/Glasgow
City Council'. This is not necessary but is unobjectionable.[3] The name,

address, gender and date of birth of the *child* should be given even if service on the child is being asked to be dispensed with, but, clearly, if the whereabouts of the child are not to be disclosed the address of the child should not be given.[4] The names and addresses of *all relevant persons* and the basis of their being 'relevant persons' within the meaning of the Children (Scotland) Act 1995, s 93(2)(b) should be stated. All known relevant persons should be mentioned. The space for the *Safeguarder* should be completed in the light of the discussion at 5.11 above. Where Form 48 is used there is a space for the name and particulars of the *local authority* to be stated. The applicant should enter against '*Principal Reporter*' the particulars of the Local Authority Reporter or Reporter Manager. Finally there should be stated particulars *of any other person whom the applicant thinks should receive notice of the application*. The forms suggest that any person actually caring for the child should be included in this list. Where particulars are given, the fullest available information should be stated, including any phone and fax numbers as well as addresses.

1 *Sic.*
2 5.13 above.
3 Cf Act of Sederunt (Child Care and Maintenance Rules) 1997, SI 1997/291, r 1.2(3).
4 See discussion at 5.22 below.

Part 2 of Form 47: 'INFORMATION ABOUT THE APPLICATION AND ORDERS SOUGHT'

5.17 '*GROUNDS FOR MAKING APPLICATION*' The applicant should here identify whether the application is being made under subsection (1) or subsection (2) of the Children (Scotland) Act 1995, s 57. It should be noted that the paragraphs within these subsections are cumulative ((a) and (b); and (a), (b) and (c) respectively) and that therefore there is no room for stating, for example, that the application is made under 's 57(2)(a)'.

5.18 '*OTHER APPLICATIONS AND ORDERS WHICH AFFECT THE CHILD*' The applicant should here mention such applications or orders as he or she knows of, including, for example: any pending proceedings under the Children (Scotland) Act 1995, Pt II; any common law court case, pending or decided, dealing with residence or contact known to the applicant; any probation order affecting the child; and, presumably also, any application or order affecting anyone, whether a 'relevant person' or not, who is close enough to the child to have an effect on the child. If the child is under the supervision of a children's hearing then this should be stated, along with as much detail as possible, including, if available, a copy of the order and the grounds of referral.

5.19 *SUPPORTING EVIDENCE* The form instances 'reports, statements or other evidence' as possible supporting evidence. Glasgow City Council's Social Work Department[1] identifies the importance of including information as to the nature, source, extent and consequences of such harm. The applicant should always keep in mind the elements in whichever of the two subsections he or she is relying upon, including, as the case may be, paragraph (b) of subsection (1) ('an order under this section is necessary to protect that child from such harm (or such further harm)') and paragraph (c) of subsection (2) ('that those enquiries are being frustrated by access to the child being unreasonably denied, the authority having reasonable cause to believe that such access is required as a matter of urgency'). Relevant to these matters will be evidence that other ways of protecting the child – voluntary work with the family, placement with relatives or friends or application for another order, for example an exclusion order,[2] have been considered and rejected. The evidence may be amplified during the hearing before the sheriff. The applicant should remember that the written 'Supporting Evidence' will be what those who are entitled to have the application served on them will see. It should therefore contain the essentials of the evidence supporting the application.

1 In *Child Protection – Procedures for Staff of the Social Work Department* (April 1997).
2 Discussed in ch 14 below.

Part 3 of Form 47

5.20   *Details of ORDER SOUGHT – TERMS AND CONDITIONS TO BE ATTACHED TO ORDER – Substantive order(s) sought*   After inserting the name of the child the applicant should here state those of the terms and conditions listed in the Children (Scotland) Act 1995, s 57(4) which he or she wishes the sheriff to grant:

> '(a) require any person in a position to do so to produce the child to the applicant;
> (b) authorise the removal of the child by the applicant to a place of safety, and the keeping of the child at that place;
> (c) authorise the prevention of the removal of the child from any place where he is being accommodated.'

Where the child is at the time of the CPO being applied for in a place which is not a place of safety – for example in the family home where he or she is exposed to the risk of significant harm – then it will generally be appropriate to apply for (a) and (b): there may be occasions where it may be thought that (a) is not essential, as where a social worker is present with the child in the home at the time or, as has happened, the social worker is accompanied by the child while making the application – it is submitted, however, that only where there is no possibility of the child being accessible should (a) not be requested. Where the child is at the time of the application within a place of safety then (c) may be requested, but it is submitted that where the child is for the time being in a place of safety which provides only temporary accommodation or accommodation which is contingent on a transient factor – for example where the child is in a hospital for treatment and is liable to be discharged – then it will be appropriate to apply for (b).

5.21   *DIRECTIONS IN RELATION TO THE EXERCISE OR FULFILMENT OF PARENTAL RESPONSIBILITIES OR PARENTAL RIGHTS*   The Children (Scotland) Act 1995, s 58(4) allows the applicant to ask for a direction as to the exercise of any parental responsibilities or parental rights in respect of the child. Section 58(5) suggests three particular categories but preserves, by the provision 'Without prejudice to the generality of that subsection', the applicant's right to apply for an order in relation to some other category. The categories suggested by s 58(5) are:

'(a) any examination as to the physical or mental state of the child;
(b) any other assessment or interview of [*sic*] the child; or
(c) any treatment of the child arising out of such an examination or assessment,
which is to be carried out by any person.'

The principles of these provisions have already been discussed.[1] The putting into practice of these principles requires careful consideration. The applicant must be satisfied that whatever examination, assessment or treatment is proposed is necessary and likely to promote the welfare of the child. As much detail as to the need for and nature of the examination etc should be stated. The Act does not specifically direct the naming of the person whom it is proposed to carry out the examination etc or the naming of the hospital or other institution. It will be for the sheriff to decide the degree of specification he or she requires. It is submitted that it is good practice to name at least the institution. An acceptable form of proposed order may be: 'Grants to the applicant local authority the parental responsibility and right to have the child medically examined within the paediatric unit of the Royal Hospital for Sick Children, Yorkhill, Glasgow by Dr AB, Paediatrician, or by a similarly qualified doctor there and to provide for and arrange for any medical treatment which such examination may show to be appropriate'.

1 At 5.07 and 5.08 above.

5.22 *ANY OTHER ORDER(S) – (a) as to non-disclosure of address or whereabouts of child; or (b) service of restricted documents on child* The Children (Scotland) Act 1995, s 57(4)(d) allows the sheriff to provide that the location of any place of safety in which the child is being kept is not to be disclosed to any person or class of person specified in the order. It is frequently necessary to specify an alleged abuser as such person. It is uncommon to specify a class of persons but an example of such a class would be the family of an alleged abuser. If the applicant wishes to specify a class of person this should be done with precision. The Act of Sederunt (Child Care and Maintenance Rules) 1997, r 3.4(2) provides that the sheriff may, on application by the applicant or on his own motion, order that a specified part of the application is not served on the child. There may be matters of which the child is unaware and ought, in the opinion of the applicant, to remain unaware. For example, the reason for the application may be the imminent return from prison of an abusing father to a household where the mother is thought to be likely to collude with the father, yet the child may be unaware that the father has been in prison: it may be thought desirable that the child should not learn of this. In such event the relevant part of the GROUNDS FOR MAKING APPLICATION and the relative SUPPORTING EVIDENCE could be excluded from the material served upon the child. A balance must always be struck between the desirability of involving the child as far as possible in matters which concern his or her life and the avoidance of unnecessary distress to the child.

Part 4 of Form 47

5.23   *DETAILS OF FIRST ORDER SOUGHT FROM THE SHERIFF*   This section draws together the formal application for a CPO, the terms and conditions mentioned in Part 3 and the directions, if any, requested in Part 3. It also asks for an order to serve on the child a copy of the application, a copy of the CPO, a notification in Form 50[1] or to dispense with service of all or any of these documents on the child. As to thus dispensing the form glosses '[*insert details of documents to be served on the child, e.g. notice in form 50 only*]'. While the reference to Form 50 is given only as an example, it is submitted that only exceptionally should Form 50 not be sent to a child who is old enough to be likely to be able to read: an example of such an exceptional situation might be where a curator or safeguarder for the child is being notified.[2] This section goes on to ask for an order for service on the persons listed in Part 1 of the application. It concludes with a request to dispense with service on the child or any other person and requires the applicant to give reasons for such a request. Similar considerations apply to considering making applications for such dispensations as apply to the consideration of serving restricted documents.[3]

1 See 6.15 below.
2 Cf 5.11 above and 6.15 below and Appendix 12.
3 Discussed at 5.22 above.

CHAPTER 6

Obtaining a Child Protection Order – appearing before the sheriff: 'Evelyn'

Representation and practical arrangements

Representation

6.01　Any application to any sheriff, including applications under the Children (Scotland) Act 1995, Pt II, may be signed by and moved for by an advocate, a solicitor advocate, or a solicitor holding a current valid practising certificate under the Solicitors (Scotland) Act 1980. Additionally the Act of Sederunt (Child Care and Maintenance Rules) 1997 ('the 1997 Rules') specifically provide for representation by any other 'representative authorised by the party'.[1] Such other representative 'must throughout the proceedings satisfy the sheriff that he is a suitable person to represent the party and that he is authorised to do so'. On fulfilment of the foregoing the representative may do all things in relation to the preparation and conduct of the proceedings as may be done by an individual on his own behalf.[2] In some jurisdictions solicitors for the local authority sign and present applications for CPOs but it is thought that sheriffs cannot insist on such representation. In most local authority areas social workers authorised by the local authority sign and present applications. Generally social workers have identification cards which include an authorisation to carry through procedures under the Act. The requirement of convincing the sheriff that a particular social worker is a 'suitable person' to represent the local authority is dealt with on a pragmatic basis. It is thought that sheriffs are entitled to (and in practice generally do) presume an authorised social worker to be 'suitable' unless the contrary appears. In practice the social worker who has prepared and signed the application will generally represent the local authority at the hearing before the sheriff. Frequently that social worker will be accompanied by a senior social worker having knowledge of the case. In Glasgow the sheriff clerk has a phone number which gives access to a social work manager at any time of the day or night in order to attempt to resolve any unforeseen problem regarding representation or the content of the order sought.

1 SI 1997/291, r 3.21.
2 SI 1997/291, r 3.21(3).

Presenting the application

6.02　If the application is presented for consideration *within working hours* – generally between 9 a m and 5 p m – the authorised social worker or other representative should advise the sheriff clerk, usually by phone, and a hearing before the sheriff will be arranged. In the larger jurisdictions such as Glasgow a 'duty sheriff' is allocated to deal with urgent applications such as CPOs and interim interdicts and that sheriff will hear the application. Should that sheriff be already engaged in a continuing urgent matter then another sheriff will be made available. In smaller jurisdictions a sheriff may have to interrupt other business to hear an application for a CPO. The special arrangements enacted to deal with the situation where it is not practicable for an application to be made or for the sheriff to consider an application are discussed later.[1] Various arrangements exist throughout Scotland for dealing with applications which require to be considered *out of working hours*. In Glasgow and Edinburgh arrangements are in position for the court to be opened and the application to be heard there – the social work department has a note of the phone number of the duty sheriff clerk who phones the duty sheriff who then attends at the court and holds the hearing in chambers. In other jurisdictions the sheriff may attend at other centres, such as local authority offices. In some jurisdictions the social workers may attend at the sheriff's home, either by arrangement with the sheriff clerk or by direct arrangement. The advantage of holding the hearing in official premises lies in the availability of copying facilities for the quite considerable documentation. It is thought that the arrangements whereby sheriffs hold the hearing in court or in other official premises does not interpose any more delay than would be involved in social workers finding and going to sheriffs' homes.

1 Chs 11 and 12 below.

What to take to court

6.03   It is essential to take to court, along with the application itself, any available documents or other written material referred to in the application (Form 47) notably in Part 2 ('GROUNDS FOR MAKING APPLICATION'; 'OTHER APPLICATIONS AND ORDERS WHICH AFFECT THE CHILD'; and 'SUPPORTING EVIDENCE').[1] For example if there is in force a supervision requirement in respect of the child, its terms should be ascertained and if possible a copy should be brought. If a conviction in a criminal court is to be relied on then some evidence as to the precise terms of the conviction and sentence should be brought. It may not always be practicable quickly to obtain an extract conviction but a copy indictment and a report of what happened at the trial may be on file and copies should be brought. In cases of particular urgency where there is not time to obtain such documentation then the best documentation available should be brought and the reason for the urgency should be stated verbally to the sheriff. In addition to documentation referred to in the application it is as well to bring the social work file if available or, in the case of a voluminous file or files, such portions as are recent and relevant. On at least one occasion the child has been brought to a hearing. Appropriate identification should be brought.[2]

1 See 5.17 ff above.
2 Cf 6.01 above.

Initial procedure where application is dealt with in court

6.04   On arriving in court the sheriff clerk will 'book' the application and will generally take it to the sheriff to look at in chambers before the hearing proper begins. The sheriff clerk may ask to see identification. The sheriff clerk will then show the social worker(s) into the sheriff's room and will usually remain during most or all of the hearing.

Principles affecting the making of a CPO

The section 16 principles

6.05 The making of a CPO is subject to the premier section 16 principle, i e that the paramount consideration for the sheriff is the welfare of the child throughout his or her childhood.[1] The principle of consulting the child and the principle of no non-beneficial order do *not* formally apply.[2] However the making of a CPO under the Children (Scotland) Act 1995, s 57(1) is subject to the sheriff being satisfied that the order is 'necessary' to protect the child[3] and a CPO under s 57(2) cannot be made unless the sheriff is satisfied that the local authority's inquiries are being frustrated by denial of access to the child and that such access is 'required as a matter of urgency'.[4] It may therefore be thought that the no non-beneficial order principle is present in all but name.[5] The principle of consulting the views of the child is absent at the stage of the application for a CPO but it is thought that the sheriff should, where practicable, ask about the child's wishes, which may well be known to the social worker, since a knowledge of these wishes will assist the sheriff in deciding if the making of the order is likely to promote the child's welfare. Moreover the principle of consulting the views of the child comes into play in the event of an application being made for the recall or variation of a CPO[6] and it is therefore sensible for the sheriff to ventilate the matter at the stage of considering the CPO application.

1 Children (Scotland) Act 1995, s 16(1).
2 C(S)A 1995, s 16(2), (3) and (4)(b).
3 C(S)A 1995, s 57(1)(b).
4 C(S)A 1995, s 57(2)(c).
5 In one case where the police had taken to a police station a child who was not suspected of any offence but had absconded from a children's home where she had resided under a supervision requirement the sheriff was told that no secure accommodation was available and that therefore the CPO would have no practical effect – the sheriff refused the application.
6 C(S)A 1995, s 16(2) and (4)(b)(ii).

Convincing the sheriff – the ground of the application

6.06 The hearing before the sheriff is not a 'proof'. The strict rules of evidence do not apply. The sheriff is entitled to have regard to hearsay evidence and will consider the whole information which has been presented and draw such inferences as common sense may suggest. The sheriff has to be 'satisfied'. The position is similar to that of the sheriff considering an application for an interim order in a family case in the civil court.[1] Nevertheless, as noted already,[2] the best available evidence should be produced so far as practicable.

1 Cf *Armstrong v Gibson* 1991 SLT 193.
2 At 6.03 above.

Convincing the sheriff – the content of the order: terms and conditions and directions

6.07 Since the paramount consideration for the sheriff is the welfare of the child throughout childhood the sheriff has potentially very considerable scope for inquiring into the steps which the applicant proposes should be taken to safeguard and promote the child's welfare. For example if the plan is to place the child or children with foster parents the sheriff may wish to hear of the experience of the foster parents and whether or not they already have children placed with them for fostering. In the case of placements being required for several children in the same family the sheriff may wish to know what efforts have been made to keep the brothers and/or sisters together, and, if this does not seem practicable, what efforts have been made to ensure the best balance of placements. If contact with a birth parent or other person is being proposed or if it is sought to limit or exclude such contact the social worker should be ready with information to justify the course proposed. In Glasgow the arrangements to contact a social work manager can be and are used if the sheriff wishes particular arrangements to be investigated. Where directions under the Children (Scotland) Act 1995, s 58(4) and (5) are sought (examination etc of child) the sheriff may ask for details of the justification for the request and may wish information as to the qualifications of the person who is to examine the child and possibly as to what is known of the child's views. It must be remembered that the sheriff is not directing that any medical examination or procedure take place, but merely conveying to the local authority the responsibilities and rights of the parent.[1] The applicant should always, of course, be ready to justify the contention that the CPO is necessary[2] or required as a matter of urgency,[3] as the case may be.

1 Cf discussion at 5.08 above and 13.15 ff below.
2 Children (Scotland) Act 1995, s 57(1)(b)
3 C(S)A 1995, s 57(2)(c).

Procedure at the hearing

The form of the hearing

6.08 Some sheriffs place the social worker or workers on oath while others simply ask questions and discuss the case without the formality of the oath. In Glasgow the latter procedure is usually adopted. The sheriff will take handwritten notes of the hearing and if the same sheriff should hear an application to vary or recall these notes will be available to that sheriff but otherwise the notes are unlikely to be referred to in any future part of the process.

Safeguarder

6.09 As noticed already, the obligation to consider the appointment of a safeguarder is not incumbent on the sheriff in relation to proceedings involved in the making of a CPO.[1] Since it is only when such an obligation attaches that a safeguarder may be appointed[2] it would seem that such an appointment at this stage is incompetent, although it will be competent and indeed obligatory for the sheriff to consider such an appointment in the event of an application for variation or recall of a CPO.[3]

1 Children (Scotland) Act 1995, s 41(2).
2 C(S)A 1995, s 41(1)(b).
3 C(S)A 1995, s 41(1).

Moving towards a decision

6.10 Hearings may last about half an hour. The sheriff will generally indicate whether or not the application is likely to be granted or if there is a problem. As noticed already,[1] some problems may be capable of resolution by a phone call to a social work manager. If and when granted, the CPO should record the time of granting in view of the provision that a CPO – other than one granted under the Children (Scotland) Act 1995, s 57(4)(c) (prevention of removal of child from a place) – shall cease to have effect where the applicant has made no attempt to implement it by the end of 24 hours after the making thereof.[2]

1 At 6.01 above.
2 Cf 6.16 below.

Scope for sheriff deferring decision or allowing applicant to withdraw application?

6.11 The 1997 Rules, rule 3.31 (1) provides: 'On receipt of an application, the sheriff, having considered the grounds of the application and the supporting evidence, shall forthwith grant or refuse it.' The word 'forthwith' does not mean 'instantly' but 'as soon as reasonably possible'.[1] There would seem to be no scope for the sheriff formally to continue consideration of the application to a later date but it is thought, however, that the sheriff may use the inherent power of the court to adjourn[2] to allow some time for further investigations to be made, provided that the adjournment did not exceed some few hours. In practice very few applications are refused. During the 12 months following the coming into force of these provisions on 1 April 1997 there were 75 hearings before the sheriffs in Glasgow of which only two were unsuccessful. It is thought that on the sheriff's indicating that he or she is not minded to grant the application the social worker may be entitled to ask leave to withdraw it and if necessary present a modified application soon after and that this may in certain circumstances be regarded as preferable to allowing the application to be refused and then lodging a further application against the background of such refusal. There have been some instances of applications being thus withdrawn.

1 Cf *A & C McLennan Ltd v MacMillan* 1964 SLT 2 per Lord Justice Clerk Grant at 3.
2 *Bruce v Linton* (1860) 23 D 85.

Scope for sheriff to hear other parties?

6.12 On at least one occasion a sheriff, presented with an application for a CPO at the instance of a mother, had reason to believe that there was relevant information, potentially readily accessible, which the de facto carer of the child could provide. The sheriff considered continuing the hearing of the application for a few hours to enable the de facto carer to be heard. In the event the sheriff decided to proceed without so doing (and refused the application on its merits) but it is submitted that it would have been in order, and consistent with the scheme of the Children (Scotland) Act 1995, which includes the avoiding of unnecessarily taking of children away from home, if the sheriff had arranged to hear from the other party.

Degree of immunity from process – the Human Rights Act 1998 – the European Convention

6.13   Although the information laid before the sheriff may not be given on oath, the deliberate giving of any false information to the court would, it is submitted, be a contempt of court. It is, however, submitted that, as the law stands at present, the social worker in giving information to the sheriff would be accorded, on the analogy of the position of a witness,[1] or counsel,[2] absolute privilege from process in respect of alleged defamation; but some of the observations of the Temporary Judge in *Russell v Dickson*[3] may indicate that the older cases may require to be reconsidered and that only qualified privilege may be available.[4] As noticed already,[5] the European Convention becomes part of the domestic law of Scotland on 2 October 2000. The local authority and its social workers are public authorities[6] and as such may not act in a way which is incompatible with Convention rights. For example they must not act so as to violate a person's rights under art 5(5),[7] and contravention of this or any other Convention right might render the social worker and the local authority liable to proceedings under the Human Rights Act 1998, s 7(1).

1 Cf *Trapp v Mackie* 1979 SC (HL) 38.
2 *Fraser v Pattie* (1847) 9 D 903.
3 1998 SLT 96, at 101H – cf discussion at 1.06 and 2.08 above.
4 For discussion of qualified privilege see 2.08 above.
5 At 1.09 above.
6 Human Rights Act 1998, s 6(3)(b).
7 'Everyone who has been the victim of arrest or detention in contravention of the provision of this article shall have an enforceable right to compensation.'

The terms of the CPO

6.14   A CPO should follow Form 49 of the 1997 Rules.[1] The form may be subjected to such variation as circumstances may require, provided that the varied version is to substantially the same effect.[2] Here is an example based upon the printed style in use in Glasgow (elements have been represented as deleted where appropriate and the variable parts, in practice handwritten, are italicised); in this case it is assumed that the sheriff had been told that a curator *ad litem* for the child was already in post in connection with pending proceedings and that no difficulty is anticipated in removing the child to the place of safety:

> Glasgow, *31 December 1997 at 11.59 p m*
>
> In the presence of *AB*, Sheriff of Glasgow and Strathkelvin at Glasgow
>
> The Sheriff being satisfied that *CD, Social Worker,* is authorised and suitable to act on behalf of the applicant and having heard ~~him~~/her on the

application Makes a Child Protection Order in terms of section 57(1) of the Children (Scotland) Act 1995 in respect of the child
Evelyn F (female), born 1 January 1989

~~The Sheriff orders that~~ ....
~~is required to produce the child to the applicant.~~

The Sheriff authorises the removal of the child by the applicant to:
[name and address of children's home]
a place of safety; and for the keeping of the child at that place.

~~The Sheriff authorises the prevention of the removal of the child from :~~
~~*The said place of safety*~~

The Sheriff orders that the locality of the place of safety should not be disclosed to:
The child's mother HF.

In terms of section 58(1) and (2) the Sheriff gives the following directions regarding contact with the child:
Prohibits contact between the child and the child's mother HF

In terms of section 58(4), (5) and (6) the Sheriff gives the following directions as to the exercise or fulfilment of parental responsibilities or parental rights in respect of the child:
Grants to the applicant Local Authority the parental responsibility and right to have the child Evelyn F medically examined within the paediatric unit of Royal Hospital for Sick Children, Yorkhill, Glasgow by Dr JK, Paediatrician, or by a similarly qualified doctor there, and to provide for and arrange for any medical treatment which such examination may show to be appropriate.

~~In terms of rule 3.4(2) of the Act of Sederunt (Child Care and Maintenance Rules) 1997 orders that this part [identifying passage] of this application be not served on the child~~[3].

Further the Sheriff Appoints the applicant to serve a copy of the order and Form 51 on the relevant person; said service to be made orally and/or personally in terms of Rule 3.15(3) of the Act of Sederunt (Child Care and Maintenance Rules) 1997; Dispenses with service on the child.

Further the Sheriff appoints the applicant to make intimation forthwith to LM, solicitor, 3 Brown Street, Glasgow, in her capacity as curator ad litem *of the child Evelyn F.*

~~For the purpose of enforcing this order warrant is granted for all lawful execution, including warrant to open shut and lockfast places.~~

(Signed) *AB*
Sheriff.

{SEAL OF GLASGOW SHERIFF COURT}[4]

1 SI 1997/291, r 3.31(2)
2 SI 1997/291, r 1.2(3).
3 This clause does not appear in Form 49 but would seem to be necessitated by SI 1997/291, r 3.4(2), as reflected in the terms of Form 47 (last line of Part 3). It is scored out in this example because of the facts of this case.
4 The impressive stamp of the relevant sheriff court is optional!

Serving a CPO[1]

6.15 Once the CPO has been granted the applicant must, unless service has been dispensed with, serve a copy of the order on the child, with a notice in the style of Form 50, and on any other person named in the application form, with a notice in the style of Form 51. The location of any place of safety may, if the sheriff agrees, not be disclosed to a particular person or class of persons. The sheriff may also specify that a part of the application not be served on the child.[2] The sheriff should not lightly dispense with service on the child. If the sheriff is considering dispensing with service on a child who is likely to be able to read but wishes to involve the child the sheriff may, in due time, appoint a curator *ad litem*.[3] The sheriff may, on the application by the applicant, or on his or her own initiative, order that a specified part of the application is not to be served on the child. It seems clear that this power may be used where the application contains material which would be detrimental to the child if it were drawn to the child's attention. The principle of the paramountcy of the interests of the child should, it is submitted, inform the sheriff's decision.[4]

1 SI 1997/291, r 3.32; Children (Scotland) Act 1995, s 57(4)(d).
2 SI 1997/291, r 3.4(2).
3 Cf discussion at 9.13 below in the context of an application to vary or recall a CPO – but in an application for a CPO the sheriff may not appoint a safeguarder – C(S)A 1995, s 41(2).
4 Cf discussion at 5.22 above.

Implementing a CPO

Timescale

6.16   As noticed already, the attempt must be made to implement a CPO within 24 hours of its having been made or it ceases to have effect.[1] This does not apply to a CPO made in terms of the Children (Scotland) Act 1995, s 57(4)(c) (i e authorising the prevention of removal of the child from the place where he or she is being accommodated): in such an application the time of implementation is the time of the obtaining of the order.[2] The statute does not expressly say so but it seems patent that when a CPO falls any directions contained in it fall at the same time.

1 Children (Scotland) Act 1995, s 60(1).
2 C(S)A 1995, s 59(5)(b).

Position where attempt to implement unsuccessful

6.17   The statute is silent as to the position where an attempt is made to implement the CPO but the attempt is unsuccessful. It is tentatively suggested that in this situation the CPO remains effective for a reasonable period, provided that persistent efforts are being made to implement it. What would constitute a 'reasonable period' would be a matter of fact.

Obligation to notify the reporter and local authority

6.18   Where the applicant is not the local authority within whose area the child resides the applicant must forthwith notify that local authority of the granting of the CPO. The applicant must always notify the reporter forthwith.[1]

1 Children (Scotland) Act 1995, s 57(5).

CHAPTER 7

Service of documents

'Service'

Definition

7.01 For the purposes of the Children (Scotland) Act 1995, Pt II 'service', in relation to the various papers and documents involved, includes any citation, intimation, or giving of notice as required by Act of Sederunt (Child Care and Maintenance Rules) 1997 ('the 1997 Rules'), Ch 3.[1]

1 SI 1997/291, r 3.1(1).

Periods of notice for service of documents – 'working day'

7.02 Unless otherwise stated in relation to a particular procedure the period of notice which must be given is 48 hours where the service is personal – i e where the document is handed to the recipient in person by a sheriff officer[1] – and 72 hours where the citation is postal.[2] Postal citation means by first class recorded delivery post.[3] In view of the consideration that the timescale is defined in hours it follows that the calculation has to be done in hours and therefore, unless otherwise stated, the hours continue to run even during Sundays and public holidays. By contrast, some of the timescales laid down in the Children (Scotland) Act 1995 are defined in terms of 'working days' – for example the rule that an application for the variation or recall of a CPO must be determined by the sheriff within three working days of the application for variation or recall being made.[4] A 'working day' means every day except Saturday and Sunday, 25 and 26 December and 1 and 2 January.[5]

1 For fuller discussion of personal service see Macphail *Sheriff Court Practice* (2nd edn, 1999) para 6.25.
2 SI 1997/291, r 3.13(1).
3 SI 1997/291, r 3.15(2)(e).
4 Children (Scotland) Act 1995, s 60(8).
5 C(S)A 1995, s 93(1) – 'working day'. For further discussion see 8.08, fn 4 below.

7.03 The periods of notice mentioned in the foregoing paragraph do not apply in relation to citations or notification made in relation to the proceedings listed in the 1997 Rules, r 3.13 (2). These proceedings are listed in r 3.13(2) as follows:

'(a) an appeal against a decision to issue a warrant for the detention of a child;
(b) a hearing in respect of an exclusion order where an interim order has been granted in terms of rule 3.36;

(c) a hearing on an application to vary or set aside a child protection order or any direction given with the order; or
(d) an application for a child assessment order.'

In the foregoing cases r 3.13(2) provides that the period of notice *and the method of giving notice shall be as directed by the sheriff.*

Calculation of periods of notice – an example

7.04   In the event of a hearing directing the reporter to make application to the sheriff for a finding as to whether grounds of referral are established,[1] the reporter having lodged an application with the sheriff clerk, the application must be heard within 28 days of its being lodged.[2] On lodgement of the application the sheriff clerk fixes a diet for the hearing of the application and issues the warrant in the style annexed to Form 60[3] in which the date and hour of the hearing and the details of the court are identified and the reporter is appointed to serve a copy of the application and warrant on the appropriate persons.

1 Children (Scotland) Act 1995, s 65(7) and/or (9).
2 C(S)A 1995, s 68(2).
3 Cf Form 33.

7.05   It is submitted that the wording 'within 28 days of its being lodged' means that in order to comply with the 28-day limit an application lodged on Tuesday, 25 June 2000 would require to be heard on Tuesday, 25 July 2000 at the latest[1]. In practice the sheriff clerk will generally fix a date near the end of the 28-day period.

1 Contrast the ambiguity of 'within a period of 3 weeks beginning with the date of the decision appealed against'. C(S)A 1995, s 51(1); discussed below at 50.09.

7.06   Whatever the date set, the rules as to the minimum periods of notice, as mentioned already,[1] come into play – 48 hours where the service is personal (i e where the document is handed to the recipient in person) and 72 hours where the citation is postal.[2] Accordingly if the hearing of the application were to be fixed for Thursday, 20 July 2000 at 10 a m the applicant reporter would require to serve on the persons by putting the application and warrant into the post by first class recorded delivery at 9.59 a m on Monday, 17 July 2000 at the latest or by effecting personal service at 9.59 a m on Tuesday, 18 July 2000 at the latest.

1 At 7.02 above.
2 SI 1997/291, r 3.13(1).

7.07   In practice reporters do not effect service at the last minute and will generally try to effect service immediately on obtaining the warrant.

Modes of service and who may ordinarily effect service

7.08   The 1997 Rules, r 3.15(2) provides:

'It shall be deemed legal service to or on any person if such service is—
(a)   delivered to him personally;

(b) left for him at his dwelling-house or place of business with some person resident or employed therein;

(c) where it cannot be delivered to him personally and he has no known dwelling-house or place of business, left for him at any other place at which he may at the time be resident;

(d) where he is the master of, or a seaman or other person employed in, a vessel, left with a person on board or connected with the vessel;

(e) sent by first class recorded delivery post, or the nearest equivalent which the available postal service permits, to his dwelling-house or place of business, or if he has no known dwelling-house or place of business to any other place in which he may at the time be resident;

(f) where the person has the facility to receive facsimile or other electronic transmission, by such facsimile or other electronic transmission; or

(g) where the person has a numbered box at a document exchange, given by leaving at the document exchange.'

A sheriff officer may effect service by any of the foregoing modes. In respect of modes (e) and (f) service may be effected by a solicitor, the sheriff clerk, the reporter or an officer of the local authority,[1] which is defined as 'including' a person authorised in terms of r 3.21 to conduct proceedings.[2] As noted already,[3] r 3.21 includes the requirement that the sheriff must be satisfied that the person is suitable as well as authorised by the local authority. It is thought that for the purpose of effecting service all that is required is authorisation by the local authority. Special procedures[4] apply where service requires to be made and there is not enough time to employ the modes specified in r 3.15(2).[5] The sheriff may in a particular case authorise a person not ordinarily empowered to effect service to do so in any of the specified modes.[6]

1 SI 1997/291, r 3.16(1).
2 SI 1997/291, r 3.16(1).
3 At 6.01 above.
4 SI 1997/291, r 3.15(3).
5 See 7.09 ff below.
6 SI 1997/291, r 3.16(1)(c).

Service as directed by the sheriff when no time for ordinary service – oral service

7.09 Some of the timescales in these procedures are very short. In such situations the sheriff may direct that service may be effected orally or in such other manner as the sheriff directs.[1]

1 SI 1997/291, r 3.15(3).

An example of a short timsescale

7.10 Where a CPO has been granted and implemented and the reporter has not exercised his or her powers to discharge the child and the reporter has not been notified of an application under the Children (Scotland) Act 1995, s 60(9) to set aside or vary the CPO, the reporter is obliged to arrange a hearing on the second working day after the CPO has been implemented.[1] Accordingly if a CPO were implemented at 11 p m on a Monday the reporter would require to arrange a hearing on the Wednesday of the same week. In practice applicants for CPOs generally anticipate this possibility by asking the sheriff to direct the applicant to serve on all parties orally. The content of the document should then be conveyed initially to the recipient by, for example, telephone,[2] with a written copy being supplied as soon as possible thereafter.

1 Children (Scotland) Act 1995, s 59(3).
2 Cf SI 1997/291, r 1.2(3).

Proof of execution of oral service

7.11 The provisions relating to proof of service[1] do not make specific reference to oral service. It is submitted that the person effecting oral service should note the time and place from where he or she effected oral service of the particular document and prepare an execution of service adapted from Form 43.[2]

1 SI 1997/291, r 3.17 and Form 43.
2 Cf SI 1997/291, r 1.2(3).

Production of certificates of execution of service

7.12 The sheriff may ask to see an execution of service. This mainly happens on the rare occasion of the sheriff's being asked to grant a warrant for the apprehension of a reluctant witness in order to secure the attendance of a reluctant witness.[1] but may also happen in the event of the sheriff's inquiring as to whether an absent party has received notice of the hearing.

1 30.34 ff below.

7.13 The 1997 Rules provide that sufficient proof of service shall be production to the sheriff of a certificate of execution of service in the style of Form 43 with, in the case of postal service, the post office receipt.[1] The rules allow that the certificate be lodged at the hearing itself unless the sheriff directs otherwise or on cause shown.[2] Proof of oral citation has been discussed already.[3]

1 SI 1997/291, r 3.17(1).
2 SI 1997/291, r 3.17(2).
3 At 7.11 above.

CHAPTER 8

Continuing, or not, the CPO: the 'initial hearing' under the 1995 Act, s 59(2)

When an initial hearing under s 59(2) has to be arranged

8.01 Where a CPO has been made and implemented[1] and the reporter has not used his powers under the Children (Scotland) Act 1995, s 60(3) to discharge the child from the place of safety[2] and, provided no notice has reached the reporter of an application to vary or set aside the CPO,[3] the reporter must arrange an 'initial hearing' in order that the hearing may decide whether it should, in the interests of the child, continue the CPO.[4] 'Implemented' means, in the case of an order requiring removal of a child, the day of the removal of the child[5] and, in the case of an order requiring the child to stay put,[6] the day of the order itself.[7]

1 Children (Scotland) Act 1995, s 59(1)(a).
2 C(S)A 1995, s 59(1)(b).
3 C(S)A 1995, s 59(1)(c).
4 C(S)A 1995, s 59(2).
5 C(S)A 1995, s 57(4)(b).
6 C(S)A 1995, s 57(4)(c).
7 C(S)A 1995, s 59(5)(b).

The decision of the reporter under s 60(3)

8.02 The Children (Scotland) Act 1995, s 60(3) provides that a child shall not, by reason of a CPO, be kept in or prevented from leaving a place or be subjected to any term, condition or direction in a CPO where the reporter, having regard to the welfare of the child, considers, whether as a result of a change of circumstances or on account of further information received by the reporter, that the conditions for the making of a CPO for the child no longer exist or that the term, condition or direction concerned is no longer appropriate. On coming to such a decision the reporter must notify the person who implemented the order and on such notification being received, the CPO or the term, condition or direction ceases to have effect. The reporter must also notify the sheriff who made the order.[1] The sheriff is properly notified by a letter to the sheriff clerk.

1 Children (Scotland) Act 1995, s 60(5).

8.03 The decision of the reporter is, as always, not governed specifically by the principles of the Children (Scotland) Act 1995, s 16 but s 60(3) in effect imports the welfare principle. Moreover, if the reporter allows a CPO to persist, then either a hearing before the sheriff on an application to vary or set aside and/or a substantive hearing under s 65(2) of the Act must follow and the s 16 principles will apply to the deliberations of the sheriff and the hearing. It follows that the reporter, when considering whether or not to exercise the s 60(3) powers, will in practice have regard to the s 16 principles as far as practicable. Relatively few cases are dealt with by reporters under s 60(3).

8.04 The Children (Scotland) Act 1995, s 60(3) in effect gives the reporter a monitoring role but prescribes that the powers conveyed may only be exercised in the event of 'a change in the circumstances of the case' or as a result of 'further information relating to the case having been received' by the reporter. It may be thought, however, that the effect of these constraints is less than it seems since if the reporter came to the conclusion that the effect of the CPO or some element in it were proving to be detrimental to the welfare of the child then it would be legitimate to regard this consideration as further information or a change of circumstances or both.

8.05 The reporter's right to give notice that he or she has exercised the powers under the Children (Scotland) Act 1995, s 60(3) flies off whenever an initial hearing begins or when an application to vary or set aside the CPO is made.[1]

1 Children (Scotland) Act 1995, s 60(4).

8.06 The Children (Scotland) Act 1995 provides that the decision to exercise or not the powers under s 60(3) is the reporter's responsibility alone and there is no provision for review. In theory the attempt might be made to challenge such a decision by judicial review but this possibility seems remote.

Arranging the initial hearing

8.07 If the reporter has not discharged the child from a place of safety by using the foregoing powers then, unless an application to vary or set aside the CPO has been lodged, an initial hearing must be arranged.[1] The general rules as to the convening of a hearing are considered later[2] but many of these rules have no application in the special circumstances of a 'second working day' hearing. The usual 48 hours' notice does not require to be given in respect of an application to vary or set aside[3] but even so, since the initial hearing must take place on the second working day after the implementation of the CPO,[4] it is not generally practicable, although theoretically possible, for an application to vary or set aside to be lodged at this stage.

1 Children (Scotland) Act 1995, s 59(2).
2 In ch 20 below.
3 1997 Rules, r 3.13(2)(c).
4 Children (Scotland) Act 1995, s 59(3), discussed at 8.08 below.

Mandatory 'second working day' provision

8.08 As already noticed, a 'working day' is statutorily defined as:

'every day except—
    (a) Saturday and Sunday;
    (b) December 25th and 26th; and
    (c) January 1st and 2nd.'[1]

The obligation imposed on the reporter is to arrange the initial hearing '*on* [emphasis supplied] the second working day after the order is implemented'.[2] Accordingly, irrespective of whether a CPO were implemented on a Friday, Saturday or Sunday, the initial hearing would require to take place on the following Tuesday (assuming that the Monday was not a non-working day), even if it were practicable to hold it earlier. If an initial hearing were not held on the second working day it would appear that the CPO and its contents would fall since only such a hearing can continue a CPO.[3] If by misfortune a second working day hearing were not to take place in circumstances wherein the child's welfare would only be served by the child's being be kept in a place of safety it is submitted that an appropriate course would be for the reporter, as 'any person', to apply for a fresh CPO under the Children (Scotland) Act 1995, s 57(1) (a)(ii) and (b),[4] or, if a sheriff were not available, under s 61(1).

1 Children (Scotland) Act 1995, s 93(1); accordingly religious holidays, such as Easter Friday, Easter Monday, Id-ul-Fitr, and Passover, local holidays, such as 'Glasgow Fair Monday', bank holidays such as 'the August Bank Holiday', and special holidays, such as the extra day at the Millennium, are working days.
2 C(S)A 1995, s 59(3).
3 C(S)A 1995, s 59(4).
4 Cf 5.01 above.

Who must be notified and how

8.09 The child, all relevant persons, certain parents having right to attend[1] and the chief social work officer of the local authority must be notified of the time and place of the hearing.[2] It is good practice to notify any safeguarder or curator *ad litem* for the child of whom the reporter has knowledge.[3] The usual requirement for seven days' notice[4] does not apply and if notice cannot be given in writing the reporter may give notice orally.[5] There is no question of fixing of a business meeting[6] at this stage.

1 Discussed at 20.12 below.
2 Children's Hearings (Scotland) Rules 1996, SI 1996/3261, rr 6(1), 7, 8 and 12(1).
3 Cf 6.12 above.
4 SI 1996/3261, r 6(1).
5 SI 1996/3261, rr 6(2) and 7(5).
6 SI 1996/3261, r 4.

Supplying of documents

8.10 The hearing may possibly not have before it any of the documents which are available to other hearings[1] and cannot expect to receive them three days before.[2] The hearing will generally be shown the same papers that were available to the sheriff, together with any later reports including any medical or other reports which have resulted from any medical examination following a direction within the CPO or otherwise.

1 Children's Hearings (Scotland) Rules 1996, SI 1996/3261, r 5(1).
2 SI 1996/3261, r 5(1).

Conduct of the initial hearing

Provisions in the Act

8.11   The provisions as to privacy,[1] prohibition of publication,[2] presumption and determination of age,[3] and, *mutatis mutandis*, attendance of child and relevant person,[4] and power to exclude relevant person(s),[5] apply to initial hearings. These provisions are discussed later.[6] The provision allowing transfer of a case to another hearing[7] can have no application. The provisions governing the conduct of a hearing considering the disposal of a child's case under the Children (Scotland) Act 1995, s 65(1)[8] do not apply to an initial hearing.

1 Children (Scotland) Act 1995, s 43.
2 C(S)A 1995, s 44.
3 C(S)A 1995, s 47.
4 C(S)A 1995, s 45.
5 C(S)A 1995, s 46.
6 In chs 22 and 23 below.
7 C(S)A 1995, s 48.
8 Discussed at 23.03 ff below.

Provisions in the 1996 Rules

8.12   There are provisions in the Children's Hearings (Scotland) Rules 1996 as to representation of children and relevant persons,[1] attendance at hearings of parents who are not relevant persons,[2] persons who may attend hearings at the chairman's discretion,[3] and as to giving the child an opportunity to indicate whether he or she wishes to express views,[4] apply to initial hearings; these provisions are discussed later.[5] A safeguarder or curator *ad litem* who has received notification of the original application may attend.[6] The provision in the 1996 Rules[7] entitling the hearing to adjourn the hearing till later on the same day would appear to apply to initial hearings, but the provisions in the 1995 Act[8] for continuation for inquiry only apply to disposal hearings and can have no application here.

1 SI 1996/3261, r 11.
2 SI 1996/3261, r 12.
3 SI 1996/3261, r 13.
4 SI 1996/3261, r 15.
5 In ch 23 below.
6 Cf 5.11 above.
7 SI 1996/3261, r 10(4).
8 Children (Scotland) Act 1995, s 69.

Persons at the initial hearing

8.13   In practice the following will generally be present: the child, unless notification of the child has been dispensed with;[1] any curator *ad litem* or safeguarder of the child; the relevant person(s) and any representative(s); the local authority per a social worker (or social workers) and the reporter.

1 Children (Scotland) Act 1995, s 45(2)(b); Children's Hearings (Scotland) Rules 1996, r 6(3).

Procedure at the hearing

8.14 Subject to those parts of the Children (Scotland) Act 1995 and the Children's Hearings (Scotland) Rules 1996 which apply to these hearings,[1] the procedure is within the discretion of the chairman to determine.[2] In practice the chairman will explain the purpose of the hearing along the lines indicated in the following paragraph and then the hearing will examine the relevant issues. It is thought that there is an obligation to consider the appointment of a safeguarder.[3]

1 Noted at 8.11 ff above.
2 SI 1996/3261, r 10(3).
3 C(S)A 1995, s 41(1); the bar on the appointment of a safeguarder imposed by s 41(2) only applies to 'proceedings under s 57 of this Act' and there would seem to be no reason to treat the initial hearing to consider a CPO granted under s 57 as 'proceedings under s 57 of this Act'.

What the initial hearing has to decide

8.15 The principal and chronologically first thing the s 59(2) hearing has to decide is whether or not the conditions for making the CPO are established. If the hearing decide that the conditions are established the hearing *may* continue the CPO, with or without variation.[1] A hearing is not a court in the sense of a forum at which evidence is adduced and witnesses are examined and cross-examined. Such a hearing is, as was the sheriff at the hearing of the application for the CPO, entitled to bring to bear its common sense on the information, written and oral, which is presented to it. Having regard to the short period of time which will have elapsed between the granting of the CPO and the holding of the s 59(2) hearing, the information before the hearing will sometimes be substantially the same as the information which was before the sheriff. Accordingly, in the absence of new information, the hearing is in effect acting as a tribunal of review of the sheriff's decision to make a CPO, subject, in certain cases, to certain terms, conditions and directions. Some hearing members may feel reluctant to 'reverse', as it were, the decision of a sheriff. In the writer's view it is no doubt right and proper that a hearing should recognise that sheriffs' decisions in relation to CPOs are not taken lightly: but the statute has given the members of the hearing the right and the duty to look at the information themselves and when appropriate they may have the duty to come to a different decision from that of the sheriff.

1 Children (Scotland) Act 1995, s 59(4).

Principles to be applied

8.16 If and when the hearing has decided that the conditions for making a CPO exist then it *may* continue the order and any s 58 direction included in it, with or without variation of the order or direction. Of the principles set out in the Children (Scotland) Act 1995, s 16, only the welfare principle formally applies, but under the Children's Hearings (Scotland) Rules 1996[1] the hearing is bound, taking account of the age and maturity of the child, to give the child the opportunity to give his or her views. It is also sensible for the hearing to have regard to the principle of avoiding unnecessary intervention in the life of the child but there is, it is submitted, no analogy here with the no non-beneficial order rule which governs the decision of a court in relation to considering parental responsibilities and other orders under s 11(1) of the Act.[2] In so far as the no non-beneficial order principle does apply it means, here as elsewhere, that the hearing should remember that it must be shown that whatever intervention is taking place or is proposed will better promote the welfare of the child than would not intervening at all. It is submitted that the hearing, unlike the reporter at the stage of considering whether or not to discharge a child by virtue of the s 60(3) powers,[3] is not bound to identify a change of circumstances or further information before changing or not continuing a CPO. However the purpose of this hearing is presumably to guard against the situation which arose in Orkney whereby there was fresh information which the reporter did not lay before the hearing which had been convened to consider renewal of a warrant for detention of the children,[4] and if there is fresh relevant information it should be given to the hearing.

1 SI 1996/3261, r 15(2)(c).
2 '[The court] shall not make any such order unless it considers that it would be better for the child that the order be made than that none should be made at all' – Children (Scotland) Act 1995, s 11(7)(a).
3 Discussed at 8.04 above.
4 *Clyde Report* para 7.61; Lord Clyde considered that the reporter 'was in error in opposing the attempts to refer to the substance of the medical examinations to the hearing' (para 13.72).

8.17 By the time the second working day hearing is taking place both the sheriff and the reporter will have been satisfied as to the necessity of the CPO in the interests of the welfare of the child. The decision as to whether to confirm it or not, or to vary it, is of course for the hearing to take but it is submitted, however, that in the absence of a material change in circumstances hearings should be cautious of deciding not to continue a CPO. The removal of the child will still be a recent event and the hearing may feel that things should be allowed to settle. There is ample opportunity for further challenge.[1] In practice initial hearings do not often refrain from continuing a CPO. However the decision is for the hearing and the hearing alone, having regard to its considered view, in the light of the information before it, of the best course to be taken to promote and maintain the welfare of the child. The chairman of the hearing may adjourn the hearing till later on the same day.[2]

1 See ch 9 ff below.
2 Children's Hearings (Scotland) Rules 1996, SI 1996/3261, r 10(4).

Decision to vary

8.18 The hearing may decide to vary a CPO or a direction therein.[1] This power is used only occasionally, generally in relation to contact.

1 Children (Scotland) Act 1995, s 59(4).

The giving of the decision

8.19 At the conclusion of the hearing the chairman announces the decision orally and may issue a written note as to the reasons for the decision.[1]

In hearings of this type, in contrast to hearings on referral or at review of a supervision requirement,[2] the rules contain no specific requirement to give reasons or issue a written note of reasons but since r 26(2)(a) requires the reporter to send to parties 'a copy of the warrant, continuation of the warrant, continuation of the order, or requirement and a copy of the statement of the reasons for the decision' it is submitted that reasons should always be stated and noted in writing. The obligation on the reporter to keep records[3] applies to these hearings as to all others.

1 For discussion of the formulation of a statement of reasons see 23.33 below.
2 Children's Hearings (Scotland) Rules 1996, SI 1996/3261, r 20(5).
3 SI 1996/3261, r 31, discussed at 22.04 below.

Appeal – recall and variation

8.20 There is no appeal to the sheriff from a decision by a hearing to continue a CPO.[1] A decision not to continue a CPO would seem to be appealable at the instance of a child, a safeguarder on the child's behalf,[2] or relevant person but not by the applicant.[3] The decision of a hearing to continue a CPO or a direction therein may be brought under review by an application under the Children (Scotland) Act 1995, s 60(7) to set aside or vary it.

1 Children (Scotland) Act 1995, s 51(15)(b).
2 Act of Sederunt (Child Care and Maintenance Rules) 1997, SI 1997/291, r 3.53(3).
3 C(S)A 1995, s 51(1).

CHAPTER 9

The motion to set aside or vary a CPO – 1995 Act, s 60(7)[1]

WHAT IS TO BE VARIED OR SET ASIDE

9.01 The CPO, whether as granted originally by the sheriff or as continued with or without variation by the hearing at a s 59(2) initial hearing, may be applied to be set aside or varied by the persons mentioned in the next following paragraph. The application to set aside or vary is always referable to the CPO and/or direction as granted by the sheriff or continued by the hearing and not to the decision of the hearing as such.

1 See also ch 10 below.

Who may apply and when

9.02 The following persons or classes of persons may apply for the setting aside or variation of a CPO and/or direction:

'(a) the child to whom the order or direction relates;
(b) a person having parental rights over the child;
(c) a relevant person;
(d) any person to whom notice of the application for the order was given by virtue of the rules;[1] or
(e) the applicant for the order made under section 57 of this Act.'[2]

1 Act of Sederunt (Child Care and Maintenance Rules) 1997, SI 1997/291, r 3.32(b); discussed at 6.14 above.
2 Children (Scotland) Act 1995, s 60(7).

Timescales

9.03 Where the application to set aside or vary is in respect of the original CPO it must be made before the commencement of the initial ('second working day') hearing[1] held under the Children (Scotland) Act 1995, s 59(2).[2] This is a very demanding timescale and such applications are rare. Where a CPO has been continued (whether with or without variation) by a hearing under s 59(2), the application to set aside or vary must be made within two working days of such continuation.[3] 'Within two working days' means that the day on which the continuation was made does not count; one then works out which is the next working day and it will follow that the last day for lodging the application is the working day immediately thereafter. The definition of 'working day' has already been discussed.[4] In the case of a continuation of a CPO made on Monday, 9 August 1999 the second working day thereafter would be Wednesday, 11 August. In the case of a continuation of a CPO made on Friday, 31 December 1999 the second working day thereafter would be Tuesday, 4 January 2000 which was not a day on which the court was open for ordinary business. In such an event it is thought that the practice allowing lodgement on the first court day after the last day would apply.[5] The application must be determined within three working days of its being made[6] – and accordingly if a continuation of a CPO was made on Thursday, 30 December 1999 and an application to set aside or vary were lodged on the same day then the hearing of the application would require to be held on or before 4 January 2000 (since 31 December 1999 and 3 and 4 January 2000, although public holidays, were working days in terms of s 93(1) of the Act).

1 Discussed at 8.08 above.
2 Children (Scotland) Act 1995, s 60(8)(a).
3 C(S)A 1995, s 60(8)(b).
4 At 8.08 above.
5 Cf the opinion of Sheriff Thomas Young in *Lanark County Council v Docherty* 1959 SLT (Sh Ct) 12.
6 C(S)A 1995, s 60(8)

SAFEGUARDER OR CURATOR *AD LITEM*

Necessary for sheriff to consider making appointment

9.04   The sheriff is bound, as soon as practicable after the lodging of an application to set aside or vary a CPO is made, to consider if it is necessary to appoint a safeguarder.[1] The general definition and function of a safeguarder, and the practice in some places of appointing a curator *ad litem* instead of a safeguarder, have already been noticed.

1 Children (Scotland) Act 1995, s 41(1); SI 1997/291, r 3.7(1)(a).

Appointing a safeguarder/curator *ad litem* – the practicalities

9.05   Where the applicant is, as is frequently the case by this stage, represented by a solicitor, it is suggested that the applicant's solicitor, immediately on receiving instructions to lodge an application to vary or recall, should advise the court by phone in order that the sheriff clerk may find a suitable diet within the strict timescale and at the same time consult the sheriff. In Glasgow the sheriff clerk will advise a sheriff in order that the process of considering the appointment of a safeguarder/curator *ad litem* may be begun as soon as possible. Ideally the sheriff who granted the CPO should be consulted. If the sheriff decides that a safeguarder/curator *ad litem* will be appropriate then the person whom the sheriff wishes to appoint should be contacted, usually by phone, to ascertain that he or she is willing to act and available on the day and at the time when the hearing of the application is to take place. The sheriff clerk should advise the applicant's agent of the identity of the person who is to be appointed – if practicable before the applicant's agent has completed the form or at the latest when the form is being lodged. The applicant's agent can then insert the appropriate name and details.

Choice of safeguarder

9.06 If a safeguarder has already received notice of the original application because of his or her appointment in connection with related proceedings[1] the sheriff should appoint that person unless on his or her own motion or on the motion of a party on cause shown the sheriff directs that another person should be appointed.[2] The same rule does not technically apply to the appointment of a curator *ad litem* but the sheriff will be mindful of the desirability of limiting the number of persons who require to interview the child and will generally appoint as curator *ad litem* the curator *ad litem* already in place. There is no obligation on the court to seek the views of parties and, accordingly, if a party wishes to show cause for the appointment of a safeguarder other than a safeguarder already in post, it would appear that that party must take the initiative. When appointing a safeguarder or curator *ad litem* the sheriff will only rarely select a named person but may ask the sheriff clerk to try to find a person appropriate to the gender or ethnic origin of the child.

1 Cf 5.11 above.
2 SI 1997/291, r 3.7(2).

Criterion for appointing safeguarder/curator *ad litem*

9.07 The test for the appointment of a safeguarder or curator is, as always, necessity, having regard to the interests of the child. It is submitted that sheriffs should be astute to recognise the advantages of the appointment of a safeguarder or curator *ad litem* at this stage. Applications to set aside or vary are comparatively few and they are likely to be taken in the more marginal and potentially contentious cases. The safeguarder or curator is, of course, a potential channel for the views of the child.[1]

1 SI 1997/291, r 3.5(2)(c).

PREPARING, FILLING UP, LODGING AND SERVING THE
APPLICATION FORM – FORM 52: 'APPLICATION TO VARY OR
RECALL[1] A CHILD PROTECTION ORDER'

The practicalities

9.08 The solicitor for the party who wishes to challenge the CPO must obtain instructions and collect as much information as possible in relation to that party's objections to the CPO itself and to any of the directions made as part of it. Since there is only a period of two working days within which to lodge the application[2] the solicitor must act quickly.[3] The reporter and the social work department will generally be ready to help by supplying papers. If a supportive affidavit can be lodged along with the application then so much the better but this may not be practicable. The applicant's solicitor should consider if any of the information, e g medical information or information from the DSS, which he or she may require may be regarded by the holder of the information as confidential to his client, in which event the client should be asked to sign appropriate mandates. If necessary, an application for full legal aid should be completed and signed.

1 The form, reproduced in Appendix 12, uses the term 'recall' although it does not appear in the Children (Scotland) Act 1995, s 60(7) or SI 1997/291, r 3.33, both of which say 'set aside'.
2 Children (Scotland) Act 1995, s 60(8).
3 Cf 10.11 below.

Part 1: 'DETAILS OF APPLICANT AND OTHER PERSONS WHO[1] THE APPLICANT BELIEVES SHOULD RECEIVE NOTICE OF THE APPLICATION'

9.09   This part of the form requires the applicant to supply information identifying: the applicant; the child; any safeguarder (if not applicant); the relevant person(s) (if not applicant(s)); the principal reporter; and 'Any other person who should receive notice of the application'. In the case of the child the name, address, gender and date of birth should be supplied. In the case of the other persons as much information as is available should be supplied, i e name, address and any phone, fax and DX numbers which may be known. Along with the information about the relevant person(s) there should be supplied the basis on which they are thought to qualify as relevant persons.[2] In relation to the other person (or presumably persons) who should receive notice of the application the form glosses: '[For example, any person who is caring for the child at the time of the application being made: insert name, address and telephone number of person and provide details of their interest in the application and/or child].' In the event of the applicant's wishing not to disclose the address or whereabouts of the child or any other person to a recipient of the application form, then, although the whereabouts must of course be indicated in Part 1, the request for non-disclosure and the reason for it should be set out in Part 3 of the form. The applicant must notify the persons mentioned in the application[3] unless, in the case of the child, service has been dispensed with.[4]

1 *Sic.*
2 Children (Scotland) Act 1995, s 93(2)(b).
3 SI 1997/291, rr 3.12(1)(b) and 3.4(1)(b).
4 SI 1997/291, r 3.4(2).

The Principal Reporter

9.10   Notification of an application to set aside or vary must always be given to the reporter.[1] The notification to the reporter should be to the office of the local reporter and it is accordingly suggested that the designation of the Principal Reporter should be given as, for example, in a

Glasgow case: c/o Reporter Manager, SCRA, 10 Bell Street, Glasgow G1 1LG (Tel 0141-567 7900, Fax 0141-567 7969).

1 Children (Scotland) Act 1995, s 60(9), SI 1997/291, r 3.12(1)(d).

Part 2: 'INFORMATION ABOUT THE APPLICATION AND ORDERS SOUGHT'

9.11   The contents of this part are similar to the contents of Part 2 of the form of application for a CPO.[1] An example, in an application by the mother, of a ground going to the root of the CPO would be:

> 'The alleged abuser AB has now left the family home and the applicant has promised not to re-admit him in any circumstances. The intervention in the children's lives represented by removing them from the family home will not better serve their welfare than leaving them at home. The CPO is accordingly unnecessary. The children CD and EF have said they want to return to their mother.'

An example of a ground seeking a variation of the order would be:

> 'The applicant is now willing to exercise contact with the children GH and IJ within the Contact Centre at [address] under the supervision of the Glasgow City Council Social Work Department and would like the prohibition on contact to be removed and replaced by a condition allowing contact under supervision at said Centre every week-day afternoon from 2 to 4 p m. The children are missing their mother.'[2]

1 Form 47, discussed at 5.17 above – 'GROUNDS FOR MAKING APPLICATION'.
2 For another example and a presentation of the practicalities at this stage see 10.12 below.

Part 3. 'DETAILS OF ORDER SOUGHT AND ANY TERMS, CONDITIONS OR DIRECTIONS'

9.12   This section of the form draws together the formal application for recall or variation of the CPO and asks for a diet to be assigned. It also contains the formal requests for authority to serve on the reporter, the local authority, the child and the other persons mentioned in Part 1 of the application. In the case of the latter two there may be dispensations from the necessity to serve.

Serving or dispensing with service on child

9.13   This part of the form also asks for an order to serve on the child a copy of the application and a notification in Form 27[1] or to dispense with service of either or both of these documents (or, presumably, parts thereof) on the child. As to thus dispensing, the form narrates: '(c) [*delete as appropriate*] Dispense with service on the child or any other person for the following reasons [*insert details*]'. It is submitted that only exceptionally should Form 27 not be sent to a child who is old enough to be likely to be able to read. As with an application for a CPO,[2] an example of such an exceptional situation would be when a safeguarder is being notified. The sheriff should not lightly dispense with service on the child. The sheriff may, in deciding on this matter, make or cause to be made such inquiries as he or she thinks fit. For example, the sheriff may ask the sheriff clerk to obtain information from the reporter, solicitor, safeguarder or curator, social worker or other person who may reasonably be expected to know what effect service of the application would be likely to have on the child.[3]

1 See 9.16 below.
2 See 5.10 above.
3 See discussion at 5.22 above.

Serving or dispensing with service on other persons

9.14   Where a dispensation is sought the reasons for requesting it must be stated.[1]

1 See discussion at 5.22 above.

Mode of service

9.15   The application to vary or set aside is one of the proceedings excepted from the general rule requiring service within 48 hours if personal and 72 hours if postal.[1] Accordingly if time does not permit any of the conventional methods of service[2] then service may be effected orally or in such other manner and by such person as the sheriff may direct.[3] The form does not contain a routine request for oral etc service but it is suggested that this should generally be requested, preferably by written request in the form, but possibly by oral request to the sheriff clerk, for onward transmission to the sheriff, when the form is lodged. If not requested the sheriff clerk may remind the applicant's agent of the possibility of oral etc service. Once the first order has been obtained then the appropriate parties must be notified in whatever way has been directed by the sheriff.[4]

1 SI 1997/291, r 3.13(1) and (2).
2 SI 1997/291, r 3.15(1) and (2).
3 SI 1997/291, r 3.15(3).
4 SI 1997/291, r 3.15(3).

Form 27. 'NOTICE TO CHILD OF APPLICATION TO VARY OR SET ASIDE CHILD PROTECTION ORDER'

9.16   The form is reproduced in Appendix 12.[1] As suggested already,[2] it is only exceptionally, for example when a safeguarder or curator is being notified, that this form should not be served on a child who may be able to read. The purpose of this form is of course to let the child know, in as ordinary language as possible, what is going on and to give him or her a chance to participate and in particular to express a view. Those responsible for choosing the words of the form had a difficult task. Research has yet to be done to see how successful they have been. It is thought that the agency responsible for the child during the currency of the CPO should take the responsibility of making sure that the child has received the form and had it explained to him or her and for arranging for the child to have such assistance as he or she may require in completing it and returning it.

1 The form refers to the Scottish Child Law Centre – the current details of such an organisation should be checked and any change, for example of phone number, should be reflected in the completed form.
2 At 9.13 above.

PREPARING FOR THE HEARING BEFORE THE SHERIFF

The local authority – social workers and local authority solicitors

9.17 In the short time[1] between the lodging of the application and the hearing before the sheriff much activity must take place. If the social workers mainly responsible for the child are not the social workers who presented the application for the CPO (which may, for example, have been prepared and presented by the Out of Hours Team) then they will require to become familiar with the recent events and make up their minds as to the appropriateness or otherwise of the CPO, any directions or conditions, and as to the appropriateness or otherwise of the application to set aside or vary: in particular, for example, the social workers should have a reasoned stance in relation to any request for contact and be ready to respond to any suggestion of supervised contact with practical proposals – keeping in mind that the decision as to contact in principle is a matter which the sheriff will decide. The local authority will generally instruct a solicitor in its legal department to conduct the proceedings before the sheriff. That solicitor should be as fully briefed as possible and ready to submit information and/or evidence in support of the conditions for making the CPO[2] and any directions.[3] An illustration of the practicalities of the work to be done by the social work department and the local authority solicitor is given later.[4]

1 Cf 9.03 above.
2 Cf Children (Scotland) Act 1995, s 60(11)(a).
3 Cf C(S)A 1995, s 60(11)(b).
4 At 10.13–10.18 below.

The reporter

9.18 The reporter must keep the case under review. The Children (Scotland) Act 1995, s 60(3) provides that a child who is subject to a CPO shall not be kept in any place of safety by such order, prevented from being removed from a place of safety, or continue to be subject to any term, condition or direction of a CPO, where the reporter, having regard to the welfare of the child, considers that, as a result of changed circumstances or further information received by the reporter, the conditions for the making of a CPO are no longer satisfied or that such term, condition or direction is no longer appropriate and the reporter notifies the person responsible for implementing the CPO. Notification under these provisions that the conditions for the making of a CPO are no longer satisfied causes the CPO to be of no effect,[1] thus rendering otiose a hearing of the application to vary or set aside. Accordingly as at the commencement of such a hearing the reporter will have already decided, at least for the time being, that the child should be retained in the place of safety. The reporter should consider the position as at the date of the children's hearing and in the light of the latest information available from the social work department and elsewhere, so as to be in a position to make appropriate submissions to the sheriff at the hearing of the motion to set aside or vary.

1 Children (Scotland) Act 1995, s 60(6)(d).

Advice hearing under s 60(10) of the Act

9.19   At any time after receiving the notice of an application to recall or vary,[1] but before the sheriff has determined the application under the Children (Scotland) Act 1995, s 60(12), the reporter may arrange an advice hearing so that such a hearing may provide the sheriff with any advice it thinks appropriate. Such a hearing may take place before or after the initial hearing under s 59 of the Act. An advice hearing under this subsection would have to observe the welfare principle[2] and the principle of consulting the child[3] but not the principle of no non-beneficial intervention.[4] Holding an advice hearing *before* the initial hearing (which must in any event be held on the second working day after the implementation of the CPO) presents practical difficulties. The usefulness of holding such an advice hearing *after* the initial hearing has examined the CPO and given its reasons for continuing it, with or without variation, is not obvious.

1 See 9.10 above.
2 Children (Scotland) Act 1995, s 16(1).
3 C(S)A 1995, s 16(2) and (4)(a)(iii).
4 C(S)A 1995, s 16(3), when read with s 16(4).

The safeguarder or curator *ad litem*

9.20   In practice the duties and rights of the safeguarder and curator *ad litem* are regarded as identical. The safeguarder is entitled to receive the whole case papers from the reporter.[1] A curator *ad litem* is in practice given the whole case papers by the reporter. In the short time available the safeguarder or curator *ad litem* may not be able to see the child before the hearing although he or she may make the attempt. The safeguarder or curator should investigate the case as fully as possible in the limited time so as to be in a position to inform the sheriff at the hearing of the s 60(7) application as to: (a) what view he or she has come to as to the interests of the child in relation to the setting aside or varying of the CPO;[2] and (b) whether or not the child wishes to express a view and how and, if the child wishes to use the curator as the channel for such view, what that view is.[3] It is thought that the curator should advise the child that the sheriff has the power,[4] should the sheriff choose to exercise it, to direct that the record of the child's views be kept confidential. An example, illustrating inter alia the role of the safeguarder/curator *ad litem* is given in the following chapter.[5]

1 SI 1997/291, r 3.8(b).
2 Children (Scotland) Act 1995, s 41(1)(a).
3 SI 1997/291, r 3.5(2)(c).
4 SI 1997/291, r 3.5(4).
5 See 10.11–10.18 below.

The solicitor for the parties

9.21 The applicant's solicitor should gather as much further evidence in the form of affidavits and medical, psychological or other reports for presentation to the sheriff at the s 60(7) hearing which has to be determined by the sheriff. The solicitor may seek to discuss the matter with the social workers who may consider that it is in the interests of the child to convey their experiences with the case and give their views on it frankly. See the following chapter for an example.[1]

1 At 10.12 and 10.13 below.

The administrative arrangements in the sheriff court

9.22 It is essential for the sheriff clerk and the Scottish Court Service to ensure that a sheriff is available within the tight timetable of 'within three working days of [the application's] being made'.[1] In the example represented in the following chapter the application for recall is lodged on Thursday, 10 April 1997. Accordingly the determination of the sheriff would have to be made on Tuesday, 15 April at the latest. In theory, since the usual periods of notice have no application[2] and since verbal service is available as directed by the sheriff[3] the hearing could take place as early as Friday, 11 April but in practice it would be unusual to fix the hearing so soon and in practice Monday, 14 or Tuesday, 15 would be fixed. If the sheriff does not determine the application to recall or vary within the prescribed time the CPO (and any ancillary directions) falls.[4] It is submitted that the ideal course is that represented in the illustration in Chapter 10, i e to fix the hearing for the second last day, in order to allow the sheriff, if minded to obtain more information, to exercise his or her power to allow 'such further procedure as he thinks fit'[5] by way of a short adjournment[6] within the timescale.[7]

1 Children (Scotland) Act 1995, s 60(8).
2 SI 1997/291, r 3.13(2)(c).
3 SI 1997/291, r 3.15(3) and 3.16(1)(c).
4 C(S)A 1995, s 60(2).
5 SI 1997/291, r 3.33(4).
6 Cf the court's inherent power to adjourn – *Bruce v Linton* (1860) 23 D 85.
7 C(S)A 1995, s 60(8).

Which sheriff?

9.23 A motion to set aside or vary a CPO is not an appeal and accordingly there is no impropriety in the sheriff who granted the CPO hearing the application to set aside or vary. In smaller jurisdictions this is the norm. In a particular case the sheriff who granted the CPO may consider that it would be preferable for another sheriff to hear the application to set aside or vary and this can be arranged. Contrariwise, the sheriff who granted the CPO may wish to deal with any s 60(7) application. The sheriff may wish to obtain parties' views on this matter.[1]

1 It is not usually possible, and indeed it would generally be constitutionally objectionable, to 'choose your sheriff': but it is common enough, in this field as in others, for consideration to be given to whether the sheriff who dealt with one stage of a case should or should not hear a later part of the case.

THE HEARING OF THE S 60(7) APPLICATION BEFORE THE SHERIFF

Procedural structure

9.24 The statutory requirements on the sheriff are set out in the Children (Scotland) Act 1995, s 60(11) which requires the sheriff, with a view to determining (a) if the conditions for making a CPO are satisfied and (b) where the application relates only to a direction under s 58, whether such direction should be cancelled or varied, to hear representations from the parties and, if he or she wishes to make representations, from the reporter. In the unusual event of the local authority not being the applicant for the original CPO it is submitted that it would be correct for the sheriff to treat the local authority as a party, by virtue of the authority's being the person having the responsibility for the child.[1] It is the clear implication of the scheme that the sheriff should have regard to the advice given following any hearing under s 60(10) of the Act.[2] Thereafter, as already noticed,[3] the sheriff may allow such further procedure as he or she thinks fit and then proceed to grant or refuse the application.[4]

1 Children (Scotland) Act 1995, s 57(7).
2 Noticed at 9.19 above.
3 At 9.22 above.
4 SI 1997/291, r 3.33(4).

The s 16 principles

9.25 In considering an application to set aside or vary a CPO the sheriff must have regard to all three of the s 16 principles;[1] but see 9.31 below for a discussion of the interpretation of the welfare principle. The sheriff must observe the principle of consulting the child by doing all that is practicable to find out if the child wishes to express a view and, if so, to find a way for that view to be expressed.[2] Apart from these necessities, the procedure is within the discretion of the sheriff. In practice the local authority is generally represented at the hearing by the local authority solicitor and the social worker(s) associated with the original application for the CPO are in attendance with the social work department file so far as relevant. See 10.14–10.19 below for an illustration of a s 60(7) hearing.

1 Children (Scotland) Act 1995, s 16(1), (2), (3) and (4)(b)(ii).
2 C(S)A 1995, s 16(2); see 9.26 below.

The views of the child at the s 60(7) hearing

9.26   The general principles and practices affecting the obtaining and recording of the views of the child have already been discussed.[1] In relation to these hearings the child may have received Form 27 with its suggestion that the child may wish to obtain legal advice via the Scottish Child Law Centre, whose free telephone number is supplied, or otherwise. If the child has consulted and instructed a solicitor then that solicitor may act as the channel of the child's views.[2] Alternatively the child, either on his or her own initiative or at the suggestion of his or her solicitor, or any safeguarder or curator or anyone else, may send in written views or come to give them personally or per any person.[3] It has already been submitted[4] that in the case of a child who is likely to be able to read, the service of Form 27 should generally not be dispensed with unless a curator *ad litem* is in post and has been notified. In any event the sheriff should be satisfied, subject to the age and maturity of the child, that a channel for the child's views is available.

1 At 4.10–4.12 above.
2 SI 1997/291, r 3.5(2)(b).
3 SI 1997/291, r 3.5(2)(a) and (d).
4 At 5.23 above.

What the sheriff has to decide

9.27   The sheriff has to determine, i e to decide, whether 'the conditions for the making *a* child protection order under section 57 of the Act *are* satisfied [emphases supplied]',[1] or, where the application relates only to a s 58 direction, whether such direction should be varied or cancelled.[2] The word 'are' suggests that the point of time which is relevant is the point of time at which the application to recall or vary is being made, and not the time when the application for the CPO was considered.[3] The word 'a' may suggest that the sheriff may not be limited to considering only the conditions relied upon in the CPO but also any other conditions which the evidence may appear to support. For discussion of the applicability of the welfare principle to the sheriff's decision as to whether or not conditions for a CPO are satisfied, see 9.31 below.

1 Children (Scotland) Act 1995, s 60(11)(a).
2 C(S)A 1995, s 60(11)(b).
3 Cf *Kennedy v B* 1972 SC 1128, 1973 SLT 38.

Relevance of a change of circumstances

9.28   It is thought that the sheriff, unlike the reporter when considering whether to continue to retain a child in a place of safety by reason of a

CPO,[1] is not bound to find change of circumstances or further information before concluding that the conditions for making a CPO are not satisfied. It is submitted that the sheriff must decide this matter on the basis of the whole information before him or her without any legal presumption in favour of the status quo. In practice, however, it may be difficult, in the absence of further information or change of circumstances, to persuade the sheriff that a different view should be taken from that which was taken when the CPO was made. Successful applications to recall are comparatively rare. Of the 73 CPOs granted in Glasgow in the year following the commencement of these provisions on 1 April 1997 12 were made the subjects of applications to recall or review, of which only three were successful.

1 Children (Scotland) Act 1995, s 60(3).

Extent of sheriff's powers on upholding CPO – is the sheriff limited to the terms of the application?

9.29   If, and only if, the sheriff has decided that the conditions for the making of a CPO are satisfied then the sheriff [emphasis supplied] *may*:[1]

> '(a) confirm or vary the order, or any term or condition on which it was granted;
> (b) confirm or vary any direction given, in relation to the order, under section 58 of this Act;
> (c) give a new direction under that section; *or* [emphasis supplied]
> (d) continue in force the order and any such direction until the commencement of a children's hearing arranged in accordance with section 65(2) of this Act.

The words 'any term or condition' in paragraph (a) refer back to the Children (Scotland) Act 1995, s 57(4).[2] Accordingly, a variation of such an element in the CPO would be competent to the sheriff at this stage. The directions which may be given under s 58 include directions as to contact[3] and as to the exercise or fulfilment of parental responsibilities or rights in relation to the child[4] – for example, in relation to medical examination. It is submitted that the 'or' highlighted in paragraph (c) is not disjunctive as amongst paragraphs (a), (b) and (c) and that the sheriff (subject always to applying the three s 16 principles) would be entitled, for example, to vary the place of safety at which the child was to be kept, vary a contact direction which had been made and make a fresh direction in relation to a medical examination. It is further submitted that the welfare principle and the consideration that technical rules 'should serve and certainly not thwart' the purpose of promotion of welfare[5] suggest that the sheriff may in appropriate circumstances follow any of these courses on motion of party or on his or her own motion, even if no such motion is contained in the application to vary or recall.

1 Children (Scotland) Act 1995, s 60(12).
2 'A child protection order may, subject to such terms and conditions as the sheriff considers appropriate, do any one or more of the following:
   (a) require any person in a position to do so to produce the child to the applicant;

   (b) authorise the removal of the child by the applicant to a place of safety, and the keeping of the child at that place;

   (c) authorise the prevention of the removal of the child from any place where he is being accommodated;

   (d) provide that the location of any place of safety in which the child is being kept should not be disclosed to any person or class of person specified in the order.'

3 C(S)A 1995, s 58(1) and (2).
4 C(S)A 1995, s 58(4).
5 Cf *W v Kennedy* 1988 SLT 583 at 585F.

Conditions for making CPO not 'satisfied'

9.30 Where the sheriff decides that the conditions for making a CPO are not satisfied the sheriff *shall* recall the CPO and cancel any s 58 directions attached to it.[1]

1 Children (Scotland) Act 1995, s 60(13).

INTERPRETATION OF THE WELFARE PRINCIPLE

9.31 As noted already,[1] the Children (Scotland) Act 1995, s 16(1) provides that where a court determines any matter with respect to a child then the welfare of that child throughout childhood shall be the court's paramount consideration. The decision of the sheriff as to whether the conditions for a CPO are satisfied is a decision based upon the sheriff's assessment of the information before him or her. A CPO will generally have been granted on the basis of perceived danger to the child[2] and the question for determination by the sheriff at the hearing on the application to recall is whether the sheriff is satisfied that the perceived dangers are real on the basis of the whole information before him or her. It has already been submitted[3] that the sheriff is not bound to identify a change in circumstances in order to entitle him or her to set aside or vary the CPO. It is submitted that the task of the sheriff is to use his or her independent judgment as to whether or not, on the most up-to-date available information and/or evidence, that the conditions for making a CPO are 'satisfied'. The sheriff is of course not considering the weight of evidence on the balance of probabilities as he or she would be at a proof, but whether or not there are, on the latest information, 'reasonable grounds to believe' etc under s 57(1) or, as the case may be, 'reasonable grounds to suspect' etc under s 57(2). This is an objective decision. If the sheriff were to conclude, for example, that there were on the information now available no reasonable grounds to believe that a CPO should be granted then the sheriff would have no option but to recall the order and cancel the CPO, even although there were other matters before the sheriff giving rise to a suspicion that the child's welfare throughout his childhood would be better promoted by the confirming of the CPO.

1 At 2.15 above.
2 See the sample case of 'Kate' in the following chapter at 10.01 and 10.15.
3 At 9.28 above.

TERMINATION OF CPO

9.32   In summary, a CPO ceases to have effect in respect of its essential order and any direction thereunder:

- where there has been no attempt made to implement the order within 24 hours of the time when the CPO was granted;[1]
- where an application to recall or vary a CPO has been made and has not been determined timeously;[2]
- where an initial hearing has not continued it;[3]
- on the person who implemented the order receiving notification from the reporter that the reporter has decided, in respect of the child who is the subject of the order, not to refer that child to a hearing arranged under the Children (Scotland) Act 1995, s 65(2);[4]
- on the reporter's giving notice that he considers, whether as a result of a change in the circumstances of the case or of further information relating to the case having been received, that the conditions for granting a CPO are no longer satisfied.[5]

1 Children (Scotland) Act 1995, s 60(1).
2 C(S)A 1995, s 60(2).
3 C(S)A 1995, s 59(4).
4 C(S)A 1995, s 60(6)(c).
5 C(S)A 1995, s 60(3).

CHAPTER 10

Application for CPO and motion to set aside or vary: 'Kate'

This chapter contains an imaginary case scenario. It is hoped that the representation of the activities of the various professionals is reasonably realistically portrayed but each acting should not necessarily be regarded as ideal practice.

BEFORE THE APPLICATION FOR THE CPO

Thursday 3 April 1997

10.01 The Social Work Department (SWD) receives information that the stepfather of Kate, now aged 11, is to be released from prison tomorrow after serving a two-year sentence for lewd and libidinous practices against Kate, and will resume residence with Kate's mother who, it is feared, will be likely to collude with the stepfather because he will intimidate her by physical assault.

Friday 4 April 1997, morning

10.02 Case conference (mother is invited but she does not attend) at which it is decided that a CPO is necessary. SWD arranges suitable foster home. Social Worker AB prepares application under the Children (Scotland) Act 1995, s 57(1) and advises sheriff clerk of imminent application for CPO. SWD advises reporter and local authority solicitor of all that has been done and of likely timetable.

THE HEARING OF THE APPLICATION BY THE SHERIFF

Friday, 4 April 1997, early afternoon

10.03 Social Worker AB and Senior Social Worker CD attend at sheriff court, argue for and obtain CPO, including authorisation to remove child and condition prohibiting contact with mother and stepfather, timed at 3.30 p m. The CPO contains a direction authorising AB to effect service by personal service and/or oral service in terms of Act of Sederunt (Child Care and Maintenance Rules) 1997, rr 3.15(3) and 3.16(1)(c).[1]

1 SI 1997/291.

AFTER THE GRANTING OF THE APPLICATION BY THE SHERIFF

Friday, 4 April 1997, late afternoon

10.04   Social workers call at mother's home and remove Kate at 4.15 p m. They record time of removal in SWD file. AB serves CPO on Kate with a notice in the style of Form 50 and serves CPO on mother with a notice in style of Form 51. They take Kate to the foster parents.

Friday, 4 April 1997, 4.45 p m

10.05   Social workers return to office and AB serves by fax the CPO with Form 51 on reporter and also phones reporter to confirm and to advise reporter of what has happened and of address of the child. Reporter notifies SWD by phone, with confirming fax, of initial hearing at 2 p m on Tuesday, 8 April. Reporter notifies Kate, and the mother, *qua* relevant person, by phone of the initial hearing and sends confirmatory letter by ordinary post.

MOTION TO VARY OR RECALL – INITIAL PREPARATIONS

Friday, 4 April 1997, later in the afternoon

10.06   The mother phones her solicitor ('MS') who advises as to the anticipated initial hearing and that the date of any such hearing will be Tuesday, 8 April. Mother asks MS to try to have the CPO recalled and in any event to have it varied so as to allow contact. MS arranges meeting with mother for Monday, 7 April. MS advises mother meantime that it would be difficult adequately to present to the sheriff the case for variation or recall of the CPO immediately because of the short timescale and that it would be preferable to await the decision of the hearing at the initial hearing and then if necessary apply to the sheriff thereafter. The mother accepts this advice.

10.07   Kate phones Scottish Child Law Centre, using the free phone number supplied in Form 50, and the procedures are explained to Kate. She is told that she could obtain services of a solicitor under the legal aid scheme for any hearings before the sheriff and get legal advice in order to present her case to the hearings. She is aware that her mother will try to have the CPO recalled and she is against this, although she would like to see her mother. She is told inter alia that she will be entitled to express a view to the children's hearing and that in the event of a hearing before the sheriff she may be able to tell the sheriff something which the sheriff may be prepared to keep secret, at least in the short term. It is suggested to her that she might want to write down a note of what she wants to tell the hearing and she is reminded that her mother would know of anything that she conveyed to the hearing. Kate indicates that she will not require legal advice or legal representation.

Monday, 7 April 1997, afternoon

10.08   The mother meets her solicitor (MS) and asks her to appear with her to ask the initial hearing not to continue the CPO and in any event to vary it so as to allow contact with mother. Mother also instructs MS that in the event of the hearing not complying with either or both of these requests she would like to take the matter to the sheriff. MS tells mother of existence of s 60(7) hearing before the sheriff and likely dates therefor – if application to set aside or vary is lodged on Thursday, 10 April it is likely that the court hearing will be on Monday, 14 April or Tuesday, 15 April. Mother informs solicitor of the names and addresses of family friends who may be willing to give affidavits supporting the mother's position by saying that the stepfather has turned over a new leaf, no longer abuses girls and never assaulted mother, and signs mandate authorising MS to obtain information from family doctor. MS explains that full legal aid may be available for any hearing before the sheriff but not for appearances before children's hearings but MS agrees to appear at the initial hearing without remuneration. MS arranges for legal aid and advice form to be completed and signed by mother.

THE INITIAL CHILDREN'S HEARING

Tuesday, 8 April 1997

Taking the child to the initial hearing

10.09   Social Worker AB goes to foster parents' house to collect Kate and take her to the hearing along with the foster parents.

At 2 p m: the initial hearing[1]

10.10   Present are: Kate, the mother, with her solicitor (MS), the reporter, AB (social worker) and the foster mother. The presence of a foster carer is not a legal essential, but may be helpful to the hearing. MS asks for CPO to be not continued or at least varied by allowing contact with the mother, and in support of this request asks mother to explain why she thinks this would be in the interests of the welfare of the child. The mother says that the information about her supposed collusion with the stepfather is incorrect but agrees that the stepfather has resumed cohabitation. AB states that she thinks the CPO should be continued and gives reasons by reference to the facts narrated in the CPO application which, she says, still exist. The reporter indicates that he intends to frame grounds of referral. AB also opposes contact and gives reasons. The foster mother reports that Kate is happy with her and will be attending school normally. The hearing chairman asks Kate for her views. Kate says she wishes to stay with the foster parents. The hearing chairman asks why and Kate says she does not wish to say why. Kate does, however, wish to have contact with her mother but not at home. Again, she does not wish to say why. AB advises that SWD can arrange for Kate to be taken to a contact centre every day after school from 4 to 6 p m. Kate agrees to this and her mother accepts it. After further discussion the hearing continues the CPO but varies it to the extent of allowing contact as agreed. The hearing chairman states as the reasons for this decision that the hearing considers: (1) that there would be danger to the child because of the information, which the hearing for the time being accepts, that the mother would be likely to collude in abuse by the step-father; (2) that the child is happy and well cared for with the foster parents; (3) that the child wished to stay with the foster parents; and (4) that it was in the child's interest to maintain contact with her mother and this accorded with Kate's expressed views. After the hearing AB takes Kate and her mother to the contact centre to introduce them and then returns Kate (not with mother accompanying) to the foster parents' home.

1 See 8.11 ff above.

MOTION TO VARY OR RECALL – FURTHER PREPARATIONS

Wednesday, 9 April 1997

10.11   MS requests copy minutes of case conference from SWD and copies of relevant reports from reporter and they agree to provide these. MS then makes appointments for family friends to come to office to swear affidavits. MS asks family doctor for letter reporting on any occasion when mother has sought medical advice regarding physical or mental effects of stepfather's violence. MS phones sheriff clerk and states that tomorrow she will be lodging an application to set aside and vary the CPO made on 4 April 1997 and continued with variation by the initial hearing on 8 April. Sheriff clerk advises the sheriff who made the CPO. Sheriff decides that a curator *ad litem* should be appointed when the application comes in and asks sheriff clerk to find out if a female solicitor on the informal list of curators is available. Sheriff Clerk phones KC ('Kate's curator') who says that she is ready to accept appointment. KC phones reporter and reporter agrees to furnish copy papers whenever appointment as curator is formalised.

Thursday, 10 April 1997

10.12   MS now has one affidavit from family friend which is to an extent supportive of mother's stance. She has also sent mandate to doctor and received verbal confirmation from doctor that mother has not received medical treatment which could be related to assault since coming to the practice. MS completes application in the style of Form 52 with the affidavit attached. She states as the 'Grounds for Making the Application': 'The abuser has reformed. In any event the child's mother is able to protect the child. The allegations in the application for the CPO, that the stepfather intimidates the applicant by assaulting her, are false. The applicant believes the child would prefer to stay in the family home. It cannot be shown that the intervention in the child's life represented by her removal from the family home would promote her welfare better than leaving her there.' MS takes the application to the sheriff clerk, obtains the first order and serves the application appropriately.[1] The sheriff clerk advises the sheriff who granted the order [who happens to be available] and the sheriff appoints KC as curator *ad litem*. The sheriff clerk then phones KC who accepts office verbally. KC then notifies MS and the reporter of her appointment, arranges to obtain the papers from the reporter and ascertains from the reporter which social worker at which office is responsible for the child's case. KC then phones SWD in order to try, if time and practicalities permit, to fix an appointment to see Kate before the s 60(7) hearing.

1 See 9.15 above.

Monday, 14 April 1997

10.13 By now MS has another affidavit and a letter from the doctor confirming the phone call. KC has seen Kate. The reporter has discussed the case again with SWD and SWD has briefed the local authority solicitor ('LAS').

THE HEARING BEFORE THE SHERIFF OF THE APPLICATION TO VARY OR RECALL

Just before the hearing in front of the sheriff

10.14 The following assemble a little before the hearing of the application by the sheriff: Kate, with foster mother and KC; the mother, with MS; the reporter; LAS and Kate's social worker, AB, and the senior social worker, CD. AB has brought the SWD file. MS hands copies of the new material (affidavits and letter from doctor) to the other parties and to the sheriff clerk. The sheriff clerk indicates that the sheriff is ready and the parties go into a small court room, not open to the public, which is being treated as the sheriff's chambers. The sheriff and the solicitors are not robed but (and practice may vary slightly from sheriff to sheriff) the atmosphere is fairly formal, with parties standing up when the sheriff comes in. The foster parent and the social workers wait outside with Kate in a private waiting room.

The s 60(7) hearing itself[1]

10.15 (Again, practice may vary slightly.) The sheriff asks the mother's solicitor (MS) to elaborate on the application and to advise as to the latest position in relation to what is in the best interests of the child. MS argues for the return of Kate by way of the CPO being set aside, which failing more generous contact (including residential). She emphasises the total lack of any medical evidence supporting the view that the stepfather assaulted the mother, thereby forcing her to collude. The sheriff then asks the reporter and then the local authority solicitor (LAS) to address her and they do, each opposing the motions. LAS says that AB would like to clarify a matter and AB is invited into the court room and speaks to a matter of fact. The sheriff offers the parties the opportunity of asking questions of AB about her statement. The sheriff then asks Kate's curator (KC): (1) the extent of her investigations; (2) her opinion, in so far as she has been able to formulate it, as to the best interests of the child; and (3) whether or not Kate wishes to express a view and, if so, how. KC replies and also opposes the motions. KC tells the sheriff that Kate does wish to express a view and wishes to speak to the sheriff directly. The sheriff asks MS if she wishes to reply and she says she wishes to say nothing beyond that her client is content that Kate should speak to the sheriff but hopes that the sheriff will be able to convey to her the substance of what Kate says. The sheriff makes no comment, beyond asking for KC to bring Kate into her chambers. The sheriff then rises and goes to her chambers with the sheriff clerk.

1 See 9.24 above.

The private interview with the child

Preliminaries

10.16 The sheriff clerk brings KC, not with Kate, to the sheriff's room and KC tells the sheriff that she, KC, has told Kate about the sheriff's power to hear from a child directly and keep a note of the information in a sealed envelope if the sheriff so decides[1] and that Kate wishes to tell the sheriff something which she has not even revealed to KC. Kate has told KC that there is 'no way' she will go back home or accept residential access but will not tell KC why. The sheriff asks the sheriff clerk to go and invite Kate into the sheriff's room. In the meantime KC withdraws. Kate arrives with the sheriff clerk who remains in the room. The sheriff explains the purpose of the meeting and tells her that her views will be taken into account but that the sheriff may not be able to do what Kate wants. The sheriff also mentions the powers which she (the sheriff) *may* be prepared to use, to keep Kate's views confidential. The sheriff explains that while theoretically a child's views can be kept confidential it may not be difficult for at least the general nature of her views to be detected by others, particularly if they are seen to have a marked effect on the sheriff's decision. The sheriff also tells Kate that the 'secret envelope' will probably be able to be opened by an appeal court in the event of an appeal but that the appeal court would probably be bound not to convey the views to anyone else, but there could be no absolute guarantee.[2] Kate says she knows and accepts this but still wishes to speak to the sheriff privately. Kate says she does not want even the sheriff clerk to be present. The sheriff explains that the sheriff clerk is a part of the court and is equally bound to confidentiality as is the sheriff herself. The sheriff says she is not prepared to hear from Kate without the sheriff clerk being present. Kate accepts this explanation.

1 SI 1997/291, r 3.5(4).
2 See 4.10 ff above.

'The views of the child – confidential' – rules 3.5(3) and 3.5(4)

10.17   Kate gives the sheriff her views in general and in particular tells the sheriff that her mother actively colluded with the stepfather and on some occasions participated in the abuse. The stepfather did not assault her mother and that was why there would be no medical evidence. Kate has never told anyone about this and does not intend to because she does not want her mother to go to prison. She still loves her mother and still wishes to see her regularly. She does not want to be adopted but would like long-term fostering. The sheriff confirms that she will record Kate's views and put them in the confidential envelope. The sheriff reassures Kate that she (the sheriff) will not disclose the information to anyone and in particular she will not promptly report her mother to the police, but warns Kate again that she cannot give an absolute guarantee of secrecy because people may be able to work out at least the essence of what Kate has said and also because at present the law is not firm and that the 'confidential' envelope may be ordered to be revealed by a superior court. Kate says that she would not mind the others being told that she has immovable objection to resuming occupancy of any household which includes the stepfather and to residential contact. Her mother and stepfather will know the reason but will obviously not tell anyone. The sheriff writes out the child's views, puts the paper in an envelope marked appropriately and seals and signs the envelope across the flap, all in the presence of Kate.[1] (The formidable legal and practical difficulties surrounding the 'confidential' views of the child are more fully discussed at 4.12 to 4.18 above. It should be emphasised that recording of the child's views in a 'confidential' envelope is a matter for the sheriff to decide upon in the exercise of his/her discretionary judgment. Not all sheriffs would adopt the course taken by the sheriff in the case of 'Kate'.)

1 For discussion of some of the legal implications of 'confidential views' see 4.13 ff above.

Closing submissions

10.18   The hearing resumes with the same persons present as before. The sheriff says that Kate has expressed immovable objection to staying in any household with the stepfather and to residential contact but is happy to continue with non-residential contact. The sheriff then asks parties if they wish to make any final remarks. MS says that the child's views, while having to be taken into account, are not to be regarded as decisive of the issues. KC accepts that this is a correct statement of the law but argues that the child is clearly articulate and mature and that, she having expressed so clear a view, it would be unreasonable not to give it great weight and that this, together with the other information and evidence, points to the refusal of the application in relation to both setting aside and varying the CPO. LAS adopts this submission. The reporter also adopts it and indicates that he intends to frame grounds of referral.

The sheriff gives her decision

10.19   The sheriff briefly gives judgment by saying that, having considered all the information and evidence, including the views of the child, she is satisfied that the conditions for making the CPO are satisfied and that the application is refused and the CPO confirmed without variation.[1] The sheriff then speaks directly to Kate's mother and emphasises that the decision was taken in Kate's interests as far as the sheriff could assess these interests on the information before her but that in these proceedings full evidence had not been led. The sheriff concludes by telling Kate's mother that, as she will no doubt have been told, the matter will now go to a children's hearing and that if the grounds are not accepted at the hearing then the matter will later come to a sheriff for full scrutiny of the evidence.

1 Children (Scotland) Act 1995, s 60(12).

CHAPTER 11

Special emergency protection of child: justice of peace authorisation

GENERAL

11.01 One of the main features of the Child Protection provisions of the Children (Scotland) Act 1995, following key recommendations in the Clyde Report, is as far as possible to confer upon the sheriff the power to order initial intervention in the life of the child. The Act recognises, however, that there will be situations wherein it is not practicable to engage these provisions, because of either difficulty of access to the sheriff or the inherent urgency of a situation in which the police are involved. The Act has addressed these situations (a) by giving to justices of the peace, in certain defined circumstances, powers to make what might be described as a 'holding' authorisation, valid for a limited period, and (b) by directly empowering the police to take the child away from the source of danger and keep him or her in a place of safety for a limited time.[1] In each case the special emergency provisions are tied to the ordinary emergency provisions in that if a CPO is not applied for within a prescribed period then the authority to keep the child falls.

1 See ch 13 below.

JUSTICE OF THE PEACE AUTHORISATION

The statutory framework

11.02 The powers are conferred on justices of the peace by the Children (Scotland) Act 1995, s 61(1)–(4) and are subject to the regulations made by virtue of s 62 of the Act, i e the Emergency Child Protection Measures (Scotland) Regulations 1996 (SI 1996/3258). 'Justice of the peace' is not defined in the Act or in the 1996 Regulations but it is thought that a justice of the peace would only have jurisdiction when operating in his or her own local authority area ('commission area').[1]

1 Cf Criminal Procedure (Scotland) Act 1995, s 6(1) and (6).

Pre-condition for application to JP – not practicable to apply to sheriff

11.03 The definition of 'sheriff' for this purpose has already been noticed.[1] Before it can be competent for a Justice of Peace Authorisation (hereinafter 'JPA') to be made, a JP has to be satisfied that it is not practicable in the circumstances for an application to be made to the sheriff for a CPO *or* for the sheriff to consider an application for a CPO.[2] The wording of this provision means, it is submitted, that the JP may be 'satisfied' if either or both of these conditions prevails, namely that it is not practicable to find a sheriff *or* that a sheriff may be accessible but it is for some reason impossible for that sheriff to consider the application because of illness or because, for example, disqualified by interest in the case. Accordingly the applicant must be ready to lay satisfactory information before the JP as to the practical unavailability of a sheriff (and it will be suggested that this explanation be recorded in the application[3]).

1 At 4.02 above.
2 Children (Scotland) Act 1995, s 61(1)(b) and (2)(b).
3 See 11.06 below.

Conditions as to which JP has to be satisfied

Application by any person – 1995 Act, s 61(1)

11.04   Where an application to a JP is made by 'any person'[1] the JP must consider (1) if the conditions laid down in the Children (Scotland) Act 1995, s 57(1) for the granting of a CPO are satisfied (reasonable grounds to *believe* that child is suffering or will suffer significant harm if not removed *and* that an order is necessary[2]) *and* (2) that it is probable that a CPO, if made, would contain an authorisation in terms of paragraph (b) ('authorise the removal of the child by the applicant to a place of safety and the keeping of the child at that place') or paragraph (c) ('authorise the prevention of the removal of the child from any place where he is being accommodated') of s 57(4). If satisfied on these points, the JP may grant the application.

1 Children (Scotland) Act 1995, s 61(1).
2 Cf 5.01 above.

Application by a local authority – 1995 Act, s 61(2)

11.05   Where an application is made to a JP by a local authority[1] the JP must consider (1) if the conditions laid down for making a CPO in the Children (Scotland) Act 1995, s 57(2) are satisfied (reasonable grounds to *suspect* significant harm, enquiries being made, *and* enquiries being frustrated because access to child being refused where there is reasonable cause to believe that access required as matter of urgency[2]) *and* (2) that it is probable that a CPO, if made, would contain the authorisation mentioned in said paragraphs (b) and (c), narrated above. If satisfied on these points, the JP may grant the application.

1 Children (Scotland) Act 1995, s 61(2).
2 Cf 5.01 above.

Style of application

11.06   Neither the Children (Scotland) Act 1995 nor the Emergency Child Protection (Scotland) Regulations 1996 make provision for how the application is made, thus in theory leaving open the possibility of verbal application. The said Regulations do, however, make provision for intimation to 'take such steps so far as reasonably practicable' on potentially interested parties.[1] It is accordingly submitted that it good practice and in accordance with the philosophy of the Act, which insists on due formality when intervening in the lives of children, that such applications should be made in writing. The following suggested style is based upon the styles of application for a CPO, but takes account of the more limited orders sought.

'APPLICATION FOR A JUSTICE OF THE PEACE AUTHORISATION BY A LOCAL AUTHORITY

Section 61 of the Children (Scotland) Act 1995

Case No: *1999 – 1*

Date submitted: *1 January 1999*

Application to *Mrs AB, Middleton Farm, Isle of Brachie,* Justice of the Peace for the local authority area of *Muirbrachlan.*

For a Justice of the Peace Authorisation under section 61(2) of the Children (Scotland) Act 1995.

Applicant: *Muirbrachlan Council, per CD, Social Worker, Social Work Office, Isle of Brachie.*

Child: *Miranda F, girl, born 30 December 1998*

Part 1. PERSONS WHOM THE APPLICANT BELIEVES SHOULD BE INFORMED

(a) Any relevant person in relation to the child [please also insert basis for qualifying as relevant person]: *Ms EF, aged 19, 3 The Cottages, Brachness, Isle of Brachie, Muirbrachlan; the child's mother.*

(b) Any person, other than a relevant person, with whom the child was residing immediately before the grant of the authorisation: *None*

(c) Where not the applicant, the local authority for the area in which the place of safety to which the child was or is to be removed is situated: *N/A*

(d) Where not falling within paragraph (c) above and where not the applicant, the local authority for the area in which the child is ordinarily resident: *N/A*

(e) Where not the applicant, the local authority for the area in which the child was residing immediately before the grant of the authorisation (where they are not the authority under (c) or (d) of this Part): *N/A.*

(f) The Principal Reporter per: *GH, Authority Reporter, Scottish Children's Reporter Administration, 79 Main Street, Muirbrachlan.*

[Note to applicant: when informing any of the above-named persons the applicant may, where he considers it necessary to do so in order to safeguard the welfare of the child, withhold from any of those persons any information tending to identify the place of safety at which the child is being kept or, as the case may be, the place at which the child is being accommodated and/or such other steps which the applicant has taken or is taking to safeguard the welfare of the child while in a place of safety.]

Part 2. INFORMATION ABOUT THE APPLICATION

REASONS WHY IT IS NOT PRACTICABLE FOR THE APPLICATION TO BE MADE TO A SHERIFF OR FOR A SHERIFF TO CONSIDER THE APPLICATION. [State why sheriff cannot be applied to and/or reasons why no sheriff able to consider an application for a CPO]:

The resident Sheriff is in Muirbrachlan and cannot reach Isle of Brachie because of stormy weather. Honorary Sheriff KL is on the island but is ill. No other sheriff is on the island.

GROUNDS FOR MAKING APPLICATION. [Applicant to provide grounds for making the application showing that the conditions for making a Child Protection Order (see section 57(1) and (2) of the Children (Scotland) Act 1995) exist *and* sufficient to satisfy the Justice of the Peace that a Child Protection Order based on these conditions, if made, would contain either a condition authorising the removal of the child by the applicant to a place of safety and the keeping of the child at that place *or* authorise the prevention of the removal of the child from any place where s/he is being accommodated]:

The child is a newly born baby. In 1997 the mother received residential treatment for clinical depression in IJ Hospital. The mother appears to be suffering from acute post-natal depression and has in the presence of the applicant Social Worker threatened to take her own life and that of the baby. The mother is without support from family or friends.

SUPPORTING EVIDENCE. [List reports, statements, affidavits or other evidence produced or explain absence]:

The Social Work file is in Muirbrachlan. It contains records in relation to the hospital treatment. The applicant produces her work diary indicating arrangements for the mother's reception into IJ Hospital in June 1997.

Part 3. DETAILS OF ORDER SOUGHT

ORDER SOUGHT: The applicant requests the Justice of the Peace to grant a Justice of the Peace Authorisation in terms of section 61(3) of the Children (Scotland) Act 1995:

(a) REQUIRING the said *Ms EF* to produce the said child *Miranda* to the applicant.

(b) ~~PROHIBITING any person from removing the said child .... from the place namely .... where he/she is being accommodated~~.

(c) AUTHORISING the applicant to remove the said child *Miranda* to a place of safety namely:[2] *The Medical Centre, Isle of Brachie* and to keep ~~him~~/her there until the expiry of the authorisation.

SIGNED: *CD, Social Worker, Social Work Office, Isle of Brachie.*
Phone: *Isle of Brachie .....;* DX: .....; Fax: ....

Date: *1 January 1999.* Time: *2.30 p m.'*

1 Emergency Child Protection (Scotland) Regulations 1996 (SI 1996/3258), reg 8.
2 It is submitted that it is good practice to state the proposed place of safety but it is not clear if the statute makes this mandatory.

Factors affecting the JP's decision – extent to which s 16 principles applicable

11.07 A JP is not, it may be contended, acting as a court when considering an application for a JPA. But a JP may not grant a JPA unless satisfied that the conditions which would entitle the sheriff to grant a CPO are present. It is accordingly submitted that the s 16 conditions apply to the deliberations of the JP to the same extent as they do to those of the sheriff.[1]

1 See discussion at 6.05 above.

Contents of JPA

11.08 A JPA may: require any person in a position to do so to produce the child to the applicant;[1] prevent any person from removing a child from a place where he or she is then being accommodated;[2] and authorise the applicant to remove the child to a place of safety and to keep the child there until the expiration of the JPA.[3]

1 Children (Scotland) Act 1995, s 61(3)(a).
2 C(S)A 1995, s 61(3)(b).
3 C(S)A 1995, s 61(3)(c).

Style of JPA

11.09 The following style, based on the CPO style,[1] is suggested:

'JUSTICE OF THE PEACE AUTHORISATION

Section 61 of the Children (Scotland) Act 1995

Authorisation by: *Mrs AB, Middleton Farm, Isle of Brachie*, ONE OF HER MAJESTY'S JUSTICES OF THE PEACE For The Local Authority Area of: *Muirbrachlan.*

In the application by [Insert name and address]: *Muirbrachlan Council per CD, Social Worker, Social Work Office, Isle of Brachie.* for a Justice of the Peace Authorisation in respect of the child [Insert name, address (unless non-disclosure is considered to be necessary in order to safeguard the welfare of the child), gender and date of birth of the child] *Miranda F, girl, born 30 December 1998.*

TERMS AND CONDITIONS {Delete or modify as appropriate}

HER MAJESTY'S JUSTICE OF THE PEACE ORDERS: that [Insert name and address of person] *Ms EF, aged 19, 3 The Cottages, Brachness, Isle of Brachie, Muirbrachlan,* is required forthwith to produce the said child to the applicant [Insert name and address of the applicant] *Muirbrachlan Council per CD, Social Worker, Social Work Office, Isle of Brachie.*

HER MAJESTY'S JUSTICE OF THE PEACE AUTHORISES: the removal of the said child by the applicant to [Insert details of the place unless non-disclosure is considered to be necessary in order to safeguard the welfare of the child]: *The Health Centre, Isle of Brachie,* a place of safety and for the keeping of the child at that place.

~~HER MAJESTY'S JUSTICE OF THE PEACE AUTHORISES: the prevention of the removal of the child from: [Insert details of the place unless non-disclosure is considered to be necessary in order to safeguard the welfare of the child]~~ ....

FOR THE PURPOSE OF ENFORCING THIS ORDER WARRANT IS GRANTED FOR ALL LAWFUL EXECUTION, INCLUDING WARRANT TO OPEN SHUT AND LOCKFAST PLACES

Signed: *AB*, one of Her Majesty's Justices of the Peace for the Local Authority of *Muirbrachlan*;
At: *Middleton Farm, Isle of Brachie, Muirbrachlan.*
Date: *1 January 1999.*
Time: *2.45 p m.*

1 SI 1997/291, Form 49.

Obligations of applicant where JPA granted

Implementation and notification

11.10   The applicant must implement the JPA as soon as reasonably practicable.[1] As soon as it has been implemented, either by the removal of the child to the place of safety or by taking steps to prevent any person from removing the child from where he or she is being accommodated, the applicant must (subject to the right to withhold information as to the child's whereabouts and any other steps which the applicant has taken or is taking to safeguard the welfare of the child while in a place of safety if that be necessary[2]) inform the persons listed in the Regulations (reflected in suggested style, 11.06, Part 1 above) that the authorisation has been granted and as to the steps which have been taken to implement it, the whereabouts or destination of the child, the reasons for the JPA and of any other steps being taken to safeguard the child's welfare.[3]

1 Emergency Child Protection Measures (Scotland) Regulations 1996 (SI 1996/3258), reg 7.
2 SI 1996/3258, reg 10 as read with reg 9(b) and (d).
3 SI 1996/3258, reg 8.

Involving and safeguarding the welfare of the child

11.11   As soon as may be consistent with the protection and welfare of the child the 'specified person' – in practice the social worker representing the local authority[1] applicant for the JPA – must, always having regard to the child's age and maturity, tell the child of the 'emergency protection measures'[2] which are being or have been taken and also of any further steps which are in contemplation. So far as practicable, before continuing with the emergency protection measures and before any further steps are taken, the child must be given an opportunity to express his or her views.[3] The applicant must also safeguard the welfare of the child, having regard in particular to the length of time during which the child is subject to the various measures.[4] If the 'place of safety' is a police station the applicant must try to find another place as soon as practicable.[5] While the child is subject to the emergency protection measures the applicant *shall* allow any relevant person and any person with whom the child was living just before the JPA and *may* allow any other person 'such contact (if any) with the child as, in the view of the specified person, is both reasonable and in accordance with the welfare of the child'.[6] As happens so often, the provisions seem to be pointing the social worker in the direction of a 'relaxed' approach to persons wishing contact with the child but placing firmly on the social worker the responsibility for the choice. It would accordingly appear that if the specified person's professional opinion was that no contact with a relevant person or a person with whom the child had been living before the JPA was 'both reasonable and in accordance with the welfare of the child' then the specified person would be entitled to deny such contact despite the 'shall allow' of Regulation 16(b).

1 Cf Emergency Child Protection Measures (Scotland) Regulations 1996 (SI 1996/3258), reg 12.
2 SI 1996/3258, reg 13(a).
3 SI 1996/3258, reg 13(b).
4 SI 1996/3258, reg 14.
5 SI 1996/3258, reg 15.
6 SI 1996/3258, reg 16.

Obligations on local authority

11.12   A child accommodated by a local authority as a consequence of the exercise of s 60(3) powers becomes a 'looked after' child[1] and accordingly the obligations under the Children (Scotland) Act 1995, s 17(1) devolve upon the local authority in respect of that child

1 Children (Scotland) Act 1995, s 17(6)(c)

JPA must be implemented within 12 hours

11.13   A JPA ceases to have effect automatically if, within 12 hours, the child 'has not been or is not being taken to a place of safety' or, as the case may be, 'arrangements have not been made to prevent the child's removal from any place specified in the authorisation'.[1] It would seem that a child could be regarded as 'being taken to' the place of safety after he or she had been removed from the family home. What is meant by 'arrangements' to keep the child in a place would seem to require, at least, that the person responsible for the 'place' be made aware of the JPA by any mode and told to observe it.

1 Children (Scotland) Act 1995, s 61(4)(a).

If implemented then maximum duration 24 hours from time of granting – control by the reporter – supersession of JPA by CPO

11.14   Where arrangements have been made to keep the child in the place or, as the case may be, once the child has been taken to a place of safety, the JPA ceases to have effect 24 hours after the time on which it was 'given'[1] or when an application for a CPO is disposed of,[2] whichever time is earlier.[3] The reporter has the authority to terminate the keeping of the child in the place of safety if he or she considers[4] that the conditions for the exercise of the power under the Children (Scotland) Act 1995, s 61(1) or (2) are not satisfied or that it is no longer in the best interests of the child that he should be so kept. If it is desired to keep the child in the place then a CPO should be applied for. On the granting of any CPO the requirements of the CPO supersede the requirements of the JPA.

1 Children (Scotland) Act 1995, s 61(4)(b)(i).
2 C(S)A 1995, s 61(4)(b)(ii).
3 C(S)A 1995, s 61(4)(b)
4 C(S)A 1995, 61(8) (a) and (b).

Must the place of safety be named in the application for a JPA which requests removal of child?

11.15   Having regard to the tight timescale, it is difficult to figure a case wherein a local authority social worker would seek a JPA without having checked that a suitable place of safety was available. The Children (Scotland) Act 1995, s 61(4)(a)(ii) does, however, use the term '*a* [emphasis supplied] place of safety'. It is submitted that it is good practice to name a particular place of safety in the application and that the indefinite article highlighted may be aimed at the possibility of the named place becoming unable to receive the child, so that the applicant in such a situation would be able to implement the JPA by taking the child to another place of safety.

No appeal

11.16   There is no provision enacted for appeal against the giving of a JPA.

CHAPTER 12

Special emergency protection of child: immediate action by the police

Criteria for immediate action by constable – the statutory provision

12.01   The Children (Scotland) Act 1995, s 61(5) provides:

'Where a constable has reasonable cause to believe that—
(a) the conditions for the making of a child protection order laid down in section 57(1) are satisfied;
(b) it is not practicable in the circumstances for him to make an application for such an order to the sheriff or for the sheriff to consider such an application; and
(c) in order to protect the child from significant harm (or further such harm), it is necessary for him to remove the child to a place of safety.
he may remove the child to such a place and keep him there.'

Circumstances in which constable may take immediate action – meaning of 'constable'

12.02   Accordingly, as with the application for a JPA,[1] it is a pre-condition of a constable's being empowered to take immediate action that it is not practicable in the circumstances for application for a CPO to be made to the sheriff or for the sheriff to consider such an application. It is the constable taking the action who has to have reasonable cause to believe that engaging the services of a sheriff is impracticable. 'Constable' means a constable of a police force within the meaning of the Police (Scotland) Act 1967.[2] A constable in any Scottish force is entitled to act as a constable throughout Scotland.[3] A special constable may act in an emergency or when assigned by the Chief Constable in order to gain practical experience.[4]

1 Discussed at 11.03 above.
2 Children (Scotland) Act 1995, s 93(1).
3 Police (Scotland) Act 1967, s 17(4).
4 P(S)A 1967, s 17(6).

Scope of constable's powers

12.03   It has been said[1] that the necessity must be immediate since otherwise a CPO or a JPA could be sought, and this appears to be logical. The matter is, however, left to the judgment of the constable. The scope for exercise of the constable's powers is potentially considerable. Social workers sometimes have to invoke the assistance of the police when carrying through their ordinary duties. There would appear to be no reason why a constable when so involved should not, at the request of the social worker or on his or her own initiative, take a child to a place of safety if the constable had reasonable cause under the Children (Scotland) Act 1995, s 61(5)(c) – and there may be occasion when it will be the constable's duty so to do.

1 Norrie, *Children's Hearings in Scotland* (1997) p 216.

Obligations of constable where child removed

Notification

12.04   As soon as reasonably practicable after removing the child, the constable (subject to withholding information where necessary to safeguard the welfare of the child[1]) shall take such steps as are reasonably practicable to inform the specified persons about the removal, the place of safety at which the child is being, or is to be, kept, the reasons for the removal and any other steps which the constable has taken or is taking to safeguard the welfare of the child.[2] The persons to be informed are:[3]

> '(a) any relevant person in relation to the child;
> (b) any person, other than a relevant person, with whom the child was residing immediately before being removed to the place of safety;
> (c) the local authority for the area in which the place of safety to which the child was removed is situated;
> (d) where not falling within paragraph (c) above, the local authority for the area in which the child is ordinarily resident;
> (e) the local authority for the area in which the child was residing immediately before being removed to a place of safety (where they are not the authority under (c) or (d) of this regulation); and
> (f) the Principal Reporter.'

Where the constable considers it necessary in order to safeguard the welfare of the child, he may withhold from persons entitled to be notified (in practice only those in classes (a) and (b)) the information in relation to the whereabouts of the child and as to steps being taken to safeguard the welfare of the child.[4]

1 See fn 4 below.
2 Emergency Child Protection Measures (Scotland) Regulations 1996 (SI 1996/3258), reg 4.
3 SI 1996/3258, reg 3.
4 SI 1996/3258, reg 5.

Involving the child and safeguarding the welfare of the child

12.05   The constable has the same responsibilities while the child is in the place of safety in relation to protecting the welfare of the child and allowing contact by parents and others as attach to the applicant for a JPA in the like situation.[1] These responsibilities have been noticed already in the context of the applicant for a JPA.[2]

1 Emergency Child Protection Measures (Scotland) Regulations 1996 (SI 1996/3258), reg 12 ('specified person').
2 11.11 and 11.12 above.

Obligations on local authority

12.06   A child accommodated by a local authority as a consequence of the exercise of the Children (Scotland) Act 1995, s 61(5) powers becomes a 'looked after' child[1] and accordingly the obligations under s 17(1) devolve upon the local authority in respect of that child

1 Children (Scotland) Act 1995, s 17(6)(c).

Limitations on duration – control by the reporter

12.07   The powers conferred by the Children (Scotland) Act 1995, s 61(5) only last for 24 hours from the time of removal of the child.[1] Moreover the reporter has the authority to terminate the keeping of the child in the place of safety if he or she considers[2] that the conditions for the exercise of the power under s 61(5) are not satisfied or that it is no longer in the best interests of the child that he or she should be so kept. If it is desired to keep the child in the place then a CPO should be applied for. The authority to hold the child by virtue of s 61(5) flies off on the disposal of an application for a CPO.[3]

1 Children (Scotland) Act 1995, s 61(6).
2 C(S)A 1995, 61(8) (a) and (b).
3 C(S)A 1995, s 61(7).

CHAPTER 13

Child assessment orders: 'Daniel'

GENERAL

13.01 In further implementation of recommendations of the Clyde Report, the Children (Scotland) Act 1995 introduced Child Assessment Orders (CAOs) which are intended to be a means whereby a local authority which has reasonable cause to suspect that a child is at risk may obtain access to that child in order to assess the state of that child's health or development with a view ultimately to enabling the local authority (and the reporter) to form an opinion as to whether compulsory measures of supervision may be necessary. At the time of writing, only a handful of Child Assessment Orders have been applied for and granted. This experience accords with the experience in England where the parallel orders are used only occasionally.

APPLYING FOR A CHILD ASSESSMENT ORDER (CAO)

Only a local authority may apply

13.02 The sheriff 'may' make a CAO only on the application of a local authority (there is no provision for application for a CAO at the instance of 'any person'), provided that the sheriff is satisfied as to the relevant statutory criteria enacted in the Children (Scotland) Act 1995, s 55(1) [emphases supplied]:

> '(a) the local authority have *reasonable cause to suspect* that the child in respect of whom the order is sought is being so treated (or neglected) that he is suffering, or is likely to suffer, significant harm;
> (b) such assessment of the child is required in order to establish whether or not there is reasonable cause to believe that the child is so treated (or neglected); *and*
> (c) such assessment is unlikely to be carried out, or be carried out satisfactorily, unless the order is granted.'

The style for an application for a CAO is Form 45 of the Act of Sederunt (Child Care and Maintenance Rules) 1997.[1]

1 SI 1997/291.

'Significant harm'

13.03   As in the case of the CPO, the concept of 'significant harm', already noticed,[1] is pivotal. In many cases wherein there is 'reasonable cause to suspect' in terms of the Children (Scotland) Act 1995, s 55(1)(a) the authority will also have 'reasonable cause to believe that access [to the child] is required as a matter of urgency' under s 57(2)(c) of the Act and that therefore a CPO is required. This may account for the comparatively few applications for CAOs. In some cases wherein the suspected significant harm appears to be caused by neglect over a period of time rather than positive harmful actions against the child, it may be that the remedy of a CAO would be regarded as more appropriate. The imaginary case of 'Daniel'[2] attempts to illustrate this.

1 At 5.03 above.
2 See 13.06ff below.

CONTENTS OF A CAO

Essentials

13.04   In addition to formal particulars a CAO should specify the date on which the assessment is to begin and require any person who is in a position to do so to produce the child to an authorised person, permit the authorised person or any other authorised person to carry out an assessment in terms of the CAO and comply with any other conditions of the CAO.[1] Once granted, the assessment should be carried out by an authorised person in accordance with the terms of the order.[2] The form of the order requires the authorised person to be named.[3] An 'authorised person' is any officer of the local authority and any person (presumably including persons who are not officers of the local authority) whom the local authority has authorised to carry out the assessment or any part of it.[4] The words of the section are consistent with more than one person being named in the order as authorised persons and the prescribed form echoes this.[5]

1 Children (Scotland) Act 1995, s 55(3)(a) and (c).
2 C(S)A 1995, s 58(3)(d).
3 SI 1997/291, Form 46.
4 C(S)A 1995, s 55(6).
5 SI 1997/291, Form 46.

Optional elements and duration

13.05   A CAO may where necessary permit the taking of the child to 'any place' for the purposes of the assessment and authorise the keeping of the child at that place or any other place for such period of time as may be specified in the CAO. The details of the place (or presumably places) should be identified in the order.[1] Where such an element is included in the order the order should specify the period (or possibly periods within the seven-day limit mentioned below) of time during which the child is to be kept at the place. Where there is provision for such a placement the sheriff may specify in the CAO any person(s) with whom he or she considers it appropriate for the child to be allowed contact.[2] The duration of the CAO must be specified in the order and must not exceed seven days beginning with the date of the order. Since a CAO is an order restricting liberty this provision must be construed in favour of liberty and therefore the date specified in the order is 'day one'. Accordingly if a CAO specified that the assessment was to begin on Sunday, 15 June 1997 and to last for seven days, the order would cease to have effect at the end of Saturday, 21 June 1997.

1 SI 1997/291, Form 46.
2 Children (Scotland) Act 1995, s 55(5).

PROCEDURE – FILLING IN THE APPLICATION FORM

Parts 1 and 2

13.06   The application form for a CAO is Form 45.[1] Part 1 of the form is identical to Part 1 of the application for a CPO.[2] Part 2 is almost identical and includes a space for: 'GROUNDS FOR MAKING APPLICATION [*applicant to provide details of grounds for making the application: including reasons why a Child Protection Order is not being sought.*]'. It is suggested that an example of an appropriate entry here, in respect of a nine-year old boy, would be:

> 'The head teacher of ~ Primary School has reported that Daniel is very withdrawn and that he refuses to mix with any of the other children. The family is well known to the Applicant Authority's Social Work Department and Daniel's older brother, Josh, whose mother is also the mother of Daniel, required to receive help from the Applicant Authority's Educational Psychologist and also from their Speech Therapist. A CAO is required because the mother, apparently feeling threatened by the intervention which has taken place in Josh's life, is unwilling to allow the child to be admitted to the ~ Unit of the Kirklenton Royal Hospital for assessment and would not even agree to this if she were to be allowed to come to the hospital with him. At the time when the case of Josh was being investigated it was noted that Josh was very uncommunicative in the presence of his mother and it was only when his mother permitted him to be assessed away from home that a proper assessment could be made. Unless such an assessment takes place it is likely that Daniel will become permanently, psychologically damaged and thus suffer significant harm. As the mother now refuses this permission, a CAO is necessary.*
>
> A CPO is not necessary at this time since there is no threat of physical injury to the child from the mother or anyone else. The Educational Psychologist and Speech Therapist believe that a diagnosis will be possible within four days.'

1 See Appendix 12.
2 See 5.15 above.

Part 3, first section: 'ASSESSMENT'

13.07   This section allows for information as to commencement, duration, names, designations and addresses of authorised persons and the name and address of the person who, on the application being granted, would be required to produce the child. It also requires the applicant to specify: 'The type of assessment is [*provide details of the type of assessment that is sought including information on health, development and/or the way the child has been treated.*]' It is submitted that an example of an appropriate entry here in relation to the case of 'Daniel' would be:

'a: The type of assessment required is: *Psychological and educational; Speech therapeutic; Social.*

b: The assessment will begin on *29 May 2000.*

c: The assessment will have effect for 4 days from that date.

d: The persons to be authorised to carry out the assessment are:
- *Ms AB, MA, M Phil, DCH, Senior Educational Psychologist, Kirklenton Town Council, Education Offices, 14 Laverock Road, Kirklenton LE6 8DV.*
- *Mrs CD, BA, DCH, Senior Speech and Language Therapist, Kirklenton Town Council, Education Offices, 14 Laverock Road, Kirklenton LE6 8DV.*
- *Mr EF, MA(SocSci), DipSW, Senior Social Worker, Social Work Department, 8 Laverock Road, Kirklenton LE6 6DV.*
- *Miss GH, MA, EdB, Head Teacher, Laverockhill Primary School, Hill Street, Kirklenton LE6 9EZ.'*

Part 3, second section: 'OTHER ORDERS'

13.08   This section allows for details of the place to which the child is to be taken, arrangements for contact and 'details and grounds for any order sought in relation (a) to non-disclosure of address or where-abouts of child; or (b) service of restricted documents on child'. In view of the provision that the mode of service and period of notice in relation to an application for a CAO are 'as directed by the sheriff',[1] it will generally be appropriate to ask the sheriff to grant an order allowing oral service of the first order. In order to effect this a paragraph in approximately the following style may be added as part of 'OTHER ORDERS':

'a: In terms of section 55(4): *to permit the taking of the child to The ~ Unit, Kirklenton Royal Hospital,*
for the purpose of assessment;
and
to authorise the child to be kept there for   4   days.

b: In terms of section 55(5) the sheriff is requested to make the following directions as to contact with the child by: *Deborah ~ , 93 Morrison Avenue, Kirklenton, LE8 4WW, the birth mother of Daniel, every day between 4.30 and 6.30 p m at the said Unit.*

(a) in relation to non-disclosure of address or whereabouts of child: *N/A*
(b) service of restricted documents on child: *N/A'*

1 SI 1997/291, r 3.13(2)(d).

Part 4: 'DETAILS OF FIRST ORDER SOUGHT FROM THE SHERIFF'

13.09 This part brings together the formal requests made by the applicant to the sheriff in relation to the contents of the 'first order'.[1] The formal
requests are: to fix a hearing; to order, subject to deletion where appropriate, service on the child along with Form 26[2] (which seeks the child's
views); to order for service of limited documents on the child; to order
service of a copy of the application and the first order on the persons listed
in Part 1 of the application together with a notice in Form 34 (formal intimation to named person[3]); any order that an address should not be
disclosed; and any dispensation with service on the child, with reasons.
The form should be signed by the applicant and dated.

1 See 4.09 above.
2 Reproduced in Appendix 12.
3 Reproduced in Appendix 12.

SAFEGUARDER/CURATOR *AD LITEM*

Necessary for sheriff to consider appointment

13.10 When an application for a CAO is made the sheriff is bound to
consider if it is necessary to appoint a safeguarder.[1] The status and powers
of the safeguarder have already been noticed.[2]

1 Children (Scotland) Act 1995, s 41(1).
2 At 4.04, 4.05 above.

Procedure

13.11 The procedures in relation to a safeguarder/curator are *mutatis
mutandis* as in an application to set aside or vary a CPO.[1]

1 See 9.04–9.07 above.

VIEWS OF THE CHILD

13.12 The principle of consulting the child applies.[1] The relevant considerations have been noticed already.[2] The child will generally receive the
appropriate form.[3] The considerations anent the views of the child in an
application to set aside or vary a CPO[4] apply here *mutatis mutandis*. It has
already been submitted[5] that in the case of a child who is likely to be able
to read, the service of form of notification, in this case, Form 26, should
generally not be dispensed with unless a curator *ad litem* is in post and has
been notified. In any event the sheriff should be satisfied, subject to the age
and maturity of the child, that a channel for the child's views is available.

1 Children (Scotland) Act 1995, s 16(2) and (4)(b)(i).
2 At 4.06 above.

3 Form 26, mentioned at 13.09 above.
4 See 9.26 above, which refers back to the discussion at 4.10–4.12 above.
5 At 9.13 above, cf 5.10, 5.11 above.

SERVICE OF PAPERS

13.13   Once the first order has been obtained the named persons should be served with the papers, subject to any restriction as to service which has been allowed. Service is in the mode and on the period of notice directed by the sheriff.[1]

1 SI 1997/291, r 3.13(2)(d); cf 13.08 above.

PREPARATIONS FOR AND ATTENDANCE AT THE HEARING BEFORE THE SHERIFF

13.14   The parties to a CAO hearing may be: the applicant local authority, generally represented legally; the child and/or any safeguarder, curator *ad litem* or legal representative; the relevant person(s), also generally with a legal representative; and the reporter. The preparations for a hearing to consider an application to recall or vary a CPO already discussed[1] are appropriate here. Similarly the hearing will take substantially the same form,[2] including the power of the sheriff to allow 'such further procedure as he thinks fit' before making an order granting or refusing the application.[3]

1 At 9.17, 9.18, 9.20 and 9.21 above.
2 See 9.24 ff above.
3 SI 1997/291, r 3.27.

BASIS OF SHERIFF'S DECISION

Section 16 principles

13.15   The s 16 principles must be observed by the sheriff.[1] As noticed already,[2] practical experience is limited but it is thought that sheriffs will generally be slow to refuse a well-prepared and apparently soundly based application. It is, however, possible to figure a case wherein important issues of principle could arise, for example where a CAO is sought because parent and/or child has a conscientious objection to medical procedures[3] and simply refuses consent to such treatment.

1 Children (Scotland) Act 1995, s 16(1), (2), (3), and (4)(b)(i).
2 At 13.01 above.
3 Cf *Finlayson, Applicant* 1989 SCLR 601.

The wording of the order

13.16 The operative parts of the CAO,[1] apparently based upon the Children (Scotland) Act 1995, s 55(3)(c), are in these terms:

'The sheriff orders that [*insert name and address*] is required to produce the child to the authorised person and permit that person or any other authorised person to carry out the assessment in accordance with this order.

In terms of section 55(4) the sheriff permits the child to be taken to [*insert details of the place*] for the purpose of the assessment, and authorises the child to be kept there for [*insert the number of days*]'.

In terms of s 55 the sheriff makes the following directions as to contact with the child by [*insert name and address of person and his or her relationship with child*] while the child is in the aforementioned place [*insert details of any directions sought as to contact with the child*].

An example, based upon the application outlined above,[2] would be:

'SHERIFF COURT OF LENTON AND MUIRBRACHLAN AT
KIRKLENTON

Case No C/101

On 22 May 2000

The Sheriff ORDERS that there shall be a: *Psychological and educational; Speech therapeutic; and Social assessment of the child* Daniel ~, male, d o b 27.02.91, *of 93 Morrison Avenue, Kirklenton, LE8 4WW.*

The assessment is to begin on   *29 May 2000 at 9 a m*   and shall have effect for   *four*   days from that date.

The persons authorised to carry out the assessment are:

- *Ms AB, MA, M Phil, DCH, Senior Educational Psychologist, Kirklenton Town Council, Education Offices, 14 Laverock Road, Kirklenton LE6 8DV.*

- *Mrs CD, BA, DCH, Senior Speech and Language Therapist, Kirklenton Town Council, Education Offices, 14 Laverock Road, Kirklenton LE6 8DV.*

- *Mr EF, MA(SocSci), DipSW, Senior Social Worker, Social Work Department, 8 Laverock Road, Kirklenton LE6 6DV.*

- *Miss GH, MA, EdB, Head Teacher, Laverockhill Primary School, Hill Street, Kirklenton LE6 9EZ.*

The Sheriff ORDERS that *Mrs Deborah ~ , 93 Morrison Avenue, Kirklenton, LE8 4WW* is required to produce the child to the authorised person and permit that person or any other authorised person to carry out the assessment in accordance with this order.

In terms of section 55(4) the Sheriff PERMITS the child to be taken to *The ~ Unit, Kirklenton Royal Hospital,*
and AUTHORISES the child to be kept there for *four* days.

In terms of section 55(5) the Sheriff makes the following directions as to contact with the child by *Mrs Deborah ~ , 93 Morrison Avenue, Kirklenton, LE8 4WW, mother of the child*
while the child is in the aforementioned place *every day (that is from 29 May till 1 June 2000 inclusive) between 4.30 and 6.30 p m, said contact to be supervised.*

For the purpose of enforcing this order WARRANT IS GRANTED to officers of court for all lawful execution, including warrant to open shut and lockfast places.

Signed: *Margaret Lorimer*
Sheriff at: *Kirklenton.'*

1 SI 1997/291, Form 46.
2 At 13.07.

THE QUESTION OF CONSENT

CPO and CAO contrasted

13.17   In contrast to a direction within a CPO,[1] the operative part of the CAO, *ex facie* at least, appears to direct that the assessment take place. However, notwithstanding the difference in wording, the withholding of consent *by the parent* is overcome in each order.[2] But what if a child of sufficient age and maturity should withhold consent? How does this equate with the language of the CAO, quoted above? Professor Norrie in his commentary[3] opines:

> 'Capacity to consent or refuse is governed by s. 2(4) of the Age of Legal Capacity (Scotland) Act 1991, and the effect of that provision is expressly preserved by s. 90 below. It follows (though it would have been better to express this) that an assessment cannot be carried out on a child who refuses to submit to it, whenever the child is of sufficient mental maturity to understand the nature and consequences of the proposed procedure. A child assessment order under this section cannot authorise what would otherwise be an assault against the child, for otherwise s. 2(4) if the 1991 Act would be compromised contrary to the express terms of s. 90 below. The order, therefore, permits an assessment to be carried out in the absence of parental consent but not in the absence of the capable child's own consent.'

1 Discussed at 5.07 and 6.14 above.
2 Cf *In re R (A Minor) (Blood Tests: Constraint)* [1998] 2 WLR 796.
3 *The Children (Scotland) Act 1995* (1998) p 99.

Does the right to consent infer the right to withhold consent?

13.18   Norries's position is predicated upon the premise that the Age of Legal Capacity (Scotland) Act 1991, by giving the child the right to consent, also ipso facto gives to the child the right to withhold consent. This is not self-evident and there is at present no authoritative decision of the Scottish courts, although in *Houston, Applicant*[1] Sheriff J McGowan stated:

> 'It seems to me illogical that on the one hand a person under the age of 16 should be granted the power to decide upon medical treatment for himself but his parents have the right to override his decision. I am inclined to the view that the minor's decision is paramount and cannot be overridden.'

In *Re W (a minor) (medical treatment)*[2] the matter was considered by the Court of Appeal in England and Lord Donaldson MR regarded the parallel provisions of the Family Law Reform Act 1969, s 8 as not giving the mature child a veto on medical treatment but rather as providing

> 'the legal "flak jacket" which protects the doctor from claims by the litigious whether he acquires it from his patient, who may be a minor over the age of 16 or a "Gillick competent" child under that age, or from another person having parental responsibilities which include a right to consent to treatment of the minor'.

In their discussion of this issue in their first edition Wilkinson and Norrie[3] describe Lord Donaldson's approach as having 'a certain cogency' and suggest that it might well find support in the Scottish courts. In the second edition,[4] however, the earlier discussion of *Re W* is omitted, although there is extensive reference to the authorities and legal literature.[5] After noting the absence of orders contained in CAOs from the list of orders in s 90 in relation to which the child's right to consent is expressly preserved, the second edition states:[6]

> 'but that omission does not, it is submitted, affect the rule that a capable child remains capable even in the face of a child assessment order. It follows from this that a child assessment order cannot be given effect to if the child refuses to submit to it and the child is of sufficient mental maturity to understand the nature and consequences of the proposed assessment. [Footnote: See further, Lockyer and Stone, *Juvenile Justice in Scotland* (1998), p. 120.]'

1 1996 SCLR 943 at 954C, D.
2 [1992] 4 All ER 627 at 635c.
3 *The Law Relating to Parent and Child in Scotland* (1993) p 185.
4 ed Norrie (1999).
5 p 260 ff
6 Ibid page 626, 627,

Suggested procedure where issue of child's consent is a live one

13.19 It is most unfortunate that this matter could come before a sheriff at short notice in a proceeding which is highly summary and from which there is no statutory right of appeal.[1] It is suggested that were such a point raised in the course of an application for a CAO the sheriff may be entitled to use the power to allow 'such further procedure as he thinks fit'[2] before making an order granting or refusing the application by setting the case out for a full hearing and appointing a safeguarder or curator *ad litem* if this had not already been done. In considering whether or not to take this course the sheriff would require to weigh the urgency or otherwise of the position and have regard to the paramountcy of the interests of the child under the Children (Scotland) Act 1995, s 16(1).

1 But see 13.23 below.
2 SI 1997/291, r 3.27.

POWER TO MAKE CPO ON AN APPLICATION FOR A CAO

The formal provisions

13.20   The Children (Scotland) Act 1995, s 55(2) enacts:

> '(2) Where—
> (a) an application has been made under subsection (1) above; and
> (b) the sheriff considers that the conditions for making a child protection order under section 57 of this Act are satisfied,
> he shall make such an order under that section as if the application had been duly made by the local authority under that section rather than this section.'

The 1997 Rules provide that in the event of the sheriff's taking this course then the relevant CPO rules[1] come into play.[2]

1 SI 1997/291, rr 3.31–3.33.
2 SI 1997/291, r 3.27(3).

Sheriff's power mandatory or discretionary?

13.21   The term 'shall' might suggest that whenever the sheriff came to the conclusion that the CPO conditions were satisfied he or she was obliged to proceed under the Children (Scotland) Act 1995, s 55(2) and grant a CPO. In the substantive provisions in relation to the granting of an application for a CPO under s 57 the operative word is 'may'.[1] The direction to the sheriff in s 55(2) is that he shall make an order under s 57 'as if the application had been made by the local authority under that section'. It is submitted that the sheriff, if satisfied that the s 57 conditions exist, is to regard the application before him or her as a s 57 application and that therefore the discretion conveyed by subsections (1) and (2) of s 57 is also conveyed to the sheriff here. In short, once the sheriff becomes convinced that the s 57 conditions are satisfied *and* that he or she should exercise his or her discretion in favour of granting a CPO, then a CPO shall be granted.[2]

1 Children (Scotland) Act 1995, 57 (1) and (2).
2 Professor Norrie comes to substantially the same conclusion by a somewhat different route – Norrie *Children (Scotland) Act* 1995 (1998) p 100, commentary on C(S)A 1995, s 55(2).

The s 16 conditions

13.22   As noted already,[1] all three s 16 principles apply when considering an application for a CAO but not when considering an application for a CPO.[2] It is submitted, based on the reasoning in the foregoing paragraph, that, once the sheriff is ready to accept that the s 57 conditions are satisfied, then he or she must regard the application before him or her as in effect a s 57 application and that therefore, strictly, only the paramountcy of welfare principle applies.[3]

1 At 13.12 and 13.15 above.

2 See 6.05 above.
3 But see discussion at 6.05 above.

The practice

13.23 The time at which the sheriff is to assess the position is, it is submitted, the time when the sheriff has the s 55(2) application before him or her and not the time when the application was framed.[1] It is therefore possible to figure a situation wherein a sudden change in the child's circumstances might amount to s 57 conditions which were not present when the application was being framed. Exercise of this power is not, however, dependent on a change of circumstances and it will always remain open to the sheriff (in appropriate circumstances) to take a different view from the framer of the application and conclude that the s 57 conditions are present. It is submitted that sheriffs should be cautious of exercising the s 55(2) powers. In practice, as already noted, applications for CAOs are rare and the writer is not aware of any exercise of the s 55(2) power.

1 *Kennedy v O* 1975 SC 308, 1975 SLT 235.

APPEAL

No statutory right of appeal – possible application to the *nobile officium* of the Court of Session

13.24 The Children (Scotland) Act 1995, s 51, which regulates appeals, proceeds, in relation to appeals against decisions of sheriffs, by way of allowing appeals either on a point of law or in respect of any irregularity in the conduct of the case and then listing the decisions of sheriffs which are appealable – the list is contained in sub-paragraphs (i)–(iii) of s 51(11). Decisions by sheriffs to grant or refuse an application for a CAO do not appear in this list. Neither do decisions of sheriffs to grant or refuse an application for a CPO[1] appear in this list – yet in s 51(15)(a) the legislature found it necessary to provide explicitly that a decision of a sheriff on an application under s 57 of the Act (the CPO provision) could not be the subject of appeal. Professor Norrie,[2] dealing with the possible argument, on the *expressio unius est exclusio alterius* principle, that this might render appealable procedural decisions in relation to proof proceedings before the sheriff which the earlier case law had held to be unappealable, advances the view that this means that s 51(15) lists decisions which are unappealable in addition to those which have long been regarded as such and that this provision was rendered necessary as a consequence of the creation of the new CPOs with their own special appeal mechanisms. This seems likely enough, but what of applications for CAOs which have no special appeal mechanisms? It is submitted that on a literal reading of s 51(11) there can be no appeal to either the sheriff principal or the Court of Session against the decision of a sheriff in relation to a CAO, that Professor Norrie's explanation of s 51(15), in so far as it deals with CPOs, is correct and that these factors, combined with the lack of special appeal mechanisms in relation to CAOs which, as indicated already,[3] may raise issues of profound importance and difficulty, constitute a *lacuna* which the Court of Session might be prepared to fill by the exercise of the *nobile officium*.

1 Children (Scotland) Act 1995, s 57.
2 *Children (Scotland) Act 1995* (1998) p 90, commentary on C(S)A 1995, s 51(15).
3 At 13.19 above.

CHAPTER 14

Exclusion orders under ss 76–80

GENERAL

The legislative background

14.01 Amongst the most controversial innovations in the Children (Scotland) Act 1995 is the Exclusion Order ('EO'), with the associated power to make an Interim Exclusion Order which may be granted with immediate effect on the basis of information submitted by one side only (what lawyers call *'ex parte* statements'), without intimation to the person sought to be excluded. The perceived advantages of the EO and the Interim EO were strongly advocated by the Scottish Child Law Centre on the basis that the child, who on any view is the innocent party, is not 'punished' by being required to leave home. Traditionalists argued against the concept of a person's 'right' to occupy his own home being removed without proof and even, in the case of an Interim EO, without the opportunity of being heard, but the advocates of the new remedy pointed out that children have rights too, and they won the day. Only a handful of EOs have been granted but it is thought that the existence of the potential remedy has deterred some abusers from attempting to return to a family home. It has been said that the existence of the EO has caused some local authority housing departments to be more willing than they otherwise might be to allocating local authority housing to potential excluded persons.

THE SCHEME OF SS 76–80

The EO and the Interim EO

14.02 It is not necessary for an EO to be preceded by an Interim EO any more than it is necessary for an interdict to be preceded by an interim interdict but, as with interdicts, there will frequently be occasions where the urgency of the situation makes the interim remedy attractive. The procedures for obtaining an EO and an Interim EO are distinct, notably in that the latter can be obtained without intimation, but it is provided that, apart from the obvious difference in relation to duration,[1] the consequences of an EO and an Interim EO are the same.[2]

---

1 Children (Scotland) Act 1995, s 76(12) 'exclusion order'.
2 C(S)A 1995, s 76(7) and (12) 'exclusion order'.

Effect of an EO

14.03   An EO has the effect, in relation to the home to which it relates, of 'suspending the named person's rights of occupancy (if any) and shall prevent him from entering the home, except with the express permission of *the local authority* which applied for the order[1] [emphasis supplied]'.

1 Children (Scotland) Act 1995, s 77(1)

Orders ancillary to EO

14.04   The applicant for an EO may, and it is thought generally will, apply for one or more of the ancillary orders provided in the Children (Scotland) Act 1995, s 77 and the sheriff may, if and in so far as he or she thinks fit, when granting the EO (and, as noticed already, this includes an Interim EO), do[1] one or more of the things listed in s 77(3) namely [emphases supplied]:

'(a)   grant a warrant for the summary ejection of the named person from the home;

(b)   grant an interdict prohibiting the named person from entering the home *without the express permission of the local authority*;

(c)   grant an interdict prohibiting the removal by the named person of any relevant item specified in the interdict from the home, except either—
(i)   *with the written consent of the local authority, or of an appropriate person*; or
(ii)   by virtue of a subsequent order of the sheriff;

(d)   grant an interdict prohibiting the named person from entering or remaining in a specified area in the vicinity of the home;

(e)   grant an interdict prohibiting the taking by the named person of any step of a kind specified in the interdict in relation to the child;

(f)   make an order regulating the contact between the child and the named person;
and the sheriff may make any other order which he considers is necessary for the proper enforcement of a remedy granted by virtue of paragraph (a), (b) or (c) of this subsection.'

The passages highlighted within (b) and (c) are interesting in the distinction drawn between permission to enter the home contrary to the order – which may be granted only by the applicant local authority – and permission to remove any 'relevant item' specified in the interdict, which permission may be granted not only by the local authority (in writing) but also by an 'appropriate person'[2] (not, apparently, necessarily in writing). A 'relevant item' is defined[3] as an article within the home which is owned or on credit sale or hire purchase which is reasonably necessary to enable the home to be used as a family residence but does not include any such vehicle, caravan or houseboat or such other structure as is mentioned in the definition of 'family home' in s 76(12) of the Act.[4] The passage highlighted above at the end of the subsection is important and gives the sheriff wide scope, which may be exercised *ex proprio motu* or on motion of a party, to provide protection for the child for whose protection the EO is being sought. For a constructive use of this provision see 15.08 below.

1 Children (Scotland) Act 1995, s 77(2).
2 Defined in C(S)A 1995, s 76(2)(c) – see discussion at 14.10 below.
3 C(S)A 1995, s 77(8).
4 C(S)A 1995, s 77(8).

Territorial jurisdiction

14.05 An application for an exclusion order or for the recall or variation of such an order or of any associated order[1] shall be made to the sheriff for the sheriffdom within which the family home is situated.[2]

1 Children (Scotland) Act 1995, s 79(2)(b) and (3), discussed at 14.46 ff below.
2 C(S)A 1995, s 80(2).

Extra-territorial jurisdiction implied by s 77(3)(e)?

14.06 Where a power of arrest[1] is attached to such an interdict, intimation must be given not only to the chief constable in whose area the family home is situated but also to the chief constable in whose area the 'step or conduct' which is 'prevented' [*sic*] is likely to take place.[2] A different police area would not necessarily be in a different sheriffdom (Tayside, Central and Fife includes three forces) but the implication may be that, at least in relation to an interdict under the Children (Scotland) Act 1995, s 77(3)(e), an extra-territorial jurisdiction is conferred

1 Children (Scotland) Act 1995, s 78 – discussed at 14.39 ff below.
2 C(S)A 1995, s 78(4).

Limitations and qualifications affecting ancillary orders

14.07 None of the foregoing, except an interdict prohibiting the named person from entering the home,[1] shall be granted if the named person satisfies the sheriff that it is unnecessary.[2] When granting a warrant for summary ejection[3] in the absence of the named person the sheriff may give directions as to the preservation of any of that person's goods and effects which are in the family home.[4] (Presumably the sheriff should here act *ex proprio motu*; and presumably the sheriff may give such directions on an application for variation, when the named person will be present.[5]) The sheriff may consider and make a contact order[6] *ex proprio motu*. The sheriff may, on the application of the named person or the local authority, make the EO or any of the ancillary remedies subject to such conditions as he or she considers appropriate.[7] No application for an EO shall be finally determined unless the named person has been afforded the opportunity of being heard either personally or through a representative and the sheriff has considered the views of any person on whom the application has been served.[8]

1 Children (Scotland) Act 1995, s 77(3)(b).
2 C(S)A 1995, s 77(4).

3 C(S)A 1995, s 77(2) and (3)(a).
4 C(S)A 1995, s 77(5).
5 See 14.49 below.
6 C(S)A 1995, s 77(3)(f).
7 C(S)A 1995, s 77(7).
8 C(S)A 1995, s 76(3) – see 14.50 below.

Power of arrest

14.08   The sheriff may,[1] on the application of the applicant local authority or *ex proprio motu*, attach a power of arrest to any interdict granted under the Children (Scotland) Act 1995, s 77(2) and (3) but this power shall not have effect until such interdict, together with the attached power of arrest, is served on the named person.[2] A power of arrest may be attached at any time during the currency of the EO, on the application of the local authority.[3] For further discussion of the procedure see 14.56 below.

1 Children (Scotland) Act 1995, s 78(1).
2 C(S)A 1995, s 78(3).
3 C(S)A 1995, s 78(2).

Power vested in sheriff to grant a CPO

14.09   If, on considering an application for an EO or an Interim EO, the sheriff considers that the conditions for making a CPO are satisfied, the sheriff may make a CPO under the Children (Scotland) Act 1995, s 57 as if the application by the local authority had been made under that section.[1] For discussion as to the exercise of this power see 14.40–14.44 below.[2]

1 Children (Scotland) Act 1995, s 76(8).
2 Cf discussion of the parallel power when the sheriff is considering a CAO – 13.20–13.23 above.

APPLYING FOR AN EO – THE BACKGROUND

The basic pre-conditions

14.10   Only a local authority may apply for an EO.[1] The basic conditions in relation to which the sheriff has to be satisfied before an EO may be granted concern:

- the child;
- the person sought to be excluded – the 'named person';[2] and
- a person in the home who is capable of caring for the child or any other person in the home who requires care – the 'appropriate person'.[3]

The basic conditions[4] may be summarised thus:

(a) the child must have suffered, be suffering or be likely to suffer significant harm as a result of any conduct, or any threatened or reasonably apprehended conduct, on the part of the named person;

(b) the making of the EO against the named person must be necessary for the protection of the child, irrespective of whether the child is for the time being residing in the family home, *and* that the making of the EO would better safeguard the child's welfare than the removal of the child from the family home; *and*

(c) the availability of a person (the 'appropriate person'), specified in the application, who is capable of taking responsibility for the provision of appropriate care for the child and any other member of the family who requires such care and who is, or will be, residing in the family home.

1 Children (Scotland) Act 1995, s 76(1).
2 C(S)A 1995, s 76(1).
3 C(S)A 1995, s 76(2)(c).
4 C(S)A 1995, s 76(2)(a),(b) and (c).

APPLYING FOR AN EO – THE PROCEDURES – FILLING UP THE APPLICATION FORM (FORM 54)

Part 1 of Form 54: DETAILS OF APPLICANT AND THE PERSONS THE APPLICANT BELIEVES SHOULD RECEIVE NOTICE OF THE APPLICATION

14.11   The form is substantially self-explanatory.[1] There may be duplication: for example, the mother may well be the 'relevant person' and the 'appropriate person'. The child will usually be resident in the family home from which it is proposed that the named person should be excluded. It is accordingly unlikely that the possibility of seeking an order not to reveal the whereabouts of the child[2] will be used frequently. In this form, as in the form applying for a CPO, there is space for details 'of any safeguarder appointed by a children's hearing or court in respect of the child.'

1 For the terms of Form 54 see Appendix 12; cf the discussion of Part 1 of the Application for a CPO at 5.16 ff above.
2 Form 54, Part 1, concluding Note; Children (Scotland) Act 1995, s 77(7).

More than one child

14.12   Although the statutory form is framed so as to refer to a single child, it is common, in an application in respect of two or more children having the same interest, to include all the children on the same form.[1]

1 Cf Interpretation Act 1978, s 6(c). Cf the discussion of Part 1 of the Application for a CPO at 5.16 ff above.

Part 2 of Form 54: INFORMATION ABOUT THE APPLICATION AND ORDERS SOUGHT

14.13   Again, see the discussion of the substantially similar part of the CPO application[1] in relation to the sub-headings in the instant form headed 'CONDITIONS FOR MAKING APPLICATION', 'ANY OTHER RELEVANT APPLICATION OR ORDER WHICH AFFECTS THE CHILD' and 'SUPPORTING EVIDENCE'. The narration by the applicant should make clear what the factual basis is for maintaining that the basic pre-conditions set out in the Children (Scotland) Act 1995, s 76(1) do indeed exist. Peculiar to the application for the EO is the space for 'PROPOSALS BY THE LOCAL AUTHORITY FOR FINANCIAL OR OTHER SUPPORT FOR THE NAMED PERSON'.[2] It is thought that the inclusion of a request for information on this subject reflects the concern of the legislature at the serious step of excluding a person, without proof of 'guilt' and indeed possibly without being heard, from his or her own house.

1 At 5.17 ff above.
2 Cf Children (Scotland) Act 1995, s 76(9) and (10)(b).

Part 3 of Form 54: DETAILS OF ORDER SOUGHT AND ANY TERMS, CONDITIONS OR DIRECTIONS

14.14

(a) ORDER SOUGHT
This section of the form includes the gloss 'The applicant requests the Sheriff to [*insert details of the order sought and any terms and conditions to be attached to the order*] in respect of the child [*insert name*]'. As there is, as will be noticed presently, a separate box for terms and conditions, it is submitted that this section may simply be used to ask for the exclusion order itself.[1]

(b) ANCILLARY OR INTERIM ORDERS SOUGHT
Such particular orders as are wanted of those listed in the Children (Scotland) Act 1995, s 77(3) (ejection, interdicts and orders for the regulation of contact) should be inserted here.

- *Ejection.*[2] A crave for ejection will only be required when the named person is resident in the house. A person may be resident in a house when voluntarily absent from it from a period, for example when temporarily away from home because of work or on holiday. It is thought that a person detained in prison is not resident in the family home which he occupied before being sentenced. It is suggested that a pragmatic approach be adopted.[3]
- *Interdict.*[4] The possible subjects for interdict are:
    prohibiting the named person from entering the home without the express permission of the applicant local authority (NB not the appropriate person);
    prohibiting the named person from removing items except with the written consent of the local authority or the appropriate person;
    prohibiting the named person from entering or remaining in a specified area near the home; and
    prohibiting the named person from taking any step of a kind specified in the interdict in relation to the child.

A crave for interdict will generally be included. It must be reasonably precise. In a case reported in 1973[5] Lord President Emslie, delivering the opinion of the First Division, said: 'the terms of the interdict must be no wider than are necessary to curb the illegal actings complained of, and so precise and clear that the person interdicted is left in no doubt what he is forbidden to do'. What constitutes precision and clarity depends on the subject matter. It is suggested that the form 'To interdict the excluded person from approaching or contacting the said children Caroline and Edward' is not totally satisfactory. This is because it can be made more precise by stating 'by speaking to them directly, telephoning or writing to them, or communicating with them directly in any other way'. An interdict in these terms makes it clear that all the possible forms of direct contact were being prohibited. It would also leave open, as is generally desirable, the possibility of indirect contact, for example by way of asking the curator *ad litem* to give a verbal message to the child. Alternatively, if it were wished to prohibit even such indirect contact, the words 'or indirectly' should be added after 'directly'. The word 'approaching', in the context of approaching a person, seems to be precise enough – it is difficult to think how it could be improved upon. But in the context of approaching a place it is thought (having regard to s 77(3)(d)) that a precise distance should be given, for example: 'To interdict the named person from entering Glebe Street, Glasgow or coming within 100 metres of the close mouth of the family home at 10 Glebe Street, Glasgow.'

- *Contact.* It is submitted that the issue of contact should be raised in the application. In a particular case the local authority may consider the danger to the child to be so great that contact should be prohibited entirely. At the other end of the spectrum, the applicant local authority may think that some limited form of contact should be allowed. If the local authority has at the time of completing the application no firm view then it may employ the formal words: 'To make such order regulating contact between the said children Caroline and Edward and the named person at such times and at such place as to the court seems appropriate.' Any conditions affecting contact should be inserted in the space 'TERMS AND CONDITIONS TO BE ATTACHED TO ORDER'. An order in relation to contact may be made by the sheriff *ex proprio motu*.[6]

(c) TERMS AND CONDITIONS TO BE ATTACHED TO ORDER

The sheriff may make an EO or any ancillary order subject to such 'terms and conditions' as he or she considers appropriate.[7] Examples of such terms and conditions would be:

> suspending the ejection for a period (unlikely since the EO may be expected generally to be sought in conditions of urgency, but it is possible to figure a situation where the children are temporarily away from home and it is desired to give the named person some time to get ready to go); and
> requiring any contact to be under supervision of the local authority (very likely).

(d) DIRECTIONS AS TO PRESERVATION OF NAMED PERSON'S PROPERTY

The sheriff may make an order prohibiting the named person from removing from the home any 'relevant item' unless and until he has obtained the written consent of the appropriate person or the applicant local authority or a subsequent permissive order from the sheriff.[8] It is thought that such an order would be sought if the householder, who may be expected generally to be the mother, were known to have threatened to damage, destroy or put away the named person's property. A 'relevant item' is a thing which is owned or hired by any member of the family concerned or by an appropriate person or which is being acquired by such under a hire-purchase or conditional sale agreement *and* which is reasonably necessary to enable the family home to be used as a family residence.[9] A 'relevant item' does not include 'any vehicle, caravan or houseboat or such other structure so used as is mentioned in the definition of "family home" in section 76(12) of this Act'.[10] In other words, the family home itself, whatever shape it takes, cannot be the subject of a preservation order in terms of s 77(3)(c).

(e) POWER OF ARREST

It is thought that a power of arrest will only be sought when the applicant local authority has reasonable grounds to suspect that the named person will be likely to breach one or more of the interdicts granted under s 77(2). If a power of arrest has not been taken originally then it can be applied for by the local authority at any time while the EO is in force.[11] Procedures in relation to power of arrest are noticed later.[12]

1 See example at 15.03 below.
2 Children (Scotland) Act 1995, s 77(3)(a)
3 Cf the cases on 'the same household', discussed at 46.16 below.
4 C(S)A 1995, s 77(3)(b), (c), (d) and (e).
5 *Murdoch v Murdoch* 1973 SLT (Notes) 13.
6 C(S)A 1995, s 77(6).
7 C(S)A 1995, s 77(7).
8 C(S)A 1995, s 77(3)(c).
9 C(S)A 1995, s 77(8) (a) and (b); cf 'Articles exempt from poinding' listed in Debtors (Scotland) Act 1987, s 16.
10 C(S)A 1995, s 77(8).
11 C(S)A 1995, s 78(2).
12 At 14.56 below.

Part 4. DETAILS OF FIRST ORDER SOUGHT FROM THE SHERIFF

General

14.15   This section of the form draws together the formal application for an EO, the ancillary orders, with any terms and conditions, mentioned in Part 3,[1] and the directions, if any, requested in Part 3.[2] *Consideration should always be given to whether or not the sheriff should be asked to make a particular order by virtue of the provision[3] allowing the sheriff to make an order which he or she may consider necessary for the proper enforcement of a remedy.* This section of the application also asks for authority to serve the application and a notice in Form 28[4] on the child, and authority to serve a copy of the application, together with a notice in Form 36, on the named person and the persons listed in Part 1 of the application, together with notice in Form 36. The form also allows for dispensing with service on the child or any other person. As to thus dispensing, the form states: '(c) *[delete as appropriate]

Dispense with service on the child or any other person for the following reasons [*insert details*]'. It is submitted that only exceptionally should Form 28 not be sent to a child who is old enough to be likely to be able to read: an example of such an exceptional situation would be where a curator or safeguarder for the child is being notified.[5] The form also allows for a request for an Interim EO.[6] It concludes with a request, which may be deleted, for a power of arrest.[7]

1 See 14.14 above.
2 See 14.14 above at (d).
3 Noticed at 14.04 above and highlighted.
4 See 14.18 below.
5 Cf 5.23 and 6.15 above.
6 Children (Scotland) Act 1995, s 76(4); see discussion at 14.21 ff below.
7 Discussed at 14.56 below.

Directions for service of documents

14.16   The general rules for citation or notice are set out in Act of Sederunt (Child Care and Maintenance Rules) 1997, r 3.15 and have been discussed already.[1] Rule 3.15(3) allows for service orally or in such other manner as the sheriff directs where service requires to be made and there is not sufficient time to employ the ordinary methods of service. If an early diet for the hearing before the sheriff is sought, as it may be where an Interim EO is applied for, then application should be made here for authority to effect service orally or in such manner as the sheriff directs.[2]

1 In ch 7 above.
2 SI 1997/291, r 3.15(3), see 7.10 ff above.

Signing and dating the form on behalf of applicant

14.17   The form should be signed and dated and the name, designation and address, with phone, DX and fax numbers supplied in legible form. The considerations noticed in relation to representation in relation to an application for a CPO[1] also apply here but in practice the local authority will generally instruct one of the solicitors in its legal department to handle an application for an EO and that solicitor will sign the application.

1 Discussed at 6.01 above.

THE VIEWS OF THE CHILD – FORM 28

14.18   As noticed already,[1] the principle of consulting the child applies when an EO is asked for. Form 28 tells the child of the application for the EO and suggests to the child various ways whereby he or she may express his or her views if desired.[2] It is competent to dispense with sending this notice to the child if the sheriff considers that notification of the child would be 'inappropriate'.[3] Only rarely should a child old enough to read not be sent the form. An example of its being inappropriate to send a mature child the form would be when the application for the EO arose out of circumstances which included one or more facts which would be damaging to the child to learn about, for example that the child's father had been in prison; in such a situation the sheriff may decide to appoint a safeguarder or curator *ad litem* who could be asked to seek the views of the child but not to inform the child of the damaging fact.[4]

1 At 4.06 ff above.
2 Cf 9.25, 9.26 above.
3 SI 1997/291, r 3.3.
4 See 15.06(b), and 15.08 below.

FORM OF FIRST ORDER –FORM 32

14.19   The first order in the style of Form 32 should:

● assign a date, time and place for the hearing of the application by the sheriff;
● appoint the applicant to serve on the persons listed in Part 1 of the application, subject to such dispensations as may be appropriate, together with the reason(s) for such dispensations;
● narrate the details of any ancillary order granted,[1] including any terms and conditions (including, it is submitted, the appointment of a safeguarder or curator *ad litem*);
● grant any interim EO, interim interdict or other interim order (including any order the sheriff may consider necessary for the proper enforcement of a remedy);[2]
● narrate, it is submitted, any special matter which the sheriff wishes to record – for example 'having been informed by the applicant's solicitor that a local authority house is available for the named person to rent';
● if necessary order under r 3.15(3) that service be effected orally or in such other manner as the sheriff directs.

The first order should be signed by the sheriff or the sheriff clerk and the place and date of signing stated.

1 See 14.14 para (b) above.
2 Children (Scotland) Act 1995, s 77(3), final provision.

PRINCIPLES AFFECTING THE MAKING OF AN EXCLUSION ORDER

The s 16 principles

14.20   All three of the section 16 principles apply when an EO, including an Interim EO, is being considered.[1] In the case of an application for an Interim EO it may not be possible to obtain information direct from the child as to whether he or she wishes to express a view but the sheriff may ask the social worker who should be prepared as far as practicable to be ready to advise the sheriff. The principle of no non-beneficial order should, it is submitted, make sheriffs cautious of exercising the power under the Children (Scotland) Act 1995, s 76(8)[2] to make a CPO in an application for an EO.

1 Children (Scotland) Act 1995, ss 16(4)(b)(i), 93(1) and s 76(12).
2 See 14.40 below.

OBTAINING AN INTERIM EXCLUSION ORDER AS PART OF FIRST ORDER

Representation and practical arrangements

14.21 The discussion of these matters in relation to the obtaining of a CPO[1] is applicable here.

1 See 6.01 ff above.

What to take to court etc

14.22 The discussion of these matters in relation to the obtaining of a CPO[1] is applicable here.

1 See 6.03 ff above.

Safeguarder/curator *ad litem*

14.23 When considering an application for an EO the sheriff is bound to consider if it is necessary to appoint a safeguarder[1] or, in practice, a curator *ad litem*. The powers and duties of, and the procedures relative to, safeguarders have already been discussed.[2] Applications for EOs have so far been, and probably will continue to be, rare and possibly controversial. They may tend to raise particularly delicate issues as to the interests of children, who may have complex feelings about the exclusion of, possibly, a parent from the home and the amount and type of contact which they should have with the excluded person. Accordingly sheriffs may tend to consider it necessary to appoint a safeguarder or curator *ad litem*.

1 Children (Scotland) Act 1995, s 41(1).
2 At 4.04 ff above.

Procedure where interim EO sought

(1) Adjournment/continuation?

14.24 Rule 3.37 provides: 'After hearing *parties* [emphasis supplied] and allowing such further procedure as he thinks fit, the sheriff shall make an order granting or refusing the application.' It is thought that this provision is intended to apply to a hearing at which 'parties' are represented, i e the 'full' hearing 'finally determining the application'[1] or the 'confirmation' hearing[2] which takes place where an interim EO has been granted, rather than a hearing in relation to an application for an Interim EO. It is thought, however, that it would be competent for the court, in exercise of its inherent power,[3] to allow a short continuation (within the day) of a hearing on an interim EO: if, for example, (1) the sheriff wished further inquiry to be made as to the ability of the proposed 'appropriate person' to carry through his or her responsibilities; or (2) the sheriff, on receiving information that the proposed 'appropriate person' was not able so to do, decided to consider granting a CPO and wished to have enquiries made as to a suitable placement for the child.

1 Children (Scotland) Act 1995, s 76(5), discussed at 14.51 ff below.
2 C(S)A 1995, s 76(5), discussed at 14.45 ff below.
3 Cf *Bruce v Linton* (1860) 23 D 85.

(2) Granting a CPO on an application for an EO

14.25 It has been suggested already[1] that this power[2] may be used cautiously. As suggested above, an example of the appropriate use of this power would be where the person proposed as the appropriate person turned out to be unwilling to act or to be otherwise unsuitable.

1 14.20 above.
2 Children (Scotland) Act 1995, s 76(8).

CONVINCING THE SHERIFF AT: THE INTERIM STAGE; THE 'CONFIRMATION' STAGE; AND ON FINAL DETERMINATION

Information and evidence

14.26 Section 76 repeatedly requires the sheriff to be 'satisfied' in relation to various matters[1] and at one point[2] the phrase 'if it appears to him' is used. Neither the Act nor the rules make any distinction in relation to the quality or quantity of information or evidence, between an interim and final EO. It is suggested, however, that while at the interim stage a high proportion of indirect and hearsay evidence will often be acceptable, the information at the final determination stage should generally be in the form of sworn testimony of witnesses having first hand knowledge. Hearsay evidence of witnesses will not be inadmissible,[3] but will often be less persuasive. Corroboration while in no way essential[4] may sometimes be desirable.[5]

1 Children (Scotland) Act 1995, s 76(1), (4)(a), (5), (8)(b).
2 C(S)A 1995, s 76(9).
3 Subject to the Civil Evidence (Scotland) Act 1988, s 2(1) – discussed at 43.08 ff below.
4 Cf *M v Kennedy* 1993 SCLR 69 at 73C.
5 Cf *M v Kennedy* 1993 SCLR 69, commentary at 80A; for further discussion on evidence see 43.08 ff below.

14.27 The procedure in relation to the confirmation stage[1] and the final determination[2] of an application for an EO is discussed later. The substantive grounds for granting an interim and a final EO are, however, identical[3] and will be dealt with here.

1 14.45 ff below.
2 14.51 ff below.
3 C(S)A 1995, s 76(12) definition of 'exclusion order'.

THE SUBSTANTIVE GROUNDS FOR AN EO

The basic pre-conditions under the Children (Scotland) Act 1995, s 76(2)

14.28 The sheriff has to be satisfied that what I have called the 'basic pre-conditions', set out in s 76(2) exist.[1] Care must be taken to ensure that the sheriff has enough information to enable him or her to be satisfied on all these pre-conditions.

1 See 14.10 above.

(1) Significant harm to the child deriving from named person

14.29 The harm must be 'significant'. The *Shorter Oxford Dictionary* tells us that 'significant' means 'important, notable' but it is thought that the courts would tend to interpret this concept as meaning material or palpable and not trivial but not quite perhaps so high on the scale as may be connoted by 'important' except in the tautological sense that any material harm to a child must be 'important'. The harm, actual or apprehended,[1] must derive from the named person and be linked with the individual child. Harm to, for example, the child's mother would not per se be enough, although if the harm to the mother affected or was likely to affect the child then this could be enough. If this were to be the argument then it should be averred in Part 2 of the application form and supported by information laid before the sheriff. If reliance were to be placed on research into the link between domestic violence and the welfare of children then the applicant should be ready to lay any such research before the sheriff. Further, the fact that harm deriving from the named person is reasonably apprehended in respect of one child in a family may not entail that harm to another child is also reasonably to be apprehended.[2]

1 The child may not have suffered harm – reasonable apprehension is enough: *McGregor v L* 1981 SLT 194.
2 See the example at 15.06 below at para (d) and at 15.08 below, in the opinion of the sheriff, second sentence.

(2) EO is necessary and a better safeguard to child's welfare than removal of child

14.30 In the case of a named person who has caused or, it is reasonably apprehended will cause, significant harm to the child *and* where there is an available 'appropriate person' (see next paragraph) it is difficult to figure a case wherein it would not be necessary to keep the named person out of the family home and to do this in preference to removing the child.

This pre-condition accordingly seems to amount to an echo of the principle of no non-beneficial order provision.[1] Nevertheless the sheriff must apply his or her mind to this condition and the local authority should be ready to advise the sheriff thereon.

1 But see discussion of granting a CPO in response to an application for an EO – 14.40 below.

(3) Availability of 'appropriate person'

14.31 It is essential, before an EO, including an Interim EO, is made, that the sheriff be satisfied that there is a person (to be named in the application) who is capable of taking responsibility for the care of the child and any other member of the family who requires such care and who is, or will be, residing in the home – an 'appropriate person'. It is submitted that local authorities should ensure that as full information as possible on this matter is available to the sheriff. It is well known that 'collusion', perhaps by 'turning a blind eye' to abuse or neglect of a child, perhaps as a result of intimidation, sometimes occurs. The sheriff will wish clear reassurance on this matter. If it is lacking, the sheriff may require to consider granting a CPO in terms of the Children (Scotland) Act 1995, s 76(8).[1]

1 Discussed at 14.40 below.

CIRCUMSTANCES WHICH GO AGAINST THE GRANTING OF AN EO

'Unjustifiable or unreasonable ... all the circumstances of the case'

14.32 If it 'appears to' the sheriff that to grant an EO would be 'unjustifiable *or* [emphasis supplied] unreasonable' having regard to 'all the circumstances of the case' then the sheriff 'shall not make an exclusion order'.[1] This gives the sheriff a wide discretion. As already noticed,[2] the s 16 principles apply and the principle of regarding the welfare of the child as the paramount consideration would appear strongly to fetter this discretion. For example, a decision by the sheriff that the order should not be granted because of the hardship it would cause to the named person would, having regard to this principle, be difficult to justify. Even observing the s 16 principles, however, the discretion remains a wide one. In *Russell v W*[3] the named person had been convicted of serious Schedule 1 offences of which he had asserted and was still asserting his innocence. Counsel for the named person did not seek to go behind the conviction. If, however, the conviction had been formally challenged, evidence would have been required to establish, to the civil standard, that the offence had taken place.[4]

1 Children (Scotland) Act 1995, s 76(9) and (9)(a).
2 At 14.20 above.
3 [1998] Fam LR 25.
4 Law Reform (Miscellaneous Provisions) (Scotland) Act 1968, s 10(2)(a).

Requirements to reside in family home mentioned in s 11

14.33 The statute proceeds to specify,[1] without prejudice to the generality of the 'all the circumstances' provision, two particular situations to which the sheriff must have regard when deciding whether an EO would be unjustifiable or unreasonable.

1 Children (Scotland) Act 1995, s 76(9)(b) and (11).

(a) Family home part of an agricultural holding

14.34 Where the family home is or is part of an agricultural holding within the meaning of the Agricultural Holdings (Scotland) Act 1991 and there is a requirement that the named person, either alone or with another person, must reside in the family home then the sheriff must have regard to this. Such a requirement might be in the form of a condition in an agricultural tenancy requiring the named person to reside in the family home as a condition of employment or as a condition of continuing occupancy or both.

(b) Tied house

14.35 Where the family home is let to the named person, whether alone or with another, as an incident of employment then the sheriff must have regard to this.

How much discretion does the sheriff have?

14.36 The sheriff is to consider the application for an EO 'having regard to' all the circumstances of the case, including the foregoing two specified matters. The sheriff must then judge if any of the circumstances to which he or she has had regard lead to the conclusion that an EO would be 'unreasonable or unjustifiable'. This decision, although it looks like an exercise of discretion, is, it is submitted, in reality an exercise of broad judgment of fact. The presence of circumstances tending to make it appear unreasonable, from the point of view of the named person, to grant the order does not by itself prevent the sheriff from making the order. Similarly, as in other situations wherein judgement of objective fact is involved, the paramountcy of the welfare of the child principle cannot apply in the sense of overriding all other interests. The sheriff has to balance the interests of the child and the named person. If it 'appears' to the sheriff, having performed this balancing process, that any disabling factor is present so as to render the EO unreasonable or unjustifiable then it appears that the sheriff has no discretion – he or she 'shall not make an exclusion order'.[1]

1 Children (Scotland) Act 1995, s 76(9).

CONTENT OF THE ORDER

Ancillary orders and terms and conditions

14.37   See the discussion at 14.14(b) above. If information, factual or scientific, is necessary to establish the necessity for a particular term or condition then that information should be made available to the sheriff.[1] The scope of 'judicial knowledge' is strictly limited.[2]

1 Cf 15.26 below – first paragraph of the Sheriff's 'Note'.
2 See discussion at 45.14, 45.15 below.

Named person's right to dispute ancillary orders

14.38   No ancillary order except the order prohibiting the named person from entering the home without the express permission of the applicant local authority may be granted if the named person satisfies the sheriff that such order is unnecessary.[1] The exception represents the consideration that an order prohibiting the named person from entering the home is only in form an ancillary order – it is of the essence of the exclusion order and the onus is of course on the applicant to satisfy the sheriff in the first place that the EO is necessary for the protection of the child. The onus is also on the named person to prove that any of the other ancillary orders are not necessary for the protection of the child.[2]

1 Children (Scotland) Act 1995, s 77(4).
2 But see 41.13 below for observations on the limitations on the evidential consequences of the rule about onus after evidence has been led.

Preservation of named person's effects

14.39   Where an ancillary order for ejection is made in the absence of the named person the sheriff may give a direction as to preservation of the named person's effects in the home.[1] There seems to be no good reason why the sheriff should not raise this matter *ex proprio motu* as well as on the motion of party.

1 Children (Scotland) Act 1995, s 77(5).

GRANTING A CPO WHERE AN EO HAS BEEN APPLIED FOR

The formal provisions – the deliberative process

14.40   The Children (Scotland) Act 1995, s 76(8) enacts:

> 'Where, —
>> (a)   an application is made under subsection (1) above; and
>> (b)   the sheriff considers that the conditions for making a child protection order under section 57 of this Act are satisfied,
>
> he may make an order under that section rather than under this section.'

It will be noted that, in contrast with the parallel provisions in relation to applications for CAOs,[1] the word 'may' is employed here. It is submitted that there is no doubt that the sheriff has a discretion whether or not to exercise the power to treat an application for an EO as an application for a CPO. The pre-conditions for granting an EO are more demanding than those for the granting of a CPO in that the local authority applicant for a CPO only requires to satisfy the sheriff that it has reasonable grounds to suspect that a child is being or will be ill-treated, that he is suffering or will suffer significant harm etc,[2] whereas the applicant for an EO has to satisfy the sheriff inter alia that the child as a matter of fact has suffered, is suffering or is likely to suffer significant harm etc, and that additionally there is an 'appropriate person' in the family home. The circumstances in which it would be open to the sheriff to treat the application for an EO as an application for a CPO include situations wherein the sheriff is satisfied as to the existence of the s 57(2) conditions and:

- there is no available 'appropriate person'; and/or
- the sheriff judges that there is present one or more of the circumstances going against the granting of an EO mentioned at 14.32 above.

If the sheriff judges that any of the foregoing applies then he or she has the discretion to treat the application as if it were an application for a CPO. That decision, being a determination of a matter affecting the welfare of a child, is subject directly to the paramountcy principle,[3] but not directly to either of the other s 16 principles, although in practice the sheriff would take account of any known views of the child as part of the circumstances. Thereafter, if the sheriff decides to consider the application as an application for a CPO, then only the paramountcy of welfare principle, strictly, applies.[4] It is difficult to figure a situation wherein the sheriff, having decided not to grant an EO and being satisfied as to the s 57 conditions, would not proceed to grant a CPO but the sheriff has a discretion to do so and would in that event presumably simply refuse the application for the EO.

1 Children (Scotland) Act 1995, s 55(2), discussed at 13.21 above.
2 C(S)A 1995, s 57(2).
3 C(S)A 1995, s 16(1).
4 But see discussion at 6.05 above.

Who should make the motion under s 76(8) and when?

14.41 It seems clear that the sheriff may act *ex proprio motu* in this matter at any time when the process is before him or her. It is thought that only exceptionally should such a motion be made at the instance of the applicant local authority at the stage of considering an application for an Interim EO: if the local authority thinks that a CPO is required it should apply for a CPO in the first place. The exceptional case might be where in the very course of the hearing in relation to the initial order the applicant received information indicating that a CPO was necessary. It is thought that at any later time the local authority may apply to the sheriff by motion should circumstances indicate that a CPO is necessary.

Can a person other than a local authority make a s 76(8) motion?

14.42 *Quaere* whether any other person, such as the reporter, the child or safeguarder/curator, any relevant person, or indeed the appropriate person may in the course of an EO process make a motion for a CPO. It seems unlikely that the legislature had this in contemplation but the possibility is not expressly excluded. Since 'any person' may apply for a CPO under the Children (Scotland) Act 1995, s 57(1), why should such person, rather than applying for a separate CPO while an EO is under consideration, not be entitled to pursue the arguably neater course of applying to convert an EO into a CPO? It is thought, however, that the possibility of such an application by any person is in practice remote. The natural first approach would be to the social work department of the local authority and such a department would be unlikely not to respond to information that a child was at risk, although differences of opinion between such departments and the children's reporter and others are not unknown.[1]

1 Cf Fife Report p 386 ff and *passim*.

Procedure where sheriff makes CPO in an application for EO

14.43 Where a sheriff, either at the interim stage or later, decides to make a CPO in the context of an application for an EO the rules explicitly provide[1] that the procedural rules[2] governing a CPO come into play.[3] Thus a CPO so granted is subject to the same provisions anent recall and variation as would a CPO granted in response to a CPO application made directly under s 57.[4] Neither the Children (Scotland) Act 1995 nor the Act of Sederunt (Child Care and Maintenance Rules) 1997 make a similar explicit reference to the position of an initial hearing under s 59(2) in the context of a CPO granted by virtue of s 76(8) but it is submitted that the intention is clear that a CPO so granted should be in all respects equivalent to a CPO made in the ordinary way and that therefore the provisions in relation to an initial hearing etc would apply.[5]

1 SI 1997/291, r 3.39.
2 SI 1997/291, rr 3.31–3.33.
3 See 6.08 ff above.
4 See chs 9 and 10 above.
5 See ch 8 above.

14.44 EOs are still reasonably infrequent. As far as the writer is aware, there has been no resort to the Children (Scotland) Act 1995, s 76(8). It may be some time before the issues raised in the preceding three paragraphs have to be addressed.

PROCEDURE FOLLOWING FIRST ORDER WHERE INTERIM EO GRANTED – 'CONFIRMATION' HEARING UNDER S 76(5)

Service of first order and notice to persons named in the application

14.45   The applicant must give notice by serving a copy of the application on the persons mentioned in the application or, as the case may be, on the persons who should receive notice thereof.[1] The ordinary mode and period of notice[2] should be employed, unless an early diet has been fixed in a situation of urgency, in which event service should be effected in such manner as has been prescribed by the sheriff[3] and on such period of notice as may be practicable.

1 SI 1997/291, r 3.12.
2 Discussed at ch 7 above.
3 SI 1997/291, r 3.15(3).

Date of s 76(5) hearing

14.46   The sheriff shall conduct a hearing of the application for an EO within such time as the rules prescribe.[1] In relation to an application in which an Interim EO has been made the hearing shall take place not later than three working days after the granting of the interim order.[2] Accordingly, if an Interim EO were granted on Saturday, 27 June 1998 the s 76(5) hearing would require to take place on Wednesday, 1 July 1998 at the latest. The rules have not prescribed a timescale in relation to an application where an Interim EO is not granted, but it is thought that it would generally be desirable to fix a reasonably early diet – within, say, a week or ten days.

1 Children (Scotland) Act 1995, s 76(5).
2 SI 1997/291, r 3.36.

Nature of hearing under s 76(5)[1]

14.47   The Children (Scotland) Act 1995, s 76(5) allows for the possibility of a hearing under this section being definitive but also provides that the sheriff may *'before finally determining the application* [emphasis supplied] confirm or vary the interim order, or any term or condition on which it was granted or may recall such order'. The words highlighted would appear to allow the hearing to be continued to a later diet. Accordingly, depending on circumstances, it may not be possible for the final determination to be reached at the first diet fixed for the s 76(5) hearing. Where the application is not substantially opposed it should be possible so to do. Where the named person is legally advised it should be possible for his solicitor to advise the local authority solicitor of whether or not the application is to be seriously opposed. Where there is to be serious opposition it will generally be necessary and desirable to allow a period of weeks for investigation, preparation and citation of witnesses.[2] In the (unlikely nowadays) event of the named person not having legal representation or if for any reason it has not been possible for the parties to agree, with the concurrence of the sheriff, that a second stage of the full hearing should be allowed after a period for preparation, then it is submitted that the local authority solicitor, and all other parties attending, should be ready with witnesses to give evidence at the first stage of the s 76(5) hearing.

1 A s 76(5) hearing may perhaps, and in this text sometimes is, referred to as a 'full hearing' which may be divided into two stages – cf 15.11 ff below, but these terms are tentative and non-statutory.
2 Cf 15.12 below.

Powers of sheriff at s 76(5) hearing

14.48 The sheriff's powers at such a hearing would appear to be:

(a) to continue to a second stage for the purpose at that stage of 'finally determining' the application and meantime confirming the interim exclusion order and the interim ancillary orders without variation;

(b) to continue to a second stage for the purpose at that stage of 'finally determining' the application, meantime confirming the interim exclusion order but varying or recalling all or any of the interim ancillary orders or any term or condition on which such order or orders were granted;

(c) to proceed immediately to final determination of the application by confirming the exclusion order without variation of any ancillary orders or any terms or conditions on which such orders have been granted;

(d) to proceed immediately to final determination of the application by confirming the exclusion order but varying one or more of the ancillary orders or the terms or conditions on which such order or orders were granted; or

(e) to proceed immediately to determine the application by recalling the interim exclusion order (and with it the ancillary orders – it seems clear from the wording of s 77(2) that 'ancillary' orders, as the term implies, are dependent for their survival on the continuing in being of the EO which they subserve).

PROCEDURE FOLLOWING FIRST ORDER WHERE INTERIM EO NOT GRANTED INITIALLY

Procedure generally

14.49 It is only where an Interim EO has been granted that a s 76(5) hearing requires to take place.[1] Otherwise the procedure is within the discretion of the sheriff.[2]

1 Children (Scotland) Act 1995, s 76(4).
2 SI 1997/291, r 3.37(1).

Power to grant an interim exclusion order after first order

14.50 Where the conditions mentioned in the Children (Scotland) Act 1995, s 76(3)(a) and (b) (named person has been given opportunity of being heard and sheriff has considered any views expressed by any person on whom notice of application served) the sheriff , by virtue of s 76(6), may at any time before the final determination of the application, grant an interim exclusion order and, it may be inferred, any ancillary order.

FINAL DETERMINATION OF APPLICATION FOR EO

General

14.51 As noticed already,[1] an application for an EO may be determined without further continuation at a s 76(5) hearing. Otherwise the final determination hearing will be the 'second stage' of the s 76(5) hearing,[2] at a hearing fixed as part of the first order[3] or at another date fixed in the course of and in accordance with such procedure as the sheriff thinks fit.[4] An interim EO made under s 76(6)[5] – and probably also an interim order made in terms of s 76(4) and confirmed in terms of s 76(5)[6] – but not an interim EO made under s 76(4),[7] may endure until it ceases to have effect on a date six months after being made.[8] But it is thought that it was not the intention of the legislature that the sheriff should allow an Interim EO to persist in this way and that the preferable practice will be for the sheriff, if there has not been a final determination in the course of the 'first stage' of a s 76(5) hearing, to fix a hearing for final determination of the application within a few weeks of the first order or the 'first stage' of the s 76(5) hearing as the case may be.

1 At 14.48 (c)–(e) above.
2 See 14.48 (a) and (b) above.
3 SI 1997/291, r 3.11 and r 3.37(1).
4 SI 1997/291, r 3.37(1).
5 Children (Scotland) Act 1995, s 76(12): definition of 'exclusion order'.
6 C(S)A 1995, s 76(12).
7 C(S)A 1995, s 76(12).
8 C(S)A 1995, s 79(1).

Preparations

14.52 The degree of preparation required for a s 76(5) hearing where there has been no advance agreement, with consent of the court, that such a hearing will not be a final determination hearing, has already been discussed.[1] Otherwise, as when preparing for the hearing of a motion to vary or recall a CPO, the parties have much to do in preparation for the full hearing. Some of the preparations, set out in the relevant chapter above,[2] apply, *mutatis mutandis*, here.

1 See 14.47 above.
2 See 9.17 ff above (excluding 9.19 which deals with advice hearings under the Children (Scotland) Act 1995, s 60(10) which have no place in EO procedures).

Citation of witnesses

14.53   Witness citation may be proved by a certificate in the style given in Form 43 and r 3.17 provides that proof of citation by lodgement of execution of service may be lodged on the day of the hearing unless the sheriff otherwise directs. It is thought that the implied instruction to lodge proof of citation within this time limit is directory only,[1] except in the event of a warrant to apprehend the witness[2] being asked for. It is submitted that there is no implication that the general rule that citation of a person as a witness is not a pre-condition of that person's being called as a witness[3] is being in any way eroded.

1 I e failure to comply with it would not be a fatal procedural flaw
2 See 30.34 ff below.
3 Evidence (Scotland) Act 1852, s 1; *Watson v Livingstone* (1902) 5 F 171; *McDonnell v McShane* 1967 SLT (Sh Ct) 61 at 63.

Arrangements within the sheriff court

14.54   Although the tight time limits in respect of an application to vary or recall a CPO[1] do not apply here, it is nevertheless important for some priority to be given to proof hearings in exclusion order cases and for them to be dealt with expeditiously.[2] Where the proof hearing is likely to last for more than one day, the days should be continuous. There is no necessity for the sheriff who presided over the early stages of the application to hear the proof. Similarly, there will generally be no reason why the same sheriff should not preside throughout.

1 Discussed in the context of sheriff court arrangements for applications to vary or recall CPOs at 9.22 above.
2 Cf *Lothian Regional Council v A & A* 1992 SCLR 376 per LP Hope at 378.

Form of the proof

14.55   The sheriff has a discretion as to the procedure.[1] The principle that the onus of proof rests with the person affirming places that onus on the local authority and while the onus of proof is not necessarily determinative of who should lead,[2] in practice the person having the onus of proof generally leads.[3] It is submitted that an appropriate order for leading any evidence and for questioning would, when parties are present or represented, generally be as follows: the local authority, the reporter, the mother *qua* relevant person and appropriate person, the named person, the child's solicitor, if any, and the child's safeguarder or curator *ad litem*, if any. The matter, however, is for the sheriff to decide and the view may be taken that the named person, as the substantial contradictor, should come last. The party leading the evidence would be entitled to re-examine. At the conclusion of the evidence parties are entitled to be heard on the evidence.

1 SI 1997/291, r 3.37(1).
2 Cf *Macfarlane v Macfarlane* 1947 SLT (Notes) 34 per LP Cooper.
3 Macphail *Sheriff Court Practice* (2nd edn) para 8-64.

POWER OF ARREST

Power may be granted at any time – onus of proof on applicant

14.56   The court may, at the time of the initial application[1] or at any time while an EO is in force,[2] attach a power of arrest to any of the interdicts granted under the Children (Scotland) Act 1995, s 77(2) and listed in s 77(3). A power of arrest does not have effect until intimated to the named person.[3] There is no statutory form specifically prescribing the style of intimation to the named person. Where the power of arrest is part of the EO then the named person will receive notice when the EO is served on him.[4] Where it is desired to ask the sheriff to attach a power later it is suggested that a procedure akin to the procedure appropriate for varying an EO under s 79 of the Act[5] may be employed. It may be, however, that an application for an EO during the pending procedures could competently be granted on the basis of an *ex parte* motion – on the reasoning that since a power of arrest can be granted in this way initially, the same should apply, particularly in a case of urgency, to an application made in the course of process. The onus of proving the need for a power of arrest would appear to be with the applicant. There is no provision parallel to the Matrimonial Homes (Family Protection) (Scotland) Act 1981, s 15(1)(b) which provides that the court must attach a power of arrest unless it appears to it that in all the circumstances of the case such a power is unnecessary.

1 Children (Scotland) Act 1995, s 78(1); 1997 Rules, r 3.35 and Form 54 Parts 3 and 4..
2 C(S)A 1995, s 78(2).
3 C(S)A 1995, s 78(3).
4 SI 1997/291, r 3.37(2).
5 Discussed at 14.63 ff below.

Notification of chief constable

14.57   Where a power of arrest is attached the local authority must, as soon as possible after the interdict and the power of arrest have been served on the named person, deliver a copy of the application for the interdict, the interlocutor granting it and the certificate of service on the named person to the chief constable of the police area in which the family home is situated. Where an interdict prohibiting the named person from taking some step in relation to the child[1] has been granted, the chief constable of the area in which the step or conduct specified in the interdict may take place then must also be notified. There is no statutory form prescribing the style of the certificate of service on the named person but it is suggested that Form 42[2] may be suitably adapted. Once the chief constable has been notified, a certificate of delivery to the chief constable in the style of Form 56 should be completed by the applicant local authority or its agent. Any variation or recall of a power of arrest must be similarly notified.[3]

1 Children (Scotland) Act 1995, s 77(3)(e).
2 'Certificate of Execution of Citation of or Notice to Child/Certificate of Execution of Notice to Person Named in Application or Any Other Person.'
3 C(S)A 1995, s 78(5).

Operating the power

14.58   A constable may arrest the named person without warrant if he or she has reasonable cause for suspecting that that person has breached an interdict to which a power of arrest has been attached.[1] If satisfied that a further breach is unlikely, the constable may release the named person 'unconditionally' and report the matter to the procurator fiscal forthwith.[2]

1 Children (Scotland) Act 1995, s 78(6).
2 C(S)A 1995, s 78(7)(a) and (9).

Procedure at the instance of the procurator fiscal

14.59   If the named person has not been released but the procurator fiscal decides to take no criminal proceedings[1] then subsections (11)–(13) of the Children (Scotland) Act 1995, s 78 come into play and the named person should be brought before the sheriff's summary criminal court on the first day, apart from week-end days and court holidays, after the apprehension.[2] The named person is then in the position of a 'custody case' in the criminal context and is entitled to have a person of his choice, a solicitor and, if he or she is a child, a parent notified.[3] The named person will also have the possibility of being represented by the duty solicitor under the legal aid scheme.

1 In the parallel situation under the Matrimonial Homes (Family Protection) (Scotland) Act 1981 it is rare for the procurator fiscal to take criminal proceedings.
2 Children (Scotland) Act 1995, s 78(11).
3 Criminal Procedure (Scotland) Act 1995, s 15(1), (2) and (4), as applied by C(S)A 1995, s 78(12), as amended by the Criminal Procedure (Consequential Provisions) (Scotland) Act 1995, Sch 4, para 97(7)(c).

Procedure in court

14.60   When a named person is brought before the sheriff under the Children (Scotland) Act 1995, s 78(11) the procurator fiscal 'shall present to the court' a petition giving statements containing particulars of the named person and the facts giving rise to the arrest, together with a request for his detention for a further period not exceeding two days. The sheriff must then consider (i) if the fiscal's statement of facts discloses a prima facie breach of interdict, (ii) whether proceedings for breach of interdict will be taken and (iii) if there is a substantial risk of violence by the arrested person against any member of the family, or the appropriate person, residing in the family home.[1] Unless it appears to the sheriff that the answer to each of these questions is in the affirmative, the sheriff must order the release of the named person from custody (unless he is in custody for something else).[2]

1 Children (Scotland) Act 1995, s 78(13)(b).
2 C(S)A 1995, s 78(13)(c).

Procurator fiscal's duties as to notification

14.61   Where a named person is liberated in terms of the Children (Scotland) Act 1995, s 78(7)(a) or is to be brought before the sheriff under s 78(11) the fiscal is obliged by s 78 (14) to inform at the earliest opportunity (i) the local authority which made the application for the interdict, (ii) the appropriate person and (iii) any solicitor who acted for the appropriate person when the interdict was granted or any other solicitor whom the fiscal thinks may be acting, that he (the fiscal) has decided that no criminal proceedings should be taken arising out of the facts and circumstances giving rise to the arrest. The subsection provides that in the case of a person to whom subsection (13)(b) applies (i e a person in respect of whom it appears to the sheriff that the fiscal's statement discloses that he or she is prima facie in breach of interdict etc – points (i), (ii) and (iii) in 14.60 above) the information should be given 'before that person is brought before the sheriff'. Taken literally, this is an impossibility: it is suggested that all the fiscal can do is to try always to advise the various parties in advance of the appearance before the sheriff and to take particular care to ensure that this is done in any case where he (the fiscal) thinks that the sheriff will take the view that points (i), (ii) and (iii) in s (13)(b) appear to apply.

14.62   When computing the two days' detention which the sheriff may impose if it appears to him that the subsection (13)(b) criteria (points (i), (ii) and (iii) above) are present, no account is to be taken 'of a Saturday, a Sunday or any holiday in the court in which proceedings for breach of interdict will require to be raised'.[1] An action of breach of interdict may be raised against a defender in the court of his domicile or in the court for the place where it is alleged that the likely breach will take place.[2] Breach proceedings may be raised by the applicant for the interdict – the local authority – or any person whom the interdict was designed to protect and who is likely to be harmed by the breach, for example, the child or the appropriate person. Breach of interdict proceedings in the sheriff court are commenced by initial writ[3] and are civil proceedings to which the normal rules apply.[4] The concurrence of the procurator fiscal should be endorsed on the initial writ.[5] If the procurator fiscal decides to initiate criminal proceedings this concurrence will not be granted and civil proceedings for breach of interdict will be incompetent.

1 Children (Scotland) Act 1995, s 78(13)
2 Civil Jurisdiction and Judgments Act 1982, Sch 8, rr 1 and 2(10).
3 See Macphail *Sheriff Court Practice* (2nd edn) para 21–96 ff.
4 *MacIver v MacIver* 1996 SCLR 225.
5 *Gribben v Gribben* 1976 SLT 266.

VARIATION OR RECALL OF EXCLUSION ORDER

The statutory provisions

14.63   The sheriff may, on the motion of the applicant local authority, the named person, an appropriate person or the spouse or partner[1] of the named person (if that spouse or partner is not excluded from the family home and is not an appropriate person), vary or recall an EO or any associated order.[2]

1 'Partners' here are 'persons who live together in a family home as if they were husband and wife' – Children (Scotland) Act 1995, s 79(4).
2 C(S)A 1995, s 79(2)(b) and (3).

14.64 An application to vary or recall an EO or any associated order made under the Children (Scotland) Act 1995, s 77 shall be in Form 57.[1] A first order in Form 32[2] is obtained, fixing a hearing and authorising and/or dispensing with service in Form 37, and service is effected in the usual way with the usual rules for dispensation and for proof of service.[3] At the hearing the sheriff, after hearing parties and allowing such further procedure as he thinks fit, makes an order granting or refusing the application.

1 SI 1997/291, r 3.40(1).
2 SI 1997/291, r 3.11.
3 SI 1997/291, rr 3.12 and 3.15–3.18, discussed in ch 7 above.

14.65 An application to vary or recall may be used for formal purposes, for example if the address of the family home is changed and it becomes necessary for the exclusion order to be changed in respect of the address of the family home. It is suggested that the 'order sought' in this situation might be:

> 'The applicant requests the sheriff to vary the exclusion order by changing the address of the children's family home from AB to CD from 1 January 1999 with the same associated orders and on the same terms and conditions as were previously attached in respect of the children EF and GF.'

14.66 Alternatively, such an application may be aimed at changing a material part of the EO and associated orders, such as a contact direction[1] or any direction anent the preservation of the named person's goods and effects within the family home.[2] In this situation it is thought that the applicant would generally have to aver a material change of circumstances. For example, a child may have expressed a wish for contact to be changed, leading to, for example, an application by the appropriate person[3] for a change in the contact arrangements. In this situation the changed circumstances may be included in Part 2 of Form 57 thus:

> 'The named person frequently fails to exercise contact with the child AB and this causes upset to her and to her mother. Accordingly AB's welfare is not promoted by the existing order regulating contact, although it remains in AB's interests to maintain some contact with the named person. There are produced herewith:
>> Affidavit by the applicant CD, the mother of AB, dated 26 June 2000; and Letter from AB dated 25 June 2000.'

In this situation Part 3 of Form 57 may include:

> 'ORDER SOUGHT: The applicant requests the sheriff to vary the order which regulates contact and specifies that contact shall take place every

Saturday between 10 a m and 6 p m by withdrawing the said specified contact and replacing it by an order allowing such contact as the appropriate person and the said child AB shall allow on receiving a telephoned request from the named person.'

1 Children (Scotland) Act 1995, s 77(3)(f).
2 C(S)A 1995, s 77(5).
3 C(S)A 1995, s 79(3).

DURATION OF EXCLUSION ORDER

The general rule

14.67 An exclusion order may contain a date for its expiry, provided that such date is within a period ending on a date six months after being made.[1] In the absence of such a specified expiry date the EO, unless earlier recalled,[2] or unless the family home ceases to be available,[3] 'shall cease to have effect six months after being made'.[4]

1 Children (Scotland) Act 1995, s 79(2)(a), read with s 79(1) – see Form 55.
2 C(S)A 1995, s 79(2)(b).
3 C(S)A 1995, s 79(2)(c), discussed at 14.69 below.
4 C(S)A 1995, s 79(1), discussed at 14.51 above.

When is an EO 'made' for the purpose of the six months' duration?

14.68 By virtue of the definition section[1] an EO includes an interim order granted under the Children (Scotland) Act 1995, s 76(4) and such an order confirmed or varied under s 76(5) and also an interim order granted under s 76(6) (i e an interim order granted in the course of process where no interim order was made as part of the first order) except that in s 76(3) and s 79 'it' (meaning an EO) does not include an interim order granted under s 76(4). The exception in relation to s 76(3) is clearly understandable – that subsection is plainly referring to the final determination of an EO. Section 76(4) deals with an interim EO granted before intimation to the named person, i e at the 'first order' stage. An interim order 'made' at that stage is therefore not to be within the definition of an EO for the purposes of s 79. This latter part of the definition section[2] does not, however, as does the earlier part of it, mention an order under subsection (4) 'and such order confirmed or varied under subsection (5) above', and this might lead to the conclusion that only a subsection (4) interim order *not* confirmed under subsection (5) was excluded from the purview of s 79 – with the consequence that the six months would not run from the date of an unconfirmed subsection (4) order but would run from an interim order made under that subsection, but only once it had been confirmed under subsection (5). This may be the answer in that it seems sensible to conclude that the date of the subsection (4) interim order, if not confirmed at the subsection (5) hearing, should not be the commencement date for the running of the six-months period, whereas if it was so confirmed then it should be. The position is, however, unclear. In *Russell v W*[3] Sheriff H Matthews QC appointed the orders he granted after the full and final hearing to run from the date of the final interlocutor and not from the date of the confirmation hearing. The matter does not seem to have been fully argued since Sheriff Matthews simply says in his opinion 'I saw no reason to order that the exclusion order should cease to have effect any earlier than six months after I made it'. Such an interpretation gives the child the maximum available protection, and, in relation to provisions which are aimed at child protection, is, it is submitted, a justifiable interpretation.

1 Children (Scotland) Act 1995, s 76(12), referred to in s 93(1).
2 '... it does not include an interim order granted under subsection (4) above;'.
3 [1998] Fam LR 25.

Home no longer available: s 79(2)(c)

14.69　By virtue of this paragraph an EO ceases to have effect in the event of any permission to occupy the relevant home given by a third party to the spouse or partner of the named person or to an appropriate person being withdrawn. This paragraph would come into play, for example, on the expiry of a lease. There is no special machinery within the Children (Scotland) Act 1995 for having termination of the EO in this way recognised or declared. It may be that the machinery for recall[1] might be used for this purpose but it seems unlikely that anyone would wish to take such a step. It is conceivable that termination of the EO by operation of s 79(2)(c) might have to be proved as a defence to any action of breach of interdict.

1 Children (Scotland) Act 1995, s 79(2)(b), discussed at 14.63 ff above.

APPEAL

Appeal to the Court of Session

14.70　The provisions for appeal against decisions of the sheriff enacted in the Children (Scotland) Act 1995, s 51(1) refer only to decisions of sheriffs on appeal from hearings, decisions of sheriffs under applications under s 65(7) or (9) and decisions of sheriffs under s 85(1) of the Act (review of establishment of grounds of referral). But appeal against the granting of an exclusion order is not expressly excluded, whereas appeal against the decision of a sheriff in relation to an application for a CPO under s 57 is expressly excluded.[1] In *Harper v Inspector of Rutherglen*[2] Lord Traynor stated: 'Every judgement of an inferior Court is subject to review, unless such review is excluded expressly or by necessary implication.' This is still the law.[3] It is submitted that it is competent to appeal against a final exclusion order to the Court of Session but probably[4] not to the sheriff principal.[5] It is thought that appeal against an interim order which had not been confirmed under s 76(5) would not be appealable but it is tentatively submitted that an interim order which had been so confirmed may be appealable to the Court of Session and that such an appeal might have to be considered if the final hearing of the proof were long delayed.

1 Children (Scotland) Act 1995, s 51(15)(a).
2 (1903) 6 F 23 at 25.
3 See Macphail *Sheriff Court Practice* (2nd edn) para 18-01 and the cases therein cited.
4 Cf discussion of appeals in Macphail *Sheriff Court Practice* (2nd edn) paras 18.01 and 25.29 ff.
5 Cf discussion of the possibility of appeal in relation to a Child Assessment Order by application to the *nobile officium* of the Court of Session – at 13.23 above.

Form of appeal to the Court of Session

14.71 It is submitted that a lawful method of initiating an appeal would be for the appellant or his agent to write the words 'The named person [or as the case may be] appeals to the Court of Session and requests the sheriff to write a note' and append his signature and the date. It is submitted that nowadays it would be good practice for a represented appellant to lodge a note of grounds of appeal.

Note by sheriff after appeal lodged

14.72 It is suggested that, as soon as practicable after the lodging of an appeal, the sheriff should write a note including a recital of the proceedings, findings in fact and findings in law and a discussion of the arguments, followed by a statement of his or her reasons – as in the opinion of Sheriff Matthews in *Russell v W*.[1]

1 [1998] Fam LR 25 – see also 15.26 below.

REPEATED APPLICATIONS FOR AN EO

14.73 There is no provision for an EO to be renewed in any way. Accordingly, if it is thought that, on the expiry of an EO, a child still requires the protection of such an order, a fresh EO has to be applied for. The interdict procedure in relation to EOs contrasts in this respect with ordinary civil procedure wherein an interdict, if undefended or granted after proof, may be in an appropriate case declared to be 'perpetual'. It may be thought unsatisfactory that there is no similar machinery in place here whereby an EO might in appropriate circumstances be extended by minimal procedure and without unnecessarily upsetting children.

CHAPTER 15

Model application for Exclusion Order: 'Samantha' and 'Edward'

Note: What follows necessarily enters into personal details to a greater extent than earlier examples. In order to avoid any suggestion of identification, the events are set in the imaginary towns of Kirklenton and Dunchrennan. It is hoped that the representation of the activities of the various professionals is reasonably realistic, but each acting should not necessarily be regarded as ideal practice. Where forms are given the 'standard' part of the form is reproduced in roman typeface, with the 'moveable' parts in italics. The family surname is represented by '~'.

THE BACKGROUND

People, places and dates

15.01

- *Dramatis personae*
  SAMANTHA ~, BORN 13 JANUARY 1987
  EDWARD ~, born 1 July 1988
  FSE (Father of Samantha and Edward), born 1960
  MSE (Mother of Samantha and Edward), born 1962
  SW, social worker, main grade, allocated to the family by Kirklenton Town Council's social work department
  CAW (child abuse worker), social worker with special qualifications and experience in work with cases involving sexual abuse of children
  Area Manager, Kirklenton Town Council's social work department
  LAS (local authority solicitor), the member of Kirklenton Town Council's legal department allocated to deal with this case
  ASW (another social worker), social worker, main grade, who has worked with SW in this case
  AR (Authority Reporter)
  CAL (curator for Samantha and Edward), solicitor (female), holding the accreditation in Child Law of the Law Society of Scotland
  SFF (solicitor for the father)
  SFM (solicitor for the mother)
- 30 August 1996. FSE, who till then has resided with his wife, MSE, and the children in the family home in the industrial town of Kirklenton in the Sheriffdom of Lenton and Muirbrachlan, is convicted after trial by sheriff and jury in the Sheriff Court of Dunchrennan, a town in the north-east of Scotland, of lewd and libidinous practices on three occasions against three girls, aged ten to 13. The children were the

159

daughters of the landlady of the house where FSE was accommodated on occasions when he required to work away from home. The sheriff at Dunchrennan calls for social work and psychiatric reports and remands FSE in custody. The reports narrate that the offender protests his innocence and consequently denies that there was any need for treatment in relation to his alleged propensity to abuse children. After considering the reports, on 20 September 1996 the sheriff sentences FSE to two years' imprisonment. FSE lodges an appeal against conviction and sentence and is granted interim liberation pending appeal.

- The social worker who prepared the court report notifies the Kirklenton social work department which refers the case to the Principal Reporter per the Authority Reporter in Kirklenton. The reporter refers the case to the local authority under s 56(4)(b) of the Children (Scotland) Act 1995.

- FSE returns to the family home in Kirklenton where his wife and children are also staying. FSE remains in the family home till his appeal is heard by the High Court of Justiciary at the end of January 1997. During this time he repeatedly protests his innocence to his wife who initially disbelieves him and accordingly makes sure that he is not alone with the children. After a month or two MSE comes to believe her husband's protestations of innocence and ceases to prevent her husband from being alone with the children. In the event, FSE makes no move to abuse either child.

- On 31 January 1997 FSE's appeal against conviction and sentence is decided by the High Court. The appeal against conviction is refused and in relation to the appeal against sentence the High Court increases the sentence from two to three years. The expected date of release is 30 August 1998.

- The Kirklenton social work department is advised of the result of the appeal and arranges for one of its staff who is a specialist in working with cases of child sexual abuse (CAW) to visit FSE in prison from time to time. CAW reports that FSE consistently maintains his innocence and consequently refuses therapy.

- MSE visits her husband during his term in prison and he continues to maintain his denial of involvement with the crimes of which he has been convicted. MSE initially continues to believe her husband but becomes less convinced later.

- In early 1998 social workers in Kirklenton, conscious of the release date of 30 August 1998, apply their minds to the question of the protective measures which may be taken in relation to Samantha and Edward. Case conferences are held which are attended by inter alia MSE and the children's reporter. The children's names are placed on the Child Protection Register because of the perceived risk to them should FSE return home on release from prison. The relative merits of applying for a CPO and an EO are considered. The social worker responsible for the family (SW) discusses the case frequently with MSE during the months leading up to the end of August 1998. In particular, she tries to assess: (a) whether MSE's statements that she is coming to accept FSE's guilt are genuine and not simply an attempt to avoid having the children removed by a CPO; (b) whether, if she is genuine, she would be likely to be able without formal intervention to keep FSE out of the house; and (c) if formal intervention should be necessary, if MSE would be ready, willing and able to secure the safety of Samantha and Edward with the support of an EO – i e would she be an appropriate 'appropriate person' and be prepared to be named as such (failing which CPO procedures would have to be considered).

- At a case discussion on 29 May 1998 MSE continues to assert, although with diminishing certitude, that her husband is innocent and consequently would pose no threat to the children. The social work department refer the matter formally to the reporter. The reporter present at this discussion returns to the office and discusses with the Authority Reporter responsible for Kirklenton the possibility that compulsory measures of supervision might be necessary on the basis that the children are, or are likely to become, members of the same household as a Schedule 1 offender.[1] The Authority Reporter discusses the matter further with the Area Manager of the social work department who indicates that an EO is being considered. The Authority Reporter notes that the social work department is monitoring the situation, and requests the department to produce background reports.
- A case conference is held on Monday, 17 August 1998. It is attended by SW, the SW Area Manager, CAW, the Reporter and MSE herself. SW reports that she is now satisfied that the mother is genuine in her acceptance of FSE's offending, that she would be unlikely to be able to keep FSE out of the house and the children safe without formal intervention, but that she would be able to take responsibility for the care and welfare of the children if an EO were in place and she is willing to be specified as the 'appropriate person' in terms of the Children (Scotland) Act 1995, s 76(2)(c). The Area Manager agrees. It is accordingly resolved to apply to the Sheriff for an EO and to this end to instruct the local authority solicitor.

---

1   Children (Scotland) Act 1995, s 52(2)(f).

OBTAINING THE FIRST ORDER, INCLUDING INTERIM EO: THE APPLICATION

Administrative arrangements in the sheriff court

15.02   On Wednesday, 26 August 1998 the local authority solicitor, LAS, phones the sheriff clerk's office to advise that an application for an EO (including an application for an Interim EO) is being prepared and will be ready for presentation to the sheriff on Friday, 28 August. LAS states that the background is complex and, having regard to the comparative novelty of such applications, may be expected to take some time. Of the three resident sheriffs in Kirklenton one is on holiday and another is engaged in a long-running jury trial which cannot be interrupted. The other resident sheriff (Sheriff Margaret Lorimer) is at present listed as dealing with the criminal custody cases and a summary trial which is expected to last for the rest of the day on Friday, 28 August. The sheriff clerk discusses the matter with the two resident sheriffs and it is decided that a resident sheriff should hear the application and that the same sheriff should hear the full hearing.[1] While it is not to be anticipated that the consideration will ordinarily require a full day, it is agreed that the novelty of the application and its importance justify a day being cleared for Sheriff Lorimer. Accordingly the sheriff clerk arranges for a 'floating' sheriff to come to deal with the summary criminal business on 28 August, thus leaving Sheriff Lorimer free to deal with the EO. The sheriff clerk also adjusts the diary so as to ensure that Sheriff Lorimer will be able to preside at the full hearing which is likely to be fixed for Wednesday, 2 September 1998.[2]

1 Children (Scotland) Act 1995, s 76(5), Act of Sederunt (Child Care and Maintenance Rules) 1997, SI 1997/291, r 3.36; discussed at 14.28 and 14.29 above.
2 SI 1997/291, r 3.36.

The application

15.03

'FORM 54

APPLICATION FOR EXCLUSION ORDER BY LOCAL AUTHORITY

Section 76 of the Children (Scotland) Act 1995

Application to the Sheriff at Kirklenton   Case No C *12/98*

for an Exclusion Order under section 76(1) of the
Children (Scotland) Act 1995   Date lodged: *28/8/98*

Part 1. DETAILS OF APPLICANT AND OTHER PERSONS WHO THE APPLICANT BELIEVES SHOULD RECEIVE NOTICE OF THE APPLICATION

APPLICANT	*Kirklenton Town Council, per SW, social worker, Social Work Department, 8 Laverock Road, Kirklenton, LE6 4DV. Tel: 012104 545 554. Fax: 012104 545 555.*
CHILDREN	*Samantha ~ , born 13.1.87, girl* *Edward ~, born 1.7.88, boy* *Both children reside at 1/1, 3 Brown Street, Kirklenton.*
THE NAMED PERSON	*FSE (Father), born 18.10.64* *1/1, 3 Brown Street, Kirklenton* *Currently detained in HM Prison, Barlinnie, Glasgow.*
SAFEGUARDER	*(Not applicable – no safeguarder known to be appointed)*
RELEVANT PERSON(S)	*MSE (Mother), born 14.3.67* *1/1, 3 Brown Street, Kirklenton.* *FSE (Father), born 18.10.64* *1/1, 3 Brown Street, Kirklenton* *Currently detained in HM Prison, Barlinnie, Glasgow.*

THE APPROPRIATE PERSON   *MSE (Mother), born 14.3.67*
    1/1, 3 Brown Street, Kirklenton.

THE PRINCIPAL REPORTER   *The Principal Reporter, c/o The Authority Reporter, Scottish Children's Reporter Administration, 17 Laverock Road, Kirklenton LE6 7EK. Tel: 012104 545 700. Fax: 012104 545 710.*

PART 2. INFORMATION ABOUT THE APPLICATION AND ORDERS SOUGHT

CONDITIONS FOR MAKING APPLICATION

1. *Before his present term of imprisonment the named person FSE lived with his wife MSE and their two children Samantha and Edward ~ at Flat 1/1, 3 Brown Street, Kirklenton.*
2. *On 30 August 1996 the named person was convicted after trial in Dunchrennan Sheriff Court of lewd and libidinous practices against three girls, A ~, V ~ and M ~, aged ten, 12 and 13 at the time of the offences, who were the daughters of the landlady of the house in Dunchrennan in which the named person was boarding while working away from home.*
3. *On 20 September 1996 the Sheriff at Dunchrennan sentenced the named person to two years' imprisonment. The named person appealed against conviction and sentence and was released on bail pending the disposal of his appeal. He returned to the family home in Kirklenton and stayed there from late September 1996 until his appeal was decided in the High Court in Edinburgh in January 1997.*
4. *On 31 January 1997 the High Court refused the named person's appeal against conviction and increased his sentence to three years' imprisonment with immediate effect. The named person's expected date of release is 30 August 1998. There will be no supervised release order or other order affecting him after release.*
5. *On 17 February 1997 the social work department of the applicant local authority was notified of the named person's conviction and sentence and on 21 February 1997 SW visited MSE to assess the position in relation to the children. MSE at this stage supported her husband. A case discussion took place in the local authority's social work department on 26 February 1997 when it was decided to monitor the situation.*
6. *From the beginning of his sentence till the date hereof FSE has maintained his innocence in relation to the charges of which he was found guilty. He has refused offers of therapy. The applicant's colleague, CAW, a specialist in sexual cases, has visited FSE in prison on four occasions to offer counselling and on each occasion the offer was refused, on the fourth occasion with acrimony when, on 20 July 1998, FSE said to CAW "I didnae dae anything so you can stuff your f——— counselling".*
7. *On 30 January 1998 a Child Protection case conference was held and it was resolved that the names of Samantha and Edward should be placed on the Child Protection Register because of the anticipated danger to them on FSE's release. The children's names were duly entered in the Child Protection Register.*
8. *Samantha and Edward are about the age of the children whom FSE was convicted of abusing in the case in Dunchrennan Sheriff Court. It is accordingly apprehended that he may abuse either or both of them if, on release from prison, he returns to stay at the family home. He has stated that he intends so to return on his release.*

9. The children have lived in the family home all their lives. MSE resides there and has looked after them very satisfactorily during the period of his imprisonment with the help of State benefits. She is not in employment and is well able to give them all appropriate attention. They are fond of their mother. They have friends locally and go to the local school. It would not be in their best interests for them to be removed from their home.

10. MSE was initially supportive of FSE, refusing to accept that he did the things of which he was convicted. She has gradually changed her attitude and at a Child Protection Procedures Review case conference held on Monday, 17 August 1998 she stated that she was now convinced that her husband had been rightly convicted, that she wanted nothing more to do with him and was now anxious to keep him out of the house and protect the children from him.

11. MSE admits, however, that if approached by her husband she might, partly because of fear of her husband and partly because of emotional blackmail, relent and let him into the house after which she could not answer for what might happen.

12. MSE has not told the children of their father's offending and they think he has been working away from home as often happened in the past. She does not wish Samantha or Edward to be told of the fact that their father has been in prison or the reason for this.

13. On 14 August 1998 the named person told SW that he intended to resume residence in the family home on his release from prison.

On the basis of the foregoing facts the applicant local authority believes that the conditions for making an Exclusion Order are satisfied in respect that:

(a) the children Samantha and Edward would be likely to suffer significant harm if the named person were to resume occupation of the family home;

(b) an Exclusion Order is necessary for the protection of the children because the named person has stated his intention to return to the family home and to reside there on his release from prison on 30 August 1998;

(c) the children have resided in the family home all their lives and are happy there. To remove them would be an unnecessary disruption of their lives. Their protection would be achieved with the least disruption to their lives if the named person were excluded from the family home;

(d) MSE is now committed to protecting and advancing the welfare of her children within the family home and is willing and able to act as the appropriate person in the event of an Exclusion Order being granted.

ANY OTHER RELEVANT APPLICATION OR ORDER WHICH AFFECTS THE CHILD

None.

Note: The reporter has decided not to state grounds of referral until the result of this application is known. In the event of an Interim Exclusion Order not being granted the Reporter intends to state grounds for referral based upon para (f) of s 52(2) of the Children (Scotland) Act 1995 (children are or are likely to become members of the same household as a Schedule 1 offender). The local authority state to the reporter that in the event of an Interim EO not being granted they intend to apply for a CPO.

SUPPORTING EVIDENCE

1. *Indictment in the case Her Majesty's Advocate v FSE.*
2. *Opinion of the Criminal Appeal Court in the appeal by FSE against conviction and sentence.*

3. *Report by Chief Social Work Officer, Dunchrennan Council to Chief Social Work Officer, North Lenton Council, dated 14 February 1997.*
4. *Minutes of case discussion within the applicant authority's social work department regarding Samantha and Edward, 26 February 1997.*
5. *Four reports by CAW on visits to named person in prison, including report dated 20 July 1998.*
6. *Child Protection Procedures Initial Report Form CP1, dated 23 January 1998.*
7. *Child Protection Procedures Initial Case Conference Minute Form CP2, dated 30 January 1998.*
8. *Child Protection Procedures Review Case Conference Minute Form CP5, dated Monday, 17 August 1998.*
9. *Report of interview by SW of FSE on 14 August 1998.*

PROPOSALS BY THE LOCAL AUTHORITY FOR FINANCIAL OR OTHER SUPPORT FOR THE NAMED PERSON

1. *FSE is a scaffolder who was in well-paid employment before being imprisoned. He expects to be able to resume his former employment near Dunchrennan and has satisfied SW that this hope is a realistic one.*
2. *At the request of the applicant local authority Dunchrennan Council has indicated that in the (likely) event of FSE finding it difficult to obtain private digs it will be able to provide hostel accommodation in the short term and, if necessary, local authority housing in the longer term.*
3. *Voluntary after-care will be available to FSE in Dunchrennan should he decide to stay there and wish to take it up.*

PART 3. DETAILS OF ORDER SOUGHT AND ANY TERMS, CONDITIONS OR DIRECTIONS

ORDER SOUGHT

The applicant requests the sheriff to grant an Exclusion Order against the named person, FSE, born 18 October 1964, in respect of Samantha ~, born 13 January 1987, and Edward ~, born 1 July 1988; and to grant said order **ad interim**.

ANCILLARY OR INTERIM ORDERS SOUGHT

In terms of section 77(3) the following Orders are sought:

1. *To grant an interdict prohibiting the named person, FSE, from entering the family home at 1/1, 3 Brown Street, Kirklenton without the express permission of the applicant local authority; and to grant said interdict* **ad interim**.
2. *To grant an interdict prohibiting the named person, FSE, from approaching the family home at 1/1, 3 Brown Street, Kirklenton; and to grant said interdict* **ad interim**.
3. *To grant an interdict prohibiting the named person, FSE, from approaching or meeting either Samantha ~ or Edward ~ outwith the family home, except in so far as such approaching or meeting may be regulated by any conditions regarding contact between the named person and either of the children in terms of any Exclusion Order granted in response to this application; and to grant said interdict* **ad interim**.
4. *To grant an interdict prohibiting the named person from communicating in any way, directly or indirectly with the said children including, without prejudice to the said generality, by written or printed card or note, by telephoning or by*

speaking directly to them or either of them; and to grant said interdict <u>ad interim</u>.

5. To make an order regulating the contact between the children, Samantha ~ and Edward ~ and the named person FSE at such times and places, if any, as the court may consider appropriate.

TERMS AND CONDITIONS TO BE ATTACHED TO ORDER

In the event of the court granting an order regulating contact between the children, Samantha ~ and Edward ~ and the named person FSE, the applicant requests in terms of section 77(7) that such contact be supervised by officers of the Kirklenton Council's Social Work Department.

PART 4. DETAILS OF FIRST ORDER SOUGHT FROM THE SHERIFF

The applicant requests the sheriff to:

(a) Fix a hearing
(b) Order the applicant to serve forthwith a copy of the Application on:
  (i) *see paragraph (c) below;*
  (ii) *the named person, together with a Notice in Form 36; and*
  (iii) *the persons listed in paragraph 1 of this Application, together with a notice in Form 36.*
(c) Dispense with service on the *children, Samantha ~ and Edward ~ for the following reasons: the children do not know of the offences committed by their father or that he is in prison; their mother does not think they should be told; moreover the applicant believes that the children are not old or mature enough to be able to cope with the knowledge that their father has offended in the way he has and that he has been imprisoned and fears that such knowledge would be detrimental to them at this time. If the named person is excluded from the family home by virtue of an Exclusion Order, interim or full, the daily lives of the children will not be materially affected since their father was away from home while imprisoned and has throughout their lives been away from home, sometimes for prolonged periods, because of his work.*
(d) Make an Interim Exclusion Order excluding the named person, *FSE, from the children's family home at 1/1, 3 Brown Street, Kirklenton* in terms of Part 2, above, on the terms and conditions set out in Part 3 above and subject to the directions sought.
(a) Grant the following Ancillary Orders *ad interim:*

1. *To grant an Interdict prohibiting the named person, FSE, from entering the family home at 1/1, 3 Brown Street, Kirklenton without the express permission of the applicant local authority.*
2. *To grant an interdict prohibiting the named person, FSE, from approaching the family home at 1/1, 3 Brown Street, Kirklenton.*
3. *To grant an interdict prohibiting the named person, FSE, from approaching or meeting either Samantha ~ or Edward ~ outwith the family home, except in so far as such approaching or meeting may be regulated by any conditions regarding contact between the named person and either of the children in terms of any Exclusion Order granted in response to this application.*
4. *To grant an interdict prohibiting the named person from communicating in any way, directly or indirectly with the said children including, without prejudice to the said generality, by written or printed card or note, by telephoning or by speaking directly to them or either of them.*
5. *To make an Order regulating the contact between the children, Samantha ~ and*

Edward ~ and the named person FSE at such times and places, if any, as the court may consider appropriate.

(f) ~~Grant a power of arrest.~~[1]

SIGNED   *LAS*   DATED: *28 August 1998*

L A S (Full name)
Solicitor
Legal Department
The Municipal Buildings
Kirklenton
AGENT FOR APPLICANT LOCAL AUTHORITY'

1 Deleted – see 15.05 below.

THE HEARING OF THE APPLICATION BY THE SHERIFF ON FRIDAY, 28 AUGUST 1998

Practical preliminaries

15.04   LAS phones the sheriff clerk at 10 a m. A hearing at 11 a m is fixed. LAS and SW arrive at the sheriff clerk's office at about 10.45 a m and lodge the application and supporting evidence with the sheriff clerk who books them and takes the papers to the sheriff for her perusal. Sheriff Lorimer reads the papers for some 20 minutes and then asks the sheriff clerk to bring LAS and SW into her chambers. The sheriff clerk brings them and remains. The hearing of the application begins.

Addressing the sheriff on the application

15.05   LAS outlines the history of the case as set out at 15.01 above, under reference to paras 1 to 13 of part 2 of the Application. SW is present throughout and supplies points of information when required but the sheriff does not administer the oath. LAS points to the contents of numbers 6 and 7 of the supporting evidence which report that the children are happy and well cared for by MSE in the family home. He stresses that the named person has been convicted of a serious offence against children around the age of puberty. He stresses that the named person has never acknowledged his guilt of the crimes and has refused to consider any form of therapy. He stresses that the named person is determined to return to the family home and may be expected to do so unless restrained by order of court and accordingly moves the sheriff to grant *ad interim* the interdict requested at 1. LAS supports the interdicts requested at 2, 3 and 4 on the basis that if allowed to approach the family home or communicate with the children FSE may be expected to cause them to persuade their mother to allow him to return, thus making her feel emotionally blackmailed. In any event such contact would imperil the children's mother's aim that they should not, at least at present, hear about their father's history. LAS submits that an Interim EO and interim interdicts are necessary because of FSE's imminent return from prison. By the same token it would be inappropriate to allow contact and accordingly the sheriff should, at least at this stage, either refrain from pronouncing an order regulating contact or, alternatively, regulate contact and fix the quantum of contact at nil. The views of the children as to the granting of the EO are not available as such since they do not know that the application is being made. It would be detrimental for them to know of this. LAS concludes by saying that the social work department does not think that a power of arrest is necessary because FSE is manipulative and devious but never violent.

The sheriff raises some issues

15.06   The sheriff asks LAS to make further submissions on certain matters.

(a) *The views of the children.* The sheriff points out that she is required by the Children (Scotland) Act 1995, s 16 to give the children an opportunity, so far as practicable, to express any views that they may care to express. SW states that their general attitude is that they are happy at home with their mother and, while no one has asked them explicitly, they would be devastated to be removed from the family home. LAS suggests that in the circumstances this complies with s 16 by conveying the children's views so far as practicable.

(b) *Dispensing with service on the children.* The sheriff says that while appreciating the motive of avoiding distress to the children, she is unhappy at the prospect of excluding the children, a girl aged about 11½ and a boy aged about ten, from such an important decision affecting their lives. The sheriff indicates that she is inclined to appoint a safeguarder or curator *ad litem*.

(c) *The suitability of MSE as the 'appropriate person'.* The sheriff refers to the mother's vacillation in relation to acknowledging FSE's offending and the impressions that she is liable to emotional blackmail and asks if she can really be trusted to 'police', as the saying goes, the order. SW, who has brought the social work file with her, finds a note by another social worker (ASW) who is satisfied about this and who has discussed the matter more deeply with the mother. The sheriff asks if ASW could be contacted and perhaps come and confirm this. SW goes out and phones the office and returns to report that ASW could come to court at 2 p m.

(d) *The risk of significant harm to Edward.* The sheriff points out that FSE's offences have all been directed against young girls and asks what information there is to suggest that Edward is at risk from his father. SW states that she thinks there is research which suggests that a male child would be at risk in this situation but she is not qualified to give an informed opinion. CAW would be able to provide this but is absent on sick leave. SW mentions that if Edward is not included in the order its aims would be frustrated.

The sheriff adjourns the hearing till 2 p m.

Social work department supplies some answers

15.07   At 2 p m. the hearing is resumed with ASW now present. He confirms that he has discussed with MSE the issue of her being able to resist any impulse to allow FSE into the family home or allow him any contact with the children and is satisfied that MSE will be willing and able to do so. As to the risk to Edward, SW cannot take matters much further although she has consulted some training notes which suggest that a boy might be in danger in these circumstances.

The decision of the sheriff in relation to the first order

15.08   After hearing the final submissions the sheriff adjourns for a short time and then calls parties back to her room to give her decision with reasons. Sheriff Lorimer stated:

> 'I am satisfied that FSE, a convicted abuser of pubescent females, would present a real risk of significant harm to Samantha if allowed to return to the family home and that therefore it is appropriate to grant an Interim EO in respect of Samantha. As to Edward, however, I do not think there was enough solid information laid before me to justify granting an order in respect of him. I will grant interim interdict prohibiting the named person from entering the family home without the express permission of the applicant local authority. I will grant interim interdict in response to crave 2 but with more exact specification, namely that the named person is not to come within 500 metres of the family home at 3 Brown Street, Kirklenton. In relation to craves 3 and 4 (interim interdict against contact or communication with the children), although I was not for granting an Interim EO in relation to Edward, I consider that, by virtue of the sheriff's powers to 'make any other order which he considers is necessary for the proper enforcement of a remedy granted by virtue of paragraph (a), (b) or (c) of this section',[1] that I would be entitled to interdict any contact or communication with Edward as well as with Samantha if it seemed that contact with Edward would be inimical to the efficacy of the order, provided of course that such a course was consistent with the welfare of Edward. I did not receive explicit evidence on these matters but I consider that it stands to reason that allowing contact with Edward would probably lead to the mother being put under pressure to allow FSE into the house. Also, common sense tells me that such contact would be likely to put Edward under emotional pressure which would be intolerable for a ten-year-old. In the circumstances I concluded that I should grant the interdicts craved. I agree that service should not be effected on the children, not so much because of their age and immaturity but rather because I am afraid that service of the application, even if parts were omitted (Act of Sederunt (Child Care and Maintenance Rules) 1997, r 3.4(2)), would be likely to bring the facts of their father's imprisonment and the reason for it to their notice and I think this would be detrimental to them at present and should be avoided so far as possible. In order to involve the children to an extent and in order to obtain their views without disclosure of the details of the current proceedings, I decided that a safeguarder or curator *ad litem* should be appointed. During the adjournment the sheriff clerk has ascertained that no safeguarder whom I regarded as suitable was available on the list[2] but CAL, who is not a safeguarder but has great experience in the law and practice affecting children and is frequently appointed by the

sheriffs here to prepare reports, is available and willing to be appointed. I am confident that CAL is an appropriate person to win the confidence of the children and I shall direct her to ascertain their views so far as can be done without revealing their father's history. No order will be made regulating contact since this would be inconsistent with the interdicts, and it seems more sensible to make no order rather than adopt the artificial formula of regulating contact at 'nil'. I agree that on the present information there seems to be no need for a power of arrest but of course if necessary such a power can be attached later in the proceedings.[3] Since the rules[4] prescribe that a s 76(5) hearing must be fixed not later than three working days after the granting of the interim order I will fix Wednesday, 2 September 1998 at 2 p m within the sheriff court here as the date and time for the full hearing. I was not asked to authorise oral or other special mode of citation.[5] I will arrange for this extempore ruling to be extended and put into the process.'

1 Children (Scotland) Act 1995, s 77(3).
2 Social Work (Panels of Persons to Safeguard the Interests of Children) (Scotland) Regulations 1984 (SI 1984/442), reg 3(1) – probably still in force in 1998 – see 17.02 below.
3 C(S)A 1995, s 78(2).
4 I e Act of Sederunt (Child Care and Maintenance Rules) 1997, SI 1997/291, r 3.36.
5 SI 1997/291, r 3.15(3).

THE FIRST ORDER

The order itself

15.09

12/98

'FORM 32

Rule 3.11

FORM OF FIRST ORDER UNDER THE CHILDREN (SCOTLAND) ACT 1995

~~Section 55 (Application for Child Assessment Order)~~
~~Section 60 (Application to vary or set aside Child Protection Order)~~
Section 76 (Application for Exclusion Order)
~~Section 79 (Application to vary or recall Exclusion Order) and~~
~~Section 67 (Application for warrant for further detention of child)~~

KIRKLENTON 28 August 1998

The court assigns   *Wednesday, 2 September 1998*   at   *2 p m*
within *the Sheriff Court of Lenton and Muirbrachlan at Kirklenton, 1 Wallace Street, Kirklenton* for the hearing of the application;
appoints the applicant forthwith to give notice of the application and hearing to the persons listed in Part 1 of the application by serving a copy of the application and this order together with notices in Forms [insert form Nos]: *36*
*dispenses with notice and service on [insert name]: *Samantha* ~ *and Edward* ~

for the following reason(s) [insert reasons]: *children do not know why FSE is in prison; it is uncertain whether children of their age and maturity would be able to handle this information without serious detriment to their welfare.*

[~~Note: Insert details of any other order granted and in an application under Section 76 for an exclusion order insert as appropriate Meantime grants an interim exclusion order; or interim interdict; or otherwise as the case may be~~]

Meantime grants an Exclusion Order in respect of the child Samantha ~ and in pursuance thereof

Grants Interdict <u>ad interim</u> *prohibiting the named person, FSE, from entering the family home at 1/1, 3 Brown Street, Kirklenton without the express permission of the applicant local authority.*
Grants Interdict <u>ad interim</u> *prohibiting the named person, FSE, from approaching within 500 metres of the family home at 1/1, 3 Brown Street, Kirklenton.*
Grants interdict <u>ad interim</u> *prohibiting the named person, FSE, from approaching or meeting either Samantha ~ or Edward ~ outwith the family home,*
Grants interdict <u>ad interim</u> *prohibiting the named person from communicating in any way, directly or indirectly, with the said children including, without prejudice to the said generality, by written or printed card or note, by telephoning or by speaking directly to them or either of them*

* Delete as appropriate

Margaret Lorimer
Sheriff'

Appointment of curator *ad litem*

15.10 The following style (non-statutory) may be followed.

Case no: C 12/98
'APPOINTMENT OF ~~SAFEGUARDER~~/CURATOR *AD LITEM*

In the Sheriff Court
At: *Kirklenton*
On: *28 August 1998*

In the Application by[1] *Kirklenton Council*
~~The Principal Reporter per~~[2]
Under Section[3] ~~51, 55, 60, 65, 67,~~ 76, ~~79, 85~~ of the Children (Scotland) Act 1995

The Sheriff appoints[4] *Mrs CAL, Solicitor, 77 White Street, Kirklenton*

As ~~safeguarder~~/curator *ad litem* in the proceedings;

Directs said ~~safeguarder~~/curator to intimate in writing to the sheriff clerk at[5] *Kirklenton*
whether or not s/he intends to become a party to the proceedings by[6] *Wednesday, 2 September 1998 at 2 p m.*

~~Further, in terms of Section 41(4) of the said Act, Directs that the expenses of the duly appointed safeguarder shall be borne by the Local Authority.~~

Margaret Lorimer
Sheriff'

1 Insert name.
2 Insert name and address of the individual Authority Reporter.
3 Delete as appropriate.

4 Insert name and address.
5 Insert name of court.
6 Insert date fixed for hearing or application in which the safeguarder/curator *ad litem* is being appointed.

Serving the spplication – lodging the certificates of execution

15.11   The applicant must now serve[1] the application on all persons mentioned in Part 1 of the form, except in so far as dispensed with.[2] The appropriate certificates[3] should be lodged in court by the time of the hearing at the latest.[4] An example would be:

Rule 3.14(3)

'FORM 42

CERTIFICATE OF EXECUTION OF NOTICE TO PERSON NAMED IN APPLICATION OR ANY OTHER PERSON UNDER THE CHILDREN (SCOTLAND) ACT 1995

KIRKLENTON: 29th day of August 1998

I, SO, Sheriff Officer, 1 Union Street, Kirklenton, hereby certify that on the 29th day of August, Nineteen Hundred and Ninety Eight, I duly gave notice to FSE (Father), by delivering a copy of the foregoing application, warrant and intimation to him personally at HM Prison, Barlinnie, Glasgow, in presence of SOW, 1 St Vincent Street, Glasgow, Witness hereto with me subscribing.

SO
Sheriff Officer

SOW
Witness'

1 SI 1997/291, r 3.12(1)(c); Form 36.
2 SI 1997/291, r 3.12.
3 SI 1997/291, r 3.14(3); Form 42.
4 SI 1997/291, r 3.17(2).

THE FULL HEARING: THE FIRST STAGE – CONFIRMATION UNDER s 76(5)

Preliminaries

15.12   On 31 August 1998 FSE, just released from prison, meets his solicitor (SFF) and instructs him to oppose the application at the full hearing stage. Legal aid papers are completed. SFF phones the solicitor for the mother (SFM) to discuss how best to proceed. The curator *ad litem* (CAL) visits the children in the family home. Thereafter all parties, i e LAS, CAL, the reporter, SFF, and SFM exchange phone calls and it emerges that the named person, FSE, intends to make a sustained challenge to the merits of the EO, asserting his innocence and arguing that in any event the EO is unnecessary. LAS will wish to present more elaborate evidence in relation to the risk to both children, including the evidence of CAW who is still indisposed. Parties agree that it will be desirable if the full hearing diet on 2 September could be continued to a date a month or so ahead, with at least three days reserved. LAS phones the sheriff clerk and explains the position. The sheriff clerk reports the position to Sheriff Lorimer.

The 'confirmation' hearing commences

15.13   On 2 September 1998 all parties' representatives (i e LAS, CAL, the reporter, SFF, and SFM) assemble before the sheriff in a small court, closed to the public, which the sheriff deems to be her chambers. FSE is present but MSE is not. SW is also present.

The local authority's stance

15.14   LAS moves the sheriff to confirm the EO and the ancillary orders under the powers conferred by the Children (Scotland) Act 1995, s 76(5). He submits that there has been no material change since the matter came before the sheriff at the hearing on 28 August and he refers to Sheriff Lorimer's note of that date which is now available to parties.

The named person's stance

15.15   SFF, for the named person, the father, states that she has instructions to bring witnesses of family members and possibly others who will say that FSE is no threat to children, and that the sheriff should finally determine that the conditions for making an EO have not been met and therefore that the Interim EO and the other interim orders should be recalled. SFF explains that she is not in a position to advance this evidence today and will require some weeks for preparation. She accordingly cannot today oppose the motion to confirm the interim EO but she asks the sheriff to vary the interim order, as s 76(5) allows, to the extent of lifting the interim orders prohibiting contact with the children and inserting an ancillary order under s 77(3)(f) of the Act, regulating contact between the children and the named person. In support of this she argues that the father did not molest his children during the period while he was on bail pending appeal and that he has made no attempt to approach or contact the family during the admittedly short period since being released from prison. The social work department has indicated that contact could take place at a contact centre under social work supervision and accordingly there could be no danger to the children even if, which her client does not admit, he had abused children. SW confirms that such arrangements could readily be made. As to further procedure, SFF submits that there will have to be a full proof and she moves the court to allow answers to be lodged if so advised.

The reporter's stance

15.16　The reporter states that at present he does not intend to state grounds for referral and expects to maintain this position provided an EO, interim or final, remains in force and continues to be obeyed by FSE. The reporter says he doubts if he has at this stage a *locus* to comment on the motion for interim contact on the part of FSE but in so far as he has any *locus* he would adopt the local authority's stance. He has no objection to the procedural proposals advanced by SFF.

The mother's stance

15.17　SFM reports that her client would prefer that there should not be an interim order regulating contact. She feels this would result in pressure upon her to allow more contact outwith the terms of the order, i e in the home, and she would prefer to have more time to get used to the idea that FSE is at liberty before allowing such contact. Samantha, as CAL will narrate, is now aware of her father's offending etc, but Edward is not and would, in the mother's and the curator's view, be quite unable to cope with it. If contact were allowed with Samantha and Edward the truth would be bound to leak out. It would be impracticable to allow contact with Samantha and not with Edward. She had no objection to the procedural proposals advanced by SFF.

The submission of the curator *ad litem*

15.18　CAL reports that she has had one meeting with Samantha and Edward together and another, longer, meeting with Samantha alone. Samantha had worked out from the arrival of legal papers in the house, the unusual length of time that her father had been away and from her observations of her mother's reactions to various events that something was seriously wrong. She had put her suspicions to her mother who, in order to avoid speculation as to something even worse, had told Samantha the truth. Samantha's reaction was complex. She was very upset at what her father had done but did not wish never to see him again. She did not think her father would try to abuse her and if he made any serious attack she would resist and tell. She did not, however, want to see her father at present as she needed 'space' to get used to the situation. She might wish to have contact in the future but not now. She was sure that Edward was far too young to understand and should not be allowed to see his father on this account alone. CAL's assessment was that Samantha was a very mature 11-and-a-half-year-old whereas Edward was a very immature ten-year-old. CAL thought Samantha's summing up of the position was correct and that accordingly contact should not be allowed at this stage and the matter could be looked at again at or after the continued full hearing. CAL accordingly, as of today at least, adopted the stance of the local authority. Samantha would be happy to see the sheriff and state her position directly. She had no view to express which she wanted the sheriff to keep secret. In the circumstances the sheriff might not think it necessary to see Samantha but if she did CAL had arranged that Samantha could come to court in the late afternoon after school. CAL did not anticipate that she would lodge answers but had no objection to answers being allowed.

The decision of the sheriff

15.19 Sheriff Lorimer asks LAS if he has anything to say in response to the submissions of the others, and he has nothing to add. The sheriff offers the other parties an opportunity to make a further submission in response to any new material but no one so wishes. After retiring for a short period, the sheriff announces that she will confirm the EO in terms of the Children (Scotland) Act 1995, s 76(5) without variation. She gives her reasons as follows:

> 'It was accepted, correctly on the information before me, that the Exclusion Order itself should be confirmed. As at the interim hearing there was today a reasonable apprehension of significant harm to the children. It remains clear that it is preferable to exclude the father rather than remove the children. It was not practicable to obtain Edward's views. I did not require to hear from Samantha directly since her views were conveyed with great clarity by the curator *ad litem*. Samantha made it clear that she did not wish contact for the time being but might come to wish contact in the future. I accepted the curator's assessment of Samantha as mature and sensible and in all the circumstances thought her wishes should be respected. I thought that the same reasons which militated at the interim stage against granting contact with Edward were still valid today. I accordingly make no variation in the Interim Exclusion Order. The second and final stage of the full hearing will take place on Monday, 28 September, with the rest of the week reserved. Of consent I shall allow parties to lodge answers if so advised. I shall have this short determination extended and put in the process.'

The formal order of court

15.20 The interlocutor following the foregoing is in these terms:
'Kirklenton, 2 September 1998

Act: LAS, for the local authority (with SW, social worker)

Alt: SFF, solicitor, for the named person (named person personally present)
SFM, solicitor, for the mother
AR for the Principal Reporter
CAL, solicitor, the curator *ad litem*, in person

The sheriff, having resumed consideration of the application and being satisfied that it has been served on the named person, the relevant persons and the principal reporter, and having heard parties' procurators, the children's reporter and the curator *ad litem* for the children, and being satisfied that the conditions mentioned in section 76(1) have been met CONFIRMS the Interim Orders granted on 28 August 1998, namely the interim Exclusion Order in respect of the child Samantha ~ prohibiting *ad interim* the named person FSE from entering the house at 1/1 Brown Street, Kirklenton without the express permission of the local authority; prohibiting *ad interim* the named person from entering or remaining within 500 metres of said house; and prohibiting *ad interim* the named person from communicating in any way, directly or indirectly, with the said children, including, without prejudice to the said generality, by written or printed card or note, by telephoning or by speaking directly to them or either of them; REFUSES the motion of the named person to vary said orders by allowing contact by the named person with the said children or either of them; on the motion of the named person, there being no objection by any party or by the curator *ad litem*, ALLOWS, if so advised, parties and the curator *ad litem* to lodge answers within 14 days of today's date and appoints any party lodging answers to intimate said answer to other parties and the curator *ad litem*; thereafter, on the motion of the applicant local authority, there being no objection, ALLOWS a hearing on the Exclusion Order and ancillary orders on Monday, 28 September and following days at 10 a m.'

Written answers for the named person

15.21   Only the named person takes the opportunity of lodging answers. On 14 September 1998 his solicitor lodges and intimates to the others the following:

'SHERIFFDOM OF LENTON AND MUIRBRACHLAN AT KIRKLENTON

ANSWERS

for

FSE, residing at 34 St Thenew Street, Kirklenton

NAMED PERSON

in the Application of

Kirklenton Town Council, The Municipal Buildings, Kirklenton

APPLICANT

for an exclusion order under s 76 of the Children (Scotland) Act 1995

ANSWERS TO APPLICATION
PART 2 – INFORMATION ABOUT THE APPLICATION AND ORDERS SOUGHT

1. Admitted under explanation that on 31 August 1998 FSE was released from prison. He now resides temporarily with his mother at the address in the instance.
2. Admitted under explanation that FSE maintained at the trial and still maintains that he is innocent of the charges libelled against him. Explained and averred that FSE has no conviction against him for abusing male children.
3. Admitted. Explained and averred that during the period of three months or thereby when FSE was at home he assisted, as he always did when at home, with the upbringing of Samantha and Edward, that the children were happy and well cared for by MSE and FSE and that no

untoward incident occurred and no allegation of any untoward incident has ever been made.

4. Admitted.
5. Not known and not admitted.
6. Admitted that on the fourth visit of CAW FSE angrily rejected the offer of counselling because he had often made it clear to CAW that he refused to accept counselling because he had not committed the offences. Denied that he used the terms quoted. *Quoad ultra* admitted.
7. Not known and not admitted.
8. Admitted that Samantha and Edward are about the age of the children whom FSE was convicted of abusing in the case in Dunchrennan Sheriff Court. Admitted that FSE has stated it as his intention to return to the family home on his release. *Quoad ultra* denied.
9. Admitted.
10. Admitted that MSE was initially supportive of FSE, refusing to accept that he did the things of which he was convicted. *Quoad ultra* not known and not admitted.
11. Not known and not admitted. Explained and averred that FSE has no intention of employing any form of 'emotional blackmail' although he would, if a lawful opportunity presented itself, attempt to convince his wife that the children have nothing to fear from him.
12. Believed to be true that MSE has not told the child Edward of his father's conviction. *Quoad ultra* not known and not admitted.
13. Admitted that FSE stated to SW on 14 August 1998 that he intended to resume residence in the family home. Explained and averred that it is no reasonable ground for the applicant to apprehend that any conduct of FSE is likely to cause significant or any harm to the children or either of them. He has never harmed them and they have never expressed any apprehension of harm from him. In any event the conviction of FSE relates to female children only. There is accordingly no ground what-ever for apprehending harm to Edward. There are no reasonable grounds for apprehending harm to either child in the event of the FSE returning home. An exclusion order is accordingly unnecessary. In any event it is of paramount importance, having regard to the welfare of the children throughout their childhood, that they continue to have contact with their father. Accordingly, in the event of an exclusion order being finally granted an order regulating contact should be made. FSE has never and will never breach an order of court. Any power of arrest is therefore unnecessary.

PLEAS-IN-LAW

1. The said children not being likely to suffer significant harm as a result of any reasonably apprehended conduct by the named person, an exclusion order should not be granted as craved.
2. An exclusion order not being necessary for the protection of the said children, it should not be granted as craved.
3. In all the circumstances an exclusion order being unjustified and unreasonable, it should not be granted as craved.
4. In all the circumstances the ancillary orders sought by the applicant in terms of section 77(3) of the Children (Scotland) Act 1995 being unjustified and unreasonable, they should not be granted as craved.
5. In the event of an exclusion order being made an order should be made under section 77(3)(f) of the said Act regulating contact between the named person and his children and that without a requirement that such contact be supervised in any way.

6. *Separatim* and in any event, there being no averment suggesting that the named person is likely to breach any order of court, the application to attach a power of arrest to any order granted should be refused.

IN RESPECT WHEREOF

(sgd) FSE

Solicitor
23 Wallace Square
Kirklenton
Agent for the Named Person'

THE FULL HEARING: THE FINAL STAGE

The proof

15.22   On 28 September 1998 the parties assemble for the proof in the same small court. The presiding sheriff is Sheriff Ralph Thomson QC, one of the permanent sheriffs in Kirklenton. Present are LAS, CAL, SFM and her client MSE, SFF and her client the named person (FSE) and AR. Sheriff Thomson indicates that, without prejudice to any matter of onus of proof, he proposes to invite the local authority to lead its evidence first, then the Authority Reporter (AR), then SFM, then SFF and finally CAL. The sheriff also indicates that he will allow cross-examination and final speeches in accordance with this sequence. He invites comments. All agree. AR indicates that he did not think it appropriate to bring witnesses but he might ask some questions. CAL indicates that she is not intending to lead evidence but expects to ask questions.

The evidence[1]

15.23   LAS leads evidence from SW, the Area Manager and CAW. He takes from the former the evidence regarding the conviction and sentence of FSE and also the history of the case as reflected in the social work records[2] up to and including the meeting with FSE on 15 August 1998. She says that, on the evidence, she apprehends significant harm if FSE is allowed admittance to the family home or unsupervised access to the children. The Area Manager supports this. CAW then gives evidence and speaks to his limited acquaintance with this particular case but also qualifies himself as an expert witness (he holds a diploma in the study of the sexual abuse of children and has considerable practical experience in USA and London as well as in Scotland) and opines that Edward would be likely to be at risk as well as Samantha. MSE gives evidence herself, saying she can supervise ('police' as the reporter puts to her) the EO and is in favour of it. She is strongly against contact for Edward. She realises that Samantha is now in favour of contact but the mother is against that since she fears FSE may use this to put pressure on her. FSE gives evidence asserting his innocence. Relations of FSE give evidence that FSE has sometimes looked after their children without any apparent untoward result. On behalf of FSE a child psychologist who has examined the papers in the case but has not interviewed Edward, because of the practical difficulties flowing from Edward's not knowing about his father's case, opines that Edward should have at least supervised contact with his father. CAL reports that Samantha would now like limited, but unsupervised, contact with her father on a non-residential basis and she has told CAL that she will not allow contact to be used by her father as a way of putting pressure on her mother. CAL says that the position in relation to Edward is unchanged. CAL's own assessment is that Edward still lacks the maturity to cope with his father's history, that he is used to his father being away for extended periods and that at present there should be no contact. The matter should be looked at again in six months' time.

1 The evidence lasts for the full five days reserved, with extensive examination, and searching cross-examination, particularly by SFF and CAL: in the interests of brevity, the evidence is only lightly touched on in this narrative.
2 Cf items 1–4 and 6–9 of the 'Supporting Evidence' in Part 2 of the Application, at 15.3 above.

The submissions[1]

15.24   Parties' representatives argue their clients' cases in accordance with the stances already outlined. SFF, while pointing out that FSE maintains his innocence, does not seek to re-open the case which resulted in his conviction. LAS is neutral on the issue of contact with Samantha. MSE is very much against it. The reporter, AR, is also against such contact. CAL says she has confidence in Samantha and that her views should be regarded.

1 Again only briefly given.

The formal determination of the sheriff

15.25

Case no: 12/98

'Application for an Exclusion Order by Kirklenton Council v FSE

Sheriff Ralph Thomson QC
LAS, solicitor, for the applicant local authority
SFM, solicitor, for the mother
SFF, solicitor, for the named person, FSE
CAL, solicitor, curator *ad litem* for Samantha and Edward ~
AR, for the Principal Reporter

Kirklenton, 6 September 1998

The sheriff having considered the application and the evidence and heard parties' procurators GRANTS said application and in terms thereof:

Makes an Exclusion Order in terms of section 76 of the Children (Scotland) Act 1995 against the named person FSE, d o b 18 October 1964, in respect of the children Samantha ~, d o b 13 January 1987 and Edward ~, d o b 1 July 1988, and excludes the said FSE from the home at 1/1, 3 Brown Street, Kirklenton;

Further, in terms of s 77(3) of said Act:

Grants an interdict prohibiting the named person FSE from entering the said home without the express permission of the applicant local authority, namely Kirklenton Council;

Grants an interdict prohibiting the named person FSE from entering or remaining within 500 metres of said house;

Grants an interdict prohibiting the named person FSE from communicating in any way, directly or indirectly, with the child Edward including, without prejudice to the said generality, by written or printed card or note, by telephoning or by speaking directly to him except in so far as any contact between the said FSE and Edward may be regulated by a children's hearing;

Refuses *in hoc statu* to attach a power of arrest to any of the foregoing orders;

Regulates contact between the said named person and Samantha by allowing unsupervised contact every alternate Saturday, commencing Saturday, 14 September 1998, between the hours of 12 noon and 6 p m, with Samantha to be collected from and returned to the Children's Centre, 14 Craigievar Avenue, Kirklenton at said times – said order to be subject to any order which may be made by a children's hearing;

On the motion of the applicant local authority, of consent of the curator *ad litem*, and there being no objection by other parties, Dispenses with intimation of said orders on the children;

Having heard parties' procurators on the commencement date of said orders, appoints said orders to run from and including today's date.

Ralph Thomson
Sheriff'

AN APPEAL IS MARKED

15.26   The named person's solicitor writes the following on the interlocutor sheets below the foregoing interlocutor:

'Kirklenton, 2 October 1998

The named person appeals to the Court of Session and requests the Sheriff to write a note.

SFF
Solicitor
Agent for the named person
Edinburgh Agents: Messrs EA, WS,
Edinburgh'

Extracts from the sheriff's note

15.27

'This is an application by Kirklenton District Council under section 76 of the Children (Scotland) Act 1995 for an Exclusion Order which would exclude from the family home at 1/1, 3 Brown Street Kirklenton, FSE (the "named person") from the home where he normally resides with his wife, MSE. The application is in respect of the two children of the marriage between FSE and MSE, namely Samantha, born 13 January 1987, and Edward, born 1 July 1988. MSE is both the "relevant person" and the "appropriate person".

On 28 August 1998 Sheriff Lorimer assigned 2 September 1998 as a diet for the hearing of the application and dispensed with service on the children on account of their age and lack of maturity. They did not know about what had happened in relation to their father. She also granted an interim exclusion order [the sheriff now rehearses the procedural history of the case including the interim orders granted and in brief the final order granted on 6 September 1998].

I found the following facts to be admitted or proved:

1. Samantha ~, born 13 January 1987, and Edward ~, born 1 July 1988, are the children of FSE and MSE who were married in June 1985. They have resided with their parents at all material times at 1/1, 3 Brown Street, Kirklenton which is an owner-occupied flat. FSE is a scaffolder and frequently worked away from home for extended periods.

2. On 30 August 1996 FSE was convicted after trial before a sheriff and jury in Dunchrennan Sheriff Court . . . [The sheriff outlines the history of the case, substantially along the lines of the summary at 15.1 above] . . .

24. The Applicant local authority, and in particular the family's social worker, SW, are apprehensive that FSE will conduct himself towards his children in the same or a similar way as he has been found to have done towards the children in the case in Dunchrennan Sheriff Court. Their concern is based on the following considerations:
    (a) FSE has not made himself available for a risk assessment in relation to offending behaviour;
    (b) in the absence of such assessment no informed opinion is available as to his preferences as to the age and gender of children;
    (c) power is one of the main motivating factors in sexual offending, with the age and gender of the children a secondary consideration. Accordingly, all children close to the offender are at risk;
    (d) FSE has not addressed his offending behaviour. He therefore has no insight into his offending behaviour and will not be able to recognise risky moods and situations and deploy appropriate strategies in order to control his behaviour.

I made the following findings-in-fact-and-in-law:

(1) The apprehensions of the appellant local authority that the named person, if he should return to the family home, may abuse Samantha and/or Edward are reasonable.
(2) Samantha and Edward, if living in family with FSE, are likely to suffer significant harm as a result of reasonably apprehended conduct of FSE.
(3) The making of an Exclusion Order is necessary for the protection of the children.
(4) The making of an Exclusion Order will better safeguard the welfare of the children than would their removal from home.

(5) It is necessary to interdict FSE from coming or remaining within 500 metres of the family home.

(6) It is necessary to interdict FSE from communicating with Edward.

(7) It is not necessary to attach a power of arrest to any of the foregoing.

(8) It is in the interests of Samantha, having regard to her welfare throughout her childhood and her views, taking account of her age and maturity, that limited unsupervised contact be allowed between Samantha and FSE and it is better for Samantha that such an order be made than that no order should be made.

Note:[1]

. . .

CAW described to me his qualifications. He is an MA (Soc Sc) of Glasgow University, with First Class Honours, holds the Diploma in Social Work granted by Dundee University and has worked in the Tavistock Clinic in London for two years where a large proportion of his caseload comprised sexual abuse cases. He has studied for one year in the USA where one of his teachers was David Finkelhor who is a recognised expert in the study of the sexual abuse of children. His evidence was to the effect inter alia that power is a main motivating factor in child sexual abuse and that age and gender are secondary. As no assessment of FSE as an individual had been possible it had to be assumed that a boy such as Edward was equally at risk as Samantha. On such a specialised matter I felt I must give great weight to CAW's evidence, which was uncontradicted. Information on these matters was not available to Sheriff Lorimer when she refused to grant an interim exclusion order in respect of Edward. I was impressed by CAW's analysis and accepted his conclusions. I therefore granted the order in respect of Edward.

. . .

SFF, for the father, pointed out, in relation to contact with Edward, that the expert evidence of the child psychologist adduced on behalf of the father was uncontradicted and suggested that in this circumstance I was bound to accept it. LAS and CAL disagreed and referred me to *Davie v Magistrates of Edinburgh* 1953 SC 34 wherein Lord President Cooper stated at 40:

> "The scientific opinion evidence, if intelligible, convincing and tested, becomes a factor (and often an important factor) for consideration along with the whole other evidence in the case, but the decision is for the Judge or jury."

I was well satisfied as to the high qualifications of the child psychologist adduced by FSE but on the foregoing authority I reject the suggestion that I am bound to follow the views of the expert. Having regard to the whole evidence, including the testimony of the mother, the views of Samantha as reported to me by the curator *ad litem*, and the curator *ad litem*'s own assessment, I was well satisfied that the interests of Edward would be best served by contact between Edward and his father being avoided for a while.

. . .

The interrelationship between an order regulating contact under s 77(3)(f) of the Act and a possible ruling on contact by a children's hearing, in the event of the reporter successfully having the case of either or both children referred to a children's hearing, was discussed. I was referred to *Aitken v Aitken* 1978 SC 297, *D v Strathclyde Regional Council* 1985 SLT 114 and *A v G and Strathclyde Regional Council* 1997 SCLR 186.[2] The discussion was to an extent academic since the children are not at present subject to a supervision requirement made by a hearing. As at present advised, my view is that the legislature having conferred on the sheriff the competence to regulate custody this is a power which the sheriff is entitled to exercise but that it cannot have been intended that there should be a collision between the exercise of this power and the pre-eminent jurisdiction of the hearing. For the avoidance of the appearance of such collision, I have worded the orders regulating contact in order to reflect this.

. . .

I was asked by all parties to make explicitly clear the commencement date of this Exclusion Order. This is important because of the terms of s 79(1) of the Act which provides that, subject to the provisions for early recall, "an exclusion order shall cease to have effect on a date six months after being made". The matter could perhaps be clearer but I think the definition of 'exclusion order' in s 76(12), in which such an order is defined as including an interim order "except . . . in section 79 of this Act", leads to the conclusion that s 79(1) must be taken as referring not to an interim order – not even an interim order "confirmed under s 76(5)" – but to an order granted after the "final determination" referred to in s 76(5). Once granted, the Exclusion Order has immediate effect. It is an order inhibiting the liberty of the subject. Accordingly the day on which the order is pronounced becomes, in my view, "day one". I have worded the order so as to reflect this.'

1 Extracts only printed here.
2 The decision of the Inner House in *P v P* 2000 SCLR 477, Extra Div, disapproving the decision of the Sheriff Principal in *A v G and Strathclyde Regional Council*, had not, of course, been made at the time of Sheriff Thomson's judgment.

Part III – The stage of the children's hearing

CHAPTER 16

Formulating the grounds of referral

DUTIES OF REPORTER

General

16.01   Once the reporter has decided to take the matter to a hearing, the bulk of the work involved in setting it up rests with him or her. Primary among these tasks, logically if not always chronologically, is the preparation of the grounds of referral. Self-evidently, these grounds form the basis in law for the hearing to assume jurisdiction over the child, and they may have to face scrutiny in the sheriff court or, on appeal, by the Court of Session: they are also of significance in that their number and content will often significantly affect the decision of the hearing as to the disposal of the child concerned.[1] It accordingly follows that the drafting of the grounds of referral should be approached with deliberation and carried through with care.

1 Martin, Fox and Murray *Children out of Court* p 177ff.

Terminology: grounds, conditions and facts; the forms – 'grounds'

16.02   The Children (Scotland) Act 1995, s 52(1) refers to, and s 52(2) of the Act lists, the *conditions* which have to be satisfied in respect of the child if the need for compulsory measures of supervision is to be established. Section 65 of the Act, which prescribes the basic rules for the conduct of hearings, defining the characteristics of cases which the reporter is to refer to a children's hearing, prescribes inter alia that the reporter must be satisfied that 'at least one of the grounds specified in section 52(2) of this Act is established'. The term 'grounds' has no statutory definition. The Act of Sederunt (Child Care and Maintenance Rules) 1997[1] do not provide a style for the reporter to use when stating grounds of referral to a hearing and in practice the forms prescribed in the old rules, The Children's Hearings (Scotland) Rules 1986[2] ('the 1986 Rules') are employed. Forms 4A and 4B, annexed to the 1986 Rules, are headed 'Form of statement by reporter of grounds for the referral of a case to a children's hearing' and refers to the child as 'being referred to a children's hearing for [local authority area] on grounds of the following conditions . . .' and then refers to the individual 'conditions' (under the Social Work (Scotland) Act 1968, s 32(2)[3]) which are being relied upon. There follows the 'Statement of Facts', being 'the facts on the basis of which it is sought to show that the condition . . . specified as aforesaid is . . . satisfied'. It is accordingly submitted that the term 'grounds' may be taken as referring to the whole complex of facts and legal inferences from these facts on which the reporter is relying to bring the child within the jurisdiction of the hearing. This assumes importance when the chairman of the hearing has to ascertain[4] 'whether these grounds are accepted in whole or in part by [the child and the relevant person]'.[5]

1 SI 1997/291.
2 SI 1986/2291.
3 Now re-enacted with significant modifications in the Children (Scotland) Act 1995, s 52(2).
4 See 23.12 ff below.
5 C(S)A 1995, s 65(4).

FORM OF STATEMENT OF GROUNDS OF REFERRAL

The (old) statutory forms – Form 4A: the child

16.03   The normal form of statement of grounds of referral is contained in Form 4A of the Schedule to the Children's Hearings (Scotland) Rules 1986. Form 4B was the variant of this form to be used when a child under care or supervision elsewhere in the United Kingdom has been notified to the reporter. The layout and detailed styles provided in these forms provide a basic framework which has functioned adequately in practice and should be followed, with such minor modifications as may be required.[1] The relevant form[2] begins with the name and address of the child. There is no explicit provision for the date of birth of the child to be stated, but in practice this is invariably included if known. A 'child' for the purposes of chapters 2 and 3 of the Children (Scotland) Act 1995, Pt II which deal with the hearings system, is defined[3] as: (a) a child who has not attained the age of 16; (b) a child over 16 who has not attained 18 and in respect of whom a supervision requirement is in force; (c) a child whose case has been referred to a children's hearing under s 33 of the Act (referral from another part of UK); and, in relation to the ground of referral founding upon failure to attend school regularly without reasonable excuse,[4] a child who is over 16 but not over school age.[5] There is no space on the form specifically provided for the information as to the capacity in which the referred child is a 'child' but in practice the reporter will supply this when necessary.

1 SCRA have adapted the old Form 4A as SCRA Form F which is reproduced as the last entry in Appendix 12.
2 Reproduced in Appendix 12 below.
3 Children (Scotland) Act 1995, s 93(2).
4 C(S)A 1995, s 52(2)(h).
5 For discussion of 'school age' see 1.10 above and 46.19 below.

Local authority area – statement of conditions of referral – statement of facts

16.04   The next element of the form states the local authority area within which the hearing is to take place. There follows the heart of the statement, namely the section stating the conditions of referral and the statement setting out the supporting facts. The statutory example figures a case in which there are three conditions and they are listed as (a), (b) and (c). These separate conditions are followed by relative statements of facts numbered (1), (2) and (3). In practice, reporters sometimes lay out the document so that each ground of referral is followed by its own statement of fact. This form of grouping (while not, of course, invalidating the document) is, it is submitted, undesirable, not only because it is without statutory warrant but because it seems more logical and convenient to have the grounds of referral grouped together at the beginning of the document so as to catch the eye, and to eliminate the risk of something being temporarily overlooked because it is over the page.

Accuracy

16.05   By the time of framing the grounds the reporter must have reached positive conclusions that the condition or conditions of referral can be established and that compulsory measures of supervision are necessary. It is appreciated that reporters may often have to act swiftly, but the test must always be whether the proposed grounds would be capable of being proved in court in the possible event of a referral to the sheriff for proof. There is now[1] provision for amendment of the *statement of facts* should the matter go to the sheriff for proof but there is no statutory provision and therefore no scope[2] for amendment of the *conditions* for referral and the reporter accordingly will have to rely on the stated conditions right throughout the case. It is therefore of great importance that the correct condition or conditions is/are selected so as to accord with the facts so far as known. Of course if important new facts become known during the course of a case then fresh grounds of referral can be stated and served.

1 SI 1997/291, r 3.48.
2 Cf *S v Kennedy* 1996 SCLR 34 at 42F where the sheriff, before the enactment of SI 1997/291, r 3.48, was held not to be entitled to amend the statement of facts: Cf *McGregor v D* 1977 SC 330.

Comprehensiveness

The legal minimum

16.06   It is not a prerequisite, if a hearing wishes to take account of a fact which might be a ground of referral, for that ground to be stated as such in the grounds of referral. In the early case of *K v Finlayson*[1] Sheriff Isobel Sinclair QC said:

> 'I find it unthinkable that a person who has denied the original grounds of referral against her – and denied them successfully in two out of three cases – should then be judged as unfit to carry out any part of her parental role (for that is really what the condition of the child's residence in an institution amounts to) on grounds which have not been stated as grounds of referral and which she has no opportunity of denying or having examined in court.'

In *O v Rae*[2] Sheriff Sinclair's decision was overruled. Lord President Hope, delivering the opinion of the court in relation to a hearing's having taken account of circumstances which could have constituted a ground of referral but which had not been included in the grounds of referral, stated:

> 'They [the hearing] are entitled to ask for and to consider information across a wide range and to obtain the views of various people, including social workers and any safeguarder, as what would be in the best interests of the child. To restrict their consideration of the child's best interests by requiring them to have regard only to what had been stated in the grounds of referral would be inconsistent with the scheme of the Act, to which the rules are designed to give effect. It would be illogical to require the children's hearing to ignore information which they were required by section 43(1) [of the Social Work (Scotland) Act] and by rule 19(2) [of the 1996 Rules] to obtain.'

On the other hand, in a case[3] wherein it was established, after a remit back to the sheriff for clarification, that the sheriff had decided that sexual abuse did not take place within the family home the hearing were held not to be entitled to proceed on the basis that the abuse had taken place within the home.

1 1974 SLT 358.
2 1992 SCLR 318 at 324A, 1993 SLT 570 at 574L.
3 *M v Kennedy* 1991 SCLR 898.

Good practice and the needs of the child

16.07   In *In the Child's Best Interests*[1] it is stated:

> 'In some cases several grounds may be framed. For example, there may be evidence of both physical and sexual abuse of a child. The physical abuse may be easily proved and accepted by the parents, the sexual abuse more difficult to prove and not accepted by the parents. If there is agreement made to remove the ground of sexual abuse to achieve parental acceptance of the physical abuse ground and to obviate the necessity of a Hearing before the Sheriff, this leads to a number of subsequent difficulties. The first will be at the Hearing, where the subject cannot be openly addressed, the second will be in the protection of the child, especially where the physical abuse is not of a particularly serious nature requiring the child to live outside the home. For the social worker supervising the child, the task of confronting parents with the reality of the abuse is made more difficult, because their denial has been given the support of the Hearing. Compulsory measures of care should always be made on the real grounds of referral.'

In the Fife Report it is stated:[2]

> 'While ... noting that in the recent case of *O v Rae* 1992 SCLR 318 the propriety of hearings' taking into account matters not appearing on the grounds of referral is endorsed, we nevertheless think that it is good practice for Reporters to state the ground of referral most relevant to the child's needs – if necessary in addition to other stateable grounds. We doubt if legislation could be employed to compel the stating of the "most relevant" ground but we **recommend**:–

It should be recognised as good practice for Reporters to state when possible the ground of referral most relevant to the child's needs, if appropriate in addition to other grounds.'

The old Form 4A, under reference to the conditions of referral set out in the Social Work (Scotland) Act 1968 states: 'Here specify **which** one or more of the **conditions** mentioned in section 32(2) of the act is or **are considered by the reporter to be satisfied with the respect to the child** [emphasis supplied]'. It is strongly submitted that good practice requires the reporter to state 'the real grounds of referral'. Mr Alan Finlayson, a now retired reporter of immense experience, in his commentary on *O v Rae*[3] (which should be read in its entirety), states inter alia:

'Ideally, grounds for referral and reasons for intervention should give as much fair notice as possible to children and parents as to why intervention is being sought. Again, ideally, the aim of the hearing process works to its optimum when there is consensus as to the matter and extent of the problems which are to be addressed ... When conflict between the ideal and the possible exists, the needs and best interests of the child are paramount and it is encouraging to note that that principle found favour with the Lord Justice-Clerk [Ross] in *Kennedy v A* [1986 SLT 358] at p. 362 – the "principles of natural justice must yield to the best interests of the child" – and was specifically adopted by the Lord President in the present case. It is to be hoped, however, that those who practise in this field will not allow such weight of judicial authority to influence them to depart from good practice and abandon some of the essential principles referred to in this commentary.'

1 (Scottish Child and Family Alliance, Edinburgh, 1991) (distributed by HMSO) eds RIM Meek & Ors at pp 28 and 29.
2 *The Report of the Inquiry into Child Care Policies in Fife* (HMSO, 27 October 1992) p 598.
3 1992 SCLR 318 at 327E:

The European dimension

16.08   It is submitted that the decision in *O v Rae*[1] may be open to criticism in view of the incorporation of the Human Rights Act 1998 into our law. In maintaining that the appellant father had not been treated unfairly by the children's hearing's having had regard to the allegation (which had been deleted when the grounds of referral were before the sheriff) that the father had sexually abused one of his children, Lord President Hope, after observing that the children's hearing had 'wide powers of investigation' and were not 'just a disposing body' stated at 324D:

'What was in issue now was the arrangements which should be made in their [the children's] best interests. The children's hearing had a duty to act fairly in relation to the appellant but that duty was fulfilled so long as they gave him a fair opportunity of correcting or contradicting what was said about him or against him in the reports. He was present at the hearing on 16 December 1990 with his solicitor and he was given the opportunity of denying that he had sexually abused his child'. It is submitted that it could be argued that the children's hearing, in addition to deciding what arrangements would best serve the interests of the children was in fact also determining their civil rights and the civil rights of the father. Article 6(3)(d) of the Convention prescribes, as one of the minimum rights for anyone charged with a criminal offence, the right 'to examine or have examined witnesses against him . . .'.

These provisions also have application in the resolution of civil disputes.[2] It may be thought that a children's hearing, which is not a body before which witnesses can be examined and cross-examined, and which, under the whole scheme of the Children (Scotland) Act 1995,[3] is not a body empowered to decide important disputed matters of fact, would no longer be regarded as being able fairly to decide this issue.

1　1992 SCLR 318.
2　*Airey v Ireland* (1979) 2 EHRR 305.
3　Cf the dictum of Lord President Hope in *Sloan v B* 1991 SLT 530 at 548E: 'The genius of this reform, which has earned it so much praise which the misfortunes of this case should not be allowed in any way to diminish, was that the responsibility for the consideration of the measures to be applied was to lie with what was essentially a lay body while disputed questions of fact as to the allegations made were to be resolved by the sheriff sitting in chambers as a court of law'.

THE LAYOUT OF THE 'STATEMENT OF FACTS'

General

16.09　The statement of facts may comprise several numbered paragraphs setting out the facts which, according to the reporter, exist in relation to the child. Often the first one or more of these paragraphs will deal with formal matters such as the relationship of the child with the parent, the averment that the parent has habitual control of the child and the like. The subsequent paragraphs will contain the substantive allegations which the reporter is making to justify his contention that the condition under the Children (Scotland) Act 1995, s 52(2) which he has set out at the beginning of the former Form 4A[1] exists in relation to the child. The importance or weight of each statement may vary and it will be open to the hearing to treat the ground of referral as accepted in part, thus enabling the hearing, if it wishes, to proceed under s 65(6) of the Act even if one or more of the inessential individual statements is not accepted.

1　Now SCRA Form F.

OFFENCE BY A CHILD CASES – 1995 ACT, s 52(2)(i)

Averments should be factual

16.10　If only one offence is alleged the facts said to constitute that offence may be set out in a single paragraph introduced by the words 'In support of condition . . . above, it is stated:'. The averments should be factual, i e should use words denoting that which can be observed ('he hit John Smith on the head with a baseball bat or similar object') and not 'legal' ('he assaulted John Smith with a baseball bat').

Permissible latitude in averring facts

16.11   The Children's Hearings (Scotland) Rules 1996,[1] r 17(2) provides, in relation to 'offence by a child' cases, that 'the statement of the facts constituting the offence shall have the same degree of specification as is required by section 138(4) of the 1995 Act [the Criminal Procedure (Scotland) Act 1995] in a charge in a complaint and the statement shall also specify the nature of the offence in question'. The Criminal Procedure (Scotland) Act 1995, s 138(4) simply gives effect to Schedule 3 to that Act.

1 SI 1996/3261.

The Schedule 3 provisions: alternative charges and verdicts

16.12   The Criminal Procedure (Scotland) Act 1995, Sch 3 is reproduced in Appendix 2. Its provisions are lucid but necessarily sometimes complex. A pleader must be aware of the whole contents of the Schedule. Sub-paragraphs 7, 8, 9, 10, and 14 prescribe alternative verdicts. One example will suffice here:

'8. — (1) In an indictment or a complaint charging the resetting of property dishonestly appropriated —
(a) having been taken by theft or robbery; or
(b) by breach of trust, embezzlement or falsehood, fraud and wilful imposition,
it shall be sufficient to specify that the accused received the property, it having been dishonestly appropriated by theft or robbery, or by breach of trust and embezzlement, or by falsehood, fraud and wilful imposition, as the case may be.
(2) Under an indictment or a complaint for robbery, theft, breach of trust and embezzlement or falsehood, fraud and wilful imposition, an accused may be convicted of reset.
(3) Under an indictment or a complaint for robbery, breach of trust and embezzlement, or falsehood, fraud and wilful imposition, an accused may be convicted of theft.
(4) Under an indictment or a complaint for theft, an accused may be convicted of breach of trust and embezzlement, or of falsehood, fraud and wilful imposition, or may be convicted of theft, although the circumstances proved may in law amount to robbery.
(5) The power conferred by sub-paragraphs (2) to (4) above to convict a person of an offence other than that with which he is charged shall be exercisable by the sheriff court before which he is tried notwithstanding that the other offence was committed outside the jurisdiction of that sheriff court.'

Appropriate degree of specification

16.13   Paragraph 2 of the Schedule, which excuses the prosecutor from stating a *nomen juris* (legal name) for the offence charged, would seem to have no application to grounds of referral, having regard to the provision[1] that the statement of facts 'shall also specify the nature of the offence in question'. It is thought that paragraphs 4 and 5, which countenance amendment of a complaint in certain circumstances and adjournment of the trial, should not be regarded as importing such procedures into the rules for the conduct of hearings.[2] The remaining paragraphs, namely 1, 3 and 4, 6, 11–13, and 15–19, deal more generally with the degree of specification which is required. The principle lying behind many of these paragraphs may be summarised as not requiring exact specification where such specification is not of the essence of the offence, provided that the degree of specification given is enough to convey the important points to the reasonable person so that he or she knows what he or she is being charged with. The paragraphs themselves, however, must be applied.

1 Children's Hearings (Scotland) Rules 1996, SI 1996/3261, r 17(2).
2 Amendment of the statement of facts at the stage of the proof before the sheriff is now permitted by SI 1997/291, r 3.48.

Alternative offences

16.14   Notwithstanding the alternatives imported automatically by sub-paragraphs 7–10 and 14 of the Schedule, it is submitted that when necessary and appropriate the alternative offences (e g robbery *or* theft *or* reset) should be set out, thus making the position clear to the child and relevant person and simplifying the task of the chairman of the hearing in putting the grounds to the child and relevant person so that, if there is an acceptance of a lesser offence, it is at least open to the hearing, if it thinks it right to do so, to treat such acceptance as a partial acceptance of grounds of referral in terms of the Children (Scotland) Act 1995, s 65(6). It must be remembered that the chairman does not, it is submitted, have any power comparable to the power, competent to the sheriff at the application stage, of finding that any other offence established by the facts has been committed.[1]

1 SI 1997/291, r 3.50.

Numbering of alleged offences

16.15   Each alleged offence should be set out in a separate numbered paragraph. Alternative alleged offences should be listed as separate sub-paragraphs within the relevant numbered paragraph and introduced by the words 'or *alternatively*'.

Nature of offence to be specified

16.16   The Children's Hearings (Scotland) Rules 1996, r 17(2) concludes by stipulating that 'the statement shall also specify the nature of the offence in question': i e the '*nomen juris*' of the offence must be stated. This is normally done by stating the legal name after the relevant factual narrative, for example:

> 'In support of condition . . . above it is stated that on 1st April 1998 between the hours of 4 and 6 p m at Glasgow Green in Glasgow he did strike John Smith, aged 15, on the head with a baseball bat: this being an offence of assault.'

When alternative offences are narrated the *nomen juris* of each alternative offence should be so stated.

16.17 The function and usefulness of specifying the *nomen juris* of an offence has been called into question, in the context of the application to the sheriff, by the Court of Session.[1] It is tentatively and respectfully submitted that the purpose of stating the *nomen juris* may be found by considering the hearing stage. The chairman has the duty of ascertaining if the child and parent accept that an offence has been committed. It may be thought to be helpful to the lay chairman of the hearing to know the specific offence alleged against the child so as to be able to find out if the child and the relevant person accepts that he committed it.

1 *McGregor v D* 1977 SC 330 at 337.

GROUNDS ALLEGING SCHEDULE 1 OFFENCES AGAINST A CHILD

No 'latitude'?

16.18 The wording of the Children's Hearings (Scotland) Rules 1996, r 17(2) imports into 'offence by a child' cases the 'latitude' provisions of the Criminal Procedure (Scotland) Act 1995, Sch 3. No such latitude is imported in the area of offences against a child – an area of at least equal and perhaps more importance from the point of view of the welfare of the child. However the approach of the courts to some such cases may suggest that some latitude would be allowed in the interests of the protection of the child. In *S v Kennedy*[1] it was argued that actings amounting to a Schedule 1 offence which took place furth of Scotland could not constitute such an offence. In rejecting this argument Lord Justice-Clerk Ross stated:[2]

> 'I appreciate that there is considerable force in the submission made by Mr Jackson [counsel for the appellant father] in relation to question 1. However, I have come to the opinion that there is no need to read the statute in the restricted manner for which he contended. In section 32(2)(d) of the Act of 1968 and Schedule 1 of the Act of 1975, Parliament has not stated expressly that the offences referred to must be offences which can be prosecuted in Scotland. In my opinion, it is doing no violence to the language used to construe "offence" in its context as including conduct amounting to such an offence.
>
> It must always be kept in mind that proceedings under Part III of the Act of 1968 are civil proceedings sui generis and that the purpose of the legislation is to provide for children who may be in need of compulsory measures of care.'

1 1996 SCLR 34.
2 At 39B.

Multiple offences

16.19 Where more than one such offence is alleged to have been committed against a child it is normal to narrate each offence in a separate numbered paragraph. If one or more alternatives is alleged this may properly be done in sub-paragraphs, as mentioned above. In Schedule 1 offence cases, as opposed to offence by a child cases, there is no explicit obligation to aver the *nomen juris* of the crime relied upon and such specification is in practice not necessarily given. It is suggested that, although not statutorily obligatory, it is nevertheless helpful, particularly to the chairman at the hearing stage, if the *nomen juris* is specified in these cases also.

Specification of name of offender in Schedule 1 cases

16.20   In cases wherein the identity of the offender is reasonably thought to be known it is submitted that the reporter, if he or she thinks the identity of the offender will be a relevant consideration in disposing of the case, ought to specify the name in the grounds of referral. Specifying the name is clearly not, however, necessary for the ground of referral to be relevantly stated.[1] If, however, the name is not specified it is incompetent, where the matter goes to the sheriff for proof, for the sheriff (in the absence of amendment, which may cause delay) to make any finding naming the offender.[2] It may be thought strange that the sheriff, who has heard evidence *in foro contentioso*, may not make such a finding while, in accordance with the rule in *O v Rae*,[3] the hearing may take account of extraneous material which may convey that name. In an appropriate case the sheriff may use the powers of amendment conveyed by r 3.48 and allow the name of the offending person to be added. When this is done it may be necessary to allow an adjournment to allow evidence in rebuttal.

1 *McGregor v AB* 1981 SC 328.
2 *S v Kennedy* 1987 SLT 667.
3 1992 SCLR 318.

MORE THAN ONE CONDITION OF REFERRAL

16.21   It frequently happens that a reporter will wish to rely on more than one condition of referral, for example, lack of parental care and one or more Schedule 1 offences. The form prescribed by the 'old' rules[1] indicates that each condition relied on should be set out in separate sub-paragraphs, for example '(a)', '(b)' and '(c)', the last sub-paragraph introduced by 'and'. In practice these conditions are sometimes set out in a continuous paragraph with the various conditions introduced by the words 'or alternatively'. As suggested above[2] averments of alternative offences are appropriate in s 52(2)(i) cases when, ultimately, only one alternative may be accepted (a person cannot, in respect of the same facts, be guilty of both theft and reset) but it is suggested that when multiple *conditions* are being relied on the statutory form should be adhered to (i e 'and' and not 'or' should be used) in case the impression is given that only one of the 'alternatives' is ultimately to be relied upon.

1 Children's Hearings (Scotland) Rules 1986, SI 1986/2291, rr 16 and 17 and Form 4A of Schedule.
2 At 16.14.

EDUCATION CASES

16.22 Should the matter go to the sheriff for proof, the reporter will require to obtain from the education authority a certificate from the head teacher certifying the attendance dates. At the stage of stating the grounds of referral, however, the reporter, although he or she will require to be satisfied that the relevant absences took place, need not yet obtain the certificate, although in practice the reporter would have previously obtained the certificate by this stage. It is, however, for the child and the relevant person to accept or not the ground of referral and the hearing would of course have no power to 'confront' the child or parent with the certificate and attempt to 'try' the case.

CHILDREN IN SAME FAMILY – SIMILAR GROUNDS

16.23 Sometimes a number of statements of grounds of referral in nearly identical terms will be necessary when the same circumstances in the family home affect a number of children. Sometimes one particular fact or set of facts will not apply to one of the children and care must be taken regarding this. When the reporter avers a ground under the Children (Scotland) Act 1995, s 52(2)(e) (child is, or is likely to become, a member of the same household as a child against whom a Schedule 1 offence has been committed) care must obviously be taken to make the position clear.

INCLUSION OF MATTER PREVIOUSLY DEALT WITH

General

16.24 The legal principle of *res judicata* provides that a matter which has been examined and ruled upon in a competent court may not, as between the same parties, be re-opened so as to seek to dislodge the original ruling. This principle has only limited application to hearings' law. Incidents which have formed part of an earlier ground of referral may be relied upon in a later referral, including a subsequent incident even when the earlier incident was made the subject of an application to the sheriff for proof under the Children (Scotland) Act 1995, s 68 and not established at that proof.[1] The later incident may be regarded as creating a new situation which requires the matter to be looked at of new: but it has been implied obiter[2] that that may not be the only circumstance in which the reporter may rely on matters which were the subject of a previous referral.

1 *McGregor v D* 1981 SLT (Notes) 97.
2 *Kennedy v S* 1986 SLT 679 per Lord Hunter at 681.

Where reporter decides not to arrange a hearing – Where sheriff sustains an appeal

16.25   If the reporter has, on investigation of the available information, decided that a children's hearing does not require to be arranged,[1] with or without referring the child to a local authority for advice, guidance or assistance under the Children (Scotland) Act 1995, Pt II, Chap 1, it is provided that the reporter 'shall not at any other time, on the basis *solely* [emphasis supplied] of the information obtained during the initial investigation referred to in that subsection, arrange a children's hearing under subsection (6) below'.[2] The sheriff may, in sustaining an appeal, 'discharge the child from any further hearing or other proceedings in relation to the grounds for the referral of the case'[3]. In either of the foregoing events it would appear that the same facts and grounds could be used again in conjunction with new facts or grounds, on the principle, mentioned above, that a new situation has been created.

1 Children (Scotland) Act 1995, s 56(4).
2 C(S)A 1995, s 56(5).
3 C(S)A 1995, s 51(5)(c)(ii).

Acceptance or establishment of grounds in application to sheriff in earlier case concerning child in same family

16.26   The extent to which an earlier determination by the sheriff may render unnecessary further proof of fact is considered later.[1]

1 See 36.17 below.

CHAPTER 17

The safeguarder at the children's hearing stage

THE STATUTORY PROVISIONS

The basic provisions

17.01 The statutory background and the arrangements for recruiting and appointing safeguarders have already been noticed.[1] The basic statutory provision is now contained in the Children (Scotland) Act 1995, s 41 which provides inter alia:

'(1) Subject to subsection (2) below [which excludes the proceedings in connection with the making of a Child Protection Order under s 57 of the Act from the safeguarder provisions], in any proceedings under this Chapter or Chapter 3 of this part of this Act either at a children's hearing or before the sheriffs —
(a) shall consider if it is necessary to appoint a person to safeguard the interests of the child in the proceedings; and
(b) if they, or he, so consider, shall make such an appointment, on such terms and conditions as appear appropriate.'

The criterion for appointment of a safeguarder is now 'necessity', as perceived by the hearing or the sheriff, and not, as in the old law,[2] an anticipated conflict of interest between parent and child.

1 At 4.04 ff.
2 Social Work (Scotland) Act 1968 (as amended), s 34A(1).

APPOINTMENT OF PANELS OF SAFEGUARDERS

The regulations

17.02 As at the time of writing no regulations have been made as to the arrangements and detailed procedures for the establishment of a panel of safeguarders as is permitted under the Children (Scotland) Act 1995, s 101, although it is understood that such regulations are being considered and are in draft form. It is accordingly, for the present, still necessary to refer to the old rules, namely the Social Work (Panels of Persons to Safeguard the Interests of Children) (Scotland) Regulations 1984[1] (hereinafter 'Safeguarders' Regulations 1984' or 'the 1984 Regulations').

1 SI 1984/1442.

Procedure for enrolling safeguarders

17.03   Each local authority area has the obligation of establishing a panel or panels of persons to act as safeguarders. The detailed provisions as to how the local authority is to carry out this function are set out in the Social Work (Panels of Persons to Safeguard the Interests of Children (Scotland) Regulations 1984, regs 1–10. The local authority may decide in advance as to the types of 'experience, aptitudes and any professional qualifications' which those appointed to a panel should have. The local authority must throughout act in consultation with the chairman of the children's panel and with the sheriff principal from whom nominations to the panel of safeguarders must be invited. The local authority may also seek nominations from other persons or bodies but must not appoint any of its own members, any person employed by itself in connection with any of its social work functions, any serving member of a children's panel or any serving member of a Children's Panel Advisory Committee. Appointments are for up to three years but a person may be re-appointed. A safeguarder may not have his office terminated prematurely unless the chairman of the children's panel and the sheriff principal are satisfied that the safeguarder concerned is unable, unfit or unsuitable to carry through his or her functions. It will be seen that the safeguarder is accorded a degree of independence and he is expected to use that independence fearlessly to protect and promote the interests of the child.[1]

1   Once a child's case comes before the sheriff the sheriff in practice may appoint a curator *ad litem* rather than a safeguarder – see discussion at 34.03 below.

Who may become a safeguarder? – Notes for Guidance from former Scottish Office

17.04   In practice persons with qualifications in law, social work and education are commonly appointed to panels of safeguarders but it must be emphasised that no formal qualification has been enacted as being either necessary or sufficient for appointment as a safeguarder. The two central desirable qualities are the ability to communicate and sympathise with children and their parents, on the one hand, and the skill and articulateness which are needed adequately to represent the interests of the child at the hearing or before the sheriff. Safeguarders from time to time require to submit written reports[1] but lack of access to secretarial assistance should not be a bar to appointment as a safeguarder: local authorities are expected to try to make such facilities available when needed and in some local authority areas this is done by the reporter's department. In 1985 the then Scottish Office issued a document entitled *Safeguarding the Interests of Children in Proceedings before Children's Hearings and Sheriffs: Notes of Guidance for Persons Appointed as Safeguarders*[2] (hereinafter referred to as the *Notes for Guidance*). Although overtaken by the enactment of the Children (Scotland) Act 1995, these are still the only 'official' guidance and are still in circulation. It is thought that the Scottish Executive is considering issuing updated guidance.

1 Children's Hearings (Scotland) Rules 1996, SI 1996/3261, r 14(4) and (at the court stage) Act of Sederunt (Child Care and Maintenance Rules) 1997, SI 1997/291, r 3.10.
2 Issued by Scottish Office in June 1985 and enclosed with Social Work Services Group Circular No SW/785 dated 24 June 1985.

The Scottish Safeguarders Association

17.05 This is a non-statutory association to which most safeguarders belong. It has issued *Practice Guidelines for Safeguarders*. These do not have the force of law but are helpful. Copies may be obtained from the Secretary of the Association.[1] It is understood that some local authorities issue them to safeguarders.

1 At the time of writing: Mr Stuart Wardrop, 100 Spoutwells Drive, Scone, Perthshire; Tel/Fax: (01738) 551985; e-mail: Stuart.wardrop@lineone.net

REMUNERATION OF SAFEGUARDER

The rules

17.06 The local authority within whose area the relevant hearing sits is bound by regulation to defray the expenses incurred by a member of a panel (of safeguarders) and to pay him 'such fees and allowances as they think fit'.[1] The local authority is bound by statute to bear a safeguarder's expenses, in so far as not 'defrayed' in terms of the regulation, in so far as reasonably incurred by him in safeguarding the interests of the child in the proceedings.'[2] The Act and Regulations contain no provision indicating how it is to be decided that a particular expense, incurred or to be incurred, is 'reasonably incurred'. In practice a solicitor employed by a safeguarder will generally be eligible for legal aid under the Legal Aid (Scotland) Act 1986, s 29[3] (as amended) and the rules enacted thereunder.[4] No doubt the prudent safeguarder, until legal aid is granted, will check with the local authority before incurring any material expense.

1 Social Work (Panels of Persons to Safeguard the Interests of Children) (Scotland) Regulations, 1984, SI 1984/1442, reg 10.
2 Children (Scotland) Act 1995, s 41(4).
3 As substituted by C(S)A 1995, s 92.
4 Act of Sederunt (Civil Legal Aid Rules) 1987; for an example of, and discussion in relation to, a grant of legal aid to a solicitor instructed by a safeguarder, see *Munro and McClure, Applicants* 2000 Fam LB 46–5.

The practical position at present

17.07 At present the local authority pays fees and expenses to safeguarders appointed by the hearing or by the sheriff and may have regard to the rates recommended by the Convention of Scottish Local Authorities ('COSLA'). The recommendations for the financial year 1999/2000 are reproduced, by kind permission of COSLA, as Appendix 11. The recommended rates are reviewed at the start of each financial year.

Function of safeguarder generally

17.08   The concept of a separate person intervening in the interests of the child – given the reporter's place in the hearings system as the person charged with acting in the interests of the child – may seem anomalous. Published research is scanty but experience suggests that the concept is of value in that the safeguarder may be seen by the child as being even more independent of 'the system' than is the reporter and as such able to resolve certain difficulties.[1] Ideally the safeguarder should be able to establish such a relationship with the child as to enable the child and assist in enabling the child's point of view and, at the appropriate stage, the child's best interests to be understood and where appropriate conveyed to the other agencies concerned in the protection of the child. The specific role of the safeguarder in conveying the views of the child[2] has already been noticed[3] in the context of the child protection provisions and will be discussed in the context of the hearing presently.[4] For discussion of the safeguarder's role at the proof and appeal stage see chs 34 and 51.

1 Cf *The Evaluation of Children's Hearings in Scotland* (Scottish Office Central Research Unit, 1998) vol 1, p 100: 'Most of those who commented on safeguarders were positive and saw them as a useful contribution to decision making, for example: "quite often the arguments will reach an impasse and the panel will go for a safeguarder to be appointed which is really quite a useful instrument in helping to clear a dispute" (reporter) ...'.
2 SI 1997/291, r 3.5 (2)(c).
3 E g at 4.10 above.
4 At 17.12 below.

Immunity of safeguarder from claim for defamation

17.09   It is submitted that any written report or oral submission by a safeguarder to a hearing or a court is absolutely privileged and that the safeguarder, like a witness, would have a complete defence to any claim for defamation.[1]

1 *Watson v McEwan* (1905) 7 F (HL) 109; *Slack v Barr* 1918 SLT 133; *Trapp v Mackie* 1979 SC (HL) 38.

THE SAFEGUARDER IN A PARTICULAR CASE

Procedure for appointing safeguarder – the law

17.10   The decision as to whether or not a safeguarder is to be appointed is a matter for the children's hearing and the obligation *ex proprio motu* to consider making an appointment is mandatory,[1] although of course it would be open to any party to move the hearing to appoint a safeguarder.

Where a safeguarder is appointed the hearing chairman shall state in writing the reasons for the hearing's decision to make that appointment.[2] There is no obligation, when a decision has been taken not to appoint a safeguarder, to make a record of this decision but in modern practice this is often done and such recording is, it is submitted, good practice. The appointment may be on such 'terms and conditions as appear appropriate'.[3] The purpose of appointing a safeguarder being to safeguard the interests of the child 'in the proceedings'[4] may suggest that it would not be appropriate to appoint a safeguarder in a case in which the hearing was about to discharge the referral.[5] This may be correct and it is difficult to envisage a hearing deciding to appoint a safeguarder in a referral which it was about to discharge, although, standing the safeguarder's right to sign an appeal by the child to the sheriff,[6] the technical possibility may exist. There is no provision in the Children's Hearings (Scotland) Rules 1996 giving the hearing the competence to appoint a safeguarder at any stage in the proceedings – contrast the explicit provision[7] that it is competent for the sheriff so to do. It is thought, however, that the reference in the Children (Scotland) Act 1995 itself to 'any proceedings'[8] is wide enough to include continued or adjourned proceedings and in practice hearings appoint safeguarders at such hearings: the provision in the 1996 Rules, r 14(5), allowing for delivery of information to a safeguarder 'regardless of the date of his appointment in the proceedings', may put the matter beyond doubt.

1 Children (Scotland) Act 1995, s 41(1).
2 Children's Hearings (Scotland) Rules 1996, SI 1996/3261, r 14(1).
3 Children (Scotland) Act 1995, s 41(1)(b).
4 C(S)A 1995, s 41(1)(a).
5 This is the view taken by Norrie in *Children (Scotland) Act 1995* (1998) p 72.
6 SI 1997/291, r 3.53(3)
7 SI 1997/291, r 3.7(1)(b).
8 C(S)A 1995, s 41(1).

Practical considerations

17.11 In practice the reporter may indicate to the children's hearing that a particular case is one where a safeguarder should be considered. If it is decided to appoint a safeguarder, the hearing will generally require to be continued[1] to enable the safeguarder to make his or her investigations and to submit a report so that it can be available in due time for the continued sitting of the hearing. The local authority makes available to the reporter the names of the panel of safeguarders and should co-operate with the reporter in ensuring that a suitable safeguarder is appointed with the minimum of delay.[2] The practical arrangements for identifying a safeguarder for a particular case vary as between local authority areas. On a safeguarder being appointed the chairman must note the decision with reasons for it.[3] It does not, however, seem to be obligatory to name the safeguarder at this stage and indeed this will rarely be possible since it is necessary to ascertain if an intended safeguarder is ready to accept appointment.

1 Children (Scotland) Act 1995, s 69(1)(a).

2 Cf *Blueprint for the Processing of Children's Hearings Cases – Inter-agency Code of Practice and National Standards* (Scottish Office Social Work Services Group, March 1999), paras 4.12 and 4.13.
3 SI 1996/3261, r 14(1).

Specific rights and duties of a safeguarder once appointed

17.12   On appointment the safeguarder becomes entitled to receive from the reporter the chairman's statement of reasons, any information or document which the reporter has made available to the chairman and the hearing members:[1] the rule indicates that this is with the exception of the copy of any report by a safeguarder. Presumably this means that when, for example, a case has gone to the sheriff for proof without a safeguarder being initially appointed by the hearing and where the sheriff has appointed a safeguarder for the proof who has submitted a report and the hearing has decided to appoint its own safeguarder, the second safeguarder is not to see the report of the first safeguarder. The safeguarder must report in writing on the child's case and prepare any further report (or, presumably, reports) as the hearing may require and give such reports to the reporter.[2] The safeguarder must receive due notification of hearings (seven days, except for hearings concerning children kept in a place of safety or secure accommodation and hearings to consider an application for the suspension of a supervision requirement or a transfer of residence under the Children (Scotland) Act 1995, s 72, when notification may be given as soon as reasonably practicable or orally[3]). A safeguarder is entitled to be present throughout the duration of any hearing of the case until the disposal of the case.[4] In the course of the hearing the hearing must discuss the case with, among others, any safeguarder and obtain his views on what arrangements would be in the best interests of the child.[5] Where a child has indicated a wish to express views one of the possible channels for such views is the safeguarder.[6] Elaine Sutherland, a distinguished commentator on Scottish family law[7] and herself a safeguarder of experience, has observed that where a child has expressed a wish to express a view the safeguarder should ascertain what that view is and:

> 'The safeguarder should then include a clear statement of the child's views in the report along with the safeguarder's own reasons for finding that they are consistent with or, more particularly, inconsistent with the child's interests. That is respecting the child's right to have his or her views taken into account. Thereafter, it is for the safeguarder to make a recommendation and the hearing to make a decision. That is giving primary consideration to the child's interests. Expression of views is a child's right, making a recommendation and taking a decision in the child's interests are an adult's responsibilities.'[8]

The safeguarder also has the right, along with the child, relevant person and the local authority, to be informed in writing of the decision of the hearing, to receive a copy of any supervision requirement and of the reasons for the decision and of the right of appeal (if competent) to the sheriff.[9] A safeguarder has the same right as the child and the relevant person to be consulted and have his or her views considered in hearings convened to give advice to a court or local authority or approved adoption society,[10] and hearings to consider suspension of supervision requirement pending appeal[11] and hearings to consider the case of a child kept in a place of safety under ss 45(7), 59(2) or 68(10) or by virtue of s 82(5) of the Act.[12]

1 SI 1996/3261, r 14(5).
2 SI 1996/3261, r 14(4).
3 SI 1996/3261, r 14(2), read with r 6(2) and r 7(5).
4 SI 1996/3261, r 14(3).
5 SI 1996/3261, r 20(3)(c).
6 SI 1996/3261, r 15(4) – see also 17.17 below, sub-para 7.
7 See her *Child and Family Law* (1999) T & T Clark.
8 Elaine E Sutherland 'The Role of the Safeguarder' in *Representing Children – Listening to the Voice of the Child* (1995) Scottish Child Law Centre.
9 SI 1996/3261, r 21(1).
10 SI 1996/3261, r 22(3)(b).
11 Children (Scotland) Act 1995, s 51(9); SI 1996/3261, r 23(3).
12 SI 1996/3261, r 6(2), read with r 7(5) and r 14(2).

More than one safeguarder?

17.13   In a case in 1991[1] a children's hearing decided that a separate safeguarder should be appointed for a particular child in a family of four children and, although in the event no separate safeguarder was appointed, no adverse comment was made on the concept of such an appointment.

1 *H v Kennedy* 1999 SCLR 961.

Power of safeguarder to sign appeal to the sheriff

17.14   The 1997 Rules, r 3.53 provides that an appeal to the sheriff against a decision of a children's hearing may be signed on the child's behalf by any safeguarder appointed by the children's hearing. It has been held in the sheriff court[1] that the parallel provision in the Act of Sederunt (Social Work) (Sheriff Court Procedure Rules) 1971 ('the 1971 Rules'), as amended, conferred upon the safeguarder a right of appeal independent of the child. In this case a report by an educational psychologist, which would have advised on whether or not it was appropriate for the child 'J' to be enrolled in a residential school, had not been available and the hearing decided not to continue the case since it was of the view that the child should attend the local school. The child's safeguarder appealed to the sheriff. The reporter did not associate himself with the appeal and challenged its competency before the sheriff. It may be inferred that the child and parent did not support the appeal either and, as the sheriff narrated, the safeguarder did not consult the child. The reporter argued that the safeguarder did not have an independent right of appeal apart from the child – the sole right of appeal under the Social Work (Scotland) Act 1968, s 49(1) being conferred on a 'child or his parent or both' – the hearing had made its decision and the safeguarder was *functus officio*. Sheriff George Crozier rejected the challenge to the competency of the appeal and, according to the report, continued the hearing of the appeal in order to obtain the psychologist's report. Having considered the report, he 'concluded that it would be in J's interests to go to a residential school', allowed the appeal and remitted to the hearing to reconsider its decision. In his opinion on competency the sheriff stated:

> 'I do not see that the safeguarder has any duty to consult an eleven-year-old child. I note from the Social Work (Sheriff Court Procedure Rules) 1971 in terms of rule 12(2) that provision is made for an appeal to be signed by the child or his parent or any safeguarder appointed by the chairman at the children's hearing on behalf of the child. Taking the terms of this rule in conjunction with the fact that the prime purpose of appointing a safeguarder is to have someone independent to look after the interests of the child, I came to the conclusion that it was competent for a safeguarder to take an appeal to the sheriff.'

Commenting on this, the learned editor of *Scottish Civil Law Reports*[2] quoted the first edition of this book at page 313 where the opinion was expressed that the safeguarder does not have a separate right of appeal and that 'an appeal signed by a safeguarder is to be treated as the child's appeal'. From the point of view of clarification of the law, it is a pity that Sheriff Crozier's decision was not taken to the Court of Session on appeal by the reporter. Even before the enactment of the Children (Scotland) Act 1995, s 16, it seems strange that the safeguarder did not at least consult the child for his views – how can one 'look after the interests of the child' without knowing and passing on his views (even if one does not agree with such views[3])? Moreover the sheriff does not appear to have been addressed on the consideration that the safeguarder appointed at the hearing, in contrast to the safeguarder appointed by the sheriff, does not have the powers of a curator *ad litem*. The writer has nevertheless some sympathy with Sheriff Crozier's approach in one respect. Under the 1995 Act, as under its predecessor, the essential purpose of having a safeguarder is, in Sheriff Crozier's words, 'to have someone independent to look after the interests of the child'. That being so, it may be thought strange such a person should not have an independent right to challenge a disposal which he or she considers to be contrary to law and against the interests of the child. It is submitted that the matter should be clarified by amending legislation.

1 *Ross v Kennedy* 1995 SCLR 1160.
2 Sheriff Alastair L Stewart QC, at 1995 SCLR 1162.
3 The writer would respectfully disagree with the learned commentator at 1995 SCLR 1163 in so far as he suggests that the child's wishes could by themselves invalidate the action of the safeguarder; the view that the entry of the child directly into the process 'overturns' the safeguarder's decisions or opinions has now been disapproved by the Inner House in *R v Grant* 2000 SLT 372 at 374A.

RIGHTS AND DUTIES OF SAFEGUARDER ONCE APPOINTED

Practical matters

17.15   The hearing which has appointed the safeguarder may well have adjourned for, say, three weeks and any written report from the safeguarder will have to be available for delivery to the hearing members at the very least three clear days before the date of the continued hearing.[1] It follows that the safeguarder must make inquiries as quickly as possible. The child or children may be in some form of detention pending disposal[2] and in that event the urgency is all the greater since the extensions which may be obtained on such periods of detention are strictly limited. If the safeguarder, in spite of everything, begins to think that it will be impracticable to deliver his report in time he should contact the reporter without delay so that the reporter may consider applying for an extension of any warrant.

1 SI 1996/3261, r 5(1)(e).
2 See ch 21 below.

17.16 The safeguarder will normally wish to visit the child, the relevant person(s) and any relevant agency before reporting to the hearing. He may also wish to interview persons, such as school teachers, social workers, child guidance consultants and the like, who have responsibilities for the care of the child. In the *Notes for Guidance*[1] issued in 1985 the Secretary for State indicated that he did not propose in the meantime to use his powers to make regulations giving safeguarders formal rights of access to information but made it clear that the government hoped that agencies would co-operate in providing safeguarders with necessary information. It is thought that in general safeguarders have been able to investigate cases on the basis of the existing legislation. Should a safeguarder consider that his or her investigations are being obstructed by an agency, he or she may wish to take the matter up with the administrative head of the agency concerned. Safeguarders may be issued with an identity document by the local authority but of course this does not confer any right of access.

1 Referred to at 17.04 above.

WRITTEN REPORT TO HEARING BY SAFEGUARDER

17.17 The form and content of such a written report are nowhere prescribed and will vary with the circumstances of each case. It is suggested that most reports of safeguarders appointed at an early stage in the proceedings will contain, as a minimum, most of the following:[1]

1. a heading containing the name, occupation if any, of the safeguarder and an address and a possible telephone number at which the safeguarder may be contacted. A safeguarder who has a professional or similar occupation will no doubt give his business address, telephone and fax number but it is thought that many safeguarders working from home may not feel it appropriate to disclose their home address and it is understood that the reporter's department may be prepared to be used as 'care of' addresses;

2. a note of the name or names and other particulars (including age) of the child or children involved in the case;[2]

3. a copy of the reasons stated by the hearing for appointment of the safeguarder;[3]
4. names and addresses of relevant persons, parents, institutions and other agencies interesting themselves in the child including identification of the person or institution having the actual care of the child;[4]
5. a summary of the inquiries made by the safeguarder, including the names and addresses of the persons interviewed, with a note of the main facts covered – a mention being made of any person whom the safeguarder would like to have seen but has been unable to see;[5]
6. a brief account of the background, if necessary by reference to other reports if any;
7. an indication of what the safeguarder has been able to gather as to the respective wishes, feelings and aspirations of the child, the parents and anyone else having responsibility for the care and upbringing of the child – focusing attention, so far as relevant, on how far these agree and how far they diverge;
8. an assessment by the safeguarder, so far as he or she feels able to make one, as to where the child's true interests lie, together with reasons. If the safeguarder thinks that further investigation is required before a final conclusion is reached then he should say so, leaving it to the hearing to consider ordering further investigation in terms of the Children (Scotland) Act 1995, s 69(1).

1 The points listed here echo only partly the list in the *Notes for Guidance*.
2 In some cases it will not be appropriate to disclose the whereabouts of the child and/or, where there are issues of domestic violence, a parent – Children (Scotland) Act 1995, s 70(6), and cf 20.16 below.
3 C(S)A 1995, s 41(3).
4 See footnote 2 above.
5 *Practice Guidelines for Safeguarders* (Scottish Safeguarders Association, February 1999) para 7.4.

SAFEGUARDER'S ATTENDANCE AT THE HEARING

General

17.18 As already noted, a safeguarder has a right to be present throughout the duration of the hearing.[1] In most circumstances a safeguarder will wish to attend although sometimes he or she may not feel it necessary to attend the hearing if his or her recommendation coincides with all other recommendations. The provision in the Children's Hearings (Scotland) Rules 1996, r 14(3) that a safeguarder appointed by a hearing 'shall be entitled to be present throughout the duration of any hearing until the disposal of that case' seems to make it now clear that the safeguarder is entitled to be present at the hearing and any continuation thereof until disposal has been decided upon.[2] It is thought that the wording would not, however, extend to a review hearing and that such a hearing would require to consider of new whether or not to appoint a safeguarder.[3]

1 SI 1996/3261, r 14(3).

2 Thus giving statutory authority to the interpretation of the position under the old regulations by Sheriff Principal (as he now is) D J Risk QC in *Catto v Pearson* 1990 SCLR 267.
3 Cf SI 1996/3261, r 14(6)(c).

Appointment of safeguarder by hearing where grounds disputed

17.19 It could be argued that since the safeguarder's basic interest is the final disposal of the child's case, it is premature to appoint one until the grounds of referral have been admitted or established. In disputed grounds, or where the child does not understand the grounds, the hearing, although considering that the appointment of a safeguarder might ultimately be necessary, may logically enough prefer to await the sheriff's decision: so to do would have the pragmatic advantage of reducing the number of investigators calling upon the family in relation to a matter which may never go ahead. Since, however, the intervention of the safeguarder in the interests of the child might by itself materially affect the subsequent development of the case, it is submitted that the preferable course in some cases will be for the safeguarder to be appointed earlier rather than later. Under the 1997 Rules a safeguarder appointed by the hearing shall be the safeguarder, if any, appointed by the sheriff unless the sheriff, on his or her own motion or on cause shown by a party, otherwise directs.[1]

1 Act of Sederunt (Child Care and Maintenance Rules) 1997, SI 1997/291, r 3.7(2); cf the references to intimation to any safeguarder in Forms 60–63.

Duties of safeguarder in relation to papers received

17.20 The safeguarder must keep papers securely, not reveal their contents except where necessary in the performance of his or her duties and must, 'when he has completed the performance of all duties associated with his appointment', return the papers to the reporter.[1] The consideration that the safeguarder must thus part with papers (some of which in a particular case might seem to the safeguarder to be important to justify, for example some expression of opinion in a possible defamation claim) may fortify, if fortification be required, the view expressed above[2] that a safeguarder is absolutely immune from such a claim alleging defamation.

1 SI 1996/3261, r 14(6).
2 At 17.09.

CHAPTER 18

Procedures prior to hearings – business meetings

INTRODUCTORY

The rationale of business meetings

18.01 There are a number of decisions which have to be taken in relation to the content of notifications of hearings sent to persons which by their nature have to be taken before such notifications are sent out by the reporter. The jurisdiction to decide as to these matters is conferred upon hearings, and not on the reporter. In earlier practice the reporter asked meetings of hearings at which the reporter, and sometimes no other party, was present to give guidance on such matters. In the early stage of the case which came to be reported as *Sloan v B*[1] such a meeting was held on the question of whether or not the child should be excused from the hearing under the provisions of the Social Work (Scotland) Act 1968, s 40(2). This practice was non-statutory but well established and received the approval of the First Division, being described by Lord President Hope, delivering the opinion of the court,[2] as 'an eminently sensible step in the procedure, even although it had no statutory basis'. But this approval was only given on the basis that all the hearing was doing was giving guidance to the reporter and that the matter would be considered again when the hearing met to perform its statutory functions. The Children (Scotland) Act 1995, s 64 gives a statutory basis for these procedures and the Children's Hearings (Scotland) Rules 1996,[3] r 4 governs the practice. The Clyde Report[4] recognised the value of 'business meetings' but considered that openness[5] pointed to the parent and child being told of the meeting and being allowed to present their stances orally or in writing. Accordingly the Rules provide for intimation and allow the presentation of written views.

1 1991 SLT 530.
2 At 540F.
3 SI 1996/3261.
4 At 18.31 and Recommendation 149.
5 And the UN Convention on the Rights of the Child, art 12(2).

Scope and composition of business meetings

18.02 When arranging a hearing the reporter may, where he or she thinks fit, arrange business meetings to determine the procedural matters set out in the Children's Hearings (Scotland) Rules 1996, r 4(2)[1] and also give such direction or guidance to the reporter in relation to the performance of the reporter's functions in relation to the proceedings as they think appropriate.[2] The meeting must be drawn from the children's panel of the appropriate local authority area,[3] but need not comprise the same members who will make up the substantive hearing. The Children (Scotland) Act 1995 makes no provision as to the composition of a business meeting, but the Rules[4] import the provision in the Act[5] which prescribes three panel members with each gender represented.

1 Discussed at 18.03ff below.
2 Children (Scotland) Act 1995, s 64(3)(b); Children's Hearings (Scotland) Rules 1996, SI 1996/3261, r 4(1)(b).
3 C(S)A 1995, s 64(1).
4 SI 1996/3261, r 4(1).
5 C(S)A 1995, s 39(5).

PROCEDURAL DETERMINATIONS COMPETENT TO BUSINESS MEETINGS

Notification of relevant persons under para (c) of definition

18.03   Under the Children's Hearings (Scotland) Rules 1996, r 7(1) the reporter is obliged to notify any relevant person having the right and duty to attend hearings in terms of the Children (Scotland) Act 1995, s 45(8). A business meeting is empowered to determine whether notice is to be given under this rule 'to any person as a "relevant person" in terms of paragraph (c) of the definition of that term in section 93(2)(b) of the Act'.[1] Since the obligation to notify any relevant person who has the right and duty to attend is mandatory, this provision cannot mean that the business meeting is here being empowered to decide whether or not a relevant person is to be notified, but must mean that the business meeting is to decide whether a person who is potentially a relevant person in terms of the said paragraph (c) is a relevant person. This is a remarkable provision in that it confers on the business meeting jurisdiction to decide a matter of mixed fact and law which is binding on the reporter (who is generally regarded as legal adviser to the hearing[2]). However it is not the only example of jurisdiction to make decisions cognate with those of a court being conferred upon bodies within the hearings system.[3]

1 '(c) any person who appears to be a person who ordinarily (and other than by reason only of his employment) has charge of, or control over, the child.'
2 See 2.11 above.
3 Cf the power of a children's hearing to decide whether the 'protestations of innocence' should be accepted or not – see the opinion of the court in *O v Rae* 1992 SCLR 318 per LP Hope at 324E and F.

Release of child from obligation to attend a hearing

18.04   Where a child has been lawfully notified of a hearing[1] a children's hearing may release the child from the obligation to attend where, in the case of an allegation concerning a Schedule 1 offence, the hearing thinks that the child's attendance is not necessary for the just hearing of the case or, in any case, where the hearing considers that the child's attendance would be detrimental to the interests of the child.[2] A decision on this point may be taken at a business meeting.[3] Such a decision, in contrast with the decision as to a person's status as a relevant person, seems entirely within the traditional jurisdiction of a children's hearing.

1 Children (Scotland) Act 1995, ss 45(1) and 42(2)(b); Children's Hearings (Scotland) Rules 1996, SI 1996/3261, r 6.
2 C(S)A 1995, s 45(2).
3 SI 1996/3261, r 4(2)(b).

Release of relevant person from obligation to attend a children's hearing

18.05   Where a relevant person has been lawfully notified of a hearing[1] a children's hearing may release the relevant person from the obligation to attend if satisfied that to require his or her attendance would be unreasonable or unnecessary for the proper consideration of the case.[2] This decision may be taken by a business meeting.[3] Like the immediately foregoing, this seems to be a decision within the traditional jurisdiction of a children's hearing.

1 Children (Scotland) Act 1995, ss 45(8) and 42(2)(b); SI 1996/3261, r 7.
2 C(S)A 1995, s 45(8).
3 SI 1996/3261, r 4(2)(c).

DIRECTIONS AND GUIDANCE TO REPORTER COMPETENT AT BUSINESS MEETINGS

18.06   A business meeting may also be arranged by the reporter for the purpose of 'obtaining any direction or guidance in relation to the performance of his functions in relation to the proceedings'.[1] It is thought that this provision is intended to refer to those discretionary procedural decisions of the reporter such as a decision as to whether persons having no legal entitlement to attend hearings should be allowed to be present. It is thought that reporters will not seek guidance from business meetings in relation to discretionary decisions such as whether or not to arrange a hearing[2] or as to possible referral of a child's case to the local authority for 'voluntary' support.[3] These decisions have long been regarded as appropriate to the professional judgment of the reporter: it seems unlikely that the legislature intended the reporter to ask business meetings for guidance in relation to these functions and reporters have shown no signs of wanting to do so.

1 SI 1996/3261, r 4(1)(b).
2 Children (Scotland) Act 1995, s 56(6).
3 C(S)A 1995, s 56(4).

CONVENING A BUSINESS MEETING – PROCEDURE

Notice and timescale

18.07   The reporter selects the date and place for the business meeting – in practice in liaison with the panel. The reporter must, not later than four working days[1] before the meeting, notify in writing the time, date and place of the meeting to the panel members involved[2] and the date only[3] of the meeting to the child, the relevant person and any safeguarder.[4] Along with the notification, the following must be sent:[5]

(i) notice of the matters as to which the determination or directions/ guidance of the business meeting is sought;
(ii) a copy of any relevant documents; and
(iii) a copy of the grounds of referral.

The reporter must, when giving notice to the child, any relevant person or safeguarder, advise that they are each entitled to make their views known on the issue in question and have these views presented to the business meeting by the reporter.[6]

1 Not defined in the Children's Hearings (Scotland) Rules 1996, SI 1996/3261, so the definition in the Children (Scotland) Act 1995, s 93(1) comes into play: 'every day except – (a)
Saturday and Sunday; (b) December 25th and 26th; and (c) January 1st and 2nd.'
2 SI 1996/3261, r 4(3).
3 Since they have no right to attend they do not need to know the time and place of the
meeting, but they do need to know the date since they have the right to make written
submissions.
4 SI 1996/3261, r 4(3)(a) and (b).
5 SI 1996/3261, r 4(3)(c).
6 SI 1996/3261, r 4(4).

Forms

18.08   The Children's Hearings (Scotland) Rules 1996, in relation to these provisions amongst others, do not provide specific forms for notification to persons of a business meeting. The Scottish Children's Reporter Administration has devised standard forms.

Views of child, safeguarder and relevant person

18.09   The reporter must make a written record of any views given to him or her other than in writing by a child, safeguarder or relevant person and shall, as soon as reasonably practicable after receiving such views, give a copy of these views in writing to the members of the children's panel who will be attending the business meeting and to the other persons who have received notice of the meeting under the Children's Hearings (Scotland) Rules 1996, r 4(3).[1]

1 Children's Hearings (Scotland) Rules 1996, SI 1996/3261, r 4(6).

THE DELIBERATIONS AND DECISION OF THE BUSINESS MEETING – PRIVACY AND APPEAL

18.10 The rules governing business meetings are set out in the Children's Hearings (Scotland) Rules 1996, r 4 and the other 1996 Rules do not apply.[1] With two exceptions, the provisions of the Children (Scotland) Act 1995 which govern children's hearings do not apply to business meetings. The exceptions are: the provisions of s 44 of the Act (prohibiting publication of proceedings at children's hearings)[2] and the appeal provisions contained in s 51, which only apply in relation to any determination of a business meeting under s 64(3)(a) of the Act, as set out in the 1996 Rules, r 4(2)(a)–(c).[3] It is difficult to figure an appeal in relation to a decision of a business meeting as to the release or not of a child or relevant person from the obligation to attend a hearing.[4] It is possible in theory to envisage an appeal on a decision as to who may be a relevant person[5] but, as far as the writer is aware, no such appeal has yet been taken.

1 Children (Scotland) Act 1995, s 64(5).
2 See 22.16 below.
3 Discussed at 18.03–18.05 above.
4 Children's Hearings (Scotland) Rules 1996, SI 1996/3261, r 4(2)(b) and (c).
5 SI 1996/3261, r 4(2)(a).

CHAPTER 19

Varieties of hearings

INTRODUCTORY

The statutory provisions

19.01   A children's hearing is a sitting of the children's panel constituted in accordance with the Children (Scotland) Act 1995, s 39(5).[1] A business meeting is not a children's hearing.[2] The enactments and rules governing the composition of hearings and the enrolment and appointment of members of hearings have already been discussed.[3]

1 Children (Scotland) Act 1995, s 39(3).
2 C(S)A 1995, s 64(5).
3 At 1.01 ff above.

Classes of hearing

19.02   Hearings may conveniently be classified with descriptions such as: 'second working day' hearings under the Children (Scotland) Act 1995, s 59(2); dispositive hearings; special hearings; and advice hearings.

'SECOND WORKING DAY' HEARINGS

19.03   The purpose of such a hearing is to determine whether or not and, if so, whether with or without variation, a Child Protection Order should be continued.[1]

1 Children (Scotland) Act 1995, s 59(2); discussed in Ch 8 above.

DISPOSITIVE HEARINGS

Hearing on referral with grounds stated

19.04   Where the reporter has decided that compulsory measures of supervision are necessary and that at least one ground of referral specified in the Children (Scotland) Act 1995, s 52(2) is established, he or she shall arrange a hearing to dispose of the case.[1] The sheriff may order the child to be detained[2] and in this event the hearing for the consideration of the child's case must in effect be held within three days.[3]

1 Children (Scotland) Act 1995, ss 56(6) and 65(1).
2 C(S)A 1995, s 68(10)(b).
3 C(S)A 1995, s 68(12).

'Eighth working day' hearing

19.05   Where a CPO has been continued at a 'second working day hearing'[1] or by the sheriff in an application to vary or recall a CPO,[2] the reporter must arrange a dispositive hearing under the Children (Scotland) Act 1995, s 65(1) on the eighth working day after the CPO was implemented.[3]

1 See 19.03 above.
2 Children (Scotland) Act 1995, s 60(12)(d).
3 C(S)A 1995, s 65(2).

Remit from the sheriff after a s 68 proof

19.06   Where the case has been sent to the sheriff for proof of grounds which have not been accepted[1] or not understood by the child[1] and the sheriff has found all or some of the grounds established and remitted the matter to the reporter to fix a hearing, then the reporter must arrange a dispositive hearing.[3]

1 Children (Scotland) Act 1995, s 65(7).
2 C(S)A 1995, s 65(9).
3 C(S)A 1995, s 68(10)(a).

Hearing on referral with grounds certified by a court

19.07   Both civil and criminal courts may in specified circumstances refer the case of a child to the reporter, specifying the condition of referral under the Children (Scotland) Act 1995, s 52(2).[1] In the event of the reporter referring such a case to a hearing the condition certified by the sheriff becomes equivalent to a ground established by the sheriff after a s 68 proof.[2]

1 For discussion of the relative provision see 3.16–3.19 above.
2 Children (Scotland) Act 1995, s 54(3)(b); Criminal Procedure (Scotland) Act 1995, s 48.

'First practicable working day' hearing

19.08   Where a child has been found pursuant upon a warrant granted under the Children (Scotland) Act 1995, s 45(4)[1] the reporter must arrange a dispositive hearing which is to take place 'wherever practicable' on the first working day after the child was found.[2]

1 See 19.10 below.
2 Children (Scotland) Act 1995, s 45(7).

Remit from criminal court for disposal

19.09   Where a criminal court has remitted a case for disposal after a child has pleaded guilty to or been found guilty of a criminal offence the reporter must arrange a hearing for disposal of the case.[1] Where the court has this power it sometimes may, and in one instance must, obtain the advice of a children's hearing.[2] On such a remit a certificate by the clerk of the remitting court is conclusive evidence for the purposes of the remit that the offence has been committed by the person remitted.[3] Where a person not subject to a supervision requirement between 16 and 17½ is remitted that person shall, for the purpose of the remit, be regarded as a child.[4]

1 Criminal Procedure (Scotland) Act 1995, s 49(1)(b), (3)(b), (4) and (6).
2 See 19.26–19.28 below.
3 Children (Scotland) Act 1995, s 50(1).
4 C(S)A 1995, s 50(2).

'WARRANT' HEARINGS, SUNDRY REVIEW HEARINGS AND HEARINGS FOR A PARTICULAR PURPOSE.

Warrant hearings

19.10   Where the reporter considers that a warrant is necessary to secure the attendance of a child at a hearing he may apply to a hearing for a warrant to find the child, to keep the child in a place of safety and to bring him or her before a dispositive hearing.[1] (Where a child fails to attend a hearing to which he or she has been duly convened, the hearing, on either its own motion or that of the reporter, may grant a like warrant.[2]) Where a child has been required[3] to attend at or reside at a place and has failed to do so a hearing may, on its own motion or on application by the reporter, grant a warrant which shall be authority to find and remove the child and take him or her to a place of safety.[4] A hearing which considers that there is reason to believe that a child will not attend a hearing or will not comply with a requirement under the Children (Scotland) Act 1995, s 69(3) (requirement to reside at a place for investigation), or that being kept in a place of safety is necessary to safeguard or promote the child's welfare, may grant a warrant which will allow detention of the child for 22 days.[5] The reporter may apply to a hearing for the extension of such a warrant.[6]

1 C(S)A 1995, s 45(3) and (4).
2 C(S)A 1995, s 45(5).
3 C(S)A 1995, s 69(3).
4 C(S)A 1995, s 69(4), (5).
5 C(S)A 1995, s 66(1)–(3).
6 C(S)A 1995, s 66(5).

Review of case of child arrested by the police

19.11   Where the reporter has been informed by a constable in accordance with the Criminal Procedure (Scotland) Act 1995, s 43(5) that charges are not to be proceeded with against a child who has been detained in a place of safety under that section, the reporter, unless he considers that compulsory measures of supervision are not required, shall arrange a hearing which shall begin not later than the third day after the reporter has received the notification.[1] If the reporter decides that compulsory measures are not required the child is released but otherwise the child may be kept in the place of safety until the commencement of the hearing. It is then for that hearing to decide under subsection (5)(a) if, applying the test of the Children (Scotland) Act 1995, s 66(2),[2] a warrant to detain the child is required, and also whether or not to direct the reporter to hold a hearing. Before deciding on this the hearing would of course have to be satisfied that at least one of the grounds of referral was satisfied and also that compulsory measures of supervision were required to secure the child's welfare. It is thought that the first of these decisions should be regarded as an intellectual exercise based on the information before the hearing while the second would be an assessment of the child's needs, with those needs being regarded as the paramount consideration.[3] It would not, for example, be open to the hearing to conclude that it was not satisfied that any of the s 52(2) conditions of referral appeared to be satisfied but that nevertheless the child's welfare would be advanced by compulsory measures and therefore the reporter should hold a hearing. It seems clear that it would be competent for the hearing to direct that a hearing should be arranged without granting a warrant. It also seems clear that the hearing could not grant a warrant and not direct a hearing. There is no power conferred on the hearing to direct the reporter not to fix a hearing and there seems no good reason to suppose that such a power, which would constitute a surprising abridgement of the reporter's discretion, is to be implied. Where the hearing does grant warrant for the detention of the child under s 63(5)[4] the child shall not remain so detained where the reporter, having regard to the welfare of the child, considers, as a result of a change in the circumstances or of further information relating to the case having been received by him or her, that the s 66(2) conditions (justifying detention) no longer obtain, or that the child is not in need of compulsory measures of supervision.[5] It is submitted that the reporter would have to come to the latter conclusion if, on further investigation, he or she concluded that no satisfactory evidence existed supporting any condition of referral under s 52(2) of the Act.

1 Children (Scotland) Act 1995, s 63(1) and (2).
2 '(a) that there is reason to believe that the child may—
   (i) not attend at any hearing of his case; or
   (ii) fail to comply with a requirement under section 69(3) of this Act.'
3 C(S)A 1995, s 16(1).
4 Children's Hearings (Scotland) Rules 1996, SI 1996/3261, r 27 and Form 8.
5 C(S)A 1995, s 63(6)(a) and (b).

Fugitive child hearing

19.12 The Children (Scotland) Act 1995, s 82 makes special provisions in relation to a 'fugitive child' which means substantially a child who 'absconds' from a place or person at or with whom he or she is required to stay or does not return to such a place or person after a 'period of leave'.[1] Such a child may be arrested without warrant in any part of the United Kingdom and 'a court'[2] which is satisfied that there are reasonable grounds for believing that such a child is in premises may grant a warrant authorising a constable to enter such premises and search for the child, using reasonable force if necessary.[3] A child so arrested may be returned to the original place or person or to a place of safety but if such place or person is unable or unwilling to receive him then intimation must be made to the reporter and the child is kept meantime in a place of safety.[4] On receiving such intimation the reporter must, if the child is the subject of a supervision requirement, arrange a review hearing or, if the child is not subject to a supervision requirement, a hearing to consider[5] whether compulsory measures of supervision are required.

1 Children (Scotland) Act 1995, s 82(1), (2) and (3).
2 Not defined but presumably including (but not exclusively) any court having a criminal jurisdiction.
3 C(S)A 1995, s 82(1).
4 C(S)A 1995, s 82(4).
5 C(S)A 1995, ss 56(6) and 82(5)(b).

Secure accommodation hearing

A 'looked after' child

19.13 The Secure Accommodation (Scotland) Regulations 1996, reg 7 provides that a child who is being looked after by a local authority under the Children (Scotland) Act 1995, Pt II, Chs 1 or 4 may, if the chief social work officer ('CSWO') and the person in charge are satisfied that compulsory measures of supervision may be required, that the secure accommodation criteria are satisfied,[1] *and* that it is in the child's best interests to be placed and kept in secure accommodation, be placed in secure accommodation.[2] When this happens the CSWO must immediately advise any relevant person and also the reporter and the reporter must be given the details of the placement together with the views of the CSWO and the person in charge as to compulsory measures of supervision and the need or otherwise for secure accommodation.[3] On receipt of such information and within 72 hours of the *placement* in secure accommodation the reporter shall proceed to consider the child's case under s 56 of the Act and if the reporter decides to refer the child to a hearing this must be convened within 72 hours[4] or at the most 72 plus 24 hours of the placement.[5] If the reporter arranges a referral the child then enters the system and a hearing may authorise the use of secure accommodation.[6]

1 Children (Scotland) Act 1995, s 70(10)(a) or (b).
2 Secure Accommodation (Scotland) Regulations 1996, SI 1996/3255, reg 6(1) – the CSWO must also check that the secure accommodation provided is appropriate to the child's needs.
3 SI 1996/3255, reg 7(2)(b).
4 Excluding Sundays and public holidays: SI 1996/3255, reg 2(2).
5 SI 1996/3255, reg 8.
6 C(S)A 1995, s 70(9), when read with s 56(6) and s 65(1): SI 1996/3255, Sch, Form 2.

Child under supervision

19.14   The Secure Accommodation (Scotland) Regulations 1996, reg 6 provides that where a child is subject to a supervision requirement, but not subject to an antecedent authorisation of secure accommodation by a hearing,[1] the chief social work officer and the person in charge of the residential establishment providing the secure accommodation, if satisfied that the secure accommodation criteria[2] exist, may place that child in secure accommodation and the CSWO must 'satisfy himself, in relation to the placing of the child in the residential establishment providing the secure accommodation, that the placement in that establishment is appropriate to the child's needs having regard to its statement of functions and objectives'. It would appear from the wording of this regulation, taken literally, that these provisions apply to all children subject to a supervision requirement under the Children (Scotland) Act 1995, s 70 and not only to children subject to a requirement to reside in a place under s 70(3)(a). (The provision that a child, even a child subject to compulsory measures of supervision, could be removed from home and placed even temporarily in secure accommodation on the opinion of the CSWO and the person in charge of a residential establishment having a secure facility may seem to be contrary to the thrust of the Child Protection provisions of the Act, driven by the concerns expressed in the Clyde Report about taking children from home without judicial scrutiny, but it is difficult to give the provisions any other interpretation and on some rare occasions it may be necessary to employ these provisions in this way. On such a placement in secure accommodation being made, the CSWO must advise the child, in a manner appropriate to his or her maturity, any relevant person and the reporter of the details and of his and the person in charge's views as to the need or otherwise for the child's detention in secure accommodation.[3] On receipt of this the reporter must fix a review hearing under s 73(8) of the Act[4] as if there had been a transfer under s 72(2) of the Act.[5] Such a review must take place no later than 72 hours[6] from the time of the *placement*.[7] Such a hearing may authorise[8] the use of secure accommodation.[9] An authorisation so given may be continued at a review hearing.[10]

1   Children (Scotland) Act 1995, s 70(9).
2   C(S)A 1995, s 70(10)(a) or (b).
3   Secure Accommodation (Scotland) Regulations 1996, SI 1996/3255, reg 6(2).
4   With s 73(8) being read as if the reference in s 73(8)(a)(iii) to a transfer under s 72(2) of the Act included a reference to a placement under reg 6.
5   SI 1996/3255, rr 6(3) and (4).
6   Excluding Sundays and public holidays: SI 1996/3255, reg 2(2).
7   SI 1996/3255, reg 6(4).
8   The Children's Hearings (Scotland) Rules 1996, SI 1996/3261, r 26(1)(c) refers to the hearing considering if it should 'issue a warrant under the 1996 Regulations': this must be a loose use of the term 'warrant' – hearings authorise secure accommodation but do not grant warrant for the conveyance of children thereto.
9   Children (Scotland) Act 1995, s 73(9)(d), read with ss 73(8)(a)(iii), 70(1), 70(3)(a) and 70(9): SI 1996/3255, Sch, Form 2.
10   Children (Scotland) Act 1995, s 73(9)(e): SI 1996/3255, Sch, Form 4.

Hearing to consider suspension of supervision requirement

19.15   Where a child or relevant person appeals to the sheriff against a decision of a hearing about a supervision requirement the child or relevant person may apply to a hearing for suspension of the requirement appealed against[1] and the reporter must 'forthwith' arrange a hearing which may grant or refuse the application.[2]

1 Children (Scotland) Act 1995, s 51(9).
2 C(S)A 1995, s 51(10).

Hearing to consider transfer of child

19.16   Where a child is required under a supervision requirement to reside in a specific residential establishment or other specific accommodation[1] the CSWO of a local authority may, in any case of urgent necessity where it is in the interests of the child or of other children in the establishment or accommodation to do so, transfer the child to another place.[2] In this event a review hearing under the Children (Scotland) Act 1995, s 73(8) must be arranged within seven days of the transfer.[3]

1 Children (Scotland) Act 1995, s 70(3)(a).
2 C(S)A 1995, s 72(1).
3 C(S)A 1995, s 72(2); cf C(S)A 1995, s 73(8)(a)(iii).

Is the family home 'specific other accommodation'?

19.17   On the basis that home is a 'specific other accommodation' – and this seems literally correct – it might be argued that the foregoing provision applies to any supervision requirement that the child is to remain at home, with the consequence that such a child subject to a 'home supervision requirement' could be removed from home by the local authority if it believed, for example, that the child was in danger there. If the phrase is regarded as ambiguous then the *ejusdem generis* rule of interpretation might exclude this possibility. Similarly, the principle of reading the statute as a whole[1] would point against such an interpretation, since to read the section so would bypass the safeguards attaching to a CPO.[2] But where there is no ambiguity it is inappropriate to invoke the canons of statutory interpretation.[3] In practice this provision is not generally interpreted as meaning that the family home is 'specific other accommodation' but it is submitted that the matter should be clarified by Parliament.

1 Discussed at 5.04 above.
2 Cf discussion at 19.14 above.
3 *Ferguson v Secretary of State for Social Services* 1989 SLT 117.

REVIEW HEARINGS UNDER THE 1995 ACT, S 73

At the instance of the local authority

19.18   A local authority may refer a child's case to the reporter for a review hearing where it is satisfied as to the circumstances set out in the

Children (Scotland) Act 1995, s 73(4) and the reporter must arrange a hearing.[1] These circumstances are:

(a) the requirement ought to cease or be varied;
(b) a condition in the requirement is not being complied with; or
(c) the best interests of the child would be served by the local authority —
  (i) applying for a parental responsibilities order under s 86 of the Act;
  (ii) applying for a freeing for adoption order under s 18 of the Adoption (Scotland) Act 1978; or
  (iii) placing the child for adoption [always given that the local authority intends to apply for such an order or so to place the child].

Where the local authority is aware that an application for adoption of a child under supervision has been or is likely to be made it must forthwith refer the child's case to the reporter.[2] Where a reporter has to hold a hearing under these provisions[3] and the reporter is advised by the adoption agency that it has determined that agreement to an application under s 16 or s 18 of the Adoption (Scotland) Act 1978 is unlikely to be forthcoming she or he must arrange a hearing to sit within 21 days of the notification from the local authority.[4]

1 Children (Scotland) Act 1995, s 73(8)(a)(i).
2 C(S)A 1995, s 73(5).
3 C(S)A 1995, s 73(8)(a)(i) – Children's Hearings (Scotland) Rules 1996, SI 1996/3261, r 22(8) refers to C(S)A 1995, s 73(8)(a)(iv) but this would seem to be a mistake.
4 SI 1996/3261, r 22(8) – but see immediately preceding footnote.

At the instance of the child or relevant person

19.19   A child or a relevant person may require a review of a supervision requirement at any time at least three months after the requirement has been made, continued or varied[1] and the reporter must fix a hearing when such a request is made.[2]

1 Children (Scotland) Act 1995, s 73(6).
2 C(S)A 1995, s 73(8)(a)(ii).

At instance of a relevant person proposing to take child to live furth of Scotland

19.20   A relevant person who proposes to take a child under supervision to live outside of Scotland must, unless such a move is already permitted by the supervision requirement or by an order under the Children (Scotland) Act 1995, s 11, notify the reporter and the local authority in writing[1] and the reporter must arrange a review hearing.[2]

1 Children (Scotland) Act 1995, s 73(7).
2 C(S)A 1995, s 73(8)(a)(iv).

Review of a supervision requirement within three months of expiry

19.21 In any event, once a supervision requirement is due to expire within three months unless continued, the reporter must fix a hearing.[1]

1 Children (Scotland) Act 1995, s 73(8)(a)(v).

Review determined by the hearing

19.22 An innovation of the Children (Scotland) Act 1995 was to allow the hearing, when making a supervision requirement, to determine that a review should be held at a specific time during the duration of the requirement.[1] Exercise of this power by a hearing does not, of course, prevent a review being requested by other parties entitled to request a review.

1 Children (Scotland) Act 1995, s 70(7); cf Children (Scotland) Act 1995, s 73(8)(a)(iii).

ADVICE HEARINGS

Variation or recall of CPO

19.23 Where a CPO has been made and an application to recall or vary has been lodged[1] the reporter may, after he or she has received notice of the application to recall or vary but before the sheriff has decided on it, arrange a hearing to give advice to the sheriff.[2]

1 Children (Scotland) Act 1995, s 57 and 60(7), discussed in chs 5, 6 and 9 above.
2 C(S)A 1995, s 60(10), discussed at 9.19 above.

Adoption proceedings and parental responsibilities orders

19.24 A hearing convened under the Children (Scotland) Act 1995, s 73(4)[1] *shall*, irrespective of any other action it may take, draw up a report providing advice on the various procedures or proposed procedures[2] and the relevant court shall consider such advice.[3] An illustration of such a report is given later.[4] It has been held that a hearing giving advice in this context should advise specifically on the degree of contact if asked to do so.[5]

1 Noticed at 19.14 above.
2 Children (Scotland) Act 1995, s 73(13).
3 C(S)A 1995, s 73(14).
4 At 56.12 below.
5 *S v Petrie* 2000 SLT (Sh Ct) 145.

Placing for adoption of child under supervision

19.25 An approved adoption society *shall* refer the case of a child who is under supervision and whom it has decided would benefit by being adopted to the reporter who must arrange an advice hearing.[1]

1 Adoption (Scotland) Act 1978, s 22A (1) and (2) (interpolated by Children (Scotland) Act 1995, Sch 2, para 15).

Criminal court considering sentencing child under supervision

19.26 Where a child under supervision has pled guilty to or been found guilty of an offence the High Court *may* and the sheriff court and the district court *shall* request that the reporter arrange an advice hearing[1] and may, except in relation to an offence the sentence for which is prescribed by law, after considering the advice, remit to a children's hearing for disposal.

1 Criminal Procedure (Scotland) Act 1995, s 49(3); Crime and Disorder Act 1988, Sch 18, para 118.

Criminal court considering sentencing child not under supervision

19.27 Where a child not under supervision has pled guilty to or been found guilty of an offence the court may request that the reporter arrange an advice hearing[1] and may, except in relation to an offence the sentence for which is prescribed by law, after considering the advice, remit to a children's hearing for disposal.

1 Criminal Procedure (Scotland) Act 1995, s 49(1)(b).

Court of summary criminal jurisdiction considering sentencing child aged 16–17½ not under supervision

19.28 Where a child (not under supervision) over 16 but not yet 17½ has pled guilty to or been found guilty of an offence which has been charged under summary procedure the court may request that the reporter fix an advice hearing[1] and may, except in relation to an offence the sentence for which is prescribed by law, *if the hearing so advise* remit to a children's hearing for disposal.[2]

1 Criminal Procedure (Scotland) Act 1995, s 49(6).
2 CP(S)A 1995, s 49(7).

Review precipitated by new grounds of referral

19.29 Under the Social Work (Scotland) Act 1968 there was no express provision requiring the review of a supervision requirement after new grounds had been stated. It was open to those entitled to ask the reporter to arrange a review hearing to arrange a review (a 'precipitated review') in order to prevent the child being subject to multiple supervision requirements. The Children (Scotland) Act 1995 introduces a provision that where a referral is made in relation to a child already subject to a supervision requirement the children's hearing, before disposing of the new referral, shall review the existing supervision requirement.[1] The obligation is to review the original requirement 'before disposing of the [new] referral …' and, since the purpose of the provision is presumably to avoid multiple supervision requirements, it is thought that the obligation to review the existing requirement only attaches once the hearing on the new referral is in a position to impose a supervision requirement, i e after the new grounds of referral have been admitted or proved.[2]

1 C(S)A 1995, s 65(3).
2 This is Professor Norrie's view in Norrie *Children's Hearings in Scotland* (1997) pp 137–139, with which the writer would respectfully concur.

CHAPTER 20

Convening a hearing

NOTIFICATION OF HEARINGS AND PROVISION OF DOCUMENTS TO HEARING MEMBERS

The general rule

20.01 Subject to the special provisions which come into play when the placement of a child in secure accommodation is in question[1] the reporter shall,[2] wherever practicable, notify the chairman and members as to the time and place of a hearing at least *seven* days before the date of the hearing and shall, as soon as reasonably practicable but not later than *three* days before it give to each of them a copy of any of the following which are available and which are relevant for their consideration at the hearing:

(a) a report of a local authority on the child and his social background;
(b) the statement of grounds of referral;
(c) any judicial remit or reference by a local authority;
(d) any supervision requirement to which the child is subject;
(e) any report prepared by any safeguarder appointed in the case;
(f) any views of the child given in writing to the reporter under the Children's Hearings (Scotland) Rules 1996, r 15(4).

1 See 19.13 and 19.14 above.
2 Children's Hearings (Scotland) Rules 1996, SI 1996/3261, r 5(1).

Last-minute information

20.02 If any other document or information which may be material, including any oral views of the child given to the reporter under the Children's Hearings (Scotland) Rules 1996, r 15, is obtained by the reporter then he or she shall make it available to the hearing members before the hearing.[1]

1 Children's Hearings (Scotland) Rules 1996, SI 1996/3261, r 5(2).

Confidentiality of documents provided

20.03 Except in relation to performing their duties in connection with the hearing procedures,[1] the hearing members must not disclose any information[2] and they must return the papers to the reporter after the hearing.[3]

1 Under the Children's Hearings (Scotland) Rules 1996, SI 1996/3261, rr 20(4) and 22(4).
2 SI 1996/3261, r 5(4).
3 SI 1996/3261, r 5(5).

Official observers

20.04   If a member of the Council on Tribunals or the CPAC or any sub-committee thereof is to attend a hearing then he or she has a like right to a copy of the papers, subject to a like duty not to disclose information and to return the papers after the hearing.[1]

1 Children's Hearings (Scotland) Rules 1996, SI 1996/3261, r 5(6) and (7).

NOTIFICATION OF HEARINGS TO CHILDREN

The general rule

20.05   Except in relation to specified urgent hearings,[1] the reporter must give the child seven days' notice in writing of the date, time and place of the hearing and tell the child of his right and obligation to attend it, unless the child's presence has been dispensed with under the Children (Scotland) Act 1995, s 45(2).[2] Such a dispensation may be effected by direction given by a business meeting.[3] Even where a dispensation has been given the child must be given notice of his or her right to attend the hearing under s 45 of the Act.

1 Noticed at 20.06 below.
2 Children's Hearings (Scotland) Rules 1996, SI 1996/3261, r 6(3).
3 Children (Scotland) Act 1995, s 64(3); SI 1996/3261, r 4(2); discussed at 18.04 above.

The urgent hearings needing only short notice

20.06   In relation to certain specified hearings the rule[1] recognises that it will generally be impracticable to give seven days' written notice, or indeed written notice at all, to the child and accordingly written notice is to be given as soon as reasonably practicable and, if such notice cannot be given in writing, the reporter may give it orally. These hearings are:

(a)   hearings to consider the case of a child in a place of safety under the following sections of the Children (Scotland) Act 1995, viz.: s 45(7) (child detained after s 45(4) warrant);[2] s 59(2) ('initial hearing' for child detained after CPO);[3] s 68(10) (child detained by order of sheriff after proof hearing);[4] by virtue of s 82(5) ('fugitive child' discovered and original person or place of safety not responsible for accepting return of child);[5]

(b)   hearings to consider child placed in secure accommodation under the Secure Accommodation (Scotland) Regulations 1996, reg 7;[6]

(c)   hearings under s 51(9) (to consider application to suspend a supervision requirement pending appeal to the sheriff);[7]

(d)   hearings under s 72 (to review case of child transferred to another place in case of urgent necessity).[8]

1 Children's Hearings (Scotland) Rules 1996, SI 1996/3261, r 6(2).
2 Noticed at 19.10 above.
3 Discussed at 19.03 above.
4 Noticed at 19.06 above.
5 Discussed at 19.12 above.
6 Discussed at 19.13 and 19.14 above.

7 Discussed at 19.15 above.
8 Discussed at 19.16 above.

The views of the child

20.07   The Children's Hearings (Scotland) Rules 1996, r 15 lists those hearings in relation to which, taking account of the age and maturity of the child, an opportunity must be given to the child, so far as practicable, to indicate whether he or she wishes to express views. These are:

(a) hearings considering whether to make, or hearings which are reviewing, a supervision requirement – i e dispositive hearings and review hearings;
(b) hearings which are considering whether to grant[1] or continue[2] a warrant;
(c) hearings considering whether to continue a CPO;[3]
(d) hearings providing advice under the Children (Scotland) Act 1995, s 60(10) (advice to the sheriff about recall or variation of a CPO);
(e) hearings considering whether to make a requirement under s 69 (3) of the Act (requirement that child reside at a place for investigation);
(f) hearings drawing up a report under s 73(13) of the Act (advice about adoption or parental responsibilities); and
(g) hearings considering whether to issue a warrant under the Secure Accommodation (Scotland) Regulations 1996.

When giving a child notice of one of the foregoing hearings the reporter must inform the child of the entitlement conferred by s 16(2) of the Act to express views; that if he or she does so wish, an opportunity will be given to him or her to express them; and that any views expressed to the reporter will be passed to the hearing, any relevant person and any safeguarder.[4] Where the child has indicated a wish to express views the chairman of the hearing may exercise any of the powers of the hearing under the Act or the Rules as is considered appropriate in order to ascertain these views and the hearing must have regard to them.[5] Without prejudice to the generality of the foregoing provision, the Act sets out possible modes whereby the child's views may be conveyed to the hearing.[6] It is also provided that a child aged 12 or more shall be presumed to be old and mature enough to form a view.[7] This does not mean that a child under 12 shall be presumed not to be old and mature enough to express a view.

1 Under the Children (Scotland) Act 1995, s 45(4) or (5), s 63(5), s 66(1) or s 69(4) or (7).
2 Under C(S)A 1995, s 66(5).
3 C(S)A 1995, s 59(4).
4 Children's Hearings (Scotland) Rules 1996, SI 1996/3261, r 6(4).
5 SI 1996/3261, r 15(3).
6 SI 1996/3261, r 15(4).
7 SI 1996/3261, r 15(5).

Form of notification of child

Child required to attend – views of child requested

20.08   As already noticed,[1] the Children's Hearings (Scotland) Rules 1996 do not supply forms of notification. The form in use by SCRA is as follows:

'To *Philippa* ~, (*d o b* 3.05.1987),
Flat 1/2, 27 Church Street,
Kirklenton, LE12 9TF

Dear *Philippa*

I have arranged a children's hearing to consider the Grounds of Referral attached to this letter.

The hearing will be held at 7 *pm* on Monday, 5 June 2000 at *Room 2, St Lenton's House, 1 Laverock Place, Kirklenton LE5 1AA.*

You have the right to attend the hearing, and it is very important for you to be there. If you do not come the hearing may arrange for you to be brought. You may be kept in a place of safety until the next hearing can be arranged. If there is a good reason why you cannot come to the hearing, such as illness, please contact my office. My address and telephone number are printed at the bottom of this letter.

There is a leaflet with this letter which will tell you about the hearing.

You may want to tell the hearing what you think would be best for you. You have the right to do that. If you do want to, you can tell me before the hearing starts or you can say it at the hearing.

You can write to me if you want. Whatever you tell me or write to me will be passed on to the panel members and also to your parents or main carers and to the safeguarder if one is appointed by the hearing. **You can either write to me on the page which is attached, or on another piece of paper.**

If you want to, you can bring someone with you to the hearing, a representative, to help you talk to panel members. Travel expenses will be paid to you and your representative.

Date: *27 May 2000*

> Signed: ~
> Children's Reporter
> *St Lenton's House*
> *1 Laverock Place*
> *Kirklenton LE5 1AA.*
> *Telephone* ~

[The accompanying page:

To the Panel Members from *Phillipa* ~, *aged 13.*

I would like you to know what I think before you make a decision at the children's hearing.

(Write what you want to say here and remember that a copy will be given to your parents or main carers and any safeguarder. You can say as much as you like but you do not have to fill the page. If you want, you can ask someone to help you write down what you want to say.)

Please bring this to the children's hearing or send it to the reporter at *St Lenton's House, 1 Laverock Place, Kirklenton LE5 1AA.*]'

1 At 18.08 above.

Papers accompanying intimation to child

20.09 The only document (apart from the explanatory leaflet) which should be enclosed with the intimation to the child is the foundation document which the hearing has before it – for example, in the case of a disposal hearing after grounds have been stated, the statement of grounds of referral.[1] The child does not receive reports etc.

1 SCRA Form 7, based upon Children's Hearings (Scotland) Rules 1986, SI 1986/2291, Sch, Form 4A.

NOTIFICATION OF CHILDREN'S HEARINGS AND PROVISION OF RELEVANT DOCUMENTS TO RELEVANT PERSONS AND CERTAIN PARENTS WITH RIGHT TO ATTEND

Relevant persons

20.10 Subject to the powers of exclusion now conferred upon hearings while in progress to exclude relevant persons from any part or parts of the hearing,[1] a relevant person has the right and duty to attend at all stages of the hearing unless the hearing is satisfied that such attendance is unnecessary for the proper consideration of the case.[2] A business meeting may be arranged to decide on this.[3] The reporter must notify in writing such a person, if his or her whereabouts are known, of his or her right and duty to attend at all stages of the hearing and of the date, time and place of the hearing.[4]

1 Children (Scotland) Act 1995, s 46.
2 C(S)A 1995, s 45(8); Children's Hearings (Scotland) Rules 1996, SI 1996/3261, r 7(2).
3 SI 1996/3261, r 4(2)(a) and (c) – discussed at 18.05 above.
4 SI 1996/3261, r 7(1).

Certain parents

20.11 The Children's Hearings (Scotland) Rules 1996, r 12(1) provides that any father of the child whose case is to be considered at the children's hearing and who is living with the mother of the child (and where they are the parents of the child according to the definition in the Children (Scotland) Act 1995, s 15(1)[1]) is *entitled* (but not obliged) to attend, but always subject to the usual provisions as to exclusion from part or parts of the hearing introduced by s 46 of the Act. The reporter must notify such a person of his right so to attend if his whereabouts are known.[2] The rule does not say in express terms that such a person has the right to be notified of dates, times and places of hearings but it may be that this may be taken as implied.[3]

1 '"parent", in relation to any person, subject to Part IV of the Adoption (Scotland) Act 1978 and sections 27 to 30 of the Human Fertilisation and Embryology Act 1990 and any regulations made under subsection (9) of the said section 30, means someone, of whatever age, who is that person's genetic father or mother.'
2 Children's Hearings (Scotland) Rules 1996, SI 1996/3261, r 7(3).
3 Since such parents are entitled to receive the documents – 1996 Rules, r 5(3)(b).

Form of foregoing notification

20.12   Once again[1] no form has been provided in the Children's Hearings (Scotland) Rules 1996 but SCRA has adapted a form.

1 Cf 20.08 above.

Time for giving foregoing notifications

20.13   Apart from in the 'urgent hearings needing only short notice',[1] the written notification to relevant persons (and presumably to 'certain parents'[2]) must be given not later than seven days before the date of the children's hearing to which it relates. In the case of the said urgent hearings, notification shall be given as soon as reasonably practicable and if written notice cannot be given then by word of mouth.[3]

1 Children's Hearings (Scotland) Rules 1996, SI 1996/3261, r 6(2) – noticed at 20.06 above.
2 SI 1996/3261, r 7(3) – noticed at 20.11 above.
3 SI 1996/3261, r 7(5).

Documents to accompany foregoing notifications

20.14   Along with notifications to relevant persons and certain parents the reporter must supply the same documents as supplied to the panel members,[1] except for documentation already supplied.[2] Where in 'urgent hearings' written notification of seven days is impracticable the documentation should be conveyed as soon as and in whatever way is practicable. The obligation which attaches to panel members and others[3] to keep the contents of documents confidential and to return them to the reporter does not attach to relevant persons or 'certain parents'.

1 Under Children's Hearings (Scotland) Rules 1996, SI 1996/3261, r 5(1) – noticed at 20.01 above.
2 SI 1996/3261, r 5(3).
3 SI 1996/3261, r 5(4)–(7).

NOTIFICATION OF HEARINGS TO CHIEF SOCIAL WORK OFFICER

20.15   The reporter must notify the CSWO of all hearings, giving the details of the child so far as known.[1]

1 Children's Hearings (Scotland) Rules 1996, SI 1996/3261, r 8.

POWER OF REPORTER NOT TO DISCLOSE WHEREABOUTS OF CHILD OR RELEVANT PERSON

20.16   When in fulfilling his or her duties in relation to notification under the Children's Hearings (Scotland) Rules 1996, rr 5 (hearing members and relevant persons), 6 (children) and 7 (relevant persons and certain parents), the reporter considers that disclosing the whereabouts of the child or the relevant person (and presumably 'certain parents') might place that person at risk of serious harm (whether or not physical harm), he or she may withhold such information as is necessary to avoid such disclosure.[1]

1 Children's Hearings (Scotland) Rules 1996, SI 1996/3261, r 9.

PRACTICAL ARRANGEMENTS

20.17 The reporter must liaise with the chairman of the Children's Panel in his or her local authority area, engaging such standing arrangements as may be in force, in order to ensure that identified hearing members are scheduled to attend individual hearings.

CHAPTER 21

Securing the presence of children at hearings – warrants

INTRODUCTORY

General

21.01 In very many cases it will not be necessary to detain a child pending the disposal of his/her case, but where a warrant is necessary the provisions of the Children (Scotland) Act 1995 and the Children's Hearings (Scotland) Rules[1] must be implemented carefully.

1 SI 1996/3261.

Child already detained

21.02 As already noticed[1] a child may be detained by virtue of the provisions of the child protection code. A reporter, in relation to a child detained under a CPO[2] must, unless the reporter has discharged him or her[3] or there has been an application to the sheriff to set aside the order[4] which has been notified to the reporter[5], arrange an initial hearing which may continue the CPO so that the child remains detained till the dispositive hearing.[6] Other cases, also already noticed, of children in detention pending a hearing are children who have been arrested by the police,[7] 'fugitive children' who have been found,[8] and children placed in secure accommodation by a local authority[9]. Once a child has been brought to such a hearing the hearing has powers[10] to detain further. The reporter may also, in advance of a hearing, obtain warrant for the detention of a child so as to bring the child to a hearing.[11]

1 Chs 5 to 9 above.
2 Children (Scotland) Act 1995, s 57(1).
3 C(S)A 1995, s 60(3).
4 C(S)A 1995, s 60(7).
5 C(S)A 1995, 59(1)(c).
6 C(S)A 1995, ss 59(4), 65(2).
7 Discussed above at 19.11.
8 Discussed above at 19.12.
9 Discussed above at 19.13 and 19.14.
10 See below 21.11 ff.
11 C(S)A 1995, s 45(4).

ANTICIPATORY WARRANT AND FAILURE TO APPEAR WARRANT

Arranging an anticipatory warrant hearing

21.03 As already noticed[1] the reporter may *if he has cause to believe that a child will not attend a hearing* apply to a hearing for warrant to find and keep a child and bring him or her to a hearing.[2] Such a warrant may be described as an 'anticipatory warrant'. An anticipatory warrant hearing is a children's hearing and not a business meeting.[3] Nevertheless the provisions in relation to notification and provision of documents contained in rr 5,[4] 6,[5] and 7[6] cannot have been intended and are not in practice regarded as having application to such hearings. Accordingly the hearing will not generally have received in advance any documents or reports. It is suggested that the rules should be amended in order to clarify the position – possibly by permitting business meetings to entertain motions to grant anticipatory warrants without intimation having been given to the child or other persons.

1 Above at 19.10.
2 C(S)A 1995, s 45(4).
3 The scope of a business meeting's powers are delimited in SI 1996/3261, r 4(2), see discussion at 18.03 ff above.
4 Which refers to the reporter arranging 'any children's hearing'.
5 Which refers to the reporter arranging 'a children's hearing'.
6 Which refers to notification for relevant persons and certain parents in relation to 'a child whose case is to be considered at a children's hearing'.

Relevant considerations: welfare and necessity

21.04 The welfare principle applies to deliberations as to anticipatory warrants. Neither of the other principles of s 16 of the Children (Scotland) Act 1995 (taking account of the views of the child and minimal intervention) applies in terms of s 16 but the provision of s 45(4) to the effect that the hearing must be 'satisfied on cause shown that it is necessary' for them to grant a warrant imports the no non-beneficial order principle in all but name and r 26(1)(a) of the Children's Hearings (Scotland) Rules 1996 places an obligation on the hearing to take steps to obtain the views of the child.[1] The reporter must be ready to try to convince the hearing that there is good cause to believe that unless a warrant is granted the child will not come. For example the child may not have come voluntarily to previous hearings, may have said that he or she does not intend to come voluntarily or there may be information that those responsible for the child will prevent or discourage him or her from coming. The information of the reporter may be in the form of reports or it may be conveyed verbally. In any event it should be specific. If given specific information a hearing will generally accept the information as true and grant warrant. The main purpose of such a warrant is to secure the attendance of this child at the hearing, not to protect the child,[2] but any information as to any degree of risk faced by the child should be mentioned to the children's hearing by the reporter.

1 See the following para for further discussion.
2 If the child is in urgent need of protection from significant harm one or other of the provisions of the child protection code should be invoked.

The views of the child and others as to the child's welfare

21.05   Although s 16(4)(a)(ii) of the Children (Scotland) Act 1995 does not include s 45(4) warrants in the list of those warrant hearings to which the principles of consulting the child and no non-beneficial order are to be applied, rule 26(1) of the Children's Hearings (Scotland) Rules includes s 45(4) warrants in the list of orders granted by hearings which are required, before taking a decision to 'take steps under rule 15 to obtain the views of the child, and endeavour to obtain the views of any relevant person and of any safeguarder, if attending the hearing, on what arrangements would be in the best interests of the child'. Rule 15(1) and (2)(b) similarly requires such a hearing to give the child an opportunity, taking account of age and maturity, to indicate if she or he wishes to express a view. Beyond asking the reporter about the child's and relevant persons' views it is uncertain what other 'steps' a hearing could take to ascertain such views. It is also difficult to figure a case wherein the child's or relevant persons' views, if against granting the warrant, would prevail against a reporter who was otherwise able (as he would require to do in any event) to show cause that the warrant was necessary in the interests of the child. It is suggested that those responsible for the rules should consider the removal of anticipatory warrant hearings under s 45(4) from the list in rr 15(2)(b) and 26(1)(a).

Form and execution of warrant

21.06   A Warrant under s 45(4) of the 1995 Act should follow the style of Form 5 of the 1996 Rules.[1] Such a warrant may be implemented as if it were a warrant for the apprehension of an accused person issued by a court of summary jurisdiction;[2] it therefore carries to the officers of law – the police – the authority where necessary to break open shut and lockfast places[3] and to use reasonable force to secure the person apprehended. Before being entitled to break open doors the officer must notify the occupants of premises of his identity and the purpose of his visit and have asked for and been refused admission.[4] The procedure after the child has been found will be discussed presently.[5]

1   SI 1996/3261, r 27.
2   Children (Scotland) Act 1995, s 84.
3   Criminal Procedure (Scotland) Act 1995, s 135(1).
4   *Renton and Brown's Criminal Procedure*, (6th edn) 5–15 and the authorities therein cited.
5   See below at 21.08.

Failure to appear warrants

21.07   Where a child fails to appear at a hearing to which she or he has been lawfully convened[1] a hearing may, on the application of the reporter or *ex proprio motu*, issue a warrant in the style of Form 5 and such warrant shall have the same effect as a warrant under s 45(4), discussed above.[2]

1   Children (Scotland) Act 1995, s 45(1); Children's Hearings (Scotland) Rules 1996, SI 1996/3261, r 6 – discussed above at 20.05 ff.
2   C(S)A 1995, s 45(5).

Child found – procedure up to first hearing

21.08   Ideally a child found as a consequence of an anticipatory warrant or a failure to appear warrant should be brought before a hearing immediately,[1] but in practice the child will usually be taken to a place of safety. In this event s 45(6) provides that the child may not be kept there by virtue of this warrant after whichever is the earlier of (a) the expiry of seven days from the date when he was *first taken there* or (b) the day on which the reporter arranges a hearing – which he is bound to do, wherever practicable – on the first working day after the child was so *found*.

1 Cf C(S)A 1995, s 45(7).

Computation of time

21.09 The maximum time of seven days during which the child may be kept in a place of safety is to begin 'on the day when he was first so taken there'.[1] It is submitted that it is clear that this means that the day the child was 'taken there' is to be 'day one', i e that where a child was taken to a place of safety in the course of a Saturday the latest time up to which she or he could be detained would be the end of the following Friday. What is meant by 'taken there' is less clear. On the face of it the words suggest that the relevant point of time would be the time when the child crossed the threshold of the place of safety: but what if Strathclyde police find a child in Arrochar at 10.30 p m on a Saturday night and decide, after consulting the duty social work manager, that rather than drive to Dunoon before midnight, they should instead drive the child directly to a children's home in Glasgow, and do so, arriving at 1 o'clock in the morning? It is tentatively suggested that the principle that statutes abridging the liberty of the subject should be interpreted in favour of freedom should rule and that the child is 'taken there' when the journey begins. Therefore, in this example, 'day one' would be the Saturday. The calculation of the 'first working day' is clearly linked to the time when the child was 'found'.

1 C(S)A 1995, 45(6)(a).

The first practicable working day hearing[1]

21.10 Such a hearing may be convened without the normal 7 days notice having been given and may even be convened verbally.[2] Even so it may not be practicable to hold the hearing on the first working day because of, e g, travelling difficulties or problems in contacting relevant persons and others. The consideration that a hearing could not be given the papers three days before the hearing[3] cannot of itself be regarded as a feature importing impracticability since this would make any first working day hearing impossible. On those occasions when the first practicable working day is late enough to allow papers to be timeously delivered to hearing members the hearing may be able to consider and dispose of the case but more frequently the first practicable working day hearing will require to continue the hearing.

1 Noticed above at 19.08.
2 SI 1996/3261, r 6(2) – discussed above at 20.05.
3 SI 1996/3261, r 5(1).

HEARING UNABLE TO DEAL WITH CASE IMMEDIATELY

Section 66

21.11   Where a case comes before a hearing for disposal and the hearing are for any reason unable to dispose of the case right away the hearing may grant warrant for the detention of the child subject to such conditions as to medical or other examination of the child and contact with specified person or class of persons as to the hearing shall appear necessary and expedient and, if they are satisfied as to the criteria under section 70(10) of the Children (Scotland) Act 1995,[1] with authorisation of secure accommodation. Such warrant may, on application by the reporter before expiry, be, on cause shown, extended for a further period not exceeding 22 days and the secure accommodation authorisation[2] may be added in at such a continuation.[3] Section 66(8) of the Act provides that a child shall not, under a warrant granted under s 66(1), be held in a place of safety or in secure accommodation for a period exceeding 66 days from the day when he was first taken to a place of safety. The position could be clearer but the result would seem to be that a hearing may continue a warrant under s 66(5) on more than one occasion provided no single continuation exceeds 22 days and provided the total time in the place of safety does not exceed 66 days.

1 Children (Scotland) Act 1995, s 66(1), (4) and (6); Children's Hearings (Scotland) Rules 1996, SI 1996/3261, r 27 Forms 12 and 13.
2 SI 1996/3261, Form 15.
3 C(S)A 1995, s 66(5); Forms 14 and 15.

Grounds not admitted

21.12   The hearing may be unable to proceed with the case for a number of reasons, such as the failure of a relevant person to appear but one of the most common reasons for the hearing not being able to deal with the case is the non-acceptance of grounds of referral by the child or a relevant person[1] or the perceived inability of the child to understand the grounds[2] and consequential direction to the reporter to make application to the sheriff for a proof under s 68. As we shall see[3] there is little likelihood in practice of the proof before the sheriff being determined within 22 days – still less within any shorter period. Accordingly, where a warrant is necessary the hearing should in the first instance grant the warrant for the maximum period of 22 days. In a case of any complexity the reporter may require to return to a hearing for one or more continuations, with or without variations, in terms of s 66(5). If the hearing has not been able to dispose of the case within the 66 days the reporter may apply to the sheriff for warrant for further detention under s 67.[4] Where a warrant is granted pending the decision of the sheriff on the grounds of referral it may be necessary and appropriate for a hearing to use its powers to require the child, subject to s 90 of the Act, to submit to any medical or other examination,[5] regulate contact[6] and to authorise secure accommodation.[7] A hearing may feel it inappropriate to use its powers to require medical examination or treatment however,[8] other than urgent treatment neces-sary in the interests of the child, which might be of the nature of investi-gating grounds of referral which have not yet been admitted. A s 66 warrant, unlike a warrant under s 69(3) (which can only be granted after the grounds have been admitted or proved), does not permit the child to be required to attend or to reside for the purposes of investigation at a hospital, clinic etc.

1 Children (Scotland) Act 1995, s 65(7).
2 C(S)A 1995, s 65(9).
3 Below at 36.05.
4 Below at 21.28 ff.
5 C(S)A 1995, s 66(4)(a).
6 C(S)A 1995, s 66(4)(a).
7 C(S)A 1995, s 66(6).
8 Always subject to the limitations imported by the provisions of the Age of Legal Capacity (Scotland) Act 1991. See discussion at 13.17ff above and elsewhere.

DETENTION OF CHILD AFTER GROUNDS OF REFERRAL ADMITTED OR PROVED: SECTION 69 OF THE CHILDREN (SCOTLAND) ACT 1995

Dispositive hearing continuing case for investigation

21.13   A dispositive hearing may always continue the case[1] to a subse-quent hearing where they are satisfied that, in order to complete their consideration of the case, further investigation is required. These investi-gations may be such as to cause the hearing to 'require the child to attend, or reside at, any clinic, hospital or other establishment during a period not exceeding twenty-two days.'[2] There must always be something further to investigate: it is not consonant with the philosophy of the system for the hearing to continue a case simply because it would like to mull over the case. Moreover, the lack of continuity of identity of hearing members mili-tates against this. However in certain cases, particularly where a child is involved in multiple referrals, a continuation may be desirable and permissible even when the further investigation amounts to seeing how the child is able to settle.

1 Children (Scotland) Act 1995, s 69(2).
2 C(S)A 1995, s 69(3).

Detention of child during continuation for investigation (Section 69(7))

21.14   Where a hearing continues a case for further investigation and is satisfied that keeping a child in a place of safety is necessary in the inter-ests of safeguarding or promoting the child's welfare or that there is reason to believe that she or he will not otherwise attend the subsequent hearing, the hearing may grant warrant valid for a period of 22 days or till the date of the continued hearing, whichever is shorter[1]. Such a warrant may also contain conditions including conditions as to contact[2], conditions requiring the child, subject to s 90 of the Act,[3] to allow medical examination or treatment[4] and conditions authorising secure accommodation.[5] It is clear[6] that this period of 22 days is in addition to the period of 66 days mentioned in s 66. Where a child is to be kept at or attends at a place under s 69(10) of the Act, the hearing may order non-disclosure of that place.[7]

1 Children (Scotland) Act 1995, s 69(2) and (5).
2 C(S)A 1995, s 69(4).
3 Which limits such orders by reference to the provisions of the Age of Legal Capacity (Scotland) Act 1991. See discussion at 13.17ff and 21.12 above.
4 C(S)A 1995, s 69(9).
5 C(S)A 1995, s 69(11); Children's Hearings (Scotland) Rules 1996, SI 1996/3261, Forms 18 and 19.
6 Because C(S)A 1995, s 66(1) opens thus: 'Without prejudice to any other powers . . .'.
7 C(S)A 1995, s 69(10).

THE OPERATION OF SECTION 69

General

21.15 The powers of hearings in relation to disposal will be discussed later.[1] In the meantime it may be observed that a hearing may continue a case to a subsequent date for further investigation.[2] No limitation is specified in section 69 of the 1995 Act but generally two or three weeks is considered appropriate. These further investigations may be carried out by social workers and/or others and embodied in further report(s).

1 See Chapter 25, particularly 25.17 ff.
2 Children (Scotland) Act 1995, s 69(2).

A requirement to reside or attend – s 69(3)

21.16 If specialised investigation is required, the hearing, when continuing to a later date, may issue a requirement to attend or reside at a clinic, hospital or other establishment during a period not exceeding 22 days.[1] Such a requirement, while it places an obligation, ultimately enforceable, on the child to comply, does not have the force of a warrant and if the child does not choose to fulfil it she or he cannot by virtue of such requirement be taken to the clinic etc. by force. Accordingly if, for example, a hearing continued consideration of the case of 'Philippa' from Wednesday 5 August 1998 till Wednesday 2 September 1998 with the condition that she reside at the Fred Stone Family and Psychiatric Unit, Yorkhill for as long as the unit should consider necessary, not exceeding 22 days, to examine and report, it would be open for Philippa to attend or not.

1 Children (Scotland) Act 1995, s 69(3); SI 1996/3261, Form 20.

Child fulfilling the requirement

21.17   If, in the example given, Philippa attended the Unit, and had only been asked to reside there for, say, 12 days, it would be open to the hearing on 2 September to continue further and to make a residential or attendance requirement for the remaining 10 days. The provision that the period of required residence or attendance is not to exceed 22 days in all would rule out a further requirement of a duration which would result in this period being exceeded.

Child failing to fulfil the requirement: s 69(4) warrant

21.18   Where the child fails to fulfil a s 69(3) requirement a children's hearing may on the motion of the reporter or *ex proprio motu* grant a warrant under subsection (4).[1] This may be done at the hearing to which the earlier hearing had continued the case or at a hearing convened for the purpose by the reporter. Such a warrant is authority to the person named in the warrant[2] to find the child, remove him or her to a place of safety and, where the place of safety is not the clinic etc. named in the s 69(3) requirement, to take the child to that establishment for the purposes mentioned in the requirement.[3] Such a warrant may also contain such conditions (subject always to the provisions of s 90 of the Act, which incorporate the relevant provisions of the Age of Legal Capacity (Scotland) Act 1991) requiring the child to submit to any medical or to other examination or treatment and conditions to regulate contact.[4] It may also, where the secure accommodation criteria are in the hearing's views satisfied, authorise secure accommodation.[5] In addition it may contain an order by the hearing that the place where the child is being kept shall not be disclosed to any person or class of person.[6] A warrant so granted shall be granted for such period as appears to the hearing to be appropriate provided that no such warrant shall permit the keeping of a child in a place of safety beyond expiry of 22 days from its date or beyond the day of the next hearing of the child's case, whichever is earlier.[7]

1 Children (Scotland) Act 1995, s 69(4); Children's Hearings (Scotland) Rules 1996, SI 1996/3261, r 27, Form 16.
2 SI 1996/3261, Form 16.
3 C(S)A 1995, s 69(5).
4 C(S)A 1995, s 69(9).
5 C(S)A 1995, s 69(11).
6 C(S)A 1995, s 69(10).
7 C(S)A 1995, s 69(6).

Continuation of s 69(4) warrant at the 'next hearing'?

21.19   There is no explicit provision for the continuation of such a warrant. The Children's Hearings (Scotland) Rules provide no form for such a continuation, although they do so provide for such forms in relation to continuations of warrants under s 66 of the 1995 Act and also for warrants under s 63, which may be continued under the authority conferred by s 66(5) which is applied to s 63 warrants by s 63(5).

Furthermore: if there were statutory authority for the hearing to continue a s 69(4) warrant one would expect that such warrants would be mentioned in s 16(4)(a)(ii) of the Act, which applies the s 16 principles of consulting the child and no non-beneficial order to specified decisions of hearings including a continuation under s 66(5). These considerations make it difficult to resist the conclusion that the 'next hearing' is powerless to continue the s 69(4) warrant even although that hearing takes place while the 22 day period in the clinic etc. specified in the s 69(3) requirement which gave rise to the s 69(4) warrant might still have some, or conceivably all,[1] of its time to run. It could surely not be intended that such a hearing had the power to issue a fresh s 69(4) warrant. If it were legitimate to issue a fresh warrant there would scarcely be any necessity for the elaborate provisions in the Act for continuations and styles for such continuations in the Rules. The answer to the foregoing problem may lie in the consideration that a 'next hearing' dealing with a child who had failed to fulfil a s 69(3) requirement, and in respect of whom a s 69(4) warrant had had to be granted and executed, would generally be a child in respect of whom the hearing would be satisfied that keeping that child in a place of safety would be necessary in the interests of safeguarding or promoting the child's welfare. In addition the hearing would generally have reason to believe that the child might not attend the subsequent hearing of the case and that therefore a warrant under s 69(2) and (7)[2], with a condition under s 69(9)(a) requiring the child (always subject to s 90) to submit to medical or other examination or treatment (at the clinic etc. mentioned in the s 69(3) requirement) was required.

1 If the child was found on the day of the 'next hearing' and taken to a place of safety which was not the specified clinic etc and then directly to the hearing.
2 Noticed above at 21.14.

Section 69(7) warrant

21.20   Where a hearing continues a case for further investigation under s 69(2) of the 1995 Act and is satisfied that keeping the child in a place of safety is necessary in the interests of safeguarding or promoting the welfare of the child or that there is reason to believe that the child may not attend the subsequent hearing of the case they may grant a place of safety warrant.[1] Such a warrant may (subject always to the provisions of s 90 of the Act, which incorporate the relevant provisions of the Age of Legal Capacity (Scotland) Act 1991) require the child to submit to medical examination or treatment and may regulate contact.[2] It may also, where the secure accommodation criteria are thought to be present, authorise secure accommodation[3] and may also contain an order by the hearing that the place where the child is to be kept shall not be disclosed to any specified person or class of persons.[4]

1 Children (Scotland) Act 1995, s 69(7); Children's Hearings (Scotland) Rules 1996, SI 1996/3261, r 27, Form 18.
2 C(S)A 1995, s 69(9).
3 C(S)A 1995, s 69(11).
4 C(S)A 1995, s 69(10).

Multiple s 69(7) warrants?

21.21 It has been said[1] that a s 69(7) warrant, although limited to 22 days in the first instance and not capable of being continued, may be granted of new at a continued hearing and that there would be, at least in principle, no limit to the number of times that such a warrant could be so granted.[2] For the reasons outlined above[3] it is submitted that this may be open to question. (The provisions in s 67(1) regarding warrant by the sheriff for further detention make it clear – by the words 'or under this subsection' that multiple warrants are competent under that section. There is no similar clarity in s 69(7).)

1 Norrie *Children (Scotland) Act 1995* (1998) at p 142; Norrie *Children's Hearings in Scotland* at 158 and 170.
2 As Norrie acknowledges in *Children's Hearings in Scotland* at 158.
3 Above at 21.19.

Form of and execution of warrants

21.22 Forms 5 to 19 of the Schedule to the Children's Hearings (Scotland) Rules 1996 are to be used.[1] The person empowered to execute the warrant is 'the applicant' whose name and address and 'where appropriate' full designation is to be provided. The wording of the form may be varied as circumstances require.[2]

1 See chart contained in SI 1996/3261, r 27.
2 SI 1996/3261, r 2(2)(b).

OTHER WARRANTS AND ORDERS INVOLVING DETENTION OF CHILD

Continuation of CPO and associated directions

21.23 Where a CPO has been granted by the sheriff[1] the initial hearing under s 59(2) of the 1995 Act may decide to continue the CPO[2] and thereby continue the detention of the child. It may also continue (or not) associated directions concerning parental responsibilities and rights.[3]

1 Children (Scotland) Act 1995, s 57 – discussed above at Chs 5, 6 and 8.
2 C(S)A 1995, s 59(4).
3 C(S)A 1995, s 59(4); Children's Hearings (Scotland) Rules 1996, SI 1996/3261, Forms 6 and 7. NB the heading of Form 7 includes a reference to 'first authorisation of removal of child to place of safety' and its para 1, which lists possible variations, reflects this ('The applicant shall be authorised to remove the child . . .'). Section 59(4) does not permit the hearing to make a direction of its own and the removal of a child seems more than a variation: how then can a s 59(4) order ever contain a 'first authoristation to remove the child . . .'?

Child arrested by police: s 63(5)(a) warrants

21.24 Where a child has been arrested by the police and kept in a place of safety but no prosecution of the child is to take place and the reporter has been informed, the reporter must first of all consider whether compulsory measures of supervision are required. If the decision is in the negative, the reporter directs that the child be no longer kept in the place of safety;[1] if the answer is in the affirmative then a hearing arranged by the reporter in terms of s 63(1) of the Act may consider granting a warrant to keep the child in the place of safety and subsections (3) to (8) of s 66 of the Act shall apply to such warrant as they apply to a s 66(1) warrant.[2] The application of subsections (3) to (8) of s 66 to s 63(1) warrants substantially equates such warrants with s 66(1) warrants, already discussed.[3] The inclusion of s 66(5) and (8) amongst the provisions applied to s 63(5)(a) warrants authorises continuations subject to a maximum over-all period of 66 days. However, exclusion of s 66(1) would seem to have the result that the reporter's right to apply to the sheriff for a warrant for further extension[4] has no application to s 63(5)(a) warrants.

1 Children (Scotland) Act 1995, s 63(1) and (3).
2 C(S)A 1995, s 63(5)(a); Children's Hearings (Scotland) Rules 1996, SI 1996/3261, r 27, Forms 8 to 11.
3 Above at 21.11 ff.
4 C(S)A 1995, s 67, discussed above.

CONSIDERATIONS RELEVANT TO THE GRANTING OF WARRANTS BY HEARINGS

The s 16 principles

21.25   When a hearing is considering whether or not to grant a warrant under s 66(1), or s 69(4) or (7) or to continue a warrant under s 66(5) [1] they are bound to have regard to all three of the s 16 principles.[2]

1 But not warrants under the Children (Scotland) Act 1995, s 45(4) – but see discussion above at 21.04.
2 C(S)A 1995, s 16(4)(a)(ii).

The views of the child: rule 26

21.26   In relation to the warrants and other orders listed in r 26 of the Children's Hearings (Scotland) Rules 1996 the hearing must 'take steps under rule 15 to obtain the views of the child, and endeavour to obtain the views of any relevant person and of any safeguarder, if attending the hearing, on what arrangements would be in the best interests of the child.'

21.27   The warrants and orders so listed are those under the following provisions of the Children (Scotland) Act 1995:
- s 45(4) and (5) – warrants to find a child, keep in a place of safety and bring before a hearing;
- s 59(4) – continuation of a CPO;
- s 63(5) – warrant to keep a child in place of safety following arrest;
- s 66(1) and (5) – warrants where children's hearings are unable to dispose of case;

- s 69(4) – warrant for fulfilment of requirement to attend or reside at clinic, hospital etc.;
- s 69(7) – warrant to take a child to and keep in place of safety while case continued under s 59(4);
- s 59(4) – to continue direction given under s 58 (direction as to parental responsibilities or parental rights when CPO made);
- warrants under the Secure Accommodation (Scotland) Regulations 1996;[1]
- s 69(3) – requirement to reside at a clinic etc.

1 SI 1996/3255.

WARRANT GRANTED BY THE SHERIFF FOR FURTHER DETENTION OF CHILD

The substantial provisions of section 67

21.28 Section 67(1) of the Children (Scotland) Act 1995 provides that where a child is being kept in a place of safety under a s 66 warrant or under s 67(1) itself the reporter may at any time prior to the expiry of that warrant apply to the sheriff for a warrant to keep the child in the place of safety after the expiry of the earlier warrant. The wording of subsection (1) makes it clear that such a warrant may be applied for on more than one occasion and indeed there is no statutory limit on the number of times such a warrant may be granted. The warrant must specify the date on which it will expire and may contain any such requirement or condition or additional orders (medical examination and treatment, contact, secure accommodation authorisation and non-disclosure of whereabouts) as may be contained in a s 66 warrant.[1] Any secure accommodation authorisation or non-disclosure order expires with the warrant.[2]

1 Children (Scotland) Act 1995, s 67(2) and (3).
2 C(S)A 1995, s 67(3).

Timing of application

21.29 An application may be made 'at any time prior to the expiry of that warrant [i e the warrant of the hearing or the warrant of the sheriff under s 67(1)]'. It therefore follows that the reporter may competently apply to the sheriff during the currency of the first s 66 warrant and it may be sensible to do this in the course of the procedure before the sheriff under s 68.

Application form and grounds for application

21.30 The style of application is provided in Form 59 of the Act of Sederunt (Child Care and Maintenance) Rules 1997. The form is substantially similar to that in the Motion to Set Aside or Vary CPO, discussed already[1] but a notable difference is that here the applicant is the reporter and not the local authority (which in hearings procedure, as opposed to child protection procedures, generally has no separate standing). The form requires the applicant to state inter alia the reason for the application: it is important for such reason to be clearly stated since such applications may only be granted 'on cause shown'. The form also seeks reasons for any order sought regarding non-disclosure of whereabouts of the child or service of restricted papers on the child.

1 See above at 9.08 ff.

Procedure before the sheriff

21.31 The sheriff, after hearing parties and allowing such further proce-dure as he thinks fit makes an order granting or refusing the application.[1] In principle the hearing before the sheriff could follow, *mutatis mutandis*, the procedures in an Application to Vary etc discussed above[2] but in prac-tice such hearings are generally associated with the proof procedures under s 68 of the Children (Scotland) Act 1995 and are comparatively brief in duration. All three of the s 16 principles apply[3] and the sheriff will consequently require to be told where the child is being held, and why further detention is necessary and if the child wishes to express a view and, if so, what that view is.

1 SI 1997/291, r 3.43.
2 Above at 9.24 ff.
3 Children (Scotland) Act 1995, s 16(1)–(4)(b)(iii).

Service on the child – the views of the child

21.32 As always when the s 16 principle of consulting the views of the child is applicable to a decision of the sheriff rules 3.3 to 3.5 of the Act of Sederunt (Child Care and Maintenance) Rules 1997 come into play.[1] Hence the possibility, mentioned already in the context of dispensing with service on the child, of appointing a safeguarder or curator *ad litem*. Where a child has indicated a wish to express a view the sheriff must give that opportunity and may take steps to facilitate their expression.[2] The views of the child may be obtained in any of the ways set out in r 3.5(2). At the stage of a s 68 proof there may be a safeguarder or curator *ad litem* in post and in that event the sheriff may look to him or her for the child's views and will pay due regard to his or her assessment of the interests of the child.

1 SI 1997/291, r 3.2.
2 SI 1997/291, r 3.5.

'Confidential' views of the child

21.33 The general implications of the provisions affecting the sheriff's obtaining the views of the child have been discussed.[1] The concept of hearing at this stage the child views which the child may wish to keep secret from other parties is an interesting one. If the sheriff receives confidential views from the child and decides to exercise the power under r 3.5(4) of the 1997 Rules to cause the written views of the child to be placed in a confidential envelope which is to be available to the sheriff only, then, in the event of the said views significantly influencing the decision, the argument that this constituted a violation of Article 6(1) of The European Convention of Human Rights would have some plausibility.[2] The hearing has no power to receive confidential views. The sheriff has no power to pass these views to the hearing or anyone else. It is however submitted that if the sheriff does receive confidential views from the child which he thinks should affect the decision as to the further detention of the child then the sheriff would be obliged to give such weight to those views as he thought right.

1 Above at 4.10 ff; see in particular the full discussion 'Interpretation of the confidentiality provisions' at 4.15.
2 *McMichael v United Kingdom* (1995) 20 EHRR 205: see especially paras 78 to 84.

CHAPTER 22

Structure of a children's hearing

HEARINGS AND WHO MAY ATTEND THEM

Children's hearings

22.01 In this chapter, unless otherwise stated, 'hearing' or 'children's hearing' is used to refer to a hearing as defined in s 93(1) of the Children (Scotland) Act 1995, i e not to a business meeting. Accordingly, when reference is from time to time made to 'all stages of the hearing' this means a hearing proper and not a business meeting. Hearings are held in private with no unnecessary persons present.

Terminology

22.02 The term 'hearing' is generally used to refer both to the tribunal of three panel members and to a sitting of the tribunal, although the 1995 Act tends to use the full term 'children's hearing' where referring to the tribunal and the term 'hearing' to refer to an individual sitting: thus in s 69(1) '... the children's hearing shall consider those grounds ... and shall – (a) continue the case to a subsequent hearing'. By contrast, the children, women and men in the Scottish street use the word 'panel' to cover both meanings: 'I had to go to the panel yesterday and they told me to come to another panel in three weeks' time'. The term hearing is also used in the Act to embrace a series of hearings dealing with the child.[1] Panel members themselves sometimes use the term 'hearing' in a broad sense to refer to the whole event: 'The hearing became much more relaxed after the child had given her views – it was a good hearing'.

1 E g in Children (Scotland) Act 1995, s 45(1): '[The child] shall – (a) have the right to attend all stages of the hearing'.

The essential components of a hearing

22.03 For a lawful hearing there have to be present three panel members, amongst whom each sex is represented, one of whom shall act as chairperson,[1] and the reporter. A hearing may consider the case of a child in the absence of the child, relevant person and representatives[2] but it would be unusual for a hearing to come to any substantive decision in the absence of the child.

1 Children (Scotland) Act 1995, s 39(5).
2 Children's Hearings (Scotland) Rules 1996, SI 1996/3261, r 20(2); cf C(S)A 1995, s 45(2).

The reporter at a hearing

22.04   The Children (Scotland) Act 1995 does not explicitly insist that the reporter be present but his duties under the Act and the Children's Hearings (Scotland) Rules 1996, notably r 31 which requires the reporter to record the proceedings, make it clear that the reporter's presence is essential. The obligations on the reporter in terms of r 31 are related to a 'children's hearing'[1] and 'children's hearing', in the 1996 Rules, means 'a children's hearing as defined in section 39(3) of the Act'[2] and not a children's hearing as defined in s 93(1) of the Act (which definition excludes business meetings). Accordingly, the reporter must be present at business meetings and report their proceedings. Section 51(12)(b) of the Act, by conferring on the reporter the right to make an appeal from the sheriff to the sheriff principal and the Court of Session 'on behalf of the children's hearing' is a statutory recognition of the reporter's relationship with the children's hearing and the reporter's function as adviser as well as clerk to the hearing, although without explicit statutory provision[3] is now well established. It must be emphasised that the hearing cannot be bound by the advice tendered to it by the reporter and that the procedural management of the hearing remains with the chairman. Nevertheless, the concept of the initiator of proceedings (even although these proceedings are in no sense to be equated with a prosecution) acting in effect as clerk and legal adviser to the tribunal remains anomalous. In *McMichael v United Kingdom* the Commission opined that a hearing was not a tribunal such as to comply with Article 6(1) of the European Convention because 'its members fail to offer the necessary guarantees of independence' but the court itself did not consider it necessary to resolve that issue.[4] The court did, however, insist on the importance of a 'fair – adversarial[5] – trial'. The non-adversarial nature of hearings procedure has been repeatedly asserted.[6] The reporter's advice is in practice available to all parties and reporters should adopt a neutral stance. It is submitted, however, that the position of the reporter as de facto legal adviser to the hearing – acknowledged in *Miller v Council of the Law Society of Scotland*[7] – as well as the person vested with the responsibility of bringing the child to a hearing is anomalous and may lead to difficulties in relation to compliance with Article 6 of the European Convention on Human Rights.

1 SI 1996/3261, r 31(1).
2 SI 1996/3261, r 2(1).
3 Cf Martin, Fox and Murray, *Children Out of Court* p 277.
4 (20) EHRR 205 at 230 and 236.
5 (20) EHRR at 237.
6 E g *in W v Kennedy* 1988 SLT 583.
7 2000 SLT 513 at 516L, noticed above at 2.11.

Panel members and individual hearings

22.05   The selection of the chairman and members of any individual children's hearings from among the generality of members of the relevant children's panel is a matter for the chairman or deputy chairman of the children's panel who may make standing arrangements, after consulting with the reporter and, if he wishes, panel members themselves.[1] If standing arrangements are made, they should be kept under review.[2] There is no legal requirement for continuity of membership between a hearing and a continued hearing although in particular cases arrangements may be made to allow one or more members of the original hearing to participate in the continued hearing.

1 Children's Hearings (Scotland) Rules 1996, SI 1996/3261, r 10(1).
2 SI 1996/3261, r 10(2).

Participants in hearings

22.06   The other persons participating in a hearing may be divided into three, sometimes overlapping, classes, namely, persons who may be placed under an obligation to attend, persons who have a right to attend and persons who may attend at the discretion of the chairman.

PERSONS WHO MAY BE PLACED UNDER OBLIGATION TO ATTEND

A child

22.07   A child whose case has been referred to a hearing and who has been properly 'notified' of the hearing, falls under an obligation to attend the hearing in terms of the notification.[1] The hearing has, in cases involving a Schedule 1 offence, the power to dispense with the child's attendance for all or part of the hearing if satisfied that his presence is unnecessary.[2] The hearing may in any case dispense with the child's presence if satisfied that such presence would be detrimental to his interest.[3] Such dispensation may be determined at a business meeting.[4] Release of a child from the obligation to attend does not take away the child's right to attend.[5]

1 Children (Scotland) Act 1995, s 45(1)(b); for discussion of 'notification' see above at 20.05 ff; for discussion of warrants see Ch 21.
2 C(S)A 1995, s 45(2)(a)
3 C(S)A 1995, s 45(2)(b).
4 C(S)A 1995, s 64(3)(a), Children's Hearings (Scotland) Rules 1996, SI 1996/3261, r 4(2)(b) – discussed above at 18.04.
5 The wording of C(S)A 1995, s 45(2) makes this clear: 'Without prejudice to subsection (1)(a) above . . .'.

Presence of child at review under s 73(8)(a)(v)

22.08   A supervision requirement expires automatically unless reviewed and continued within one year of the date on which it was made or continued.[1] Where a supervision requirement is due to expire within three months the reporter must fix a review.[2] If a child who has been properly convened fails to appear, a warrant may be granted under s 45(1) of the Children (Scotland) Act 1995 so that his or her presence may be secured at a later hearing. In the event, however, of the expiry date being imminent and the child absenting himself from the review, it is thought that it would be lawful for the hearing to consider the merits of the case and, if they thought it appropriate to do so, continue or terminate the requirement in the absence of the child[3] provided they were satisfied that the reporter had taken all practicable steps to effect notification under rule 6 of the Children's Hearings (Scotland) Rules 1996 and generally to secure the child's attendance.

1 Children (Scotland) Act 1995, s 73(2).
2 C(S)A 1995, s 73(8)(a)(v).
3 Children's Hearings (Scotland) Rules 1996, SI 1996/3261, r 20(1).

Relevant person(s)

22.09   The definition of 'relevant person' has already been noticed.[1] A relevant person in respect of a child is obliged to attend at all stages of the hearing unless the 'hearing are satisfied that it would be unreasonable to require his attendance, or that his attendance would be unnecessary for the proper consideration of the case'.[2] The relevant person[3] must be notified in writing.[4] The definition of a relevant person includes 'any person who appears to be a person who ordinarily (and other than by reason only of his employment) has charge of, or control over, the child'.[5] The reporter must judge as to whether such a person is a relevant person within the meaning of the section and that person, once notified, will come under a prima facie obligation to attend. The reporter may seek guidance from a business meeting on this point.[6] The relevant person's obligation to attend all stages of the hearing persists 'unless the hearing are satisfied that it would be unreasonable to require his attendance or that his attendance is unnecessary for the proper consideration of the case'.[7] Such a dispensation may be determined at a business meeting.[8] A relevant person who has been required to attend and who fails to attend is guilty of an offence punishable by a fine on summary conviction.[9] The Act is silent on who has the duty to report, or at least to consider reporting, an offending relevant person to the procurator fiscal. It is submitted that this has been impliedly left to the discretion of the reporter. In practice such prosecutions are very rare. It is not stated in the Act that non-attendance, to be an offence, has to be wilful but it is thought, on the analogy with contempt of court by non-attendance,[10] that this must be so. It is hardly conceivable that any parent would be prosecuted under this provision if any reasonable excuse were known.

1 Above at 1.20 ff.
2 Children (Scotland) Act 1995, s 45(8)(b).
3 As discussed at 1.20ff.
4 Children's Hearings (Scotland) Rules 1996, SI 1996/3261, r 7(1).
5 C(S)A 1995, s 93(2)(b).
6 C(S)A 1995, s 64(3)(a), SI 1996/3261, r 4(2)(a) – discussed above at 18.03.
7 C(S)A 1995, s 45(8)(b).
8 C(S)A 1995, s 64(3)(a), SI 1996/3261, r 4(2)(c).
9 C(S)A 1995, s 45(9).
10 Cf *Pirie v Hawthorn* 1962 JC 69.

PERSONS WHO MAY ATTEND AS OF RIGHT

The child

22.10 A child who has been lawfully convened to a hearing has an unqualified right to attend at all stages of the hearing, i e at the first hearing and at any continuation thereof until disposal. As already noticed[1] the obligation of the child to attend may be dispensed with, but the right of the child to attend cannot be removed. Commenting on the parallel provisions in the Social Work (Scotland) Act 1968, Lord President Hope, delivering the opinion of the Court in the Orkney case, stated[2]:

> '.... what we have been doing is to analyse where the balance lies between the two important provisions for their [children's] protections which Parliament has laid down in the Act. The protection against harm or distress, which is what s 40(2) is all about, is as important as the protection against a determination of the case until the grounds for referral have been accepted or established, which is what s 42(1) is designed to achieve. . . . . . . The discretion which if given to the children's hearing on s 40(2) may seem at first sight to involve a denial of rights to the children. But properly understood its true purpose is that of protection where the children's hearing are satisfied that this is required, and it is important that the opportunity to provide that protection where it is most needed should not be denied to them.'

Having regard to the thrust of these observations it is submitted that releasing the child from the obligation to attend is not, in the case of a child who is not so young or manifestly otherwise unable to contribute to the deliberations of the hearing, a decision which should be taken lightly. Of course where real detriment to the child is in prospect she or he should not be required to attend, but otherwise the consideration that the child has a 'right' to attend is not a complete answer: the release of the obligation to attend may give the message to the child that his or her attendance is not expected.

1 Above at 22.06.
2 *Sloan v B* 1991 SLT 530 at 549 I and J.

Very young children

22.11 The Children (Scotland) Act 1995, like the Social Work (Scotland) Act 1968, and the Children's Hearings (Scotland) Rules 1996, like the 1986 Rules which preceded them, do not recognise any category of 'very young children', i e, those who not only could not understand grounds of referral, but those who are too young to make any valid contribution at all to the consideration of their cases. The practicability of having very young children (e g, the baby in *McGregor v L* 1981 SLT 194) physically present at a hearing may be doubtful. The value of such a child's being present when in any event the hearing (unless they decide to discharge the referral) will be bound to direct an application to the sheriff for a finding (because the child is incapable of understanding what is going on[1]) is not obvious. The language of s 45(1) of the 1995 Act, in referring, for example, to the child being 'under obligation to attend those stages in accordance with the notice' appears to presuppose a child old enough to be aware of being 'under obligation' and therefore inappropriate in relation to babies and very young children. It is submitted that, while it may be good practice to try to have even very young children brought to the sitting of the hearing, even for only part thereof, the failure to bring a baby or very young child to a hearing when it was difficult and pointless so to do would not be fatal to the legality of the proceedings. In a case of doubt the reporter may seek a determination at a business meeting.[2]

1 Children (Scotland) Act 1995, s 65(9)(a).
2 SI 1996/3261, r 4(2)(b).

Relevant Person(s) – when relevant person may be excluded

22.12   Under s 45(8) of the Children (Scotland) Act 1995 a relevant person has the right, subject to the right of the hearing to exclude persons under s 46, to attend 'at all stages of a children's hearing who are considering the case of a child'. It is submitted that 'consider' is not here being given a narrow construction but should be broadly construed so that, for example, the parent is given a right to attend a hearing, even if convened only for the limited purpose of considering whether a warrant to detain a child should be granted, or as the case may be continued, under s 45(4), s 66(1), s 69(4), s 69(7) and s 63(5)(a) of the Act. A relevant person may be excluded by the chairman for so long as is necessary in the interests of the child where the hearing are satisfied that they must do so in order to obtain the views of the child or where that person's presence is causing or is likely to cause significant distress to the child. After re-admission of the excluded person the chairman must explain to him or her the substance of what has happened in his or her absence. The hearing does not have the power of the sheriff[1] to preserve the confidentiality of the child's views.

1 Act of Sederunt (Child Care and Maintenance Rules) 1997, SI 1997/291, r 3.5(4) – discussed above at 4.12.

Safeguarder and curator *ad litem*

22.13   Any safeguarder appointed by a children's hearing is entitled to attend all stages of a hearing till disposal.[1] A safeguarder or curator *ad litem* appointed by the sheriff is not strictly entitled to attend *qua* safeguarder and would be admitted either as a person assisting the child or as a person whose presence was, in the opinion of the chairman, justified.[2]

1 Children's Hearings (Scotland) Rules 1996, SI 1996/3261, r 14(3).
2 SI 1996/3261, r 11(1), r 13(d).

Representatives of child and relevant persons(s)

22.14   Any child or relevant person attending any stage of a hearing may, in addition to being personally present, each be accompanied by one person (it may be the same person or one each) and that person may assist in the discussion.[1] The representative of the relevant person is subject to the same possibility of exclusion etc[2] as the relevant person. There is no provision allowing for the 'representative' to be present in the absence of the parent or child, but a hearing would allow and, in the writer's opinion, would be entitled to allow representations, e g by a solicitor, to be made on behalf of a parent or child genuinely incapacitated from attending.

1 Children's Hearings (Scotland) Rules 1996, SI 1996/3261, r 11(1) and (2).
2 Above at 22.12.

Council on Tribunals

22.15 A member of the Council on Tribunals, or of the Scottish Committee of that Council may attend and be provided with the appropriate documents in his or her capacity as such.[1]

1 Children (Scotland) Act 1995, s 43(3)(a); SI 1996/3261, r 5(6).

The media

22.16 The Children (Scotland) Act 1995 provides that a bona fide representative of a newspaper or news agency may attend but always subject to the hearing's power to exclude such a person if satisfied that it is necessary to do so in the child's interests so as to obtain the child's views or if they think the presence of the media is causing or is likely to cause significant distress to the child.[1] This provision is a direct result of the Orkney case and is in contrast to the provisions of s 35(3) of the Social Work (Scotland) Act 1968 which, bracketing in the same subsection the press and the Council on Tribunals, provided that nothing in s 35(1) and (2) (the privacy and minimum number of persons provisions) should authorise the exclusion of bona fide representatives (plural) of a newspaper or news agency. The reader is referred to Lord Clyde's narration and comments at paras 12.38–12.56 and 18.35–18.38 of his report. It is submitted that hearings should be astute to protect the interests of the privacy of children and have regard to Article 16 of the UN Convention on the Rights of the Child.[2] Where the hearing has exercised its power to exclude, the chairman may, after the exclusion has ended, disclose to the media representative the substance of what has taken place in his or her absence.[3] Section 44 of the 1995 Act prohibits the publication of any information which is intended to or is likely to identify any child,[4] child's address or the school of any child concerned in the proceedings. Breach of this prohibition is an offence subject to a statutory defence.[5] The Scottish Ministers may waive this prohibition in relation to proceedings before hearings where such dispensation is in the interests of justice.[6]

1 Children (Scotland) Act 1995, s 43(3)(b) and (4)(a) and (b).
2 '1. No child shall be subjected to arbitrary or unlawful interference with his or her privacy, family, home or correspondence, nor to unlawful attack on his or her honour and reputation.
2. The child has the right to the protection of the law against such interference or attacks.'
3 C(S)A 1995, s 43(5).
4 Not only the referred child, but any child involved – *McArdle v Orr* 1993 SLT 463.

5 The sheriff and the Court of Session may dispense with these requirements of s 44(1) in relation to proceedings before them – see s 44(5)(a) and (b); for further discussion of the practicalities in relation to the media see below at 23.04.
6 As applied to the Scottish constitutional framework by virtue of the Scotland Act 1998, ss 52(3) and 53(1) and (2)(b).

Social worker

22.17   The presence of the child's or family's social worker is also nowhere stated to be essential but it is clearly implied[1] that his or her presence is expected. A hearing would not normally countenance the possibility of proceeding in the absence of the social worker but if, in an exceptional situation, the social worker did not arrive the proceedings would not thereby be rendered void. In practice the reporter would make telephone enquiries and the chairman could adjourn the case until later in the day under rule 10(4) of the Children's Hearings (Scotland) Rules 1996 or to a later date under rule 10(4) when read with r 10(3), and make such interim decision in relation to the child as seemed best on the available information.

1 Children's Hearings (Scotland) Rules 1996, SI 1996/3261, r 8.

Legal representation at the hearings stage

22.18   There is nothing to prevent the 'representative' of the child or parent at the hearings stage from being a qualified lawyer. This is unusual though by no means rare – a number of solicitors are prepared to represent children for no or nominal remuneration. Full legal aid to cover the actual attendance of a lawyer at the hearing (as opposed to proceedings before the sheriff on application or appeal) is not available, although, under Part II of the Legal Aid (Scotland) Act 1986, limited free legal advice may be available to help the parent and/or child to prepare and present their case to the hearing.

Desirability of increased legal representation?- The UN and European Conventions – The rôle of the legal representative

22.19   Nowadays a court may not normally impose a sentence of imprisonment on any person who has not previously been sentenced to imprisonment or detention unless that person has had access to legal representation after being found guilty and before being sentenced.[1] Compulsory supervision with or without a residential requirement may reasonably be regarded (and certainly is regarded by parents and children) as at least a partial deprivation of liberty,[2] and it could, subject of course to appeal and review, at least in theory, endure for a very long time, and such a disposal may be imposed without the parents or child being legally advised at any stage.[3] The perception that legal representation was unavailable led to the unhappy event of the United Kingdom's reservation[4] in relation to the hearings system to the United Nations Convention on the Rights of the Child. When the European Convention on Human Rights becomes part of Scots domestic law in October 2000 it may well be arguable that effective legal representation is a right by virtue of Article 6 of that Convention.[5] As mentioned by Mr Andrew Lockyer and Professor Fred Stone[6] the argument mounted by defenders of the hearings system against legal 'representation' is not against lawyers being present but against the concept of lawyers presenting the child's or the relevant person's 'case' instead of allowing parties to speak for themselves. As Lockyer and Stone acknowledge, Mrs Barbara Reid, herself a former Chairman of Strathclyde Panel, has noted:

> 'In fact, in recent years the legal profession has become aware of the difference between courts and hearings and most lawyers have adopted the discursive and constructive role required by the hearing forum.'[7]

The Law Society of Scotland has now in place procedures for accrediting solicitors as specialists in the law affecting children.[8] It is submitted that only by developing and ultimately universalising the availability of expert legal assistance – supported by free legal aid – that Scotland's obligations, as part of the United Kingdom, under the UN and European Conventions can be purified. The present principal reporter has emphasised, correctly in the writer's view, the importance of the child's being able to communicate directly with the hearing.[9] As recognised in the words quoted from Mrs Reid, the assistance of a well-qualified legal adviser should not inhibit this. It has been questioned whether a legal representative is entitled, having regard to the confidentiality provisions, to take notes when attending a hearing. In the writer's clear view the professional legal representative must be taken to be aware of his or her professional duties and is entitled to take notes.

1 Criminal Procedure (Scotland) Act 1995, s 204(1).
2 *H and H v McGregor* 1973 SC 95 at 100.
3 Although of course there is the possibility of appeal to the sheriff at which legal representation is available and, in practice, is the norm.
4 CRC/C/2/Rev 4, [Convention on the Rights of the Child Treaty Series No 44 (1992)] p 31. The reservation was withdrawn on 18 April 1997.
5 *Benham v United Kingdom* (1996) 22 EHRR 293; *Airey v Ireland* (1979) 2 EHRR 305; *Artico v Italy* (1980) 3 EHRR 1.
6 Lockyer, A and Stone, F *Juvenile Justice in Scotland* (1997) at 256.
7 Reid, B *Panels and Hearings* in *Juvenile Justice in Scotland* at 195.
8 Noted in Cleland A and Sutherland E E *Children's Rights in Scotland*, 1996, at 4.52.
9 Alan Miller, *The Children's Hearings System and the European Convention: Threat, Challenge or Opportunity?* (May 2000) 45 JLSS 25.

Unmarried father

22.20 The father of a child who is living with the mother where both the father and the mother are parents of the child as defined in s 15(1) of the Children (Scotland) Act 1995 is entitled to attend and is also subject to the provisions anent exclusion in s 46.[1] An unmarried father who is not qualified as a relevant person should consider applying to the court for an order conferring parental responsibilities under s 11(2)(b) of the C(S)A 1995.[2]

1 Children's Hearings (Scotland) Rules 1996, SI 1996/3261, r 12(1).
2 *P v P* 2000 SCLR 477 at 488E.

Escort of person in custody

22.21   A constable, prison officer or other person duly authorised who has in his lawful custody a person who has to attend a hearing is entitled to attend for escort purposes.[1]

1 Children's Hearings (Scotland) Rules 1996, SI 1996/3261, r 12(2).

PERSONS WHO MAY ATTEND AT CHAIRMAN'S DISCRETION

22.22   Children's hearings are to be conducted in private[1] and with a minimum number of persons present.[2] Subject to this the chairman has discretion to admit:

1.   the chairman and members and the clerk of the local CPAC;
2.   trainee panel members and their instructors;
3.   social work students and researchers into the children's hearing system; and
4.   'any other person whose presence at the hearing may in the opinion of the chairman be justified by special circumstances'.[3]

Chairmen exercise a sensible discretion in the number and character of any extra persons they allow to be present: often, for example, the presence of a school teacher or a carer from a children's home is helpful.

1 Children (Scotland) Act 1995, s 43(1).
2 C(S)A 1995, s 43(2).
3 Children's Hearings (Scotland) Rules 1996, SI 1996/3261, r 13.

RECORD OF PROCEEDINGS OF CHILDREN'S HEARINGS

22.23   Rule 31 of the Children's Hearings (Scotland) Rules 1996 imposes upon the reporter the duty of causing a report of the proceedings to be kept. The rule makes certain specific requirements as to what must be recorded, and also prescribes that the reporter may in addition record such other information regarding the proceedings as he thinks appropriate.

22.24   The information which it is obligatory for the reporter to include in his record of proceedings is:

1.   particulars of the place and date of the hearing;

2. the full name and address of the child, and his or her sex and date of birth;
3. the full name and address (so far as these can be obtained) of the father, the mother and any other relevant person in relation to the child;
4. a record as to which (if any) of the persons mentioned in heads (2) and (3) above was present;
5. the full name and address of any representative attending the hearing;
6. the full name and address of any safeguarder;
7. the terms of any decision disposing of the case of the child, or of any decision to issue a warrant, made by the children's hearing or any other course of action taken by them with respect to the child; and
8. in any case where the hearing proceed in accordance with s 65 of the Children (Scotland) Act 1995 –
   (a) particulars of the grounds of referral which are accepted or, as the case may be, not accepted, and by whom;
   (b) a record of any direction under subsection (7) or (9) of s 65 to make application to the sheriff for a finding under that section; and
   (c) a record of whether the children's hearing proceeded to consider the case at a hearing.

22.25   The chairman requires to make or cause to be made a written statement of the decision and the reasons for it and must sign this. The appropriate formulation of reasons is discussed later.[1]

1 Below at 23.31ff.

CHAPTER 23

Conduct of hearing: general

THE RÔLE OF THE CHAIRMAN OF THE HEARING

The chairman of the hearing

23.01 'Except as otherwise provided by these Rules and any other enactment, the procedure at any children's hearing shall be such as the chairman shall in his discretion determine'. The words of rule 10(3) of the Children's Hearings (Scotland) Rules 1996 indicate the key position of the chairman of the hearing and underline the wide discretion accorded to the chairman in controlling the proceedings at a children's hearing. Of course women and men are equally entitled to chair hearings: the Children (Scotland) Act 1995 and the Rules refer always to 'chairman' and that statutory term will be used here. There are no qualifications specially prescribed but in practice chairmen of hearings are experienced panel members. The selection of chairmen for hearings is one of the responsibilities of the chairman of the Children's Panel for a particular local authority area.[1]

1 SI 1996/3261, r 10(1).

Duties of chairman – general

23.02 The chairman's right to regulate procedure and to decide on the persons who may at his discretion be admitted to the hearing and his duty to explain the grounds of referral mean that he in effect takes the lead in the discussion of the child's case but the chairman enjoys no legal primacy. The considerable responsibility of explaining the grounds of referral calls for a fund of legal knowledge and an ability to communicate. The reporter is available to advise[1] but a good chairman will not wish to rely too much on the reporter's support. Hearings sometimes come to a divided decision and in this event the chairman's vote is equal to the vote of each of the other hearing members. More usually, however, there is no split and it is for the chairman, after allowing full discussion, to judge when to bring the discussion to a conclusion and interpret the will of the hearing. Hearings should be conducted openly and fairly, in compliance with the rules of procedure and in a manner which is, so far as possible and consistent with honesty and straightforwardness, friendly and relaxed. It is for the chairman to lead the hearing in trying to achieve, in Barbara Reid's phrase 'the desired atmosphere of openness and co-operation'.[2]

1 Cf above at 22.04.
2 Reid, B *Panels and Hearings* in *Juvenile Justice in Scotland* (1997) at 197.

PRELIMINARIES

23.03   The first main duty of the chairman is to explain the grounds of referral but before embarking on this the chairman should introduce the parties[1] and then ensure that all the rules governing the make-up of the hearing are observed. He should:

- introduce himself and the other hearing members by name and make sure that all present know who else is present – perhaps, so far as necessary, asking people to say who they are;
- take all reasonable steps to ensure that the number of person present is kept to a minimum;[2]
- admit to the hearing all persons having a right and/or duty to attend, i e the child,[3] the relevant person(s),[4] representative(s) of the child and relevant person(s),[5] any member of the Council on Tribunals,[6] a social worker,[7] any escort of a person in custody[8] and a bona fide representative of the media[9] (see next paragraph).
- decide upon who should be admitted of those who may be admitted at discretion – CPAC, panel members being trained, students of the system, and 'any other person whose presence at the hearing may in the opinion of the chairman be justified by special circumstances'.[10] The latter category is helpfully wide and enables the chairman to admit (and, it is thought, allow to participate in the discussion) persons such as carers or teachers who are aware of the needs of the child; and
- keep in mind the reporter's recording duties[11], if necessary asking the reporter if there is any detail he would like to be clarified.

1 Hallet et al (1998) *The Evaluation of Children's Hearings in Scotland*, vol 1 notes at p 42: 'Introductions appeared to be most successful when, once panel members had been introduced, everyone else at the hearing introduced themselves'.
2 Children (Scotland) Act 1995, s 43(2).
3 C(S)A 1995, s 45(1)(b) – discussed above at 22.07, 22.08, 22.10, 22.11.
4 C(S)A 1995, s 45(8)(b) – discussed above at 22.09, 22.12.
5 Children's Hearings (Scotland) Rules 1996, SI 1996/3261, r 11(1) and (2) – discussed above at 22.14.
6 C(S)A 1995, s 43(3)(a) – discussed above at 22.15.
7 Cf SI 1996/3261, r 8 – see discussion above at 22.17.
8 SI 1996/3261, r 12(2).
9 C(S)A 1995, s 43(3)(b).
10 SI 1996/3261, r 13.
11 SI 1996/3261, r 31 – listed above at 22.25.

The media

23.04   It is rare for the media to want to attend but should there be public interest in the case there is likely to be competition. Lord Clyde tells us in relation to the Orkney case (governed by s 35(3) of the Social Work (Scotland) Act 1968, which allowed 'representatives' of the media): 'The press arranged among themselves that some only of their representatives should be present in the room where the hearing sat on 5th March since there was quite inadequate space for all of them'.[1] The current legislation does not say so in express terms but it would seem that where several representatives of the media are interested in attending the chairman must take the responsibility of deciding who the media representative is to be. Publishing information which could identify any child or an address or school is prohibited.[2] The media representative may be excluded by the chairman if this is in the child's interests and the chairman may (or may not) reveal to the media representative what took place during such exclusion.[3]

1 Report of the Enquiry into the Removal of Children from Orkney in February 1991 (the Clyde Report) (HC Papers (1992–93), no 195), para 12.43 – cf above at 22.16.
2 Children (Scotland) Act 1995, s 44 – discussed above at 22.16.
3 C(S)A 1995, s 43(4) and (5).

Defect in notification of party attending?

23.05 It is good practice for the chairman to check that those who are attending in response to a compulsory notification from the reporter have been properly and timeously notified.[1] Should there be any defect in notification, for example insufficient notice, he may, in consultation with the reporter, consider how best to repair any informality. It is thought that a defect in intimation, in contrast to a failure to explain the grounds of referral when the mandatory provisions in s 65(4) of the Children (Scotland) Act 1995 apply,[2] is a defect which may be remedied and that the remedy would be to allow the party aggrieved such further time, if any, as he may reasonably require for further preparation and investigation. It is submitted that the provisions of r 10(3) and (4) of the Children's Hearings (Scotland) Rules 1996 are ample to provide the chairman with the power so to do.

1 Children's Hearings (Scotland) Rules 1996, SI 1996/3261, rr 6 and 7 – discussed above at 20.05–20.13.
2 Cf *Sloan v B* 1991 SLT 530 at 546G.

Defect in notification of absentee?

23.06 If a person who seems to have a right or duty to attend is not present the chairman should check with the reporter that such a person has been duly notified. If this does not occur, and if his or her whereabouts are known it is submitted that this would be a fundamental defect which, if not rectified, would imperil the legality of the proceedings and that therefore it would be essential for the chairman to allow a continuation in order to allow proper notification to be effected. Care and tact are necessary when only one parent appears as the relevant person. The chairman should try to make sure that the other parent, if any, has been properly notified and that there has not been a recent separation resulting in one parent not receiving a letter sent to the family home.

EXPLAINING THE PURPOSE OF THE HEARING

The statutory provision

23.07   In a children's hearing under s 65 of the Children (Scotland) Act 1995 or at a review of a supervision requirement under s 73(8) of the Act the chairman, unless the children's hearing is considering the case in the absence of the child, any relevant person and any representative, must explain the purpose of the hearing to those present.[1] Thereafter, in the case of a hearing in a referral under s 65(1) he shall 'explain to the child and relevant person, at the opening of proceedings on the referral, the grounds stated by the principal reporter for the referral in order to ascertain whether these grounds are accepted in whole or in part by them'.[2]

1 Children's Hearings (Scotland) Rules 1996, SI 1996/3261, r 20(2).
2 Children (Scotland) Act 1995, s 65(4).

The explanation of the purpose of the hearing

23.08   The matters which should be covered include:

- There is an allegation that the condition of referral exists.
- The hearing is not a court to 'try' the case but can only deal with the child's case if the grounds are accepted by the child and the relevant person(s) or established at a trial-like enquiry held in private by the sheriff.
- The grounds can only be properly accepted if sufficient facts are admitted to support the condition of referral. If some facts are accepted and some not then the hearing may, if the facts accepted are enough to amount to the condition of referral, accept the partial admission and proceed to deal with the case. There will often be discussion of the facts which may constitute the grounds of referral. The amount and detail of such discussion is a matter for the judgment of the hearing under the guidance of the chairman.
- If and when the grounds of referral have been accepted by the child and the relevant person or established by the sheriff then the hearing will be able to have a discussion involving the child, the hearing members, the relevant person(s), social workers and others to see if there is some underlying problem which has contributed to the offence and, if so, if there is any likely way whereby that problem might be resolved.
- The powers of the hearing include imposing compulsory measures of supervision which may involve the child staying at home, with or without a condition as to some form of treatment, but which might also involve the child being required to live elsewhere, e g with a relative, a foster parent or in a residential establishment, even if the child and/or the relevant person(s) are against such a course of action. In an appropriate case the possibility of the hearing authorising secure accommodation[1] may have to be mentioned in the interests of openness. It may also be appropriate to make reference to the

Rehabilitation of Offenders Act 1974 (see following paragraph). It may also be appropriate to refer to the power of the hearing to discharge the referral. How much these matters should be stressed is a matter for judgment – the reporter will be able to assist.

The explanation of the purpose of the hearing and of the grounds of referral need not be repeated at a continued hearing to persons who were present at the original hearing.[2]

1 Children (Scotland) Act 1995, s 70(9) – discussed as a potential disposal below at 25.30ff.
2 *C v Kennedy* (4 July 1986, unreported).

Rehabilitation of Offenders Act 1974

23.09   The general purpose of this Act is to provide various periods of time after the expiry of which a person convicted of an offence becomes a 'rehabilitated person' as defined in s 4 of the Act and subject to the limitations set out in s 7. Being 'rehabilitated' means, in broad terms, that the 'spent' conviction need not be revealed by the rehabilitated person. Section 3 of the 1974 Act[1] provides that the admission or proof of a ground of referral under s 52(2)(i) of the Children (Scotland) Act 1995 (offence by a child) is to be treated for the purpose of the 1974 Act, but not in any other context, as a conviction. Section 5(3) of the 1974 Act provides that the rehabilitation period shall be six months when a hearing, where the s 52(2)(i) ground has been admitted or proved, decides to discharge the referral in terms of s 69(1)(b) and (12) of the Children (Scotland) Act 1995. Section 5 of the 1974 Act also provides that the rehabilitation period for the imposition of a supervision requirement imposed under the Children (Scotland) Act 1995 shall be one year from the imposition of the requirement or the period throughout which the requirement endures, whichever period is longer. Section 7(2)(c) of the 1974 Act provides, in effect, that the expiry of the rehabilitation period shall not prevent the discharge under s 69(1)(b) and (12) or the imposition of a supervision requirement being referred to in other hearings or in the other types of care proceedings listed in s 7(2)(c) of the 1974 Act.

1 Amended by the Children (Scotland) Act 1995, Sch 4, para 23.

UNDERSTANDING OF GROUNDS AND CHAIRMAN'S EXPLANATION

Child must understand the grounds and chairman's explanation

23.10   Section 65(9) of the Children (Scotland) Act 1995, provides:

> 'Where a children's hearing are satisfied that the child –
> a) for any reason will not be capable of understanding the explanation of the grounds for the referral required under subsection (4) above; or
> b) has not understood an explanation given under that subsection,
> they shall either direct the Principal Reporter to make an application to the sheriff for a finding as to whether any of the grounds of the referral are established or discharge the referral.'

No difficulty should arise when the child is obviously mature and sensible enough to understand what is going on or when it is obvious that a child is too immature to understand what is happening. The difficulties will generally arise at the margin or when in the course of the discussion it may emerge that what seemed to be clear acceptance of the grounds was not a true acceptance. An example would be a child charged with breach of the peace who has accepted this ground but it turns out that all he was accepting was being present and not taking part. In a doubtful case the hearing, unless minded to discharge the referral, under s 65(7), should direct the reporter to make application to the sheriff for a proof hearing under s 68 of the Act. 'The right to dispute the grounds of referral is an essential part of the system'[1] and the denial of that right would imperil the proceedings[2] whereas a referral to the sheriff which proved to be 'unnecessary' (in the sense of the ground being admitted before the sheriff and the sheriff being prepared to hold the grounds established without hearing evidence under s 68(8) of the Act[3]) would not. No pressure or appearance of pressure should be applied towards securing acceptance of grounds of referral in whole or in part and the possibility of a proof before the sheriff should be represented as what it is, that is a safeguard of the rights of the child. The reporter will assist the hearing members and try to ensure that no ground of referral is accepted or denied by the child or relevant person owing to a misunderstanding.

1 Per Lord President Hope delivering the opinion of the court in the Orkney case, *Sloan v B* 1991 SLT 530 at 548F.
2 In contrast to the position in *Sloan v B* 1991 SLT 530 where the possibility that an error had been made was held to be irrelevant since the case was bound to go to the sheriff: 'An acceptance by the children of the grounds would simply have confirmed the necessity for the case to go to the sheriff in view of the parents' denial' – per Lord President Hope at 549F.
3 Discussed below at Chapters 27–40.

Relevant person must understand the grounds and chairman's explanation

23.11   The possibility that a relevant person may be unable to understand the grounds of referral after the chairman's explanation is not explicitly addressed by the Children (Scotland) Act 1995. Since, however, the acceptance by the relevant person(s) of the grounds of referral is a pre-condition of the hearing's being entitled to deal with the case (other than by discharge) and since one cannot 'accept' what one cannot understand it follows that the chairman on behalf of the hearing must be satisfied that any relevant person present does understand the grounds of referral before he can proceed to ascertain whether the grounds are accepted in whole or in part.

Position if grounds or chairman's explanation not understood, not accepted, or not accepted and not understood

23.12   Where a children's hearing are satisfied that a child is for any reason not capable of understanding the grounds of referral or has not understood the explanation given by the chairman then the hearing, unless they are in favour of discharging the referral, must direct the reporter to make application to the sheriff for a finding as to whether any of the grounds are established.[1] If a relevant person present has not understood then that person cannot have accepted the ground and the hearing should direct the reporter to apply to the sheriff for such a finding.[2] Where a relevant person or a child has not accepted the grounds of referral, then, unless there has been a partial acceptance which the hearing are prepared to accept and work with (see following paragraphs) the hearing, unless in favour of discharging the referral, shall direct the reporter to make application to the sheriff for a finding on the non-accepted grounds.[3] It is not uncommon for grounds to be not accepted by a relevant person and not understood by the child, in which event, unless the hearing is in favour of discharging the referral, the hearing should direct the reporter to make application to the sheriff both under s 65(7) and s 65(9) of the Children (Scotland) Act 1995.[4]

1 Children (Scotland) Act 1995, s 65(9).
2 C(S)A 1995, s 65(7)(a).
3 C(S)A 1995, s 65(7).
4 Paying the travelling expenses of children (unless already 'looked after' by the local authority), relevant persons, and witnesses for attending at the proceedings before the sheriff is not the responsibility of the local authority but SCRA may pay witnesses' expenses and the chairman may mention this to parties and refer them to the reporter for fuller details.

ACCEPTANCE OF GROUNDS IN WHOLE OR IN PART

The statutory provisions

23.13   Section 65 of the Children (Scotland) Act 1995 provides:

'(5) Where the chairman has given the explanation required by subsection (4) above and the child and the relevant person accept the grounds for the referral, the children's hearing shall proceed in accordance with section 69 of this Act.
(6) Where the chairman has given the explanation required by subsection (4) above and the child and the relevant person accept the grounds in part, the children's hearing may, if they consider it appropriate to do so, proceed in accordance with section 69 of this Act with respect to those grounds which are accepted.'

Accordingly, in the event of partial acceptance of grounds the hearing has the option of proceeding 'in respect of the grounds so accepted' or, unless they decide to discharge the whole referral, directing the reporter to make application to the sheriff for a finding.

Partial acceptance of grounds of referral

23.14   A 'partial' acceptance to be valid must of course leave standing enough within the statement of facts to amount to the condition said to

constitute the condition of referral. For further discussion of partial acceptance in relation to particular grounds of referral see below 24.09ff.

Position if a child admits to offence not alleged in a s 52(2)(a) case

23.15   For example, in the event of it emerging during the hearing that the
commission of the offence alleged was not admitted by the child or relevant person, but that another offence would be admitted, then the children's hearing has no power similar to that of the sheriff's power at the
proof stage,[1] to find that another offence has been committed and admitted. Accordingly the children's hearing must then either discharge the referral or send the matter to the sheriff for proof on the basis that the stated
grounds have not been accepted.[2] In the event of an application to the sheriff , the sheriff may, on the motion of parties or at his own hand, amend the
application.[3] Reporters try to avoid this situation by careful preparation in
the first place.

1 Act of Sederunt (Child Care and Maintenance Rules) 1997, SI 1997/291, r 3.50.
2 Children (Scotland) Act 1995, s 65(7)(a).
3 SI 1997/291, r 3.48.

ABSENCE OF RELEVANT PERSON AT DISPOSITIVE HEARING

The statutory provision

23.16   Section 65(10) of the Children (Scotland) Act 1995 provides: 'The
acceptance by the relevant person of the grounds of the referral shall not
be a requirement for a children's hearing proceeding under this section to
consider a case where that person is not present'. This provision reflects
the position of the hearing's having no power to compel the presence of
the relevant person and prevents the relevant person from frustrating the
progress of the referral by not turning up.

Practice

23.17   The desirability of an agreed approach, when this can be achieved,
lies at the heart of the system and the co-operation of the relevant person
should be obtained if reasonably practicable. If there is an informal indication that the relevant person would like to come but is temporarily
unable so to do then an adjournment of the hearing[1] may be appropriate.
Where the child does not accept the grounds of referral and the hearing
direct the reporter to make application to the sheriff then the relevant
person will be entitled to receive notice of the proceedings before the
sheriff[2] and attend them if so inclined. Accordingly where the child does
not accept the grounds and the relevant person is absent the hearing may
be content to send the case to the sheriff without an adjournment.

1 Children's Hearings (Scotland) Rules 1996, SI 1996/3261, r 10(3) and (4).
2 Act of Sederunt (Child Care and Maintenance Rules) 1997, SI 1997/291, rr 3.45(1),
   3.12(1)(f) and Form 39.

PROCEDURE AFTER ACCEPTANCE OR NOT OF GROUNDS ASCERTAINED

Acceptance of grounds by child and relevant person

23.18 The acceptance of the grounds by the child and any relevant person attending is a pre-condition of the hearing's proceeding to consider a child's case.[1] Where the child and relevant person have understood and accepted the grounds of referral the children's hearing may proceed to consider the child's case.

1 Children (Scotland) Act 1995, s 65(5).

Discharge of referral where grounds not accepted (child not already under supervision)

23.19 Such disposals are relatively uncommon, although of course competent.[1] Reasons for such a disposal include a material change of circumstances – but the hearing members may simply think that, even if the condition for referral exists, there is no necessity for compulsory measures of supervision at that time.

1 Children (Scotland) Act 1995, s 65(7) and (9) (last few words of each subsection).

Discharge of referral where grounds not accepted (child already under supervision)

23.20 Multiple referrals are common enough and a hearing may take the view that a further referral would not add to the support being given to the child. However it is recognised that the grounds most appropriate to the needs of the child should be brought explicitly to the hearing[1] and it is submitted that hearings should not lightly discharge a referral in these circumstances.

1 See discussion above at 16.06 ff.

Discharge of referral where grounds accepted (child under supervision)

23.21 For the reasons mentioned in the foregoing paragraph it is submitted that hearings should not lightly discharge a referral where the grounds are accepted and the child is under supervision.

Discharge or not of referral by hearing: appeal provision?

23.22 A decision by a hearing not to discharge a referral under their powers under s 65(7) or (9) of the Children (Scotland) Act 1995 is not a 'decision' within the appeal provisions of the Act.[1] The reporter has no right of appeal against a decision of a hearing[2] but it is thought that a child aggrieved by a hearing's decision not to press on with a case or discharge the referral may be appealable at the instance of the child, perhaps per his or her safeguarder.[3]

1 *H & H v McGregor* 1973 SC 95, interpreting the Social Work (Scotland) Act 1968, s 49(1).
2 Children (Scotland) Act 1995, s 51(1).
3 Act of Sederunt (Child Care and Maintenance Rules) 1997, SI 1997/291, r 3.53(3); cf *Ross v Kennedy* 1995 SCLR 1160, discussed above at 17.14.

CONSIDERATION OF THE CASE

The background

23.23   The relevant persons(s) and any father who is living with the mother where both are parents[1] as well as the hearing members will have received the papers in the case in advance of the hearing, including any views in writing given to the reporter under r 15(4) of the Children's Hearings (Scotland) Rules 1996. The child does not enjoy this right – it may be that the non-provision of papers to children, having regard to their age and maturity, may have to be re-considered in the light of the provisions of Article 6 of the European Convention on Human Rights.[2]

1 Children's Hearings (Scotland) Rules 1996, SI 1996/3261, r 5(3).
2 Cf *McMichael v United Kingdom* 1995 (20) EHRR 205; *Kraska v Switzerland* (1993) 18 EHRR 188.

The Act's provisions

23.24   On arranging a disposal hearing the reporter shall, if he has not previously done so, request a report from the local authority or information supplementary to what has already been provided.[1] The hearing, once the grounds of referral are accepted or established must consider those grounds and any reports obtained.[2] They may then:

1.   continue the case to a subsequent hearing where they think they require further information;
2.   discharge the referral;
3.   or make a supervision requirement under s 70 of the Children (Scotland) Act 1995.

1 Children (Scotland) Act 1995, s 56(7).
2 C(S)A 1995, s 69(1).

The Rules' provisions

23.25   Rule 20(3) of the Children's Hearings (Scotland) Rules 1996 provides that the hearing shall:

1. consider the social enquiry report and any judicial remit or any other relevant document or information available to them;
2. consider any report from the manager of a residential establishment in which the child is required to reside;
3. discuss the case with the child, and any relevant person, any safeguarder and representative attending; and
4. take steps under r 15 to obtain the views of the child and also the views of any relevant person and safeguarder attending as to what arrangements would be in the best interests of the child.

Rule 20(4) obliges the chairman to inform the child and any relevant person of the substance of the reports etc if it appears to him that they are relevant to disposal and that their disclosure would not be detrimental to the interests of the child.

The developing discussion

23.26 The foregoing bald rehearsal of the formal requirements gives little impression of the reality of a constructive hearing. There is in the Rules, surprisingly given the development of the system and the consideration of the many reports involving aspects of the hearings system since the 1986 Rules, still no mention of involving the reporter or the social worker in the discussion. In practice both will generally be able to make useful contributions. There are no topics specifically prescribed. The home and school and peer group background will generally require to be discussed and any psychological or educational problems mentioned in the reports will have to be addressed. The social worker[1] and the reporter will be able to advise on the resources available and the hearing members may have strong views as to what resources should be made available. If a residential placement, with or without authorisation of secure accommodation, is in prospect it is essential that this be openly discussed.

1 Cf the responsibilities of the local authority towards a child who, by virtue of a supervision requirement, becomes a 'looked after child'; Children (Scotland) Act 1995, s 17(1) and 6(b).

Further investigation required?

23.27 In many cases the hearing will be able to make their decision on the basis of the information initially available but is some cases – the more complex cases – further investigation may be required. A continuation may be allowed under s 69(2) of the Children (Scotland) Act 1995 and there would seem to be no limitation as to the duration or number of such continuations unless, under s 69(3) of the Act, the hearing require the child to attend or reside at any clinic, hospital or other establishment in which case a limit of 22 days, not apparently necessarily consecutive days, is set. The powers of the hearing in relation to granting warrants to ensure compliance with a s 69(3) requirement have already been discussed.[1]

1 Above at 21.13 ff.

THE DECISION OF THE HEARING

Moving towards a decision

23.28   The discussion of the decision to be taken must be held openly and in the presence of the child. While the obligation of the child to attend may be dispensed with[1] the child's right to be present throughout every stage of the case is clear.[2] The relevant person should if possible also be present at the discussion: s 46 of the Children (Scotland) Act 1995, which allows for the exclusion of the relevant person, may in a particular case allow exclusion of the relevant person from the discussion when the child is giving his or her views, but so far as practicable the relevant person should be allowed to stay in order that the necessary participants can be achieved.

1 Children (Scotland) Act 1995, s 45(2).
2 C(S)A 1995, s 45(1)(a).

The decision of the hearing

23.29   It is now well established that a decision may be taken by a majority although such decisions are still comparatively unusual. If the dissentient wishes to give reasons he should do so.

Essential preliminaries as to certain disposal

23.30   A disposal involving placing the child with a person who is not a relevant person shall not be made unless a report has been obtained from the local authority commending such a disposal and confirming that the provisions of reg 15 of the Fostering of Children (Scotland) Regulations 1996 have been observed and satisfied.[1]

1 Ie SI 1996/3263: Children's Hearings (Scotland) Rules 1996, SI 1996/3261, reg 20(6).

Announcement of decision: the rules

23.31   Once the decision has been taken the chairman shall inform the child, any relevant person, any safeguarder and any representative of:

1. the decision of the hearing;
2. the reasons for the decision; and
3. the right of the child and the relevant person under s 51(1) of the Children (Scotland) Act 1995 to appeal to the sheriff against the decision and, where the appeal is against a decision relating to a supervision requirement, to apply to the children's hearing for suspension of the requirement appealed against.[1]

1 Children's Hearings (Scotland) Rules 1996, SI 1996/3261, r 20(5).

'REASONS FOR THE DECISION'

Reasons should be self-sufficient

23.32 In stating the reasons the hearing should specify the facts and circumstance which caused it to make the decision. It is not enough to rehearse the statutory requirement, e g, 'we were satisfied that compulsory measures of supervision were required in the child's own interests' or merely to narrate that the statutory procedures had been followed.[1] In the important case of *H v Kennedy*,[2] the hearing had had to consider whether the parallel provisions of the Social Work (Scotland) Act 1968 had been complied with. There were two statements of reasons in relation to two sets of siblings. The decisions to which the statements of reasons were appended were amongst many in a series of hearings concerning the family. The First Division rejected the main argument that this statement was inadequate. Lord President Hope stated:

> 'The statement must be intelligible to the person to whom it is addressed and it must deal with all the substantial questions which were the subject of the decision'.

Lord Mayfield, with whom the Lord President and Lord Allanbridge expressly concurred, laid stress on the way in which the decisions had been reached and the continuing nature of the process of which they formed part. Lord Mayfield stated:

> 'I have referred to the informality of procedure, where discussions are reached and verbal decisions made in the presence of the parents, a safeguarder and the parent's agent. All those present have the opportunity to participate in those discussions. Furthermore, it is not appropriate to consider the decision of the children's hearing on 10 October in isolation. It was, as I have suggested, part of a continuing process and, indeed, the decision on 10 October followed from a continued hearing on 22 August. The adequacy or otherwise of the two statements of reasons given is therefore to be considered against the background of the knowledge on the part of the parents as to what was being considered; and the opportunity given to them, their agent and safeguarder to have their say, as it were, and express any views.'

The Lord President however rejected a subsidiary argument to the effect that since the reasons had to be given before the hearing was concluded those present had had a sufficient opportunity to object and ask questions if they thought the reasons not intelligible. The Lord President, pointing out that the written reasons had to be notified to persons not necessarily present and had to be included in the papers lodged by the reporter in the event of an appeal to the sheriff, said:

> 'Accordingly the reasons must be sufficiently clear to be intelligible to persons who, although fully informed about the circumstances, were not present at the Hearing. And the fact that no objection was made to the adequacy of the reasons given at the Hearing is not to be taken as conclusive of the question whether the reasons set out in the statement of reasons are adequate.'

It is not easy completely to reconcile the Lord President's approach with that of Lord Mayfield and it is submitted that in so far as there is a difference between the two opinions the approach of Lord President Hope is to be preferred. It is more consistent with our obligations under Article 6 of the European Convention[3]and therefore hearings should aim at making statements of reasons as self-sufficient as possible.[4]

1 Cf *K v Finlayson* 1974 SLT (Sh Ct) 51 at 54 (overruled, but not on this point in *O v Rae* 1992 SCLR 318, 1993 SLT 570.
2 1999 SCLR 961.
3 Cf *McMichael v United Kingdom* 1995 (20) EHRR 205; *Kraska v Switzerland* (1993) 18 EHRR 188.
4 Cf *R v Kennedy* 1995 GWD 7–354, 2nd Div.

Reasons should make clear hearing's attitude to pivotal considerations

23.33   In *Kennedy v B*[1] children had been made subject to a home supervision requirement with conditions restricting their being left alone with a person in respect of whom grounds involving allegations of sexual abuse had been held as established in earlier referral proceedings. Subsequently the person was acquitted by a jury in respect of criminal charges arising out of the same alleged incidents. A review hearing renewed the supervision requirement but removed the conditions. Their reasons included a statement that 'supervision was a safeguard for the children and gave the Social Work Department the right of access to them' and the statement that 'the Social Work Department see their ongoing rôle as a monitoring exercise'. On appeal the sheriff thought the hearing had given insufficient consideration to the acquittal and remitted for reconsideration. On appeal the Court of Session reversed the sheriff in so far as he had held that the decision of the hearing was not justified. Lord Justice-Clerk Ross, giving the opinion of the court, stated:

> ' … it is not clear to what extent, if any, they attached weight to the fact that the first respondent had been acquitted. They did not state expressly that they attached any weight to that factor. Nor did they make it clear that they applied their minds to the question of whether a supervision requirement was necessary in the children's interest and in particular what might be achieved as a result of such supervision. To that extent the approach of the children's hearing appears to us to be open to question.'

1 1992 SCLR 55, 2nd Div.

Conclusion

23.34   The proper approach may thus be summarised as being that the reasons should include reference to any pivotal matter, positive or negative, which has governed the hearing's deliberations in coming to the decision in question. There can however be no mechanical test. What constitutes a pivotal factor will always be a matter for judgment: in *Kennedy v M*[1] a hearing had information before it that the local authority had a long-term plan for the freeing for adoption of the child; the hearing, in deciding to leave access by the parent to the child to the discretion of the

Social Work Department, made no reference to these plans in their reasons. Lord President Hope said at 99A:

> 'That no reference was made here to the long-term plan that the child should be freed for adoption is a sufficient indication that the children's hearing did not regard this as a factor which affected the way in which the discretion about access was currently being exercised by the Social Work Department. In my opinion there was no need for the children's hearing to make reference to this point in these circumstances, as the whole tenor of their decision was that the present arrangements were working satisfactorily and that they should remain in place for the time being'. [2]

1 1995 SCLR 88.
2 1995 SCLR 88 at 99A. Cf *C v Kennedy* (4 July 1986, unreported) – discussed below at 53.68 – wherein a defect in a notification of a continued hearing (the purpose of the continued hearing was not correctly described) was held to be immaterial since the parent had been present at the original hearing and therefore knew the purpose.

Written notice of decision

23.35 Section 21(1) of the Children's Hearings (Scotland) Rules 1996 must be observed in relation to notification of the decision to the child, any relevant person any safeguarder and the local authority. Notable is the requirement, except where the decision is in relation to a continuation of a supervision requirement where an appeal is blocked by s 51(7) of the Children (Scotland) Act 1995 to advise the child and relevant person of the right of appeal. Notification of a decision must be given to any person with whom the child is residing, and where the referral has been initiated by a police report, to the chief constable.[1] Where a decision is taken to make or terminate a supervision requirement in relation to a child of 16 or over the chief constable of the child's area of residence must be informed.[2]

1 SI 1996/3261, r 21(2).
2 SI 1996/3261, r 21(3); cf 1.26 and 3.20 above.

Announcement of decision: good practice

23.36 The foregoing matters must be covered. In addition it is good practice to deal with the following:

- If a residential placement is being required it should be identified and described.
- The concept of being a 'looked after' child should, where applicable, be explained.
- The implications of the Rehabilitation of Offenders Act 1974 [1] should when applicable be explained.
- The availability of free Legal Aid should be explained clearly.
- If applicable it should be mentioned that the notice 'Now that a supervision requirement has been made' will be sent out.

1 See above at 23.08.

CHAPTER 24

Conduct of hearing: specialities in certain types of hearing

OFFENCE BY A CHILD CASES

24.01 Such cases still comprise the numerical majority of referrals.[1] They have the appearance of being simpler than cases based upon the 'care and protection' grounds and while exact statistics are not available experience indicates that they still occupy proportionately less time than the latter. There are, however, indications that discussion of disposal of such cases is occupying more and more of the time of hearings and that hearing members are becoming more searching in their quest for appropriate disposals. The preparation and presentation of care and protection cases, both to children's hearings and to sheriffs, is very demanding of reporters' time and expertise.

1 40,080 out of 65,104 in 1997/98 according to statistical Report in Annual Report 1997/98 of SCRA.

EXPLAINING THE GROUNDS OF REFERRAL IN AN OFFENCE BY A CHILD CASE

The statutory provision

24.02 Where a child's case has been referred to a hearing for consideration and determination on the merits[1] it is the duty of the chairman 'to explain to the child and the relevant person, at the opening of proceedings on the referral, the grounds stated by the principal reporter for the referral in order to ascertain whether these grounds are accepted in whole or in part by them.'[2] This provision is subject to the qualification that acceptance by a relevant person not present is not to prevent the hearing proceeding to consider the case[3] and to the provisions,[4] which will be discussed presently, in relation to the child not understanding the grounds or the explanation.

1 Children (Scotland) Act 1995, s 65(1).
2 C(S)A 1995, s 65(4).
3 C(S)A 1995, s 65(10).
4 C(S)A 1995, s 65(9).

Explaining the nature of the alleged offence – the rôle of the reporter

24.03 The chairman and other hearing members (in common with the child and relevant person) will each have a copy of the statement of grounds of referral[1] stating that one or more offences have been committed by the referred child and narrating the Statement of Facts which is relied upon by the reporter as constituting the offence or offences. The rules provide for the offence to be identified.[2] The chairman should define the offence concerned and relate the statement of facts to that offence and indicate the essential facts which would make up the offence and which would, therefore, require to be accepted (by both child and relevant person) before the grounds could be recorded as having been accepted by the child and the relevant person.[3] If alternative offences are alleged the chairman should explain each and also explain that the child or relevant person cannot accept that the child has committed both. If alternative offences have not been spelled out and a possible alternative is admitted the chairman does not have any power parallel to that of the sheriff in a proof under s 68 of the Children (Scotland) Act 1995 to find that any other offence established by the facts has been committed and admitted[4]. The reporter will be ready to assist the chairman throughout.

1 Children's Hearings (Scotland) Rules 1996, SI 1996/3261, r 5(1)(b).
2 SI 1996/3261, r 17(2) – discussed above at 16.14 and 16.15.
3 SI 1996/3261, r 31(h); for a modern and systematic exposition of the substantive criminal law see Gordon, G H *The Criminal Law of Scotland* (2nd edn) (Edinburgh, 1978) and Supplement – the third edition is in preparation; Macdonald, J H A, *A Practical Treatise on the Criminal Law of Scotland* (5th edn) (Edinburgh, 1948) is still referred to and remains useful although out of date.
4 See discussion above at 23.15.

Art and part

24.04   The chairman must keep in mind that it is possible to commit a crime or offence not only as the principal actor but also as an accomplice – 'acting in concert' or 'art and part'. Where acting in concert is being relied upon this should, ideally, be reflected in the Statement of Facts. For a person to be guilty on an art and part basis there must be participation in the offence – mere presence is not enough. The chairman must be ready to explain and apply this concept.[1]

1 For a discussion of art and part, see *Gordon* Ch 5.

CRIMINAL INTENT AND DEFENCES

Mens rea

24.05   Most offences at common law, of which assault, theft and fraud are representative samples, cannot be committed without there being a degree of criminal intent or '*mens rea*' in the mind of the offender. Breach of the peace is conduct which disturbs public order or is likely to cause such a disturbance and *mens rea* in any real sense does not require to be present: all that has to be proved is that the conduct was deliberate and that the alleged offender was an active participant. Some offences, such as malicious damage to property, may be committed recklessly. Some statutory offences, such as exceeding the speed limit, can be committed without *mens rea*. Some statutory offences, such as knowingly allowing oneself to be driven in a vehicle which has been unlawfully taken and driven away, contrary to s 178(1)(b) of the Road Traffic Act 1988, require a limited degree of *mens rea* in that it has to be proved that the alleged offender knew that the vehicle had been unlawfully taken away.

Affirmative defences

24.06 Certain circumstances which may appear at first sight to constitute an offence may not truly be offences because of the presence of circumstances constituting a 'defence' – generally amounting to the absence of *mens rea* – available to the alleged offender. For example the external signs of assault may be present on an alleged victim but there may be facts and circumstances indicating that the alleged offender was not engaged in an unjustifiable physical attack upon another but was resisting, using reasonable force, an attack on himself or another which there was no other way of avoiding (e g by escape). The foregoing would amount to self-defence. The presence or absence of *mens rea* and the possible presence of a defence are not matters which a child or relevant person can be assumed to have considered and the chairman should be ready to explore, in such depth as may be necessary, that the parent and relevant person are aware that the necessary degree of criminal intent was present and that any possible defence was absent.

Rehabilitation of Offenders Act 1974

24.07 This Act provides various periods of time after the expiry of which a person convicted of an offence becomes a 'rehabilitated person'. The details of this Act have already been discussed.[1] The chairman may wish to explain the relevant provisions of the 1974 Act in as simple terms as possible before ascertaining whether the grounds of referral are to be admitted by the child and the relevant person.

1 See above at 23.09.

Partial acceptance of an offence allegedly committed by a child[1]

24.08 A valid partial acceptance of an offence could be constituted by an acceptance of one of the elements of the offence and not another. For example where in an offence by a child case the child was alleged to have stolen jeans and training shoes from a shop ('this being the offence of theft') and the child admitted taking the jeans but not the shoes then this would constitute a partial acceptance which would allow the hearing, if so minded, to proceed. If on the other hand it was alleged that the child 'did shout, swear, brandish a knife and commit a breach of the peace' and it emerged that the child, although apparently admitting to a breach of the peace did not admit to any of the individual actions of shouting, swearing or brandishing a knife, then this could not be regarded as partial acceptance since the child was not admitting having performed any of the actions which amounted to the breach of the peace. Examples of misleading partial 'acceptances' could be multiplied.[2] It is very important for the chairman to ensure not only that the child and relevant person understand the legal definition of the crime and the actions and intentions which compose it but also to be satisfied that the relevant person and the child accept that the actions and motives which are being accepted amount to the crime alleged. The reporter should be astute to advise the hearing on such matters.

1 For general discussion of partial acceptance see above at 23.12.
2 See Martin F and Murray K (eds), *Children's Hearings*, p 121 for further examples; Cf Hallet J et al *The Evaluation of Children's Hearings in Scotland* (Vol 1), pp 43, 44.

Partial acceptance: to proceed or not to proceed?

24.09   Whether or not to proceed on a partial acceptance is a matter for the judgement of the hearing.[1] It is suggested that the test should generally be whether or not the partial acceptance will be sufficiently comprehensive for the hearing adequately to address the whole needs of the child. In the 'breach of the peace' example given in the foregoing paragraph a hearing might be reluctant to accept a partial acceptance which excluded the reference to the knife on the grounds that unless the knife element were proved or, as the case may be, not proved, the true character of the offence and therefore of the needs of the offender would not be known.

1 Children (Scotland) Act 1995, s 65(6).

CARE AND PROTECTION CASES

Complicated grounds of referral

24.10   The complexity of the grounds of referral will vary but sometimes the apparent simplicity of a ground of referral may conceal, or at least encourage one to overlook, vital considerations. For example, when it is alleged as a formal ground of referral that the child 'is likely – (i) to suffer unnecessarily; or (ii) be impaired seriously in his health or development, due to a lack of parental care' there will be alleged in support of that ground a number of individual facts and circumstances (e g a parent under influence of drink on a certain occasion, a child left alone in the family home in a hungry and dirty condition on another occasion, etc). In this type of case it must be kept in mind that the heart of the matter is that one or more of these circumstances have taken place *and* that as a consequence of this it is proper to infer that as a consequence of a lack of parental care the child is likely to suffer unnecessarily or be impaired seriously in his or her health or development. The concept of likelihood of course involves a forward-looking assessment, but the facts on which that assessment is made are the facts available at the time of the session of the children's hearing. It is accordingly important for the chairman to make clear to the parent and the child that the factual aspect (i e at least one of the alleged facts) *and* the inference that unnecessary suffering etc is likely to arise in the light of the admitted facts must *both* be admitted if the ground of referral is to be treated as accepted. On some occasions, a relevant person or a child will be prepared to admit that certain individual events took place but will not accept that the inference that unnecessary suffering etc is the likely result. The hearing must be satisfied that both of these arms of the ground of referral are fully and knowingly accepted by both the child (in cases where the child is able to understand) and the relevant person. If the hearing are doubtful as to whether there has been such an acceptance, the hearing should, (unless satisfied that there has been a sufficient and satisfactory partial acceptance on which they are prepared to proceed or minded to discharge the referral) hold that the grounds have not been fully accepted and direct the reporter to have the matter brought before the sheriff for proof.[1]

1 Children (Scotland) Act 1995, s 65(7).

Multiple conditions of referral – common factual basis

24.11 As already discussed[1] a reporter may often be well advised to aver two or more conditions of referral even if these are supported by common factual grounds. In practice these may be averred alternatively, i e separated by 'or' or cumulatively, i.e. separated by 'and'. At the stage of ascertaining if the grounds of referral are accepted the chairman will require to make sure that he finds out the attitude of the parents and, if able to understand, the child, to all of the several conditions averred. If one or more of the several conditions is *not* accepted, but provided at least one of the conditions is accepted, the hearing will have to decide (unless they are going to discharge the referral) whether to proceed on the ground accepted or to direct the reporter to make application to the sheriff for a finding.

1 Above at 16.06 ff.

24.12 *Partial acceptance in care and protection cases.* The legal acceptability, as the law stands at present following the decision in *O v Rae*[1], of the hearing's dealing with the case on the basis inter alia of material information not contained within the grounds of referral which have been considered by the sheriff at a proof has already been noticed and discussed.[2] The consideration that a matter not within the grounds of referral may form part of the hearing's deliberations as to what is in the best interests of the child does not, it is submitted, make it appropriate for a hearing to proceed on the basis of a partial acceptance while intending to have regard to the matter not within the scope of that partial acceptance. In the first edition of this book it was stated[3] that the basis for the decision as to whether or not to proceed on a partial acceptance 'ought to be one of straightforwardness and pragmatism'. If the precise condition accepted is not likely seriously to affect the hearing's disposal, then it may not matter if a particular condition among several is not accepted. The hearing should avoid keeping in mind, as it were, the unadmitted condition when deciding on disposal. It is suggested that where there is a doubt the safe, and in the long run the more satisfactory, course will be to direct an application to the sheriff for a finding, in order to "clear the air." ' It is submitted that such a course does not conflict with the decision in *O v Rae*.

1 1992 SCLR 318, 1993 SLT 570.
2 Above at 16.06 ff.
3 At p 122.

HEARINGS ON REFERENCE FOR ADVICE BY COURT[1] OR LOCAL AUTHORITY[2] OR APPROVED ADOPTION SOCIETY[3]

Procedure generally

24.13 In these hearings (i e all 'advice' hearings except a hearing to give advice to the sheriff in relation to an application to vary or recall a CPO[4] for which no explicit rules have been made – see discussion below[5]) the procedure to be followed[6] is parallel to that of the hearing on referral. The chairman has the same obligation to explain the purposes of the hearing to the child and relevant person(s), if present, and to discuss the case of the child and afford the child, the relevant person(s), any safeguarder and any representative the opportunity of taking part in the discussion and giving their views on the case. The hearing must also 'take steps on [sic] rule 15 to obtain the views of the child, and endeavour to obtain the views of any relevant person, and of any safeguarder if attending the hearing, on what arrangements with respect to the child would be in the best interests of the child.'[7] Although rule 22 of the Children's Hearings (Scotland) Rules 1996 does not mention unmarried fathers[8] as being entitled to participate in the discussion it is well established in practice that any person in this category will, where known, generally be notified of the hearing, supplied with documents and permitted to participate in the discussion.

1 Children (Scotland) Act 1995, s 73(13); Criminal Procedure (Scotland) Act 1995, s 49(3), s 49(1)(b), s 49(6).
2 C(S)A 1995, s 73(13).
3 C(S)A 1995, s 73(13); Adoption (Scotland) Act 1978, s 22A(1) and (2) (interpolated by C(S)A 1995, Sch 2, para 15).
4 C(S)A 1995, s 60(10).
5 Below at 24.21.
6 Children's Hearings (Scotland) Rules 1996, SI 1996/3261, r 22.
7 SI 1996/3261, r 22(3)(c).
8 Cf SI 1996/3261, r 5(3)(b).

Disclosure of information contained in the documentation

24.14 The hearing will on such an occasion, in addition to the usual background papers, have the reference by the local authority, adoption agency, or the court and any supervision requirement which exists in relation to the child. The relevant person(s) and any unmarried father who has been notified will also have these documents.[1] Rule 22(4) of the Children's Hearings (Scotland) Rules 1996 provides that the chairman 'shall inform the child and each relevant person whose whereabouts are known of the substance of any reports, documents and information mentioned in paragraph (3)(a) if it appears to him that this is material to the advice that will be given and that its disclosure would not be detrimental to the interests of the child'. The reference to 'each relevant person whose whereabouts are known', is inapt in the context of a hearing in progress. The bracketing of such persons with the child as persons to whom matters may be disclosed if not detrimental to the interests of the child is misleading having regard to the consideration that such persons should have received copies of all the documents available to the hearing members.[2]

1 Children's Hearings (Scotland) Rules 1996, SI 1996/3261, r 5(3)(a).
2 SI 1996/3261, r 5(3).

Content of reports

24.15 Neither the Children (Scotland) Act 1995 nor the Children's Hearings (Scotland) Rules 1996 indicate what the contents of the reports or notes of advice might be. In the case of reports on applications for parental responsibilities and in connection with adoptions the reports should not replicate the social enquiry and other reports – which will available to the local authority or agency – but should give the hearings' view as to whether or not the proposed application is in the best interests of the child. Reasons must be given.[1]

1 Children's Hearings (Scotland) Rules 1996, SI 1996/3261, r 22(6); for discussion of 'reasons' see above at 23.32 ff; for an illustration see below at 56.11.

Content of advice to courts

24.16 When giving advice to a court the court should be told whether the hearing thinks the hearings system has anything useful to offer the child or young person concerned. In the event of the hearing coming to this conclusion, it should, it is submitted, clearly indicate to the court the type of disposal it had in mind. In the event of the hearing advising a court that the case should be dealt with by the court it is now generally accepted that it is appropriate for hearings, if so minded in a particular case, to direct the court's attention to a specific fact or circumstance which might assist in assessing an appropriate sentence or even to express a more general view. An example might be in relation to a possible disposal, such as community service, which would be open to the court but not to a hearing. Once again, reasons must be given.[1]

1 Children's Hearings (Scotland) Rules 1996, SI 1996/3261, r 22(6).

Notification of advice

24.17 After considering the case the hearing must tell those present the advice they intend to give.[1] There is no explicit provision obliging the chairman to state reasons at the time but it is generally good practice for this to be done. As soon as reasonably practicable after the hearing the chairman must make (or cause to be made) and sign a written report telling what the advice is and stating reasons.[2] Within 7 days of the determination the reporter must send a copy of the foregoing to the court, the local authority or the approved adoption agency as the case may be and also to the child, any relevant person and 'any safeguarder appointed in the proceedings'.

1 SI 1996/3261, r 22(5).
2 SI 1996/3261, r 22(6).

Form of report/advice

24.18 The Children's Hearings (Scotland) Rules 1996 prescribe no specific form.[1] In practice, the report/advice is usually handwritten on the record of proceedings by the chairman or other hearing member. The chairman must sign[2] or, if he is unavailable, the document may be authenticated by a member of the relevant hearing.[3]

1 But see illustration at 56.11 below.
2 Children's Hearings (Scotland) Rules 1996, SI 1996/3261, r 22(6).
3 SI 1996/3261, r 29(1).

Is a hearing subsequently bound by its own advice?

24.19   When a court sends a case to the hearing for disposal after having received advice from the hearing, it may be assumed that the hearing will dispose of the case along the lines indicated in the advice to the court. There is, however, nothing in the Children (Scotland) Act 1995 compelling it so to do and, particularly in the event of a change of circumstances, a change of mind might be necessary and desirable. In the absence of a change of circumstances, a change of mind would be hard to justify and could constitute the foundation for an appeal against disposal to the sheriff under s 51 of the Act.

Majority and minority advice?

24.20   There is no provision for the advice of the hearing to be stated as 'by a majority', with an accompanying 'minority' opinion, but in practice these are regarded as competent in advice to courts.

Advice to sheriff under s 60(10) on whether to vary or recall CPO

24.21   This type of advice hearing is not covered by r 22[1] nor by any of the rules (rr 16 to 21) of Part IV of the Children's Hearings (Scotland) Rules 1996. Parts II and III of the 1996 Rules would however seem to be applicable where relevant. Such advice hearings are rare. It is thought that they should be conducted as nearly as possibly as if r 22 applied except that, as noticed above,[2] it would seem that such a hearing may appoint a safe-guarder.

1 SI 1996/3261, r 22(1).
2 See 24.15.

HEARING TO CONSIDER SUSPENSION OF SUPERVISION REQUIREMENT PENDING APPEAL

Pre-hearing procedures

24.22 The decision of a hearing as to disposal is subject to appeal to the sheriff. When the disposal has included any form of supervision require-ment, the child or his parent may, after lodging the appeal,[1] make appli-cation to the children's hearing under s 51(9) of the Children (Scotland) Act 1995 for the suspension of the supervision requirement appealed against. Such an application should be made in writing to the principal reporter and it then becomes the duty of the reporter to arrange a chil-dren's hearing 'forthwith' to consider that application.[2] Notification of such a hearing should ideally be given in writing[3] separately to the child and relevant person(s) but if such notice cannot be given in writing the reporter may give notice orally.[4]

1 Children's Hearings (Scotland) Rules 1996, SI 1996/3261, r 23(6).
2 Children (Scotland) Act 1995, s 51(10); SI 1996/3261, r 23(1).
3 SI 1996/3261, r 23(2).
4 SI 1996/3261, rr 6(2)(c) and 7(5).

Procedure during the hearing

24.23 Such a hearing, being a proceeding under Chapter 2 of the Children (Scotland) Act 1995, must consider if it is necessary to appoint a safeguarder.[1] The appellant, his representative and any safeguarder attending must be given an opportunity of being heard.[2] (Although the rule does not expressly say so, the reporter and the local authority's social worker[3] will in practice be given the opportunity of being heard.) The chairman must inform the applicant at the conclusion of the hearing as to the decision of the hearing and the reasons therefor.[4] There is no obliga-tion for the chairman to explain the purpose of the hearing, nor is there any right reserved to the child or the relevant person to receive a state-ment in writing of the reasons for the decision as there would be in a prin-cipal hearing. (Nor is there any obligation on the chairman to advise the child or the parent of any right of appeal and as any appeal from a decision of a hearing to refuse to suspend a supervision requirement pending appeal would overlap the substantive appeal it is thought that such an appeal would be incompetent[5].) In the event that the applicant fails to attend the hearing, then application to suspend the supervision requirement shall be treated as abandoned.[6] *Quaere* if, on an application for suspension being treated as abandoned, a fresh application for suspension, timeously lodged, would be competent.

1 Children (Scotland) Act 1995, s 41(1).
2 Children's Hearings (Scotland) Rules 1996, SI 1996/3261, r 23(3).
3 Cf SI 1996/3261, rr 8 and 13(d).
4 SI 1996/3261, r 23(4).
5 Cf *H and H v McGregor* 1973 SC 95.
6 SI 1996/3261, r 23(5).

Relevant considerations

24.24   The principle of the paramountcy of the welfare of the child throughout childhood applies[1], subject to the statutory derogation in favour of protecting the public from serious harm, physical or otherwise,[2] but beyond that neither the Children (Scotland) Act 1995 nor the Children's Hearings (Scotland) Rules 1996 supply criteria to be applied by hearings in deciding on suspension and the absence of the possibility of reported decisions and the non-availability of appeal makes the development of case law virtually impossible. The matter will usually arise in the context of a supervision requirement with a condition of residence outside of the home. In general the obvious criteria may properly be applied, namely, the degree of urgency which, in the hearing's opinion looking at the matter from the point of view of the best interests of the child, attends the removal of the child from the home and the degree of urgency of his obtaining treatment in the place where he has been required to reside. It is now clear that it may be in the child's own interests to be compulsorily restrained from further offending.[3]

1 Children (Scotland) Act 1995, s 16(1).
2 C(S)A 1995, s 16(5)(a).
3 *Humphries v S* 1986 SLT 683.

CHAPTER 25

Disposal and Review of Case by the Hearing

SECTION 16(1)[1] – THE WELFARE PRINCIPLE

Section 16(1) – the paramountcy principle

25.01 Section 16(1) of the Children (Scotland) Act 1995 provides:

> 'Where under or by virtue of this Part of this Act, a children's hearing decide, or a court determines, any matter with respect to a child the welfare of that child throughout his childhood shall be their or its paramount consideration.'

Section 43(1) of the Social Work (Scotland) Act 1968 provided:

> 'When a children's hearing have considered the grounds for the referral of a case, accepted or established under the last foregoing section, the report obtained under section 39(4) of this act and such other relevant information as may be available to them, they shall proceed in accordance with the subsequent provisions of this section to consider on what course they should decide in the best interests of the child.'

Lord President Emslie described the relevant provisions of the 1968 Act as being 'intended to secure the well-being of children in need of care'.[2] In *Kennedy v A*[3] Lord Justice-Clerk Ross opined that the principles of natural justice must yield to the best interests of the child and this opinion was quoted with approval in the opinion of the court delivered by Lord President Hope in *O v Rae*.[4] Accordingly, in so far as s 16(1) enacts that the welfare of the child is to be the paramount consideration, it does little more than give statutory authority to the approach of the courts to the earlier legislation. The English case of *Re P (a child) (residence order: restriction order)*[5] constitutes a strong re-affirmation of the paramountcy principle. In this case the Court of Appeal, interpreting the parallel (although not identical) provisions of the Children Act 1989[6] held that the provisions of that Act contained no provision which could displace the welfare of the child as the paramount consideration. Dealing with the argument that it was 'almost unthinkable' that the child should, other than in an emergency, be removed from her religious heritage, Butler-Sloss LJ, refusing to interfere with the decision of the judge of first instance, said: 'But N's religious and cultural heritage cannot be the overwhelming factor for the reasons set out by the judge nor can it displace other weighty welfare factors'. Ward LJ referred to and adopted the passage in *J v C*[7] wherein Lord McDermott, formulating the scope and meaning of welfare being the paramount consideration, stated: 'I think [these words] connote a process whereby, when all the relevant facts, relationships, claims and wishes of parents, risks, choices and other circumstances are taken into account and weighed, the course to be followed will be that which is most in the interests of the child's welfare as the term has now to be understood'.

1 Cf discussion above at 2.17 ff.
2 *McGregor v D* 1977 SC 330 at 336.
3 1986 SLT 358 at 362A.
4 1992 SCLR 318 at 324E.
5 [1999] 3 All ER 734 per Butler-Sloss LJ at 746h and per Ward LJ at 755f ff; (leave to appeal to the House of Lords was refused by the Court of Appeal and by the Appeal Committee of the House of Lords).
6 Section 1(1): '... the child's welfare shall be the court's paramount consideration'.
7 [1969] 1 All ER 788 at 820–821, 1970 AC 668 at 710–711.

Section 16(1) – 'the welfare of the child throughout his childhood'

25.02   It was thought, however, that hearings could not concern themselves with the longer term interests of the child and this obtained some support from the opinion of Lord Hunter in *R v Children's Hearing for the Borders Region* in which the imposition by a hearing of a supervision requirement with a condition that a child should reside in a 'pre-adoptive home' was described[1] by his Lordship as 'an oblique purpose'.[2] The Sinclair Report[3] considered this matter in the context of adoptions and parental rights orders under s 16 of the Social Work (Scotland) Act 1968 and recommended[4] that hearings be given the power to advise courts on such matters.[5] The Fife Report recommended generally that consideration should be given to conferring upon hearings the right and duty to consider the long-term interests of the child when appropriate.[6] Accordingly the inclusion of the words 'throughout his childhood' in s 16(1) of the Children (Scotland) Act 1995 represent a significant clarification of the considerations which are to affect hearings in relation to their decisions on any matter with respect to a child.

1 *R v Children's Hearing for the Borders Region* 1984 SLT 65 at 67; cf the decisions of the sheriffs in *A v Children's Hearing for Tayside Region* 1987 SLT (Sh Ct) 126, *M v Children's Hearing for Strathclyde Region* 1988 SCLR 592 and *Kennedy v M* 1995 SLT 717.
2 The prohibition of the course taken by the hearing in the case of *R v Children's Hearing for the Borders Region* 1984 SLT 65 was removed by the Law Reform (Miscellaneous Provisions) (Scotland) Act 1985, s 27.
3 *Review of Scottish Child Care Law*, Report of the Working Group under the chairmanship of Mr J W Sinclair CBE, 1990, Edinburgh, HMSO ('the Sinclair Report').
4 Sinclair Report, Recommendations 71–73.
5 Now enacted – discussed above at 24.11.
6 *The Report of the Inquiry into Child Care Policies in Fife* (HMSO, 27 October 1992), p 434, para 25.

Derogation from the welfare principle: s 16(5)

25.03   This sub-section provides:

'If, for the purpose of protecting members of the public from serious harm (whether or not physical harm) –
a) a children's hearing consider it necessary to make a decision under or by virtue of this Part of this Act which (but for this paragraph) would not be

consistent with their affording paramountcy to the consideration mentioned in subsection (1) above, they may make that decision; or

b) a court considers it necessary to make a determination under or by virtue of Chapters 1 to 3 of this Part of this Act which (but for this paragraph) would not be consistent with its affording such paramountcy, it may make that determination.'

No such provisions were contained in the Social Work (Scotland) Act 1968, but it had long been recognised by the courts that the 1968 Act's phrase 'in the best interests of the child' should not be interpreted narrowly and that, for example, it could be consistent with the best interests of the child, properly understood, to detain the child in a place of safety, which will tend to prevent him from committing offences.[1] Accordingly, once again, the provisions of the Children (Scotland) Act 1995 give statutory authority to the approach of the courts.

1 *Humphries v S* 1986 SLT 683; cf per Lord President Emslie in *McGregor v D* 1977 SC 330, 1977 SLT 182 at 185: 'The scheme of the Act is the search for a solution which will be in the best interests of the delinquent child and other children in need of care.

Apparent derogation from the welfare principle: authorising secure accommodation

25.04   A child who is being looked after by a local authority under chapters 1 or 4 of Part II of the Children (Scotland) Act 1995 may be placed in the secure accommodation of a residential establishment if the Chief Social Work Officer (CSWO) and the person in charge of the residential establishment consider that the secure accommodation criteria exist and that the child may be in need of compulsory measures of supervision.[1] Such a placement, if it is to persist for more than 72 hours, must be ratified at a hearing.[2] A hearing may also, as part of a supervision requirement, authorise such in advance provided they are satisfied that placement in a residential establishment is required and that the secure accommodation criteria exist and that the child may be in need of compulsory measures of supervision under Part II of the Act.[3] The secure accommodation criteria are that the child:

a) having previously absconded, is likely to abscond unless kept in secure accommodation, and, if he absconds, it is likely that his physical, mental or moral welfare will be at risk; or

b) is likely to injure himself or some other person unless he is kept in such accommodation

The criterion mentioned in sub-paragraph (a) is clearly capable of justification on a 'welfare of the child' basis. On the other hand the element in sub-paragraph (b) which refers to the contingency that the child is 'likely to injure . . . other persons' does not on the face of it rely on 'the best interests of the child' for its justification. It may be, however, that it would be thought to be, in the long term, in the best interests of the child that he should so far as practicable be prevented from injuring others, just as it was held to be 'in his own interest' to be prevented from offending.[4]

Accordingly the apparent derogation from the welfare principle constituted by the secure accommodation provisions is more apparent than real.

1 Secure Accommodation (Scotland) Regulations 1996, SI 1996/3255, reg 7.
2 See above at 19.13 for discussion of the procedure.
3 Children (Scotland) Act 1995, s 70(9) and (10).
4 Cf *Humphries v S* 1986 SLT 683.

Punishment and welfare

25.05   Punishment is an unwelcome and in some sense painful condition
imposed on a person and validated by the proven fact that that person has
committed a crime and principally justified by appeal to the concepts of
retribution, deterrence and reform. It is also linked with the concept that
by declaring certain acts punishable society 'denounces' these acts and the
consideration that, when punishment takes a custodial form, society is, at
least for the time being, protected from being harmed by the offender.
Reparation for the victim is increasingly recognised as a valid element in
the content of the punishment.[1] With the exception of the s 16(5) and the
secure accommodation provisions the Children (Scotland) Act 1995 avoids
explicit invocation of any of the elements of punishment as criteria which
could or should guide hearings as to how they might dispose of cases. It
has been remarked, however, that 'a fairly common view among critics is
that hearings are in fact allowed to punish but not to call it "punishment" '.[2]

1 The literature on the concept of punishment and its 'justifications' is extensive. A compre-
  hensive statement and discussion of the classic doctrines is contained in *Punishment – The
  Supposed Justifications* by Ted Honderich, Hutchinson, 1969 Pelican books, 1971: see also
  H L A Hart *Punishment and Responsibility*, Oxford 1968.
2 Andrew Lockyer, 'Justice and Welfare' in Martin and Murray (eds), *The Scottish Juvenile
  Justice System* (1982) p 179.

Punishment as retribution

25.06   The 'pure' theory of punishment as retribution is summed up by
Immanuel Kant thus:

> 'Juridical punishment can never be administered merely as a means for pro-
> moting another good, either with regard to the criminal himself or to civil
> society, but must in all cases be imposed because the individual on whom it
> is inflicted has committed a crime... The principle is that of equality or tal-
> ion which should be carried out in the spirit. Even if civil society were on the
> point of being dissolved with the consent of the members, as for example if
> a people dwelling on an island resolved to separate and scatter to all parts of
> the world, they would be bound first of all to execute the last murderer in
> their prisons, so that each may meet with that fate which his deeds deserve
> and the guilt of blood may not rest upon the people.'[1]

It may be conceded that punishment in this sense is foreign to the hearings' system, even including the provisions of 16(5) and the secure accommodation provisions.

1 Immanuel Kant, *Philosophy of Law*, translated Hastie (1887), p 115.

Punishment as rehabilitation

25.07   It does not follow, however, that punishment in all its aspects need be excluded from the framework of the hearings' system. Barbara Wootton presents a view of punishment far removed from that of Kant:

> '... a sentencing policy which makes the prevention of crime its primary objective is not necessarily to be equated with one that is "soft". Such a policy is non-punitive in the sense that it neither regards punishment as an end in itself nor evaluates crimes and those who commit them in terms of what each is thought to deserve. But, while adhering to the principle of minimum action, it does not rule out the use of penalties or discard deterrence altogether. For everyone knows that human beings respond to a variety of stimuli; and that the responses vary both as between one individual and another and in the same individual in different circumstances. One man may make rich use of opportunity where another may be shocked into change by the loss of cherished privileges. One responds to psychotherapy, another to strict discipline, while for a third perhaps the only hope is an extremely liberal and rewarding regime.[1]'

The philosophical nihilism in relation to the possible reformation of offenders which flourished in the 1970s and the 1980s[2] is now in at least partial recession. In 1998, Bill Whyte, after reviewing some more recent studies, observes:

> 'The evidence from such reviews offers cautious optimism that many approaches to working with young people who offend can be effective in reducing offending. It provides support for those who claim that juvenile offenders' anti-social attitudes can be amended, self-esteem can be boosted, skills can be acquired for making better pro-social decisions for resisting pressures to commit offences and for better self-management'.[3]

There is an element of punishment, in the sense defined at the outset – imposition of an unwelcome and to an extent painful condition validated by the fact that the person punished has committed an offence – in any compulsory measurers of supervision and that element is only more visible when residence in an establishment is insisted upon. The justification in accordance with the philosophy of the Children (Scotland) Act 1995, and its predecessor the Social Work (Scotland) Act 1968 must lie in the belief that the compulsory measures are directed to the promoting the welfare of the child not only because 'it would be better for the child to remain in a place of safety than to be left to his own unprotected devices'[4] but also on the basis that the compulsory measures of supervision – in whatever form they may take, are those to which the offender is entitled in his or her interest.[5]

1 Barbara Wootton (Baroness Wootton of Abinger) *Crime and the Criminal Law: Reflections of a Magistrate and Social Scientist* Hamlyn Lectures for 1963, p 116.
2 E g Martinson, R (1974), '*What Works? Questions and answers about prison reform'*, *The Public Interest*, 10 – referred to in Whyte, B, *Rediscovering Juvenile Delinquency*, in Lockyer, A and Stone, F H *Juvenile Justice in Scotland*, 1998, Edinburgh, T & T Clark.
3 Whyte, B, *Rediscovering Juvenile Delinquency*, in Lockyer, A and Stone, F H *Juvenile Justice in Scotland*, 1998, Edinburgh, T & T Clark, p 207.

4 Per Lord President Emslie delivering the opinion of the court ordering the detention of a child pending investigation of his case in *Humphries v S* 1986 SLT 683 at 684K.
5 Cf Lockyer, A (1982) *'Justice and Welfare'* in Martin, F and Murray, K (eds) *The Scottish Juvenile Justice System*, Scottish Academic Press.

Derogation from the welfare principle – potentially unlimited ambit

25.08   While the derogation from the welfare principle imported by s 16(5) of the Children (Scotland) Act 1995 must be primarily aimed at children referred under s 52(2)(i) and (l)[1] of the Act, it is expressed wholly generally. It is not difficult to figure cases under s 52(2)(a) of the Act,[2] which might necessitate the invocation of the derogation, and possibly there could be cases under a 52(2)(j) or (k).[3] It is more difficult to figure cases under any of the other sections where it would not have been appropriate for the reporter to found upon a ground under s 52(2)(i) and/or (l). However, the derogation imported by s 16(5) is not limited to any ground of referral. Moreover, standing the decision of the Court of Session in *O v Rae*,[4] it would appear to be open to a hearing to invoke the derogation and, say, authorise secure accommodation, if information emerged during the course of a hearing or series of hearings (on any ground) that the public required to be protected from serious harm (whether or not physical harm) or where others might otherwise be injured, even where there was no risk of injury to the child and it was not in the interests of the child to make such an authorisation. The writer's concerns as to the general fairness of this and as to its effect on our obligations under the UN and European Conventions have already been expressed'[5]

1 Offending child and child in local authority accommodation requiring special measures of supervision in the interests of child or others.
2 Child 'beyond the control of any relevant person'.
3 Misuse of alcohol or drug or of volatile substance.
4 1992 SCLR 318, discussed above at 16.06 ff.
5 Above at 16.06 ff.

Limits of the paramountcy principle

25.09   Section 16(1) of the Children (Scotland) Act 1995 is expressed so as to refer to a hearing deciding or a court determining *'any* [emphasis supplied] matter with respect to a child'. It is submitted that it is clear that this provision, while *ex facie* universal in its application by virtue of the use of the indefinite article, is nothing of the sort. It is submitted that it has two effects. In the first place it identifies the welfare of the child throughout childhood as the general focus of concern for hearings. In the second place it guides hearings as to disposal of cases. It does not mean that every decision of a hearing can be made by asking and answering the question 'what do we think is in the best interests of the child?' Hearings have many quasi-judicial functions. Under s 65(9) of the 1995 Act a hearing, if satisfied that a child has not understood the explanation of the grounds of referral given by the chairman shall, unless they decide to discharge the referral, direct the reporter to apply to the sheriff for a finding. It is submitted that it is clear that the decision as to whether or not the child has understood the grounds is a decision which must be made on an objective assessment of the facts. It would be quite wrong for the hearing to reason as follows: 'We find it difficult to assess if the child has really understood the grounds of referral, but he has said that he understands and accepts them and we are convinced it would be in the interests of the child throughout his childhood to be under our jurisdiction, and therefore we will hold that the child has understood the grounds and in the child's interests we will accept that and deal with the case'.

Limits of the paramountcy principle – the interests of others

25.10   In the case of *O v Rae*, where an allegation that a named person had sexually assaulted a child had been made in a report which was available to the hearing, Lord President Hope, delivering the opinion of the court, emphasised that the hearing must treat the alleged offender fairly:

> 'The children's hearing had a duty to act fairly in relation to the appellant [the alleged abuser (who was the child's father)], but that duty was fulfilled so long as they gave him a fair opportunity of correcting or contradicting what was said about him or against him in the reports.'[1]

This reflects the proposition that the paramountcy of the interests of the child does not exclude other interests – in this instance the interests of the alleged abuser to protest his innocence. Of course it may be remarked that it could never be in the true interests of the child to be dealt with on the basis of allegations which had not been thus tested[2] and that what is being said here amounts to no more than a caveat against the unduly facile application of the paramountcy principle. This may be so but it is as well to be explicit.

1 *O v Rae* 1993 SLT 570 at 575C, D.
2 Cf the discussion of best practice at 16.17 above.

THE SECTION 16 PRINCIPLES – THE NO NON-BENEFICIAL ORDER PRINCIPLE

The statutory provision

25.11   Section 16(3) of the Children (Scotland) Act 1995 provides:

> 'In the circumstances mentioned in subsection (4)(a)(i) or (ii) or (b) of this section, no requirement or order so mentioned shall be made with respect to the child concerned unless the children's hearing consider, or as the case may be the sheriff considers, that it would be better for the child that the requirement or order be made than that none should be made at all.'

Meaning of the sub-section (3) provision – terminology – no non-beneficial order

25.12 This principle has been said to be the 'minimum intervention principle'[1] and is often referred to[2] as the 'no order' principle. The minimum, or minimal, intervention principle may be thought to entail that the disposal which is least invasive is always to be preferred.[3] Sub-section (3) merely states that no determination or order shall be made unless the hearing or the court is satisfied that it would be better for the child that the order or determination being considered will be more beneficial for the child than no determination or order at all. The sub-section gives no guidance as between two or more orders which a hearing may be considering. For example, if a hearing had concluded that a child required special educational support and were considering whether or not this should be delivered by a requirement that he should remain at home and attend an establishment or by a requirement, which might be regarded as more invasive, that the child should reside in a residential establishment which provided educational support, the sub-section would not require the hearing to adopt the former course of action. Accordingly the phrase 'the minimum intervention principle' will not be used here. The phrase 'the no order principle' is fairly well established but seems negative and lacks sufficient content. The more informative, although less neat, 'no non-beneficial order principle' is preferred.

1 Norrie *Children (Scotland) Act 1995* (W Green, 1996), p 17.
2 E g in Lockyer A and Stone F H *Juvenile Justice in Scotland* (T & T Clark, 1998), p 106.
3 Cf Ross S and Bilson A (1989) *Social Work Management and Practice* (Jessica Kingsley Publishers, London) p 80: 'A further practice development of a systemic approach is the idea of "creative resolution" of problems. The phrase means that the social worker's action should be brief and direct to help maximise the resources of the client in her system. The social worker's interventions should be the minimum required to bring about an acceptable change and must be aimed at resolving rather than "curing" the problem.'

Avoiding unnecessarily invasive intervention

25.13 Having recognised that the words of the sub-section do not import the principle of minimal intervention into the statutory framework it must be acknowledged that it will often be good practice to avoid a more invasive intervention when the indications are that a less invasive intervention is likely to be equally effective. Barbara Reid observes[1]: 'The child's welfare being paramount, the requirement to seek and take account of children's views and to minimise intervention are each to be found embedded in established practice under the 1968 Act'. Accordingly the writer would not disagree with Professor Norrie's discussion of sub-section (3)[2] where he describes the practical effect of the sub-section as being 'that the onus lies with the person seeking intervention by court order or decision of the children's hearing to justify why intervention is necessary: that justification will nearly always lie in the protection or enhancement of the child's welfare': but the sub-section does not require hearings or courts to adopt an approach which might be summarized as 'the less intervention the better'.

1 In *Panels and Hearings* in Lockyer, A and Stone, F H *Juvenile Justice in Scotland* (1998, Edinburgh, T & T Clark) p 196.
2 *Children (Scotland) Act 1995* (1996, W Green) p 17.

SECTION 16(2) – THE CONSULTING THE CHILD PRINCIPLE

The statutory provision

25.14   Section 16(2) of the Children (Scotland) Act 1995 provides:

> 'In the circumstances mentioned in subsection (4) below, a children's hearing or as the case may be the sheriff, taking account of the age and maturity of the child concerned, shall so far as practicable –
> a)   give him an opportunity to indicate whether he wishes to express his views;
> b)   if he does so wish, give him an opportunity to express them; and
> c)   have regard to such views as he may express;
> and without prejudice to the generality of this subsection a child twelve years of age or more shall be presumed to be of sufficient age and maturity to form a view.'

Sub-section (4) applies this principle inter alia to a hearing which is considering whether to make a supervision requirement and to review hearings.

Conveying the child's views

25.15   By the time the hearing has come to the stage of considering disposal, the child, even if his obligation to attend the hearing has been dispensed with, should have received notification of the hearing including notification that if he wishes to express views then an opportunity will be given to allow this to happen[1] The child may attend the hearing and give his views in person without the assistance of a representative or safeguarder, or the views may be conveyed by the child in writing, on audio or video tape or through an interpreter or by any safeguarder attending the hearing.[2]

1 Children's Hearings (Scotland) Rules 1996, SI 1996/3261, r 6(3) and (4); r 6(4)(c) requires the reporter to convey, before the hearing takes place, any views so expressed to the hearing members, any relevant person and any safeguarder.
2 SI 1996/3261, r 15.

Considering the child's views

25.16   Hearings and judges have long had regard to the views and aspirations of children. In the first edition of this book the safeguarder's rôle in enabling the child's views and aspirations to be conveyed was noticed[1] and in the context of applications for 'custody and access', as the concepts were then known, judges have been astute to consult children.[2] In 1980

Lord Dunpark, in an address to the Scottish Child Law Group,[3] stated that interviewing even quite young children was helpful. Accordingly the provisions of sub-section (2) of section 16 may, like the provisions of sub-sections (1) and (3), be said to give legislative approval to previous good practice: but these provisions systematise and make obligatory what was previously discretionary and unregulated and perhaps constitute the most innovative of the s 16 principles.

1 At pp 47 and 52.
2 See for example *Fowler v Fowler* 1981 SLT (Notes) 9, wherein Lord Stott 'allowed Denise [aged 10] in effect to decide the issue for herself' and *Macdonald v Macdonald* 1985 SLT 245 wherein Lord Dunpark took a similar course but failed to give the parents their say and was reversed on that account.
3 Referred to in *Wilkinson and Norrie on Parent and Child* (1st edn) (1993, W Green) p 255, foot-note 46.

Weight to be given to the views of the child

25.17 It is for the hearing to assess the maturity of the child. A child of 12 and over is presumed to be mature enough to express a view unless the contrary appears. The hearing members may rely largely on their common-sense but may, it is submitted, rely on any expert opinion which may be available.[1] Section 16(2) does not say and must not be interpreted as mean-ing that a child aged under 12 is presumed not to be mature. There are many reported examples,[2] and many more unreported examples, of courts and hearings having regard to the evidence and views of children well under the age of 12 and treating such evidence and views as decisive of crucial matters. Conversely, it does not follow that a child over the age of 12 must necessarily be judged mature. The presumption of maturity is not irrebuttable: however a hearing must have good reason to hold that a child over 12 was not entitled to express a view to which the hearing should pay some regard. How much regard a hearing pays to the views of any child is a matter for the judgement of the hearing members: clearly having regard to a child's views is not to be equated with doing what the child wants.

1 Cf *Cameron v Cameron* 1996 SCLR 552 at 553C-E wherein Lord Hamilton heard directly from a girl just under the age of eight, after having regard to reports of two psychologists who opined that the child was confident and articulate, and proceeded to hold that she had nevertheless not attained a sufficient degree of maturity to entitle the court to take account of her views under the Child Abduction and Custody Act 1985 Schedule 1, art, 13. (For an example of careful arrangements made by the judge in relation to speaking to the child see Lord Hamilton's opinion at 553D ff.).
2 E g *Fowler v Fowler* 1981 SLT (Notes) 9 and *Cameron v Cameron* 1996 SCLR 552.

DISCHARGE

Discharge – when competent

25.18 Where a children's hearing decide not to make a supervision requirement under section 70 of the Children (Scotland) Act 1995 they shall discharge the referral.[1]

1 Children (Scotland) Act 1995, s 69(12) – see also s 65(7) and (9).

Discharge – when appropriate

25.19 It will be appropriate for the hearing to discharge the case under s 69(12) of the Children (Scotland) Act 1995 when, for one reason or another, they consider that no further action by them is required. On the other hand the hearing may take a different view from that which first commended itself to the reporter and conclude that the whole circumstances do not justify the imposition of compulsory measures of supervision. The hearing may simply disagree with the reporter or, more likely, have more extensive or up-to-date information than was originally available to the reporter. The hearing may not, of course, discharge the referral because they do not really believe that the condition or conditions of referral exist: where grounds have been appropriately accepted or held as established by the sheriff these grounds must be taken as a *datum* by the hearing. A decision to discharge the referral under s 69(12) is most commonly met with when the hearing is dealing with a child already under supervision and the hearing decides that the form of supervision the child is undergoing does not require to be changed.

Effect of discharge under s 69(12): Rehabilitation of Offenders Act 1974 – further referral

25.20 A discharge of this type is to be contrasted with the discharge of a referral by the hearing in terms of s 65(7) or s 65(9) and the discharge by the sheriff under s 68(9) the 1995 Act. The former represents the hearing simply dismissing the case from it and the latter amounts to the sheriff quashing the referral completely. Both such discharges are or ought to be equivalent to returning the child to the legal position he would have been in if the referral had never been made in the first place. A discharge under s 69(12), however, recognises the existence of the referral and leaves it on the record. In a referral based upon s 52(2)(i) of the Act it is analogous to the 'absolute discharge' imposed by a court and, like an absolute discharge attracts in such cases a six months rehabilitation period under s 5(3) of the Rehabilitation of Offenders Act 1974.[1] A discharge under this section, like any other disposal, is appealable to the sheriff although, as it is the minimal disposal available to the hearing, such appeals are rare. It is thought that discharge of a referral by a hearing under this section does not operate so as to bar a reporter from founding on the facts of such a referral as *part* of the facts founded upon in a later referral which also includes new factual allegations.[2]

1 See above at 23.09 for further discussion of Rehabilitation of Offenders Act 1974.
2 Cf *McGregor v D* 1981 SLT (Notes) 97; *Kennedy v S* 1986 SLT 679 at 681; the writer is indebted to Professor Norrie for his discussion of this matter in *Children's Hearings in Scotland* (1997) at 111.

SUPERVISION REQUIREMENTS

Supervision requirement without special condition

25.21 Where the hearing are satisfied that compulsory measures of supervision are necessary in respect of a child they may make a supervision requirement. A supervision requirement may have attached to it certain conditions, which will be discussed presently, but it may simply place the child under the supervision of the CSWO of a local authority.[1]

1 Children (Scotland) Act 1995, s 70(1), Children's Hearings (Scotland) Rules 1996, SI 1996/3261, r 25(1), Form 1.

Consequences of any supervision requirement: duties of local authority

25.22   A child who is subject to a supervision requirement becomes a 'looked after' child of the relevant local authority, i e the local authority of the children's panel whose members made up the hearing which imposed the requirement.[1] The basic obligations of a local authority in respect of a child looked after by a local authority are set out in s 17(1) of the Children (Scotland) Act 1995. The local authority is required, in such manner as the Scottish Executive may prescribe,[2] to:

a)   safeguard and promote his [the child's] welfare (which shall, in the exercise of their duty to him be their paramount concern);
b)   make such use of services available for children cared for by their own parents as appear to the authority reasonable in his case; and
c)   take such steps to promote, on a regular basis, personal relations and direct contact between the child and any person with parental responsibilities in relation to him as appear to them to be, having regard to their duty to him under paragraph (a) above, both practicable and appropriate.

The duty under s 17(1)(a) is elaborated in s 17(2) so as to make clear that it includes a duty of providing the child with advice and assistance with a view to preparing him for when he ceases to be looked after by the local authority. Section 17(1)(a) in effect imports the paramountcy principle but s 17(5) provides in effect that if, in order to protect the public from serious harm, physical or otherwise, the local authority thinks it necessary to exercise their powers in such a way as would run counter to the paramountcy principle so imported then it may do so. Before deciding on how to use their powers the local authority shall so far as is reasonably practicable find out the views of the child, his parents, any person having parental rights and any other person whose views the local authority consider relevant and shall have regard to the child's views, if any, taking account of his age and maturity, and have regard to any views expressed by the others they have consulted.[3] The local authority must also have regard to the child's religious persuasion, racial origin and cultural and linguistic background.[4] But none of these factors may operate so as to override the paramountcy principle, imported by s 17(1)(a).[5]

1 Children (Scotland) Act 1995, s 17(6)(b).
2 The Arrangements to Look After Children (Scotland) Regulations 1996, SI 1996/3262, noticed below at 25.23.
3 C(S)A 1995, s 17(3) and (4)(a) and (b).
4 C(S)A 1995, s 17(4)(c).
5 Cf *Re P (a child) (residence order: restriction order)* [1999] 3 All ER 734, discussed above at 25.01.

The Arrangements to Look After Children (Scotland) Regulations 1996[1]

25.23 These Regulations, made by virtue inter alia of s 17(7) of the Act, prescribe the day to day obligations of the local authority in respect of a looked after child. They include obligations (subject always to the requirement to obtain the consent of the mature child enacted by the Age of Legal Capacity (Scotland) Act 1991) to procure medical examination of the child on placement and obligations to ensure that ordinary health care services are provided.[2] They also make provision for procedures on the death of a looked after child[3] and for the circumstances in which a looked after child may be cared for by parents[4] – see discussion below.

1 SI 1996/3262.
2 SI 1996/3262, reg 13.
3 SI 1996/3262, reg 15 – see also s 28 of the Social Work (Scotland) Act 1968, as amended by the Children (Scotland) Act 1995, Sch 4, para 12.
4 SI 1996/3262, r 16.

Effect of a supervision requirement

25.24 It would appear that the purpose of the foregoing provisions is to enable the local authority to be in effect the parent of the child for the duration of the supervision requirement. The obligation to give advice and assistance to the child with a view to preparing him for life when no longer looked after is important and is consonant with the provision that no child shall be subject to a supervision requirement for longer than is necessary for promoting or safeguarding his welfare.[1] The provisions of s 17(1) (a) and (b) of the Children (Scotland) Act 1995 regarding safeguarding and promoting the child's welfare and making use of services available for children being cared for by their own parents, when read with regulation 13 of The Arrangements to Look After Children (Scotland) Regulations 1996 would seem to entitle a local authority to authorise, always subject to the provisions of the Age of Legal Capacity (Scotland) Act 1991 s 2(4), routine medical and dental treatment of a child under supervision, thus rendering it unnecessary for hearings to insert conditions as to treatment under s 70(5)(a) of the 1995 Act in order to permit such routine treatment. These provisions would also seem to convey to the local authority the power to decide matters in relation to the education of the child. These powers are conveyed to the local authority by the making of any supervision requirement – not only by the making of a supervision requirement with a condition requiring residence away from home. It is however unusual, although not unknown, for a local authority to exercise such powers under a supervision requirement which does not contain a condition of residence outside of the home.

1 Children (Scotland) Act 1995, s 73(1).

SUPERVISION REQUIREMENT WITH RESIDENTIAL CONDITION

The provisions

25.25   A supervision requirement may (but need not) contain a condition requiring the child to reside at any place or places specified (i e named) in the requirement.[1] The place or places may be in England or Wales, and in that event shall be authority for the person in charge of such a place to restrict the child's liberty to the extent set out in the Children (Scotland) Act 1995.[2] Since the definition of 'residential establishment' includes a reference to 'a place in Northern Ireland'[3] and since the provisions of s 70(4) about placements in England and Wales are 'without prejudice' to the generality of s 70(3), it would seem that a placement in a residential establishment in Northern Ireland would be competent and could in a particular case where the interests of the child so demanded, be appropriate. A placement in the British Islands other than Scotland, England, Wales or Northern Ireland would not seem to be competent.[4] The hearing may order that any place at which they require the child to reside shall not be disclosed to any person or class of persons specified in the requirement.[5]

1 Children (Scotland) Act 1995, s 70(3); a requirement under s 44(1)(b) of the Social Work (Scotland) Act 1968 which failed to name the establishment was held by the sheriff to be invalid: *R v McGregor* Glasgow Sheriff Court (Sheriff J Irvine Smith) 25 August 1976; see also *R v Children's Hearing for the Borders Region* 1984 SLT 65 at 66.
2 C(S)A 1995, s 70(4).
3 C(S)A 1995, s 93(1).
4 Interpretation Act 1978, s 5, Sch 1: the definitions of 'British Islands' and 'United Kingdom' appear to exclude the Isle of Man and the Channel Islands from the United Kingdom.
5 C(S)A 1995, s 70(6).

Placement at home

25.26   The 'place' may be the child's home provided the local authority is not providing accommodation for the child under s 25 of the Children (Scotland) Act 1995, and that the child is not returned to the care of a parent from which he had been removed by any order, authorisation or warrant.[1] In 1986 a condition under s 44(1)(a) of the Social Work (Scotland) Act 1968 requiring a child to reside with the mother but not under the same roof as the father was upheld by the Court of Session.[2]

1 Arrangements to Look After Children (Scotland) Regulations 1996, SI 1996/3262, reg 16.
2 Cf *C v Kennedy* Court of Session, 4 July 1986 (unreported).

The Fostering of Children (Scotland) Regulations 1996[1]

25.27   These regulations specify investigative procedures which a local authority must comply with in order to check the suitability of a person who is not a relevant person with whom it is proposed to place a child. The local authority must also check that the child is suitable for the person or persons with whom he is to be placed, and that placing the child with the proposed foster parents will be in the child's best interests. Regulation 15 provides that before a local authority may recommend that a children's hearing should place a child under the care of a person who is not a relevant person these procedures must have been carried out. A hearing accordingly must not make a supervision requirement under s 70(3)(a) of the 1995 Act unless it has received a report from the local authority as to the child's needs and the suitability towards meeting those needs of the place and the person or persons who are to have charge or control of the child and the local authority have confirmed that they have carried out the procedures and gathered the information as required by this regulation.[2]

1 SI 1996/3262.
2 Children's Hearings (Scotland) Rules 1996, SI 1996/3261, r 20(6).

Types of residential placement – deciding on the appropriate placement

25.28 A child may be placed in a residential establishment as defined in s 93(1) of the 1995 Act, with approved foster carers, with relatives, or with friends of the family (and at home, as discussed above, 25.23). Except where the child is placed with a relevant person the provisions of the Fostering of Children (Scotland) Regulations 1996 mentioned in the previous paragraph apply.

Placement in a residential establishment

25.29 Any placement away from home constitutes a material intervention in the life of the child but it should not be facilely assumed that placement in a residential establishment is particularly to be avoided. Sir William Utting observed in 1991:[1]

'With residential care widely regarded as a placement of last resort staff are said – not unreasonably – to be in a low state of morale. At the same time, every exploration of residential care, every piece of research, every inspection continues to unearth examples of excellent practice. And young people themselves speak of the advantages and benefits of life in a residential home as compared with foster care.'

In 1997 Scottish Office issued guidance including the following:[2]

'Whether it is appropriate to place a child in a residential home, rather than other types of support or provision, depends on the individual circumstances of the child. It may be suitable in emergency situations and necessary on a longer term basis where a family placement is ruled out for any reason. It has particular advantages for grouping specialist services on the same site. It can provide a suitable setting for looking after brothers and sisters together.'

The decision of the hearing will be affected by the resources available and the ideal may often be unattainable because of lack of resources, but the aim ought always to be to meet as fully as possible the needs of the individual child or children and not to implement any pre-conceived dogma.[3] A requirement to reside in a residential establishment may of course be accompanied by such other condition or conditions as may be thought appropriate.[4]

1 Utting, Sir W *Residential Child Care in England*, HMSO 1991, p 15, para 77.
2 *Scotland's Children – The Children (Scotland) Act 1995 – Regulations and Guidance* vol 2, p 70 para 3.
3 Cf the approach of the House of Lords to the question of the rights of the genetic parent: 'This is a matter which must be decided not by applying any presumption but upon an evaluation of the evidence' – per Lord Hope of Craighead in *Sanderson v McManus* 1997 SCLR 281 at 289F.
4 Children (Scotland) Act 1995, s 70(3)(b).

Practical considerations

25.30   A hearing should not normally impose a requirement to reside in a named establishment unless it is clear from the report before them that a named residential establishment is available and prepared to take the child in. There is, however, no statutory limitation on the hearing's power in this regard and the hearings may, and sometimes do, decide that this form of disposal is appropriate even when such a course is not recommended in the available reports and even when no immediate arrangements are on hand for the child's reception at the establishment. The hearing may make an order under s 70(3)(a) of the Children (Scotland) Act 1995 provided they name an establishment in the order. If, in the event, 'the relevant local authority are unable to make immediate arrangements for his reception in that establishment or place' the local authority may arrange for the child to be temporarily accommodated in some suitable place, other than that specified in the requirement for any period not exceeding twenty-two days commencing on the day of the hearing.[1] If arrangements still cannot be made the reporter must arrange for a review hearing within specified timescales.[2]

1 Children's Hearings (Transmission of Information etc) (Scotland) Regulations 1996, SI 1996/3260, reg 4(1).
2 SI 1996/3260, reg 4 (2) and (3).

Authorisation of secure accommodation

25.31   If, when ordering a placement in a residential establishment, the hearing are satisfied that there exists one or other or both of the identifying criteria indicating the need for a disposal involving secure accommodation (see 25.04 above) they may (not must) make it a condition of the supervision requirement that the child 'shall be liable to be placed and kept in secure accommodation in that establishment during such period as the person in charge of that establishment, with the agreement of the chief social work officer of the relevant local authority considers necessary'.[1] The formal order should follow Form 2.[2] 'Secure accommodation', in this context, means 'accommodation provided in a residential establishment, approved by the Secretary of State [now the Scottish Executive] in accordance with regulations made under section 60(1)(bb) of the Social Work (Scotland) Act 1968 or under paragraph 4(2)(i) of Schedule 4 to the Children Act 1989, for the purpose of restricting the liberty of children.[3] It should be noted that the hearing does not 'order' the child to be held in such accommodation but merely authorises or licenses the manager of the establishment, with the agreement of the CSWO, to hold the child there as he thinks necessary.[4] A hearing will not normally grant such authorisation unless the practical possibilities have been adequately explored in the reports before them.

1 Children (Scotland) Act 1995, s 70(9).
2 Children's Hearings (Scotland) Rules 1996, SI 1996/3261, r 25(2).
3 C(S)A 1995, s 93(1).
4 The Secure Accommodation (Scotland) Regulations 1996, SI 1996/3255, reg 6.

SUPERVISION REQUIREMENT WITH 'ANY' CONDITION

Conditions as to counselling etc

25.32 A supervision requirement may require the child to comply with any condition.[1] The social worker may have prepared a scheme whereby the child may attend for drug or alcohol counselling and if this advice is accepted the particular form of counselling or therapy should be specified in the requirement.

1 Children (Scotland) Act 1995, s 70(3)(b).

Supervision requirement with conditions – special and routine treatment

25.33 This matter has been discussed already.[1]

1 Above at 25.23.

Supervision requirement with conditions – contact

25.34 Hearings are also specifically empowered to 'regulate the contact with the child of any specified person or class of persons'.[1] The hearing is under obligation to consider whether a condition of this type should be attached.[2]

1 Children (Scotland) Act 1995, s 70(5)(b).
2 C(S)A 1995, s 70(2).

'Compulsory measures of supervision' – definition

25.35 The statutory definition is somewhat circular: '"compulsory measures of supervision" means, in respect of a child, such measures of

supervision as may be imposed upon him by a children's hearing'.[1]
Compulsory measures of supervision may reasonably be seen as having
some of the characteristics of a probation order issuing from a court,
with the important differences that a probation order can never be made
'unless the offender expresses his willingness to comply with the
requirements thereof"[2] and that any residential requirement attached to
a probation order can only endure for twelve months[3] whereas the duration of a supervision requirement is governed by s 73(2) and (9) of the
Children (Scotland) Act 1995. There is some analogy between variation
of a supervision requirement and amendment[4] of and breach of probation[5] in the power and duty of the local authority to refer the case to the
reporter if satisfied that variation is required or that a condition is not
being complied with.[6]

1 Children (Scotland) Act 1995, s 93(1).
2 Criminal Procedure (Scotland) Act 1995, s 228(5).
3 CP(S)A 1995, s 229(3)(b).
4 CP(S)A 1995, s 231 and Sch 6.
5 CP(S)A 1995, s 232.
6 C(S)A 1995, ss 71(2) and 73(4)(a) and (b) – discussed below at 25.46ff.

Transfer of child subject to supervision requirement in case of necessity – Act s 72

25.36   Where a child is required by a supervision requirement imposed
under s 70(3)(a) of the 1995 Act to reside in a specific residential establishment or other specified accommodation then if it is in the interests of that
child or other children in that establishment or accommodation in a situation of 'urgent necessity' the CSWO of the relevant local authority may
direct that the child be transferred to another place[1]. Any child so transferred must have his case reviewed by a children's hearing *within seven
days of the transfer.*[2] It has already been submitted that the family home
should not be regarded as 'specific other accommodation'.[3]

1 Children (Scotland) Act 1995, s 72(1).
2 C(S)A 1995, s 72(2).
3 See 19.17 above.

MISCELLANEOUS PROVISIONS AFFECTING SUPERVISION REQUIREMENTS

Views to be ascertained and taken into account

25.37   Before making any decision in respect of a child whom they are
looking after, or are proposing to look after, a local authority shall, so far
as reasonably practicable, find out the views of: the child (should he wish
to express them); the child's parents; any person (not a parent) who has
parental rights; and any other person whose views the authority consider
to be relevant and take such views into account.[1]

1 Children (Scotland) Act 1995, s 17(3); as already noticed (above at 25.13) the s 16
  'consulting the child principle' applies anyway.

The child's religious persuasion, racial origin and cultural and linguistic background

25.38 In making a decision with respect to a child the local authority shall, so far as practicable, have regard to the child's religious persuasion, racial origin and cultural and linguistic background.[1] Note that it is the child's religious persuasion etc that are to be taken into account.[2] As already noticed the Arrangements to Look After Children (Scotland) Regulations 1996[3] prescribe the duties of a local authority when a child is being or is to become a looked after child. As already noticed[4] the paramount concern of the local authority is to safeguard and promote the welfare of the child.[5]

1 Children (Scotland) Act 1995, s 17(4)(c).
2 Cf The United Nations Convention on the Rights of the Child, article 14(1): 'States Parties shall respect the right of the child to freedom of thought, conscience and religion'; and article 9 of the European Convention: '1. Everyone has the right to freedom of thought, conscience and religion ...'; see discussion at 25.01 above of *Re P (a child) (residence order: restriction order)* [1999] 3 All ER 734.
3 SI 1996/3262.
4 See discussion above at 25.22.
5 Children (Scotland) Act 1995, s 17(1)(a).

Coming into effect of supervision requirement

25.39 Under the Social Work (Scotland) Act 1968 a children's hearing was empowered, if satisfied that such a course was proper, to postpone the operation of the requirement.[1] There is no such provision in the Children (Scotland) Act 1995 and it is thought that no such power is now accorded to a hearing.

1 Social Work (Scotland) Act 1968, s 44(3).

Special educational needs; special mental health needs

25.40 Under the Social Work (Scotland) Act 1968 a children's hearing which considered that a child might require special education in terms of s 63 of the Education (Scotland) Act 1962 (re-enacted as s 60 of the Education (Scotland) Act 1980) was expressly empowered, in addition to any other course they might take, to send a report to that effect to the education authority concerned.[1] The same Act also provided that where a hearing took the view that an application for admission to hospital or a guardianship application under Part V of the Mental Health (Scotland) Act 1984 should be made to the sheriff they were to report accordingly to the mental health officer concerned.[2] These provisions are not re-enacted in the Children (Scotland) Act 1995. The duty of the local authority to prepare a care plan for a child who is to become a looked after child[3] should embrace these issues and the local authority's plans should be laid before the hearing in their background report. The hearing may make appropriate conditions based on the information they have received. If a hearing wishes further information they may, as already noticed,[4] continue the case for further investigation.[5]

1 Social Work (Scotland) Act 1968, s 44(4).
2 SW(S)A 1968, s 46.
3 Children (Scotland) Act 1995, s 17(1) and (7); Arrangements to Look After Children (Scotland) Regulations 1996, SI 1996/3262, reg 6 and Sch 2, Part I.
4 Above at 21.11 ff.
5 C(S)A 1995, ss 69(2) and 73(9)(a).

Implied limitations on conditions to supervision requirements: and practical considerations

25.41   While the scope for imposing imaginative 'conditions' in respect of supervision requirements is, in theory, considerable, any condition must be in the interests of the child and, it is thought, should be seen to be so without using any elaborate or far-fetched reasoning. It might, for example, be argued that a particular offending child would be 'better' for making financial recompense to his victim but it is to be doubted whether it would be in the spirit of the Children (Scotland) Act 1995 for a hearing to require a child to take on a part-time job and make reparation out of the proceeds. It might be proposed, in an appropriate case, that a hearing should impose a condition involving practical reparation, eg by repainting a vandalised wall or the like. It is, however, submitted that the advisability of such disposals must be regarded with reserve and, in any event, their effectiveness would depend on firm enforcement and there is no specific machinery for such enforcement within the law or the practice of the hearings system.

Rehabilitation of Offenders Act 1974

25.42   The effect of this Act in relation to a supervision requirement in an offence by the child case has already been discussed.[1]

1 Above at 23.09.

Child under supervision: 'looked after' by the local authority

25.43   As already noticed,[1] a child subject to a supervision requirement becomes a 'looked after' child in terms of s 17 of the 1995 Act.

1 Above at 25.22.

Supervision requirements and parental responsibilities orders under s 86 of the Act

25.44   Under s 16 of the Social Work (Scotland) Act 1968, when read with s 44(5) of that Act a child's being subject to a supervision requirement for three years probably constituted a ground entitling a local authority to resolve to assume parental rights.[1] The s 16 provisions have now been swept away and their approximate equivalent are the provisions for parental responsibilities orders under s 86 of the Children (Scotland) Act

1995. Having been under supervision for three years is not a ground for dispensing with the consent of the relevant person under s 86(2)(b) of the 1995 Act and the court in considering whether or not to make a parental responsibilities order is bound by the s 16 principles.[2] The existence or not of a supervision requirement is simply one matter amongst others for the sheriff to take into account when considering an application for a parental responsibilities order.

1 *Strathclyde Regional Council v B* 1998 Fam LR 142.
2 Children (Scotland) Act 1995, s 16(1)–(4)(b)(i).

Supervision requirement and freeing for adoption

25.45   When a child is under supervision the local authority, as adoption agency, may apply to the court for a dispensation from obtaining the consent of the parent or guardian of the child in any application for freeing for adoption.[1] The court which is making a freeing order in relation to a child subject to a supervision requirement may terminate the supervision requirement.[2]

1 Adoption (Scotland) Act 1978, s 18.
2 A(S)A 1978, s 18 as amended by Children (Scotland) Act 1995, Sch 2, para 11.

DURATION AND REVIEW OF SUPERVISION REQUIREMENTS

25.46 No supervision requirement shall endure for any period longer than is necessary in the interests of promoting or safeguarding the welfare of the child.[1]

1 Children (Scotland) Act 1995, s 73(1).

Referral for review at the instance of the relevant local authority

25.47   A local authority must refer the case of a child under supervision to the reporter for review where satisfied or, as the case may be, aware of any of the following:

- that the supervision requirement ought to cease to have effect or be varied;
- that a condition in the supervision requirement is not being complied with
- that the best interests of the child would be served by the local authority's
  i. applying for a parental responsibilities order under s 86 of the Children (Scotland) Act 1995;
  ii. applying for a freeing order under s 18 of the Adoption (Scotland) Act 1978; or
  iii. placing the child for adoption;
and they intend so to do;[1]

- that an application has been made and is pending, or is about to be made, for adoption under s 12 of the Adoption (Scotland) Act 1978.[2]

1 C(S)A 1995, s 73(4).
2 C(S)A 1995, s 73(5).

Application for review at the instance of child or relevant person

25.48 A child or relevant person may require a review at any time at least 3 months after the making or continuing, with or without variation, of a supervision requirement.[1]

1 Children (Scotland) Act 1995, s 73(6).

Other sources of reviews

25.49 Reviews under s 70(7) of the Children (Scotland) Act 1995 and reviews arising from a transfer of a child under s 72(2) have already been noticed.[1] A relevant person intending to take a child under supervision to live outwith Scotland must give the reporter 28 days' notice with a view to a review being held.[2]

1 Above at 19.18 and 19.16.
2 Children (Scotland) Act 1995, s 73(7).

Reporter's duties

25.50 On receiving any of the foregoing notifications or requisitions the reporter must arrange a review hearing and make any arrangements incidental thereto.[1]

1 Children (Scotland) Act 1995, s 73(8).

Powers of the hearing at review

25.51 A hearing on review has all the powers of a disposal hearing,[1] including the power to continue for investigation,[2] in which event the provisions of s 69(3) to (10)[3] of the 1995 Act apply to such a continuation as they would to the continuation of a disposal hearing by virtue of s 69(1)(a).[4] A hearing may terminate, vary or continue a requirement, with or without variation.[5] The hearing may direct that the address of any specified place or places should not be disclosed to any person or class of persons and specify the same in the requirement.[6] If a hearing convened to consider the case of a child whose supervision requirement will expire in three months and they decide that a supervision requirement is no longer 'required' they may direct the local authority to provide such supervision or guidance as the child may be willing to accept.[7] When considering a referral under s 73(4)(c) or s 73(5) of the 1995 Act,[8] the hearing, irrespective of the substantive disposal under s 73(9), must draw up a report to advise the court which the court must consider before deciding the matter.[9] The timescales prescribed in r 22(7) and (8) of the Children's Hearings (Scotland) Rules 1996 must be observed.

1 Children (Scotland) Act 1995, s 73(9)(d).
2 C(S)A 1995, s 73(9)(a).
3 Discussed above at 21.13 ff.
4 C(S)A 1995, s 73(10).
5 C(S)A 1995, s 73.
6 C(S)A 1995, s 73(11).
7 C(S)A 1995, s 73(8)(a)(v) and (12).
8 Noticed above at 25.44.
9 C(S)A 1995, s 73(13) and (14).

Limits on duration of a supervision requirement

25.52 Unless varied or continued under s 73(9) of the 1995 Act a supervision requirement expires at the end of a period of one year.[1] A supervision requirement which is in place on the child becoming 18 ceases to have effect on that date;[2] but the reporter must arrange a hearing within three months of the date on which a supervision requirement is due to expire.[3] Accordingly, it is unlikely in practice that a supervision requirement will be allowed to expire simply by the child reaching 18. A condition of a supervision requirement expires when the sheriff allows an appeal and directs that the condition shall cease to have effect.[4] A supervision requirement expires when the sheriff sustains an appeal and discharges the child from any further hearing.[5] It must however be remembered that in the event of an appeal being taken against the decision of the sheriff the supervision requirement or condition is re-instated.[6] Accordingly discharge of a referral by a sheriff 'cannot be operative until expiry of the 28 appeal days under s 50(2) [of the 1968 Act]'.[7]

1 Children (Scotland) Act 1995, s 73(2).
2 C(S)A 1995, s 73(3).
3 C(S)A 1995, s 73(8)(a)(v).
4 C(S)A 1995, s 51(5)(b).
5 C(S)A 1995, s 51(5)(c)(ii).
6 *Kennedy v M* 1995 SCLR 88 at 94D ff; *Stirling v Grieve* 1995 SCLR 460 at 463G – 465A.
7 *Stirling v D* 1995 SCLR 460 at 464C, 1995 SLT 1089; cf C(S)A 1995, 51(b).

Review of supervision requirement containing authorisation of secure accommodation

25.53 Where a secure accommodation authorisation under s 70(9) of the 1995 Act has been imposed or continued the reporter must arrange a review within 3 months of the condition under s 70(9) being made or continued.[1] Where a child has been made subject to a s 70(9) authorisation and has not in the preceding 6 weeks been placed in secure accommodation by virtue of that authorisation then the child or relevant person may require a review which the reporter must arrange within 21 days.[2] Such a review counts as a review under regulation 11(1) of the Secure Accommodation (Scotland) Regulations 1996.

1 Secure Accommodation (Scotland) Regulations 1996, SI 1996/3255, reg 11(1).
2 SI 1996/3255, reg 12.

No longer any residual power of government to terminate a supervision requirement

25.54   The Social Work (Scotland) Act 1968 provided that the Secretary of State, if satisfied 'in all the circumstances of a case and in the interests of a child' that any supervision requirement should be terminated might by order terminate it.[1] This provision has been repealed[2] and has no equivalent in the Children (Scotland) Act 1995.

1 Social Work (Scotland) Act 1968, s 52.
2 Children (Scotland) Act 1995, Sch 5.

CHAPTER 26

Procedural obligations of reporter and local authority on disposal of case

DUTIES OF REPORTER

Notification to parties etc

26.01   Any decision on disposal of the case whether on initial referral or on review of a supervision requirement must be notified by the reporter in writing to the child, any relevant person, any safeguarder and the local authority.[1] Such notification shall include details of the supervision requirement, a copy of the statement of reasons for the decision, and, except in the case wherein the sheriff has ruled that no subsequent appeal against a supervision requirement shall lie until 12 months have elapsed,[2] it must advise as to the right of appeal to the sheriff under s 51 of the Children (Scotland) Act 1995. These obligations to notify are expressly made subject to the provisions in ss 70(6) and 73(11) of the Act empowering hearings not to disclose the address of the child when making or continuing placements in foster homes or residential establishments.[3] Where a hearing have made a decision disposing of a child's case the reporter is obliged to notify as soon as practicable any person with whom the child is residing.[4]

1 Children's Hearings (Scotland) Rules 1996, SI 1996/3261, r 21(1).
2 Children (Scotland) Act 1995, s 51(7).
3 SI 1996/3261, r 21(1).
4 SI 1996/3261, r 21(2)(a).

Notification to police of disposals and of making and termination of supervision requirements of over 16s

26.02   In a case originating with the police[1], notification of a disposal must be sent 'to the chief constable of the police area'[2] – presumably the police area within which the hearing is situated, but possibly the police area of the notifying officer. Where a supervision requirement is made or terminated in relation to a child who has reached the age of 16 the reporter must notify the chief constable of the area within which the hearing is situated and, if the child resides in another police area, the chief constable of that area.[3]

1 Cf above at 1.25ff.
2 Children's Hearings (Scotland) Rules 1996, SI 1996/3261, r 21(2)(b).
3 SI 1996/3261, r 21(3); cf 19.26 to 19.28 above and 26.03 below.

Child under supervision reaching 16

26.03   Where a child subject to a supervision requirement reaches 16 the reporter must advise the chief constable of the police area[1] – presumably the police area of the child's residence.

1 Children's Hearings (Scotland) Rules 1996, SI 1996/3261, r 33.

26.04   Where a children's hearing decide on the disposal of a child's case the reporter must notify any person with whom the child is residing.[1] In practice if the effect of the decision is that a person ceases to be responsible for the child, then the reporter must give notice of the decision to that person as soon as possible. If the child is to be placed in a residential establishment, then the notification must be given to the person in charge of that establishment.

1 Children's Hearings (Scotland) Rules 1996, SI 1996/3261, r 21(2)(a).

DUTIES OF LOCAL AUTHORITY

Sending social background report to carer

26.05   When a child has been made subject to a supervision requirement and the person in charge of the child is other than the local authority itself, the local authority is empowered, if it thinks that any report which was put before the hearing would assist that person in caring for the child, to make such report available to that person as soon as practicable after it has received the notification mentioned in para 26.01.[1] The local authority may also furnish any relevant information to the carer of a child subject to a supervision requirement.[2]

1 Children's Hearings (Transmission of Information etc) (Scotland) Regulations 1996, SI 1996/3260, reg 3.
2 SI 1996/3260, reg 3.

Local authority unable to effect immediate residential placement

26.06   As already noted,[1] where a supervision requirement contains a residential condition (whether in a residential establishment or elsewhere) and the place of residence is unable to accommodate the child right away, then the local authority may arrange for the child to be temporarily accommodated 'in some suitable place' for a period not exceeding 22 days commencing with the making of the relevant supervision requirement or continuation or variation thereof.[2] In the event of the 22 day period being insufficient to enable the child to be placed then the local authority should, before the expiry of the 22 days, refer the case to the reporter under s 73(4) of the Children (Scotland) Act 1995 for review.[3] Such a hearing has to take place as soon as is reasonably practicable and in any event within 7 days of the reporter receiving the reference by the authority.[4] If the hearing takes place outwith the 22 days then the child may be kept in the temporary accommodation until the sitting of the hearing.[5] It would seem from these time limits that a child is not to remain in temporary accommodation under these provisions for a period exceeding 29 days.

1 See above at 25.30.
2 Children's Hearings (Transmission of Information etc) (Scotland) Regulations 1996, SI 1996/3260, reg 4(1).

3 SI 1996/3260, reg 4(2).
4 SI 1996/3260, reg 4(3)(a).
5 SI 1996/3260, reg 4(3)(b).

Conveyance of child to place

26.07 It is also the duty of the local authority when a child has to be conveyed to a residential establishment or other place as a result of a supervision requirement having been imposed (or under the provisions of s 82(1), (3) or (5) of the 1995 Act anent fugitive children), to ensure that the child is conveyed to that place.[1]

1 Children's Hearings (Transmission of Information etc) (Scotland) Regulations 1996, SI 1996/3260, reg 5.

Monitoring of placement

26.08 When a child is placed in accommodation the local authority must advise the relevant education and health authorities, keep the placement monitored in accordance with fixed time limits and if necessary promote a review of the supervision requirement.[1]

1 Arrangements to Look After Children (Scotland) Regulations 1996, SI 1996/3262, regs 7, 13 and 18.

Termination of placement

26.09 The duty imposed on a local authority[1] to advise all persons who received notice of the placement applies to a termination of placement in consequence of the termination of a supervision requirement.

1 By the Arrangements to Look After Children (Scotland) Regulations 1996, SI 1996/3262, reg 19(2).

Part IV
The application to the sheriff for a finding

CHAPTER 27

The application to the sheriff: general

THE SEPARATION OF ADJUDICATION OF FACT FROM DISPOSAL

The Kilbrandon origins

27.01 The Kilbrandon report recommended that the 'adjudication of the allegation issue' should be a matter for the court whereas 'consideration of the measures to be applied' was to be the responsibility of the new institution which the report referred to as 'the panel'.[1] This body 'would thus exercise jurisdiction on the basis of facts established either by the acceptance of the child in the parents' presence and with their agreement, or after adjudication in a court of law'.[2] This separation of function has been described by Lord President Hope as 'the genius of this reform'.[3]

1 *Children and Young Persons: Scotland* (1964) Cmnd 2306 ('the Kilbrandon Report'), para 72.
2 Kilbrandon Report, para 73.
3 *Sloan v B* 1991 SLT 530 at 548E.

Statutory basis for sheriff's function

27.02 The function of the sheriff now derives from s 65 (7) and (9) of the Children (Scotland) Act 1995. The detail of these sub-sections will be discussed presently but broadly they provide that unless the grounds of referral are accepted by the relevant person(s) and by a child who is able to understand them then the matter must go the sheriff for proof unless the hearing are prepared to discharge the referral there and then.

Terminology

27.03 While the applications to the sheriff for proof derive from the provisions of s 65 (7) and (9) of the 1995 Act the principal provisions affecting these proofs are contained in s 68. Accordingly proofs and other procedures in relation to applications to the sheriff will here be identified under reference to s 68.

THE RULES AND THE FORMS

The 1997 Rules

27.04 The procedural rules governing applications to the sheriff are enacted in Chapter 3 of the Act of Sederunt (Child Care and Maintenance

Rules) 1997 (hereinafter 'the 1997 Rules').[1] The forms in the Schedule to the 1997 Rules may be varied as circumstances may require.[2]

1 SI 1997/291, reproduced in Appendix 5.
2 SI 1997/291, r 1.2(3).

The body of the application

27.05   The initiating writ in this procedure is, by virtue of r 3.45 of the 1997 Rules, in the style of Form 60 of these Rules. The application consists of a heading identifying the sheriff court to which application is made, followed by a recital of the procedure before the hearing. The form requires the applicant reporter to identify the child, the relevant person and any safeguarder appointed by the hearing and to state whether the application is made under 'section 65(7) **or** 65(9)' [emphasis supplied]. It seems clear that the 'or' is not disjunctive and in practice it is very common for applications to be made relying on both subsections as when the relevant person did not admit the grounds of referral (s 65(7)) and the hearing were satisfied that the child was not capable of understanding, or did not in fact understand the explanation of grounds of referral (s 65(9)). Thereafter there must be narrated which conditions/statements are not accepted and by whom. It is important that this part of the application be filled up so as accurately to reflect what happened at the hearing. This was not achieved in the Orkney case and this resulted in criticism by the Court of Session.[1] The form goes on to state that the application is accompanied by the Statement of Grounds of Referral[2] and the report of any safeguarder.[3]

1 *Sloan v B* 1991 SLT 530 at 547H ff.
2 For style of this Statement see above at 16.03 and 16.09.
3 For the rôle of the safeguarder at the children's hearing see above at Chapter 17.

The formal craves

27.06   The form concludes with the formal craves to the court:

> 5. The Principal Reporter therefore makes application to the sheriff to find whether the grounds of referral not accepted by the said* *[insert name of child]* or *[insert name of relevant person or persons]* * or not understood by the said child are established.
> 6. The Principal Reporter requests the sheriff to remove the obligation on the child to attend the hearing in view of *[insert reason(s)]*. And to dispense with service on *[insert name and give reasons]*.*
> *delete as appropriate

The form is to be signed by a reporter and dated and the name, designation, address, telephone number, fax number and DX code of the reporter should also be supplied.

Meaning of 'reporter' on forms

27.07   As noticed already[1] the Children (Scotland) Act 1995 adopts the device of using the term 'the principal reporter' to include all to whom the principal reporter's powers under the Act are delegated. The forms of course reflect this scheme. In practice the reporter who signs Form 60 and other forms will be a reporter manager, an authority reporter or other reporter employed by SCRA. The forms in relation to the proceedings before the sheriff are court papers and it appears to be accepted that the signing reporter must be qualified to practise in the court in these proceedings either by being a Scottish solicitor holding a current practising certificate or a member of the Faculty of Advocates, or by virtue of one year's experience as a depute reporter[2] under regulations 3 and 4 of the Reporters (Conduct of Proceedings before the Sheriff) (Scotland) Regulations 1997.[3] It may be thought desirable for the signing reporter to be the reporter who was present at the children's hearing but this is not necessary. Nor is it necessary, although it is desirable, for the reporter conducting the application before the sheriff to be the signing reporter or the reporter who was present at the children's hearing. There seems no reason why one qualified reporter could not sign on behalf of another.

1 Above at 2.03 to 2.06, discussing the Children (Scotland) Act 1995, s 40(5) and 93(1).
2 A reporter who qualifies under this provision who is also on the Roll of solicitors of the Law Society of Scotland does not require to hold a practising certificate: *Miller v Law Society of Scotland* 2000 SLT 513.
3 It might be argued that SI 1997/291, r 3.21 allowed the principal reporter to be represented by an 'other representative authorised by the party' provided the sheriff was satisfied that such representative was suitable. In practice this provision is not relied upon by the principal reporter and no machinery exists for identifying 'suitable' persons. In any event the existence of the Reporters (Conduct of Proceedings before the Sheriff) (Scotland) Regulations 1997 suggests that the legislature did not intend r 3.21 to be invoked by the principal reporter.

Jurisdiction of reporter

27.08   Since individual reporters derive their powers by delegation by the principal reporter it would now seem clear that all appropriately qualified reporters have right of audience before all the sheriffs of Scotland. The issue of right of audience before sheriffs principal is discussed later.[1]

1 Below at 54.20.

Dispensing with the obligation of the child to attend

27.09   The child has an unqualified right to attend the hearing of a s 68 application,[1] and, unless his attendance is dispensed with, is under obligation to attend.[2] The obligation to attend may be dispensed with by the sheriff in an application in which the ground of referral is based on the 'child-abuse' type conditions contained in paras (d), (e), (f) or (g) of s 52(2) of the 1995 Act and the sheriff is satisfied that the attendance of the child 'is not necessary for the just hearing' of the application.[3] The child's obligation to attend may be dispensed with in any application where the sheriff is satisfied that 'it would be detrimental to the interests of the child for him to be present at the hearing of the application'.[4] Where dispensation is sought the reporter should complete para (6) of Form 60 appropriately.

The appropriate time for consideration of these issues is when the application is lodged under r 3.45 of the 1997 Rules.[5] No formal procedures have been enacted but it is submitted that the reporter should draw any such crave to the attention of the sheriff clerk on lodgement of the application and the sheriff clerk should place the matter before the sheriff who should make such enquiries, if any, as he or she may consider appropriate before deciding on whether or not to make the dispensation. Since dispensation from the obligation to attend may be misinterpreted as a discouragement to attend or even as an abridgement of the right to attend the sheriff in some cases may wish to be assured that the child is aware of his rights. In any event such a dispensation is an important step in the procedure and the reporter should be ready to justify it to the sheriff. It will often be desirable for even a young child to be present – the sheriff may wish to see the child.[6] Having regard to the unqualified right of the child to attend it is submitted that the sheriff, even if dispensing with the obligation to attend, should not dispense with service on the child unless satisfied that the child is too young to be able to read the application. If the sheriff were to consider that part of the application should not be served on the child he has power, on application by the applicant or *ex proprio motu* to order that a specified part of the application is not served on the child.[7]

1 Children (Scotland) Act 1995, s 68(4)(a).
2 C(S)A 1995, s 68(4)(b).
3 C(S)A 1995, s 68(5)(a).
4 C(S)A 1995, s 68(5)(b).
5 *Quaere* if it would be in order for the sheriff so to dispense at a later stage, e g where at the proof the child had not turned up. It is tentatively submitted that this would be lawful, although only in special circumstances – e g where information had become available, after the lodging of the application, which was detrimental to the interests of the child concerned in the application. The sheriff would require to be assured that the child had been made aware of his right to attend.
6 Cf *Kennedy v B* 1972 SC 128 at 130, which indicates that the sheriff to an extent relied upon his observations of the child in court.
7 SI 1997/291, r 3.4(2).

Dispensing with service on other persons

27.10   The other persons (apart from the child) who should be served with the application are the relevant person(s)[1] and any 'safeguarder appointed by the sheriff'.[2] (The implication of Form 60 para 'a' iii is that there is no obligation to serve on a safeguarder appointed by the hearing but since any safeguarder appointed by the hearing is one of the 'persons named in the application'[3] it is thought that a safeguarder appointed by the children's hearing should also be served.) It is thought that service on any safeguarder who has been appointed should never be dispensed with. It is difficult to figure a situation wherein it would be right to dispense with service on a relevant person whose whereabouts was known.

1 SI 1997/291, r 3.12(1)(f) – Form 39.
2 SI 1997/291, r 3.12 (1)(f) and Form 60 para 'a' ii and iii.
3 Cf SI 1997/291, r 3.12(1).

CONDITIONS, FACTS AND GROUNDS: 'ACCEPT THOSE GROUNDS IN PART'[1]

'Grounds of referral'

27.11   As noticed already[2] the Children (Scotland) Act 1995 seems to regard the 'grounds of referral' as being a condition or conditions listed in s 52(2) on which reliance is being placed *together* with the facts alleged in support of the condition or conditions. It appears therefore that where the Act refers in s 65(6) and (7) to 'grounds' being accepted 'in part' it may be taken as meaning equally partial acceptance of conditions (i e accepting one condition and not another) or partial acceptance of alleged facts, or both.

1 Discussed more fully above at 23.13 ff.
2 Above at 16.02 ff.

Non-acceptance, or only partial acceptance of grounds

27.12   Unless the child, being a child who is mature enough and has understood the chairman's explanation of the grounds, and the relevant person(s) accept entirely the grounds of referral stated by the reporter then, unless the hearing decide to discharge the referral or, in the case of a partial acceptance, decide that they can proceed on the basis of what has been accepted, the hearing must direct the reporter to make application to the sheriff 'for a finding as to whether such grounds for the referral as are not accepted by the child and [sic – but surely an error – 'or' must surely have been intended] the relevant person are established'.[1]

1 Children (Scotland) Act 1995, s 65(7).

Partial acceptance – the practicalities

27.13   In practice the reporter who signs Form 60 makes a hand-written note, such as 'Not accepted by child' against the appropriate averment. It is now clear that at the proof any acceptance, partial or otherwise, may be retracted at the s 68 proof.[1]

1 *Kennedy v R* 1992 SCLR (Notes) 546, sub nom *Kennedy v R's curator ad litem* 1993 SLT 295 – discussed below at 36.09 ff.

Grounds not understood

27.14   Where the hearing are satisfied that the child for any reason will not be capable of understanding or has not understood the chairman's explanation of the grounds of referral then they must direct an application to the sheriff for a finding or discharge the referral.[1] The 1995 Act does not explicitly deal with the situation wherein the relevant person does not understand the explanation of the grounds, but clearly a person who has not understood the explanation of grounds cannot be regarded as having accepted them and non-acceptance would have to be recorded.

1 Children (Scotland) Act 1995, s 65(9).

CHAPTER 28

Jurisdiction of the sheriff

THE SHERIFF AND THE SHERIFFDOMS

The office of sheriff

28.01   In Scotland the sheriff is the judge presiding in the local court. He or she is a legally qualified judge holding the Royal Warrant. A sheriff is removable only if the Lord President of the Court of Session and the Lord Justice-Clerk have, after investigation, advised the Scottish Ministers that the sheriff is unfit for office by 'inability, neglect of duty or misbehaviour' and the Scottish Ministers have laid before the Scottish Parliament an order which the Parliament does not annul.[1] Sheriffs (except honorary sheriffs) must be advocates or solicitors of at least ten years' standing. The use of temporary sheriffs appointed under s 11(2) of the Sheriff Courts (Scotland) Act 1971 has been discontinued following the decision of the Court of Session in *Starrs v Ruxton*.[2] The sheriff court has a wide civil and criminal jurisdiction. In civil matters actions for payment of any amount are competent, as are actions for divorce, separation, and actions declaring the rights and responsibilities for children. In criminal matters the sheriff may, when sitting with a jury, try all serious crimes except those reserved to the High Court of Justiciary, namely, treason, murder, rape, breach of duty by magistrates and certain statutory offences such as offences under the Official Secrets Act 1911.[3] The sheriff may impose up to three years' imprisonment or, in a case wherein such disposal is thought to be inadequate, remit the accused to the High Court for sentence. When sitting alone the sheriff may try less serious criminal charges and may, in relation to certain common law offences, impose up to six months' imprisonment and, in relation to certain statutory offences, may impose up to twelve months' imprisonment. The sheriff also has numerous administrative responsibilities.[4] In judicial status the office of sheriff in Scotland is parallel to that of circuit judge in England.

1 Sheriff Courts (Scotland) Act 1971, s 12, Scotland Act 1998, s 53(2)(3); for definition of 'inability' see *Stewart v Secretary of State for Scotland* 1998 SC (HL) 81.
2 2000 JC 208, 1999 SCCR 1052, 2000 SLT 42.
3 *Renton & Brown's Criminal Procedure* (W Green, 6 edn, ed Gordon) 2-08.
4 See *Macphail on Sheriff Court Practice* (W Green, 2 edn, ed Nicholson and Stewart) (Edinburgh 1998) Chapter 26.

The sheriffdoms

28.02   There are six sheriffdoms: Grampian, Highland and Islands; Tayside, Central and Fife; Lothian and Borders; Glasgow and

Strathkelvin; North Strathclyde; and South Strathclyde, Dumfries and Galloway. Except for Glasgow and Strathkelvin each sheriffdom is divided into sheriff court districts each with its individual court. For a description of the extent of these districts the reader may consult *Index to Sheriff Court Districts in Scotland* by Charles McCaffrey.[1] A more up-to-date and highly 'user friendly' text is *Scottish Courts Companion – A Guide for Busy Professionals* by the late Temporary Sheriff David T Crowe LLB WS.[2]

1 W Green, 1981.
2 T & T Clark, Edinburgh, 1998.

STATUS AND FUNCTION OF SHERIFF IN CHILDREN'S REFERRAL PROCEEDINGS

Privacy – discretion of sheriff as to who may be present

28.03　The proceedings before the sheriff are heard 'in chambers',[1] which implies a degree of privacy. The exact degree of privacy is not defined and the categories of persons mentioned in s 43 of the Children (Scotland) Act 1995 and rules 11, 12 and 13 of the Children's Hearings (Scotland) Rules 1996 (the 1996 Rules)[2] have no explicit application to the sheriff. However, since the privacy accorded to children and families may be abridged at the hearing stage by the presence of the persons mentioned in rule 13 of the 1996 Rules (CPAC members, potential panel members in training, persons studying the system etc and 'any other person whose presence at the hearing may in the opinion of the chairman be justified by special circumstances') it would seem illogical if similar categories of person were not to be regarded as in principle admissible to the proceedings before the sheriff. Ultimately the sheriff has a discretion as to whom he will admit to chambers (see the observations of Lord President Hope in the following paragraph). This discretion must be exercised reasonably and in accordance with the tone of the 1995 Act and article 16 of the UN Convention on the Rights of the Child which entered into force for the United Kingdom on 15 January 1992. The implications of article 16 will be discussed in the following paragraph. The presence of sheriffs as part of their training is unobjectionable. The writer has approved the presence of bona fide students of the system. It will always be appropriate to notify parties and witnesses and obtain their reaction to the possibility of outsiders being present. In particular the views of the child, ideally with the advice of a solicitor, curator *ad litem* or safeguarder, should be taken into account. But the 'permission' of parties should not be regarded as decisive, since it may be given as a result of an imagined impression that the sheriff will be displeased if it is withheld. The overriding objective is the interest of the child to be accorded a fair hearing. If the sheriff considers that the presence of an outsider would prejudice the achievement of this objective he should exclude such outsider.

1 Children (Scotland) Act 1995, s 93(5).
2 Discussed above at 22.10 ff.

Presence of representative of the media – the position in 1991

28.04   In the Orkney case evidence was not led but extensive argument took place and on the following day the sheriff read out a judgement which dealt with points of competency and also[1] revealed the contents of productions which would presumably have been part of the evidence had a proof taken place. Until the lunch break on the first day the press were not present but after lunch, 'having been advised that none of the counsel for the curators or for the parents had any objections'[2] the sheriff admitted representatives of the press to be present. The press were also present during the reading of the judgement on the following day. On appeal to the Court of Session it was argued that the provision in s 42(4) of the Social Work (Scotland) Act 1968 that the proceedings should be held 'in chambers' carried the implication that only persons with a right or duty to attend should have been admitted. Rejecting this submission Lord President Hope, delivering the opinion of the First Division, after noting that bona fide representatives of the press were entitled as of right to be present at a session of a children's hearing under s 35 of the 1968 Act, stated:

> 'It does not seem logical that they can attend proceedings of a children's hearing, but must be excluded from the sheriff's chambers when he is dealing with the same matter under s 49(1) on appeal. No doubt there will be cases, especially where the sheriff is hearing evidence under s 42(4), where the press should not be allowed to attend at all. But by providing that the proceedings are to be in chambers, Parliament has done what was necessary to allow him to decide this matter as he thinks fit. It is a matter for his discretion and thus subject entirely to his control as to who, other than those who have a duty or right to be there, may attend, and for how long they may remain.'[3]

1 Inappropriately, as was subsequently held in *Sloan v B* 1991 SLT 530 at 551J ff.
2 *Sloan v B* 1991 SLT 530 at 543I.
3 *Sloan v B* 1991 SLT 530 at 551F, G.

The 1995 Act and privacy

28.05   Section 43(4) of the Children (Scotland) Act 1995, in contrast to s 35 of the Social Work (Scotland) Act 1968, does not accord to the press an unqualified right to be present at a children's hearing, but empowers the hearing to exclude the media, if the hearing are satisfied that:

a)   'it is necessary to do so in the interests of the child, in order to obtain the child's views in relation to the case before the hearing; or

b)   the presence of that person is causing, or is likely to cause, significant distress to the child.'

After such exclusion the chairman 'may' explain to the person excluded the substance of what has taken place in his absence.[1] Other provisions in the 1995 Act and subordinate legislation give ambiguous signals in relation to privacy. On the one hand there is the power conferred upon the sheriff to obtain the views of the child and hold them as confidential.[2] On the other hand there is the provision, precipitated by the *McMichael* case,[3] that all the reports etc which are to be considered by the hearing must be given to relevant persons.[4] The prohibitions on identification of any child involved in hearings' proceedings, which we shall examine presently, are more stringent than those in the 1968 Act. On balance, it is submitted that the tone of the 1995 Act, with its strongly child-centred approach, is inimical to any factor which might detract from the child being dealt with in as unthreatening an atmosphere as possible.

1 Children (Scotland) Act 1995, s 43(5).
2 Act of Sederunt (Child Care and Maintenance Rules) 1997, SI 1997/291, r 3.5(4).
3 *McMichael v United Kingdom* (1995) 20 EHRR 205.
4 Children's Hearings (Scotland) Rules 1996, SI 1996/3261, r 5(3).

The European Convention on Human Rights and the UN Convention on the Rights of the Child

28.06   Article 8 of the European Convention provides:

1.   Everyone has the right to respect for his private and family life, his home and correspondence.
2.   There shall be no interference by a public authority with the exercise of this right except such as is in accordance with the law and is necessary in a democratic society in the interests of national security, public safety or the economic well-being of the country, for the prevention of disorder or crime, for the protection of health or morals, or for the protection of the rights and freedoms of others.

The court is a public authority[1] and as from 2 October 2000 the existing law will require to be interpreted in the light of this and the other provisions of the Convention. Article 16 of the UN Convention has similar provisions specifically in relation to children.

1 Human Rights Act 1998, s 6(3)(a).

Persons who may be present – the position now

28.07   As made clear in the remarks of Lord President Hope in the Orkney case the sheriff has a wide discretion in relation to whom he admits to chambers. Not only was no criticism made of the sheriff for exercising his discretion in favour of admitting the press but the Lord President also went on to say, 'and for what it is worth we think he was right to exercise his discretion as he did in the exceptional circumstances of this case ...'. The Lord President did however recognize that there would be cases, once the stage of hearing evidence was reached, when it might be appropriate to exclude the press. It is submitted that the developments since 1991 have pointed the sheriff towards being very cautious indeed before admitting the press to proof hearings.[1] Giving and listening to evidence on many of the matters which form the subject matter of s 68 proofs is a daunting enough experience which may be made more daunting by the presence of the media. The provisions enabling the evidence of children to be presented by live television link[2] recognise the daunting quality of giving evidence. Where the sheriff has decided to exercise the power[3] to exclude 'any person' from proceedings while any child is giving evidence there is no obligation on the sheriff to inform that person of the substance of what the child has said – in contrast to the position of a relevant person who has been excluded (who must, where not legally represented, be so informed).[4]

1 The writer finds himself, somewhat to his surprise on such a topic, to differ, at least in emphasis, from the view of Professor Norrie who states 'Given the limitations on what may be reported it may be that sheriffs ought usually to permit journalists to be present unless there is good reason why they should not be.' – Norrie *Children's Hearings in Scotland* (1997) p 82.
2 Act of Sederunt (Child Care and Maintenance) Rules 1997, SI 1997/291, r 3.22.
3 SI 1997/291, r 3.47(6).
4 SI 1997/291, r 3.47(7).

Prohibition of publication of proceedings

28.08 Stringent restrictions are imposed on the reporting in relation to any application to the sheriff under ss 57 (CPO), 60(7) (recall etc of CPO), 65(7) or (9) (proof proceedings under s 68), 76(1) (EO), 85(1) (application to open up case in which grounds have been established) and any appeal under Part II of the Children (Scotland) Act 1995. No media report may contain material which is intended to or is likely to identify any child involved or an address or school as being that of such a child.[1] This prohibition extends not only to the child who is the subject of the referral but also to any child witness.[2] Contravention of this prohibition is an offence punishable on summary conviction by a fine of up to 'level four' – at present £2,500 – for each contravention.[3] 'Publish' is defined so as to include causing material to be published,[4] with the consequence that any person who passes on any information or document intending that it be published or in a situation where publication is a likely consequence of so doing may be committing the offence. It is a defence for the accused to prove that he did not know, and had no reason to suspect, that the published matter was intended, or was likely to identify the child, the address, or the school.[5] The ban on publication may, 'in the interests of justice', be dispensed with by the sheriff, the Court of Session on appeal, or by the Scottish Executive 'to such an extent as the sheriff, the Court or the Secretary of State as the case may be considers appropriate.[6] *Quaere* if the decision of a sheriff or the Court of Session as to whether it is in the interests of justice to make this dispensation is one to which the paramountcy principle of s 16(1) of the Act applies. Professor Norrie[7] considers that this principle does apply but is then compelled to read the sub-section as meaning 'in the interests of justice *to the child*' and he accepts that, except on the application of a child who wanted to clear his name it is difficult to figure a situation where it would be in the interests of the child to lift the ban.

The writer strongly sympathises with the thrust of Norrie's view – the whole scheme of the Act, like its predecessor the Social Work (Scotland) Act 1968 is (subject to the reservation to the Lord Advocate of the right to prosecute children) to deal with children in accordance with their needs and welfare. The writer is nevertheless inclined to think that the view might be taken (a) that the decision as to whether publication is 'in the interests of justice' is a matter of legal judgement, in the same category as a decision as to sufficiency of evidence,[8] and (b) that the plain meaning of the provision is that the court is bound to consider 'the interests of justice' at large without the qualification 'to the child'. In construing the paramountcy principle in s 1 (1) of the Children Act 1989[9] the English courts have treated the issue of the decision as to publication as a 'balancing exercise'.[10] Of course as Ward LJ stated,[11] in relation to the less absolute paramountcy principle in the Children Act 1989:

> 'If welfare is not paramount because a question of upbringing is not being determined, then welfare must be balanced against freedom of publication'.

But even on the basis that welfare should dominate the decision his Lordship stated:[12]

> 'Although the welfare of the child is paramount in the sense that it rules upon and determines the course to be followed, that does not mean that when this is the test, the freedom of publication is not to be weighed in scales at all. Of course it is. It is one of the relevant facts, choices and other circumstances which a reasonable parent would take into account. We do not live in a vacuum and our choices have to be made for ourselves as well as for our children in the realisation that we sometimes have to sacrifice self for the greater good of the social order.'[13]

As noted already, however,[14] the pre-2 October 2000 law may have to be re-examined in the light of the European Convention on Human Rights.

1 Children (Scotland) Act 1995, s 44(1).
2 *McArdle v Orr* 1994 SLT 463.
3 C(S)A 1995, s 44(2).
4 C(S)A 1995, s 44(4).
5 C(S)A 1995, s 44(3).
6 C(S)A 1995, s 44(5).
7 *Children (Scotland) Act*, (1998 Revised Edition) p 77.
8 Cf discussion of the limits of the paramountcy principle above at 2.17 and elsewhere.
9 '1. – (1) When a court determines any question with respect to –
  (a) the upbringing of a child; or
  (b) the administration of a child's property or the application of any interest arising from it,
  the child's welfare shall be the court's paramount consideration'.
10 *Re Z (a minor) (freedom of publication)* [1995] 4 All ER 96.
11 [1995] 4 All ER 96 at 983e.
12 [1995] 4 All ER 96 at 982d.
13 See also *Oxfordshire County Council v L and F* [1997] 1 FLR 235.
14 Above at 28.06.

28.09 It is to be hoped that, if and when an application to dispense with the ban on publicity is made, there will be full argument on the issue. Standing the principle, now recognised in relation to children's hearings' law, that an appeal suspends the order of the sheriff and that the possibility of an appeal should not be negated by immediate implementation,[1] it may be that the media would not be entitled to act on such an order by the sheriff until the expiry of the 28 day appeal period prescribed by s 51(13) of the 1995 Act. It is submitted that, for the avoidance of doubt, a sheriff or sheriff principal who is minded to dispense with the prohibition of publication in terms of s 44(5)(a) of the Act should suspend the operation of his order for 28 days. The prohibition on publication by the media does not expressly embrace the reporting of an application to the *nobile officium* of the Court of Session but in practice it would be difficult to report on such a case without reflecting the proceedings before the sheriff or the hearing out of which the application to the *nobile officium* had arisen, thus bringing any publication within the scope of the prohibition. The Scottish Ministers would not be bound by the paramountcy principle in considering whether to dispense with the prohibition on disclosure. It appears that no dispensation by the Secretary of State was granted by virtue of the parallel provisions of the Social Work (Scotland) Act 1968.[2]

1 *Stirling v D* 1995 SCLR 460 at 461C.
2 See the speech of the Earl of Lindsay before the House of Lords Committee of the Whole House, June 7, 1995, col. 95 – referred to in Norrie *Children (Scotland) Act 1995* (2 edn 1998) p 77.

Judicial character of proceedings

28.10 The proceedings before the sheriff are 'of an informal nature'[1] but there is no doubt that they are of a judicial character and that the sheriff is acting as judge and not in any other capacity: ' … what Parliament has enacted is that the disputed issue is referred to the sheriff *qua* sheriff in his court for judicial determination.'[2] The description of the sheriff's role as 'simply a piece of fact-finding machinery for the benefit of the children's hearing' has been disapproved.[3] The sheriff is not merely making findings in fact. He is deciding as to whether or not grounds of referral are established by evidence or by sufficient admission by parties. In so doing he is directing his mind to whether or not it can be affirmed, not only that certain facts exist, but that the existence of these facts leads to the conclusion in law which the reporter seeks to draw. That conclusion is that one or more of the twelve conditions of referral listed in s 52(2) of the 1995 Act has been made out so as to give a children's hearing jurisdiction to make decisions affecting the relevant child. The sheriff's powers include, as we shall presently see: the power, under s 68(9) of the Act, to dismiss the application and discharge the referral; the power, under r 3.48 of the Act of Sederunt (Child Care and Maintenance) Rules 1997, to allow amendment of the statement of facts supporting the grounds for referral; and the power, under r 3.50, to find on the facts that any offence (other than the offence named) established by the proven facts has been committed. These are characteristically judicial functions and differ entirely from, for example, the purely supervisory and administrative function which the sheriff exercises over discretionary decisions of public officials – e g the appeal to the sheriff against the refusal of a chief constable to grant a firearms certificate.[4]

1 Per Lord Justice-Clerk Grant in *Kennedy v B* 1972 SC 128 at 133.
2 Per Lord Justice-Clerk Wheatley in *Kennedy v O* 1975 SC 308 at 315.
3 1975 SC 308 at 314, 315.
4 See the discussion of the administrative jurisdiction of the sheriff in such cases as *Kaye v Hunter* 1958 SC 208.

'Civil proceedings sui generis'

28.11   The rôle of the sheriff, although clearly a judicial role is of a special nature, as has been repeatedly emphasised by the Court of Session on appeal.[1] The application is 'to be treated as a civil proceeding'[2] and 'the ordinary codes of civil and criminal procedure do not apply' since the proceedings are 'civil proceedings *sui generis*'.[3] Although 'the basic rules of evidence must be observed'[4] the code of procedure is to be found only in the Children (Scotland) Act 1995 and the Act of Sederunt (Child Care and Maintenance Rules) 1997. Lord President Emslie, interpreting the substantially identical provisions of the earlier legislation, stated the matter in these clear terms:[5] '. . . the ordinary code of civil procedure of the sheriff courts has been expressly excluded by the Act of Sederunt.'[6] In *WW v Kennedy*[7] Lord Sutherland, delivering the opinion of the First Division, stated:

> '. . . the proceedings in front of the sheriff on referral are self-contained civil proceedings *sui generis* in which it must be borne in mind at all times that the principal purpose is to ascertain what is necessary to be done in the interests of the child. In our opinion it would be quite wrong for this objective to be thwarted by the application of rigid rules of evidence or procedure just because such rigidity may be appropriate in other kinds of proceedings.'

1   Eg *McGregor v T and P* 1975 SC 14 and *McGregor v D* 1977 SC 330.
2   *Kennedy v O* 1975 SC 308 at 315.
3   *McGregor v D* 1977 SC 330 at 336.
4   Per Lord Justice-Clerk Grant in *Kennedy v B* 1972 SC 128 at 133.
5   In *McGregor v D* 1977 SC 330 at 336.
6   The Act of Sederunt reference is to the Social Work (Sheriff Court Procedure Rules) 1971, Sl 1971/92, (the 'Sheriff Court Procedure Rules') rule 27(1) and Pt I of Sch 2.
7   1988 SCLR 236 at 239.

The proof

28.12   The hearing of evidence before the sheriff in relation to an application under s 68 of the Children (Scotland) Act 1995 is referred to as a 'proof' (which is the term in Scots legal language for the sitting of a court when evidence is led in order to establish facts usually, but not exclusively, in the civil context) but the term has no authority either in the Act or in any of the subordinate legislation.

TERRITORIAL JURISDICTION OF SHERIFF

Offence by a child cases: offence committed in other sheriffdom(s)

28.13   It is provided that where one of the grounds for referral is an offence by the child the application must be made to a sheriff who would have jurisdiction if the child were being prosecuted.[1] The territorial jurisdiction of the sheriff is set out in s 4 of the Criminal Procedure (Scotland) Act 1995 which provides inter alia that where an offence is alleged to have been committed in one district in a sheriffdom it shall be competent to try that offence in any sheriff court within that sheriffdom. Section 9 of the same Act provides inter alia that where offences in more than one sheriffdom are alleged then the accused may be tried in any of the sheriffdoms concerned. Accordingly where a child is alleged to have stolen a car in Wick and driven without license or insurance from there to Stranraer then an application to a sheriff for proof may be made to any of the sheriffs through whose jurisdiction the child is said to have passed.

1 Children (Scotland) Act 1995, s 68(3).

Care and protection cases

28.14 It is unfortunate that the issue of which sheriff has jurisdiction in 'care and protection' applications is not made clear, but, on the principle that if the statute had intended to mention this situation it would have done so and not merely mentioned the 'offence by the child' type of case, the proper conclusion is probably that 'care and protection' applications (including applications based on grounds of referral alleging a Schedule 1 offence) should be made to the sheriff within whose jurisdiction the hearing took place. In the event of a change of residence occurring after a direction by the hearing in terms of s 65 (7) or (9) of the Children (Scotland) Act 1995 but before the proof in a care and protection case, it is submitted that the sheriff should accept jurisdiction on the basis that the 'terms of the section are sufficiently wide'[1] to enable him to do so.[2] The sheriff would then, if sustaining the ground of referral, remit the matter to the reporter who would have to fix a hearing, and it would then be for that hearing to decide whether or not to exercise its powers under s 48(1) to request a transfer.

1 *L v McGregor* 1980 SLT 17 at 20.
2 Cf the discussion of the jurisdiction of the children's hearing in *Mitchell v S* 2000 SLT 524 at 526J ff.

JURISDICTION OF SHERIFF NOT EXCLUDED BY EARLIER ABORTIVE APPLICATION

28.15 If the reporter lodges an application and, through no fault of the reporter's, it is not heard by the sheriff within the 28 days prescribed by s 68(2) of the Children (Scotland) Act 1995 it is probable that the reporter may raise fresh grounds of referral on the basis of the same conditions and facts. When the grounds are still not accepted and a further application to the sheriff is required, the lodging and not proceeding with of the earlier application will not bar the sheriff from hearing the second application.[1]

1 *McGregor v L* 1983 SLT (Sh Ct) 7.

JURISDICTION OF SHERIFF NOT EXCLUDED BY EARLIER FINDING

28.16   An earlier finding by the court in a previous application in relation to a fact forming *part* of a ground of referral does not constitute *res judicata* (ie a matter which, having once been decided cannot be reopened).[1]

1 *McGregor v D* 1981 SLT (Notes) 97; *Kennedy v S* 1986 SLT 679, particularly per Lord Hunter at 681.

CHAPTER 29

Limited scope for preliminary challenge to application before sheriff

COMPETENCY AND RELEVANCY

Competency

29.01   It is inseparable from the exercise of jurisdiction by any court that that court is satisfied on the papers before it that the action is 'competent', that is to say that it seeks a remedy or order which it is within the power of the court to grant; that it is set out in a form which, on the face of it, displays that the body of law, whether statutory or common law, which is invoked as the source of the court's authority, has been properly invoked; and that the procedural requirements laid down by such body of law have been complied with in acceptable fashion. The court also has to be satisfied that it has jurisdiction in the sense of being the appropriate forum.

Relevancy

29.02   The concept of the competency of the application must be clearly distinguished from the concept of the relevancy of the factual averments within the application. 'Relevancy' in Scots legal language means the logical connection between the facts averred and the legal proposition derived from those facts. Therefore, an application is factually relevant provided that at least one of the 'facts' which are alleged within the application would, if proved to be true, result in the ground of referral linked with that fact being sustained. An application would be irrelevant if, even on all of its factual assertions being proved by evidence, this did not 'add up' to the establishment of any of the condition or conditions of referral relied upon. In the practice of our civil courts there are well established formal procedures for testing the competency of an action and the relevancy of averments by means of debates on preliminary pleas. Therefore the court is not obliged to hear evidence in relation to an action which is radically incompetent or in relation to averments which, even if proved, would not afford to the litigant the remedy which he was seeking.[1]

---

1 The famous civil case *Donoghue v Stevenson* 1932 SC (HL) 31 (the 'snail in the bottle' case) went to the House of Lords not after proof of any facts but simply on the argument as to whether the averments in the written pleadings (that an opaque bottle of ginger beer, allegedly containing the decomposed remains of a snail, which had been bought from a café in Paisley) were relevant to an action of damages by the consumer against the manufacturer of the ginger beer in the bottle.

Preliminary pleas?

29.03　In ordinary civil procedure matters of competency, jurisdiction and relevancy may be notified by preliminary pleas and settled in advance of hearing the main evidence in the case either by legal debate or sometimes, in the case of a challenge to jurisdiction, by a preliminary proof. It has, however, been emphasised again and again in the Court of Session that the normal code of civil procedure does not apply to applications to the sheriff in relation to the children's hearings system. Accordingly any procedural device has to be founded upon the legislation, primary and subordinate, enacting that system.

Preliminary pleas to the competency and jurisdiction

29.04　In both the cases of *L v McGregor*[1] and *McGregor v L*[2] preliminary challenges were made, in the first case to jurisdiction and in the second case to the competency, and in each of these cases the sheriff saw fit to hear preliminary debate. This was a course which, at least in *L v McGregor*, appeared to be acquiesced in by the Court of Session (*McGregor v L* was not appealed). In *H v Mearns*[3] an objection to the competency of the proceedings on the basis that the hearing of the application had not commenced within 28 days of the lodging of the application was argued before the sheriff as a preliminary matter. It was held, on appeal, that the application was incompetent. In *Kennedy v O*,[4] which was decided before the Reporters (Conduct of Proceedings before the Sheriff) (Scotland) Regulations 1975 was enacted, the argument as to whether a non-legally qualified reporter was entitled to represent the reporter was treated as an appropriate matter for preliminary debate. In *Merrin v S*[5] the Court of Session held (unanimously on this point) that the sheriff had been correct to treat the issue of whether a child under eight years of age was, in law, capable of committing an offence in terms of s 32(2)(g) of the Social Work (Scotland) Act 1968 as one on which the sheriff was entitled to rule on after hearing preliminary argument. In *Mitchell v S*[6] the referred child had not been in Scotland at the date when the case was formally referred to a children's hearing and the sheriff dismissed an application for a s 68 proof as incompetent. Holding that the sheriff had been correct to do so Lord Justice-Clerk Cullen, delivering the opinion of the court, observed: 'It is well recognised that the sheriff is entitled to dismiss an application where it is incompetent.'[7]

1　1980 SLT 17.
2　1983 SLT (Sh Ct) 7.
3　1974 SC 152.
4　1975 SC 308.
5　1987 SLT 193.
6　2000 SLT 524 – discussed above at 1.15.
7　2000 SLT 524 at 528F.

No preliminary challenge on ground of relevancy of the Statement of Facts

29.05　In the case of *McGregor v D*[1] the Court of Session declared emphatically that it was the duty of the sheriff to hear the evidence tendered by the reporter in support of the application even if the sheriff were convinced that even if all the factual allegations were to turn out to be true there would still be no ground of referral established in relation to the child. In short, the court ruled that what lawyers call the 'debate on the relevancy' had no place in the applications procedure. In reaching its conclusion the court laid stress on the words in s 42(6) of the Social Work (Scotland) Act 1968 which refers to the situation in which in an application 'the sheriff is satisfied on the evidence before him that any of the grounds ... has been established'.[2] It also stressed the mandatory words of rule 8 of the Social Work (Sheriff Court Procedure Rules) 1971, as amended, which provided inter alia that the sheriff 'shall, in relation to the grounds of referral which are in dispute, hear evidence tendered by or on behalf of the reporter'.[3] The court regarded the absence of preliminary debate on relevancy as being not merely a necessary inference from the words of the statute and the statutory instrument but integral to the whole nature of the application before the sheriff. Lord President Emslie regarded the possibility of debates on relevancy as being inimical to the simplicity and informality of the procedure in these applications. He recognised that in a few cases which were plainly irrelevant some time might be wasted in establishing facts which could never amount to a ground of referral but regarded this simply as 'the price to be paid for the desired simplicity and informality.'

1 1977 SC 330.
2 Cf 1995, the Children (Scotland) Act 1995, s 68(10): 'Where the sheriff, after hearing any evidence or on acceptance in accordance with sub-section (8) above, finds that any of the grounds for the referral to which the application relates is, or should be deemed to be, established – (a) he shall remit the case to the Principal Reporter ...'.
3 Cf Act of Sederunt (Child Care and Maintenance Rules) 1997, SI 1997/291, r 3.47(1): '... the sheriff shall, in relation to any ground of referral which is in dispute, hear evidence tendered by or on behalf of the Principal Reporter, including evidence given pursuant to an application granted under rule 3.23 [evidence of children by television link].'

Preliminary matters of competency and relevancy should generally be reserved

29.06 In the Orkney case[1] there were a number of applications. The reporter came to the proof hearing before the sheriff ready to adduce evidence. The legal representatives of the parties raised preliminary matters arising out of the procedural history of the case. The presence of the children at the session of the children's hearing for the explanation of the grounds of referral had been dispensed with at a preliminary hearing, which was a non-statutory but at the time well established procedure equivalent to the business meeting now enacted under s 64 of the Children (Scotland) Act 1995. Moreover the record of proceedings narrated, incorrectly, that an explanation had been given to the children which was not understood. The sheriff heard argument and, after considering the matter, held the applications to be incompetent on the ground of fundamental nullity. On appeal to the Court of Session it was held that any irregularity had been capable of correction and that it is only when an irregularity is incapable of correction – as in the case of *Merrin v S*[2] (child aged 7 accused of offence) – that the sheriff would be entitled to hold the proceedings to be incompetent because of fundamental nullity.[3] Lord President Hope, delivering the opinion of the First Division, stated:[4]

> 'Unless he [the sheriff] was in a position to repel the plea there and then he should have reserved his decision on it until he had made a finding based on the evidence as to whether or not the grounds for the referral were established.'

1 *Sloan v B* 1991 SLT 530.
2 1987 SLT 193.
3 *Sloan v B* 1991 SLT 530 at 546F–K.
4 *Sloan v B* 1991 SLT 530 at 546K.

Sheriff's obligation to hear the evidence adduced by the reporter

29.07   In *P v Kennedy*[1] a father who was identified in grounds of referral as a Schedule 1 offender had moved the sheriff to restrict the proof by not allowing the reporter to adduce evidence from the complainers in relation to the alleged Schedule 1 offences for which the father had not then been tried. The sheriff declined so to restrict the proof and her decision was upheld by an Extra Division on appeal where it was stated that the sheriff had no power to restrict the evidence of the reporter. It was also observed that the apparent assumption by the appellant that criminal proceedings against a parent should take precedence over referral proceedings had been rejected.[2]

1 1995 SCLR 1, 1994 Fam LB 13-5.
2 In *Ferguson v MP* 1989 SC 231, 1989 SCLR 525, 1989 SLT 681.

Preliminary matters raised before the sheriff: the appropriate course in practice

29.08   It is submitted that when a challenge is made to the very legality of the proceedings before the sheriff, the sheriff has little option but to hear debate on these matters and to rule appropriately. It would be absurd if the sheriff were bound to entertain proceedings which were legally defective merely because they were headed 'Application to the sheriff under section 65(7) of the Children (Scotland) Act 1995 '. It is now very clear, however, that sheriffs should be (and indeed are) slow to throw out cases on technical matters of competency and jurisdiction when there is any colourable argument in favour of jurisdiction being exercised. As has been pointed out, the application to the sheriff is intended to provide an expeditious and informal method of resolving mainly factual disputes. Just as the sheriff, if doubtful as to the admissibility of evidence before him, should admit it under reservation as to its relevancy and competency,[1] similarly it is submitted that when it seems that an application is doubtfully competent (as opposed to obviously incompetent) the sheriff should reserve the matter of competency and proceed to hear the application. This would leave it open to the aggrieved party to take the case to the sheriff principal or Court of Session but would avoid the risk of the time wasting necessity of a remit back in order to hear evidence.[2]

1 Thus getting the evidence 'on the record' so that its admissibility can be ruled upon by the Appeal Court – see per Lord President Emslie in *McGregor v T and P* 1975 SC 14 at 23.
2 This was the course which the sheriff indicated he would have followed (if he had sustained the plea to the competency) in *McGregor v L* 1983 SLT (Sh Ct) 7; cf *Constanda v O* (27 October 2000, unreported) Sheriff Principal E F Bowen QC, Glasgow Sheriff Court.

Possible challenge to relevancy at 'warrant' stage?

29.09   In the case of *McGregor v AB*[1] the sheriff had sustained the appeal against the granting of a warrant on the ground, among others, that in the circumstances of the case the consideration that the mother had not been named in grounds of referral based upon a Schedule 1 offence rendered the detention of the child inappropriate. The Court of Session, on the basis of the arguments laid before it by counsel for the reporter, treated the sheriff's decision as being based upon the view that for a Schedule 1 offence case to be relevantly averred the identity of the offender would require to be specifically averred by the reporter. The court rejected this proposition and held that, the essence of the ground being the assault upon the child and not the individual who administered the assault, specification of the name of the individual was unnecessary. The case is interesting from our present point of view, however, in that it seems to be implicit in the approach to the case by the Court of Session that in principle the sheriff was justified in considering the relevancy and specification of the grounds of referral in an appeal against the granting of a warrant based on these grounds. It is submitted that sheriffs should be very cautious in applying this principle.

1 1981 SC 328, sub nom *McGregor v K* 1982 SLT 293.

AMENDMENT OF STATEMENT OF FACTS NOW COMPETENT

29.10   Amendment of pleadings is, in ordinary civil procedure, frequently effected as a prelude to the proof. Under the rule 3.48 of the Act of Sederunt (Child Care and Maintenance Rules) 1997 the sheriff may at any time, on the motion of any party or on his own motion, allow amendment of the Statement of Facts. There is no provision for amendment of or addition to the Conditions of Referral. It is however thought that a deletion from the Conditions of Referral is competent. An example would be in relation to a Condition of Referral under s 52(2)(b) of the 1995 Act – 'is falling into bad associations or is exposed to moral danger'. It is submitted that the sheriff would in an appropriate case be well entitled to allow deletion of one or other of the alternatives and the acceptability of deletions of this type are well recognised in practice.

CHAPTER 30

Preparations for proof

PROVISIONS AFFECTING THE REPORTER

Status and functions of reporter in relation to proof

General position of reporter

30.01 When an application comes before the sheriff the reporter should normally be ready with his witnesses and other evidence so that the sheriff may hear that evidence.[1] A reporter who is a solicitor or an advocate has of course an automatic right of audience in the sheriff court. A reporter who is not an advocate or solicitor is entitled to conduct referral proceedings before the sheriff provided he has held his appointment for at least one year.[2] The primary responsibility for setting up the proof rests with the reporter although, of course, the child and the safeguarder and the relevant person(s), may also have preparations to make and evidence to lead, and their responsibilities will be examined later.[3] It is appropriate first to examine the preparation for the proof from the reporter's point of view, but it will be appreciated that some of the procedures described in this chapter, eg for enforcing the attendance of relevant witnesses, for recovering evidence in the hands of others, and application for evidence of children to be taken by television link, are equally available to other parties.

1 Cf *P v Kennedy* 1995 SCLR 1, 1994 Fam L B 13-5.
2 Reporters (Conduct of Proceedings before the Sheriff) (Scotland) Regulations, 1997, SI 1997/714, reg 3. As already noticed (above at 27.07 (footnote 3)) the enactment of these Regulations suggests that the legislature did not expect the principal reporter to invoke the permissive representation principle embodied in r 3.21 of the Act of Sederunt (Child Care and Maintenance) Rules 1997, SI 1997/291.
3 Chapters 33 and 34 below.

30.02 It is the function of the reporter to present the case to the sheriff by making such introductory remarks as may be required, calling the witnesses and examining them, cross-examining the child's or relevant person's witnesses, if any, and presenting the necessary legal argument to the court. Although under a duty to present the reporter's side of the case with vigour, thoroughness and skill, the reporter in court should not be partisan in the sense of trying to 'win' at all costs: on the contrary, if there is an inconvenient fact or apparently unfavourable piece of relevant case law he is under a duty to present the fact and mention the case and distinguish it if possible. It is the presupposition of the reporter's case that the child is truly in need of compulsory measures of supervision by virtue of one or more of the 'conditions' set out in s 52(2) of the Children (Scotland)

Act 1995 and, in relation to such a child, he must see to it that the children's hearing has the opportunity of considering the child's case. By the same token the reporter has no duty or interest to encumber the system with children who do not come into the Act's categories and he therefore would be acting contrary to his true function if by suppression of evidence or argument he sought to represent that a child *not* in one of the categories was in such a category.

30.03   The reporter is not a prosecutor and, as already noted, the procedures under the 1995 Act are civil rather than criminal,[1] but the reporter's duty to the court resembles that of the Lord Advocate and his deputes and the procurator fiscal and his deputes as this has evolved in Scotland. This function has been well described by Sheriff (as he now is) A V Sheehan:[2]

> 'The qualities required by the prosecutor are thoroughness, courage, fairness, and most of all, impartiality. In court he must be candid and frank. He must not withhold evidence or knowingly misquote the substance of a document, a witness's testimony, an opposing argument, a textbook or a decision. He has a primary duty not of securing a conviction but of assisting the court and trying to secure that justice is done. He must not press the prosecution case unduly. . . . For the Crown to persist in a charge in the knowledge of reliable evidence proving the innocence of the accused would 'constitute a violation of every tradition observed by the Crown Office'.'[3]

1 *McGregor v D* 1977 SC 330 at 336.
2 *Criminal Procedure in Scotland and France* (HMSO, Edinburgh, 1975) at p 114.
3 This final quotation is from an article in Northern Ireland Legal Quarterly Vol 19 No 3, September 1968, by Sir Gerald H Gordon QC (as he now is) himself a former procurator fiscal depute, and later a professor of Criminal Law, a Sheriff, and Temporary Judge.

Reporter's duty to investigate

30.04   The reporter has a double interest in marshalling the facts of the case. He is, in the context of the application, by definition the proponent of the proposition that there are specific grounds, as averred in the grounds of referral annexed to the application, justifying a children's hearing dealing with the child by means of compulsory measures of supervision. He must therefore be ready to present the facts which provide the basis for this view. The reporter also has a direct concern with the interests of the child – as is shown by his continuing power, at any stage in the application before the announcement of the sheriff's decision, to abandon the application in whole or in part.[1]

1 Act of Sederunt (Child Care and Maintenance) Rules 1997, SI 1997/291, r 3.46.

30.05   How much independent investigation the reporter should make into the facts of the case will vary according to circumstances and will often be affected by the time available for preparation. However, the reporter should be astute to ensure that all material grounds of referral are investigated and stated. In cases of offences by the child the reporter will generally rely on the statements submitted by the police.[1] However, in those 'care and protection' cases wherein the grounds of referral include any reference to the well-being of the child, the evidence of social workers and the medical evidence should be carefully examined and, if necessary, further investigations made.[2]

1 Cf Children (Scotland) Act 1995, s 53(2)(a) and s 53(4)–(7).
2 The local authority may have carried out its own investigations (C(S)A 1995, s 53(1)) but the reporter may wish to make further initial investigation (s 56(1)). The reporter must keep in mind the necessity of proving his case by legally sufficient evidence: for a discussion of some of the relevant principles of the law of evidence see Chapters 41 to 45 below.

Specific duties of reporter

30.06 Whenever a children's hearing have given a direction to the reporter to apply to the sheriff for a finding it becomes the duty of the reporter to apply to the sheriff for a finding. The application is in Form 60.[1] This form states the name and address of the reporter and the child and recites the history of the case. It mentions the reason for the direction by the hearing – non-acceptance of grounds and/or lack of understanding by the child – and in the former event specifies the conditions/statements not accepted. A copy of the statement of the grounds for the referral is attached and in practice any conditions accepted or, as the case may be, not accepted, by relevant person and child are noted by handwritten marginal note. Where a safeguarder has been appointed by the hearing the reporter must intimate this to the sheriff clerk and lodge any safeguarder's report along with the application.[2]

1 Act of Sederunt (Child Care and Maintenance Rules) 1997, SI 1997/291, r 3.45(1).
2 SI 1997/291, r 3.45(2).

Lodgement of application – computation of time etc

30.07 Rule 3.45(1) of the Act of Sederunt (Child Care and Maintenance Rules) 1997 ('the 1997 Rules') provides: 'Within a period of seven days beginning with the date on which the Principal Reporter was directed in terms of section 65 of the Act to make application to the sheriff, he shall lodge with the sheriff clerk an application in Form 60'. The writer takes the view that this form of wording may mean that the day following the day of the direction is to be treated as the first of the seven days[1] This, however, is not the universal view[2] and the safe course is to assume the date of the direction to be 'day one' so that a direction given on Wednesday, 19 January, 2000 would have to be followed up by an application lodged on Tuesday, 25 January 2000 at the latest or it would be time-barred.[3]

1 Cf *McCormick v Martin* 1985 SLT (Sh Ct) 57; *B v Kennedy* 1992 SLT 870. See discussion of the principles relating to the computation of time in 22 *Laws of Scotland: Stair Memorial Encyclopaedia* para 822 and in the writer's judgement in *Tudhope v Lawson* 1983 SCCR 435.
2 Cf the decision by Sheriff S O Kermack in *S, Appellants* 1979 SLT (Sh Ct) 37 interpreting the similarly worded s 49(1) of the Social Work (Scotland) Act 1968.
3 For further discussion of computation of time see above at 7.04.

30.08 It has been held by a sheriff that if the application miscarries without fault on the part of the reporter and is not heard by the sheriff then it remains open to the reporter to convene another children's hearing, which can then issue a further direction for an application to be made to the sheriff.[1]

1 *McGregor v L* 1983 SLT (Sh Ct) 7.

The first order

30.09 On the application being lodged it becomes the responsibility of the sheriff clerk, as soon as practicable after lodgement of the application, to assign a diet for the hearing of the application and to issue the appropriate warrant.[1] The diet fixed must be within twenty-eight days of the lodgement of the application.[2] The warrant should, subject to such variation as circumstances may require,[3] be in the style of Form 33:

[Place and date]

The court

1. Assigns [date] at [hour] within the [name court] in chambers at [place] for the hearing of the application;

2. Appoints the Principal Reporter forthwith

to cite AB [name of child];

to give notice/intimate to BB [insert name of relevant person or persons] whose whereabouts are known[4] and to [AB] (name and design) the safeguarder appointed by the sheriff,

by serving a copy of the application and relative statement of grounds of referral;

3. Grants warrant to cite witnesses and havers.

4.* Dispenses with notice and service on [insert name] for the following reason(s) [insert reasons].

5* Dispenses with the obligation to attend of [insert name of child] for the following reason(s) [insert reason(s)].

....

*delete as appropriate   *Sheriff or sheriff clerk

On receiving the warrant from the sheriff clerk the reporter must serve it on the parties named therein in the style of Form 39.[5]

1 Act of Sederunt (Child Care and Maintenance Rules) 1997, SI 1997/291, r 3.11.
2 Children (Scotland) Act 1995, s 68(2).
3 SI 1997/291, r 1.2(3).
4 If the whereabouts are not known the form should be suitably adapted.
5 Act of Sederunt (Child Care and Maintenance Rules) 1997, SI 1997/291, r 3.12(1)(f).

Consideration by sheriff of appointment of safeguarder

30.10 The sheriff shall, as soon as reasonably practicable after the lodging of the application, consider if it is necessary to appoint a safeguarder.[1] A safeguarder may also be appointed later.[2] Any safeguarder appointed by the hearing should, if the sheriff decides that it is necessary to appoint a safeguarder, be appointed by the sheriff as such unless the sheriff, *ex proprio motu* or on motion of party on cause shown[3], decides otherwise. In Glasgow the application is shown to a sheriff when lodged and he or she, after making such enquiry as he or she thinks appropriate, appoints or not a safeguarder or curator *ad litem*. The enquiries may take the form of phone calls by the sheriff clerk on behalf of the sheriff to the reporter, any safeguarder appointed by the hearing or any solicitor(s) known to be acting for the child or relevant person.

1 Act of Sederunt (Child Care and Maintenance Rules) 1997, SI 1997/291, r 3.7(1)(a).
2 SI 1997/291, r 3.7(1)(b).
3 SI 1997/291, r 3.7(2).

PROVISIONS AFFECTING REPORTER AND OTHER PARTIES

Service of documents

Dispensing with service on child

30.11 Under the Children (Scotland) Act 1995 itself the child has an unqualified right to attend the hearing of a s 68 application.[1] The child will generally also be under a duty to attend.[2] The sheriff has the power to dispense with the obligation on the child to attend in a case where the condition of referral is a condition under s 52(2)(d),(e),(f) or (g) of the Act – i e those conditions involving Schedule 1 offences – where the sheriff is satisfied that the presence of the child is not necessary for the just hearing of the case.[3] The sheriff may also dispense with the obligation on the child to attend in any case in relation to which he thinks that the presence of the child would be detrimental to the interests of the child.[4] Rule 3.3 of the 1997 Rules states:

> 'Where the sheriff is satisfied, taking account of the age and maturity of the child, that it would be inappropriate to order service on the child, he may dispense with –
> a)   service on the child; and
> b)   the attendance of the child at the hearing of the application.'

It cannot have been intended that this rule should take away the right of the child to attend the hearing of the s 68 application if he so wished but by allowing for dispensation from service on the child the rules run the risk of implying that an application concerning the child could be held with the child not being aware of the place and date. It is submitted that service on the child should only be dispensed with when there is information that the child is too young or immature to participate in the proceedings. No form is prescribed for informing the child of the diet where his obligation to attend has been dispensed with but SCRA has adapted a form.

1 Children (Scotland) Act 1995, s 68(4)(a).
2 C(S)A 1995, s 68(4)(b).
3 C(S)A 1995, s 68(5)(a).
4 C(S)A 1995, s 68(5)(b).

Dispensing with service on other persons

30.12   The sheriff, subject to the provisions in relation to service on the child,[1] may on cause shown dispense with service on any person named.[2] If, say, a relevant person's whereabouts are unknown then service on such person should be dispensed with. Perhaps also if service on such a person were likely to be difficult and the cause of undue delay then service may be dispensed with. However, it is submitted that great caution should be observed by the sheriff before acceding to a motion to dispense with service on a relevant person whose whereabouts are known or reasonably ascertainable.

1 Act of Sederunt (Child Care and Maintenance Rules) 1997, SI 1997/291, r 3.3.
2 SI 1997/291, r 3.18.

30.13   Once this warrant has been granted the child, the relevant persons, the reporter and any safeguarder who has intimated that he intends to become a party to the proceedings, acquire the right,[1] using the appropriate methods,[2] to cite to the court 'witnesses and havers'. In addition the reporter incurs the duty of citing the child[3] and intimating the application to any relevant person whose whereabouts are known.[4]

1 Act of Sederunt (Child Care and Maintenance Rules) 1997, SI 1997/291, r 3.14(1)(a).
2 As prescribed in SI 1997/291, rr 3.15, 3.16 discussed above at 7.09.
3 SI 1997/291, r 3.4(1) (f).
4 SI 1997/291, r 3.12(1)(f).

'Witnesses and havers'

30.14   By 'witness' is intended not merely an eye-witness but any person who is in a position to give relevant verbal testimony including, for example, an expert medical witness. The legal term 'haver' means holder and its presence in the words of style reminds us that the holder of a piece of written evidence is under an obligation, if lawfully cited as a haver and required to bring the document, to come to court with the document concerned.

Persons at the same address

30.15   Individuals residing at the same address should be notified/cited separately in separate envelopes.

Position when parental responsibilities vested in local authority under s 86 of Act

30.16   In this event the local authority is a relevant person and should be notified as such per the Chief Social Work Officer.

Citation of witnesses and havers

30.17   The purpose of citing is to compel presence at court. Citation of a witness is not a pre-condition of that person's being called as a witness[1] but in practice and as a matter of professional duty a reporter or other party must regard citation of essential witnesses and havers as a necessary preliminary to a properly presented case.

1 Evidence (Scotland) Act 1852, s 1; *Watson v Livingstone* (1902) 5 F 171; *McDonnell v McShane* 1967 SLT (Sh Ct) 61 at 63.

Forms of citation and intimation

30.18 The rules provide appropriate forms of notice to the child,[1] the relevant persons,[2] and the safeguarder[3] and for citation of witnesses and havers[4]. If a citation or intimation is being posted there should be printed on the front of the outside of the envelope words to the following effect:

> 'This letter contains a citation to or intimation from [specify the court]. If delivery of the letter cannot be made, it is to be returned immediately to The Sheriff Clerk, Sheriff Court House [specify the address]'[5]

1 Act of Sederunt (Child Care and Maintenance Rules) 1997, SI 1997/291, Form 31.
2 SI 1997/291, Form 39.
3 SI 1997/291, Form 40.
4 SI 1997/291, Form 41.
5 The Citation Amendment (Scotland) Act 1882, s 4, para (4) as amended in the Sheriff Court Procedure Rules, Sch 2, Part II.

Modes of citation and intimation

30.19 These are set out in r 3.15 of the 1997 Rules and have already been noticed.[1]

1 Chapter 7, in particular 7.10 ff.

Period of notice for citation and intimation

30.20 Any citation or intimation in relation to the application procedure 'shall be made not later than forty-eight hours, or in the case of postal citation, seventy-two hours, before the date of the diet to which the citation or notice relates'.[1] It will be noted that the periods stated run back from the 'date of the diet' and not from the time of the diet. It is submitted that, for a diet at 10 am on Friday 13 November 1998 , the last time for effecting personal service would be the end of the day on Tuesday 10 November 1998 and that the last time for effecting postal citation would be the end of the day (or, more realistically, when the post office closes) on Monday 9 November 1998. The foregoing provisions do not apply to appeals against warrants, hearings on the granting of interim EOs, hearings on applications to vary or set aside CPOs, or applications for CPOs where the period and mode of intimation are 'as directed by the sheriff'.[2]

1 Act of Sederunt (Child Care and Maintenance Rules) 1997, SI 1997/291, r 3.13(1).
2 SI 1997/291, r 13(13)(2).

Special considerations concerning citation and intimation by post

30.21 Section 7 of the Interpretation Act 1978 provides:

> 'Where an Act authorises or requires any document to be served by post (whether the expression 'serve' or the expression 'give' or 'send' or any other expression is used) then, unless the contrary intention appears, the service is deemed to be effected by properly addressing, pre-paying and posting a letter containing the document and, unless the contrary is proved, to have been effected at the time at which the letter would be delivered in the ordinary course of post.'

It could accordingly be argued, assuming that 'made' in the rule is to be treated as meaning the same as 'effected' in the Interpretation Act 1978, that the citation is 'made' not at the time when the document is handed in at the post office but at the time when 'in the ordinary course of post' it would be delivered. This would mean, in the example just given, that the document would require to be handed in at the post office, at the latest, on Saturday 7 November 1998 and sent first class post since only thus could it, in the ordinary course of post, be expected to be delivered before the end of the working day on Monday 9th. Alternatively it could be argued that by prescribing seventy-two hours for postal citation as opposed to forty-eight hours for personal citation the rule was displaying the 'contrary intention' to the provision in s 7 of the Act, thus entitling service to be timeously made by handing in to the post office before the end of the working day on the Monday. The writer inclines to the latter view but since the allowance of a mere twenty-four hours for the extra time involved in postal as opposed to personal delivery may, in modern conditions, be regarded as rather meagre it is suggested that to be on the safe side the more liberal allowance of time as envisaged by the Interpretation Act 1978 should, it is recommended, be made whenever practicable.

Sundays and holidays

30.22 Whether citation be personal or by post the 72 hours or 48 hours, as the case may be, do not cease to run during Sundays or holidays: '. . . over a period of four centuries there seems no recognition and certainly no general recognition, of the idea of *dies non* being excluded from the calculation of procedural time.'[1]

1 *S v McGregor* (8 July 1980, unreported) Court of Session; discussed further below at 50.10, footnote 1.

Persons entitled to effect service of citation or intimation

30.23 These are set out in r 3.16 of the Act of Sederunt (Child Care and Maintenance Rules) 1997, already noticed.[1] If service is effected postally or via document exchange, fax or other electronic transmission then this may be done by a solicitor, the sheriff clerk, the Principal Reporter or an officer of the local authority.[2] An officer of the local authority includes any officer authorised to conduct proceedings by virtue of the provisions in the rules, already noticed,[3] in relation to representation. The Principal Reporter has the same meaning as in s 93(1) of the 1995 Act[4] – i e including all reporters to whom the principal reporter has delegated his functions. The provision of r 20(2) of the Social Work (Sheriff Court Procedure Rules) 1971 as amended which provided that a reporter, in order to be entitled to effect service or notification, required to have held his appointment for one year by virtue of the Reporters (Conduct of Proceedings before the Sheriff) (Scotland) Regulations 1975 has no parallel in the current rules. It would therefore appear that any reporter, however recently engaged[5], may sign a citation or notification of a party or a witness.

1 Chapter 7, in particular 7.08 ff.
2 Act of Sederunt (Child Care and Maintenance Rules) 1997, SI 1997/291, r 3.16.
3 SI 1997/291, r 3.21(1) – discussed above at 6.01 ff.
4 SI 1997/291, r 1.2(1).
5 Reporters, of course, receive appropriate training.

Proof of citation and intimation

30.24 The rules provide that lodgement of the execution of service may be effected at the hearing of the application unless the sheriff otherwise directs or on cause shown.[1] Forms 42 and 43 of the 1997 Rules provide the styles of Certificate of Citation which, where properly completed, is sufficient evidence that service was duly made. Where there has been postal citation the post office receipt should be produced. If the child or witness fails to appear production of the Certificate will be essential if warrant is sought for detention of the child[2] or apprehension of the missing witness.[3]

1 Act of Sederunt (Child Care and Maintenance Rules) 1997, SI 1997/291, r 3.17.
2 See below at 32.01 ff.
3 See below at 30.32.

Witnesses

Parent as witness in care and protection cases

30.25 It has been authoritatively held under the Social Work (Scotland) Act 1968 that the parent is a competent and compellable witness for the reporter in application proofs.[1] It may be presumed that the same principle would be applied in relation to a 'relevant person', parent or otherwise, under the 1995 Act. The parent is occasionally used by the reporter as a witness in offence by a child cases but more frequently in care and protection cases. If the reporter (or any other party) intends to adduce evidence from a parent or other relevant person he must cite that person as a witness and not merely count on his attending the proof voluntarily in response to an intimation of the diet of proof.

1 *McGregor v T and P* 1975 SC 14.

Precognition of parent/relevant person by reporter?

30.26 In any case wherein the parent/relevant person is being accused, either of lack of parental care, or of an offence, that person, it is submitted, should not be precognosced by the reporter. In general one should not cite a witness without having his precognition but in the case of an accused parent/relevant person it is proper to cite him provided there is reasonable cause to believe that if prepared to testify[1] his evidence will be relevant. In cases wherein the parent/relevant person is not accused there could be no impropriety in the reporter precognoscing him.

1 See below 37.09 to 37.12 for a discussion of the special position of the witness being asked to testify on a matter which would tend to incriminate himself.

Citing witnesses who have not been precognosced

30.27 It is thought that the general professional rule that a witness should not be cited without precognition would, moreover, be applied less rigidly in the cases of witnesses in care and protection cases than in other forms of litigation. The interests of the child may demand that a witness whom it has not been practicable to precognosce but who is reasonably believed to be able to give relevant evidence should be cited. In offence by a child cases the reporter, in modern practice, following that of the procurator fiscal in summary criminal procedure, will not generally precognosce police witnesses when satisfactory police statements are available. The issue of when it may and may not be competent to adduce the referred child as a witness for the reporter is discussed later.[1]

1 Below at 37.09.

Duties arising from reporter's public interest role: all material witnesses to be cited

30.28   As already noted[1] the reporter is under a duty to make available to the court all the seemingly relevant information. It follows that *all* the witnesses who have anything relevant and significant to contribute should be cited. In the event of the reporter finding out that a potential witness has something important and relevant to say which might assist the parent's side of the case then that witness, it is submitted, should be cited by the reporter. It would not be enough, in the writer's opinion, for the reporter to mention, say, to the unrepresented child or parent/relevant person that a given witness may have helpful evidence from the 'defence' point of view and suggest that the child or parent/relevant person may care to bring that witness to the proof. Where the child or parent/relevant person is legally represented it would be sufficient for the reporter to advise the legal representative of such witness.

1 Above at 30.02 ff.

Exchange of lists of witnesses – obtaining evidence from the prosecuting authorities

30.29   If the child, relevant person or safeguarder request a list of the reporter's witnesses, or a sight of the reporter's productions, if any, then this should be provided. If the child and relevant person are not legally represented then the reporter should give assistance in the citation of any witness reasonably required for the 'defence'. These obligations have no specific statutory origin but flow from the responsibility of the reporter to act in the general public interest and in the interests of the child. In practice, in the interests of speed, the reporter will often be willing to provide the 'defence' with a sight of his precognitions and reports. Similarly it is good practice for the legal representatives of other parties to advise the reporter of intended witnesses. The reporter may ask the prosecuting authorities to supply any relevant evidence lawfully obtained in the course of a criminal investigation and the prosecutor shall furnish this unless he reasonably believes it is necessary to retain it.[1] The Lord Advocate may direct that such information be supplied without the necessity of a request.[2] In practice the reporters, Crown Office, and the procurators fiscal enjoy a good working relationship.

1 Children (Scotland) Act 1995, s 53(4) and (5).
2 C(S)A 1995, s 53(6).

Reporter's witnesses to be available for precognition by 'defence'

30.30 It is sometimes genuinely believed by persons who have given a statement or precognition to the 'authorities' that it is undesirable, or even illegal, for them to be interviewed by those representing the other side of the case. This is quite wrong as indicated by these words of Lord Justice-Clerk Macdonald in 1893:

> 'It seems to me that nothing could be done more prejudicial to either side, than that in a criminal case before a jury, the advisers of a party should direct their witnesses not to allow themselves to be precognosced. I think it is a grievous mistake. . . . I have been asked to express my view, and it is that every good citizen should give his aid, either to the Crown or to the defence, in every case where the interests of the public in the punishment of crime, or the interests of a prisoner charged with crime, call for ascertainment of facts.[1]'

These observations were made over a century ago in relation to expert medical testimony in a murder case but they have, it is submitted, equal relevance today in relation to cases under the 1995 Act.

1 *HM Advocate v Monson* (1893) 21 R(J) 5 at 11.

Practice in precognition-taking

30.31 Whether or not he or she is prepared to give a precognition is a matter for the witness to decide and there is no power vested in the reporter, the defence solicitor or any other party to these proceedings to compel any person to attend for precognition. It is suggested that reporters should, when appropriate, and certainly if asked, make clear to witnesses the position as set out by Lord Justice-Clerk Macdonald. It should perhaps be added that the witness should only be asked to make himself *reasonably* available. It is for the precognition-taker to suit the convenience of the witness and not the other way around.

Precognoscing children – desirability of as few interviews as possible with a child

30.32 Where children are to be precognosced a particular duty rests upon the reporter, curator *ad litem* and solicitor to use the utmost discretion. Scotland is fortunate in having a growing number of solicitors who have expertise in children's law – some accredited by the Law Society of Scotland as specialists in this field. It is not generally regarded as appropriate practice for the investigation of cases under the hearings procedures to be delegated to precognition agents and assistants who are not experienced in the delicate task of communicating with potentially distressed children. In 1924 a solicitor was subjected to disciplinary action arising out of inept precognition-taking. Finding the solicitor guilty of professional misconduct Lord Skerrington, delivering the opinion of the First Division said[1]:

> 'The painful position in which the respondent now stands is due primarily to his having delegated the performance of an important professional duty – the precognoscing of witnesses for the pursuer – to a person who had received no training as to how this duty ought to be performed. In adopting

this course the respondent deviated from what I understand to be the ordinary practice of the legal profession, and his evidence in the present petition shows that he did not appreciate the reasons upon which that practice is based. As was pointed out by Lord Halsbury, L C, in *Watson v M'Ewan*,[2] 'the preliminary examination of witnesses to find out what they can prove' is 'a step towards, and is part of, the administration of justice.' The course of justice may be seriously and even irretrievably obstructed, if a person with a vivid imagination and with little respect for the truth is turned loose upon the witnesses.'

It is now well recognised that being interviewed many times may be stressful for a child and accordingly, so far as practicable, interviews should be kept to a minimum. Sometimes it may be appropriate for the legal representatives of parties to arrange with a curator *ad litem* to advise them of the substance of the evidence likely to be given by the child.

1 *Writers to the Signet v Mackersy* 1924 SC 776 at 783.
2 (1905) 7 F (HL) 109, at 111, [1905] AC 480 at 487.

Absolute privilege of witnesses

30.33 Witnesses sometimes express the fear that what they say in precognition or in court may result in their being liable in defamation. Such fears are groundless. Statements by witnesses in court[1] or in precognition[2] are absolutely privileged. In *Russell v Dickson*[3] Temporary Judge J G Coutts QC, while holding himself bound by the old cases asserting the absolute privilege of the judiciary, cast doubt on the applicability of these cases in modern times. Whatever may be the merits of his Lordship's comments in relation to the privilege of the judiciary they should not, it is submitted, be regarded as detracting from the absolute privilege of witnesses. If a witness should appear to be abusing this privilege the court should intervene.[4]

1 *Mackintosh v Weir* (1875) 2 R 877; *Slack v Barr* (1918) 1 SLT 133.
2 *Watson v M'Ewan* (1905) 7 F (HL) 109.
3 1997 SC 269, 1998 SLT 96, OH.
4 Cf *Falconer v Brown* (1893) 1 Adam 96.

Procedure for enforcing attendance of reluctant witness

30.34 Where a witness who has been duly cited fails to appear at a diet,[1] the sheriff, on production of a certificate of citation, may grant warrant for the apprehension of the witness and for bringing him or her to court. The rule containing this provision is the only one of the Ordinary Cause Rules which has application to children's hearings procedures in the sheriff court.[2]

1 See above 30.24.
2 Ordinary Cause Rules 1993, SI 1993/1956, as amended, r 29.10(1). Rule 29.10 is preserved for hearings procedures in Act of Sederunt (Child Care and Maintenance Rules) 1997, SI 1997/291, r 3.24 and Sch 3; see *Macphail on Sheriff Court Practice* (2nd edn, 1998), 16.15 and 16.06 for general discussion.

30.35 It would appear that there is no provision for granting warrant, in advance of the proof, for the apprehension of a witness on the ground that the witness is reasonably believed to be unlikely to attend.

30.36 The granting of a warrant is a matter for the reasonable discretion of the sheriff who will wish to be satisfied that, as far as can be ascertained, the absence of the witness is wilful. A warrant will not readily be granted if there is a reasonable doubt as to whether the witness received his citation and accordingly citation of the witness personally by a sheriff officer should normally be attempted before a warrant is asked for. A warrant may not be granted where the witness has not been suitably funded in advance: the amount required to be given will clearly vary according to the distance of the witness's residence from the court.[1]

1 Cf *Gerard, petitioner* 1984 SLT 108: this was a criminal case and it involved a warrant for the apprehension of a witness in England, which is not competent in civil sheriff court procedure, but the case is of interest in that it indicates circumstances in which the High Court held that a sheriff had acted reasonably in ordering the detention of a witness until the trial as opposed to releasing him on caution being lodged – the witness when cited had been given a cheque for £40 to enable him to get to Dumfries from Manchester.

30.37 Once a warrant has been obtained the sheriff clerk should be asked to continue the diet and sheriff officers should be instructed to apprehend the witness and bring him to the continued diet.[1] The warrant may be executed anywhere in Scotland without endorsation.[2] The provisions of the Ordinary Cause Rules in relation to imposing a penalty on a witness in respect of whom a warrant has been granted,[3] although technically applicable, are not, it is thought, frequently employed in referral cases.

1 See brief discussion of operating a warrant to apprehend as opposed to using the ordinary sheriff court process (no longer available in children's hearings procedures in the sheriff court) of letters of second diligence at p 9 of *Constanda v O* Sheriff Principal EF Bowen QC, Glasgow Sheriff Court (27 October 2000, unreported).
2 Ordinary Cause Rules 1993, r 5.8.
3 Ordinary Cause Rules 1993, r 29.10(2).

30.38 As discussed already[1] article 5(5) of the European Convention on Human Rights gives any person who has been the victim of unlawful arrest or detention an enforceable right to compensation. Sheriffs and judges have long been astute to observe the due process of law so as not to abridge the liberty of the citizens unlawfully, but this provision underlines the need to ensure that this the due process is seen to have been observed and that this is properly recorded. It is accordingly suggested that the interlocutor embodying a warrant should narrate the process fully. A suggested style comprises Appendix 10.

1 At 1.09 above.

Child witnesses

30.39 It is presumably competent to grant a warrant for the apprehension of a child to secure the attendance of a child witness at court, but it is thought that the sheriff would be slow to grant warrant for the apprehension of a child without taking steps to ascertain if the failure to attend was wilful or not. The sheriff might wish to fix a hearing to which the parents or carers for the child would be invited to attend.

Expenses?

30.40 In ordinary civil business the expenses of obtaining and operating the letters may be awarded against the recalcitrant witness but it would seem that the general exclusion of awarding expenses in relation to these procedures[1] would also exclude awarding expenses in relation to letters. It is thought that, in s 68 proofs as in other civil business in the sheriff court,[2] there is no method whereby the attendance of a witness from furth of Scotland can be compelled.

1 Act of Sederunt (Child Care and Maintenance Rules) 1997, SI 1997/291, r 3.19.
2 See *Macphail on Sheriff Court Practice* (2nd edn, 1998), 16.17.

Recovery of documents and other evidence prior to proof

The statutory background

30.41   The Administration of Justice (Scotland) Act 1972 was enacted after the promulgation of the rules relating to s 42 applications under the Social Work (Scotland) Act 1968. The provisions in the 1972 Act allowing application to the court for inspection and production of documents and other evidence relevant to any existing or likely proceedings[1] may be invoked by a party to an application, existing or likely, under s 68 of the Children (Scotland) Act 1995. It is submitted that the provisions of the 1972 Act, as now amended, entitling the court to order any person to disclose such information as he has as to the identity of any persons who might be witnesses in any existing or likely proceedings may be invoked in s 68 application proceedings.[2]

1 Administration of Justice (Scotland) Act 1972, s 1(1).
2 AJA 1972, s 1(1A).

Time for lodging motion

30.42   The rules prescribing the procedure to be followed in the sheriff court[1] are presumably not applicable to s 68 procedures but the absence of procedural rules need not prevent the court from giving effect to substantial rights of parties[2] and it is thought that a party may proceed by application to the sheriff in the form of a motion. Technically such a motion would be competent whenever an application to the sheriff for a s 68 proof was 'likely' – presumably from the moment when the chairman of the hearing directed the reporter to make the application.[3] In practice it is thought that an application under s 1 of the 1972 Act would generally not be lodged until the application to the sheriff for a s 68 proof had itself been made, and the following proceeds on this assumption.

1 Sheriff Courts (Scotland) Act 1907, First Schedule, as substituted by Act of Sederunt (Ordinary Cause Rules, Sheriff Court) 1993 SI 1993/1956 (hereinafter 'OCR') Chapter 28, rr 28.1 to 28.7.
2 Cf *Killen v Killen* 1981 SLT (Sh Ct) 77 (a decision of Sheriff Macphail).
3 Children (Scotland) Act 1995, s 65(7) and (9).

Initial procedure

30.43   In spite of the non-applicability of the ordinary sheriff court rules to s 68 procedures it is thought that the court would be guided by, and would follow as closely as possible subject to such modifications as would seem reasonable having regard to the exigencies of s 68 procedure, the ordinary sheriff court rules.[1] It is suggested that application should be made to the court by motion accompanied by a description of the documents or other property sought to be recovered – a 'Specification of Documents' or 'Specification of Property'. On lodgement in court the sheriff clerk should fix a hearing and order intimation on the other parties,[2] including any safeguarder who has intimated an intention to become a party to the proceedings. It is suggested that at least two clear days' notice should be given of such a diet and that the date for the hearing should be fixed so as to allow for this.

1 OCR rr 28.1 to 28.7.
2 Cf OCR 28.2.

Crown immunity on ground of public interest

30.44 The Crown cannot be compelled to disclose information if in the opinion of a minister of the Crown, such disclosure would be injurious to the public interest.[1] It is thought that applications for production of documents will most frequently be considered in order to obtain hospital records of a hospital within the national health service framework. In that event intimation must be made to the Lord Advocate[2] as representing the Crown and the sheriff will regard proof (by production of an execution with recorded delivery slip or by letter of consent from the Lord Advocate's Department) of timeous intimation on the Lord Advocate as an essential pre-condition of granting any order. Parties may be prepared to accept service in order to expedite the procedure.

1 Crown Proceedings Act 1947, s 47 as preserved in relation to these procedures by Administration of Justice (Scotland) Act 1972, s 1(4).
2 Addressed thus: The Right Honourable AB, QC (or as the case may be), Her Majesty's Advocate, Crown Office, 25 Chambers St, Edinburgh EH1 1LA.

Procedure where haver wishes to resist production

30.45 The Lord Advocate[1] and, it is thought, where the motion is made under s 1 of the Administration of Justice (Scotland) Act 1972,[2] a non-party haver,[3] are entitled to be heard and may appear and argue against the granting of the motion.[4] The procedure which a non-party haver wishing to resist production should adopt in relation to a motion where s 1 of the 1972 Act is not invoked is noted presently.

1 Cf OCR r 28.2(5).
2 The provisions of which do not detract from the plea of confidentiality: Administration of Justice (Scotland) Act 1972, s 1(4).
3 Who is in such a case entitled to notification: OCR r 28.2(3)(b).
4 Cf discussion in *Macphail on Sheriff Court Practice* (2nd edn, 1998), 15.60 and 15.89.

Public interest immunity limited to Crown

30.46 'Public interest as a ground of refusal of recovery has not yet been upheld in Scotland where proposed by a body other than a government department'.[1] The records of Social Work Departments have been ordered to be produced in summary applications.[2]

1 *Macphail*, 15-54, citing *Higgins v Burton* 1968 SLT (Notes) 52 and *Strathclyde Regional Council v B* 1997 Fam LR 142.
2 *Strathclyde Regional Council v B* 1997 Fam LR 142; *A v G* 1996 SCLR 787 (Sh Ct).

Operating the court's order

30.47   Where a motion has been successful the sheriff will grant commission and diligence for the recovery of the documents or other material. Broadly the order may be served on the haver and the haver must (under the 'optional procedure'[1]) produce the documents or other material to the sheriff clerk or a Commissioner may be appointed to hold a hearing at which the commission may be executed.[2]

1 OCR, r 28.3.
2 OCR, r 28.4.

Privilege of witnesses and havers and confidentiality of information

30.48   The provisions in relation to ordinary cause procedure are contained in the relative rule.[1] Broadly the person claiming confidentiality may place the confidential material in a sealed packet and any person seeking to have the sealed packet opened may lodge a motion with the sheriff, intimate such motion to the haver, and both may appear or be represented before the sheriff to argue the point. The issue of confidentiality in the context of cases involving the interests of children is discussed by the sheriff in *A v G*[2].

1 OCR r 28.8.
2 1996 SCLR 787 – the sheriff was reversed, but not in relation to this point, in *A v G and Strathclyde Regional Council* 1997 SCLR 186 (Sh Ct).

Status of the recovery procedure – Possibility of appeal?

30.49   The recovery procedure, if initiated after the lodgement of an application for a s 68 proof arising out of a direction under s 65(7) or (9) of the Children (Scotland) Act 1995, would appear to be part of the s 68 application procedure and not an ordinary proceeding of the sheriff court. *Quaere* however if it can have been intended that a decision of the sheriff to grant or not to grant an order under s 1 of the Administration of Justice Act 1972 should be appealable to the sheriff principal or the Court of Session by stated case under s 51(11) of the Children (Scotland) Act 1995, with the consequent delay which such a form of appeal would involve. The wording of s 51(11) may suggest that an appeal 'on an application' refers only to a substantial decision on the disposal of the application. Appeals against procedural disposals by hearings were held not to be competent under the provisions of the Social Work (Scotland) Act 1968[1]. Yet, as the case law[2] reveals, delicate and important legal issues can arise in connexion with applications for the recovery of documents in children's cases. It is tentatively suggested that s 51(11) of the 1995 Act does not allow appeal by stated case in relation to a decision of the sheriff on a motion under s 1 of the 1972 Act. It is further suggested therefore that there is a lacuna in the statutory provision and any review of a sheriff's decision would require to be attempted by application to the *nobile officium* of the Court of Session.[3] In the unlikely event of the recovery procedure preceding the s 68 application it would seem that the recovery procedure would be by summary application under s 50 of the Sheriff Courts (Scotland) Act 1907, with the consequent possibility of appeal to the sheriff principal or the Court of Session.[4]

1 *H v McGregor* 1973 SC 95, 1973 SLT 110.
2 *Strathclyde Regional Council v B* 1996 Fam LR 142; *A v G* 1996 SCLR 787 (Sh Ct).
3 Cf *F v Constanda* 1999 SLT 421 at 423D–G.
4 Cf *Macphail on Sheriff Court Practice* (2nd edn, 1998) 25.29 ff.

Application for evidence of children by television link

30.50 In any proceedings under Part II of the Children (Scotland) Act 1995 any party may make application in the style of Form 44 to allow the giving of evidence by a child by live television link.[1] Such application should be lodged, unless special cause can be shown, not later than 14 days before the hearing at which the child is to give evidence. The sheriff shall order intimation on the other parties and hear the application on the earliest practicable date. In dealing with such an application the sheriff shall hear parties, allow such further procedure as he thinks fit, and thereafter grant or refuse the application.[2] Not all sheriff courts have the necessary equipment and accordingly when granting the application the sheriff may transfer the whole case to another sheriff court in the same sheriffdom or hear the whole case or part thereof in such another court.[3] The stringent provisions of criminal procedural law regarding the pre-conditions which must be met before the live link is authorised have no application here but parties arguing for or against the granting of an application should be aware of these provisions[4] and of the case law.[5]

1 Act of Sederunt (Child Care and Maintenance Rules) 1997, SI 1997/291, r 3.22(1) and (2).
2 SI 1997/291, r 3.23(1).
3 SI 1997/291, r 3.23(2).
4 Criminal Procedure (Scotland) Act 1995, s 271(5).
5 *Brotherston v HM Advocate* 1995 SCCR 693 – see discussion in *Renton & Brown* (6th edn, 1996) at 24-144 ff.

CHAPTER 31

Possible parties to the proof: representation

INTRODUCTORY

'Party'

31.01   A 'party' to litigation may be defined as a person who has a right or duty to appear before a judge in connexion with the resolution of his or her rights or duties in relation to the criminal or civil law. A party may be a legal person (a natural legal person such as Mr Smith or Mrs Mackay or an artificial legal person such as a limited company or a statutory body like a local authority) who, by virtue of a legal interest claimed by or against that person in the subject matter of a litigation, enters the process of that litigation and plays a more or less active part in it. The procedures under the Social Work (Scotland) Act 1968 have been described as 'proceedings which are essentially non-adversary, non-party proceedings'[1] but while this may correctly define the essential philosophy of the hearings system it is in practice important to be able to identify who may be 'parties', as defined in the foregoing – recognising, for example, that an unmarried father who has not acquired parental responsibilities, will not have right of audience before a hearing or the subsequent proceedings before the sheriff.[2] The possible parties, in accordance with this definition, in relation to the proceedings before the sheriff, are as set forth in the rest of this chapter and where relevant the provisions and practices in relation to the representation of parties by lawyers and others are also discussed.

1 *W v Kennedy* 1988 SLT 583 at 585I per Lord Sutherland, delivering the opinion of the First Division.
2 Cf *A v G* 1996 SCLR 787; *A v G and Strathclyde Regional Council* 1997 SCLR 186. As to how an unmarried father may acquire the right to appear: see below at 31.13.

THE CHILD

Child as party

31.02   The child is a party to the proceedings. The child has an unqualified right to be present[1] and comes under an obligation to be personally present at the proof unless his presence has been dispensed with.[2] The child's presence can be compelled.[3]

1 Children (Scotland) Act 1995, s 68(4)(a).
2 C(S)A 1995, s 68(4)(b) and (5) – see discussion above at 30.10.
3 C(S)A 1995, ss 65(8) and 68(6); cf Act of Sederunt (Child Care and Maintenance Rules) 1997, SI 1997/291, r 3.4(1)(f) and Form 31.

Legal representation of child: cases focusing on conduct of child

31.03   Section 68(4) of the Children (Scotland) Act 1995, in providing that the child, 'without prejudice to his right to legal representation', may be represented by a person other than a legally qualified person recognises the child's right to be legally represented. In cases wherein the conduct of a child living in family are the grounds of referral legal representation is often arranged by the parent and the solicitor appointed by the parent would then take his instructions from the child and the parent jointly. Should a conflict of interests arise – as may well be the case in relation to the ground specified in s 52(2)(a) of the Act[1] – the solicitor would require to withdraw from acting for the child or the parent and would, it is thought, be under a professional duty to take reasonable steps to assist the person for whom he was ceasing to act, to obtain legal representation. Children now commonly enough, particularly in the larger centres of population, instruct solicitors directly, sometimes with the assistance of the Scottish Child Law Centre[2] or Childline Scotland.[3] The right of a child under sixteen who has a general understanding of what is involved in instructing a solicitor to instruct a solicitor in civil proceedings is now secured by statute and a child over twelve is presumed to be of sufficient age and capacity to do so.[4] Where the parent neglects to arrange legal representation in a case wherein such representation seems desirable the sheriff may continue the case to enable legal representation to be obtained.[5]

1 '... beyond the control of any relevant person'.
2 Available on the phone at 0800 317 500 any time between 9 a m and 5 p m Monday to Friday.
3 Phone: 0800 1111.
4 Age of Legal Capacity (Scotland) Act 1991 (as amended), s 2(4A) an d (4B).
5 See Chapter 34 below.

Legal representation of children: cases where the child is the victim

31.04   In 'care and protection ' cases there will frequently be the possibility of conflict of interest between parent and child. Before the implementation of the safeguarder provisions in s 34A of the Social Work (Scotland) Act 1968[1] separate representation for the child was sometimes arranged by the reporter's department taking the initiative and requesting the social work department to secure the services of a solicitor for the child and in practice legal aid was granted to such a solicitor. Alternatively, if this had not been done, some sheriffs, if it seemed that separate representation for the child was needed would, either *ex proprio motu* or at the suggestion of the reporter or the parent's solicitor, appoint a named solicitor to act for the child in the course of the application procedure as a curator *ad litem*. Nowadays a safeguarder or a curator *ad litem* may be appointed.[2] The solicitor for the child may, of course,[3] instruct counsel for the hearing before the sheriff, as may the reporter (although representation by counsel at the hearing before the sheriff is infrequent).

1 Now contained in the Children (Scotland) Act 1995, s 41.
2 See discussion in Chapter 34 below.
3 Legal Aid permitting!

Representation of child by a non-lawyer

31.05   As noted in the foregoing paragraph a child may have with him a family member or a person unconnected with the family. Such a person must be able to satisfy the sheriff that he is a suitable person to represent the child and that he is authorised to do so.[1] It is thought that the sheriff would be entitled, if he thought it appropriate, to ascertain some matters in connexion with a proposed representative. For example the sheriff may wish to satisfy himself that a close relative was ready to give independent advice and that, say, a child representative was mature enough to represent the referred child adequately. The sheriff, as presiding judge in his own chambers, has the right to exclude any person who does not behave with appropriate decorum. If a child's representative has to be excluded on this basis it is thought that the sheriff would be entitled either to adjourn the hearing so as to try to find another representative or to proceed without an adjournment depending on the sheriff's view as to where the interests of the referred child lay.[2] The parent has the statutory right to act as the child's legal representative,[3] but since this right is only conferred in order to enable the parent to fulfil his parental responsibilities in relation to the child[4] it would be inappropriate for the parent to exercise this right in the event of conflict of interests, e g where the parent was accused of neglecting the child or was alleged to be involved in any way in the condition of referral.

1   Act of Sederunt (Child Care and Maintenance Rules) 1997, SI 1997/291, r 3.21(2).
2   For a robust exposition of the discretion of the sheriff in procedural matters, see *G v Scanlon* 1999 SLT 707, 2000 SCLR 1.
3   Children (Scotland) Act 1995, s 2(1)(d); cf *McGregor v T and P* 1975 SC 14 at 22; it was pointed out in the same case that the position of the parent as 'guide and counsellor' does not prevent the parent being a competent and compellable witness for the reporter and 'against' the child.
4   C(S)A 1995, s 2(1).

THE REPORTER

Reporter as party

31.06   Although not a 'litigant' in the sense of a person raising or defending an action in the ordinary civil courts the reporter, on the basis of the foregoing definition, is a party to the application, and a necessary party in that his failure to be present or properly represented at the proof may result in the application being dismissed.[1] If the reporter's failure to proceed with the application is caused by circumstances beyond his control it is probably competent to start the referral proceedings again.[2]

1   *Kennedy v O* 1975 SC 308.
2   *McGregor v L* 1983 SLT (Sh Ct) 7.

Representation of the principal reporter

31.07   The reporter may be represented at proof by a reporter who is a suitably qualified reporter, either by being a Scottish solicitor holding a current practising certificate or a member of the Faculty of advocates or by virtue of the Reporters (Conduct of Proceedings before the Sheriff) (Scotland) Regulations, regulations 3 and 4.[1] In practice the reporter who has taken the case at the hearing stage frequently sees the case through to the application stage and to any appeal to the sheriff. It has been questioned if a reporter who is not a solicitor holding a valid practising certificate or a member of the Faculty of Advocates is entitled to conduct an appeal before the sheriff principal.[2]

1 Representation by an 'other representative authorised by the party' under r 3.21 of the Act of Sederunt (Child Care and Maintenance Rules) 1997, SI 1997/291, is not in practice regarded as referring to the reporter – see above para 27.07 (footnote).
2 *Templeton v E* 1998 SCLR 672, *SN v The Children's Hearing Reporter*, Sheriff Principal D J Risk QC, Fort William (5 November 1998, unreported) – see discussion at 54.23 below; cf *Miller v Law Society of Scotland* 2000 SLT 513, discussed above at 27.07.

SAFEGUARDERS AND CURATORS *AD LITEM*

The safeguarder

31.08   A safeguarder may be regarded as a party to the proceedings in that he has the powers of a curator *ad litem* and may appear personally or instruct a solicitor or counsel.[1] The detailed provisions as to safeguarders at the hearing stage have already been discussed.[2] If the children's hearing has appointed a safeguarder that safeguarder, as such, does not become a party to the proceedings before the sheriff. The detailed provisions in relation to the proceedings before the sheriff are discussed later.[3]

1 Act of Sederunt (Child Care and Maintenance Rules) 1997, SI 1997/291, rr 3.8(a) and 3.9(1).
2 Chapter 17 above.
3 Chapter 34 below.

The curator *ad litem*

31.09   The term curator *ad litem* does not appear in Chapters 2 and 3 of Part II of the Children (Scotland) Act 1995, although it is mentioned in the 1997 Rules.[1] The sheriff's power to appoint a curator *ad litem* is based on common law. The law and practice as to the curator *ad litem* are discussed later.[2]

1 Act of Sederunt (Child Care and Maintenance Rules) 1997, SI 1997/291, r 3.5(2)(c).
2 Chapter 34 below.

RELEVANT PERSONS

Relevant persons as parties

31.10   The definition of 'relevant person' has already been discussed.[1] They have a clear interest in the proceedings and the same statutory rights of representation as the child at the application stage.[2] They would accordingly appear to qualify to be regarded as 'parties' and this description has been approved in the Court of Session.[3], albeit tentatively, in relation to parents under the Social Work (Scotland) Act 1968.

1 Above at 1.25 to 1.28.
2 Children (Scotland) Act 1995, s 68(4). cf *Kennedy v O* 1975 SC 308 at 314.
3 *McGregor v T and P* 1975 SC 14 at 21.

Entitlement to attend and be represented

31.11   Relevant persons are *entitled* to attend at any diet in the application proceedings. They are not, *qua* relevant persons, *obliged* to attend the proof – although they may, of course, come under obligation to attend the proof if cited as witnesses. They may, whether personally present at the proof or not, be represented by a solicitor or counsel and additionally, it would appear, by a lay representative also[1] although such dual representation is rare.

1 Children (Scotland) Act 1995, s 68(4); cf C(S)A 1995, s 65(8).

Biological parents whose parental rights and responsibilities have been transferred – unmarried fathers

31.12   Since s 86 of the Children (Scotland) Act 1995 provides for the transfer of 'all parental rights and responsibilities' relating to the child (apart from rights in relation to adoption proceedings which do not concern us in this context) it would seem that biological parents whose whole rights and responsibilities have been so transferred could not become a party to the s 68 application while such order is in force. Section 86(5) allows the sheriff to 'impose such conditions as he considers appropriate'. In *P v P*[1] Sheriff J K Mitchell held, correctly in the writer's respectful view, that the sheriff could not properly use s 11(2)(e) of the Act to make a specific issue order entitling a person who was not otherwise entitled to appear at a children's hearing to appear at such a hearing. It may be, however, that s 86(5) may allow the sheriff to impose a condition reserving to a biological parent the right to attend children's hearings proceedings. Section 86(5) also allows such an order to be varied on the application of the local authority, the child, a person who was a relevant person immediately before the making of the order, or any other person claiming an interest. In *P v P*[2] it was observed that a father who is not married to the child's mother may make application for parental responsibilities and rights under s 11 of the 1995 Act.

1 1999 SCLR 679 at 691ff (reversed, but not on this point in *P v P* see below.
2 2000 SCLR 477 at 488E ff – see discussion below at 56.08.

The local authority as relevant person

31.13   On the transfer of parental rights and responsibilities to a local authority under s 86 of the 1995 Act it would seem clear that, subject to any special condition adjected to the order by the sheriff[1], the local authority concerned, embodied by the Chief Social Work Officer, may be a party to the proof in substitution for the parent whose parental rights and responsibilities have been transferred. In the event of the parental rights and responsibilities of only one parent having been transferred it seems clear that the other parent would be a competent party to application proceedings.

1 Children (Scotland) Act 1995, s 86(5).

Representation of local authority

31.14   It is thought that the provisions of s 68(4) of the 1995 Act allowing relevant persons to be represented by persons other than legally qualified persons would entitle the local authority to be represented by the Chief Social Work Officer or a member of his or her department, but a local authority will generally be represented by one of its solicitors.

Wide scope of 'relevant person'

31.15   It must be kept in mind that in the context of hearings procedures 'relevant person' includes 'any person who appears to be a person who ordinarily (and other than by reason only of his employment) has charge of, or control over, the child'.[1] For discussion of whether or not, where a child is placed with foster parents under a supervision requirement, that foster parent becomes a relevant person see discussion above at 1.23.

1 Children (Scotland) Act 1995, s 93(2).

CHAPTER 32

Presence of child and relevant person at the proof diet and throughout course of proof

THE CHILD AT THE PROOF

Obligation on child to attend – warrant to apprehend

32.01   On receiving a lawful citation[1] from the reporter the child comes under obligation to attend, unless his attendance has been dispensed with,[2] and should he fail to attend the sheriff may grant an order to 'find and keep' the child.[3] The Children (Scotland) Act 1995, in dealing with warrants, is faithful to the 'welfare' approach and makes no distinction between children who have to be brought to a proof on ground of the child's conduct and children to whom the 'care and protection' categories are alleged to apply.

1 Act of Sederunt (Child Care and Maintenance Rules) 1997, SI 1997/291, r 3.4; Form 31.
2 Children (Scotland) Act 1995, s 68(5) – discussed above at 27.09.
3 C(S)A 1995, s 68(6).

Procedure where warrant to apprehend child granted

32.02   A child apprehended on an order granted because of his failure to attend the proof shall not be detained by virtue of that order for more than fourteen days or till the disposal of the application by the sheriff, whichever is the shorter period.[1] On the warrant being executed the child is brought before the sheriff as quickly as possible and a fresh diet of proof is fixed. It is submitted that the sheriff may simply ordain the child to appear at the continued proof, in effect recalling the warrant. If the sheriff takes this course then the proof need not be fixed within the fourteen day period. Alternatively the sheriff may in effect continue the warrant, in which event the child is to remain in detention and the diet of proof should be fixed for a date within fourteen days of the day when the warrant was executed (counting that day as 'day one'). The reporter will advise the sheriff of his view as to whether the child should continue to be detained under the warrant and the reasons for this view. There is no provision for notification of the relevant person, safeguarder, or curator *ad litem* of the hearing before the sheriff to consider the position of a child detained under a warrant, but in practice the reporter will try to notify such persons and any solicitor known to be acting for the child. It is also thought that the sheriff should allow any such persons or their representatives to attend and be heard should they so wish. The sheriff is not, when considering granting an order or how to deal with a child who has been 'found' after implementation of an order under s 68 of the 1995 Act[2] strictly bound by the 'consulting the child principle' or by the 'no non-beneficial order' principle. In practice, however, the sheriff will seek the views of the child where it is practicable to do so, having regard to the child's age and maturity. The sheriff is bound by the paramountcy principle[3] but should apply it having regard inter alia to the interest of the child to have his case dealt with expeditiously.[4]

1 Children (Scotland) Act 1995, s 68(6) and (7).
2 As opposed to when considering granting a warrant under C(S)A 1995, s 67 – see s 16(4)(b)(iii).
3 Children (Scotland) Act 1995, s 16(1).
4 Cf *F v Constanda* 1999 SLT 421 and *G v Scanlon* 1999 SLT 707, 2000 SCLR 1.

Presence of child not always a pre-condition of the legality of the proof

32.03   The provisions relating to dispensing with the presence of the child at the proof have already been discussed.[1] The child has an unqualified right to be present and if a child who is old enough to read has not received notification of the proof it is submitted that the sheriff should not generally allow the proof to proceed.[2] An explanation of the failure should be obtained and, if the matter can be put right,[3] a further diet of proof should be fixed and the opportunity given for the child to be appropriately notified. There is however nothing in the 1995 Act or the 1997 Rules enacting explicitly that the presence of a child who has been properly notified of the diet is a pre-condition of the legality of the proceedings even where the child's obligation to attend has not been dispensed with.

Proofs in 'care and protection' cases are commonly conducted, at least in large part, in the absence of the child, particularly when the child is very young: frequently the child's interests will be represented by a safeguarder or curator *ad litem*. In cases wherein the child's conduct or behaviour is the foundation of the ground of referral – i e always in relation to conditions (h), (i), (j), (k) and (l) and generally in relation to conditions (a) and (b) of s 52 of the 1995 Act – it would be wrong for the proof to proceed in the absence of the child since a just disposal of the case requires that the child be confronted with the evidence as to his conduct or behaviour and given the opportunity to attempt to rebut it.

1 Above at 27.09.
2 Cf discussion at 27.09 above.
3 Cf *Sloan v B* 1991 SLT 530 at 546G.

Exclusion of child from part of proof

32.04   Rule 3.47(5) of the Act of Sederunt (Child Care and Maintenance Rules) 1997 provides:

'Where the nature of the case or of any evidence to be given is such that the sheriff is satisfied that it is in the interests of the child that he should not be present at any stage of the proceedings, the sheriff may exclude the child

from the hearing during that stage and in that event any safeguarder
appointed and the relevant person or representative of the child shall be
permitted to remain during the absence of the child.'

The sheriff's decision on this point is governed by his view of where the
interests of the child lie. It is submitted that this power should be used
sparingly – usually when delicate medical or psychological evidence is
being adduced, either in relation to the parent or the child or when the
parent is being called to speak to his own shortcomings, such as drunken-
ness or the like. Since the purpose of the provision appears to be to avoid
upsetting the child by having imparted to him information that is likely to
be harmful then presumably any person representing the child should be
directed not to impart the information to the child after the conclusion of
the proceedings. This may not be necessary in the case of a legal representative, safeguarder or curator *ad litem* (who may be presumed to be aware
of this consideration), but may be necessary in the case of a non-profes-
sional representative. It is clear that it would be inappropriate for the child
to be excluded when evidence in support of the allegations of misconduct
or misbehaviour on the part of the child is being led in support of conditions under s 52(2)(a),(b) and (h) to (l) of the 1995 Act.

THE RELEVANT PERSON AT THE PROOF

Attendance at proof

32.05   The relevant person as such has no positive duty to attend the
proof and any party requiring a relevant person's attendance at a proof for
the purpose of giving evidence should cite him as a witness. The relevant
person has, however, a right to attend.

32.06   The sheriff may exclude any person, including a relevant person,
while *any* child is giving evidence 'if the sheriff is satisfied that this is
necessary in the interests of *the* [emphasis supplied] child.'[1] It is thought
that the context indicates that 'the' child refers to the child witness since
the rule goes on to provide that this action is to be taken in order to obtain
the evidence of the child or when the presence of the person or persons in
question is causing or is likely to cause significant distress to the child.
Where the relevant person has been excluded under the foregoing provisions *and is not legally represented* the sheriff must inform the relevant
person of the substance of any evidence given by the child and give the
relevant person an opportunity to respond 'by leading evidence or otherwise'.[2] The 'or otherwise' would appear to permit the relevant person to
respond only by argument or by an unsworn statement on which he could
not be cross-examined. The sheriff should include all material points
which have been made during the relevant person's absence. The sheriff,
depending on the length and complexity of these points, may wish to
adjourn for a short period to prepare a note of what he intends to say. The
writer generally makes a written note in his notebook as a permanent

record in the event of challenge. The main discussion of taking evidence from witnesses is contained in Chapter 37.

1 Act of Sederunt (Child Care and Maintenance Rules) 1997, SI 1997/291, r 3.47(6).
2 SI 1997/291, r 3.47(7).

Exclusion of relevant person where other vulnerable witness giving evidence?

32.07   There is no rule whereby a relevant person may be excluded while a person who is not a child is giving evidence, but in a case in Glasgow the sheriff excluded a relevant person where a 17 year old girl had indicated that she was too nervous to give evidence in the presence of the relevant person (whom she alleged had raped her).[1] The sheriff, relying materially on the evidence so given, held the grounds of referral to be established. There was no appeal. In *T v Watson*,[2] Lord Sutherland, delivering the opinion of an Extra Division on the now superseded provisions in relation to the exclusion of the referred child under r 8(4) of the Act of Sederunt (Sheriff Court Procedure Rules) 1971, expressly reserved the issue of the extent of the sheriff's power at common law to exclude persons.

1 *S children* (10 April 2000, unreported) Glasgow Sh Ct, Sheriff L Ruxton.
2 1995 SLT 1062.

CHAPTER 33

Duties of representative of relevant person and child

REPRESENTING THE CHILD AND RELEVANT PERSON

'Representative'

33.01 In practice the representative of parent, other relevant person, or child at the proof stage will be a solicitor, a solicitor advocate or counsel on the instructions of a solicitor. We shall accordingly, in this context, assume legal representation, although some of the following observations will apply *mutatis mutandis* to the position of a lay representative.

Instructing the solicitor

33.02 The whole relevant law regarding parent and child is complex and cannot be set out here.[1] The parent,[2] as part of his parental responsibilities, may act as the legal representative of the child,[3] and the parent's duty to provide direction and guidance[4] entitles the parent to arrange legal representation when appropriate.[5] The child if of sufficient maturity is entitled to instruct a solicitor directly.[6] In practice the parent will frequently arrange any legal representation. Legal aid will generally be available.[7]

1 For a comprehensive study of Scots family law see the continuously up-dated *Scottish Family Law Service*, (1995–), Butterworths, Edinburgh. For family law generally see J M Thomson, *Family Law in Scotland* (3rd edn, 1996), Butterworths, Edinburgh. The standard modern textbook is A B Wilkinson and K McK Norrie, *The Law Relating to Parent and Child in Scotland* (2nd edn, 1999) W Green/Sweet & Maxwell, Edinburgh. Elaine Sutherland, *Child and Family Law* (1999) T & T Clark, Edinburgh, is another comprehensive and highly readable text.
2 Defined in C(S)A 1995, s 15(1).
3 Children (Scotland) Act 1995, ss 1(1)(d) and 2(1)(d).
4 C(S)A 1995, s 1(1)(b).
5 Cf discussion at 31.04 above.
6 Age of Legal Capacity (Scotland) Act 1991 (as amended) s 2(4A) and (4B) – discussed above at 31.03 – cf the interesting observations, of Sheriff A M Bell, in the context of a civil action for 'access' in private civil proceedings, on the usefulness or otherwise of a child becoming a party to such an action and appearing through a solicitor, and the commentary thereon by Alison Clel and, solicitor, in *Henderson v Henderson* 1997 Fam LR 120.
7 See below at 33.04.

Conflict of interest between parent and child

33.03 In cases wherein the conduct of the child is the foundation of the condition of referral the solicitor may take instructions from the parent and child jointly and frequently no problem will arise. In taking instructions as to whether the ground is to be admitted or denied, however, the child's own stance must be ascertained and his instructions followed. In the event of a parent or other relevant person disagreeing with the child's instructions the solicitor would be unable to act for both.[1] It is submitted that the correct course would be for the solicitor in this situation to try, in the interests of the child and so as to minimise possible delay, to act for the child and to advise the parent to instruct another solicitor. As indicated in the immediately following section hereof it would seem that legal aid would, in an appropriate case, be available for both. Should the existence of such a conflict emerge in the course of his discussions or investigations of a case the solicitor cannot continue to act for both relevant person and child. In some cases the conflict will be obvious as when the condition of referral is that the child is beyond the control of his parent and the parent makes allegations as to the conduct of the child which are not accepted by the child. In appropriate cases the best course may be to invite the court to appoint a safeguarder or curator *ad litem*. The matter should be drawn to the attention of the court as soon as possible. No formal procedures have been enacted to bring application for the appointment of a safeguarder or curator *ad litem* to the notice of the court in advance of the proof. In practice a letter to the sheriff clerk, with a copy to the other parties, would be an appropriate way of raising the matter.[2] In Glasgow the sheriff clerk, on receiving the application under s 65(7) or 65(9) of the Children (Scotland) Act 1995, will pass the papers to the duty sheriff to consider if a safeguarder or curator ad litem should be appointed. The court should be informed clearly as to whom, as between relevant person and child, any solicitor appearing is representing.[3] A safeguarder may be appointed at any stage in the proceedings[4].

1 Cf R M Webster and J H Webster, *Professional Ethics and Practice for Scottish Solicitors*, (1984) Law Society of Scotland, Edinburgh, 2.07.
2 For further discussion of safeguarders and curators ad litem see Ch 34 below.
3 Cf *Kennedy v S* 1986 SLT 679 per Lord Hunter at 681.
4 Act of Sederunt (Child Care and Maintenance Rules) 1997, SI 1997/291, r 3.7(1)(b). As to the appointment by the sheriff of a safeguarder or curator *ad litem*, see below at 34.03ff.

Legal Aid

33.04   Legal aid for s 68 applications is available 'to a child and any relevant person'[1] by application to the sheriff and may be granted if the sheriff is satisfied:

> '(a) that *it is in the interests of the child* [emphasis supplied] that legal aid be made available; and
> (b)   after consideration of the financial circumstances of the child and his parent that the expenses of the case cannot be met without undue hardship to the child or his parent or the dependants of either'.[2]

It is submitted that the 'or' in 'to a child or his parent' is not to be treated as disjunctive since there will be occasions (infrequent but not rare) when the interests of justice and the interests of the child demand separate representation for parent and child. Applications for legal aid in this context must be made in such form, being in writing, as the sheriff may require.[3] When legal aid is applied for on behalf of a child application may competently be made 'by his parent or guardian or by any person in whose care he is, or by a person acting for the purpose of any proceedings as his tutor or curator.[4] It is thought that a child may competently make application on his own behalf. The refusal of legal aid by the sheriff may be the subject of judicial review.

1 Legal Aid (Scotland) Act 1986 (as amended by s 92 of Children (Scotland) Act 1995), s 29(2) and (4).
2 LA(S)A 1986, s 29(4).
3 See Legal Aid (Scotland) (Children) Regulations 1987, SI 1987/384, reg 4.
4 SI 1987/384, reg 6.

TAKING INSTRUCTIONS

Solicitor's task generally: the importance of speed

33.05 Unless the solicitor has been involved in the case at the children's hearing session itself (which would be unusual although not rare) the first intimation the solicitor will receive of a pending application for a section 68 proof will be the child and/or the parent coming to the office with the service copy application and warrant[1] which will contain a date less than four weeks away on which the proof has to take place. The period may be substantially less than four weeks if, as frequently happens, parties have not moved promptly. Even allowing for the possibility that the sheriff may be persuaded to adjourn the proof[2] the plain intention of the statute[3] is to secure an expeditious decision. It is therefore the solicitor's duty to act as swiftly as is consistent with the proper performance of his professional duties. A sheriff's decision not to adjourn the proof will not easily be overturned.[4]

1 Act of Sederunt (Child Care and Maintenance Rules) 1997, SI 1997/291, rr 3.4 and 3.12 and Forms 31 and 39.
2 SI 1997/291, r 3.49.
3 Children (Scotland) Act 1995, s 68(2).
4 *G v Scanlon* 2000 SCLR 1, 1999 SLT 707.

Preliminary examination of application

33.06 The solicitor should examine the recitals contained in the first part of the application both in order to discover the reason for the hearing's having directed the application – i e whether the direction has been made because of non-acceptance of the grounds by child or relevant person, or the not understanding of grounds by child, or both – and in order to check that the application is lawful, that time limits have been complied with and the like. Objections to competency and jurisdiction are rare.[1]

1 For discussion of possible preliminary challenges, see above at Ch 29.

Initial discussion of case with client

33.07 The solicitor should find out the attitude of the child, if of sufficient age and maturity, and of the relevant person, to the grounds of referral. In this respect the solicitor's task will be similar to that of a solicitor taking instructions in other forms of legal process. Certain individual features arise from the special nature of these cases. It is not possible to list them all but some can be mentioned.

Understanding the system

33.08   The parties will wish to know the likely outcome of any decision to accept grounds of referral. Explanations should already have been given but if not fully understood a parent may think (for example) that accepting grounds of referral will automatically result in the child being taken into the physical care of the local authority. Clearly the solicitor cannot predict the hearing's disposal of a case but he may require to set out the general structure of the hearing's system and clear away any misunderstandings. In particular the solicitor should advise the clients that parties are not bound by the stance taken at the hearing stage,[1] that if the grounds are denied before the sheriff the reporter will require to lead evidence to attempt to prove his/her case and that the sheriff has discretion, in the event of the grounds being admitted in court, to dispense with the hearing of evidence and hold the grounds established.[2]

1 *Kennedy v R* 1992 SCLR 546 (IH); sub nom *Kennedy v R's Curator ad Litem* 1993 SLT 295.
2 Children (Scotland) Act 1995, s 68(8) – see below at 36.09ff.

Interests of the child

33.09   While the welfare of the child is the ultimate objective of the hearings' system, it is not the immediate concern of the solicitor when taking instructions. His concern at this stage is, initially, to find out if the grounds of referral are to be accepted or not.

CASES FOUNDED ON THE CONDUCT OF THE CHILD

Section 52(2)(i)

33.10   Offence by the child cases normally come before the sheriff because all or part of the grounds have been disputed by the child or parent or both. In the majority of such cases the solicitor will take instructions in the same way as from a client accused of an offence under criminal procedure. It is the solicitor's duty to make sure that his client understands the charge and to clarify any misunderstandings. Just as in criminal practice the solicitor should not accept instructions to admit that the offence has been committed unless he is satisfied that the client knows what he is admitting. For example, merely being present with a group some of whom are committing a breach of the peace may not of itself render the person concerned guilty of breach of the peace. In some cases the client will require to be advised as to whether or not acceptance of grounds would be appropriate or not and it may be that the solicitor, in certain of these cases, will require to investigate the facts before he can properly tender such advice.

Section 52(2)(i): partial acceptance of grounds

33.11 Discussion with the child and parent may reveal that although some components of the offence are denied sufficient are admitted to constitute commission of the offence in principle or, alternatively, that the parent and child are prepared to admit to any modification of the alleged offence which the sheriff would be entitled to hold as established under s 68(8) of the 1995 Act when read with rule 3.50 of the 1997 Rules.[1] In such circumstances the solicitor should inform the relevant reporter immediately in order to find out if the reporter is content to accept the proposed modifications so that parties may jointly ask the sheriff to hold the thus modified grounds of referral as established. The reporter may be prepared to offer to amend.[2]

1 For discussion of Act of Sederunt (Child Care and Maintenance Rules) 1997, SI 1997/291, r 3.50 see 39.05 ff below.
2 SI 1997/291, r 3.48.

Section 52(2)(i) cases: grounds not accepted

33.12 In the event that the relevant person or child maintains the position of non-acceptance of the grounds of referral then the solicitor must proceed with the preparation of the defence.[1] It should be noted that where the parent does not accept that the child committed the offence then, even where the child does so accept, the sheriff would not be entitled to dispense with the hearing of evidence.

1 See below at 33.25 ff.

Section 52(2)(j) (misuse of alcohol or drugs) and (k) (misuse of volatile substance)

33.13 Special considerations may apply to these cases.[1]

1 See below at 46.22 ff.

Section 52(2)(h) (failure to attend school regularly without reasonable excuse)

33.14 As further discussed later[1] the head teacher's certificate is presumed accurate unless the contrary can be proved.[2] Thereafter the onus passes to the child to establish reasonable excuse. It should be noted that if the absence from school has been caused by exclusion the reporter will require to prove that the child was excluded as a result of the child's conduct.[3]

1 Below at 46.19 ff.
2 Education (Scotland) Act 1980, s 86.
3 *JD v Kennedy* 1988 SCLR 30.

CASES FOUNDED ON CONDUCT OF CHILD IMPLYING CONFLICT WITH RELEVANT PERSONS

Section 52(2) (a) ('beyond control'), (b) ('bad associations'/'moral danger') and (l) (child with local authority requiring special measures)

33.15 Special considerations apply to such cases and particular ethical difficulties may arise. In general the duty of the solicitor for the child will be directed towards securing that the child's stance and wishes are adequately presented. Since there may often be a conflict between the wishes of the child and the interests of the child it will often be necessary for a safeguarder or curator *ad litem* to be appointed. The meaning and implications of these grounds of referral are discussed later[1].

1 Below at 46.03 ff.

GENERAL CONSIDERATIONS AND CARE AND PROTECTION CASES

Grounds originally not accepted

33.16 In some cases the initial refusal to accept grounds may have been based upon a misunderstanding either as to the nature of the grounds or as to the consequences of accepting the grounds and the solicitor must try to ensure that the client understands the position. In some care and protection cases, as in offence by the child and other types of case, investigation by the solicitor into the facts of the case will be necessary before the solicitor can advise his client properly as to whether or not grounds should be accepted.

Grounds, conditions and facts

33.17 When the possibility of accepting grounds is being discussed the distinct concepts of grounds, conditions, and facts[1] must be kept in mind. It should be carefully checked that the child/relevant person accepts that the condition of referral has been satisfied as well as that the facts in the statement of facts are admitted. For example when it is alleged as a condition of referral that a child is likely to suffer unnecessarily or be impaired seriously in his health or development due to a lack of parental care, and a number of facts are averred in support of this condition, it is clearly not enough that the child/relevant person accepts the averments of fact as true. They must also accept the inference, embodied in the condition, that, as a consequence of the existence of these facts, it is indeed likely that the child will suffer unnecessarily and/or be impaired seriously in his health or development. The function of the court should not be overlooked and the court may in a particular case accept the uncorroborated statement of a parent to infer that a condition of referral does not exist.[2]

1 See above at Chapter 16.
2 Cf *Kennedy v B* 1972 SC 128; and *Kennedy v M* 1989 SCLR 769, 1989 SLT 687.

Advising in relation to acceptance of grounds

33.18 The unnecessary raking over, at proof, of unhappy family history should, when possible, be avoided and, if appropriate, the client may be advised to accept the grounds of referral but a client must not be persuaded to accept grounds when he is unhappy about so doing. In some cases it will be possible to give stronger advice than in others. In particular in cases relying upon conditions which the reporter may demonstrably be able to prove, such as the allegations that the child is or is likely to become a member of the same household as a person who has committed a Schedule 1 offence,[1] it may be appropriate to give fairly firm advice that the grounds of referral ought to be accepted.

1 Children (Scotland) Act 1995, s 52(2)(f).

Partial acceptance of grounds

33.19 As in offence by the child cases the solicitor, if it emerges that the child and the relevant person are ready to offer a partial acceptance of grounds which is ample enough to justify the condition being held to be established, should contact the reporter as soon as possible to see if he is prepared to agree to the grounds thus modified.

Limitation on scope of 'negotiations' in care and protection cases? – *O v Rae*

33.20 The reporter may or may not feel inclined to accept this modified position which really represents a scaling down of his case by omission of a fact or condition from the grounds of referral. However in the case of *O v Rae*[1] the First Division held that the hearing was entitled to have regard in its deliberations to information in relation to a fact which had been deleted from the grounds of referral as originally framed. Standing this decision it may be that there will be situations wherein the relevant person should not be advised, in a case where there are facts alleged which he denies, to 'settle' by having the averments with which he disagrees deleted from the statement of facts. Rather he should put the matter to proof and attempt to obtain a definite finding by the sheriff, as happened in *M v Kennedy*,[2] that the averment which he disagrees with is unfounded. It is submitted that this situation is unsatisfactory, producing as it does the possibility of wholly unnecessary and distressing evidence being examined in a situation where the reporter may no longer be convinced that the disputed averments are relevant or even capable of being proved. In practice reporters do not rely on the reasoning in *O v Rae* in order to introduce into the discussions of cases facts which are not included in the stated grounds of referral[3] and it is understood that hearings do not in practice rely on 'deleted facts'. The decision in *O v Rae* has been criticised[4] and defended.[5] It may be vulnerable to criticism as possibly being in conflict with article 6 of the European Convention.[6] It may require to be considered by a fuller bench. Until it is, the possibility remains that the sensible 'settlement' of some care and protection cases may be impeded.

1 1993 SLT 570, 1992 SCLR 318 – discussed above at 16.06 to 16.08.
2 1993 SLT 431.
3 See discussion above at 16.07.
4 By Sheriff J Kenneth Mitchell in *Children's Hearings System – Children (Scotland) Act 1995*, 1997 SCOLAG 9 at 11 ff.
5 By Professor Kenneth McK Norrie in *In Defence of O v Rae* 1995 SLT (News) 353.
6 See discussion above at 16.08.

Absence of formal procedure enabling court to take advance notice of 'settlement' of application

33.21   The consequence of successful 'settlement' discussions may be amendment of one or more of the factual averments in the statement of facts under rule 3.48, or the abandonment of one or more of the conditions of referral under rule 3.46 of the Act of Sederunt (Child Care and Maintenance Rules) 1997, or both. If, as a consequence of such discussions a ground of referral which was hitherto denied is now to be accepted, there will require to be a motion to the court to dispense with hearing proof.[1] No formal procedure has been enacted enabling the court to consider in advance whether proof can be dispensed with, and therefore attendance of witnesses at court avoided, although in practice this may sometimes be achieved by an informal approach to the sheriff (via the sheriff clerk)[2] and the proof diet will become a formality.[3] Parties should not cancel witnesses on the unchecked assumption that the sheriff will dispense with evidence. Alternatively, it is submitted that, at any time before the proof diet, it is competent to ask the court to accelerate the proof diet and, when agreement has been reached such a motion may be made, usually jointly. The sheriff may then consider whether or not to grant the motion and deem the grounds of referral to be established. The procedure in relation to dispensing with the hearing of evidence is principally discussed later.[4]

1 Children (Scotland) Act 1995, s 68(8).
2 The principal discussion of the sheriffs dispensing power appears at 36.09 ff below.
3 But it must be a properly convened diet – contrast *H v Mearns* 1974 SC 152, 1974 SLT 184.
4 Below at 36.09 to 36.16.

Grounds not understood by child (and parent accepts grounds)

33.22   Where the child has not understood the explanation of the grounds of referral the hearing, unless they decide to discharge the referral, must, even if the relevant person accepts the grounds, direct the reporter to lodge an application with the sheriff for a proof.[1] Yet, perhaps surprisingly, the acceptance by the relevant person before the sheriff entitles the sheriff, unless satisfied that the evidence should be heard, to deem the grounds to be established without hearing evidence.[2] Where this possibility is in prospect the solicitor should contact the reporter to discuss the position as soon as possible.

1 Children (Scotland) Act 1995, s 65(9).
2 C(S)A 1995, s 68(8).

Liaison with safeguarder or curator ad litem

33.23   There is reason to believe that safeguarders and curators *ad litem* are seen by families as being particularly worthy of trust as being independent of 'the system'. Accordingly where settlement of the application procedures by agreement is under discussion any safeguarder or curator *ad litem* should be brought into the discussion.

Grounds still denied

33.24   If it appears that the parent or child are still maintaining a denial of the grounds then active preparations for the proof must begin.

PREPARING FOR PROOF

General

33.25   The extent and depth of necessary investigation and preparation will vary. The preparation of many offence by the child cases will often be parallel to the investigation of simple criminal charges on summary complaint. Many care and protection cases, and some offence cases, may involve elaborate preparation.

Interviewing client and witnesses

33.26   As well as taking statements from his own clients the solicitor will require to become aware of the strength of the reporter's case. The reporter, although under no obligation to do so, will normally be willing to supply a list of witnesses and may often be prepared to let the solicitor for a parent or child see his witnesses' statements. How far he can rely on statements taken by another as opposed to having the witnesses seen individually is a matter for the solicitor's judgement having regard to the difficulty of the case and the importance of speed already mentioned.

Precognition of reporter's witnesses by 'defence' in care and protection cases

33.27   In many care and protection cases it will be necessary for the solicitor for the child and the solicitor for the relevant person to interview consultants, social workers and others, including sometimes other children, regarding intimate personal details of the family history. Busy solicitors nowadays frequently employ precognition clerks or instruct independent precognition-taking agencies. A solicitor, however, remains responsible for the precognition taker[1] and it is therefore the responsibility of the solicitor to make sure that the precognition taker is made aware of the full background to the case before starting out and is capable of acting with the skill, tact and discretion which the subject matter of such cases demands. Scotland has a growing number of solicitors who are expert in family and child law, who are experienced in communicating with children and dedicated to their welfare. Such solicitors regard it as proper practice to conduct such interviews personally or at least entrust the work to a suitably trained and experienced assistant.

1 *Society of Writers to HM Signet v Mackersy* 1924 SC 776 at 784.

Citing of witnesses and havers: recovery of documents etc.

33.28   The procedures for citation of witnesses and havers and for recovery of documents and other evidence have already been examined in the context of the reporter's duties[1] and these apply *mutatis mutandis* to the defence solicitor and any safeguarder appointed by the sheriff who has elected to become a party.

1 See above at Ch 30.

Notification to other parties of special lines of evidence

33.29   There is no statutory obligation on the 'defence' to intimate 'special' defences (such as, in offence cases, self-defence, alibi, or incrimination). The principle of fair notice, however, demands that where a substantial defence of this nature is to be advanced the reporter and any other party having an interest should be given reasonable notice so as to be able to prepare and, if necessary, investigate. It is submitted that the same principle applies to any affirmative line of defence such as a defence of reasonable excuse for failing to attend school regularly or evidence of a material change in the home circumstances directed to supporting the argument that lack of parental care is no longer likely to cause a child to suffer unnecessarily or be impaired seriously in his health or development. If reasonable advance notice is not given the additional delay and inconvenience of an adjournment of the proof may be incurred. In 1972 Lord Justice-Clerk Grant stated:

> 'Where, as here, there is a danger of prejudice to the reporter (and indeed a risk of injustice) as a result of a surprise last moment disclosure of what the respondents case is, I think the sheriff can and should adjourn the case so that the reporter may lead further evidence to meet that case and the respondents, if so advised, may lead evidence to support it.'[1]

In cases wherein the relevant person and child are separately represented or wherein a safeguarder or curator *ad litem* has been appointed the party proposing to lead the affirmative 'defence' evidence should, it is submitted, intimate his intention not only to the reporter but to the other parties.

1 *Kennedy v B* 1972 SC 128 at 133 per Lord Justice-Clerk Grant.

Adjournment of proof

33.30 The difficulty of investigating and obtaining medical evidence at short notice may make it advisable to consider applying to the court for a short adjournment of the diet of proof. The lack of any procedural machinery for preliminary or incidental motions to the sheriff leaves parties without any formal machinery for obtaining an early ruling on whether an adjournment is to be granted and in the early case of *H v Mearns*[1] an informal arrangement to postpone the hearing of an application came to grief essentially because what should have been the beginning of the hearing of the application was treated as a mere formality. It is thought, however, that when all parties are represented it would be proper, if it were clear that full investigation of the case would not be practicable in time for the proof date, for a joint informal approach to be made to the sheriff to ascertain if he would be prepared to indicate whether, when the application called for proof, he would be prepared to adjourn the proof. Certainly such a procedure would tend to reduce the number of occasions when witnesses turn up for proofs which have to be adjourned. Adjournment of the proof is always a matter within the discretion of the sheriff.[2]

1 1974 SC 152.
2 *G v Scanlon* 1999 SLT 707, 2000 SCLR 1.

CHAPTER 34

The safeguarder and curator *ad litem* at the s 68 application stage

THE CONCEPT OF THE SAFEGUARDER

The safeguarder: legislative background

34.01   England's Children Act 1975[1] was used as the vehicle for introducing into Scottish hearings law the concept of appointing persons 'for the purpose of safeguarding the interests of the child' but the provisions lay unimplemented till 30 June 1985 when the Act of Sederunt[2] amending the Sheriff Court Procedure Rules of 1971 so as to provide for the appointment of such persons came into force as did the Social Work (Panels of Persons to Safeguard the Interests of Children) (Scotland) Regulations 1984[3] ('the Safeguarders Regulations 1984'). The current provisions are contained in s 41 of the Children (Scotland) Act 1995 and s 101(1)(c) of the Act empowers the Secretary of State (now the Scottish Ministers) to make regulations but at the time of writing this power has not been used. It may be that by the operation of s 17 of the Interpretation Act 1978 the Safeguarders Regulations 1984, which provided inter alia for the local authority to enrol persons to act as safeguarders, are still in force and in practice they are so regarded. The duties of the safeguarder at the children's hearing stage have already been discussed.[4] The rights and duties of the safeguarder in the proceedings in the sheriff court are contained in rr 3.6 to 3.10 of the Act of Sederunt (Child Care and Maintenance Rules) 1997 ('the 1997 Rules'). The application of these rules in relation to the child protection code has already been discussed.[5]

1 Sections 66 and 78.
2 Act of Sederunt (Social Work) (Sheriff Court Procedure Rules 1971) (Amendment) 1985, SI 1985/781.
3 SI 1984/1442.
4 Above at 17.12 ff.
5 Above at 9.04 ff.

Definition

34.02   The term 'safeguarder' is not defined in the 1995 Act.[1] Nor is the term defined in the 1997 Rules – in contrast to the Children's Hearings Rules 1996, which define a safeguarder as 'a person appointed by a children's hearing under s 41(1) of the Act for the purpose of safeguarding the interests of the child in the proceedings'.[2] The term may be taken to have a similar meaning in the 1997 Rules with the gloss that these Rules sometimes require to differentiate between a safeguarder appointed by a children's hearing and a safeguarder appointed by a sheriff. The rights, powers and duties of the safeguarder will be discussed presently. They include, in the case of a safeguarder appointed by a sheriff (but not in the case of a safeguarder appointed by a children's hearing) 'the powers and duties at common law of a curator ad litem in respect of the child'.[3]

1 The term only appears once in the Children (Scotland) Act 1995 – in the heading to s 101.
2 SI 1997/291, r 2(1).
3 SI 1997/291, r 3.8(a).

SAFEGUARDER AND CURATOR *AD LITEM*

Curator *ad litem*

34.03   Before the arrangements for the appointing of safeguarders came into force sheriffs occasionally, when the interests of the child seemed to require it, appointed a person, usually a solicitor practising in the relevant court, as curator *ad litem* and legal aid was available for the person so appointed. The person so appointed would then appear personally in court to conduct the child's case. The sheriff's authority for making such an appointment was and is the common law. The enactments introducing the safeguarder do not abolish this power and it remains available. In current legal aid practice a safeguarder who is also a solicitor is not eligible for legal aid[1] whereas a curator *ad litem* who is a solicitor may be so entitled. Accordingly the practice has grown up in some courts, when the sheriff considers that the interests of the child will be best safeguarded by a legally qualified person – possibly a particular legally qualified person or a legally qualified person within a range of particular persons – of appointing such a person as a curator *ad litem*. In the following discussion it may be assumed, except where the context indicates otherwise, that reference to a safeguarder includes a reference to a curator *ad litem* appointed on this basis

1 Cf *Murphy, pet* (15 December 1986, unreported) Glasgow Sh Ct.

APPOINTMENT OF SAFEGUARDERS

Criterion for appointment of safeguarder

34.04   The requirement under s 34A(1)(c)(i) of the Social Work (Scotland) Act 1968 for there to be a possible or actual conflict of interest between parent and child before a safeguarder could be appointed has been removed. Section 41(1) of the 1995 Act provides that in any proceedings before a children's hearing or the sheriff under chapters 2 and 3 of the Act, except for the application to the sheriff for a Child Protection Order, the hearing or the sheriff:

a)   shall consider if it is necessary to appoint a person to safeguard the interests of the child in the proceedings; and

b) if they, or he, so consider, shall make such an appointment, on such terms and conditions as appear appropriate.

What is meant by 'necessary' is not spelt out in the 1995 Act, but decisions in relation to the appointment or not of a safeguarder are governed by the paramountcy of welfare of the child principle enacted in s 16(1) of the Act.

Indicators suggesting appointment: conflict of interest

34.05 Although the presence of a conflict of interest has been removed as a pre-condition the sheriff may regard the presence of such a conflict as an indicator. The ideas of child and relevant person to what constitutes the best interests of the child may differ. A child who is residing at home may demonstrate this conflict by running away from home or appearing to defy his parents' wishes in other ways. A child who is in the physical care of a local authority may do so by running away from whatever establishment he is being lodged in and taking refuge, perhaps, in his parents' home.

Other indicators suggesting appointment

34.06 Another indicator may be any information tending to suggest that the views of the child will be particularly important in the disposal or management of the case. In s 68 proofs the main concern of the court is the decision on the evidence as to whether of not the grounds of referral are established. There will be cases wherein the interests of the child may demand an investigation of a particular line of evidence. There will be cases wherein it may not be in the interests of the child that a particular procedural step be taken, e g an adjournment of the proof pending further investigations.[1] Another example would be a case wherein a child is claimed by the parent to be beyond the parent's control and the matter has been referred to the sheriff because the child is too young to understand the ground of referral. In such a case, if the sheriff is asked by or on behalf of the relevant person to dispense with the hearing of evidence in terms of s 68(8) of the 1995 Act, the sheriff may wish to appoint a safeguarder to assist him to decide whether or not to exercise his discretion in favour of dispensing with evidence. There will be cases wherein the sheriff may wish the child's interests to be represented in a particularly sensitive way. In one case,[2] an exclusion order was granted and the sheriff wished that the children should be informed of the general nature of the proceedings, but not for the time being told that their father had served a prison term, and consequently appointed a particular curator *ad litem* whom he was confident would handle the case with appropriate sensitivity. In one case[3] where foster carers were alleged to have assaulted a child the hearing appointed a safeguarder who was in turn appointed by the sheriff. When the matter came to the sheriff for the s 68 proof the safeguarder took the view that the child's interests were best served by resisting these allegations and instructed a solicitor who acted as effective contradictor of the reporter's stance by cross-examining and leading evidence. Safeguarders are appointed in care and protection cases more frequently than in offence by the child cases but they are from time to time appointed in the latter. For example where it may appear that the relevant person may adopt a rigidly punitive stance in relation to the child and that this may adversely influence the relevant person in exercising his right[4] to act as the child's legal representative.

1 Cf *G v Scanlon* 1999 SLT 707.
2 *Russell v W* 1998 Fam LR 25.
3 *Cunninghame v JD and CD* 2000 Fam LB 46–5.
4 Children (Scotland) Act 1995, s 2(1)(d).

PROCEDURE FOR APPOINTING SAFEGUARDER

Duty of sheriff to consider appointment of safeguarder – more than one safeguarder

34.07   The wording of the rule enjoining the sheriff, as soon as reasonably practicable after the lodging of the application, to consider whether it is necessary to appoint a safeguarder appears to place upon the court the duty of considering the matter *ex proprio motu*.[1] There is, however, as we shall presently see, nothing to prevent the reporter on the one hand or the parent or relevant person's representative on the other from raising the matter with the sheriff by written or verbal motion requesting the court to appoint a safeguarder or at least consider so doing. It is helpful when this is done since the sheriff, unless a safeguarder has already been appointed by the hearing and lodged a report,[2] will generally have no background knowledge of the case. Initially there was some scepticism in some quarters as to the rôle of the safeguarder but for some time now reporters have been ready to make the motion or to indicate by a brief note along with the application that an appointment may be appropriate. Generally, where the appointment of a safeguarder is made, it will be appropriate to appoint the same person for all the referred children in the family, but it would seem that, exceptionally, a separate safeguarder for an individual child may be competent, although not obligatory.[3] The decision of a hearing to appoint more than one safeguarder is not binding on a subsequent hearing[4] and presumably the same principle applies to a decision of a sheriff.

1 Act of Sederunt (Child Care and Maintenance Rules) 1997, SI 1997/291, r 3.7(1)(a).
2 SI 1997/291, r 3.45(1) and Form 60 and r 3.45(2).
3 Cf *H v Kennedy* 1999 SCLR 961, 1992 GWD 14–270.
4 1999 SCLR 961, 1992 GWD 14–270.

Practicalities

34.08   The requirement for prompt consideration of the issue is observed in Glasgow by the application being placed before a sheriff immediately on lodgement. In the event of there being no indication or motion from the reporter or other party, and if a safeguarder has not already been appointed by the children's hearing[1] the sheriff, unless he has had some prior involvement with the case – e g in relation to considering a CPO,[2] may have little to go on except the grounds of referral. Sometimes this may be enough to allow the sheriff to make a decision but it is submitted that it is always open to the sheriff to direct the sheriff clerk to ask, by phone or other fast means of communication, the reporter and any known legal representatives of the child and relevant persons, if they have any observation. Should the sheriff decide not to appoint a safeguarder at this stage this decision would be a decision made *in hoc statu*, i e, it would not bind the court if, later on, the same or another sheriff in the same application decided that a safeguarder should be appointed.[3]

1 Below at 34.11.
2 Unusual (though not unknown) in Glasgow, where there are 22 resident sheriffs and 4 Glasgow-based 'floating' sheriffs – more likely in smaller courts.
3 See below at 34.10 and 34.15.

Formalities

34.09 The appointment of the safeguarder is recorded in an interlocutor attached to the application. The interlocutor should not be signed before the sheriff clerk has checked that the proposed safeguarder is willing to act. It is thought that it is not necessary for the sheriff to administer the oath *de fideli administratione* in relation to an individual appointment.

Safeguarder may be appointed at any time

34.10 While, as noticed, the rules underline the need for prompt consideration of a possible appointment, the rules also empower the sheriff 'if he thinks fit' to appoint a safeguarder 'at any later stage of the application or proceedings'.[1] The safeguarder appointed by the sheriff is required, after making the necessary enquiries (which will be noticed presently) to intimate in writing to the sheriff clerk without delay and in any event before the proof, 'whether of not he intends to become a party to the proceedings'.[2] No specific procedure has been enacted for bringing the matter to the notice of the court before the proof but it would seem that the court is being encouraged by these rules to try to appoint a safeguarder in advance of the proof and it is submitted that the sheriff should, in the interests of expedition and flexibility, be prepared at any stage to entertain in chambers an application for the appointment of a safeguarder.[3] It is submitted that it is incumbent on all, including the sheriff, to try to secure that active and early consideration is given to the appointment of a safeguarder in order to avoid the issue being first seriously canvassed on the day of the proof.

1 Act of Sederunt (Child Care and Maintenance Rules) 1997, SI 1997/291, r 3.7(1)(b).
2 SI 1997/291, r 3.8(e).
3 Cf the approval accorded by the Inner House in the Orkney case to the (then) wholly non-statutory procedure whereby a children's hearing could be convened as a 'business meeting' to issue guidance on preliminary matters – *Sloan v B* 1991 SLT 530 at 540F.

Safeguarder already appointed by children's hearing

34.11   Where a safeguarder has been appointed by a children's hearing intimation of that appointment, together with any report the safeguarder has made, must be lodged by the reporter along with the application to the sheriff.[1] There is no obligation to lodge with the sheriff the reasons stated by the chairman under r 14(1) of the Children's Hearings (Scotland) Rules 1996 for the hearing's having appointed the safeguarder but it is suggested that this should be done. It is thought that where the children's hearing have appointed a safeguarder the sheriff will generally wish to do likewise. It is now provided that where a safeguarder has been appointed by a children's hearing and the sheriff is minded to appoint a safeguarder, then the sheriff, unless he *ex proprio motu* or on motion of party on cause shown directs otherwise, shall appoint the same person.[2] It is to be noted that this rule, while requiring a party to show cause why a different safeguarder should be appointed, does not make the same condition of the sheriff acting *ex proprio motu*. It is submitted however that the desirability of keeping to the minimum the number of persons whom the child requires to go over the facts of the case with may often point to keeping to the same safeguarder. On the other hand the sheriff may wish the skill, legal and/or otherwise of a particular range of safeguarders or curators *ad litem*, or even, in an exceptional case, of a particular individual, to be available in the interests of the child.

1 Act of Sederunt (Child Care and Maintenance Rules) 1997, SI 1997/291, r 3.45(2).
2 SI 1997/291, r 3.7(2).

STATUS AND FUNCTION OF SAFEGUARDER: PROCEDURE

The general rights and duties of safeguarder and curator ad litem

34.12   The safeguarder's powers are set out in r 3.8 of the 1997 Rules. He has 'the powers and duties at common law of a curator *ad litem* in respect of the child.'[1] A curator *ad litem* is an officer of court appointed by the court to secure that the case for the 'ward' (here the child) is properly conducted[2] and must exercise his judgement independently.[3] He has no control over the person of the ward.[4] At common law where the ward was a minor (i e a female child over 12 or a male child over 14) the minor was '*dominus litis*' (in charge of the litigation) and accordingly the curator did not have the power to settle an action without the ward's concurrence.[5] On the conclusion of the proceedings the appointment terminates.[6] The law affecting the powers and duties of curators *ad litem* is discussed more fully in the standard works.[7]

1 Act of Sederunt (Child Care and Maintenance Rules) 1997, SI 1997/291, r 3.8(a).
2 *Maclaren on Court of Session Practice* p 184.
3 *Drummond's Trs v Peel's Trs* 1929 SC 484 per Lord President Clyde at 496 and per Lord Hunter at 504.
4 *Docherty v McAllen* 1983 SLT 645 at 647.
5 *Stephenson v Lorimer* (1844) 6 D 377; *Dewar v Dewar's Trs* (1906) 14 SLT 238.
6 Cf *Catto v Pearson* 1990 SLT (Sh Ct) 77, 1990 SCLR 267.
7 *Macphail on Sheriff Court Practice* (2nd edn, 1998)) 4.23 to 4.28; *Wilkinson & Norrie on Parent and Child* (2nd edn, 1999) 15.60–61; *Gloag and Henderson on The Law of Scotland*, (10th edn, 1995) 49.17.

Specific initial rights and duties of safeguarder

34.13 The safeguarder is entitled under the rules to receive from the reporter copies of the application, the productions, and the papers which were before the hearing.[1] Subject to any orders[2] which the sheriff may have made towards ascertaining the views of a child who has indicated a wish to express views the safeguarder should 'determine' whether the child wishes to express views in relation to the application and, if the child does so wish, ascertain what these views are and 'transmit his [the child's] views to the sheriff'.[3] The safeguarder shall make such enquiries as he considers appropriate[4] and then, without delay, and at the latest before the proof, notify the sheriff clerk in writing as to whether or not he intends to become a party to the proceedings.[5]

1 Act of Sederunt (Child Care and Maintenance Rules) 1997, SI 1997/291, r 3.8(b).
2 SI 1997/291, r 3.5(1)(a).
3 SI 1997/291, r 3.8(c).
4 SI 1997/291, r 3.8(d).
5 SI 1997/291, r 3.8(e).

Scope of safeguarder's initial enquiries: the safeguarder's decision as to whether or not to become a party

34.14 The first decision the safeguarder has to take is whether or not he or she intends to become a party to the proceedings[1] and the safeguarder should aim to make sufficient enquiries at the outset to enable him to decide on this. If the safeguarder decides not to become a party he must prepare a written report to the sheriff on the extent of his enquiries and his conclusion as to the interests of the child in the proceedings.[2] It is interesting to note that the decision as to whether to become a party is the safeguarder's decision and not the decision of the children's hearing or the sheriff as the case may be. No procedure exists for obtaining a ruling from the sheriff. It may be that the sheriff could fix a hearing at which parties and the safeguarder would be invited to attend – but there is no statutory authority for this. It is however submitted that if, where a safeguarder had decided not to become a party to the proceedings and the sheriff took the view that the continuing presence of a safeguarder or curator *ad litem* in the process was necessary having regard to the best interests of the child, then the sheriff would be entitled to appoint another safeguarder or curator ad litem.

1 Act of Sederunt (Child Care and Maintenance Rules) 1997, SI 1997/291, r 3.10(1).
2 SI 1997/291, r 3.10(1).

Late entry by safeguarder into proceedings

34.15 A safeguarder appointed by the sheriff who has intimated a decision not to become a party to the proceedings must nevertheless receive intimation from the sheriff clerk of all interlocutors subsequent to his appointment.[1] It is now clear that a safeguarder who has intimated his intention not to become a party may subsequently seek leave to become a party.[2] Where a safeguarder becomes a party after evidence has been led the sheriff may order the evidence to be reheard in whole or in part.[3] It is submitted that this provision applies equally to a safeguarder appointed 'late' by the sheriff as to a safeguarder who has initially declined to become a party but has later decided so to become. It is more tentatively submitted that, in the event of the sheriff deciding to appoint a (non-statutory) curator *ad litem*, then the sheriff would be entitled, if the interests of the child seemed so to demand, to entertain a motion for the re-hearing of all or part of the evidence.

1 Act of Sederunt (Child Care and Maintenance Rules) 1997, SI 1997/291, r 3.10(2).
2 SI 1997/291, r 3.10(3).
3 SI 1997/291, r 3.47(8).

SAFEGUARDER NOT BECOMING A PARTY TO THE PROCEEDINGS

Report of safeguarder not becoming party

34.16   Rule 3.10 of the 1997 Rules provides that the safeguarder, when intimating the decision not to become a party 'shall at the same time report in writing to the sheriff on the extent of his enquiries and his conclusion as to the interests of the child in the proceedings.' The sheriff, at the stage of the s 68 application, has no substantive[1] decisions to take as to what constitutes 'the interests of the child': that is a matter, if the grounds of referral are sustained by the sheriff, for consideration and determination by a children's hearing[2] – and any pre-empting of the hearing's function is to be deprecated.[3] As the law stands at present it is submitted that the safeguarder must comply with the requirement of the rules and summarise 'the extent of his enquiries', which may involve narration of factual information received. He must also give 'his conclusion as to the interests of the child in the proceedings', which would seem to involve forming an opinion as to the reliability of information received and a value judgement as to the appropriate disposal. As noted already[4] a safeguarder may adopt a view as to the interests of the child which will significantly affect the course of the proceedings before the sheriff.

1 The sheriff may have procedural decisions to take to which the interests of the child will be relevant, e g decisions as to delaying the proof (cf *G v Scanlon* 1999 SLT 707) and on whether or not to delay matters by disqualifying himself (*F v Constanda* 1999 SLT 421), but a safeguarder's report would not address such matters.
2 Children (Scotland) Act 1995, s 68(10)(a).
3 *M v McGregor* 1982 SLT 41 at 44; and *Kennedy v A* 1986 SLT 358.
4 Above at 34.06.

The sheriff's use of the safeguarder's report – 'Confidential' information supplied by child to safeguarder

34.17   The use which the sheriff makes of such a report is a matter for the sheriff. It is suggested that the sheriff should examine the report whenever it arrives. It is clear that the sheriff may use it as 'a check on the view which he had formed on the evidence'.[1] It has been observed in the Court of Session that a written report of a safeguarder should not be relied upon by the sheriff until it has been spoken to in evidence.[2] It is tentatively submitted, however, that once such a report has been so spoken to, the report of the safeguarder may be regarded also as an independent source of evidence. It is also, even more tentatively, submitted that the provisions permitting the sheriff to withhold views conveyed by the child inter alia by the safeguarder[3] may permit the sheriff to use such evidence without disclosing it to parties. This important matter has already been discussed in general at 4.15 and following paragraphs and the discussion there should be read in connexion with this paragraph. It is submitted that, if a safeguarder is informed by the child in giving 'views' of any matter which the child wishes to be kept secret, then the safeguarder should note this, include it in his report, and identify it as being material which the child does not want to be disclosed. It will then be for the sheriff to consider using the powers[4] to direct that this written record of the child's views should be kept in a sealed envelope, kept in the process without being recorded in the inventory of process, and available to and openable by the sheriff only and not borrowable by any party. In relation to information not so identified, it is suggested that the sheriff should reveal it to parties and, if there is an element within it which the sheriff thinks significantly contradicts the stance of one or more of the parties, allow such party or parties the right to respond.

1 *Kennedy v M* 1989 SLT 687 per Lord Brand at 689D.
2 *AR v David Walker* 1999 SCLR 341 at 346C, Ex Div.
3 Act of Sederunt (Child Care and Maintenance Rules) 1997, SI 1997/291, r 3.5(2)(c).
4 SI 1997/291, r 3.5(4).

SAFEGUARDER BECOMING A PARTY TO THE PROCEEDINGS

Safeguarder's position as to citing and examining witnesses

34.18 A safeguarder who elects to become a party to the proceedings has all the powers and duties at common law of a curator *ad litem* in respect of the child[1] and may appear personally in the proceedings or instruct an advocate or a solicitor to appear on his (the safeguarder's) behalf.[2] Should the safeguarder be an advocate or solicitor himself he is not to act as advocate or solicitor for the child in the proceedings.[3] It seems clear that a safeguarder who is a solicitor or an advocate may be entitled in his capacity as safeguarder to call, examine and cross-examine witnesses in so far as he thinks necessary in order properly to safeguard the interests of the child.[4]

1 Discussed above at 34.12.
2 SI 1997/291, r 3.9(1). For discussion of the function and powers of a curator *ad litem* in the context of Court of Session practice see Maxwell *The Practice of the Court of Session* Part VIII, Ch 8.
3 SI 1997/291, r 3.9(2).
4 SI 1997/291, r 3.47(4); cf *Murphy, petitioner* 15 December unreported (Glasgow Sh Ct).

Limited obligation on sheriff clerk to notify party safeguarder of interlocutors

34.19 The wording of rule 3.10(2) of the 1997 Rules, in contrast to the old rule[1] does not require the sheriff clerk to intimate subsequent interlocutors to a safeguarder who has elected to become a party to the proceedings. Presumably the reasoning is that a party to the proceedings has a general duty to take note of the development of the case. The sheriff clerk must however send to the safeguarder a copy of the interlocutor containing the decision of the sheriff.[2]

1 Social Work (Sheriff Court Procedure Rules) 1971, r 4A(6).
2 SI 1997/291, r 3.51(2)(c).

Written Report?

34.20   There is no provision for the safeguarder who has become a party to the proceedings lodging a written report but in practice such safeguarders sometimes do lodge wide-ranging reports concluding with recommendations as to the disposal of the child's case. This practice receives implicit approval in the Notes for Guidance[1] but is non-statutory. It has been doubted if a sheriff is entitled to have regard to the contents of a report of a safeguarder until it has been spoken to.[2]

1 *'Safeguarding the Interests of Children in Proceedings before Children's Hearings and Sheriffs: Notes for Guidance for Persons appointed as Safeguarders'*, issued by Scottish Office in June 1985 and enclosed with SWSG circular No SW7/85 dated 24 June 1985: see para 23(2).
2 *AR v Walker* 1999 SCLR 341 Ex Div, at 346C.

APPEAL BY SAFEGUARDER TO SHERIFF PRINCIPAL AND COURT OF SESSION – PARTICIPATION BY SAFEGUARDER IN APPEALS TO THE COURT OF SESSION BY OTHER PARTIES

Right of safeguarder to appeal

34.21   Appeals are dealt with in Part VII of this book. It is thought[1] that a safeguarder, *qua* curator *ad litem*, has the competency (like a curator *ad litem*) to appeal on the child's behalf to the sheriff principal and the Court of Session under s 51(11) of the 1995 Act. It is clear that a safeguarder has the right to be a party to such an appeal by one of the other parties to the application.[2]

1 Although 'safeguarder' is not specifically mentioned in s 51(12) of the Children (Scotland) Act 1995.
2 *R v Grant* 2000 SLT 372 at 373L – 374C; this case is more fully discussed below at 54.07.

SAFEGUARDER INSTRUCTING LEGAL ADVICE

Duty to take legal advice when appropriate

34.22   The non-lawyer safeguarder may frequently be a person having considerable knowledge of the law affecting children, but it is submitted that such a safeguarder ought to be astute to consider whether he should at some stage arrange legal representation or at least obtain legal advice. The safeguarder has the right to do so under 1997 Rules, r 3.9 (1). It is thought that the reasonable expense of so doing should be borne by the local authority by virtue of s 41(4) of the 1995 Act but in practice it may be prudent for the safeguarder to check with the local authority first.[1] Cases involving safeguarders will often be cases of difficulty which have potential implications in law on which the child is entitled to expect to be legally advised. In particular it may be thought that, in any application having a material legal content wherein legal advice has not already been obtained, professional legal advice should be obtained as to the advisability or otherwise of an appeal to the sheriff principal or to the Court of Session. A legally qualified safeguarder, or a solicitor instructed by a safeguarder, may, in a particularly complex or difficult case, require to consider instructing counsel. Again it will be prudent to obtain in advance the sanction of the local authority.

1 The writer has been told of a local authority's having refused to sanction the instruction of a solicitor by a safeguarder and that the safeguarder subsequently obtained the services of a solicitor who was granted legal aid. This may be a practical answer to the problem but the writer maintains his view that instruction of a solicitor may in an appropriate case be a 'reasonable expense' in a particular case and that any decision by a local authority to refuse to meet such expense may be open to challenge, e g by judicial review.

DURATION OF OFFICE

Powers of sheriff

34.23 Once a safeguarder appointed by the sheriff has intimated his intention of becoming a party to the proceedings there are no rules providing for his subsequently resigning office or, at the conclusion of his responsibilities, being discharged from his responsibilities by the court. Nor are there any provisions for initial declinature of office or for resignation owing to illness or other cause. It is thought, however, since the safeguarder on appointment acquires the powers and duties at common law of a curator *ad litem*, the sheriff would be entitled to deal with many of these problems by analogy with the law affecting curators. It is submitted, for example, that the sheriff would be entitled to accept a safeguarder's resignation through illness or other cause and appoint a successor.

Termination of office of safeguarder appointed by sheriff

34.24 On the analogy of the position of a curator *ad litem*, it is thought that the responsibilities of the safeguarder appointed by the sheriff who has become a party to the proceedings will cease when the '*lis*' to which he is a curator has come to an end.[1] In practice this would be when the sheriff had disposed of the application either by dismissing it and discharging the referral or by sustaining it – subject, as noted already to the right of the safeguarder to appeal on behalf of the child and represent the interests of the child in an appeal by another party. The instruction by a referred child of an independent legal representative does not operate so as to displace the safeguarder or absolve the safeguarder from his/her responsibilities.[2]

1 *Drummond's Trustees v Peel's Trustees* 1929 SC 484 at 505; cf *Catto v Pearson* 1990 SLT (Sh Ct) 77, 1990 SCLR 267.
2 *R v Grant* 2000 SLT 372, discussed below at 54.07.

Position of safeguarder who has not elected to become a party

34.25   The provision that a safeguarder who has not elected to become a party is to receive subsequent interlocutors[1] implies a continuing interest in the content of these interlocutors. A safeguarder who has intimated his intention not to become a party to the proceedings may subsequently seek leave so to become.[2]

1 Act of Sederunt (Child Care and Maintenance Rules) 1997, SI 1997/291, r 3.10(2).
2 SI 1997/291, r 3.10(3).

CONFIDENTIALITY OF DOCUMENTS PROVIDED TO SAFEGUARDER

34.26   A safeguarder appointed by a children's hearing who obtains documents from the reporter under the appropriate rule[1] comes under obligation to keep these documents in a secure place, not to disclose them in any unauthorised context, and to return them to the reporter after he has completed performance of all the duties associated with his appointment.[2] No such obligations are imposed on a safeguarder appointed by the sheriff but in practice safeguarders appointed by sheriffs act in accordance with them.

1 Children's Hearings (Scotland) Rules 1996, SI 1996/3261, r 14(5).
2 SI 1996/3261, r 14(6).

IMMUNITY OF SAFEGUARDER

34.27   It is thought that, as the law stands at present,[1] the safeguarder enjoys absolute immunity from process in defamation. In court, as curator, he will have the same personal immunity as counsel[2] and, so far as the contents of his report is concerned, it would seem logical to regard them as having the same absolute privilege as is accorded to the statements of a witness to a court or other legally established tribunal.[3]

1 The coming into force of the Human Rights Act 1998 may qualify the authority of the pre-Human Rights Act cases. If a safeguarder or curator *ad litem* were to be regarded as a 'public authority' then the obligation to observe the relevant provisions of the Act would attach and breach of such provisions might give a victim a remedy. *Quaere*, however, if either a safeguarder or a curator *ad litem* is a 'public authority'. But: 'This functional way

of determining when a public authority is not a public authority for the purposes of the Act will probably give rise to much uncertainly and litigation': John Wadham & Helen Mountfield, *Blackstone's Guide to the Human Rights Act 1998* (London, 1997), p 37.
2 *Fraser v Pattie* (1847) 9 D 903.
3 *Trapp v Mackie* 1979 SC (HL) 38.

REMUNERATION OF SAFEGUARDER

34.28 The provisions[1] and practicalities[2] have already been discussed. As mentioned later motions have been made, and sometimes granted, for the approval of an additional fee for a legally aided solicitor to the safeguarder or curator *ad litem*, although there are conflicting decisions as to the competency of granting such motions.[3]

1 Children (Scotland) Act 1995, s 41(4), discussed above at 17.06, 17.07.
2 Above at 34.22.
3 Below at 39.10ff.

CHAPTER 35

The proof – our adversarial tradition and the basic procedural framework

THE ADVERSARIAL APPROACH

Adversarial and Inquisitorial

35.01 Methods of judicial enquiry may broadly be categorised as 'inquisitorial' on the one hand and 'adversarial' (or 'accusatorial') on the other. 'Inquisitorial' in this context implies a judge, or tribunal chairman, taking the initiative by questioning witnesses and calling for evidence in order to seek out the truth in what appears to be a direct fashion. The adversarial system is conducted by arranging for the case on one side to be vigorously advocated by the representative for that side and vigorously attacked by the representative of the other side. In both civil and criminal cases in the jurisdictions of the British Isles, the Commonwealth of Nations and the United States of America the adversarial approach is followed. The European jurisdictions, in the tradition of the Code Napoléon, generally adopt the inquisitorial approach. An effective inquisitorial system requires the support of well organised investigative facilities which are not available to any of the ordinary courts here.

The adversarial approach – an English perspective

35.02 Enthusiasts for the adversarial system make high claims for it; for example Lord Justice Denning (as he then was), in a case in 1957, stated:

> 'In the system of trial which we have evolved in this country, the judge sits to hear and determine the issues raised by the parties, not to conduct an investigation or examination on behalf of society at large, as happens, we believe, in some foreign countries. Even in England, however, a judge is not a mere umpire to answer the question 'How's that?' – His object above all is to find out the truth and to do justice according to the law'.[1]

1 *Jones v National Coal Board* [1957] 2 QB 55 at 63.

The classic Scottish definition

35.03 A less exalted view was expressed by Lord Justice-Clerk Thomson in 1962:

> 'It is an essential feature of the judge's function to see that litigation is carried on fairly between the parties. Judges sometimes flatter themselves by thinking that their function is the ascertainment of truth. This is so only in a very limited sense. Our system of administering justice in civil affairs

proceeds on the footing that each side, working at arm's length, selects its own evidence. . . It is on the basis of two carefully selected versions that the judge is finally called upon to adjudicate. He cannot make investigations on his own behalf; he cannot call witnesses; his undoubted right to question witnesses who are put in the box has to be exercised with caution . . . A litigation is in essence a trial of skill between opposing parties conducted under recognised rules, and the prize is the judge's decision. We have rejected inquisitorial methods and prefer to regard our judges as entirely independent. Like referees at boxing contests, they see that the rules are kept and count the points.'[1]

It will be seen that these observations are made in the context of wholly civil procedure wherein a pleader with the special rôle of the reporter or the procurator fiscal is absent. It remains true, whether one adopts the more idealistic approach of Lord Denning represented in the first quotation, or the more caustic approach of Lord Justice-Clerk Thomson as evinced in the second, that our civil and criminal tradition has emphasised the detached aspect of the judicial function and has discouraged any tendency to involve the judge in any actively investigative role. More recently there has been a shift towards the judge taking a more active part in the court process. The Commercial Court in the Court of Session and the 'Options Hearing' in the Sheriff Court Ordinary Cause Rules[2] of 1993 are examples. The rôle of the sheriff in referrals cases was perhaps a forerunner of this shift.

1 *Thomson v Glasgow Corporation* 1962 SC (HL) 36 at 51, 52 per Lord Justice-Clerk Thomson.
2 Ordinary Cause Rules 1993, r 9.12.

SPECIAL CHARACTERISTICS OF THE PROCEDURES OF THE CHILDREN'S HEARING SYSTEM

'Civil proceedings *sui generis*'

35.04 In the early leading case of *McGregor v D*[1] Lord President Emslie described the procedures under Pt III of the Social Work (Scotland) Act 1968 as 'civil proceedings sui generis'. In later cases further observations have been made on the procedures of the system. In *W v Kennedy*[2] Lord Sutherland, delivering the opinion of the First Division in 1988, quoted with approval in relation to the procedures of the children's hearings system the words of Lord Widgery CJ who described the English juvenile court's jurisdiction in care proceedings as 'proceedings which are essentially non-adversary, non-party proceedings'.[3] Lord Sutherland went on to observe that it had to be remembered that the purpose of the proceedings was to ascertain what is necessary to be done in the interests of the child and stated: 'It would be quite wrong for this objective to be thwarted by the application of rigid rules of evidence or procedure just because such rigidity may be appropriate in other kinds of proceedings'.

1 1977 SLT 182 at 185.
2 1988 SCLR 236 at 239.
3 *Humberside County Council v R* [1977] 1 WLR 151; cf *F v Kennedy (No 2)* 1993 SCLR 750 at 755A.

The sheriff's rôle

35.05 While the sheriff must never act so as to detract or appear to detract from his or her impartial and independent position the obligation to have paramount regard to the interests of the child and the other provisions, where relevant, of s 16 of the Act, entitles the Sheriff, *where there is a discretion,* to intervene more freely than would be the case in other forms of litigation to secure that the interests of the child are properly regarded, that the views of the child who wishes to express them are obtained and paid due regard to and that the making of any order is more beneficial for the child than making no order would be. The words 'where there is a discretion' have been emphasised – not even in referral cases should the court disregard the due process of law.[1]

1 *Sloan v B* 1991 SLT 530 at 582E; cf *Constanda v M 1997* SCLR 510 per Lord President Rodger at 512E.

Offences alleged to have been committed by or against a child

35.06 There is nothing in the rules governing application procedure[1] explicitly conferring on the sheriff any investigative function let alone any investigative powers. There is, however, rule 3.50 of the Act of Sederunt (Child Care and Maintenance Rules) 1997:

> 'Where in a ground of referral it is alleged that an offence has been committed **by or against** [emphasis supplied] any child, the sheriff may find that any other offence established by the facts has been committed'.

Rule 10 of the Social Work (Sheriff Court Procedure Rules) 1971 were in substantially the same terms.[2] In *McGregor v D*[3] Lord President Emslie, interpreting rule 10 in the context of an alleged offence by a child case, stated:

> 'This rule, in my opinion, admits of no ambiguity and places the emphasis where the statute intended it to be placed, namely, on the statement of what, in fact, the child is alleged to have done in the search to discover in a disputed case, after proof of the facts alleged, whether he has committed an offence. So to read r 10 preserves full protection for a child who is not in need of compulsory measures of care against incompetent proceedings before a children's hearing for, if the alleged facts proved in evidence do not disclose any offence, he may reasonably expect the sheriff to discharge the referral at the close of the reporter's evidence. If, however the sheriff errs at that stage an appeal to this court lies under s 50 of the principal Act.'

By whom is the 'search' referred to by the Lord President to be conducted? Not, presumably, only by the reporter who has already averred the offence he considers is relevant. In the case of an offence against the child this could be explored by the child's representative, if any, or by any safeguarder. It is submitted that both in cases where an offence is alleged to have been committed by the child and in alleged offence against a child cases these remarks of Lord President Emslie support an interventional role for the sheriff. Rule 3.50, of course, has no application in cases other than those involving an alleged offence by or against the child.[4]

1 As opposed to the rules governing appeals to the sheriff against hearings' decisions – see below at 52.10.
2 'Where the grounds of referral are alleged to constitute an offence or offences or any attempt thereat the sheriff may find on the facts that any offence established by the facts has been committed': SI 1971/92. This wording embraced offences against a child as well as offences by a child – *McGregor v A* 1982 SLT 45 at 47 – and the wording of the current rule gives this approach statutory authority.
3 1977 SC 330 at 336.
4 Even in offence cases the decision as to whether or not to apply rule 3.50 is a matter for the discretion of the sheriff – for fuller discussion see below at 39.06ff.

Conclusion

35.07   As the law now stands the adversarial framework at the application and appeal stage must be observed. The reporter, of course, as noticed already[1] must try to present the 'whole' case to the court but, subject to that, each party and representative must prepare and present his side of the case with all due care and with the maximum amount of vigour as is consistent with fairness and propriety.

1 Ch 30, above.

CHAPTER 36

The course of the proof: I – procedural preliminaries

GENERAL

The over-all picture

36.01 The sheriff's *prima facie* primary responsibility at the proof stage is to hear the evidence tendered by the reporter.[1] The sheriff may in certain circumstances dispense with the hearing of evidence.[2] It follows that at an early stage the sheriff will have to decide whether any question of dispensing with the hearing of evidence arises in a particular case. The sheriff will also have to consider the possibility of the appointment of a safeguarder[3] or curator *ad litem* unless an appointment has already been made, to check as to legal and/or other representation for the relevant person(s) and the child, and deal with any motion, expressed by the reporter or suggested by the parents or by the child to have the proof adjourned for any reason[4] to a later date. Any one or more of these decisions may influence and/or be influenced by the decision on one of the other points. The approach in this chapter is to take these issues in what seems to be the logical and may, in some cases, be the chronological order but the sheriff must use his discretion as to how far he pursues certain matters and in what order the various points should be taken.

1 Act of Sederunt (Child Care and Maintenance Rules) 1997, SI 1997/291, r 3.47(1); *McGregor v D* 1977 SC 330 at 334.
2 Children (Scotland) Act 1995, s 68(8) – discussed below at 36.09 ff.
3 C(S)A 1995, s 41(1); SI 1997/291, r 3.7(1).
4 E g a late application on special cause shown to allow a child to give evidence by live television link under SI 1997/291, r 3.22(3), discussed above at 30.50.

Summary nature of proceedings

36.02 The proof proceedings are conducted summarily,[1] i e the evidence is not recorded verbatim and the only formal record of proceedings is the very bare record of proceedings contained in the formal interlocutor prepared by the sheriff clerk and signed by the sheriff at the close of proceedings or, if the proceedings last for more than a day, at the close of each day's proceedings. Such an interlocutor could well record only the place and date of the proof, the names of parties' solicitors, the names of parties who were present, a narration of the procedure that had taken place (e g 'proof led and closed') and a formal record of the decision of the court (e g 'the court held the grounds of referral to be established and remitted the case to the reporter to make arrangements for consideration and determination of the case').

1 Act of Sederunt (Child Care and Maintenance Rules) 1997, SI 1997/291, r 3.20.

No formal provision for Notes of Evidence

36.03   The sheriff will take handwritten notes of the proceedings but these are not available to parties. Reporters and other professional representatives of parties should try to take as full handwritten notes as possible not only for use in the course of the proof (e g in concluding submissions) but so that if an appeal is taken the sheriff's draft stated case can be subjected to informed scrutiny and, if necessary, appropriate adjustments to it proposed. In one case the sheriff arranged for that part of the proceedings during which he was examining the child as to her competency to give evidence to be noted by another person.[1] In another case it appears that one of the parties had instructed a shorthand writer and the extended notes were made available to the Court of Session on appeal.[2]

1 *M v Kennedy* 1993 SLT 69 – not reported on this point but the sheriff narrated this in the stated case.
2 *S v Kennedy* 1996 SCLR 34 – see 41D.

Representation

36.04   If the family is legally represented the sheriff will be able to proceed more rapidly to other preliminary considerations. If no legal representative appears the sheriff may have to consider whether it would be proper to adjourn the proof in order to allow time for legal representation to be obtained. The family should have been advised at the hearing on procedure and the availability of legal aid. The sheriff may wish to satisfy himself that the relevant person(s) and (where appropriate) the child have understood what has happened and the meaning of what has been said to them.

Adjournment of proof for legal representation or further preparation – generally

36.05   Legal representation is not of course mandatory but where a party or parties is unrepresented the sheriff may adjourn before the hearing of the evidence begins in order that a party or parties should be allowed a further opportunity to obtain the services of a solicitor. Similarly an adjournment to a later date may be sought where, as happens frequently enough, a legal representative has not had enough time to prepare. The decision is one for the discretion of the sheriff. In *G v Scanlon*[1] the sheriff refused a motion by the agent for a relevant person accused of a Schedule 1 offence against a child (not the referred child) on the ground that this was a matter of fact in relation to which the reporter's witnesses were present and that it was more in the interests of the referred child for the proof to proceed speedily than that the proof should be adjourned to allow further preparation. On appeal to the Court of Session the sheriff's decision was upheld. Lord Prosser, dealing with the contention that the sheriff's refusal of an adjournment was unreasonable stated:

'The contention appeared to rest rather on two more special aspects of what had occurred. First, some emphasis was placed on the reasons for unpreparedness. The sheriff notes that Mr and Mrs G had had notice of the hearing since about 5 December 1996, and says that as far as his notes go, there was no explanation given as to why neither agent was prepared for the hearing. He is however saying that no explanation was given, not that any explanation given was so bad or unconvincing that it altered his decision. He appears quite simply to have seen the want of preparation as not necessitating an adjournment, when weighed against the need for a speedy decision. In principle, we see nothing wrong with that.'

The argument that it was in the interests of the child as well as of the accused relevant person that there should be a 'fair hearing' had been addressed to the Court of Session *and accepted* but the Court took the view that the sheriff's conclusion on balancing of the interests of the child with the interests of the accused relevant person to secure an adjournment for further preparation did not amount to unfairness. Lord Prosser continued:

'Refusing adjournment to a future date in no way ruled out the possibility of less extreme steps being taken, during the proceedings, to meet any actual problems which might arise from lack of preparation.'

1 1999 SLT 707, 2000 SCLR 1.

Adjournment for legal representation or further preparation – the child

36.06 Article 37 (d) of the UN Convention on the Rights of the Child[1] provides:

'Every child deprived of his or her liberty shall have the right to prompt access to legal and other appropriate assistance, as well as the right to challenge the legality of the deprivation of his or her liberty before a court or other competent, independent and impartial authority, and to a prompt decision on any such action.'

The application to the sheriff will generally, to a greater or lesser extent, involve considerations which have a direct or indirect bearing, on the liberty of the child. It is accordingly submitted that, if compliance with article 37(d) is to be secured beyond doubt, the child will require to be represented by a lawyer who has had enough time and resources properly to represent the child. Accordingly, it is submitted that it would be difficult for the sheriff to resist a request for an adjournment where a child was not legally represented – even if there had been dilatoriness on the part of those responsible for the child (and/or on the part of the child himself). It could scarcely be argued that the consequence of this dilatoriness should be visited on the child by denying him access to legal representation. Indeed it is thought that the court should consider an adjournment in this situation *ex proprio motu*. Similarly it is submitted that where the agent for the child submits that he or she requires more time for preparation the court, notwithstanding the decision of the Court of Session in *G v Scanlon*, should not readily refuse such motion. The provisions of article 6 (1) of the European Convention on Human Rights, which will become part of our domestic law when the Human Rights Act 1998 comes into force on 2 October 2000, will, it is thought, reinforce the arguments advanced in this paragraph.

1 Discussed above at 22.19.

Appointment of safeguarder or curator *ad litem*

36.07   If the possibility of appointing a safeguarder has not already been considered by a sheriff, then the sheriff should consider, apparently on his own initiative, if such an appointment may be appropriate.[1] If a safe-guarder or curator *ad litem* is appointed at this stage an adjournment will presumably be necessary.

1 See above at 34.07 to 34.09.

Safeguarder's report already lodged

36.08   If a safeguarder, whether appointed by the hearing or by the sheriff in advance of the proof, has lodged a written report the sheriff should, it is now submitted, read that report before hearing the evidence.[1] The comment that the report of the safeguarder may be by the sheriff as 'a check on the view he *has formed* [emphasis supplied] of the evidence'[2] should not, it is submitted, be taken literally in relation to timing so as to prevent the sheriff from looking at the report at this time. The report may alert the court as to matters which should be clarified, or even raised for the first time, with witnesses. If the sheriff is proposing to use the report in this way he should make this clear to parties. If the sheriff is proposing to use the contents of the report of the safeguarder as a source of primary evidence the safeguarder should be available to speak to the report and parties should be given the opportunity of cross-examining.[3] (The issue of any 'confidential' content in the safeguarder's report has already been discussed[4]).

1 See above at 34.17 for a discussion of the status of safeguarder's written reports.
2 *Kennedy v M* 1989 SLT 687 per Lord Brand at 689D.
3 Cf *AR v David Walker* 1999 SCLR 341 at 346C.
4 Above at 34.17.

ASCERTAINING THE STANCE OF CHILD AND RELEVANT PERSON – CONSIDERING DISPENSING WITH PROOF

Inquiring as to the stance of the child and relevant person

36.09   There is no explicit provision requiring the sheriff to ask the child and the relevant person as to their current stance in relation to the grounds of referral but this is clearly implied in the provision[1] relative to dispensing with the hearing of the evidence. In practice parties' agents will generally volunteer the information. If the stance of parties is not volunteered then the sheriff should ascertain this. It is now clear that parties are not bound by the stance adopted at the children's hearing.[2] Depending on the stances adopted by child and relevant person at the outset of the proof the sheriff may in certain circumstances dispense with the hearing of evidence.[3] If the acceptance is intimated after the commencement of the proof the sheriff may dispense with hearing further evidence.

1 Children (Scotland) Act 1995, s 68(8).
2 *Kennedy v R* (IH) 1992 SCLR 546 (Notes).
3 C(S)A 1995, s 68.

Grounds originally not accepted by relevant person or child

36.10   In an application which has been directed for this reason and, in the course of the proceedings before the sheriff, the child and the relevant person accept any of the grounds in respect of which the application has been made the sheriff 'shall' dispense with the hearing of evidence relating to that ground 'unless he is satisfied that, in all the circumstances of the case, the evidence should be heard'.[1] In common with applications based upon the child not understanding the grounds of referral the dispensing power here is in the last analysis within the discretion of the sheriff – and if the sheriff is satisfied that 'in all the circumstances' the evidence should still be heard he would not be entitled to dispense with hearing proof. In contrast, however, with the dispensing power when the application is based on the child's not understanding the ground, the word 'shall' is used and the exception (hearing the evidence) is expressed negatively. The legislature therefore appears to envisage that cases of the sheriff insisting upon proof when grounds formerly denied are now accepted will be rare. In practice it is difficult to figure a case wherein, in an application made to the court pursuant upon a direction under s 65(7) of the Children (Scotland) Act 1995, the sheriff would insist on hearing evidence where genuine acceptance of the grounds is tendered by relevant person and child.

1 Children (Scotland) Act 1995, s 68(8)(a).

Sheriff to check if acceptance of grounds genuine

36.11   It is submitted that the sheriff should check with the child and relevant person and their legal representatives as to exactly what the parent or child thinks he is accepting and such enquiries may establish that the ground is not truly being accepted at all, e g, a purported acceptance of the offence of reset may turn out to be no more than acceptance of possession of the stolen property but without the essential ingredient of guilty knowledge. Clearly it would be improper to dispense with hearing evidence in such a situation since the purported acceptance could not be a true acceptance. It is the practice of the writer, with formal consent of legal representatives, to discuss this directly with parties since without such discussion it seems impossible properly to exercise the discretion vested in the court. The extent of such discussion is of course a matter for the discretion of the sheriff. *Quaere* if such a discussion may take place in the absence of the consent of parties' legal representatives. In practice such consent is not withheld and if it were then it would remain within the power of the court to insist on hearing the evidence.

Application of r 3.50 at this stage?

36.12   Rule 3.50 of the 1997 Rules enables the sheriff, where it is alleged that an offence has been committed by or against a child, to find that any other offence established by the facts has been committed. In the event of an agreement by child and relevant person as to the existence of facts averred in the Statement of Grounds for Referral sufficient to constitute an offence other than the alleged offence there would seem to be no reason why the sheriff should not be entitled to dispense with proof and to deem the ground of referral to have been established under s 68(8) of the 1995 Act by virtue of the commission of the other offence. In any event the sheriff now has power to amend under r 3.48 and in practice the reporter would generally ask the sheriff to use these powers in these circumstances.

Advisability of caution

36.13   It is submitted that the court should be particularly scrupulous before dispensing with evidence where the child is not legally represented. Having regard to the considerations discussed in 36.06 above it may be inappropriate for the court to allow an unrepresented child to accept grounds and, there being no 'duty solicitor' scheme in relation to children's referrals, to appoint a safeguarder or curator *ad litem*.

Child not understanding explanation of ground of referral[1]: position where relevant person is absent from hearing before the sheriff

36.14   In an application which has been directed for this reason the sheriff may dispense with the hearing of evidence relating to that ground where the relevant person accepts the ground in the course of the hearing before the sheriff and 'if it appears to him reasonable to do so'. In this situation the dispensing power is introduced by the word 'may' and the sheriff is never under any compulsion to dispense with proof. Moreover, the condition of dispensing with the hearing of evidence is expressed positively 'if it appears to him . . .', thus perhaps suggesting a more stringent test than is to be applied in cases referred to proof under s 65(7) of the 1995 Act. In any event the last seventeen words of s 68(8) add the further consideration that the proof is to go on if the sheriff is satisfied in all the circumstance of the case that the evidence should be heard. It is thought, where the relevant person is absent from the proof before the sheriff, that the sheriff, having regard to the wording of s 68(8)[2] is not entitled to hold the relevant person's absence as consent and therefore may not, even where the relevant person has accepted the grounds at the children's hearing, dispense with the hearing of evidence.

1 Children (Scotland) Act 1995, s 65(9).
2 'Where in the course of the hearing of the application . . .'.

Considering dispensing with evidence in cases directed under s 65(9): non-applicability of the paramountcy principle

36.15 The provision that proof may be dispensed with (provided the relevant person accepts the grounds of referral before the sheriff) in cases wherein the reason for referring the matter to the sheriff was that the child was unable to or did not in fact understand the grounds of referral is, on the face of it, paradoxical, in that the apparent purpose of s 65 (7) and (9) of the 1995 Act is to require a proof in cases wherein consent either is not or, through lack of capacity in the child, cannot, be given. The sheriff is to be guided by what is 'reasonable', but 'reasonable' against what yardstick or in order to accomplish what end? And on what basis of fact or information is this 'reasonable' decision to be founded? – not, presumably, upon evidence since it is the hearing, or not, of evidence which is in question. The purpose of enacting these provisions was presumably to avoid the unnecessary expenditure of time and energy involved in leading evidence on matters which are a foregone conclusion. While well appreciating the delicacy of having a judicial decision depend on matters not directly before the court in evidence it is nevertheless difficult, looking at the situation realistically, to escape the conclusion that the legislature is inviting the court to base its decision as to whether or not to dispense with hearing evidence at least partly on the court's impression, on such information as is available, as to whether or not the condition of referral exists or not. The purpose in requiring, through the operation of s 65(9), this decision to be made by the sheriff and not by a children's hearing, may be the conviction on the part of the legislature that this decision is a judicial decision of a type which it would be inappropriate for the hearing to be asked to make. It is submitted that it would not be 'reasonable' for the sheriff to dispense with proof if the information before him suggested that the grounds of referral were unlikely to be established even if it indicated, in a general way, that it was in the interests of the child that he should be subjected to compulsory measures of supervision. The issue of the appropriate disposal of the child's case is not a matter which is for decision by the sheriff in a s 68 proof[1] and accordingly the principle of the paramountcy of the welfare of the child would not be legitimately used to support such an approach.[2]

1 Except, indirectly, in the anomalous ground under s 52(2)(l) of the Children (Scotland) Act 1995.
2 Cf discussion above at 2.17, 14.36 and 25.09.

Conclusion

36.16 It is submitted, therefore, that it could never be reasonable for the sheriff to dispense with hearing evidence unless he was satisfied, after making enquiries from all the parties present and considering any other available source of information, that the reporter would be able to prove his case as set out in the grounds of referral and that there was not present some feature which makes it appropriate that evidence should be heard. Some situations will be easier to decide on than others, e g, in a s 52(2)(e) case the production of an extract conviction relative to the Sch 1 offence coupled with reliable information as to where the child was staying or was likely to stay would go far to satisfying the sheriff that formal proof was not required. The decision that it is unnecessary to hear evidence is a serious one, not lightly to be taken, and it is submitted that if there is a lingering doubt the correct course is to allow the evidence to be heard not only because the doubt might prove to be well-founded but also on the basis that, in the marginal case, it is preferable for justice to be done openly. In practice, where children and relevant persons are represented by experienced solicitors and/or an experienced curator *ad litem*, it is unusual for difficulties to arise in relation to dispensing with the hearing of evidence.

When decision in previous proceedings sufficient proof of grounds

36.17   Once an essential matter of fact has been established by evidence heard by the sheriff then the same or similar evidence need not be repeated in another application in respect of children of the same household.[1] On the other hand where there has only been an admission before the sheriff of grounds in an earlier case and grounds are now denied, then evidence of fact must be led.[2]

1 *McGregor v H* 1983 SLT 626 per Lord President Emslie at 629; discussed further below at 36.21.
2 *M v Constanda* 1999 SCLR 108 per Lord McCluskey at 114F: '... it might well be appropriate, in circumstances such as obtained in this case, for him [the reporter] to adduce as a witness the mother of the child and to obtain her evidence as to how and why she came to accept the relevant facts on the earlier occasions but is not prepared to accept them now'.

Advice from a safeguarder as to dispensing with proof

36.18   The views of any safeguarder or curator *ad litem* who had elected to become a party to the application should be sought. Ideally the safeguarder or curator *ad litem* should be personally present.

Alleged offence by the child cases

36.19   The reason for applying to the sheriff for proof in such cases will nearly always be because the grounds have been disputed rather than because the child cannot understand the grounds. The sheriff, if satisfied after discussion with the child and his agent that the child and relevant person now understand the nature of the alleged offence and accept that the child committed it, the sheriff would be entitled, unless there were some feature present which satisfied him that evidence should be heard, to dispense with evidence and deem the grounds to be established. Where the child is unrepresented and wishes to accept that he or she committed the offence alleged against him or her, the sheriff must, before dispensing with evidence, be sure that the child and relevant person understood the offence and accept that the child committed it.

CONJUNCTION OF APPLICATIONS

The position generally

36.20   There is nothing in the Children (Scotland) Act 1995 or in the Act of Sederunt (Child Care and Maintenance Rules) 1997 providing for the conjoining of applications in the sense of allowing applications in respect of more than one child to be laid in front of the sheriff at the same time and treating the evidence as common to all the conjoined applications. There are, however, powerful practical arguments in favour of allowing this to be done, particularly in 'care and protection' cases wherein identical evidence will be relevant to support identical, or nearly identical, grounds of referral in respect of a number of children.

Conjunction in 'care and protection' cases

36.21   In *McGregor v H* the child's baby brother had been referred to a hearing on the ground that a Schedule I offence had been committed against him, and the reporter sought to refer the child to a hearing on the basis of being of the same household as her baby brother. In holding that a certified copy of the interlocutor in the earlier application (which had gone to proof and been sustained before the sheriff) was capable of proving that the offence against the brother had taken place, Lord President Emslie said:

> 'If, however, separate referrals of each child come to be made it is absurd to suppose any intention on the part of Parliament that the common basis of each referral must be proved by direct evidence in each and every application relating to child members of the same household. In a very real and practical sense a series of applications in referrals of children of the same household under s 32(2)(d) falls to be regarded as if each application were part of a single process designed to secure the achievement of the laudable objectives of the Act in the least burdensome way. Upon that view of the matter it is we think plainly implied that the factual basis common to all applications in the series, once it has been established in the first of them, may be sufficiently proved in subsequent applications by production of a certified copy interlocutor, pronounced in the first application of the series, which holds the common factual basis to have been made out to the sheriff's satisfaction'.[1]

It is now well accepted that this approach justifies the practice whereby applications in care and protection cases which have a common factual basis are heard simultaneously by the sheriff whenever this is possible. Conjunction of such cases is commonplace. There should be a motion to conjoin which, when granted, is recorded in an appropriate interlocutor but conjunction is sometimes effected by implication.

1 1983 SLT 626 at 629.

Conjunction in 'alleged offence by the child' cases

36.22   In the case of *McGregor v T and P*[1] the principal question before the court was the competence and compellability of a child's mother as a witness for the reporter in a case under s 32(2)(g) of the Social Work (Scotland) Act 1968 but as it happened there were two children involved owing to the fact that, in relation to some of the offences alleged, the two children were 'acting together'. The sheriff on the motion of all parties agreed to the hearing of the applications simultaneously and there was no adverse comment on this when the case came before the Court of Session.

1 1975 SC 14.

Possible problems in conjoining 'alleged offence by the child' cases

36.23   In referrals based on an alleged offence by the child, complications could arise if, for example, one referred child wished to call the co-referred child as a witness and the co-referred child was advised not to give evidence. It is accordingly submitted that caution be exercised where a motion for conjunction is made in such cases. No dispute regarding conjoining has yet been reported and the foregoing comments are accordingly tentative; but, following the approach of the Court of Session in *McGregor v H*[1] it would seem that conjunction would be sustained unless there were risk of injustice.

1 1983 SLT 626.

DISJOINING OF CONJOINED APPLICATIONS

36.24   Should it appear that the conjunction of applications is in a particular case leading to the risk of injustice it would appear that disjunction is competent. In the event that such disjunction may require re-hearing of evidence the risk of injustice occurring as a consequence of the re-hearing of the evidence would have to be weighed against the risk of injustice in allowing the conjunction to continue. The interests of the children in achieving an early decision should be given due consideration.[1]

1 Cf the discussion in *G v Scanlon* 2000 SCLR 1, 1999 SLT 707, discussed above at 36.05.

The course of the proof: II – the leading of evidence – the evidence for the reporter and others

LEADING EVIDENCE: THE REPORTER'S POSITION

37.01 It is the task of the reporter to lay before the court the evidence, verbal, written and material, which may enable it to arrive at the findings in fact which should lead to the conclusion in law which the reporter is bound to commend to the court, that is that the grounds of referral contained in the application are to be sustained. The informality of the hearing before the sheriff may discourage a too rigid application of the normal courtroom practices affecting the presentation of evidence, but the reporter remains an advocate and the essence of advocacy is the art of persuasion. It follows that even if formal procedural practices may not be meticulously enforced by the court,[1] they ought still to be regarded as a guide in that they have evolved from experience of what has been found to be the fairest and most effective way of persuading the court to come to an appropriate conclusion. While the following observations are made principally with the reporter's duties in mind they of course apply *mutatis mutandis* to the representatives of other parties.

1 Cf the observations of Lord Sutherland, already noticed, in *W v Kennedy* 1988 SLT 583 at 585L.

EXAMINATION-IN-CHIEF

Definition

37.02 Examination-in-chief is the process of taking evidence from one's own witnesses as opposed to cross-questioning or cross-examining the witnesses adduced by another party. The aim of examining-in-chief is to enable the witness to give his account of the events in his own words, hence the rule against using 'leading' questions, at least in the first instance. If a case has been well prepared the questioner will have a reliable precognition of the witness and will not be surprised by what the witness says. It is often said that no question should be asked in chief which the questioner does not know the answer to: this is the ideal, not always attainable in practice.

'Leading' questions

37.03 In ordinary speech people sometimes say 'Ah, that's a leading question' meaning that a crucial or revealing matter is being probed. In legal terminology the phrase 'leading question' has a different and quite specific meaning: it means a question which suggests or tends to suggest the answer to the person being questioned. Leading questions vary in their degree of 'leadingness' and an extreme example would be: 'And then he punched you on the nose, didn't he?' A less blatant but still leading question would be: 'And was it a *red* car?'. The fundamental objection to such questions is that they discourage the witness from speaking for himself and therefore tend to rob the testimony of the spontaneity and conviction which the witness's own words might be expected to possess: indeed, the court in disallowing leading questions may use some such phrase as 'Please let the witness speak for herself!' In general, leading questions should be avoided in examination-in-chief except when covering agreed material or once the stage has been reached when the witness is clearly denying, or at least not supporting, a line of evidence which the examiner wishes to establish and in relation to which he may be leading further evidence. Once that point has been reached, the examiner should lay before the witness the set of facts which he proposes to prove so that the witness may react to it: thus at that stage it may be permissible to ask 'And isn't it the case that he then *did* punch you on the nose?'.

Examining in chief a shy or immature witness

37.04   Another example of where leading questions may be justified is when the witness is too immature or even too shy to speak openly about the subject matter. This can often occur when child witnesses are involved. The technique requires great skill and delicacy. One does not plunge into the subject right away by asking, for example, in an indecent assault case, 'He then took your blouse off, didn't he?'. Instead one starts at the edge of the subject, 'What was everyone wearing?' then, next, 'What were you wearing?' then perhaps, 'Were you wearing that all the time?' and then, assuming a negative answer, 'How did it come about that you were not wearing it?' and then, if the witness has been too shy to answer directly, one might ask, 'Did it fall off?' and so on until, by a process of elimination, the leading question, 'Did X take it off?' is seen not as a clumsy attempt to put words into the witness's mouth but as the formulation in positive terms of what the witness has been implying by her answers to the earlier questions.

Taking evidence from a very young child – general

37.05   Dickson, writing in 1887, stated:

> '... in criminal cases, where the facts are usually simple, and justice requires full investigation, children, however young, may be examined on facts within their comprehension, although they may not be old enough to understand the nature of an oath. Under this rule children of four and five, six, and seven years of age have been admitted; and it is daily practice to examine witnesses who are still in pupillarity.'[1]

Walker and Walker, in 1964, said:

> 'A child is admissible if he appears to be able to understand what he has seen or heard and to give an account of it and to appreciate the duty to speak the truth. It is for the judge to determine whether a child should be examined, after a preliminary interrogation of the child and, if necessary hearing other evidence.[2]

In a footnote, Walker and Walker comment:

> 'Modern scientific opinion is that children develop earlier than they used to, and account may have to be taken of this.'[3]

1 *Dickson on Evidence* (3rd edn) para 1544 ('in pupillarity' then meant under 12 for a girl and under 14 for a boy).
2 *Walker and Walker on Evidence* para 349.
3 *Walker and Walker on Evidence* para 349, footnote 25.

The 'competency requirement' – the court's 'examination' of an under-age child

37.06   The rule is that children under 12 are not required to take the oath or affirmation but children between 12 and 14 may, in the judge's discretion, be sworn. Children over 14 are generally sworn. Children, however young[1], who are not sworn must be 'examined' by the judge who must decide whether the child is a 'competent' witness, i e that he knows the difference between speaking the truth and telling lies.[2] The child may not be able to speak, but provided he can communicate with the sheriff (e g by shaking and nodding of the head in answer to questions from the sheriff) this may be sufficient.[3] The question for the court is: 'Is the child likely to give trustworthy evidence?'[4] The sheriff has a very wide discretion on this issue and the appeal court does not lightly interfere with the exercise of this discretion.[5] In one case the sheriff took several hours – spread over two consecutive days – to conduct the examination and, in spite of some of the responses being confusing and unsatisfactory his decision to hold the child's evidence as admissible was not displaced on appeal.[6] The sheriff should however ask questions which enable him to test the trustworthiness of the child's evidence and should not simply rely on an affirmative response by the child to a question as to whether the child knows the difference between truth and falsehood – even when there is supporting information from others who know the child.[7] The sheriff may hear evidence from others regarding the child's competence as a witness.[8] It is not yet clear whether hearsay evidence of a person who has (e g by a stroke) become unable to testify may be admissible. The possibility has been left distinctly open.[9] It appears that the time at which the child is adduced as a witness at the proof is the time at which his or her competence is to be examined.[10] Once satisfied that the child is a competent witness the sheriff admonishes the child to tell the truth.

1 *Macdonald on the Criminal Law of Scotland* (5th edn), pp 285–286, quoted with approval in *M v Kennedy* 1993 SCLR 70 at 76C.
2 *Rees v Lowe* 1989 SCCR 664, 1990 SLT 507; *Kelly v Docherty* 1991 SCCR 312, 1991 SLT 419; *P v HM Advocate* 1991 SCCR 933; *M v Kennedy* 1993 SCLR 69; *AR v David Walker* 1999 SCLR 341.

3 *M v Kennedy* 1993 SCLR 69 at 74D to 77A.
4 *M v Kennedy* 1993 SCLR 69 at 76D; *L v L* 1996 SCLR 11 at 18E.
5 *S v Kennedy* 1996 SCLR 34 at 41G ff and 44D, but see *AR v David Walker* 1999 SCLR 341.
6 *M v Kennedy* 1993 SCLR 69 at 74C and 77A.
7 *AR v Walker* 1999 SCLR 341 at 346 B–E.
8 *M v Kennedy* 1993 SCLR 69 at 78D; see also Lilian Edwards *'Better Heard and Not Seen'* 1994 SLT (News) 9.
9 *M v Kennedy* 1993 SCLR 69 at 78E, 78F.
10 *L v L* 1996 SCLR 11 at 16C; but cf Sheriff Kelbie's comment at 1996 SCLR 24E: 'It is, however, difficult to see the relevance of an examination of a ten-year-old girl as to her present understanding of truth and falsehood to a statement which was made when she was four years old and may well have forgotten. It would appear that evidence of what a small child has said is inadmissible but one only has to wait until she is old enough and it becomes admissible, although its value remains unchanged or even diminishes.' Lord Hamilton himself says at 18F: 'It may be that consideration requires to be given to whether the existing law is satisfactory in relation to statements made by children extra-judicially, particularly in relation to sexual abuse cases'.

Position if child is not tendered as a witness

37.07 It has been held that if a child's statements are to have the force of evidence the child must be tendered as a witness and examined by the court.[1] But it has now been held by the House of Lords that a child's prior statement in a particular situation 'was simply another aspect of the child's behaviour which the court was entitled to take into account when having regard to his welfare'[2] In a recent case wherein the relevant person and the safeguarder for the referred children were legally represented and the safeguarder adopted the stance of substantial contradictor of the reporter, the reporter intimated that she was not proposing to adduce a three-year old child as a witness. All parties however moved the sheriff to examine the child in order to set up her hearsay evidence as evidence apt to prove its content.[3] While the text was in proof, a court of five judges held that the hearsay evidence of a child was admissible for what it may be worth without the need for the child to 'pass' the competency test.[4]

1 *F v Kennedy* 1992 SC 28; *L v L* 1996 SCLR 11 at 19A, OH: but see the discussion in *N v Ferguson* 1994 Fam LB 9-10, IH.
2 *Sanderson v McManus* 1997 SCLR 281 at 287B per Lord Hope of Craighead.
3 *Cunninghame v JD and SD* 2000 Fam LB 46–5, the sheriff examined the child (in the home of her emergency carer) and decided that she was not a competent witness; the session of the court at which this examination took place was held, by consent of all parties recorded in a joint minute, in the absence of parties. It is thought that this procedure could not competently have taken place without the consent of parties.
4 *T v T* (10 November 2000, unreported) Court of Five Judges (overruling *F v Kennedy* 1992 SC 28).

Taking evidence from a young child – the practicalities

37.08 The possibility of very young children being invited to testify is not a novel one and in referral cases it is often the difficult duty of pleaders to try to adduce evidence from very young children. Sheriff Macphail, summarising certain recommendations of the Thomson Committee,[1] has stated: ' . . . a greater responsibility rests on the legal profession in this matter, and advocates should never be aggressive in their examination or cross-examination of children.'[2] The presiding sheriff should do all he can to put the child at ease. Any appearance of being in a hurry should be avoided. In jurisdictions wherein proofs are normally held in large rooms the presiding sheriff may be prepared to adjourn to more homely surroundings for the purpose of hearing evidence from a very young child.[3] The sheriff must try to hold the balance between allowing the child's evidence to be adequately tested under cross-examination and avoiding unnecessary distress to the child witness. A friendly relative or social worker may be permitted to sit near the child while the child is giving evidence. Children may give evidence by way of television link where this has been permitted by the court.[4] As already noticed the sheriff has a discretion to exclude any person, including a relevant person, while the child is giving evidence or making a statement.[5] The pleader should be aware of the Memorandum by Lord Justice-General Hope on Child Witnesses dated July 26, 1990. This is reproduced as Appendix 9.

1 Departmental Committee on Criminal Procedure in Scotland (Second Report) (1975, Cmnd 6218).
2 Cf *Macphail on Evidence* para 3.29.
3 In Glasgow Sheriff Court there is a very 'child friendly' crèche and there would seem to be no objection to the sheriff's taking a very young child's evidence there rather than in the adjoining 'chambers'. In *M v Kennedy* 1993 SCLR 70 Sheriff Mitchell conducted his examination as to the competency of the child witness in the crèche.
4 The procedure is discussed above at 30.47.
5 Act of Sederunt (Child Care and Maintenance Rules) 1997, SI 1997/291, r 3.47(6) discussed above at 32.06.

Child should not be called as witness 'against' self in s 52(2)(i) cases

37.09   It is commonplace for the parent to be called as a witness for the reporter in care and protection cases and in an ordinary civil proof the pursuer can call the defender as a witness for the pursuer. This frequently happens in the typical damages case in the ordinary civil courts. It is also common enough for the reporter to call the child as a witness in a care and protection case. In offence by the child cases, however, it is thought that the 'sacred and inviolable principle of the criminal jurisprudence of Scotland, that no man is bound to incriminate himself'[1] would, in spite of the 'civil' and '*sui generis*'[2] nature of these proceedings, be held to apply. Therefore the child should not be regarded as a competent and compellable witness for the reporter in such a case.[3]

1 *Livingston v Murrays* (1830) 9 S 161 per Lord Gillies at 162.
2 *McGregor v D* 1977 SC 330 at 336 per Lord President Emslie.
3 Sheriff Sir Gerald Gordon states in Martin and Murray (eds) *Children's Hearings* (1976) at p 27 that it is 'not clear' if a child can be called on to give evidence against himself and in the 5th edition of Renton and Brown, *Criminal Procedure according to the Law of Scotland* (1984) he says, at 19-73, 'The parents are competent and compellable witnesses for the reporter, and there seems no reason why this should not be true of the child as well.' In the former work, however, Sheriff Gordon also observed, 'No reporter has yet, so far as I know, had the temerity to call the child as a witness in an offence referral': ten years on, the present writer is also unaware of any example of such 'temerity'. In *Constanda v M* 1997 SCLR 510 at 516E Lord President Rodger appears to regard it as clear that the safeguards of the criminal procedural code are to be regarded as applying where a child is referred to a hearing on the basis of an offence allegedly committed by that child. *Quaere* a child would be a competent and compellable witness in a case wherein the condition of referral,

while not an offence by the child, is a condition which might infer fault on the part of the child (such as misusing a volatile substance, alcohol or drugs or absenting self from school without reasonable cause).

The advantages of first hand i e not 'hearsay' evidence: the 'best evidence'

37.10   In cases where the condition of referral is an alleged offence by a child the criminal standard of proof ('beyond reasonable doubt') must be attained.[1] All other applications are governed by the code of evidence[2] which imports the standard of 'the balance of probability'. Until 1988 hearsay evidence was generally not admissible to prove the truth of its contents in both civil and criminal cases. In consequence of the Civil Evidence (Scotland) Act[3] of that year hearsay evidence became admissible to prove the truth of its contents in civil cases only. Accordingly in referral cases involving all grounds except alleged offence by the child grounds, the civil code applies and hearsay is admissible. The 1988 Act allows for hearsay of any degree, eg where A tells the court what C told to B and B passed on to A. It remains true, however, that the best evidence will almost always be more persuasive and that therefore first hand evidence should be led where practicable and where this is not practicable, then the evidence nearest to first hand should be adduced.[4]

1 Children (Scotland) Act 1995, s 68(3)(b).
2 Cf Civil Evidence (Scotland) Act 1988, s 9 – definition of 'civil proceedings'.
3 CE(S)A 1988, s 2(1).
4 See below at 37.20 ff for further discussion of admitting evidence.

Reference to child's previous offences? – procedure when introducing 'character evidence'

37.11   Sheriff Sir Gerald Gordon (as he now is) has raised the question of whether the reporter would be entitled, in an application to the sheriff, to make reference to previous offences committed by the child.[1] There is no specific ruling on this matter in the Children (Scotland) Act 1995 or the 1997 Rules, but it is submitted that the protection afforded in criminal procedure to accused persons against having previous offences revealed to the court by the prosecutor must also extend to children in s 68 applications.[2] Similarly it is thought that, as in criminal procedure, any attempt by the 'defence' either to impugn the general moral character of the reporter's witnesses or to set up positively the good character of the child would entitle the reporter, subject to the discretion of the court, to introduce evidence or to direct questions towards obtaining admissions as to previous offences by the child. Equally, it is submitted, that if the reporter does decide to introduce such matters it would be proper to intimate to the court that this line is about to be taken since the allowance or otherwise of this approach is always a matter for the discretion of the presiding judge whose fundamental consideration must be the securing of fairness in the conduct of the proceedings.[3]

1 See Martin and Murray (eds) *Children's Hearings* at p 27.
2 Cf discussion above in footnote 3 to para 37.09.
3 Cf *O'Hara v H M Advocate* 1948 JC 90 at 99.

'Warning' of witnesses against self-incrimination

37.12 Sheriffs, out of regard for the 'sacred and inviolable principle'[1] against self-incrimination 'warn' witnesses in s 68 applications that they need not answer questions if the answer might tend to incriminate the witness in respect of any offence. There is no statutory basis for this, as there is in relation to Fatal Accident Inquiries,[2] but the practice has been approved by the Court of Session.[3] It is not clear if answers to such questions could later be used to incriminate the witness.[4] *Quaere* if it would be proper for the sheriff, out of regard for the primacy of the interests of the child who is subject of the pending application, in a case wherein possibly self-incriminatory evidence is essential to the reporter's case, to consider telling the witness that he need not answer except on the express direction of the court and then, in an appropriate case, direct the witness to answer. It could then be argued (if necessary) at any future trial of the witness that the witness's answer, not being voluntarily given, could not be evidence against him.

1 See *Livingston v Murrays* (1830) 9 S 161 at 162 per Lord Gillies.
2 Fatal Accidents and Sudden Deaths Inquiry (Scotland) Act 1976, s 5(2).
3 *W v Kennedy* 1988 SLT 583 at 584I.
4 Contrast *Banaghan v HM Advocate* (1888) 1 White 566, and *M'Giveran v Auld* (1894) 1 Adam 448 (answers in prior civil proceedings held admissible in subsequent criminal trials) with *HM Advocate v Fleming* (1885) 5 Coup 552 (answers by bankrupt in his compulsory examination on sequestration held inadmissible at his trial for embezzlement of the funds to which the examination related).

Duty of pleader to advise court when adducing 'self-incriminating' witness

37.13 It is proper practice for the reporter or agent on posing a question which might extract a self-incriminating statement, to mention this to the court in advance, so that the sheriff may decide on whether or not to 'warn' the witness and, if so, in what terms.

The leading of evidence – the principle of fair notice

37.14 It is a central principle of any civilised legal system that a person whose interests are going to be affected by legal process should have fair notice of the case which he has to answer so that he may prepare any response. Similarly the defence side must give notice of lines of defence (such as contributory negligence or alibi) which have a highly positive content and which are peculiarly within the knowledge of the defence side. In s 68 applications similar considerations apply. Under the Social Work (Scotland) Act 1968 it was held that the reporter's side was limited to establishing facts on the basis of 'evidence tendered which is relevant to the grounds for referral set out by the reporter'.[1] Amendment of the Statement of Facts, but not of the Conditions of Referral, is now competent.[2] The court may allow amendment on motion of a party or *ex proprio motu*. The matter is one for the discretion of the sheriff and the sheriff should not allow a significant amendment without giving the opportunity to the other side to lead evidence in relation to the new matter, even if adjournment of the diet is required.[3] In alleged offence by the child cases the sheriff may find that any other offence established by the facts has been committed.[4] There is no statutory obligation on the defence side to intimate 'special' or affirmative lines of defence but it is good practice to give such notification.[5] Failure to give reasonable notice of an affirmative line of defence could lead to the court adjourning in order to enable the reporter to present evidence in rebuttal.[6]

1 *McGregor v D* 1977 SC 330.
2 Act of Sederunt (Child Care and Maintenance Rules) 1997, SI 1997/291, r 3.48.
3 SI 1997/291, r 3.49.
4 SI 1997/291, r 3.50 see below at 38.04 ff.
5 For discussion of some 'affirmative defences,' see above at 33.29.
6 Cf *Kennedy v B* 1972 SC 128 at 133.

CROSS-EXAMINATION AND RE-EXAMINATION

General

37.15   The reporter's witnesses may be cross-examined by the 'defence' side and the 'defence' witnesses may in turn be cross-examined by or on behalf of the reporter. A safeguarder appointed by the sheriff who has elected to become a party to the proceedings may cross-examine.[1] It is submitted that a safeguarder who supplies evidence to the court by written report or in oral form may be cross-examined by or on behalf of other parties.

1 Act of Sederunt (Child Care and Maintenance Rules) 1997, SI 1997/291, r 3.9(1).

Cross-examination as challenge

37.16   The most characteristic feature of cross-examination is testing the evidence of the witness by asking questions designed to undermine its acceptability and credibility. Thus it may be the duty of the cross-examiner to explore the confusion of the confused witness; to see how far the apparently exaggerating witness is prepared to exaggerate; and to test the apparently confident and solid witness by exploring his evidence and, if possible and appropriate, obtaining his reaction to contradictory evidence which has been or may be brought out from other witnesses.

Cross-examination as confrontation – laying the foundation for later evidence

37.17   Cross-examination may also be used as a means of 'putting to' a witness a version of events which the cross-examiner wishes to establish in relation to a matter which appears to be within the witness's knowledge. Thus, for example, it will be the duty of the person representing the child in a case based on an alleged offence by that child wherein self-defence is being alleged to suggest to the person injured that he was the aggressor and to put before him exactly what he is alleged to have done. Failure to do this does not make it incompetent for the cross-examiner to lead evidence in favour of his version of events later on, but such failure will tend to take away from the convincing quality of the later evidence and may be commented on adversely. Failure to 'put' the opposing case to witnesses is a frequent error by pleaders. Leading questions are permissible in cross-examination but even in cross-examination it may frequently be advisable to let the witness speak for himself.

Order of cross-examining

37.18   The sheriff has a discretion as to the order in which he invites parties to cross-examine. It is usual practice to allow the substantial contradictor to cross-examine last, but sometimes the safeguarder or the curator *ad litem* is invited to cross-examine last.

Re-examination

37.19   When a witness has been cross-examined the party adducing the witness may ask further questions – re-examine – in order to clear up any matters which have been put in doubt by answers given in cross-examination. Re-examination should not be used to re-iterate evidence in chief which has not been cross-examined on. It is improper to employ re-examination in order to introduce new matter but this rule is not strictly applied in application procedure since the court will not wish the interests of the child to be prejudiced because of a pleader's technical failure: if the court does allow new matter to emerge in re-examination it should allow re-cross-examination. Failure to re-examine when a witness has made an important concession in cross-examination may entitle the court to draw a conclusion adverse to the examiner in chief's contentions.[1]

1   Cf *Gibson v BICC Co Ltd* 1973 SC (HL) 15 at 22, per Lord Reid.

OBJECTIONS TO ADMISSIBILITY OF EVIDENCE – GENERAL

Admission of evidence 'subject to relevancy and competency'

37.20   If objection is taken to the admissibility of evidence in the course of the proof and the sheriff is minded to sustain the objection, it is normally proper practice for the sheriff to allow the evidence to be given 'under reservation of competency and relevancy'. The sheriff may then decide, after full argument at the end of the proof whether he is prepared to treat the evidence as admissible. Dealing with the matter in this way has the advantage that, even if the sheriff decides that the evidence is not admissible and does not take it into account in making factual findings, the evidence is available. In the event therefore of an appeal to the Court of Session, the appellate court can, if so minded, rule that the evidence is admissible and take account of it without the necessity of a remit back to the sheriff to hear evidence.[1]

1 *McGregor v T and P* 1975 SC 14 at 23, cf *Sloan v B* 1991 SLT 530 at 546L.

Sheriff may exclude obviously irrelevant evidence

37.21   The sheriff, as judge in charge of his court, retains the radical right to refuse to allow a line of questioning to be pursued if he considers it to be plainly improper.[1] When considering this course of action the sheriff should ascertain if the line of questioning is going to be followed up by evidence. The ground of refusal should be minuted.[2]

1 *Falconer v Brown* (1893) 1 Adam 96; cf *Reid v Guild* 1991 SCCR 71, *McAllister v Normand* 1996 SLT 622.
2 See discussion in *Renton and Brown*, 6th edn, at 24-157.

Importance of taking timeous objection to possibly inadmissible evidence

37.22   'Scots practice requires that if an objection to the line of the evidence is to be taken on the ground of incompetency it should be taken at the first available time.'[1] While the simple and non-technical nature of the application procedures[2] may be thought to confer a discretion on the court not to apply this practice with utmost vigour it is important, particularly for the professional pleader, to intimate even tentative objection as soon as possible. By so doing he not only avoids the risk of having his line of objection treated as waived but also assists the court and the other parties in focusing attention on the essential points of the case.[3]

1 *McGlone v British Railways Board* 1966 SC (HL) 1 per Lord Guest at 14. Cf *Skeen v Murphy* 1978 SLT (Notes) 2.
2 Cf *McGregor v D* 1977 SC 330 at 339 per Lord Cameron.
3 Cf *Skeen v Murphy* 1978 SLT (Notes) 2.

OBJECTIONS TO ADMISSIBILITY OF EVIDENCE – 'TRIAL-WITHIN-A-TRIAL'

The legal background

37.23   In *Chalmers v HM Advocate*[1] it was held by a Court of Five Judges that where, in a criminal jury trial, a question arose as to whether or not a statement made by the accused was admissible or not by reason of the unfairness to the accused as to the circumstances in which the statement was obtained, the evidence as to such circumstances should be heard by the judge in the absence of the jury and the admissibility of such evidence should be ruled upon by the judge on the basis of this evidence. The process by which this evidence was taken became known in Scotland as a 'trial-within-a-trial'.[2] In subsequent cases, notably *Balloch v HM Advocate*,[3] this procedure was discouraged but not overruled. In *Thomson v Crowe*[4] a Court of Five Judges, overruling *Balloch*, re-established the 'trial-within-a-trial' and extended its application to summary criminal procedure.

1 1954 JC 66, 1954 SLT 177.
2 The procedure is not unique to Scotland. In common law jurisdictions the analogous process is known as *voir dire* – cf *Wong Kam-ming v The Queen* [1980] AC 247, [1979] 2 WLR 81.
3 1977 JC 23, 1977 SLT (Notes) 29.
4 1999 SCCR 1003.

The present law in criminal proceedings

37.24   Where objection is taken to the admissibility of evidence tendered by the prosecution and a factual issue has to be resolved before a properly informed decision can be taken, the defence may move the judge to hold a trial-within-a-trial at which the circumstances surrounding the obtaining of the evidence may be explored and such a motion should generally be granted.[1] It is then for the judge to hear all the evidence tendered, both for the prosecution and the defence and decide the issue after hearing submissions.[2] The onus is on the prosecution to prove that the evidence is admissible, e g by satisfying the judge that a statement was made freely and not obtained by unfair or improper means.[3] The standard of proof to which the prosecution must attain in the trial-within-a-trial is probably the balance of probabilities.[4] However, since the prosecution must prove the guilt of the accused beyond reasonable doubt it would appear that in a case wherein an essential part of the prosecution case against the accused is a confession statement and the judge admits the evidence after the trial-within-a-trial then the prosecution will still require to prove to the tribunal of fact beyond reasonable doubt that the circumstances in which it was obtained did not make it unreliable.[5] During the trial-within-a-trial the accused and any witnesses on his behalf may give evidence and be cross-examined by the prosecutor. Since the judge gives his decision immediately after the trial-within-a-trial procedure it follows that, in the event of the judge deciding that the evidence (usually of a confession statement) is inadmissible, (i e that the confession is not available to the prosecutor) if the confession is an essential element in the prosecution case, the defence will be able to argue 'no case to answer' under s 97 of the Criminal Procedure (Scotland) Act 1995 (solemn procedure) or s 160 of that Act (summary procedure). In the event of the trial proceeding then any evidence given by the accused during the trial-within-a-trial procedure cannot be founded on by the prosecutor to prove his guilt. However, in certain circumstances the accused and his witnesses, if they give evidence, may be cross-examined if their evidence during the trial itself differs materially from what they said at the trial-within-a-trial.[6] In solemn criminal procedure the trial-within-a-trial takes place in the absence of the jury and, if the trial judge admits the controversial evidence, the crown witnesses have to be invited to go through it again in the presence of the jury. Where the trial-within-a-trial procedure is engaged in summary criminal procedure it is thought that it is the practice for a similar procedure to be adopted, that is (where the challenged statement has been held to be admissible and the trial proceeds) the prosecutor will call again the prosecution witnesses to speak to the statement by the accused and the examination and cross-examination of these witnesses will be substantially repeated.

1 *Thompson v Crowe* 1999 SCCR 1003 at 1035F and 1043E.
2 1999 SCCR 1003 at 1043F–1044A.
3 1999 SCCR 1003 at 1033F and 1043F.
4 1999 SCCR 1003 at 1033F–1034C.
5 *Cf* commentary by Sir Gerald Gordon to *Thompson v Crowe* 1999 SCCR 1003 at 1050D.
6 *Thompson v Crowe* 1999 SCCR 1003 at 1043E–F.

Applicability of the trial-within-a-trial procedure to s 68 proof on grounds of referral under s 52(2)(i) of the 1995 Act

37.25 It is submitted that the trial-within-a-trial procedure should be adopted in proofs where an offence by a child is alleged. Where such an offence is alleged the ground of referral must be proved to the criminal standard[1] and, it is submitted, this carries the implication that the allegation of an offence by a child is only to be proved by the rigorous standards of our criminal procedure. This was the approach which was adopted by Lord Justice-General Rodger in *Constanda v M*.[2] It is accordingly submitted that where in a s 68 proof, where the ground of referral is under s 52(2)(i) of the 1995 Act, it will be open to the child and probably to any relevant person to ask for a 'trial-within-a-trial' or rather a 'proof-within-a-proof' which will substantially accord with the procedure in summary criminal proceedings as outlined above. It is submitted that a decision of the sheriff to exclude evidence of, say, a confession by the referred child after a trial-within-a-trial, on ground of, say, unfairness, would not contravene rule 3.47(1). The obligation under that rule is surely only to hear admissible evidence and 'the basic rules of evidence must be observed.[3] There is no authoritative decision applying the trial-within-a-trial procedure to s 68 applications and the sheriff may wish to hear arguments on the matter.

1 Children (Scotland) Act 1995, s 68(3)(b).
2 1997 SC 217, 1997 SCLR 510, 1997 SLT 1396.
3 *McGregor v D* 1977 SC 330 per Lord President Emslie at 336.

Non-applicability of the trial-within-a-trial procedure in s 68 proof on grounds other than under s 52(2)(i) of the 1995 Act?

37.26   It is however submitted, in cases wherein the condition of referral concerns in essence the conduct of others towards the child,[1] that the trial-within-a-trial procedure has no application. Such grounds do not require to be proved to the criminal standard and there is no possibility of arguing 'no case to answer'. In the event of objection being taken to the admissibility of a confession statement by, say, a relevant person it is submitted that the sheriff, if not minded to repel the objection, should allow the evidence under reservation of competency and relevancy.[2] Similarly it is thought that the procedure may not be appropriate in those cases where the conduct, not necessarily in the form of offending, of the child, forms the condition of referral,[3] since these grounds need not be proved to the criminal standard and do not attract a 'no case to answer' submission. It may be, however, that an argument could be figured that a child who was alleged to have made a 'confession' inferring that he had done something which would entitle the court to hold such a ground established should be entitled to have the opportunity of giving evidence on the matter of the 'confession' heard as a 'proof-within-the-reporter's-proof'. This would enable this evidence to be heard and ruled upon without the child requiring to give evidence and then be cross-examined at large.

1 I e conditions (c), (d), (e), (f), (g) of s 52(2) of the Children (Scotland) Act 1995.
2 Cf *McGregor v D* 1977 SC 330; *Sloan v B* 1991 SLT 530.
3 I e conditions (a), (b) (perhaps), (h), (j), (k) and (l) of s 52(2) of C(S)A 1995.

CHAPTER 38

The course of the proof: III – 'no case to answer' and allied matters

'NO CASE TO ANSWER'

Rule 3.47(2) of the 1997 Rules

38.01   This rule provides, in relation to cases based upon s 52(2)(i) of the Children (Scotland) Act 1995 (alleged offence by a child), that the sheriff, in a case where the ground of referral is disputed, shall at the close of the evidence led by the reporter:

> '... consider whether sufficient evidence has been led to establish that condition is satisfied and shall give all the parties an opportunity to be heard on the question of sufficiency of evidence.'

Where the sheriff is not so satisfied he is to make a finding to that effect[1] and will consequently dismiss the application and discharge the referral in relation to that condition.[2]

1   Act of Sederunt (Child Care and Maintenance Rules) 1997, SI 1997/291, r 3.47(3).
2   Children (Scotland) Act 1995, s 68(9).

'Sufficient evidence'

38.02   Whether evidence is sufficient in law will depend on whether on any reasonable construction of the evidence, taken at its most favourable for the reporter ('taken at its highest'), the legal conclusion contended for by the reporter could be made out. It is to be noted that when this matter is being considered the evidence is taken as true ('*pro veritate*') and it is therefore inappropriate, when arguing for or against a submission of 'no case to answer' to make reference to the supposed reliability or otherwise of any of the witnesses.[1] Equally it is inappropriate at this stage to debate the weight of the evidence beyond mere sufficiency e g by submitting that the court should be influenced by, say, an alleged preponderance of points in the reporter's case which favour the 'defence'. The sole matter before the court is whether there is a bare sufficiency of evidence which, if believed, would result in the ground of referral being sustained.

1   *Williamson v Wither* 1981 SCCR 214; for full discussion of the 'no case to answer' provisions in the context of criminal practice, solemn and summary, see *Renton and Brown* (6th edn) 18-74 ff and 21–27.

'No case to answer' – submitted by motion of party – raised by sheriff ex proprio motu

38.03   In general where parties are represented the submission of 'no case to answer' will, where appropriate, be submitted by agent or agents. The wording of r 3.47(2) and (3) makes it clear that the sheriff should, even in the absence of motion by party, consider the question. Rule 3.47(2) provides that the Sheriff '*shall* [emphasis supplied] give all parties an opportunity to be heard on the question of sufficiency of evidence'. In many cases it will be clear whether a discussion of no case to answer will or will not be appropriate and it is thought that where all parties are represented and the issue is clear then the sheriff would be entitled to assume, in the absence of a motion from parties, that the opportunity to make submissions was not being taken up. Where, however, any party is not represented it is submitted that the sheriff should state his or her view one way or the other and invite submissions.

FINDINGS AS TO GROUNDS NOT AVERRED

Relevance of rule 3.50 at this stage

38.04   As already noticed[1] this rule empowers the sheriff, where it is alleged that an offence has been committed by or against any child, to find that any other offence established by the facts has been committed. This provision only has effect where an offence is alleged. The decision as to whether or not to find that some other offence has been committed is within the discretion of the sheriff: 'Rule 10 [the parallel provision in the old rules] only permits the sheriff to find that the facts establish some other offence. The rule does not require him to do so'.[2] If a party intends to move the sheriff to apply rule 3.50 of the 1997 Rules it is good practice to notify the court and other parties as soon as possible.

1   Above at 36.12.
2   *McGregor v A* 1982 SLT 45 at 47.

No power to substitute new condition of referral

38.05   There seems to be no power vested in the sheriff to substitute for the condition averred by the reporter a ground of referral which he thinks may be justified by the facts which have been proved. If, for example, the sole condition of referral is the allegation, under section 52(2)(b) of the 1995 Act that the child was falling into bad associations and there were no facts proved tending to support such a conclusion but there was evidence that the child was beyond the control of a relevant person, it would not be open to the sheriff to sustain the application on the basis that the condition contained in section 52(2)(a) of the Act had been proved. The powers of amendment are expressly limited to 'amendment of any statement supporting the conditions of the grounds for referral'.[1]

1   Act of Sederunt (Child Care and Maintenance Rules) 1997, SI 1997/291, r 3.48.

EFFECT OF INTRODUCTION OF TRIAL-WITHIN-A-TRIAL PROCEDURE

38.06   As already noticed,[1] the trial-within-a-trial procedure has, it is submitted, its place in proofs where the ground of referral is a condition under s 52(2)(i) of the 1995 Act (but probably not in relation to proofs on the other conditions). Before the introduction of the trial-within-a-trial procedure the solicitor for the child, if wishing to challenge the admissibility of the confession by evidence would generally require to call the child as a witness, thereby exposing him to cross-examination on the whole facts of the case. The introduction of the trial-within-a-trial procedure enables the accused child and any witnesses to give evidence interpolated into the reporter's proof and requires the sheriff to rule on the admissibility of disputed evidence right away. Where the sheriff rules such evidence, such as a confession statement, inadmissible, then, where this statement appears to be an essential part of the reporter's case, the motion that there is 'no case to answer' will be fortified. If successful, the child will of course not require to be called again.

1 Above at 37.23 ff.

CONCLUSION OF REPORTER'S CASE

38.07   By the close of the evidence for the reporter the whole evidence which has come to the notice of the reporter relevant to the grounds of referral[1] should have been made available to the sheriff. After the conclusion of the reporter's case the other parties have their opportunity to lead evidence.

1 See discussion of reporter's responsibilities in relation to the leading of evidence above at 30.25 ff.

CHAPTER 39

The course of the proof: IV – the cases for the child and relevant persons; concluding speeches; application of rule 3.50

THE CASES FOR THE CHILD, THE RELEVANT PERSON(S) AND THE SAFEGUARDER (OR CURATOR *AD LITEM*)

Sheriff's duties at close of reporter's case – position where persons have been excluded

39.01   Rule 3.47(4) of the Act of Sederunt (Child Care and Maintenance Rules) 1997 provides in effect that, where the sheriff has not disposed of the case on the basis of there having been no case to answer, the child, the relevant person and any safeguarder may give evidence and call witnesses. The obligation on the sheriff under the old rules[1] to tell parties of their rights has been removed but where any parties are not represented the sheriff will in practice advise them of their rights and give such guidance as to procedure as he thinks appropriate. The right of parties under the old rules to 'make a statement' has also been removed, although, somewhat paradoxically, it is provided that where a relevant person who has been excluded from the hearing by the operation of r 3.47(6) and where the relevant person is not legally represented, the sheriff is to tell the relevant person the substance of the evidence given in his absence and give such person 'an opportunity to respond by leading evidence *or otherwise* [emphasis supplied]'. It is not clear whether this preserves to the relevant person the right to make a statement (on which he might not be subject of cross-examination) or simply allows such person to respond by evidence and/or by argument.

1   Act of Sederunt (Social Work) (Sheriff Court Procedure Rules) 1971, SI 1971/92, r 8(2).

Evidence led by or on behalf of child, relevant person, or safeguarder

39.02   The relevant considerations concerning the leading of evidence have already been discussed above in Chapter 37.

CONCLUDING SPEECHES

Order of speeches

39.03   After all the evidence has been led the reporter should sum up his or her case in fact and in law. Thereafter any safeguarder and the representatives of the relevant person and child should do likewise. It is thought that the substantial contradictor should be given the opportunity of speaking last, but the sheriff may allow the safeguarder or curator *ad litem* to speak last.[1] In the event of an important matter being raised for the first time in a later speech the sheriff may allow a right of reply. Where the relevant person and/or the child is unrepresented the sheriff should attempt to explain the purpose of the summing up and should invite the child, if of sufficient maturity, and the relevant person to state their respective stances in relation to the evidence which has been led.

1 Cf the position as to order of cross-examination, see above at 37.14.

Purpose and content of closing speeches – reference to authority

39.04   The concluding speeches should draw to the sheriff's attention the main evidence of the case. In many cases it may be possible for this to be done briefly. The sheriff's attention should be drawn to any relevant law which is known to the pleader. Cases apparently adverse to the pleader's stance should of course be cited and the reason for distinguishing or not following them explained. The particular provision of any Act of Parliament should be stated. Any piece of primary or subordinate legislation or bye-law not reprinted in the Parliament House Book should be produced. In modern practice it is increasingly common to supply the bench with an indexed bundle of copies of authorities which are to be referred to in detail.

Written submissions

39.05   In a case of length and complexity the sheriff may, where parties are legally represented, invite written submissions. The lodgement of written submissions has become more frequent in recent times and it has been judicially commended.[1] Such submissions may be of great help to the court in disposing of the case expeditiously. In practice parties may exchange such submissions in advance of the hearing on the evidence and the hearing itself may thereby be considerably shortened.

1 E g by Sheriff Sir Gerald Gordon (as he now is) in *Bank of Scotland v Richmond & Co* 1997 SCLR 303 at 305A and by Sheriff Principal CGB Nicholson QC in *Rose v Bouchet* 1999 SCLR 1004 at 1005E.

APPLICATION OF RULE 3.50 AT STAGE OF THE CLOSING SPEECH

Parties should adopt a clear stance

39.06   It is particularly important for the parties, and in particular the reporter, to make clear to the court in what way, if at all, the sheriff is being asked to exercise the discretion under rule 3.50 of the 1997 Rules by identifying the offence other than that mentioned in the ground of referral which the sheriff is being asked to hold as established. For example, if breaking into railway premises and stealing the contents thereof were averred as house-breaking and theft, a reporter might wish specifically to ask the sheriff to make a finding of reset if he considered that the full crime of house-breaking and theft had not been established. Alternatively, the reporter might care to make clear to the court when he is *not* inviting the court to exercise this discretion. For example, in the instance just cited, the reporter would have to consider whether, if the court were not minded to hold even reset established, he wished the court to go on to consider, on the available evidence, whether the more obscure and less criminous (although potentially highly dangerous) offence of trespassing upon railway property in terms of the relevant railway statutes had been committed. It will be submitted that the sheriff's decision on this matter will be subject to the paramountcy principle in s 16(1) of the Children (Scotland) Act 1995 and that therefore the reporter's decision on this would be governed by his view as to whether to do so would best promote the welfare of the child. Should the reporter intend to make such a submission he would require to direct the court's attention to the specific section of the railway statutes allegedly contravened. It has been observed that 'rule 10 [the parallel provision in the old rules] only permits the sheriff to find the facts establish some other offence. The rule does not require him to do so.'[1] If the reporter does not canvass the possibility of such an alternative finding, he can hardly complain later on that the sheriff has not made it. In practice where the reporter wishes to found upon a statutory contravention, he will generally mention it specifically in the statement of facts.

1 *McGregor v A* 1982 SLT 45 at 47.

Criterion for exercise of sheriff's discretion

39.07 The rules and the case-law give no explicit guidance as to the criteria the sheriff should have regard to in deciding whether or not to exercise this discretion. It would seem that the sheriff's decision would be a determination on 'any matter with respect to a child' and would accordingly be subject to the s 16(1) paramountcy principle. It was submitted in the first edition of this book that 'the general thrust of the application procedure[1] points clearly against the sheriff being entitled to consider any matter bearing upon the ultimate interests of the child when deciding if the grounds of referral have been established.' The limited application of the paramountcy principle when determining matters of law has already been noticed.[2] This decision is, however, a matter of the sheriff's discretion and it is now submitted that the enactment of s 16(1) operates so as to involve the sheriff in welfare considerations at this stage. It is submitted that the sheriff should invite submissions from parties on the matter. In particular the reporter and any safeguarder or curator *ad litem* should be asked for their views as to where the best interests of the child lie. The 'consulting the child' and 'no non-beneficial order' principles of s 16(2) and (3) of the 1995 Act have no formal application to such a decision.[3] In

E v Kennedy[4] the sheriff held that the decided cases, when read with rule 10 of the 1971 Rules, entitled the court to hold that evidence of facts amounting to an offence, even although furth of Scotland, amounted to a Schedule 1 offence. In *M v Kennedy*[5] it was observed that where the evidence indicated that one of two possible Schedule 1 offences had been committed but did not enable the court to decide which one then rule 10 would operate so as to allow the court to hold that a Schedule 1 offence had been committed. In *B v McGregor*[6] the amount of evidence required to establish an allegation of the crime of reset was considered.

1 *Cf M v McGregor* 1982 SLT 41; see also *S v Kennedy* (27 February 1987, unreported) Court of Session, per Lord Justice-Clerk Ross, 'What the sheriff has to determine is whether the grounds of referral have been established ...' and *McGregor v D* 1977 SC 330 at 341 per Lord Cameron, 'Further it is to be observed that [the sheriff's] function is of a very limited character, namely, to make a finding as to whether the grounds of referral are established, that and no more.'
2 Above at 2.17.
3 The whole problem will of course be avoided if the reporter is able to follow the good practice of listing in the grounds of referral the alternative charges on which he may be seeking to rely: see above at 16.12. Of course there may be times when late information requires the reporter to rely on r 3.50.
4 1992 GWD 25-1402 (2 June 1992, unreported) Ayr Sh Ct.
5 1996 SLT 434, 1996 GWD 2–70, 1st Div.
6 3 February 1983, unreported (Court of Session).

AMENDMENT OF THE STATEMENT OF FACTS

Amendment of Statement of Facts now competent

39.08   As already noticed,[1] amendment of the Statement of Facts is now competent.[2] The reporter or other party may at the stage of addressing the sheriff ask for leave to amend the Statement of Facts in order to bring the Statement in line with the evidence led. If the evidence has been led without objection, or has been led subject to an objection which has been repelled, then the sheriff may be ready to allow amendment without further procedure. If, however, there has been an objection to the evidence in question resulting in the evidence having been received under reservation then the sheriff should generally deal with the objection before considering the motion to amend. It is thought that the sheriff should be slow to refuse outright a motion to amend in such circumstances but, where he considers that the proposed amendment is radical, allow parties the opportunity of leading additional evidence and be prepared to grant a short adjournment if this should be required in the interests of the child or in the interests of justice.

1 Above at 29.10.
2 Act of Sederunt (Child Care and Maintenance Rules) 1997, SI 1997/291, r 3.48.

Scope of amendment

39.09   Professor Norrie states: 'The sheriff should, however, be careful in exercising these powers to ensure that the grounds of referral found established do not indicate a substantially different case from that which was originally put to the child and relevant person at the previous children's hearing. The power to amend a statement of fact does not, it is submitted, include the power to change the condition the statement of facts is designed to support.'[1] If all that is meant by this is that the grounds must not be amended so as to change the condition of referral (under s 52(2) of the Children (Scotland) Act 1995) relied upon then the writer would agree. If, however, it were suggested that there is a statutory inhibition on the sheriff's discretion to allow an amendment which included new allegations of fact then the writer would have doubts about this. In relation to ordinary civil practice it has been said: 'Amendments have been allowed which required fairly substantial changes in pursuer's averments of fact.'[2] In *McGregor v D*[3] Lord President Emslie, in the context of rule 10 of the Act of Sederunt (Social Work) (Sheriff Court Procedure Rules) 1971, rejected the notion that the necessity of stating a *nomen juris* for the offence alleged inhibited the court from finding that another offence had been committed. Lord Emslie observed that the statute was concerned primarily with whether a child was in need of care, 'and to that end merely, so far as a s 32(2)(g) case is concerned, to ascertain whether he had committed "an offence"'. His Lordship went on to say that the emphasis of the Social Work (Scotland) Act 1968 was placed 'on the statement of what, in fact, the child is alleged to have done in the search to discover in a disputed case, after proof of the facts alleged, whether he has committed any offence'. It is to be noted that the *nomen juris* of the original alleged offence would be that which the hearing had considered. The case of *D* was of course decided before the powers of amendment were introduced. In the writer's view, however, the spirit of his Lordship's approach supports the view that provided no unfairness is occasioned to the child or the relevant person then even a fairly substantial amendment may be allowed. It will, as suggested in the immediately preceding paragraph, generally be possible to avoid any unfairness by allowing the child or relevant person an opportunity, by adjournment or otherwise, to prepare a reply to any new matter. It may be said that this will cause delay and administrative inconvenience – but it is submitted that more delay and adminstrative inconvenience would generally be caused if the referral required to be discharged and a fresh referral raised.

1 Norrie *Children's Hearings in Scotland* (1997) p 93;
2 *Macphail on Sheriff Court Practice* (2nd edn) para 326 – and see the cases therein cited.
3 1977 SC 330 at 337, 338.

MOTION TO SHERIFF FOR ADDITION TO LEGAL FEES

The statutory background

39.10   It is not competent for the court to award expenses in favour of or against any party to these procedures.[1] The fees which a solicitor may render to his client (frequently, in practice, to the legal aid fund) are fixed by Act of Sederunt.[2] Under these rules the sheriff has the discretion to allow 'a percentage increase in the fees authorised by the Table of Fees' where a motion is made 'not later than seven days after the date of any interlocutor disposing of expenses'. In substance the basis for making such an increase is the length, complexity and difficulty of the case.[3] In cases wherein a party is legally aided legal aid may be granted under s 29(2)(c)(i) of the Legal Aid (Scotland) Act 1986.[4] The fees payable are governed by the Civil Legal Aid (Scotland) (Fees) Regulations 1989,[5] regulation 3(1) of which provides: 'These Regulations shall regulate the fees and outlays allowable to solicitors, and the fees allowable to counsel, from the Fund in respect of Legal Aid under the Legal Aid (Scotland) Act, other than criminal legal aid, upon any taxation in accordance with Regulation 12'. Regulation 5(4) of the General Regulations provides as follows:

> 'In all Court of Session proceedings a fee, additional to those set out in Schedules 1 or 3, may be allowed in the discretion of the Court to cover the responsibility undertaken by a solicitor in the conduct of the proceedings. In the sheriff court, in proceedings of importance or requiring special preparation, the sheriff may allow a percentage increase in a cause on the Ordinary Roll, not exceeding 50 per cent, and in a cause on the Summary Cause Roll, not exceeding 100 per cent, of the fees authorised by Schedule 2 or 3 to cover the responsibility undertaken by the solicitor in the conduct of the proceedings. The Court of Session in deciding whether to allow an additional fee and the auditor in determining that fee or the sheriff in fixing the amount of a percentage increase shall take into account the following factors: [listing the eight categories importing additional responsibility].

1 Act of Sederunt (Child Care and Maintenance Rules) 1997, SI 1997/291, r 3.19.
2 Act of Sederunt (Fees of Solicitors in the Sheriff Court) (Amendment and Further Provisions) 1993, SI 1993/3080. [The Act of Sederunt is reproduced in Section A (p 242) of the Parliament House Book].
3 SI 1993/3080, Schedule 1 ('General Regulations') reg 5(b) (i) to (vii).
4 As substituted by s 92 of the Children (Scotland) Act 1995.
5 SI 1989/1490.

Interpretation of the statutory provisions – L Petitioners (No 3)

39.11   These provisions have been considered by the First Division in *L, Petitioners (No 3).*[1] In this case, which was one of the cases following Sheriff Colin Miller's inquiry, on the instructions of the Court of Session, into the allegations that new evidence had become available in relation to 'the Ayrshire case',[2] the Division had to consider (1) whether to exercise the *nobile officium* in order to allow late applications for legal aid; and (2) if so whether, in the context of an application for an increase in fees, Sheriff Miller's proceedings were to be regarded as proceedings in the Court of Session or in the sheriff court. The court decided that the legal aid applications should be allowed late. Turning to the question of whether the proceedings before Sheriff Miller should be regarded as Court of Session or sheriff court proceedings for the purpose of Regulation 5(4) of the General Regulations, Lord President Hope, delivering the opinion of the court, stated:

> 'That question can only admit of one answer in view of what we have said about the application of s 29 to this case. In our opinion the proceedings

before the sheriff were proceedings in the sheriff court for the purposes of reg 5(4), and we are of that opinion that irrespective of the basis on which legal aid was made available to the petitioners for the time being. It follows that it must be for the sheriff to determine what percentage increase should be allowed. Counsel for the first and second petitioners pointed out that, as proceedings under Pt III of the Social Work (Scotland) Act 1968 are sui generis, they could not with complete accuracy be described as proceedings as a cause on the ordinary roll. She suggested that it was unclear how the provisions of reg 5(4) were to be applied in this case. In our opinion these proceedings are sufficiently similar to proceedings on the ordinary roll for it to be appropriate for 50 per cent to be regarded as the maximum percentage increase which the sheriff may allow. We should add that counsel for the [Legal Aid] board did not suggest that it was inappropriate for a percentage increase to be allowed in this case.'

1 1996 SLT 928.
2 See *L v Kennedy* 1993 SCLR 693, sub nom *L, Petitioners* 1993 SLT 1310.

Subsequent cases

39.12 Notwithstanding the foregoing there have been differing decisions in the sheriff court as to whether application for a percentage increase in fees ('uplift') under Regulation 5(4) is competent having regard to the wording of the Regulation and in particular to the references to the 'Ordinary Roll' and the 'Summary Roll'. In *MC v Walker*[1], Sheriff Principal G L Cox, QC, sustaining the sheriff at Kirkcudbright, held that an application for uplift was incompetent, and stated:

'To anyone who has a detailed knowledge of the procedure in the sheriff court it is apparent that these proceedings would not be described as 'a cause on the Ordinary Roll' nor 'a cause on the Summary Cause Roll'. Regulation 5(4) although referring broadly to 'proceedings of importance and requiring special preparation' then apparently narrows its application to causes on the 'Ordinary Roll' and on the 'Summary Cause Roll'. The use of capital letters makes the references very specific. It appears to permit the sheriff to allow a percentage increase only in such causes. It follows that it is not competent for him to grant an increase in any other civil cause which may come before him'.

Later on in his opinion Sheriff Principal Cox observes that when the Act of Sederunt (Fees of Solicitors in the Sheriff Court) 1989 were replaced by the Act of Sederunt (Fees of Solicitors in the Sheriff Court) (Amendment and Further Provisions) 1993 (SI 1993 No 3080), Schedule, paragraph 5, the reference to the ordinary roll and summary roll was omitted. He states:

'The fact that Parliament has by subordinate legislation changed one set of regulations and not the other must be interpreted as meaning that Parliament has been deliberate in differentiating between causes in which fees can be increased in legal aid cases on the one hand and on the other hand proceedings in which a solicitor is privately instructed.'

The case of *MC v Walker* was followed by Sheriff H S Neilson[2] (who, as a sheriff sitting in South Strathclyde Dumfries and Galloway was bound by it) and by Sheriff A W Noble, sitting in Glasgow.[3] However in the case of *SH or D,*[4] Sheriff I D Dunbar, sitting in Dundee, declined to follow *MC v Walker* and held the application to be competent. Faced with the argument that the case of *L Petitioners* was 'quite extraordinary' and therefore could not be regarded as of general application, Sheriff Dunbar stated:

> 'There is an illogicality about Mr Shearer's [the solicitor representing the Scottish Legal Aid Board] argument that the regulations have a precision and cannot apply to cases of this type while, on this view, the statement in *L Petitioners* that regulation 5(4) ought to be applied only to *L Petitioners* because it was exceptional which suggests a scope for discretion which would not be present in a precise situation. If there is precision there should be no room for exceptional cases. Accordingly, I would take the view that the statement of the Lord President is a general statement and that I am bound by the decision in *L Petitioners* and will grant the increase. There is nothing in the report of the case to indicate that Lord President Hope meant anything other than the general rather than the specific. I do not have the benefit of the arguments and must interpret the decision as reported.'

1 A decision of the Sheriff Principal of South Strathclyde Dumfries and Galloway, sitting at Airdrie, 1 September 1998, unreported.
2 *AF v A Children's Hearing* 22 September 1999, unreported (Hamilton Sh Ct).
3 *D J Martin, Applicant*, 2 November 1999, unreported (Glasgow Sh Ct).
4 28 May 1999, unreported (Dundee Sh Ct).

Conclusion

39.13 In the writer's respectful view there is no need to interpret Regulation 5(4) in the restrictive way adopted by Sheriff Principal Cox, and, indeed, if the proper canon of statutory interpretation is applied, it may be wrong so to do. Sheriff Principal Cox, by his reference to the use of upper case lettering and the presumed intention of Parliament in relation to the amendment of the Act of Sederunt (Fees of Solicitors in the Sheriff Court) 1989, evidently regarded the interpretation of Regulation 5(4) as a matter of some difficulty. In invoking the principle that failure to amend one piece of subordinate legislation in a particular way leads to the conclusion that another piece of subordinate legislation should be interpreted in the other sense Sheriff Cox says that this failure 'must' be interpreted in the way which Sheriff Cox ultimately favours. It is respectfully submitted that this is incorrect. The canon of interpretation relied on by Sheriff Cox has no pre-eminence. It is also a canon of statutory interpretation that a statute should be read as a whole in order to understand the meaning of any part.[1] It appears to be the intention of the Civil Legal Aid (Scotland) (Fees) Regulations 1989, and in particular of Regulation 5(4) thereof, that solicitors should receive reasonable remuneration for work done and that, where that work exceeds the norm there should be a higher fee than that prescribed in the table of fees, a degree of 'uplift' may be allowed. Where there are two constructions open to the court then, it seems to the writer, the meaning more consistent with the rest of the enactment is likely to be correct. It is now trite that cases affecting the welfare of children are important. The thrust of Regulation 5(4) is to recognise that such cases may involve additional difficult work which should be remunerated additionally. This is made clear in relation to work in the Court of Session. It accordingly seems reasonable, in the opinion of the writer, that the provision in relation to the sheriff court should be interpreted as allowing 'uplift' in all sheriff court cases, subject to the broad limitation in Ordinary Cause cases the uplift should be restricted to 50 per cent and that in Summary Cause cases the limit should be 100 per cent. Cases not falling within these categories are not specifically dealt with but it seems reasonable to deal with them on the basis of treating the cases which have more affinity with ordinary causes as governed by the 50 per cent limitation and those which have more affinity with summary causes should be dealt with under the 100 per cent limitation. This pragmatic view was that which commended itself to Lord President Hope in the *L* case and the writer sees no reason to differ.[2]

1 *Attorney General v Prince Ernest Augustus of Hanover* [1957] AC 436 at 463.
2 For a fuller discussion of the writer's views see *Munro and McClure Applicants* 2000 SCLR 920, 2000 Fam LB 46–5.

The position in practice – timescale and procedure

39.14 According to the regulations affecting privately charged fees such a motion is to be made, 'not later than seven days after the date of any interlocutor disposing for expenses.'[1] Since there is in referrals cases no 'interlocutor disposing of expenses' there can therefore be no application for uplift and one might argue that in such cases the rules regarding 'uplift' had no application. This argument is submitted it would fall to be rejected on the basis that a provision merely limiting the time within which a right is to be exercised (in effect within seven days of the final interlocutor) should not be interpreted as limiting the substantial right conveyed. The Civil Legal Aid (Scotland) (Fees) Regulations 1989 contain no such time limitation. In practice such a motion is generally made at the conclusion of the proof. Where such a motion is made under the Legal Aid Regulations the sheriff should fix a hearing and order the party making the motion to intimate to the Scottish Legal Aid Board in order to allow the Board to make representations or to appear. The motion should be accompanied by an account of expenses and a statement of the grounds relied upon, although such motions have been entertained without lodgment of the account.

1 Act of Sederunt (Fees of Solicitors in the Sheriff Court) (Amendment and Further Provisions) 1993, SI 1993/3080, Schedule 1, reg 5(b).

Petition of safeguarder or curator *ad litem*

39.15 There is no enacted power in the sheriff to assess or increases the fee payable to a curator *ad litem* or to assess or increase the fee payable to a safeguarder, (whether he be a solicitor or not[1]) whose remuneration is a matter for the local authority.[2]

1 *Murphy, Petr* (15 December 1986, unreported, Glasgow Sh Ct).
2 Children (Scotland) Act 1995, s 41(4).

CHAPTER 40

The course of the proof: V – the decision of the court

PRONOUNCING THE DECISION: THE RULES

Giving the judgment

40.01 The rules provide that the sheriff 'shall give his decision orally at the conclusion of the hearing'[1] and that the sheriff *may*, when thus giving the decision, or within 7 days thereafter, issue a note giving reasons for the decision.[2] There is no provision for reserving judgment, but sheriffs may and often enough do take time to decide and, if it seems appropriate, to write upon a case, by using the power of adjournment conveyed by r 3.49[3] of the Act of Sederunt (Child Care and Maintenance Rules) 1997 and delivering judgment at the adjourned hearing. In the great majority of cases an extempore judgment is given at the close of the hearing and no note issued. (It is the writer's normal practice, when giving his decision at the end of the proof, to mention specifically, as one of the purposes of the proof the necessity of the reporter establishing, openly and above board, that proof to the appropriate legal standard exists for the alleged grounds of referral.)

1 Act of Sederunt (Child Care and Maintenance Rules) 1997, SI 1997/291, r 3.51(1).
2 SI 1997/291, r 3.51(3).
3 '... the sheriff ... on his own motion may continue the hearing ... for any other necessary cause, for such reasonable time as he may in the circumstances consider necessary.'

Notifying parties

40.02 The sheriff clerk must forthwith send a copy of the interlocutor to the child, unless service on the child has been dispensed with, any relevant person whose whereabouts are known, any safeguarder appointed by the sheriff and to the reporter.[1] Where the sheriff has issued a note of reasons the sheriff clerk shall send a copy to the foregoing parties at time of issue.[2]

1 SI 1997/291, r 3.51(2).
2 SI 1997/291, r 3.51(3).

Essential contents of decision

40.03 The object of the hearing of the application is to obtain a finding from the sheriff as to whether such grounds as were not accepted by the child or relevant person, or not understood, or capable of being understood, by the child are established.[1] The sheriff's determination, embodied in the formal interlocutor, must include findings deciding these issues. The possibilities are:

- that none of the grounds for referral is established with the consequence that the sheriff dismisses the application and discharges the referral;[2]
- that one or more of the grounds is, or is deemed to be, established,[3] with the consequence that the sheriff remits the case to the reporter to make arrangements for a children's hearing to consider and decide what is to be done.[4]

1 Children (Scotland) Act 1995, s 65(7) and (9).
2 Children (Scotland) Act 1995, s 68(9).
3 Cf Children (Scotland) Act 1995, s 68(8).
4 C(S)A 1995, s 68(10)(a).

Consequences of decisions

40.04   Where the sheriff dismisses the application and discharges the referral 'he shall dismiss the application, discharge the referral to the children's hearing in respect of those grounds and recall, discharge or cancel any order, warrant, or direction under this Chapter of the Act which relates to the child in respect of those grounds'.[1] The dismissal of the application therefore terminates a relative Child Protection Order. Where the sheriff upholds the grounds of referral in whole or in part the sheriff remits to the reporter who must arrange a hearing for disposal of the case.[2]

1 Children (Scotland) Act 1995, s 68(9).
2 C(S)A 1995, s 68(10).

Additional possible contents of decisions – detention of child

40.05   Where the sheriff is satisfied, on upholding the referral, that keeping a child in a place of safety is necessary in the child's bests interests or that there is reason to believe that the child will run away before the hearing then he may grant an order for the detention of the child in a place of safety. If either of the secure accommodation criteria is fulfilled, the sheriff may provide that the child shall be liable to be placed and kept in secure accommodation within a residential establishment at such times as the person in charge of the establishment, with the agreement of the chief social work officer of the relevant local authority, considers necessary.[1] Such an order expires within three days, (beginning with the day on which the child is so kept), or when the hearing considers the child's case, whichever is the earlier. In this provision 'three days', not three working days, is enacted and, since the liberty of the subject is involved, the first day on which the child is so held – which will presumably be the day of the order – counts as 'day one'. Accordingly such an order made by the sheriff at 4 p m on Thursday 31 December 1998 will cease to have effect at the end of Saturday 2 January 1999 unless a hearing has been held in the meantime.

1 Children (Scotland) Act 1995, s 68(10) and (11).

Form of interlocutor – partial establishment of grounds

40.06 By definition the application has come before the sheriff either because the child is unable to understand, or has not understood, the ground of referral or because the child or parent has not accepted the ground of referral. In either of these events, it is submitted that it is important for the court not only to reach a just and accurate decision but for this to be openly seen to be done and carefully recorded. Clearly where the sheriff has held one or more conditions of referral to be established but has held one or more not to be established this must be reflected in the interlocutor. In the case of *M v Kennedy*[1] it was held that a hearing, in disposing of the case, were not entitled to have regard to an alleged fact which had been expressly rejected by the sheriff at the proof. It accordingly seems clear that where any statement of fact is being held not to have been proved – even where the condition of referral is being held to have been established by other facts – then the sheriff's not having held as established a particular allegation should be recorded in the interlocutor.

1 1993 SLT 431.

Amendment of Statement of Facts

40.07 It was recognised under the former rules that the sheriff in giving judgment had power to effect minor emendations provided these were either in effect deletions or were minor. Material emendations were not competent. The sheriff may now amend the statement of facts[1] but should not effect a material amendment without giving parties the opportunity to be heard.

1 Act of Sederunt (Child Care and Maintenance Rules) 1997, SI 1997/291, r 3.48, discussed above at 29.10 and 39.08ff.

PRONOUNCING THE DECISION: THE PRACTICE

Possibility of issuing Note stating reasons

40.08 Under the former legislation the sheriff's function in these applications was described as being 'of a very limited character, namely to make a finding as to whether the grounds of referral are established, that and no more'[1]. The current provisions for the sheriff to issue a note of reasons are permissive only.[2] The sheriff must accordingly still assess to the best of his judgement as to whether or not to issue a Note, and, if so, as to what it should contain.

1 *McGregor v D* 1977 SC 330 at 341 per Lord Cameron.
2 The only formal occasion he would have to do this in relation to an application would be in the event of an appeal by Stated Case: see below at 54.17.

Note giving reasons as to a relevant legal issue

40.09   It may be thought appropriate to append a Note dealing with any difficult or novel legal problem which has arisen in the course of the application[1]. When this is done parties may appreciate the reasons for the decision and thus, if they are good reasons, perhaps be in a better position to accept the decision. Alternatively, if parties disagree with the decision they will be in a better position to decide on whether to appeal.

1 Cf the decision of Sheriff Neil Gow QC in *L v McGregor*, discussed above at 28.14.

Note giving reasons as to factual issue

40.10   In *S v Kennedy*[1] the Grounds of Referral had alleged that a child had been sexually abused but had not named the alleged abuser. The sheriff upheld the grounds of referral. The decision of the sheriff was appealed to the Court of Session on several grounds but in arguing the appeal counsel for the appellant submitted only that the sheriff should not have made in the stated case a finding identifying the offender. Upholding the appellant's argument, Lord Justice-Clerk Ross stated:

> 'A sheriff should not make unnecessary findings' and commented 'No doubt a children's hearing might find it useful to have information on all kinds of issues, but it is not a sheriff's function in an application made to him under s 42(2)(c) or s 42(7) to make all findings which may assist the children's hearing; what the sheriff is required to do, and all that he is required to do, is to determine whether the grounds of referral have been established'.

Lord Dunpark, agreed but stated:

> 'Counsel for the reporter pointed out that it was very important for the subsequent hearing to know the name of the person who had been found by the sheriff to have committed the offence, as the hearing would have to decide under s 43(1) of the Act what course should be taken in the best interests of the child. I agree of course, that it is important for the hearing to have all relevant information before it, but, as the reporter will be in possession not only of the findings but also of the sheriff's note, he will presumably place these before the hearing.'

Reading Lord Dunpark's observations along with the decisions of the Court of Session in *O v Rae*[2] and *M v Kennedy*,[3] both already discussed,[4] it may be that sheriffs may be more ready than formerly to append Notes. It is submitted, nevertheless, that a Note should not contain matter relative to what could have formed the subject of averment by the reporter in the Statement of Facts. The proper course is to consider allowing amendment of the Statement of Facts under r 3.48 of the 1997 Rules. Where stating conclusions on a factual issue the sheriff should not, in a care and protection case, use the terminology of 'beyond reasonable doubt'.[5]

1 1987 SLT 667.
2 1992 SCLR 318.
3 1991 SCLR 898.
4 Above at 16.06, 16.07, 16.08 and 39.09.
5 *P v Kennedy* 1995 SCLR 1.

Note in offence by a child case

40.11 Similarly in such a case the hearing may wish to know, for example, in a case of assault wherein self-defence has been alleged but rejected, that the sheriff took the view that, although self-defence had not been made out, a substantial degree of provocation had existed. It is submitted that the sheriff may legitimately add a Note to make such matters clear.

Note explaining basis of decision: submissions on whether appropriate

40.12 Although only concerned to make a determination as to the existence or not of the grounds of referral the sheriff need not ignore the wider context and may, it is submitted, ask parties to address him as to the appropriateness of a Note in a particular case.

Sheriff should not make suggestions as to disposal

40.13 It is inappropriate for the sheriff to make suggestions as to disposal in any Note appended to a decision following a proof. This is clearly contrary to the scheme of the 1995 Act: the Court of Session has deprecated any observation by the sheriff tending to 'pre-empt the disposal of the case by the children's hearing'.[1]

1 *M v McGregor* 1982 SLT 41 at 44.

Reference in final interlocutor to report by safeguarder?

40.14 If a safeguarder has been appointed by the sheriff and has lodged a report the sheriff may be asked to incorporate some reference to the safeguarder's report in the final interlocutor. The sheriff has no power to 'approve' the safeguarder's report or to order its production to the hearing[1] and there appears to be no provision warranting that a reference to the report in the final interlocutor is permissible. It is tentatively submitted that the sheriff should hear parties on such a motion being made and grant it where it is in the interests of the child *and* the interests of justice so to do. It may be that if the sheriff decided that the hearing should have the report he or she could 'give' it to the reporter as relevant information which the reporter would require to make available to the hearing and others.[2]

1 Cf *F v Kennedy* 1991 GWD 8–434 and *M v Stirling* 1991 GWD 6–381, 1993 2 Fam LB 2–3 and commentary in Fam LB 'The safest course is to copy everything to the hearing unless it is clearly immaterial.'
2 Children's Hearings (Scotland) Rules 1996, SI 1996/3261, r 5(2).

Correction of interlocutors

40.15   It is proper practice for parties to scrutinise interlocutors soon after they have been signed. There is no provision in the 1995 Act or the 1997 Rules for changing an interlocutor once it has been signed. However a party who considers that a mistake has been made should advise the sheriff clerk immediately. The sheriff, if satisfied that there has been an error, will, it is thought, be guided by the rules of ordinary practice in the sheriff court.[1] Where the error is clerical and insubstantial the sheriff may be ready to correct it without a hearing and intimate the change to other parties. Where the error is substantial and the interlocutor does not properly reflect the decision it is thought that the sheriff should, through the sheriff clerk, ascertain if there is agreement amongst parties and if there is such agreement, authorise the change.[2] In the absence of such agreement the sheriff may be willing to fix a hearing, but should there still be no agreement it must be doubted if an alteration would be competent. It is thought that the sheriff may not change an interlocutor in order to reflect a change of mind.[3]

1 See *Macphail on Sheriff Court Practice* (2nd edn) 5.87 to 5.90.
2 '... it is thought that it might be difficult to ground a practical objection to the sheriff's making a correction of which he approves, de recenti and of consent of parties, in circumstances analogous to those of a reported Court of Session decision' – *Macphail on Sheriff Court Practice* (2nd edn) 5.89.
3 *Macphail on Sheriff Court Practice* (2nd edn) para 5.87, citing *Mutual Shipping Corporation v Bayshore Shipping Co Ltd* [1985] 1 WLR 625 at 632, 633.

REPORTER'S RIGHT TO ABANDON APPLICATION

The rules

40.16   Rule 3.46 of the 1997 Rules provides:

> 'At any stage of the proceedings before the application is determined the Principal Reporter may abandon the application, either in whole or in part, by lodging a minute to that effect or by motion at the hearing.'

Any minute of abandonment must be intimated to the child, except where service on the child has been dispensed with, on any relevant person whose whereabouts are known and to any safeguarder appointed by the sheriff.[1]

1 Act of Sederunt (Child Care and Maintenance Rules) 1997, SI 1997/291, r 3.46(2).

The procedures

40.17 This rule appears to presuppose that the application has been lodged and, accordingly, the right to abandon appears to run from the moment of lodging the application until the moment when the sheriff pronounces his decision. If abandonment is carried through by written motion then the sheriff, on seeing the motion, with appropriate executions of service, is bound to grant it and any diet fixed for the hearing of the application would fall. In practice a written application to abandon is frequently lodged at the date of the proof and is supported by a verbal motion. The relevant person and child on whom notice of abandonment has been served, may attend the diet proof to hear the motion being granted, but their presence is not necessary and, if the notice of abandonment has been effectively served, is almost unknown in practice.

The practicalities – evidence turning out to be insufficient

40.18 Should it emerge in the course of further investigation that the reporter will not be able to prove his case with the witnesses he is able to call then the reporter should abandon or amend in order to delete the unsupportable averment, and should not, it is submitted, press on in the hope that the other side will admit the grounds of referral or, alternatively, supply the missing evidence by testifying. The following remarks of Lord Carmont in 1955, although made in the context of summary criminal procedure, are relevant:

> 'As I understand the matter in this case, had the accused not gone into the box, the Crown would have failed to make out a case against him, and it was only in respect that the Crown took the risk of getting and got an admission from the accused in regard to the matter charged that the case can be held proved against him. I cannot commend the practice to prosecutors and I hope that that practice, if it is a practice, will not be extended'.[1]

1 *M'Arthur v Stewart* 1955 JC 71 at 75.

The practicalities – application overtaken by other referrals

40.19 It could happen that, while awaiting the conclusion of the hearing of an application in relation to one alleged offence by a child, the reporter receives a remit from the sheriff for disposal in respect of several similar offences. In such a situation it is submitted that the reporter should consider abandoning the earlier referral. The criterion would be the reporter's assessment of which course would best promote the welfare of the child. There may be cases where the earlier case should be maintained but it may frequently be considered that there is no point in going to the trouble and expense of pursuing an application merely in order to add one offence.

Part V
Some basic concepts of the law of evidence

CHAPTER 41

The onus of proof

THE AFFIRMER MUST PROVE THAT WHICH IS AFFIRMED

The fundamental principle – onus on affirmer – onus on reporter

41.01 The Latin phrase *affirmanti incumbit probatio* means literally 'on the affirmer rests [the burden of] proof'. With some minor exceptions, most of which are more apparent than real, this principle applies to all court proceedings, including applications under the Children (Scotland) Act 1995, section 68. The burden of presenting full legal proof lies with the reporter at the outset. Even in s 52(2)(i) cases wherein the child has indicated that there is a 'special defence' such as alibi, incrimination or self-defence, this does not in any way detract from the onus on the reporter who must still prove his own case to the requisite standard of proof. The intimation of an intended 'special defence' must be treated only as fair notice that a particular line of evidence or cross-examination may be adopted by the child. Failure to prove a routine but crucial fact may be fatal to the reporter's case.[1] It has been said: 'But in the end, when all the evidence has been brought out, it rarely matters where the onus originally lay: the question is which way the balance of probability has come to rest.'[2] For further discussion of discharging the onus of proof, see 42.08 and 42.09 below.

1 *Ferguson v S* 1992 SCLR 867, 1992 GWD 26–1455, Extra Div.
2 *M'Williams v Sir William Arrol & Co and Anr* 1962 SC (HL) 70 per Lord Reid at 83.

Sufficiency of evidence and weight of evidence

41.02 The foregoing principle demands that evidence *sufficient in law* to permit the court to draw the appropriate legal inference must be adduced before the court may hold the fact averred as established. But more may be needed. Evidence which is sufficient in law may not be enough to persuade the court. The affirmer must go on to persuade and ultimately convince the court that it should draw the inference which (legally sufficient evidence having been led) is open to the court. A case can be sufficient in law and may fail because it lacks weight and persuasiveness. A pleader who has been rightly preoccupied with making sure that the evidence passes all the strictly legal tests should guard against being so concerned with this that he or she omits to remember that his or her ultimate task is the human one of persuading another person that a given state of facts can, applying the appropriate standard,[1] safely be said to exist.

1 See ch 42.

Available evidence not adduced

41.03   Where evidence which might have been led is not led the sheriff is not bound to reject the evidence which has been led.[1] In *M v Kennedy*[2] it was held that the evidence of one doctor giving evidence outwith his speciality was sufficient in law to establish sexual abuse of a child even although two other medical witnesses who were in a position to give relevant evidence were not called. It is, however, always a matter for the judgement of the pleader as to how much evidence should be led in order to persuade the court.[3]

1 *K v Kennedy* 1992 SCLR 386 (Note), Extra Div.
2 1993 SCLR 69 at 72E, F.
3 Cf the commentary by Sheriff A L Stewart QC on *M v Kennedy* 1993 SCLR 69 at 80E: 'Although the fact that Dr Day consulted Dr McEwan, as the sheriff said, "in no way undermined the reliability of Dr Day's conclusion", if Dr McEwan's evidence had been led, it might very well have reinforced that reliability and would not in any way have been superfluous. One might have thought that, especially since Orkney, reporters would be anxious to produce evidence which is as full as possible to the sheriff in any case where sexual abuse is alleged'; see also *Kennedy v H* 1992 GWD 7-340, 22 January 1992, 1st Div, where it was held that the sheriff had been entitled to prefer the expert evidence of one witness and the evidence of the parent against the evidence of a number of expert witnesses.

Presumptions

41.04   Sometimes the amount of proof which the person having the *onus of* proof may require to present may be quite substantially reduced by the inferences which the law allows to be drawn from certain facts, once these facts have been established. The rules regarding 'presumptions' are discussed later.[1]

1 At 45.07 ff below.

AFFIRMATIVE DEFENCES IN OFFENCE CASES

'Special' defences

41.05   If the 'defence' side proposes to advance a positive line of defence then this does not take away the original onus of proof on the reporter but it leaves it open to the 'defence' side, if it wishes, to adduce evidence or advance argument in favour of the affirmative defence. The defences of this nature, sometimes called 'special' defences, commonly encountered in alleged 'offence by the child' cases are self-defence, alibi and incrimination. The defence, to be successful, need not 'prove' anything by full legal proof: it need only create in the mind of the court, in relation to the special defence concerned, a reasonable doubt as to the guilt of the accused child in relation to the offence alleged against him.[1]

1 *Lambie v HM Advocate* 1973 JC 53.

Insanity at the time of the offence

41.06 The special defence of insanity at the time of the alleged offence is not often encountered in hearing applications. Such a defence would raise special considerations discussed fully in Gordon on *Criminal Law* paras 10-01 to 10-41. It seems unlikely that such a defence would be relevant where a person is alleged to have committed an offence against a child, since the happening of the events might be regarded as sufficient to demonstrate an offence in the context of the overall scheme of the Children (Scotland) Act 1995 to protect children.[1] In a case wherein this defence appeared to be a possibility the reporter would generally consider the possibility of averring additionally grounds based on lack of parental care.

1 Cf *S v Kennedy* 1996 SCLR 34, 1995 GWD 38-1924, [1996] Fam LB 19-9, 2nd Div and the reasoning of the sheriff in *E v Kennedy* 1992 GWD 25-1402 (2 June 1992), Sheriff N Gow QC, Ayr Sheriff Court.

Incrimination

41.07 Such an affirmative defence alleges that the offence was committed by another named person whose name and address, if known, should be given.

Alibi

41.08 Such an affirmative defence alleges that the child was not at the place alleged by the reporter but at some other specified place. Notice should be given to the reporter in advance. It can happen that a general defence of denial can, if the child gives evidence, develop into an allegation that he was at another place, although perhaps so nearby that it has not occurred to the defence to give notice. The reporter may be entitled to ask for an adjournment of the proof to investigate such a late-emerging line of defence.

Self-defence

41.09 Before self-defence can be sustained, all three of the following elements must be present, namely: *immediate* personal danger to the accused person (or a person whom the accused person is lawfully defending[1]); absence of means of escape or retreat;[2] and the use of only reasonable force by the accused, as opposed to 'cruel excess'.[3] If the accused person believes he is endangered he is entitled to defend himself and does not lose his right to claim self-defence even if he was not in danger, provided that his belief was not unreasonable.[4] In considering whether or not the retaliation has been reasonable, allowance must be made for the heat of the moment. The position has been expressed thus:

'You do not need an exact proportion of injury and retaliation; it is not a matter that you weigh in too fine scales ... Some allowance must be made for the excitement or the state of fear or the heat of blood.'[5]

1 *HM Advocate v Carson* 1964 SLT 21.
2 *McBrearty v HM Advocate* 1999 SCCR 122.
3 *Fenning v HM Advocate* 1985 JC 76 at 81, approved in *Friel v HM Advocate* 1998 SCCR 47.
4 *Owens v HM Advocate* 1946 JC 119.
5 *HM Advocate v Doherty* 1954 JC 1 at 4.

Provocation

41.10   Provocation by words can probably never justify retaliation by blows.[1] In criminal practice the judge will normally regard provocation as a mitigating factor in sentencing. In a referral proof the sheriff could not regard provocation as entitling him to dismiss the application but, as already noticed,[2] the sheriff might, in an appropriate case, add a note to his interlocutor indicating the presence and degree of provocation since this may be a very relevant matter for the hearing which has to dispose of the case.

1 See discussion in Sheriff Gordon's *Criminal Law* (2nd edn) paras 25-09 to 25-39, particularly 25-26 ff.
2 At 40.11 above.

Defence of reasonable excuse in cases under the Children (Scotland) Act 1995, s 52(2)(h) ('truanting')

41.11   In these cases the relevant documentary evidence may 'prove itself',[1] i e be sufficient evidence of the matters therein stated unless there is evidence to the contrary. The most common example is a certificate signed by the head teacher of the school, certifying the attendance of the child. Once such a certificate has been produced it is then for the child or parent either to attempt to disprove its terms (which is very rare indeed) or to lead evidence of reasonable excuse for the child not attending school.[2] This would appear to be one of the few cases wherein it is correct to say that, once the initial burden of proof has been discharged by the accuser, the onus then passes to the defence side.[3]

1 Education (Scotland) Act 1980, s 86.
2 *Kennedy v Clark* 1970 JC 55.
3 *Kennedy v Clark* 1970 JC 55 at p 57; for discussion of the special position in relation to *onus* of proof in education cases as opposed to others see Sheriff Gordon's commentary on *Earnshaw v HM Advocate* 1981 SCCR 279 at 285; see also *Kiely v Lunn* 1983 SLT 207 and *D v Kennedy* 1988 SLT 207.

CHAPTER 42

The standard of proof

INTRODUCTORY

Standards of proof

42.01 The law recognises that scientific certainty cannot be achieved in the law courts where the ascertainment of the details of human conduct is the subject matter. In the absence of absolute certainty there is always a risk of injustice: damages may be wrongly awarded, or a penalty may be imposed on an innocent person – but as society is not prepared to accept that civil wrongs should remain unrighted or that crime continue unpunished, the effort to deal with these problems has to be made and some risk of injustice taken in order to avoid anarchy and private revenge. In the criminal sphere it is the accepted view that the risk of punishing a person wrongly must be avoided at all reasonable cost and accordingly a higher degree of certainty must be attained in criminal than in civil matters.

REFERRALS UNDER s 52(2)(i)

42.02 In applications to the sheriff arising from referrals based upon the allegation that a child has committed an offence, the sheriff is statutorily bound to apply to the evidence relating to that ground of referral 'the standard of proof required in criminal proceedings'.[1] It follows that the reporter must seek to attain to the standard of proof 'beyond reasonable doubt' and that the sheriff, in dealing with an application relating to a referral on this ground, will apply the standard of proof appropriate when exercising criminal jurisdiction.

1 Children (Scotland) Act 1995, s 68(3)(b).

'Beyond reasonable doubt'

42.03 Proof to this standard requires the court to be very satisfied – not 100 per cent certain since such certainty is not attainable in such matters – but sure beyond any doubt to which a reason can be assigned. 'It is difficult to conceive of a higher [standard] which could ever be applied in practice.'[1] A reasonable doubt is one which would cause one to hesitate or pause before making an important decision in one's own affairs.[2]

1 *Brown v Brown* 1972 SC 123 at 126 per Lord Emslie at 145.
2 *MacDonald v HM Advocate* 1995 SCCR 663.

Welfare and rights

42.04   The case of *Constanda v M*[1] enabled Lord President Rodger to discuss the principles underlying the requirement of the criminal standard of proof in cases involving alleged offences by children. In this case the condition of referral was that of falling into bad associations or exposure to moral danger. The entire evidence led before the sheriff came from one source – evidence from the female victim that her male cousin had performed lewd and libidinous practices. The reporter argued that this conduct entitled the court to infer that the child was exposed to moral danger and that as this was not a ground under the Social Work (Scotland) Act 1968, s 32(2)(g) corroboration was not required. The First Division, sustaining the sheriff, held that the evidence of the offences alone did not by itself warrant the conclusion that the child was exposed to moral danger and that where offences by a child *and nothing else* is alleged then the reporter must employ s 32(2)(g) and adduce corroborated evidence. Lord President Rodger stated at 512D:

> 'In this case counsel for the reporter accepted that she could not prove the commission of the offence to that criminal standard since there was no corroboration of the girl's account. In enacting section 42(6) Parliament must have envisaged that precisely such an eventuality would occur and that, if it did, the condition could not be established. But for that very reason a reporter cannot avoid the result which Parliament intended by simply seeking to prove exactly the same matters and nothing more under another condition. To hold otherwise would be to deprive the child of the safeguard which Parliament provided in section 42(6). That cannot be allowed, even although the reporter may have acted with the best of intentions and may consider that in seeking to avoid the difficulties posed by section 42(6) she is trying to help the child.'

1 1997 SCLR 510.

Rehabilitation of Offenders Act 1974

42.05   Section 5 of this Act imposes on the child a rehabilitation period of six months or more in the event of a finding that a condition under the Children (Scotland) Act 1995, s 52(2)(i) has been established in relation to the child. The requirement of proof beyond reasonable doubt secures to the child a crucial element of the due process of our criminal law before this consequence can follow.

CASES UNDER CONDITIONS OTHER THAN s 52(2)(i) OF THE ACT

42.06   It has been said again and again in the Court of Session that 'the basic rules of evidence must be observed in applications before the Sheriff'.[1] It is also well accepted that the procedure has more affinities with civil than criminal jurisdiction.[2] In *S v Kennedy*[3] Lord Justice-Clerk

Ross and the other judges sitting reserved their opinions as to whether in referral proceedings the sheriff was entitled to hold that a named individual had committed a criminal offence if the evidence merely established the fact on a balance of probabilities. In *Harris v F*[4] the issue thus reserved had to be decided. In this case the sheriff had rejected a ground of referral based on the Social Work (Scotland) Act 1968, s 32(2)(dd) (the child is or is likely to become a member of same household as a person who has committed a Schedule 1 offence) because he was not satisfied beyond reasonable doubt that the named person had so offended. An Extra Division, after reviewing the authorities, including *S v Kennedy*, held that the appropriate standard was the balance of probabilities. Lord Justice-Clerk Ross, delivering the opinion of the Division, stated:[5]

> 'It must be recognised that if a standard of proof on a balance of probabilities is applied to a ground of referral under section 32(2)(dd), and the higher criminal standard of proof applies to the trial of the person concerned in a criminal court for the offence referred to in the ground of referral, the result may be that the sheriff in the application under section 42 has held that the person has committed the offence in question whereas subsequently that person is acquitted of committing that offence in the criminal court. In my opinion, however, that does not constitute an anomaly. The purpose of a ground of referral such as section 32(2)(dd) is to advance the welfare of the child and to protect the child. A decision upon whether a ground of referral has been established may well have to be taken before criminal proceedings against the person concerned can be completed, particularly where that person is pleading not guilty. There are strong public policy considerations for holding that it is appropriate at the stage of holding the ground of referral to be established to apply the standard of proof on a balance of probabilities because it is often difficult to prove beyond reasonable doubt that sexual offences of this kind have been committed. Protection of the child is, in my opinion, a justification for applying the lower standard of proof in applications under section 42 and they still are a justification even if the person concerned is ultimately acquitted of the offence in the criminal courts.'

In *Kennedy v B*[6] the situation envisaged by Lord Ross in *Harris v B* came to pass and the Second Division held that the subsequent acquittal of an alleged abuser should not be regarded, for referral purposes, as decisive of the factual issue.

1 *McGregor v D* 1977 SC 330 at 336 per LP Emslie.
2 Cf *McGregor v T and P* 1975 SC 14; *Kennedy v O* 1975 SC 308; and *W v Kennedy* 1988 SCLR 236, 1988 SLT 583.
3 1987 SLT 667.
4 1991 SCLR 124.
5 At 1991 SCLR 128D–F; cf the discussion of the justification of the standard of the balance of probabilities by Lord Dunpark in *B v Kennedy* 1987 SLT 765 at 768.
6 1992 SCLR 55.

42.07 It now appears clear from the foregoing cases that the authorities which suggest that a standard of proof more demanding than a balance of probabilities is appropriate where a crime is alleged in the course of a civil litigation, epitomised by the words 'In proportion as the offence is grave, so ought the proof to be clear',[1] has no application to proofs in referral cases. It likewise seems clear that the suggestion obiter in *M v McGregor*[2] of a 'standard of being satisfied' can have no application.

1 *Blyth v Blyth* [1966] AC 643 at 669. See also *Bater v Bater* [1951] P 35; *Arnott v Burt* (1872) 11 M 62 at 74; *Wink v Speirs* (1867) 6 M 77 at 80; and *B v Kennedy* 1987 SLT 765, 1987 GWD 21-789.
2 1982 SLT 41.

'The balance of probabilities'

42.08 The writer would adopt Sheriff Macphail's words:

> 'The expression is no doubt open to the comment that it may suggest that to satisfy the standard one need only introduce enough evidence to disturb a balanced pair of scales; but in practice that is not so. If one party gives a little evidence and the other none, the former will not necessarily succeed, because his assertion may be inherently improbable and failure to contradict an assertion does not necessarily make it credible. What is being weighed in the "balance" is not quantities of evidence but the probabilities arising from the acceptable evidence and all the circumstances of the case.'[1]

In *Re H and Others (Minors) (Sexual Abuse: Standard of Proof)* [1986] AC 536 Lord Nicholls of Birkenhead stated at 585D *et seq*:

> 'The balance of probability standard means that a court is satisfied an event occurred if the court considers that, on the evidence, the occurrence of the event was more likely than not. When assessing the probabilities the court will have in mind as a factor, to whatever extent is appropriate in the partic- ular case, that the more serious allegation the less likely it is that the event occurred and, hence, the stronger should be the evidence before the court concludes that the allegation is established on the balance of probability. Fraud is usually less likely than negligence. Deliberate physical injury is usually less likely than accidental physical injury . . .'

This does not mean that there is a higher standard of proof where an offence against a child is alleged, but only that the court must, in 'balancing' the probabilities have regard to the antecedent likelihoods as part of the whole picture.

1 Macphail, *Evidence* para 22.30.

Possibility of case 'not proved'

42.09 As already noticed[1] it is unusual, when all the evidence has been brought out, to decide a case on the basis of where the onus originally lay. However the possibility remains. This was recognised by Lord Justice- Clerk Alness in *Mitchell's Administratix v Edinburgh Royal Infirmary* 1928 SC 47 at 54 wherein his Lordship adopted the words of Lord Dunedin in an earlier case thus:

> 'I respectfully refer, in connection with the doctrine of onus, to what was said by Lord Dunedin in *Robbins* [citing 1927 AC 515] at p 520, and in

particular to these words: "Onus as a determining factor of the whole case can only arise if the tribunal finds the evidence pro and con so evenly balanced that it can come to no such conclusion. Then the onus will determine the matter." I think the onus determines the matter here.'

Accordingly the court may, in cases where the evidence is finely balanced, sometimes require to hold that the onus of proof has not been discharged.[2]

1 Above 41.01, citing *M'Williams v Sir William Arrol & Co* 1962 SC 70 per Lord Reid at 83.
2 An example of such a decision where there were very serious allegations of assault on a child is *Cunningham v SD and JD* 2000 Fam LB 46–5.

CASES UNDER s 52(2)(j) (CHILD MISUSING ALCOHOL OR DRUG) AND s 52(2)(k) (CHILD MISUSING VOLATILE SUBSTANCE)

42.10 Since such cases are not within the category of 'the condition referred to in section 52(2)(i)',[1] it would appear that the criminal standard of proof would not be required in such cases. This conclusion may gain some support from the consideration that a finding against a child in relation to such grounds does not fall with the Rehabilitation of Offenders Act 1974, s 5, referred to above.[2] It may, however, be a question if the reporter would be entitled to employ such grounds where the conduct of the child amounted to an offence such as the possession of a controlled drug in contravention of the Misuse of Drugs Act 1972, s 5: in such a circumstance might not the observations of Lord President Rodger in *Constanda v M,* quoted above,[3] come into play?

1 Children (Scotland) Act 1995, s 68(3).
2 At 23.09.
3 At 42.04.

APPLICATIONS TO THE SHERIFF UNDER THE EMERGENCY CHILD PROTECTION PROCEDURES[1]

42.11 As argued already,[2] the sheriff court proceedings in relation to these provisions are civil. It is further submitted that such proceedings are 'proceedings in the ordinary courts of law' under the Civil Evidence (Scotland) Act 1988, s 9,[3] and that the civil standard of proof applies even where an offence by a person against a child is in issue. The words of Lord Justice-Clerk Ross in *Harris v F*[4] provide the principled justification for this view.

1 Children (Scotland) Act 1995, ss 55, 57–61, and 76–80.
2 At 4.03 above.
3 Definition of 'civil proceedings' – cf discussion of 'the ordinary roll' in *Munro and McClure, Applicants* 2000 Fam LB 46–5.
4 At 42.06 above.

EUROPEAN CONVENTION ON HUMAN RIGHTS

42.12　The European Court of Human Rights has said, in relation to the European Convention on Human Rights, art 6:

> '... it is not within the province of the European Court to substitute its own assessment of the facts for that of the domestic courts and, as a general rule, it is for these courts to assess the evidence before them. The Court's task is to ascertain whether the proceedings in their entirety, including the way in which evidence was taken, were fair.'[1]

It is submitted that this indicates that the employment of the civil standard of proof in relation to the proof of alleged offences against children is not inconsistent with our obligations under the Convention.

1 *Edwards v United Kingdom* (1993) 15 EHRR 417 at 431, para 34.

CHAPTER 43

Sufficiency of evidence: I – proof of fact and admissibility of evidence

PROOF OF FACT

Facts and evidence

43.01 A fact may be something that someone has done, or something that someone has not done, or something that someone has said, or something that someone has had done to him, or something that someone has heard. It may be a lot of other things as well: a fact is simply something which has happened. Proof of fact in court is effected by the oral testimony of witnesses and by the inferences which are to be drawn from written records and material things connected with the past events. These oral statements, written records or objects are pieces or adminicles of evidence. The law of evidence in relation to proof of facts is composed of the rules which the courts apply in deciding how many and what kind of pieces of evidence are required before a fact can be regarded as established.

Crucial or essential facts

43.02 The core of any ground of referral is the existence of a fact or of a number of facts. The fact may be an offence – whether by the child or by the parent or someone else – or a fact or set of facts from which the conclusion may properly be drawn that one of the non-offence conditions of referral exists. The crucial or essential facts are those which are central to the condition of referral and must be proved by sufficient evidence of acceptable quality and to the appropriate standard. These elements are referred to as the crucial or essential facts (*facta probanda* – the facts to be proved). A comparatively simple matter may be an essential fact. In a referral based on the Social Work (Scotland) Act 1968, s 32(2)(dd) (child member of or likely to become member of same household as Schedule 1 offender) there was no evidence as to where the child was living at the material time and no other relevant evidence other than the daughter/father relationship, and the reporter's case was held to be fatally deficient.[1]

1 *Ferguson v S* 1992 SCLR 866.

Essential facts – proving a crime

43.03 The definition of the essential elements in crimes is the province of the positive criminal law and the reader is referred to *The Criminal Law of Scotland* (2nd edn) by Sheriff Sir Gerald Gordon QC (as he now is) which is the only modern systematic study of this subject. One example may be given here as an illustration. The crime of theft consists in the unlawful taking of the moveable property of another with the intention of keeping it from the true owner. This divides up into the following elements:

1   'Unlawful': the thief, as opposed to the police officer lawfully collecting evidence or the sheriff officer lawfully selling a debtor's property, has no right to remove the property.
2   'Taking' (*amotio*): the goods have to be physically moved before the theft is complete. The movement may only be slight, but merely laying a hand on an article without moving it would not be theft although it might amount to attempted theft.
3   'Of another': the goods must belong to a person other than the person accused: one cannot steal one's own property.

The foregoing three elements make up the criminal act ('*actus reus*') of theft. In addition to these there must be present:

4   Intent to keep the property from the true owner permanently or at least indefinitely. Theft, like most crimes having their origin in the common law and not created by statute, has, as an essential feature, an aspect which relates to the offender's state of mind – there must be criminal intent (*mens rea*) and, in theft, this means the intent to deprive the true owner of his property. It is not theft, for example, to appropriate one's neighbour's lawnmower without permission if the intention is merely to use it to mow the lawn and then return it.[1] (It may, however, be theft to detain an article from the true owner for some ulterior, improper, purpose, such as attempting to put pressure on him to pay money.[2])

Each of the foregoing four elements must be established by full legal proof before the offence of theft can be held as established. It must be remembered, however, that the same evidence or tract of evidence may well contain adminicles pointing to all four elements. For example, the store detective deponing to seeing the offender looking up and down the shop, grabbing the article from the counter, pocketing it and leaving the shop without paying would be a source of evidence of the existence of all of the four essential facts.

1 This *may* constitute *furtum usus* but it is doubtful if this is an offence in Scots law: see Gordon, *Criminal Law* paras 15-47 and 15-48.
2 Cf *Kidston v Annan* 1984 SCCR 20; *Black v Carmichael* 1992 SCCR 709 at 719 per LJ-G Hope.

ADMISSIBILITY OF EVIDENCE

Foundation in statement of facts

43.04   All the evidence tendered by the reporter must be founded on averments in the statement of facts accompanying the grounds of referral. In 1977, when amendment of the statement of facts was not competent, it was authoritatively stated:

'... no decision is to be taken on the application until, at the earliest, the conclusion of such evidence as the reporter has tendered *within the limits permitted by the statement of facts contained in the grounds of referral* [emphasis supplied] to which the basic rules of evidence apply.'[1]

Later in the same case it was stated:

'The only limit which rule 10[2] imposes is that proof of the offence must come from the facts found and not necessarily from the facts alleged, though presumably these facts found are those which have emerged from evidence tendered which is relevant to the grounds for referral set out by the reporter'.[3]

1 *McGregor v D* 1977 SC 330 at 337 per LP Emslie.
2 Of the Act of Sederunt (Social Work) (Sheriff Court Procedure) Rules 1971, now Act of Sederunt (Child Care and Maintenance Rules) 1997, SI 1997/291, r 3.50, discussed at 39.06 ff above.
3 *McGregor v D* 1977 SC 330 at 343 per Lord Cameron.

Fair notice and the possibility of amendment

43.05 The insistence that the evidence must emerge from the aver-ments in the statement of facts is simply the application to this form of procedure of the universal rule in Scottish legal procedure that suitably fair notice of any line of evidence must be given and that what may be proved is limited by what has been averred. Although the court now has a discretion to allow amendment of the statement of facts, such amendment, if material, may entitle any party affected to an adjourn-ment for investigation.[1]

1 SI 1997/291, rr 3.48 and 3.49, noticed at 29.10, 39.09 ff and 40.07 above.

The 'res gestae'

43.06 When an incident is referred to in a statement of facts then it becomes competent to lead evidence in relation to all that happened in connection with that incident. Sometimes questions arise as to whether matters preliminary to the incident are relevant or in relation to whether remarks or exclamations made immediately after the incident are admissible. The test as to the admissibility of such evidence is whether it can reasonably be said to be part of the things which happen (*res gestae*: the things which have been done). The concept has been defined thus:

'*Res gestae* is the whole thing that happened. Exclamations uttered or things done at the time by those concerned are part of the *res gestae*, and may be spoken to by those who heard or saw them. But an account given by anyone, whether child or adult, on going home, or at any time thereafter, is an account only, and not *res gestae*.'[1]

The effect of evidence justified as being part of the *res gestae* will be discussed presently.[2]

1 *Greer v Stirlingshire Road Trs* (1882) 9 R 1069 per Lord Young at 1076.
2 At 43.13 below.

The 'best evidence rule'

43.07   In 1887 Dickson on *Evidence*[1] stated that a

> '. . . party must adduce the best attainable evidence of the facts he means to prove. This rule is founded on the presumption, that one who tenders the less trustworthy of two kinds of proof within his reach, does so in order to produce an impression which the better proof would not create; for, if they would lead to the same result, he would probably not select the less convincing of them.'

As a statement of law this can no longer be sustained. In *F v Kennedy (No 2)*[2] it was decided that a previous statement on a matter which had not been put to the witness when giving evidence was nonetheless evidence in the cause although not the 'best evidence'. This is the law but the court emphasised that the matter was entirely one for the presiding sheriff:[3] that being so, the pleader, it is submitted, should be cautious of pre-judging that the sheriff will, in the absence of better available evidence, be prepared to accept secondary sources in a difficult case. It is accordingly thought that the logical rationale of Dickson's statement still has force and, as suggested already,[4] parties should be cautious of leading minimal evidence or second best evidence on a controversial matter. Sheriffs Macphail and Ruxton have summarised the position thus:

> 'While there is no general rule that secondary evidence is excluded when primary evidence can be adduced, if a party chooses to rely on secondary evidence when primary evidence is available, the judge of the facts may not be disposed to attach weight to the secondary evidence upon the view that it has probably been presented in the hope that it will produce a better impression than the primary evidence would create.'[5]

1 W G Dickson *A Treatise on the Law of Evidence in Scotland* (3rd edn, 1887).
2 1992 SCLR 750, 1993 SLT 1284, 1992 GWD 25-1401, 2nd Div; cf *Stewart v J* 1992 GWD 1-5, 4 Dec 1991, Extra Div.
3 1992 SCLR at 752F, 755F and *passim*.
4 At 41.03 above.
5 'Evidence' 10 *Stair Memorial Encyclopaedia* para 778; the joint authors cite W J Lewis *A Manual of the Law of Evidence in Scotland* (1925) p 256.

HEARSAY EVIDENCE, SECONDARY SOURCES OF EVIDENCE, THE CIVIL EVIDENCE (SCOTLAND) ACT 1988

Hearsay evidence – primary and secondary hearsay – terminology

43.08   'Hearsay evidence is evidence of what another person has said.'[1] If, for example, a police officer were to depone 'Mr Smith told me that he saw Willie Brown drive his car from his driveway at 6 p m on 1 March' then this evidence would, apart from the provisions of the Civil Evidence (Scotland) Act 1988, be inadmissible[2] and, if accidentally admitted, would not go any way towards proving the truth of the allegation that Willie Brown had stolen the car in these circumstances. As we shall see presently, the fact that something was said can itself be evidence. In that event the reported speech is sometimes called 'primary hearsay' or 'original evidence'.[3] Reported speech regarded as conveying information (e g the example cited in the foregoing paragraph) is termed secondary hearsay. 'Hearsay' alone generally means 'secondary hearsay'. 'Secondary evidence' is evidence which is less than the best available.

1 Macphail *Evidence* para *19.02.
2 Except possibly as evidence that the statement was made by Mr Smith – see 43.11 below.
3 Macphail and Ruxton 'Evidence' 10 *Stair Memorial Encyclopaedia* para 706.

Section 52(2)(i) grounds and the other grounds

43.09   The main provisions of the Civil Evidence (Scotland) Act 1988 (hereinafter 'the 1988 Act') are those abolishing the need for corroboration in civil causes, those permitting in civil causes the use of hearsay evidence to prove its content and those relaxing the rules in relation to the use of copy documents. The hearsay and corroboration provisions for civil cases alone introduce a sharp difference in the law of evidence applicable on the one hand to s 52(2)(i) cases, which are not civil proceedings under the 1988 Act, and on the other hand to cases based on the other conditions of referral, which are civil causes under the 1988 Act.[1] It should be noted that cases based on offences *against* children are of course civil causes for the purposes of the 1988 Act.

1 Civil Evidence (Scotland) Act 1988, s 9, as amended by Children (Scotland) Act 1995, Sch 4 para 44: definition of 'civil proceedings'.

The admissibility of hearsay under the 1988 Act and otherwise

43.10   As will be more fully discussed presently the admissibility of hearsay as evidence of its content is, under the Civil Evidence (Scotland) Act 1988, confined to hearsay of persons whose direct oral evidence would be admissible.[2] Moreover, the provisions of the Act do not extend to referrals on ground of an offence by a child.[1] It is accordingly still necessary to survey the law of admissible hearsay without regard to the provisions of the 1988 Act.

1 Civil Evidence (Scotland) Act 1988, s 2(1)(b).
2 CE(S)A 1988, s 9: definition of 'civil proceedings' in para (a).

MAIN CATEGORIES[1] OF HEARSAY WHICH MAY BE ADMISSIBLE APART FROM THE PROVISIONS OF THE 1988 ACT

'Primary hearsay' or ' original evidence' – hearsay establishing that something was said

43.11   Hearsay may be admissible to establish that something was said. For example, if it is put to a witness that he is concocting a story it may be competent to prove that someone heard him give the same account at an early stage.[2] In an important case an accused was held entitled to depone, in support of a defence of duress in a charge of illegal possession of firearms, that someone had threatened to kill him.[3] In *B v Harris*[4] there was evidence that the child had called her mother a 'bastard'. The report does not reveal how this evidence came to be a finding in fact of the sheriff but as the child was very young it is likely that the evidence consisted of a witness telling the court what the child had said. This would be a good example of 'primary hearsay' or hearsay as 'original evidence' since what was important was not the truth of what the child had said but the fact that she had said it.

1 The following list is not exhaustive, dealing only with the categories which seem likely to arise in s 68 proofs. For full examination of the various categories see *Walker and Walker on Evidence* Ch 29 and Macphail *Evidence* paras *19.22 ff; Macphail and Ruxton 'Evidence' in 10 *Stair Memorial Encyclopaedia* paras 705–718; Field and Raitt *The Law of Evidence in Scotland* (1996), Ch 8.
2 Cf *Burns v Colin McAndrew and Partners Ltd* 1963 SLT (Notes) 71, OH, per Lord Milligan.
3 *Subramaniam v Public Prosecutor* [1956] 1WLR 965 at 969, 970.
4 1989 SCLR 644.

Evidence of deceased person

43.12   In the case of a deceased person it is competent to prove what he said and use that statement as evidence as to the truth of what it contains.[1] Such a statement may not be admitted if there is reasonable suspicion that it is one-sided.[2] Before the statement of a deceased person may be used, prima facie evidence of the death must be led.

1 Cf *Moffat v Hunter* 1974 SLT (Sh Ct) 42.
2 Cf *William Thyne (Plastics) Ltd v Stenhouse Reed Shaw Scotland Ltd* 1979 SLT(Notes) 93 and the cases therein cited.

Statement forming part of the circumstances of the incident – the *res gestae*

43.13   As already noticed[1], the law recognises that events can, so to speak, overflow into speech and when some narrative has been made at a time so close to the events of the case as to feel almost part of these events, then such a statement may be admissible in evidence as forming part of the substantive event – part of the *res gestae*. The status and value of statements admissible as such is a complex matter and is discussed in the text-books.[2] In general, statements admissible by reason of forming part of the *res gestae* cannot be regarded as providing independent corroboration of the evidence of another as to what happened but there may be certain circumstances where such a statement may so provide. Sheriffs Macphail and Ruxton state:[3]

> 'Statements which are admissible under the *res gestae* exception may be used to prove the truth of their contents, and thus provide corroboration of other evidence. It is thought that the maker of the statement must be unknown,[4] or at the time of trial be unavailable as a witness[5] or deceased:[6] otherwise he should be adduced as a witness at the trial.'[7]

1 At 43.06 above.
2 See Macphail *Evidence* paras *19.69 ff and Field and Raitt *The Law of Evidence in Scotland* paras 8.20 ff.
3 'Evidence' 10 *Stair Memorial Encyclopaedia* para 710.
4 See *Ewing v Earl of Mar* (1851) 14 D 314. See also 10 *Stair Memorial Encyclopaedia*, para 711.
5 See *Harvy* (1835) Hume *Commentaries* II, Bell's *Notes* 293, and *O'Hara v Central SMT Co Ltd* 1941 SC 363, 1941 SLT 202.
6 *Ewing v Earl of Mar* (1851) 14 D 314. See 10 *Stair Memorial Encyclopaedia*, para 711.
7 J H A Macdonald *The Criminal Law of Scotland* (5th edn, 1948, ed J Walker and D J Stevenson) (reprinted 1986) p 316; *R v Andrews* [1987] AC 281 at 302, [1987] 1 All ER 513 at 521, HL.

De recenti statements

43.14 A statement made after the incident but not being part of the *res gestae* may be admissible if it was made only shortly after the incident. What is 'shortly' depends on circumstances but it may extend to days.[1] A *de recenti* statement cannot be evidence of the truth of its contents but can only be used to enhance (or, as the case may be, diminish) the reliability of the witness's testimony.[2] This matter is discussed more fully in the text-books.[3]

1 *Walker and Walker on Evidence* para 376.
2 *Begg v Tudhope* 1983 SCCR 32 at 39.
3 Macphail *Evidence* para *19.45; Macphail and Ruxton 'Evidence' 10 *Stair Memorial Encyclopaedia* para 707; Field and Raitt *The Law of Evidence in Scotland* paras 8.28 ff.

PROVISIONS ONLY OR PRINCIPALLY AFFECTING s 52(2)(i) CASES

Previous statements by witnesses in s 52(2)(i) cases

43.15 The Criminal Procedure (Scotland) Act 1995, s 263(4) provides:

> 'In a trial, a witness may be examined as to whether he has on any specified occasion made a statement on any matter pertinent to the issue at the trial different from the evidence given by him in the trial; and evidence may be led in the trial to prove that the witness made the different statement on the occasion specified.'

Technically, the rules of criminal practice have no application to referrals law – a s 68 proof is not a 'trial'. It is, however, thought that, having regard to the importation of 'the standard of proof required in criminal proceed-ings' to such proofs,[1] the court would be guided by the foregoing section when considering the admissibility of an earlier statement in a s 52(2)(i) referral. This provision does not apply to a precognition, unless a precog-nition on oath.[2] In certain specified circumstances (see 43.17 below) the contents of such a statement may be admissible to prove the truth of its contents: otherwise such a statement is only admissible in relation to credibility.

1 Children (Scotland) Act 1995, s 68(3)(b).
2 For discussion of precognition on oath see *Renton and Brown* (6th edn) para 13-03.

Previous statements by the referred child in s 52(2)(i) cases

43.16   Once again the criminal evidence code does not, technically, apply to s 68 proofs. A referred child is not an 'accused'. Nevertheless it is thought that the court would be guided by the criminal cases governing the admissibility of accused persons. The law on this subject is complex and only a survey of some frequently encountered situations will be addressed here. The most up-to-date authoritative survey is the passage in *Renton and Brown* (6th edn) paras 24-31 to 24-64, headed 'Evidence of Statements by Accused'.

Admissibility of prior statements of witnesses in s 52(2)(i) cases

43.17   Apparently following the principle in *Jamieson v HM Advocate*,[1] the Criminal Procedure (Scotland) Act 1995, s 260 introduced procedures enabling the statements of witnesses prior to the trial to be adopted into the evidence at the trial even when the witness was no longer ready to give evidence to the same effect as the earlier statement. The section must be studied but in essence it provides that a prior statement shall be admis-sible as evidence of its contents where direct oral evidence of the witness would be admissible, provided that certain conditions are satisfied. The conditions are:

(a) that the statement is contained in a document;
(b) that the witness in the course of his testimony indicates that the state-ment in the document was made by him; and
(c) that the witness would have been a competent witness at the time when the statement was made.

The section also provides that the foregoing limitations do not apply to a precognition on oath or to a statement made in connection with other proceedings in the United Kingdom or elsewhere, which statements have to be sufficiently authenticated before they are admissible. If the applica-bility of s 260 to referral cases were to be challenged it may be that in prac-tice the matter could in some cases be resolved by the sheriff applying the non-statutory principle in *Jamieson*, which seems to have been the inspira-tion of s 260. In *W v Kennedy*[2] (decided in January 1998, before the coming into force of the Civil Evidence (Scotland) Act 1988 and before the case of

Jamieson) a witness in a proof under the Social Work (Scotland) Act 1968, s 42 admitted making a statement to the police but declined to say if the contents of the statement were true. The contents of the statement supported the evidence of the referred child who had said that the witness had committed lewd and libidinous practices against her. Lord Sutherland, delivering the opinion of the First Division, said at 584L 'The statement is accordingly incorporated in the witness's evidence and is no longer merely hearsay by the police' and consequently held that the evidence of the referred child was sufficiently corroborated.[3]

1 1994 SLT 537.
2 1988 SLT 583.
3 In order to clarify the law, Lord Sutherland proceeded, to consider the position on the basis that the witness's statement was indeed hearsay and held that, on this assumption and in the special context of a s 42 proof, the statement, although hearsay, was capable of going towards proving the truth of its contents. It was decided in *F v Kennedy (No 1)* 1992 SCLR 139, 1993 SLT 1277, 2nd Div, noting that the Civil Evidence (Scotland) Act 1988 was now in force, that the admissibility of hearsay must now fall to be determined by the provisions of that Act. However, while undermining that part of the opinion in *W* which held that the hearsay was capable of proving the truth of its contents, this does not appear to take away from that part of the decision in *W* which held that the witness's statement was not hearsay and was capable of going towards proving the truth of its contents.

Previous 'self-serving' or 'mixed' statement by an accused person

43.18 An earlier statement – for example in reply to caution and charge – by an accused person which exculpates him or supports a line of defence may generally be relied upon by that person to support any evidence given by him by showing that he has consistently told the same story, and unless part of the *res gestae* such a statement cannot be relied upon by the accused to prove the truth of its contents; but a 'mixed' statement which partly inculpates and partly exculpates the accused may be admissible for the truth of its contents.[1] The law relating to such statements is complex and the pleader should be ready to cite the latest authorities.[2]

1 *Morrison v HM Advocate* 1990 SCCR 235 at 247, 248, discussed by Macphail and Ruxton in 'Evidence' 10 *Stair Memorial Encyclopaedia* para 720.
2 E g *Scaife v HM Advocate* 1992 SCCR 845; *Robertson v HM Advocate* 1995 SCCR 152 – see *Renton and Brown* (6th edn) para 24-64 and the cases therein cited.

Statements to the police: the rule against unfairness

43.19 As we have seen,[1] the right of the citizen in Scotland not to be required to incriminate himself is well entrenched. The courts have accordingly recognised that when a person is being tried any confession allegedly made to the police after charge or while the accused was a suspect must, to be admissible, have been emitted freely and not obtained unfairly. It has been recognised as a corollary of this that a statement can scarcely be said to have been emitted freely or fairly obtained if, when making it, the accused person was unaware of his right to remain silent. Equally, even if formally advised of his right to remain silent, the statement will be regarded as inadmissible if improper pressure was put upon the accused to make the statement. In order to inform the suspect of his rights the police should administer what is called the 'common law' caution. The import of the caution is that the accused person is about to be charged, that he need not say anything in reply but that if he does say something that will be taken down in writing and used in evidence. In order to try to secure that improper pressure is not employed, the courts try to ensure that a statement is truly voluntary before accepting it in evidence.

1 At 37.12 ff above.

Interpretation of these principles

43.20   In *Tonge v HM Advocate* Lord Justice-General Emslie said:

> 'Now, as is pointed out in Walkers' *Law of Evidence in Scotland*, p 39, para 45: "It is proper practice that, when a person is charged with a crime, the caution should be given, since, without it, the reading of the charge may be interpreted by the accused as a question, or as an invitation to reply, in which case any statement then made is not spontaneous and voluntary." I go further and say that the proper practice is now so long and so well entrenched that it may be taken that a full caution before a charge is made is a requirement of the law itself. The reading of a charge is calculated to provoke a response from the accused and it is quite essential that he should know, in advance, of his right to silence, and of the use which may be made of any response which he chooses to make. To charge an accused person without cautioning him is to put pressure upon him which may induce a response and I have no doubt that by accusing Gray, although not in the formal language of a charge, the accusation was clearly calculated, as a formal charge is calculated, to induce a response from the person accused.'[1]

Not long thereafter Lord Justice-General Emslie gave the classic statement of the fundamental principle in *Lord Advocate's Reference (No 1 of 1983)*:[2]

> 'A suspect's self-incriminating answers to police questioning will indeed be admissible in evidence unless it can be affirmed that they have been extracted by unfair means. The simple and intelligible test which has worked well in practice is whether what has taken place was fair or not. (see the opinion of the Lord Justice-General (Clyde) in *Brown v HM Advocate* [1966 SLT 105] at p 107). In each case the admissibility of answers by a suspect to police questioning becomes an issue it will be necessary to consider the whole relevant circumstances in order to discover whether or not there has been unfairness on the part of the police resulting in the extraction from the suspect of the answers in question. Unfairness may take many forms but "if answers are to be excluded they must be seen to have been extracted by unfair means which place cross-examination, pressure and deception in close company" (see my own opinion in *Jones v Milne*, 1975 SLT at p 5).'

1 *Tonge v HM Advocate* 1982 SLT 506 at 512.
2 1984 SLT 337 at 340.

Application of these principles

43.21   It is important to note, as was pointed out in the case of *Tonge*, that the consideration that a person has been detained under the Criminal

Justice (Scotland) Act 1980, s 2 (which empowers a police constable, among other things, to detain a suspect and put questions to him) the same rules as to admissibility of evidence apply, with the result that if a suspect, detained under s 2, makes an incriminating reply that reply will not constitute evidence against him unless it is preceded by a full 'common law' caution and is not obtained unfairly. It would, as Lord Justice-General Emslie stated, 'have been proper practice to caution a suspect in Gray's position before he was allowed to proceed with a statement and, in my opinion, nothing in section 2 of the Act of 1980 excuses compliance with that practice'.[1]

1 *Tonge v H M Advocate* 1982 SLT 506 at 513.

43.22 It does not even follow that *any* statement made even after a caution is admissible. The court has also to be satisfied that no improper pressure was put on the accused after the caution was administered. Thus any 'gross and bullying cross-examination'[1] would clearly render the confession inadmissible. Failure to administer a proper caution to a person who is in police custody as a suspect is now, following *Tonge v HM Advocate*,[2] probably fatal to the admissibility of the 'confession'. Provided that a caution has been administered, then it is a matter, when jury trial is not involved, for the presiding judge to decide whether, in all the circumstances, there has been unfairness in the form of improper pressure, threats of violence, actual violence or the like, which has given rise to the 'confession' and on his decision as to whether there has been such unfair pressure will the admissibility of the evidence of the 'confession' depend.

1 *Hartley v HM Advocate* 1979 SLT 26 at 28 per Lord Avonside.
2 1982 SLT 506.

Witnesses of limited maturity or intelligence

43.23 It has been said correctly that the court must be particularly vigilant in considering a confession of a very young person or a person of limited intelligence,[1] but in *Hartley v HM Advocate*[2] a confession of murder made at 2.30 a m by a mentally disordered 17 year-old-boy, after having been in police custody for 12 hours during which he was seen by police officers from time to time, was not regarded, by virtue of these facts, as being inadmissible: the matter was left for the jury to decide and the jury, by finding the accused guilty, must be assumed to have decided the matter in the Crown's favour.

1 Field and Raitt *The Law of Evidence in Scotland* (1996) para 14-36, citing *B v HM Advocate* 1995 SLT 961 and *HM Advocate v Gilgannon* 1983 SCCR 10: cf *HM Advocate v Rigg* 1946 JC 1.
2 1979 SLT 26.

43.24 The law regarding admissibility of confessions made to the police by accused persons in police custody on suspicion of the crime concerned may be, very broadly, summarised as requiring an affirmative answer to the two questions 'Was a caution duly administered before the statement was made?' and 'Was everything that happened done fairly in respect of the accused person?' The subject can, however, be an intricate one and it broadens out into consideration of the admissibility of sundry 'stray' comments made by accused persons in custody and in the course of criminal investigation. In a marginal case the pleader should be ready to cite up-to-date authorities.[1] The concept of a 'trial within a trial' in order to establish the admissibility or otherwise of a disputed confession has already been noticed.[2]

1 See the discussion of this matter in *Renton and Brown* (6th edn) paras 18-21 to 18-45; Sheriff Gordon's commentary on *Tonge v HM Advocate* 1982 SCCR 313 at p 352; ch 20; Macphail *Evidence* and Field and Raitt *The Law of Evidence in Scotland* (1996) ch 14.
2 *Thomson v Crowe* 1999 SCCR 1003. See above 37.23.

Statements by accused to persons other than the official investigators

43.25   Statements by the accused to persons other than police officers, Inland Revenue officers and other official investigators are generally admissible to prove their contents.[1]

1 *Renton and Brown* (6th edn) paras 24-52 to 24-55 and the cases therein cited.

Incriminatory statement by co-accused

43.26   A statement made by a co-accused incriminating the accused may be admissible against the *accused when made in the presence of and acquiesced in by the accused* in circumstances wherein the accused could reasonably be taken to know that his silence might be taken to imply acquiescence.[1] Although in referral cases there cannot technically be a 'co-accused', there would seem to be no reason why a statement of a witness apparently jointly implicated in an offence (whether by or against a child) should not be evidence against the other alleged joint offender, provided that the foregoing conditions are satisfied. The 'engineering' of one accused into the presence of another in order to be present when the other accused is likely to make a reply incriminating the first accused will not produce admissible evidence against the first accused.[2]

1 E g *Annan v Bain and Hamill* 1986 SCCR 60.
2 *HM Advocate v Davidson* 1968 SLT 17.

Evidence obtained by illegal or irregular means – trial within a trial

43.27   It is thought that in s 68 proofs the court would be guided by the general principles laid down by Lord Justice-General Cooper in the leading case of *Lawrie v Muir:*[1]

> 'From the standpoint of principle it seems to me that the law must strive to reconcile two highly important interests which are liable to come into conflict – (a) the interest of the citizen to be protected from illegal or irregular invasions of his liberties by the authorities, and (b) the interest of the State to secure that evidence bearing upon the commission of crime and

necessary to enable justice to be done shall not be withheld from Courts of law on any merely formal or technical ground. Neither of these objects can be insisted upon to the uttermost. The protection of the citizen is primarily protection for the innocent citizen against unwarranted, wrongful and perhaps high-handed interference … Irregularities require to be excused, and infringements of the formalities of the law in relation to these matters are not lightly to be condoned. Whether any given irregularity ought to be excused depends upon the nature of the irregularity and the circumstances under which it was committed.'

There is a discussion of this matter with full citation of authority in *Renton and Brown* (6th edn) para 24-143 and in Macphail *Evidence* paras *21.05 to S21.06A. The mode of having the sheriff decide on any disputed issue as to the admissibility of evidence in a proof based on a s 52(2)(i) condition by means of a trial within a trial has already been discussed.[2]

1 1950 JC 19 at 26, 27.
2 At 37.19 ff above.

Reference to medical and other reports and records in s 52(2)(i) cases

43.28   In the absence of agreement, original records should be obtained and spoken to in s 68 proofs where the ground of referral is an offence by the child.

EFFECT OF CIVIL EVIDENCE (SCOTLAND) ACT 1988 ON VALUE OF HEARSAY IN NON-s 52(i) CASES

The statutory provision

43.29   The Civil Evidence (Scotland) Act 1988 provides inter alia:

'2.—(1) In any civil proceedings—
 (a) evidence shall not be excluded solely on the ground that it is hearsay;
 (b) a statement made by a person otherwise than in the course of the proof shall be admissible as evidence of any matter contained in the statement of which direct oral evidence by that person would be admissible; and
 (c) the court, or as the case may be the jury, if satisfied that any fact has been established by evidence in those proceedings, shall be entitled to find that fact proved by the evidence notwithstanding that the evidence is hearsay.
(2) Nothing in this section shall effect the admissibility of any statement as evidence of the fact that the statement was made.'

Even before the enactment of this provision the courts were amenable to a liberal interpretation of the hearsay rule in order to facilitate the use of the evidence of children.[1] However following this provision there have been several important decisions[2] which have radically changed the effect of hearsay evidence in cases other than those based on an alleged offence by a child.[2] While this text was in proof a Court of Five Judges held (in *T v T* (10 November 2000, unreported) Court of Session) that the hearsay statement of a child was admissible to prove its facts even although the child had not been found to be a competent witness, thus overruling *F v Kennedy (No 1)* 1992 SC 28.

1 Cf *W v Kennedy* 1988 SCLR 236, but see *F v Kennedy (No 1)* 1992 SCLR 139, 1993 SLT 1277, discussed at 43.17 above, n ff.
2 For example: *F v Kennedy (No 1)* 1992 SC 28, 1993 SLT 1277, 1992 SCLR 139; *F v Kennedy (No 2)* 1993 SLT 1284, 1992 SCLR 750; *Ferguson v S* 1993 SCLR 712; *M v Ferguson* 1994 SCLR 497; *M v Kennedy* 1993 SCLR 69; *L v L* 1996 SLT 6767, 1996 SCLR 11; *Sanderson v McManus* 1997 SC 55, HL.

Wide scope of these provisions – but some limitation

43.30   The provisions extend to hearsay consisting of written matter, but unless the written material is covered by a rule of court – for example, the provision for affidavit evidence in ordinary family causes[1] or is a part of a business record docquetted in accordance with the Civil Evidence (Scotland) Act 1988, s 5(1)– the written evidence will require to be spoken to by someone (not necessarily the author) who can identify it as being what it purports to be. The Act also provides:

> '6.—(1) For the purposes of any civil proceedings, a copy of a document, purporting to be authenticated by a person responsible for the making of the copy, shall, unless the court otherwise directs, be –
> (a) deemed a true copy; and
> (b) treated for evidential purposes as if it were the document itself.'

1 Ordinary Cause Rules, r 29.3(1). This rule has, of course, no application to referral cases; Act of Sederunt (Child Care and Maintenance Rules) 1997, Sch 3.

Preservation of the competency requirement

43.31   As already noticed,[1] it is a prerequisite of any witness's giving evidence that he or she be a 'competent' witness. The inclusion of the words 'of which direct evidence by that person would be admissible' in the Civil Evidence (Scotland) Act 1988, s 2(1)(b) have the effect of requiring that the witness whose hearsay is sought to be relied upon is a competent witness. Accordingly where hearsay evidence was led in relation to a child witness who, when called to give evidence, said nothing at all, it was held on appeal that the provisions of s 2(1)(b) had not been satisfied in respect that, since it had been impossible for the presiding sheriff to ascertain if the child knew the difference between truth and telling lies, it had not been shown that direct evidence from the child would have been admissible.[2] In the same case it was observed that the more flexible approach to hearsay evinced in *W v Kennedy*[3] could no longer be regarded as acceptable since the admissibility of hearsay has now been regulated by the 1988 Act and that accordingly the provisions of that Act must be complied with. As noticed above at 43.29 *F v Kennedy (No 1)* has been overruled by a Court of Five Judges in *T v T*. This case did not, however, do away with the 'competency requirement' in relation to a child *giving evidence*, although the remarks of Lord Bonomy at para [13] of his opinion give some support for the view that the competency requirement itself may required to be reconsidered.

1 At 37.06 above.
2 *F v Kennedy (No 1)* 1992 SC 28, 1992 SCLR 139, 1993 SLT 1277, 2nd Div.
3 1988 SCLR 236 at 239, 240.

Operation of s 2(1)(b) – retraction of earlier statement

43.32   Once, however, the competency requirement has been met, the operation of this provision is impressive. As already noticed,[1] it has been held by the Second Division that a sheriff was entitled to prefer hearsay evidence to evidence given in court even although the witness had not been asked about the matter in court: and notwithstanding, as was also held, that valid criticisms were made as to the way in which the hearsay evidence had been obtained. The provision is of particular importance in connection with the retraction of earlier statements – a frequently encountered situation in child abuse cases. In *K v Kennedy*[2] the evidence before the sheriff had included evidence of a previous statement by the child to the police and the retraction by the child of that statement when giving evidence before the sheriff against a background of there being other witnesses who might have given evidence but were not called. The sheriff relied on the evidence contained in the retracted statement. Lord Sutherland, delivering the opinion of the Division, stated:

> 'The sheriff has to proceed on the basis of the evidence that is before him and is not bound to refrain from relying upon it just because there might have been other evidence which could have been of assistance one way or the other. It is clear from his note that the sheriff considered the evidence very carefully in this case and it is also clear that he did not lightly take the step of proceeding on the basis of the original statement by the girl which was subsequently retracted ... While there is no doubt that the evidence in this case was thin, we are of opinion that it could not possibly be said that no sheriff was entitled to take the course which the sheriff did in this case.'

1 At 43.07 above; see *F v Kennedy (No 2)* 1993 SLT 1284, 1992 SCLR 750.
2 1992 SCLR 386.

Confession or statement by party to litigation

43.33   At common law a statement made by a party to a litigation will, if otherwise relevant, not be inadmissible merely by reason of being hearsay. If 'against interest' i e if in the nature of a confession or an admission which will go against the person in the current litigation, then his statement, if not otherwise objectionable, will be admissible against him and will be evidence tending to establish as true the contents of the statement.[1] The importance of this common law exception to the hearsay rule has been almost eliminated by the operation of the Civil Evidence (Scotland) Act 1988, s 2(1)(b). A parent has been held to be a party under the Social Work (Scotland) Act 1968.[2]

1 It has been held in England that as care proceedings under the Children and Young Persons Act 1969, s 1 are non-adversarial the statement of a third party who *de facto* had control of the child was admissible to prove the truth of the statement: see *Humberside CC v DPR (infant)* [1977] 3 All ER 964. In *W v Kennedy* 1988 SLT 583 Lord Sutherland followed this case but, as already noticed, in *F v Kennedy (No 1)* 1992 SCLR 139, 1993 SLT 1277 it was held that after the passing of the Civil Evidence (Scotland) Act 1988 the ratio of *W v Kennedy* ceased to apply.
2 *McGregor v T and P* [1975] AC 14 at 21.

OTHER ASPECTS OF ADMISSIBILITY OF EVIDENCE

Evidence irregularly obtained – care and protection cases

43.34   In the context of care and protection cases the court might not consider itself to be bound by the restrictions of this branch of the law, which has its principal application in criminal trials. In *F v Kennedy (No 2)*[1] evidence of statements by children were adduced and it appeared that the 'Cleveland' guidelines had not been observed by those interviewing the children. Lord Justice-Clerk Ross observed: '. . . but the mere fact that the guidelines had not been followed did not mean that the sheriff was not entitled to accept the evidence of the children as reliable.' It is submitted, however, that the dictum 'irregularities require to be excused' is of general application and that therefore the pleader in a referral proof desiring to found on irregularly obtained evidence should come prepared to explain and try to excuse the irregularity.

1 1993 SLT 1284, 1993 SCLR 750.

Material evidence lost or unavailable

43.35   When original evidence has been destroyed or lost or is otherwise unavailable, then it is essential to lead evidence explaining how it has come to be lost or whether there is a good reason for its being unavailable. It will then be a matter for the court to decide in the first place whether the reason for non-production is acceptable and then, if it is acceptable, to consider whether or not the missing material is so essential to the proof as to be fatal from the point of view of the person having the *onus* of proof. In 1942 Lord Justice-General Normand put the matter thus:

> 'The question in each case is whether the real evidence is essential for proving the case against the accused. In a case of forgery I conceive it would be very difficult to prove the charge unless the document alleged to be forged was in court, but even in that case I am not satisfied that the proof would be impossible.'[1]

But there may be cases wherein it will be essential in the interests of justice for the defence to have access to the original evidence.[2]

1 *Maciver v Mackenzie* 1942 JC 51 at 54.
2 *Anderson v Laverock* 1973 SLT 12 at 14.

Material evidence not produced but inessential

43.36   In 1980 this matter was considered by the High Court. An accused had been convicted in the district court of stealing 78 newspapers from a common close. The accused appealed on the ground that the proceedings were vitiated by the failure to produce the newspapers. The High Court rejected this argument and observed:

> '... there is a very frank and proper concession by counsel that actual production of the newspapers themselves was not essential to the proof of the charge against his client. Nor, indeed, was he able to explain what particular purpose in the interests of his client, or in the administration of justice, would have been served by the production of a bundle of innominate journals, to the number of 100 or 102. In these circumstances we are clearly of the opinion that production of these newspapers, which we understand to have been delivered in accordance with the daily needs of the customers, was neither necessary nor in any event convenient or practicable in this particular case.'[1]

1 *Hughes v Skeen* 1980 SLT (Notes) 13.

Witness refreshing memory from notes – s 52(2)(i) cases

43.37   It is not acceptable for a witness in the course of his or her testimony to consult a precognition: the courts have long recognised that a precognition represents the version of what the witness will say filtered through the mind of the precognition taker.[1] It is, however, acceptable for a witness, to refresh his memory by consulting notes which he has made at the time of an event. When this is desired to be done a foundation should be laid by having the witness confirm that the notes which he wishes to consult were made at the time of the incident and not later. A police officer's notebook is prima facie confidential and unless the police witness actually produces his notes in the witness box in order to refresh his memory then production of the notes cannot be insisted upon by the other side.[2]

1 *Kerr v HM Advocate* 1958 JC 14 at 53.
2 *Hinshelwood v Auld* 1926 JC 4; it is not clear whether the notes of a witness who could not claim such confidentiality (i e not a police officer) would enjoy this immunity, particularly if, for example, the witness agreed that he had consulted his notes beforehand in order to refresh his memory.

Reference to medical and other reports and records in care and protection cases

43.38   In practice a medical report is frequently lodged and spoken to by the verbal testimony of the doctor who prepared it: but permitting a doctor to give his or her evidence in this way may be undesirable and in a case where the medical evidence is crucial the original records, or an acceptable copy thereof,[1] should be lodged and spoken to. In general, social work reports may be lodged and spoken to by their authors but in a case where their contents are controversial, it may be important, in the absence of agreement, to have the original records, or acceptable copies, spoken to by the person who compiled them in order that they may have the fullest possible persuasive effect.

1 Civil Evidence (Scotland) Act 1988, s 6(1).

Lodging of productions – presentation of productions: good practice

43.39   There is nothing at all in the Children (Scotland) Act 1995 or the various rules requiring advance lodging of productions or indeed pre-scribing any formalities in relation to productions. Proceedings are to be conducted summarily[1] and simplicity and informality[2] are important considerations. In practice the procedures of summary criminal trials tend to be adopted in relation to the lodging of productions as to other aspects of these proofs, and this seems reasonable. Following the anal-ogy with such trials, there is no necessity for either side to lodge pro-ductions in advance and it is sufficient for them to be produced at the proof and spoken to by the haver. It is also convenient to adopt from criminal procedure the convention of separately numbering written productions, including such items as photographs, from material or 'labelled' productions such as knives or articles of clothing or items which have been stolen and which will be referred to as 'Label No 1' etc. The practice of having witnesses sign labels 'in lieu of' produc-tions, such as motor cars, which for reasons of convenience cannot nor-mally be produced in court, is followed in these proofs as it is in summary trials. In a cases wherein there are more than a few written productions it is good practice to present them in good order, for example in an indexed ring-book.

1 Act of Sederunt (Child Care and Maintenance Rules) 1997, SI 1997/291, r 3.20.
2 Cf per LP Emslie in *McGregor v D* 1977 SC 330 at 336.

Notifying productions – good practice

43.40   Although there is no formal requirement to intimate productions in advance, it may be appropriate, in a case where important conclusions may fall to be drawn from productions, whether produced by the reporter or other party, for advance warning to be given: the court will not normally look with favour on the element of surprise and, recognising the short period of preparation which is often a feature of these proofs, may feel compelled out of fairness to allow an adjournment in the event of surprise evidence of this type. As already noticed, it is also good practice for all 'sides' to exchange witness lists.

Evidence in the possession of a prosecutor

43.41   The Children (Scotland) Act 1995, s 53(4)–(7) enacts important new provisions entitling the reporter, after the lodging a s 68 application, or the lodgement of an application under s 85 of the Act[1] who has made such application, to apply to any prosecutor to supply him with any evidence lawfully obtained in the course of investigating a crime or suspected crime, being evidence which may assist the sheriff in determining the application. A prosecutor, on receiving such a request, must comply with it unless he reasonably believes he must retain it. The Lord Advocate may direct that evidence be supplied without a request from the reporter in any specified case or in a class of cases. Even before the enactment of these provisions, reporters generally received all reasonable co-operation from the procurators fiscal of Scotland and in practice this continues, usually without formal resort to s 53.

1 Discussed at ch 57 below.

Parents, relevant persons and spouses as witnesses

43.42   It was decided in proceedings under the Social Work (Scotland) Act 1968 that the position of a parent as confidential adviser of the child did not impinge upon the general rule that a parent was a competent and compellable witness for the reporter when an offence by the child was alleged[1] and it is thought that the position of a parent as having the responsibility for direction and guidance of the child[2] would not prevent a parent from being a competent and compellable witness in a case with ground of referral under the Children (Scotland) Act 1995, s 52(2)(i). It is thought that a relevant person would likewise be competent and compellable. It is also seems clear that in a s 68 proof a spouse would be a competent and compellable witness in relation to evidence tending to incriminate his or her spouse.[3]

1 *McGregor v T and Anr* 1975 SLT 76 at 82.
2 Children (Scotland) Act 1995, s 1(1).
3 Cf *Bates v HM Advocate* 1989 SLT 701.

CHAPTER 44

Sufficiency of evidence: II – corroboration in s 52(2)(i) cases

THE NECESSITY FOR CORROBORATION[1]

Historical background

44.01 The insistence on evidence from more than one source in respect of essential matters of fact is a distinctive feature of the Scots legal tradition. Lord Stair, writing in 1693 regarded this as a universal principle founded upon divine authority:

> 'In all controversies witnesses are adhibited to determine, as a common rule among all nations; which is confirmed by the word of God, "In the mouth of two or three witnesses let every word be established:" ... thence also it followed, that one witness cannot make sufficient probation, whatsoever be the quality or veracity of that witness ...'[2]

As noticed in the previous chapter, the Civil Evidence (Scotland) Act 1988 abolished the need for corroboration in civil causes, but in criminal matters, with one or two exceptions which do not concern us here,[3] evidence from more than one source is still necessary to prove essential facts. The 'basic rules of evidence' apply and there is no rule more basic than that requiring corroborated evidence before a person may be convicted in a criminal court. The necessity for corroboration of the committing of an offence by a child was recognised, and indeed presupposed without argument, in *D v Kennedy*.[4]

---

1 Part VIII of *Renton and Brown* (6th edn), edited by Sheriff Sir Gerald H Gordon QC, and regularly updated, contains the most valuable, comprehensive and up-to-date discussion of evidence in the criminal sphere and no pleader arguing an evidential point in a criminal context can afford not to consult it.
2 *Institutions of the Law of Scotland* IV, 43, 1 and 2; cf *Deuteronomy* cxix, v, 15.
3 E g Parking offences.
4 1974 SLT 168.

Essential facts

44.02 It must be kept in mind that the insistence upon corroborated evidence does not mean that two witnesses must speak to every incidental fact making up the case. Nor does it imply that two eyewitnesses to, say, the commission of an offence must always be produced – there may be circumstantial evidence such as fingerprints or bloodstains. Only the essential facts require to be proved by corroborated evidence. The concept of essential facts has been discussed already.[1]

---

1 At 43.03 above.

What amounts to corroboration – general[1]

44.03   There must be conjunction or convergence of testimony[2] – it is not enough, for example, for there to be two witnesses speaking to, say, a punch but each giving a substantially different account of the surrounding circumstances.[3] Where there is one witness whose testimony provides one source of evidence of the essential fact under consideration then the court may find corroboration in any evidence which confirms or supports that account.[4] The statement of a witness to the police, if admissible to prove its contents, may provide sufficient corroboration.[5]

1 This is a big subject – see discussion in *Renton and Brown* (6th edn) paras 24-69 ff.
2 *Fox v HM Advocate* 1998 JC 94, 1998 SLT 335, 1998 SCCR 115.
3 Cf *Young v HM Advocate* 1997 SLT 405.
4 *Fox v HM Advocate* 1998 JC 94, 1998 SLT 335, 1998 SCCR 115.
5 See 43.17 above; cf *W v Kennedy* 1988 SLT 583.

Weight of evidence

44.04   The importance of leading evidence of sufficient weight, as opposed to the legal minimum, has already been noticed.[1]

1 At 41.02 above.

CONFESSIONS – JUDICIAL AND EXTRA-JUDICIAL

Terminology

44.05   A plea of guilty in criminal proceedings is a judicial confession and is conclusive against the maker without evidence being led. Similarly, the acceptance by child and parent may be accepted by the hearing and, at the s 68 stage, by the sheriff, unless satisfied that evidence should be heard. A confession to the police or others is an extra-judicial confession.

Corroboration of extra-judicial confession

44.06   While the law is astute to protect any accused person, including of course an accused child, from any improper or unfair pressure towards producing a confession,[1] the court, once it has been established that a confession has been freely made in circumstances to which no irregularity can be attributed, attaches a high evidential value to such an admission, provided it is in unambiguous terms. Accordingly in some circumstances the amount of corroboration of such a confession in order to establish an essential fact may not be great,[2] but 'There is, however, no rule of law that very little is needed to corroborate an unequivocal confession'.[3] Repeated confessions do not, of course, afford corroboration, since a person cannot corroborate himself. The making of a confession, unless a circumstantial (or 'special knowledge') confession (see 44.07 to 44.09 below) does not require to be corroborated,[4] although it is common practice, where two police officers have been present when a confession is said to have been made, to adduce both officers.

1 *Cf Hartley v HM Advocate* 1979 SLT 26 and the cases referred to therein – see discussion at 43.22 and 43.23 above.
2 *Sinclair v Clark* 1962 JC 57 at 62.
3 *Renton and Brown* para 24-78, citing *Meredith v Lees* 1992 SLT 802.
4 *Mills v HM Advocate* 1935 JC 77 and the cases cited in *Renton and Brown*, para 24-78 n 1.

Circumstantial ('special knowledge') confessions

44.07   When a confession, as well as admitting to the crime involved, contains a significant amount of detail in relation to matters so intimately connected with the commission of the crime and it can reasonably be inferred that the accused had no reason to be aware of these matters unless he was guilty of the crime then, provided it is clear that he had no other way of knowing of these matters, the adducing of independent evidence as to these points of detail will itself constitute the required corroboration. One of the institutional authorities on Scottish criminal law, Sheriff Sir Archibald Alison, put the matter thus in 1832:

> 'If a person is apprehended on a charge of theft and he tells the officer who seized him, that if he will go to such and such a place and look under such a bush, he will find the stolen goods; or he is charged with murder or assault, and he says that he threw the bloody weapon into such a pool, in such a river, and it is there searched for and found; without doubt, these are such strong confirmations of the truth of the confession, as renders it of itself sufficient, if the *corpus* is established *aliunde* [i e by independent testimony] to convict the prisoner.'[1]

Confessions of this kind are sometimes called 'self-corroborating' confessions but this expression is misleading and should be avoided since, as the passage from Alison makes clear, it is the leading of independent evidence as to the truth of the detail in the confession which gives the confession its peculiarly strong value. The term 'circumstantial confession', used by Sheriff Sir Gerald Gordon,[2] is perhaps the neatest expression but the term 'special knowledge confession' is frequently used. The principle has been restated in modern times in the case of *Connolly v HM Advocate*[3] and in the well-known case of *Manuel v HM Advocate*.[4] In *McAvoy v HM Advocate*[5] Lord Justice-Clerk Wheatley formulated the principle thus:

> 'The fact that the appellant admitted knowing of these things when otherwise he had no reason to be aware of them was sufficient to provide the requisite corroboration [of the accused's confession].'

1 Alison *Criminal Law* vol 2 p 584.
2 E g in *Renton and Brown* para 24-82 (qv).
3 1958 SLT 79.
4 1958 JC 41.
5 1983 SLT 16 at 18.

Characteristics of circumstantial confession

44.08   The presentation in court of a circumstantial confession requires care. There can be no circumstantial confession if the specialised information has been conveyed to the accused person – for example by being informed by the police in detail of the nature of their inquiries – or if the charge which has been preferred against the accused is so detailed as to suggest the specialised matters. Care must therefore be taken, when investigating the case, to make sure that the knowledge has not been imparted to the accused by some other agency. Once this has been confirmed then care should be taken when presenting the evidence in court to make this aspect clear to the court.

Corroboration in relation to the making of a circumstantial confession

44.09   When a circumstantial confession is to be relied on as the only substantial evidence in the case, the making of the confession itself should be proved by corroborated evidence.[1] As to proof of the matters spoken of in the circumstantial confession, *Renton and Brown* state: 'The position is not absolutely clear, but it seems that that evidence, unlike the evidence of the making of the confession, does not need to be corroborated.'[2]

1 *Low v HM Advocate* 1993 SCCR 493. Cf *Mitchell v HM Advocate* 1966 SCCR 917.
2 Paragraph 24-82, citing *Smith v HM Advocate* 1978 SCCR (Supp) 203.

CORROBORATION BY CONNECTED CRIMINAL ACTS – THE 'MOOROV DOCTRINE'

44.10   The writer would respectfully adopt the words of the Sheriffs Walker:

> 'Where an accused is charged with two or more crimes and only one witness implicates him in each, they afford mutual corroboration if the crimes are so inter-related by character, circumstances and time as to justify an inference that they are parts of a course of criminal conduct systematically pursued by the accused.'[1]

This principle is generally referred to as the '*Moorov* doctrine', a reference to the leading case of *Moorov v HM Advocate*.[2] In this case the accused was charged with a number of sexual assaults on women which were only spoken of by the victims themselves. It was held that it was permissible to regard each individual act as corroboration of the other, provided that (a) the crimes were of the same kind, (b) they were committed in similar circumstances, and (c) they were committed at times reasonably close to each other, so that all these factors taken together yielded the inference that the acts 'were truly connected or related as parts or incidents of a persistent campaign of lustful indulgence pursued by the [accused] at the expense of his female employees'.[3] The doctrine is frequently invoked in cases involving sexual assault but it is by no means confined to such cases and can be, and frequently is, relied upon in cases covering the entire spectrum of crime.[4] It can be applied when only two offences are alleged.[5] An incident where there has not been positive identification of the accused person cannot constitute one of the offences in a 'Moorov' pattern.[6] While there is no absolute rule, there appears to be no case in which the *Moorov* doctrine has been applied where the interval between offences was three years or more.[7]

1 *Walker and Walker on Evidence* p 409.
2 1930 JC 68.
3 Per LJ-G Clyde in *Moorov* at 77.
4 See the discussion of the doctrine in *Walker and Walker on Evidence* p 410, in Macphail *Evidence* at para 23.32 ff, in Macphail and Ruxton, 'Evidence' in 10 *Stair Memorial Encyclopaedia* para 769, and in Field and Raitt *The Law of Evidence in Scotland* paras 7–66 to 7–82.
5 *M'Cudden v HM Advocate* 1952 JC 86.
6 *M'Rae v HM Advocate* 1975 JC 34
7 *Russell v HM Advocate* 1990 SCCR 18.

IDENTIFICATION OF THE ACCUSED CHILD

44.11   Identification of the person accused is always an essential fact as to which evidence from more than one source must be adduced.[1] Where a person identifies an accused at the time or at an identification parade but does not identify in court then the proof of the prior identification is sufficient in law to constitute one source of evidence identifying the accused person.[2] Identification may be by voice[3] or by reference to a video recording.[4]

1 *Morton v HM Advocate* 1938 JC 50; for up-to-date discussions of this important principle see *Renton and Brown* paras 24-73 and 24-74 and Field and Raitt *The Law of Evidence in Scotland* paras 7-25 to 7-47.
2 *Muldoon v Herron* 1970 JC 30.
3 *McGiveran v Auld* (1894) 1 Adam 448; *Burrrows v HM Advocate* 1951 SLT (Notes) 69.
4 *Bowie v Tudhope* 1986 SCCR 205.

CHAPTER 45

Sufficiency of evidence:
III – miscellaneous

PROOF OF CRIMINAL CONVICTIONS IN CARE AND PROTECTION CASES[1]

The statutory provisions

45.01 The Law Reform (Miscellaneous Provisions) (Scotland) Act 1968, s 10 provides inter alia as follows:

'(1) In any civil proceedings the fact that a person has been convicted of an offence by or before any court in the United Kingdom or by a court-martial there or elsewhere shall (subject to subsection (3) of this section) be admissible in evidence for the purpose of proving, where to do so is relevant to any issue in those proceedings, that he committed that offence, whether he was so convicted upon a plea of guilty or otherwise and whether or not he is a party to the civil proceedings, but no conviction other than a subsisting one shall be admissible in evidence by virtue of this section.

(2) In any civil proceedings in which by virtue of this section a person is proved to have been convicted of an offence by or before any court in the United Kingdom or by a court- martial there or elsewhere—
   (a) he shall be taken to have committed that offence unless the contrary is proved, and
   (b) without prejudice to the reception of any other admissible evidence for the purpose of identifying the facts which constituted that offence, the contents of any document which is admissible as evidence of the conviction, and the contents of the complaint, information, indictment or charge-sheet on which the person in question was convicted, shall be admissible in evidence for that purpose.

   ...

(4) Where in any civil proceedings the contents of any document are admissible in evidence by virtue of subsection (2) of this section, a copy of that document, or of the material part thereof, purporting to be certified or otherwise authenticated by or on behalf of the court or authority having custody of that document, shall be admissible in evidence and shall be taken to be a true copy of that document or part unless the contrary is shown.'

It is now well established that referral proceedings (except, for the purposes of the Civil Evidence (Scotland) Act 1988, ss 1(1) and 2(1), where the condition of referral is s 52(2)(i)[2]) are civil proceedings and it is clear that the sheriff is entitled, for example, to treat an extract conviction (i e the formal document issued by the clerk of court certifying the details of a conviction) as sufficiently (but not irrebuttably, as we shall see presently) proving that the conviction took place.[3] The provisions of s 10 accordingly go a long way to simplifying the reporter's task of proving convictions but the application of these provisions is not free from difficulty. For an extensive discussion of some of the problems see Macphail *Evidence* paras 11.05 to S11.17. What follows here merely highlights some of the main points.

1 Any s 68 proof will almost invariably precede the trial of an alleged offender against the referred child in respect of the current referral, but there may be averments in the statement of facts to earlier alleged offences and these will require to be proved.
2 Civil Evidence (Scotland) Act 1988, s 9: definition of 'civil proceedings' – see discussion at 43.09 above.
3 *McGregor v H* 1983 SLT 626 at 629.

Certificate 'proves itself'

45.02   By providing that the person 'shall be taken to have committed that offence' the section makes it clear that the production of the certificate is, of itself, sufficient evidence that the offence was committed.

Certificate may be rebutted

45.03   By providing that a person 'shall be taken to have committed that offence unless the contrary is proved' the section makes it clear that evidence in rebuttal may be tendered.[1] The evidence in rebuttal could well consist in the alleged offender or anyone else, even the child, giving credible evidence in the referral proof that the offence narrated in the conviction was not truly an offence, perhaps by reason of some matter which had not been ventilated at the criminal trial. It is accordingly important for any party who seeks to rely on an extract conviction to be as ready as practicable to prove the facts of the offence independently.

1 In *Russell v W* [1998] Fam LR 25, a case concerning an Exclusion Order under the Children (Scotland) Act 1995, s 76 of the Act, counsel for the excluded person did not seek to re-open the evidence in relation to the criminal conviction of that person, but the possibility of such a challenge exists, with the consequential possibility of evidence having to be led (to the civil standard of proof) of the offence allegedly committed against the child.

Possible challenge – the practicalities

45.04   Challenges to previous convictions are rare. If parties are all represented the person relying on the extract should try to ascertain in advance if the other side is seeking to challenge that the offence took place. If a challenge is made without notice then the side relying on the extract conviction should consider asking the sheriff to adjourn so that independent evidence can be adduced.

Linking of extract conviction to the child offended against

45.05   Where the ground of referral is that a Schedule 1 offence has been committed against the referred child or against a child in a household of which the referred child is or is likely to become a member, or that the child is, or is likely to become, a member of the same household as a Schedule 1 offender, it will normally be necessary to lead sufficient independent evidence to establish that the offence narrated in the extract conviction is linked to the child offended against. If parties are represented, then this might be made the subject of agreement in advance, preferably by joint minute,[1] but in the absence of such advance agreement the person relying on the extract conviction should cite the relevant witnesses to the proof.

1 For discussion of the joint minute of admissions, see 45.18 and 45.19 below.

Linking of extract conviction to the person to whom extract conviction refers

45.06   It will, of course, sometimes not be necessary for the person who has committed an offence against the child to be identified.[1] The reporter will, however, generally wish to have the identity of the offender against the child established.[2] Where the identity of the offender has been averred by the reporter then, in the absence of agreement, evidence will have to be adduced in order to link the offender named in the extract conviction with the person named as the offender against the child in the statement of grounds of referral.[3]

1 *McGregor v A B* 1981 SC 328; *Kennedy v F* 1985 SLT 22.
2 See discussion at 16.20 above.
3 For discussion of the case law on this subject see Macphail *Evidence* at paras *11.17 and S11.17.

'Certified or otherwise authenticated by or on behalf of the court or authority having custody of that document'

45.07   It has been held in the sheriff court in circumstances where an extract of old convictions was 'no longer available' that a list certified by a police officer satisfied this requirement.[1]

1 *Kennedy v M* 1993 SCLR 164 (Notes), 1992 GWD 2-283, 22 October 1993, Sheriff N Gow QC, Ayr Sheriff Court.

INFERENCES WHICH THE COURT IS ENTITLED TO DRAW FROM CIRCUMSTANCES[1]

'Presumptions' and inferences

45.08   It is sometimes said that the proof of certain circumstances gives rise to a 'presumption' of guilt – 'so as to throw upon him [the accused] the onus of providing an explanation ... which is consistent with his innocence, and which the court or the jury is prepared to accept as true, or at least as raising a reasonable doubt in his favour'.[2] Sheriff Macphail has argued,[3] correctly in the writer's view, that it is incorrect to regard these principles as strict 'presumptions' in the sense of imposing a legal burden of proof on the accused, i e in the sense of binding the court to find the accused guilty unless he adduced evidence putting a reasonable doubt in the mind of the court. The burden of proof is always on the affirmer but in cases involving so-called 'presumptions' the law simply recognises that the court may, in some well-known and often recurring areas of evidence, and in the absence of acceptable explanation by the accused, be *entitled* (but not bound) to draw an inference of guilt.

1 For full discussion see Macphail and Ruxton 'Evidence' in 10 *Stair Memorial Encyclopaedia* paras 749–752 (civil cases) and paras 753–757 (criminal cases).
2 *Walker and Walker on Evidence* para 68.
3 *Evidence* para *22.15.

Recent possession

45.09   A person found in possession of goods which had recently been stolen may be reasonably inferred to be guilty of the theft at least on an 'art and part' (as an accomplice) basis. The principle is summed up in common-sense terms by Alison:[1]

'Possession of the stolen property recently after the theft is the circumstance of all others which most strongly militates against a panel [i e an accused]; and, unless explained by him in some way consistent with his innocence, almost always leads with sensible juries to conviction'.

The inference is at its strongest when the three following conditions concur: (a) the stolen goods are found in the possession of the accused; (b) the interval between the theft of the goods and their discovery is short, depending on circumstances; and (c) there are 'other criminative circumstances' over and above the bare fact of possession. In relation to these conditions Lord Justice-General Cooper stated in 1948:

'... if all these conditions are not present – if, for instance, the interval between the theft and the discovery is prolonged, or if the accused has only had temporary possession of the goods and has parted with them normally and openly – the facts which can be proved may well constitute ingredients (*quantum valeant*) in the case, and may combine with other factors to enable the crown to establish guilt but, unless all three conditions concur, the accused cannot be required to accept the full onus of positively excluding every element of guilt. Even when they concur, the weight of the resulting presumption, and the evidence required to elide it will vary from case to case'.[2]

It has been said that while recent possession of stolen property may be regarded as sufficient proof of all forms of theft, it may not be sufficient proof of a crime involving the use of personal violence.[3] Failure of the accused to make any reply when cautioned and charged, and failure to give evidence on his own behalf, do not constitute 'criminative circumstances'.[4]

1 *Principles of the Criminal Law of Scotland* vol 1 p 320.
2 *Fox v Patterson* 1948 JC 104 at 108.
3 *Christie v HM Advocate* 1939 JC 72 at 75.
4 *Wightman v HM Advocate* 1959 JC 44.

'Art and part' guilt – acting in concert

45.10 A person who participates positively in the commission of an offence may properly be said to have committed the whole offence even although he did not play the principal part. For example, the boy or girl who stands in the doorway of the shop looking up and down the road for the police with the intention that his or her companion may not be disturbed while breaking into and stealing from a shop may equally be found to have committed the offence of theft by housebreaking.

Limitations on 'art and part' – degrees of participation

45.11 A person is *not*, however, to be held responsible for an action of his accomplice which goes beyond the project which the participants have, or may be inferred to have, plotted together. For example, in the situation just quoted, if the violator of the shop were unexpectedly to come upon a member of staff within the shop and assault him, the 'watcher', in the absence of clear evidence of agreement to participate in assault and robbery, would not be regarded as having committed the aggravated offence of assault and robbery. A classic exposition of the concept of acting in accordance with a common plan is contained in the case of *HM Advocate v Lappen*[1] and the wider implications of the concept are extensively discussed in Gordon *Criminal Law* (2nd edn) ch 5. Merely standing by while a breach of the peace is taking place may not be enough, but each situation must be considered on its merits. For recent discussions of the requisite degree of participation see: *Stillie v HM Advocate*[2] and *White v Macphail*.[3]

1 1956 SLT 109 per Lord Patrick at 110.
2 1990 SCCR 719 (authorities reviewed).
3 1990 SCCR 578. Cf *K v Kennedy* 1992 GWD 19-953, Extra Division, 5 March 1992.

Age of child in under-age driving

45.12 It is submitted that when under-age driving is averred as a ground of referral the reporter should adduce evidence from at least one source (e g by reference to a birth certificate or from a parent) as to the age of the child and should not attempt to rely on the presumption of age in the Children (Scotland) Act 1995, s 47.

LIMITATIONS ON INFERENCES TO BE DRAWN FROM EVIDENCE

45.13 Lord Justice-General Cooper, discussing the doctrine of recent possession of stolen goods, said 'If its limitations are not observed, the cardinal presumption of innocence may easily be transformed into a rash assumption of guilt'.[1] It is submitted that these cautious words have a general application to circumstantial evidence and pleaders should be aware of its limitations. It was held in 1965[2] that merely being aware of the disposal of stolen property and not taking any steps to inform the authorities was not enough to give rise to an inference of 'connivance' with the thief or of being 'privy' to the detention of the property from the true owner so as to entitle a conviction for reset. In *Hipson v Tudhope*[3] this principle was followed in the situation of a person being found in a stolen car and it was held that mere presence in such a car as a passenger which had been driven past police officers' signals to stop, coupled with failure by the accused person to dissociate himself from the other occupants of the car, did not raise a prima facie inference of guilt of reset of the car.

1 *Fox v Patterson* 1948 JC 104 at 107.
2 *Clark v HM Advocate* 1965 SLT 250.
3 1983 SLT 659.

MATTERS OF FACT PECULIARLY WITHIN THE KNOWLEDGE OF THE ACCUSED PERSON

45.14   In *Milne v Whaley*[1] it was established at the trial of an accused person that when stopped by the police and asked to produce his driving licence and certificate of insurance he replied that he had neither. No evidence was led to corroborate this admission. The appeal court in its opinion stated:

> 'All the Crown has to do is to demonstrate *prima facie* the absence of entitle-ment to drive, and the Crown has amply done that in this case by proving the circumstances in which the charge was brought. Thereafter, if an accused person wishes to displace the *prima facie* inference, which is all the Crown has to show, it is for him to do. After all, the possession of a licence and insurance cover are facts peculiarly within the knowledge of an accused person, and it would be absurd and quite unworkable if one were to expect or require the Crown to prove the negative, particularly in the matter of insurance.'

Where a threat to use a knife was alleged as part of the offence the accused may be convicted even when the threat itself is uncorroborated.[2] Where an accused admitted to having an article which was not per se an offensive weapon his admission that he had it for the purpose of physical violence was held to be sufficient to bring the article within the category of an offensive weapon. This area of the law of evidence is a complex one (see Macphail *Evidence* paras *22.14–22.18) and raises matters which will not often be encountered in referral proofs.

1 1975 SLT (Notes) 75.
2 *Yates v HM Advocate* 1977 SLT (Notes) 42.

MATTERS OF FACT WITHIN JUDICIAL KNOWLEDGE

45.15   Judges are entitled to 'know' certain matters of fact without the necessity of having heard evidence thereon. It is suggested that it should never be too readily assumed that the sheriff will regard any matter as being within judicial knowledge and that when in doubt evidence should be led. The scope and limitations on judicial knowledge are discussed in the textbooks.[1]

1 *Walker and Walker on Evidence* paras 52 and 53; Macphail *Evidence* paras *2.01–2.09; Macphail and Ruxton 'Evidence' in 10 *Stair Memorial Encyclopaedia* paras 510–512; and Field and Raitt *The Law of Evidence in Scotland* ch 4.

45.16 It is thought that judicial notice will be taken of the well-known matters of mixed fact and law relating to road traffic law and practice, for example that persons under the age of 17 are disqualified by age from holding a driving licence (except for a moped of 50 cc or below, where the age is 16) and that a person disqualified from driving, whether by reason of being under age or as a result of disqualification imposed by the court, cannot be lawfully insured for the purposes of the road traffic legislation.

PROOF OF SUBORDINATE LEGISLATION

45.17 A court is bound to take note of statute law and in practice take note of statutory instruments.[1] Pleaders should, however, have available for production, if necessary, the Stationery Office copy of any statutory instrument which is to be founded upon as part of the evidence in case any dispute should arise as to its terms. Where there is no statutory method of certifying the terms of a byelaw a witness will be required to prove the accuracy of the copy produced.[2]

1 Macphail *Evidence* para *11.02.
2 *Walker and Walker on Evidence* para 200.

EVIDENCE BY JOINT MINUTE OF ADMISSION

Legal basis

45.18 In civil and criminal procedure there are provisions allowing facts to be admitted by joint minute of admissions, i e by way of a document setting out the agreed facts with the narrative that these facts are, for the purpose of the pending case, to be held as admitted. The document is signed by the legal representatives of both parties. In criminal procedure this practice has a statutory basis[1] and in Court of Session practice it is authorised by rule of court.[2] In civil sheriff court practice, however, the very well established practice of allowing minutes of admissions is based not upon statutory provision but on use and wont.[3] In practice joint minutes of admission are accepted by the court in referral proofs and it is submitted that this is entirely in order when the 'defence' side is legally represented. It seems to the writer that there is a strong argument, in logic, to the effect that a joint minute can only bind those parties on whose behalf it is signed and that therefore, for example, in a care and protection case wherein the parents but not the child are represented the usefulness of the joint minute would be of limited value. It may be that a safeguarder appointed by the sheriff who has become a party to the application would be entitled, as curator *ad litem*, to instruct legal representation and that the legal representative would be empowered to sign a joint minute which would 'bind' the child. It may be a question whether a safeguarder who was not himself or herself legally qualified would be entitled to sign such a joint minute.

1 Criminal Procedure (Scotland) Act 1995, s 256.
2 RCS 1994, r 36.7.
3 See discussion in Macphail *Sheriff Court Practice* (2nd edn) pp 527 ff paras 16.28–16.30.

Form and content of joint minute.

45.19 Any joint minute must make clear what is being admitted. If an individual fact is being admitted it should narrate (for example) that, 'for the purpose of the present action, it is admitted that the shop premises at 552 High Street, Glasgow were locked and secured at 5.00 p m on 2 January 1999'. If a medical or other report is being agreed it should be made clear whether it is simply being agreed that the contents of the report represent the credible testimony of the expert concerned – thus leaving it open to parties to lead other and contradictory expert evidence if so advised: alternatively, it may be agreed that a given report is true. Once a fact has been unequivocally admitted as true it is probably incompetent to lead additional evidence on the matters admitted.[1]

1 *Walker and Walker on Evidence* para 48(b).

CHAPTER 46

The grounds of referral

GENERAL PRINCIPLES

The conditions of referral and the historical background

46.01 The conditions of referral are set out in the Children (Scotland) Act 1995, s 52(2), the terms of which are reproduced in Appendix 1. The United Kingdom Parliament has long been attentive to enact special provisions for the protection of children and concepts such as being 'beyond control' and 'falling into bad associations' and 'being exposed to moral danger' are of some antiquity. A list of offences against children was present in the Children and Young Persons (Scotland) Act 1937, Sch 1 and incorporated in the original Social Work (Scotland) Act 1968. In 1975 the list, in modified form, was enacted as the Criminal Procedure (Scotland) Act 1975, Sch 1. The present Schedule 1, further modified, is part of the Criminal Procedure (Scotland) Act 1995 and offences as described in conditions (d), (e) and (f) continue to be conditions of referral. Condition (g) extends the unnecessary incest provision (unnecessary because incest, as a Schedule 1 offence, is already covered by condition (f)) to male children. The 12 conditions in s 52(2) of the 1995 Act include one fresh condition – '(j) has misused alcohol or any drug, whether or not a controlled drug within the meaning of the Misuse of Drugs Act 1971' – but beyond that the conditions, subject to some tidying up, substantially reproduce those in the Social Work (Scotland) Act 1968, s 32(2). In the case of ground (c) the tidying up is elaborate and the old '(c) lack of parental care is likely to cause him unnecessary suffering or seriously to impair his health or development' becomes

'(c) is likely—
   (i) to suffer unnecessarily; or
   (ii) be impaired seriously in his health or development,
   due to a lack of parental care.'

Interpretation of the conditions – '(a)' and '(c)'[1]

46.02 In general the cases interpreting the conditions enacted in the former legislation will be relevant in the interpretation of the conditions in the Children (Scotland) Act 1995. The interpretation of conditions (a) and (c), however, will require to be approached carefully, not principally because of the changes in the grammatical structure of condition (c) but because parental rights in relation to the care and control of a child have now been expressly defined by s 2(1) of the Act in terms of the parental responsibilities set out in s 1, and supersede any analogous rights at common law.[2] Moreover it is provided that a person exercising these rights shall so far as practicable have regard to such views as the child concerned may express, always taking into account the child's age and maturity.[3] Thus, for example, the invocation by the parent of the right to chastise a child as a 'defence' in a ground based upon the Schedule 1 offence of assault involving bodily will require to be considered in the light of parental rights as defined in s 2(1).[4]

1 For a comprehensive discussion of the modern law affecting parental responsibilities and rights see Wilkinson and Norrie *Parent and Child* (2nd edn) ch 8.
2 Children (Scotland) Act 1995, s 2(5).
3 C(S)A 1995, s 6(1).
4 See commentary by Sheriff David Kelbie to *DG v Templeton* 1998 SCLR 180 at 185.

CHILDREN REQUIRING COMPULSORY MEASURES OF SUPERVISION

'(a) is beyond the control of any relevant person'

The statutory provisions

46.03   Under the Social Work (Scotland) Act 1968, s 32(2)(a) the ground was stated in terms of the control of the parent and 'parent' was widely defined[1]. The question of who was a 'parent' was a matter of fact.[2] The Children (Scotland) Act 1995 has introduced the concept of the 'relevant person'.[3] The degree of control which a relevant person ought to expect to exercise must, it is submitted, first of all be judged on the basis of how far such exercise conforms to the rights, so far as relevant, conveyed by s 2(1), i e the rights:

(a) to have the child living with him or otherwise to regulate the child's residence;
(b) to control, direct or guide, in a manner appropriate to the stage of development of the child, the child's upbringing.

As already noticed, these rights must be exercised 'in order to enable [the relevant person] to fulfil his parental responsibilities in relation to the child',[4] i e the responsibilities set out in s 1(1) of the 1995 Act, including the responsibility 'in so far as compliance with this section is practicable and in the interests of the child':

'(a) to safeguard and promote the child's health, development and welfare;
(b) to provide, in a manner appropriate to the stage of development of the child—
    (i) direction;
    (ii) guidance;
    to the child'.

Regard will also have to be paid to the 1995 Act's provision to the effect that in reaching any major decision which involves fulfilling parental responsibilities and rights regard must be had, so far as practicable, to the child's views, should he or she wish to express them, taking account of the child's age and maturity and also to the views of any other person having parental responsibilities or rights in relation to the child, all as provided in s 6(1).

1 Social Work (Scotland) Act 1968, ss 30(2), 94(1).
2 *C v Kennedy* 1991 SCLR 166
3 Discussed at 1.20-1.22 above.
4 Children (Scotland) Act 1995, s 2(1).

Application in practice

46.04 The application of these principles in practice is to be judged by the standard of the reasonable relevant person, as opposed to the unreasonable relevant person. Unreasonableness has been described as 'sentimentality, romanticism, bigotry, wild prejudice, caprice, fatuousness, or excessive lack of commonsense'.[1] The degree of control which a relevant person may reasonably expect to exercise over a child varies with circumstances, including the age and maturity of the child.[2] A common example of a child's appearing, prima facie, to be 'beyond control' is staying out overnight without permission. It is submitted that evidence of serious misbehaviour at school would be relevant to establish this ground on the basis that the relevant person is entitled to expect the child to behave properly at school.

1 *Re W* [1971] AC 682 at 699, 700; cf *D v Kelly* 1995 SLT 1220 at 1223L, 1224A.
2 Cf *Gillick v West Norfolk and Wisbech Area Health Authority* [1986] AC 112, [1985] 3 All ER 402; cf *D v Kelly* 1995 SLT 1220.

'(b) is falling into bad associations or is exposed to moral danger'

46.05 The Children (Scotland) Act 1995 does not define 'bad associations' or 'moral danger' and there is a dearth of authority. It would seem that any associations which would be likely to harm the child significantly might be 'bad'. An example would be a child who is associating with persons who are abusing drugs. It has been said that examples of exposure to moral danger might include 'an adult's use of a child under the age of 8 to act together with him in carrying out the commission of a criminal offence; young children going regularly to a house of a stranger without the approval of their parent and receiving gifts of sweets or money there; "rent boys" or girls running away from home and seen soliciting or keeping company with known prostitutes'.[1] An isolated sexual offence against a child would probably not be sufficient to constitute exposure to moral danger.[2] The moral danger and the character of the bad associations frequently have a sexual context but there may well be other contexts. An example in the context of involving a child in crime would be the experiences of the hero in *Oliver Twist*, but participation in crime per se may not always necessarily entail exposure to moral danger.[3] When assessing whether there has been exposure to moral danger regard must be paid to the established customs and practice of the society to which the child belongs,[4] but some experiences to which a child is subjected may be so repugnant as to justify the application of this sub-paragraph in any event.[5] The matter is one of mixed fact and law. In a case wherein the child was proved on the civil standard of proof to have committed a number of offences it was held, in the absence of evidence linking these offences to exposure to moral danger, that there was insufficient evidence to prove this ground.[6] Moral danger is an objective concept and may exist without fault on the part of the relevant persons. The condition is stated in the alternative: ' . . . is falling into bad associations *or* [emphasis supplied] is exposed to moral danger'. The statement of facts may include material relevant to either or both elements, but the condition will be capable of being held as established if only one element is proved to the satisfaction of the court. It is submitted that the interlocutor should record whether both or only one of the elements has been sustained.

1 Meek et al *In the Child's Best Interests* (1991) p 28.
2 *B v Kennedy* 1987 SLT 765.
3 *Cf Mohamed v Knott* [1968] 2 All ER 563 at 568, 569, interpreting the Children and Young Persons Act 1963, s 2(1).
4 *Mohamed v Knott* [1968] 2 All ER 563 at 568B-E.
5 *Mohamed v Knott* [1968] 2 All ER 563 at 568C; cf Wilkinson and Norrie (2nd edn) para 19-14.
6 *Constanda v M* 1997 SCLR 510.

'(c) is likely—(i) to suffer unnecessarily; or (ii) be impaired seriously in his health or development, due to a lack of parental care'

46.06 'Care' is no longer defined in terms of 'protection, control, guidance and treatment' as it formerly was[1] but these concepts may still be usefully regarded as elements in care. Failure by a relevant person in respect of any one of these elements on a single occasion, if the facts are serious enough, may be enough to satisfy this condition.[2] The facts must be sufficient to support the conclusion that appropriate care is probably not being provided and reasonable inferences may be drawn from the parent's previous conduct in relation to other children.[3] For this condition to have application there must be evidence that the lack of care is indeed likely to cause unnecessary suffering or serious impairment to health or development.[4] Failure to provide necessary treatment for a physical disease may constitute sufficient evidence[5] but 'health and development' does not merely refer to bodily health but embraces emotional and intellectual development.[6] The test is an objective one[7] and the condition may apply if the carrying through of these intentions is adjudged to be likely seriously to endanger the child, even if the relevant person has the best of intentions,[8] or, presumably, where the relevant person is unable, because of physical or other disability, to supply the appropriate care.[9] Some specific source of likely[10] serious impairment to health or development should be identified and if necessary proved: it is not enough merely to establish that the child would be better off remaining with foster parents.[11] Where relevant persons are doing their best, taking and following appropriate advice and delivering the degree of care which might reasonably be expected of the reasonable parent, then this condition may not apply: 'It is want of the reasonable parental care which is to be expected of a reasonable parent which is in contemplation, not failure to attain perfection or success in parental care, nor indeed absence of some ingredient which might be provided by others.'[12] As already noticed,[13] the provisions of the Children (Scotland) Act 1995, ss 1, 2 and 6 now fall to be considered when interpreting 'care'.

1 Social Work (Scotland) Act 1968, s 32(3): these concepts are now included in 'supervision' – Children (Scotland) Act 1995, s 52(3).
2 *Kennedy v S* 1986 SLT 679 at 682F and 682K.
3 *McGregor v L* 1981 SLT 194.
4 Cf *H v Lees; D v Orr* 1993 SCCR 900, 1995 SCCR 380.
5 *Finlayson, Applicant* 1989 SCLR 601.
6 Cf *F v Suffolk County Council* [1981] 2 FLR 208.
7 *M v McGregor* 1982 SLT 41 at 43.
8 *Finlayson, Applicant* 1989 SCLR 601 at 605.
9 Cf *D v Kelly* 1995 SLT 1220 at 1223L, 1224A.
10 In England 'likely' has been interpreted as referring to a 'real possibility' of harm – *Re H and ors (Minors) (Sexual Abuse: Standard of Proof)* [1996] 1 All ER 1.
11 *H v Harkness* 1998 SLT 1431, 1998 GWD 12-582 1st Div.
12 *D v Kelly* 1995 SLT 1220 at 1224C.
13 At 46.02 above.

'(d) is a child in respect of whom any of the offences mentioned in Schedule 1 to the Criminal Procedure (Scotland) Act 1995 (offences against children to which special provisions apply) has been committed'

Statutory source

46.07 Ground (d)[1] refers to offences known as 'Schedule 1 offences'. These are as set out in the Criminal Procedure (Scotland) Act 1995, Sch 1, which provides:

> 'OFFENCES AGAINST CHILDREN UNDER THE AGE OF 17 YEARS TO WHICH SPECIAL PROVISIONS APPLY.
> 1. Any offence under Part I of the Criminal Law (Consolidation) (Scotland) Act 1995.
> 2. Any offence under section 12, 15, 22 or 33 of the Children and Young Persons (Scotland) Act 1937.
> 3. Any other offence involving bodily injury to a child under the age of 17 years.
> 4. Any offence involving the use of lewd, indecent or libidinous practice or behaviour towards a child under the age of 17 years.'

1 Children (Scotland) Act 1995, s 52(2)(d) (amended by the Criminal Procedure (Consequential Provisions) (Scotland) Act 1995, Sch 4, para 97(4)).

Extra-territoriality

46.08 A Schedule 1 offence may take place even when the events involved happen outside Scotland.[1]

1 *E v Kennedy* 1992 GWD 25-1402; *S v Kennedy* 1996 SCLR 34.

(1) Criminal Law (Consolidation) (Scotland) Act 1995, Pt I

46.09 The offences are set out in detail in the Criminal Law (Consolidation) (Scotland) Act 1995, Pt I. They may be grouped under these headings:

incest (s 1);
intercourse with step-child (s 2);
intercourse of person in position of trust with child under 16 (s 3);
intercourse with girl under 16 (s 5);
indecent behaviour towards girl between 12 and 16 (s 6);
procuring (s 7);
abduction and unlawful detention (s 8);
permitting a girl to use premises for intercourse (s 9);
seduction, prostitution etc of girl under 16 (s 10);
trading in prostitution and brothel-keeping (s 11);
allowing child to be in a brothel (s 12);
and certain homosexual offences (s 13).

'Position of trust' in relation to s 3 is not defined and is a matter of fact for the court to decide. Presumably a teacher or child-minder would be included, but would, say, a taxi-driver? The question may be academic since intercourse with a person under 16, male or female, is an offence anyway.[1]

1 Criminal Law (Consolidation) (Scotland) Act 1995, ss 5 and 13.

(2) Children and Young Persons (Scotland) Act 1937 ('the 1937 Act'), ss 12, 15, 22 and 33 (as amended)

46.10   These sections create offences under the headings 'Cruelty to persons under sixteen',[1] 'Causing or allowing persons under sixteen to be used for begging', 'Exposing children under seven to risk of burning', and 'Prohibition of persons under sixteen taking part in performances endangering life or limb'.

1 Children and Young Persons (Scotland) Act 1937, s 12, as amended by the Children (Scotland) Act 1995, s 105(4) and Sch 4, para 4(7).

46.11   *Children and Young Persons (Scotland) Act 1937, s 12 as amended.* This is the most complex and the most frequently used of these sections. It provides that any person aged 16 or over who has parental responsibilities for a person under 16 or has charge or care of such a person commits an offence if he 'wilfully assaults, ill treats, neglects, abandons, or exposes him or causes or procures him to be assaulted, ill-treated, neglected, abandoned, or exposed, in a manner likely to cause him unnecessary suffering or injury to health (including injury to or loss of sight, or hearing, or limb, or organ of the body, and any mental derangement)'. 'Wilful' in s 12 means 'not by accident or inadvertence, but *so that the mind of the person who does the act goes with it* [emphasis supplied]'.[1] Since assault is a crime requiring *mens rea* the use of this epithet in relation to assault in s 12 is redundant in relation to assault, but not in relation to the other offences within the section. Wilfulness may be present even when there is no intent to harm.[2] The right of 'any parent, teacher or other person having lawful control or charge of a child' to administer punishment to a child is preserved by subsection (7). Punishment must be moderate and not imposed vindictively,[3] but anger on the part of the punisher does not necessarily infer the *mens rea* of assault.[4] The considerations governing reasonable chastisement are considered in the case law.[5] In *G v Templeton*[6] Sheriff Principal D J Risk QC, sustaining the sheriff, reviewed the authorities and held on the facts that the defence of reasonable chastisement was not made out. But it must be remembered that the exercise of the parental right to chastise may only be exercised in order to discharge the parental responsibilities set out in the Children (Scotland) Act 1995, s 1(1).[7] The question of what constitutes 'reasonable chastisement' is not straightforward. In a much-publicised case Sheriff Dan Russell in Hamilton held that the repeated smacking of a child on the bare bottom in a health centre waiting room was not reasonable chastisement.[8] Teachers may no longer use physical punishment.[9] What constitutes 'charge or care' is a matter of fact and may be widely interpreted.[10] More than one person may be liable at a particular time, for example, both parents.[11] *The Children and Young Persons (Scotland) Act 1937, s 27, as amended*,[12] enacts *presumptions in favour of 'charge' and 'care'*. 'Neglect' has been described as 'the want of reasonable care, that is the omission of such steps as a reasonable parent would take, such as are usually taken in the ordinary experience of mankind'.[13] There must be evidence from which the likelihood of harm may be inferred.[14] There are statutory provisions which enact, read short, that neglect is to be inferred if adequate food, clothing, medical aid or lodging are not provided or if a child under three dies from suffocation as a result of sharing a bed with a drunken adult.[15] 'Abandon' means leaving the child to his or her fate,[16] even in circumstances which suggest that the child may be cared for,[17] but probably does not include leaving a child with a person who has parental responsibilities, even if that person is known to be unwilling or unable to look after the child.[18] For any action to constitute an offence under this section it must be done 'in a manner likely to cause [the child] unnecessary suffering or injury to health . . .'.[19] Any injury etc less than this is not enough,[20] but the section defines the offence in terms of actings 'likely' to cause unnecessary suffering etc and makes it clear that it is no defence if actual injury etc 'was obviated by the action of another person'.[21] In 1954 the First Division held that failure by an absent father to maintain a child financially constituted a breach of s 12(1).[22] In modern times, having regard to the changed social security arrangements, including the operation of the Child Support Agency, it may be that such failure might not be thought to be 'likely' to cause unnecessary suffering etc and that therefore a conviction would not be appropriate (unless, perhaps, it were argued that the intervention of the Department of Social Security and/or the Child Support Agency constituted 'action by another person'). The matter would be one of fact for the court to determine.

1 Per Lord Russell CJ in *R v Senior* [1899] 1 QB 283 at 291.
2 *Clark v HM Advocate* 1968 JC 53.
3 *Scorgie v Lawrie* (1883) 10 R 610; *McShane v Paton* 1922 JC 26; *Brown v Hilson* 1924 JC 1; *Gray v Hawthorn* 1964 JC 69.
4 *B v Harris* 1989 SCCR 644.
5 E g *Stewart v Thain* 1981 SLT (Notes) 2; *Guest v Annan* 1988 SCCR 275; *Peebles v Macphail* 1990 SLT 245; *B v Harris* 1989 SCCR 644; *Byrd v Wither* 1991 SLT 206.
6 1998 SCLR 180 (see Sheriff Kelbie's commentary at 185, 186).
7 See discussion at 46.02 above.
8 See the illuminating discussion of this case by Paul and Sadie Spink *What is reasonable chastisement?* 1999 JLSS vol 44 no 6 pp 26, 27.
9 Education (Scotland) Act 1980 (as amended), s 48A.
10 *Liverpool Society for the Prevention of Cruelty to Children v James* [1910] 3 KB 813; *R v Drury* (1975) 60 Cr App R 195.

11 See *R v Watson and Watson* (1959) 43 Cr App R 111.
12 By Children (Scotland) Act 1995, Sch 4.
13 *HM Advocate v Clarks* 1968 SLT 161 at 163 per LJ-C Grant, quoting with approval the charge to the jury of a sheriff substitute at Edinburgh .
14 *H v Lees; D v Orr* 1993 SCCR 900; *McF v Normand* 1995 SCCR 380.
15 Children and Young Persons (Scotland) Act 1937, s 12(2).
16 *Mitchell v Wright* (1905) 7 F 568; *R v Boulden* (1957) 41 Cr App R 105. There must be more than temporary dereliction of duty: *McGregor v A* 1982 SLT 45.
17 *R v Whibley* [1938] 3 All ER 777; *R v Boulden* (1957) 41 Cr App R 105.
18 Cf *McLean v Hardie* 1927 SC 344.
19 CYP(S)A 1937, s 12(1).
20 *R v Whibley* [1938] 3 All ER 777; *R v Hatton* [1925] 2 KB 322; contrast *Kennedy v S* 1986 SLT 679.
21 CYP(S)A 1937, s 12(3)(a).
22 *Henderson v Stewart* 1954 JC 94.

46.12   *The 1937 Act, ss 15, 22 and 33.*   The Children and Young Persons (Scotland) Act 1937, s 15 makes it an offence respectively for any person to cause or procure, and any person over 16 who has parental responsibilities or charge or care of a child to allow, a child to engage in begging. Section 22 makes it an offence for any person over 16 who has parental responsibilities for or charge or care of a child under seven to allow the child to be in a room with an open fire grate which is not sufficiently protected against the risk of burning or scalding. It would seem that burning injury to a child caused by, say, an unprotected electric fire would not fall within this section and that the concepts of neglect or exposure in the 1937 Act, s 12(1) would have to be invoked in an appropriate case.[1] Section 33 prohibits the participation of a child in any performance to which the Children and Young Persons Act 1963, s 37(2) applies and in which life or limb is endangered and makes it an offence for any person over 16 to procure or any parent or guardian to allow a child to take part in such a performance. A 'child' for the purpose of s 33 means a person not over school age.[2] Grounds based on facts which would constitute an offence under these sections are not often encountered.

1 It would seem that when CYP(S)A 1937, s 12 is invoked the accused person would have available the defence that the neglect or exposure was not wilful – a defence not available under s 22, which appears to create an offence of absolute liability.
2 Children and Young Persons (Scotland) Act 1937, s 37(a), as amended by the Employment Act 1989, Sch 3, Pt III, para 13.

(3) 'Any other offence involving bodily injury to a child under the age of 17 years'

46.13   In general, assault need not involve injury:[1] but before an assault may qualify as a Schedule 1(3) offence, actual bodily injury must be involved. An indecent assault upon a child does not per se involve bodily injury.[2]

1 For full discussion see Gordon *Criminal Law* (2nd edn, 1978) pp 815 ff.
2 *F v Kennedy* 1988 SLT 404; *B v Kennedy* 1987 SLT 765.

(4) 'Any offence involving the use of lewd, indecent or libidinous practice or behaviour towards a child under the age of 17 years'

46.14   This provision fills the gap in the existing law exposed in the case of *F v Kennedy*[1] wherein an unsuccessful attempt had been made to have indecent but not injurious acts categorised as offences involving bodily injury.

1 1988 SLT 404.

46.15 *Civic Government (Scotland) Act 1982, s 52(1) and (7).* The Civic Government (Scotland) Act 1982, s 52(1) creates new offences of taking, or permitting to be taken, distributing, possessing or publishing indecent photographs of children under 16, and s 52(7) of the same Act[1] enacts that references to offences mentioned in the Criminal Procedure (Scotland) Act 1975, Sch 1 shall, include references to such offences. This reference to the Criminal Procedure (Scotland) Act 1975 was not brought up to date in the Children (Scotland) Act 1995. It may be arguable, having regard to the flexible attitude of the court where the interests of children are involved,[2] that the court might regard this amendment as being implied, but the case of *F v Kennedy*,[3] wherein the attempt to have indecent but not injurious acts categorised as offences involving bodily injury was unsuccessful, may suggest otherwise. It is submitted that the Scottish Parliament ought to remedy this seeming oversight without delay.

1 When read with the Criminal Justice Act 1988, Sch 15, para 89.
2 Cf *W v Kennedy* 1988 SCLR 236, 1988 SLT 583; *S v Kennedy* 1996 SCLR 34, 1996 SLT 1087; *E v Kennedy* 1992 GWD 25-1402.
3 1988 SLT 404.

'(e) is, or is likely to become, a member of the same household as a child in respect of whom any of the offences referred to in paragraph (d) above has been committed'

Definition of 'household'

46.16 'Household' for this purpose means a family unit – a group which generally lives together even if some members come and go.[1] The decision is one of fact and degree and there must be sufficient evidence. Ties of affection or occasional overnight contact may not be enough to create a household and 'likely' should not be given a strained or artificial meaning.[2] It has been said:

> '... the important question in deciding whether a person was a member of a household was whether the ties of affection and regular contact which held the parties together as a group still continued, and the fact that persons were separated temporarily or only due to the intervention of the authorities would not generally mean that they were not members of the same household.'[3]

There is no presumption that a child is a member of the same household as his or her parent.[4]

1 *McGregor v H* 1983 SLT 626; *A v Kennedy* 1993 SCLR 107.
2 *Templeton v E* 1998 SCLR 672
3 *Kennedy v R's Curator ad Litem* 1993 SLT 295 per LP Hope at 299L ff
4 *Ferguson v S* 1992 SCLR 866.

'(f) is, or is likely to become, a member of the same household as a person who has committed any of the offences referred [to] in paragraph (d) above'

46.17   While identification of the offender is not necessary for a ground under the Children (Scotland) Act 1995, s 52(2)(d)[1] identification is necessary under this subsection, at least to the extent of establishing that the alleged offender is or is likely to become a member of the household. In practice this will mean that the alleged offender must be named or otherwise identified in the statement of facts. As already noted, there is no presumption that a child is a member of the same household as a parent.[2]

1 *S v Kennedy* 1987 SLT 667.
2 *Ferguson v S* 1992 SCLR 866.

'(g) is, or is likely to become, a member of the same household as a person in respect of whom an offence under sections 1 to 3 of the Criminal Law (Consolidation) (Scotland) Act 1995 (incest and intercourse with a child by step-parent or person in position of trust) has been committed by a member of that household'

46.18   Since the Criminal Law (Consolidation) (Scotland) Act 1995, ss 1–3 deal with offences which are Schedule 1 offences this ground seems otiose since all such offences are already included in grounds (d), (e) and (f). Reporters, when framing grounds of referral have to decide which of the grounds are the most appropriate.

'(h) has failed to attend school regularly without reasonable excuse'

School age – proof of failure and defences

46.19   This condition presumably applies only to children of school age, which is defined in the Education (Scotland) Act 1980, s 33 which provides inter alia that the upper limit of school age is 16. This section also provides that a child whose 16th birthday falls on or after 1 March but before 1 October in any year is deemed to have reached 16 on the summer leaving date (31 May) and that a child whose 16th birthday falls on or after 1 October but before 1 March of the next year is deemed to have reached 16 on the winter leaving date (the first day of the Christmas holidays for a child actually attending school and 21 December for any other child). Absence may be established by certificate which stands unless successfully challenged.[1] Once failure to attend regularly has been established the onus of proving reasonable excuse falls to the relevant person or child.[2] It is a reasonable excuse when a child has been excluded from school by reason of misconduct which has been only alleged and not proved[3] but not necessarily if the allegation had been proved.[4]

1 Education (Scotland) Act 1980, s 86.
2 *Kennedy v Clark* 1970 JC 55, cf discussion at 41.11 above.
3 *D v Kennedy* 1988 SLT 55.
4 *D v Kennedy* 1988 SLT 55 at 57F.

Special features of the Education (Scotland) Act 1980

46.20 The Education (Scotland) Act 1980, ss 35-44 contain provisions which define, for the purpose of the 1980 Act, the obligation of parents and persons having parental responsibilities in relation to, or the care of, a child to ensure the attendance of such child at school. These sections extend, for the purpose of the 1980 Act, the concept of failing without reasonable excuse to attend school regularly so as to make this concept include certain other facts and circumstances which might not, by themselves, necessarily amount to failure by the child regularly to attend school without reasonable excuse, as this has been interpreted by the court.[1] For example s 35(2) of the 1980 Act provides that a child who has been suspended from school for non-compliance with school rules is to be regarded as having failed without reasonable cause to attend school regularly. The children to whom these provisions apply are children 'of school age' in terms of s 33 of the 1980 Act. In the event of a child within its jurisdiction failing to attend school regularly without reasonable excuse the local authority, 'where no requirement arises under s 53(1) of the Children (Scotland) Act to give information about the child to the Principal Reporter under this subsection may provide the Principal Reporter with such information'.[2] *The children's reporter requires to consider* if there are facts sufficient to draw the inference that the child has failed without reasonable excuse to attend school regularly in terms of s 52(2)(h) of the 1995 Act since the 1995 Act does not re-enact for its purposes the definitions contained in ss 35-44 of the 1980 Act. If proceedings are taken under s 35 (failure to secure regular attendance at school), s 41 (failure to comply with an attendance order) or s 42(3) (failure to permit examination of child) of the 1980 Act and the court is satisfied that one or more of these conditions exists the court *may* (my emphasis) refer the matter to the reporter, specifying that a condition of referral under the Children (Scotland) Act 1995, s 52(2)(h) exists. Thereafter the reporter shall make such investigations as he thinks appropriate and then, if he considers that compulsory measures of supervision are necessary, arrange a hearing under s 69 of the 1995 Act at which the specified condition will count as a ground established.[3]

1 Cf *Kiely v Lunn* 1983 SLT 207.
2 Education (Scotland) Act 1980, s 36(3), as amended by Children (Scotland) Act 1995, Sch 4, para 28.
3 Children (Scotland) Act 1995, ss 54(2)(d) and 54(3); cf *D v Kennedy* 1988 SLT 55.

'(i) has committed an offence'

46.21 This is still the most frequently invoked ground of referral. The standard of proof for this ground, *in contrast to all other grounds*, is the criminal standard.[1] A child under the age of criminal responsibility, namely eight, may not be the subject of this ground.[2] In relation to a child over eight, it has been said[3] that any difficulty created by old authority, to the effect that a pupil child may not be guilty of a crime on an 'art and part' basis if he or she acted on instructions, would be elided by employing the Social Work (Scotland) Act 1968, s 32(2)(b) (now the Children (Scotland) Act 1995, s 52(2)(b)) – 'is falling into bad associations or is exposed to moral danger'. This seems valid but the pleader would require to submit that there was a causal link between the offences and the bad associations or moral danger.[4]

1 Children (Scotland) Act 1995, s 68(3)(b); see 42.02-42.05 above.
2 *Merrin v S* 1987 SLT 193.
3 By *Wilkinson and Norrie* at para 19.26.
4 *Constanda v M* 1997 SC 217, 1997 SCLR 510, 1997 SLT 1396.

'(j) has misused alcohol or any drug, whether or not a controlled drug within the meaning of the Misuse of Drugs Act 1971'

46.22   The essence of ground (j) would appear to be 'misuse' as opposed to 'use' and therefore a child consuming a moderate amount of alcoholic beverage which can be regarded as reasonable having regard to his or her age and maturity, or treating himself or herself in good faith with drugs which are legally available without prescription, is not, presumably, at risk under this ground. The use of the term 'misuse' may appear to imply a reference to the Misuse of Drugs Act 1971. The relationship, if any, between this condition and the provisions of the 1971 Act may have to be explored by the courts. The Act of 1971 does not define offences in terms of 'misuse' but defines categories of controlled drugs and creates offences by enacting, for example in s 5(1), that 'Subject to any regulation under section 7 of this Act [which allows for bona fide possession of drugs by doctors etc] for the time being in force, it shall not be lawful for a person to have a controlled drug in his possession'. Offences under the 1971 Act, if committed by children, may, like any other statutory offences, be referred to hearings under the Children (Scotland) Act 1995, s 52(2)(i) (alleged offence by a child). On the analogy of *Constanda v M*[1] it would be inappropriate to use ground (j) to bring a child into the system in respect only of an offence or offences under the 1971 Act. It would also, it is submitted, be inappropriate to make any exact analogy between offences involving controlled drugs and 'misuse' of alcohol by, for example, regarding possession of drugs or alcohol as itself constituting a sufficient factual basis for this condition.[2] This ground is a reflection of the United Kingdom's obligations under the United Nations Convention on the Rights of the Child, art 33.[3] It also appears to be consequent upon part of Recommendation 53[4] of the *Review of Scottish Child Care Law*[5] the discussion of which[6] makes it clear, by analogy with the then existing ground based on the misuse of volatile substances, that the principal purpose of the recommendation was to protect the child from the harmful consequences of inappropriate consumption of alcohol and drugs, but it may be competent to use this condition where a child is believed to be (perhaps innocently) concerned in the illegal supply of drugs. It would be competent nowadays, it is submitted, to refer to the said Convention and the said *Review* as an aid to the construction of this provision if it were argued that its meaning was ambiguous.[7]

1 1997 SC 217, 1997 SCLR 510, 1997 SLT 1396.
2 Similarly in relation to possession with intent to supply: cf PG Wodehouse 'The Purity of the Turf' in *The Inimitable Jeeves* (Herbert Jenkins Ltd, London, 1923) p 175:

Jeeves: 'Before Mr Little left, I persuaded him to invest a small sum for the syndicate of which you were kind enough to make me a member, sir, in the Girls' Egg and Spoon race.'

Bertie: 'On Sarah Mills?'

Jeeves: 'No, sir. On a long-priced outsider. Little Prudence Baxter, sir, the child of his lordship's head gardener. Her father assures me she has a very steady hand. She is accustomed to bring him his mug of beer from the cottage each afternoon, and he informs me she has never spilled a drop.'

3 'States Parties shall take all appropriate measures, including legislative, administrative, social and educational measures, to protect children from the illicit use of narcotic drugs and psychotropic substances as defined in the relevant international treaties, and to prevent the use of children in the illicit production and trafficking of such substances.'

4 'Section 32(2)(gg) [of the Social Work (Scotland) Act 1968] should be amended to read: "He has misused drugs or alcohol or a volatile substance or has engaged in conduct which has caused or is likely to cause serious harm".'

5 (HMSO, 1990).

6 In the *Review* itself at 13.9.

7 Cf *Pepper* v *Hart* [1993] AC 593.

'(k) has misused a volatile substance by deliberately inhaling its vapour, other than for medicinal purposes'

46.23 'Glue-sniffing' and other forms of 'solvent abuse' are not per se offences although in particular circumstances such conduct may be so alarming as to constitute a breach of the peace.[1] This ground of referral was accordingly interpolated into the Social Work (Scotland) Act 1968, s 32(2)[2] and is now re-enacted here.[3]

1 *Taylor v Hamilton* 1984 SCCR 393.

2 By the Solvent Abuse (Scotland) Act 1983, s 1.

3 For an examination of the facts of solvent abuse among the young see Dr Joyce M Watson *Solvent Abuse – The Adolescent Epidemic?* (Croom and Helm Ltd, 1986).

'(l) is being provided with accommodation by a local authority under section 25, or is the subject of a parental responsibilities order obtained under section 86, of this Act and, in either case, his behaviour is such that special measures are necessary for his adequate supervision in his interest or the interest of others'

'In his interest or the interest of others'

46.24 A child who is provided with accommodation by a local authority is a 'looked after' child under s 17(6)(a) of the Children (Scotland) Act 1995. This ground gives explicit recognition to the 'interest of others' but since it has long been recognised, for example, that it can be in a child's interests to be detained in order to prevent him from worsening his position by committing further offences, this innovation is more apparent than real.[1] There is no reported case discussing this ground or its predecessor in the Social Work (Scotland) Act 1968.[2] Once again the consequences of the provisions of the Children (Scotland) Act 1995, ss 1, 2 and 6[3] must be kept in mind.

1 *Humphries v S* 1986 SLT 683.

2 Social Work (Scotland) Act 1968, s 32(2)(i).
3 Discussed at 46.02 above.

'Supervision'

46.25   The Children (Scotland) Act 1995, s 52(3) provides that, for Pt II of the Act, 'supervision' in relation to compulsory measures of supervision 'may include measures taken for the protection, guidance, treatment or control of the child'.

Part VI
Appeals to the sheriff

Powers of the sheriff at appeal stage: general nature of the sheriff's jurisdiction

THE STATUTORY BACKGROUND

The current provisions

47.01   The Children (Scotland) Act 1995, s 51 regulates both appeals from decisions of the hearing to the sheriff and appeals from the sheriff to the sheriff principal and to the Court of Session. The jurisdiction of the sheriff on appeal from the hearing rests principally on s 51(1) of the Act which provides that 'within a period of three weeks beginning with the date of any decision of a children's hearing', a child or a relevant person, or relevant persons, or both (or all) may 'appeal to the sheriff against that decision' and that, where such an appeal is made, it shall be heard by the sheriff. The Act is silent as to what may constitute appropriate reasons for such an appeal. The sheriff may hear evidence from parties and may examine the reporter, examine the authors or compilers of reports or statements and call for any further report which he or she considers may assist in the deciding of the appeal.[1]

1 Children (Scotland) Act 1995, s 51(3).

The former provisions and their interpretation

47.02   The provisions of the Social Work (Scotland) Act 1968 governing appeals to the sheriff from decisions of hearings were in substantially the same terms.[1] In the first reported case on the scope of the sheriff's appellate jurisdiction[2] under the 1968 Act a hearing had decided, apparently with some hesitation, that residential supervision was required, although the social worker, while recognising that this form of supervision had to be considered, had in the event advised against it. Between the time of the hearing and the appeal diet some apparent improvements took place in the home situation and Sheriff Mowat allowed the appeal to the extent of remitting the case back to the hearing,[3] stating:

> 'In these circumstances, I consider that the fact that it is now five months since the boy's last offence, and the existence of indications that the truancy may have ceased and that the family are waking up to their responsibilities, justify me in allowing the appeal so that these indications may be fully investigated and the hearing can reconsider the decision in all the present circumstances. I would emphasize that this result is not an indication that the hearing acted improperly in any way, or that a residential

requirement may not still be the proper determination of the case in the end of the day.'

The interest of this case lies not only in the disposal but in Sheriff Mowat's analysis of the scope of the sheriff's appellate jurisdiction:

> 'In approaching this case I had a firm view that the procedure for appeals against determinations of a children's hearing made it clear that a sheriff should not interfere with a determination simply because he felt another form of treatment might be preferable. That conclusion seems to me to follow from the fact that, although in practice a hearing had a choice between only two effective methods of supervision, a sheriff who finds one method is not justified is still not entitled to substitute the other method. Accordingly, I consider that a sheriff should not allow an appeal unless there was some flaw in the procedure adopted by the hearing or he was satisfied that the hearing had not given proper consideration to some factor in the case.'

In adopting this approach Sheriff Mowat was substantially following a long-established attitude of appellate courts to the decisions of administrative tribunals. For example in 1950 Lord Chief Justice Goddard, in an appeal arising out of a local authority's refusal to grant a licence for a camp site, said:

> '... where the duty to hear and determine a question is conferred on a tribunal of any kind, or on a local authority, they state their reasons for their decision, and the reasons which they state show that they have taken into account matters which they ought not to have taken into account, or they have failed to take matters into account which they ought to have taken into account, the court to which an appeal lies can and ought to adjudicate on the matter.'[4]

It is to be noted, however, that Sheriff Mowat *did* have regard to events which had taken place *after* the hearing.

1 The Social Work (Scotland) Act 1968, s 49 provided inter alia: '(1) A child or his parent or both may, within three weeks beginning with the date of any decision of a children's hearing, appeal to the sheriff in chambers against that decision, and the child or his parent or both shall be heard by the sheriff as to the reasons for the appeal ... (3) The reporter, whether or not he is conducting the proceedings, may be examined by the sheriff; and the sheriff may examine the reporter and the authors or compilers of any reports or statements, and may call for any further reports which he considers may assist him in deciding the appeal.'
2 *D v Sinclair* 1973 SLT (Sh Ct) 47.
3 Under SW(S)A 1968, s 49(5)(b).
4 *Pilling v Abergele UDC* [1950] 1 KB 636 at 637.

THE DEVELOPMENT OF THE LAW UP TO THE CHILDREN (SCOTLAND) ACT 1995

Approach of the courts to the interpretation of the appeal provisions in the Social work (Scotland) Act 1968

47.03 The provision in the Social Work (Scotland) Act 1968, s 49(3), enacting that the sheriff 'may examine the reporter and the authors or compilers of any reports or statements, *and may call for any further reports* *which he considers may assist him in deciding the appeal'*[1] [emphasis supplied] gave rise to a view that the sheriff had more sweeping powers than indicated in *D v Sinclair*.[2] In the comparatively early case of *K v Finlayson*[3] the sheriff, although not examining the scope of the sheriff's powers on appeal, adopted a broadly interventional stance. In *Humphries v S*[4] the sheriff rejected the view 'that the decision of the hearing could only be interfered with if it was manifestly wrong in light of the evidence available' and sustained an appeal by sending it back to the hearing with the observation that it would be worthwhile to consider returning the child to his mother, as opposed to placing him with a foster parent in accordance with its original decision. In the more recent case of *Kennedy v A*[5] the sheriff had allowed an appeal and remitted back to the hearing with observations and directions inter alia indicating that the hearing should now 'make long term decisions' as to the child's future. The Court of Session, on appeal, held that the sheriff had no power to make observations or give directions to a hearing: he simply had to give reasons for his decision.[6]

1 For further discussion of the meaning of this provision see 52.10 below.
2 1973 SLT (Sh Ct) 47.
3 1974 SLT (Sh Ct) 51 disapproved in *O v Rae* 1992 SCLR 318, 1993 SLT 570.
4 (8 September 1980, unreported) Inverness Sheriff Court, (Sheriff Fulton).
5 1986 SLT 358.
6 For further discussion of *Kennedy v A* see 53.06 below.

The 'restrictive approach'

47.04   The restrictive approach of Sheriff Mowat in *D v Sinclair* has not been expressly ruled upon by the Court of Session but in *O v Rae*[1] Lord President Hope may have given it some countenance by observing:

'If the decision is one which no reasonable hearing would have taken on the information that was properly before them, then the sheriff has power under section 49(5) [of the 1968] Act to intervene on the ground that it is not justified in all the circumstances of the case'.

1 1992 SCLR 318 at 325, 1993 SLT 570.

Children (Scotland) Act 1995, s 51(5)(c)(iii)

47.05   This provision entitles the sheriff, on upholding an appeal, to 'substitute for the disposal by the children's hearing any requirement which could be imposed by them under section 70 of the Act'. In the case of *D v Sinclair*[1] Sheriff Mowat expressed the view that the sheriff was not entitled to substitute one disposal for another simply because he felt that such disposal was better. It may therefore be a question as to how far the new provision should lead to a change of attitude by sheriffs as to their powers on appeal. It is submitted, however, that there are still two stages in considering an appeal. In the first place the sheriff must address the issue posed in the first few words of subsection (5), i e whether he or she 'is satisfied that the decision of the children's hearing is not justified in all the circumstances of the case'. These words are identical to those in the Social Work (Scotland) Act 1968, s 49(5). It may therefore be that sheriffs may still follow the approach of Sheriff Mowat by not being prepared to be satisfied that the decision is not justified 'unless there was some flaw in the procedure adopted by the hearing', or, where 'satisfied that the hearing had not given proper consideration to some factor in the case'. On this reasoning, it would only be when the sheriff was so satisfied, that it would be open to him or her to consider sustaining the appeal by substituting his or her own disposal or otherwise.[2]

1 1973 SLT (Sh Ct) 47.
2 For further discussion of exercise of the sheriff's appeal powers see ch 53 below.

CHAPTER 48

Appeals from decisions of the hearing to the sheriff: appealable decisions

THE STATUTORY PROVISIONS

Children (Scotland) Act 1995, s 51

48.01   This section provides inter alia:

'(1) Subject to subsection (15) below, a child or a relevant person (or relevant persons) or both (or all)—
  (a) may, within a period of three weeks beginning with the date of any decision of a children's hearing, appeal to the sheriff against that decision; and
  (b) where such an appeal is made, shall be heard by the sheriff.
  ...
(4) Where the sheriff decides that an appeal under this section has failed, he shall confirm the decision of the children's hearing.
(5) Where the sheriff is satisfied that the decision of the children's hearing is not justified in all the circumstances of the case he shall allow the appeal and—
  (a) where the appeal is against a warrant to find and keep or, as the case may be, to keep a child in a place of safety, he shall recall the warrant;
  (b) where the child is subject to a supervision requirement containing a condition imposed under section 70(9) of this Act, he shall direct that the condition shall cease to have effect; and
  (c) in any case, he may, as he thinks fit—
    (i) remit the case with reasons for his decision to the children's hearing for reconsideration of their decision; or
    (ii) discharge the child from any further hearing or other proceedings in relation to the grounds for the referral of the case; or
    (iii) substitute for the disposal by the children's hearing any requirement which could be imposed by them under section 70 of this Act.
  ...
(9) Where a child or a relevant person appeals under subsection (1) above against a decision of a children's hearing in relation to a supervision requirement, the child or the relevant person may make application to a children's hearing for the suspension of the requirement appealed against.'

Only substantial decisions appealable

48.02   Although the Children (Scotland) Act 1995, s 51(1) confers a right of appeal against 'that decision', i e 'any decision of a children's hearing', it is clear that decisions on procedural matters are not to be treated as 'decisions' within the meaning of the subsection: in short, they are not appealable. This is the clear inference from the case of *H and H v McGregor*.[1] In this case, decided under the Social Work (Scotland) Act 1968, the grounds of referral were not accepted and the hearing 'decided' not to discharge the referral[2] and directed the reporter to make application to the sheriff for a finding. The parents appealed to the sheriff who dismissed the appeal on the basis that there had been no appealable decision. On further appeal by the parents to the Court of Session the decision of the sheriff was upheld. Lord Justice-Clerk Wheatley stated:

> 'But the provisions of sub-para (c) are primarily directed towards the procedure to be followed when the facts are in dispute, and the instruction thereanent is peremptory. The exception to that mandatory procedure is that the hearing may decide to discharge the referral without the disputed facts being determined. The fact that the hearing were of the opinion that, without prejudice to the manner in which it would be ultimately disposed of, the referral could not be decided until the facts were determined, and were consequently not treating the case as one to which the exception applied, did not, in my view, constitute a "decision" within the meaning of section 49(1).'

Lord Wheatley also pointed out that the same reasoning would cover a 'decision' not to proceed on the basis of a limited number of admitted facts when this situation arises under s 42(2)(b) of the 1968 Act. 'In both cases', he said, 'it is just a decision to have the full facts ascertained and determined before a decision on the proper method of disposal can be considered.' Lord Wheatley then added: 'In neither case is it a disposal of the referral, and *it is a decision on the disposal of the referral at which in these circumstances section 49(1) is aimed*' [emphasis supplied].

1 1973 SC 95, 1973 SLT 110.
2 Social Work (Scotland) Act 1968, s 42(2)(c).

Specific appealable decisions

48.03   On the basis of the foregoing analysis, appealable decisions include:

(1) The granting or renewal of any warrant for the apprehension or detention of a child, i e:
   (a) where a child has been notified of a hearing under the Children (Scotland) Act 1995, s 45 and the hearing is satisfied on cause shown that it is necessary to grant a warrant to secure the attendance of the child at the hearing:[1]
   (b) where a child has been notified under s 45 but has failed to attend the hearing;[2]
   (c) where a hearing have granted a warrant to find and keep a child under s 45(4) of the Children (Scotland) Act 1995;
   (d) where a children's hearing has been arranged under Pt II of the Act and the hearing is unable to dispose of the case *and* is satisfied that there is reason to believe that the child may not attend a hearing *or* may fail to comply with a requirement under s 69(3) of the Act [attend at a place (clinic etc) for up to 22 days] *or* that it is

necessary that the child should be kept in a place of safety in order to safeguard or promote the child's welfare;[3]

(e) where a hearing has exercised its power to continue such a warrant for a further period;[4]

(2) a decision to make a supervision requirement;[5]

(3) a decision to continue, with or without variation, a supervision requirement;[6]

(4) a decision to discharge a referral under either s 65(7), s 65(9)(b) or s 69(1)(b) of the Act; and

(5) a decision to terminate a supervision requirement.[7]

1 Children (Scotland) Act 1995, s 45(4).
2 C(S)A 1995, s 45(5).
3 C(S)A 1995, s 66(1) and (2).
4 C(S)A 1995, s 66(5).
5 C(S)A 1995, s 70(1).
6 C(S)A 1995, s 73(9)(c)-(e).
7 C(S)A 1995, s 73(9)(b).

Appeal against decision not to impose supervision requirement?

48.04   In theory there seems to be no reason why an appeal should not be competent at the instance of a relevant person, child, or possibly by a safeguarder in the interest of the child, against a decision of a hearing *not* to impose a supervision requirement.[1]

1 *Stirling v D* 1995 SCLR 460, 1995 SLT 1089 was an appeal by a reporter and a safeguarder against the discharge of a referral by the sheriff on the ground that the children's hearing had no power to make or continue a supervision requirement only for the purpose of enabling unsupervised access to take place. The appeal was refused on other grounds, but no point was made as to the participation of the safeguarder in the appeal. See also *Thomson v Principal Reporter* 1998 SCLR 898 for an unusual attempt to re-instate a supervision reqirement.

Secure accommodation and appeals

48.05   A hearing may, where granting warrant for detention of child,[1] or where making a supervision requirement which requires a child to reside at a specified place or specified places,[2] if satisfied that any of the criteria set out in the Children (Scotland) Act 1995, s 70(10) is satisfied,[3] decide that the child shall be liable to be placed and kept in secure accommodation. Such a decision is appealable as part of the decision to grant the warrant or to impose the supervision requirement. In the case of an appeal against such a supervision requirement the sheriff may remove the 'secure accommodation' condition although otherwise refusing the appeal.[4]

1 Children (Scotland) Act 1995, s 66(6).
2 C(S)A 1995, s 70(1), (3)(a), and (9)(a).
3 C(S)A 1995, ss 66(6) and 70(9)(b).
4 C(S)A 1995, s 51(5)(b). For further discussion see 53.03 below.

No appeal to sheriff from decision of hearing competent to reporter

48.06   The Act gives the reporter no right of appeal to the sheriff from any decision of a children's hearing. This is consistent with the whole philosophy of the Children (Scotland) Act 1995 which is to vest in the hearing the decision as to the treatment of children in need of compulsory measures of supervision. The reporter's duty is to bring the child to the hearing and lay the facts before the hearing to which the child's case, once the grounds of referral are admitted or proved, stands referred: once this is done, and if the hearing should decide that no further action is necessary and that the referral should be discharged, then the reporter has no further legal interest to pursue the matter.

CHAPTER 49

Grounds of appeal – types of appeal

STATUTORY GROUND OF APPEAL

49.01   The sheriff may sustain an appeal when he or she is 'satisfied that the decision of the children's hearing *is not justified in all the circumstances of the case*'[1] [emphasis supplied]. This very broad provision would seem to indicate that the categories of appeal can never be closed. This chapter, accordingly, only seeks to identify the main areas wherein grounds of appeal may exist. It does not claim to be exhaustive. The types of appeal tend to overlap.

1 Children (Scotland) Act 1995, s 51(5).

TYPES OF APPEAL

Appeal against warrant

49.02   The Children (Scotland) Act 1995 itself identifies an appeal 'against a warrant to find and keep or as the case may be, to keep a child in a place of safety'.[1] Appeals against the granting of warrants are reasonably familiar and generally raise matters of fact and degree.

1 Children (Scotland) Act 1995, s 51(5)(a).

Appeal against supervision requirement

49.03   This is the most common type of appeal. Once again, such appeals generally turn on matters of fact and degree.

Appeal against supervision requirement with a secure accommodation condition

49.04   In such appeals the sheriff, if minded to sustain the appeal, shall direct that the secure accommodation condition shall cease to have effect.[1]

1 Children (Scotland) Act 1995, s 51(5)(b).

Appeal on basis of an alleged irregularity in the conduct of a case

49.05   This ground is expressly recognised in the rules.[1]

1 Act of Sederunt (Child Care and Maintenance) Rules 1997, SI 1997/291, r 3.56(3)(a).

EVIDENCE IN APPEALS

49.06   Whatever the ground of appeal, under the present legislation, evidence may be led.[1]

1 Act of Sederunt (Child Care and Maintenance) Rules 1997, SI 1997/291, r 3.56(3).

APPEAL GROUNDS ALLEGING PROCEDURAL IRREGULARITY

Irregularity must be 'material'

49.07   Any irregularity may require to be excused[1] and if all the procedural steps are not duly performed and notifications duly given this may provide prima facie grounds for an appeal: for an appeal based on such grounds to succeed, however, it would seem that the defect must be 'material' in the sense of causing real prejudice to the person affected by the irregularity[2] or, presumably, to the interests of the child. In the Orkney case[3] the absence of the children from the hearing was not held to be a material irregularity because no prejudice could accrue to the children since the parents were disputing the grounds of referral.[4] In *McGregor v A*[5] the reporter had stated grounds of referral by reference to the Children and Young Persons (Scotland) Act 1937, Sch 1, which had been repealed by the provisions of the Criminal Procedure (Scotland) Act 1975 but reenacted in terms which were, so far as material, identical.[6] The sheriff had heard proof and discharged the referral inter alia on the ground that the condition alleged had no meaning in law. On appeal by the reporter the Second Division, although refusing the appeal on other grounds, disapproved the reasoning of the sheriff on this point on the basis that the mistake in the referral was 'so technical and so lacking in any prejudice that it cannot be held to constitute a fundamental nullity'.

1 Cf per LJ-C Cooper in *Lawrie v Muir* 1950 JC 19 at 27.
2 *C v Kennedy* (4 July 1986, unreported) Court of Session.
3 *Sloan v B* 1991 SLT 530.
4 *Sloan v B* 1991 SLT 530 at 547L-548 I.
5 1982 SLT 45.
6 The minutiae of the statutory history are set forth in 1982 SLT at 46.

Ultra vires acting by hearing

49.08   A children's hearing, being a statutory creation, must act within the powers of the statute which set it up. *In R v Children's Hearing for the*

Borders Region[1] a hearing had varied a supervision requirement so as to include a 'condition of residence in a pre-adoptive home chosen by the local authority'. On appeal Lord Justice-Clerk Wheatley said:

> 'I have no doubt that the power under s 44 (1)(a) to make a condition speci-fying where the child is to reside confers a wide discretion on the children's hearing ... I do not consider, however, that this discretion extends to the children's hearing divesting itself of the responsibility of specifying where that residence has to be, and delegating the selection to a third party subject to a restriction on the type of home, such as was prescribed here ... In my view the delegation of choice to a third party and the lack of specification take the condition in this case beyond the permissible bounds of statutory competence into the category of ultra vires.'

1 1984 SLT 65; see also following paragraph.

Acting by hearing contrary to statute

49.09 The foregoing case is also illustrative of an action which was ultra vires by reason of contravention of another statute. The Adoption Act, 1958, s 29(1), as amended, prohibited, with certain exceptions which did not arise in that case, the making of arrangements for adop-tion by any person other than an approved adoption society or a local authority and s 57(2) of that Act makes it clear that making an arrange-ment for an adoption is to include causing another to do this. Both the sheriff and the First Division of the Court of Session expressed the opinion that the hearing's action in paving the way for adoption contra-vened these sections.[1]

1 This prohibition, in relation to the (current) Adoption (Scotland) Act 1978 has now been modified by the Law Reform (Miscellaneous Provisions) (Scotland) Act 1985, s 27, which amends the Adoption (Scotland) Act 1978, s 65(3), so as to provide that a hearing, merely by placing a child in a way which facilitates adoption is not to be regarded as making arrangements for adoption: however the basic principles decided in *R v Children's Hearing for the Borders*, remain valid.

Failure by hearing to comply with hearings rules

49.10 Failures in the sheriff court to convene lawfully or comply with a statutory timetable have been held to be fatal irregularities.[1] Presumably similar actings by hearings would prima facie constitute a ground of appeal on irregularity. Irregular, even incompetent, actings alleged on the part of the hearing may be challenged on appeal and where this was not done the Court of Session has refused to permit resort to the *nobile offi-cium*.[2] It may be that a decision by a chairman to admit a person to a hearing[3] would be open to challenge on appeal if it could be said that it was not appropriate to admit that person and that admitted person had influenced the decision to the prejudice of the appellant.

1 *H v Mearns* 1974 SC 152; and *S v McGregor* (8 July 1980, unreported) Court of Session, discussed at 50.10 below.
2 *CM v Kennedy, BM v Kennedy* 1995 SCLR 15, 1995 SLT 123.
3 Children's Hearings (Scotland) Rules 1996, SI 1996/3261, r 13(d).

Imperfect notification

49.11   Any non-timeous or otherwise imperfect notification of any hearing or other diet may prima facie constitute a ground of appeal on the ground of irregularity but an appeal on such ground alone is unlikely to succeed unless real prejudice has been caused.[1]

1 *C v Kennedy* (4 July 1986, unreported) Court of Session.

Failure by hearing adequately to state reasons etc

49.12   As noticed already,[1] the hearing chairman must, at the end of a dispositive hearing,[2] announce the decision of the hearing and the reasons for it, and advise those present of their rights, and thereafter there must be notification by the reporter in writing.[3] It is, as already mentioned,[4] well established that a statutory statement of reasons of this type must be a true statement of reasons and not simply an assertion that the statutory procedures were complied with. It must therefore be properly informative and not merely formal. Failure satisfactorily to state reasons will therefore be a prima facie ground of appeal on the basis of irregularity of procedure. For discussion of adequate reasons see above at 23.32. Failure properly to notify would likewise constitute a stateable ground of appeal.

1 At 23.31 ff above.
2 There would appear to be no such obligations in a 'warrant' hearing although in practice the decision is announced.
3 Children's Hearings (Scotland) Rules 1996, SI 1996/3261, rr 20(5), 21 and 26(2).
4 At 23.32 ff above.

GROUNDS OF APPEAL OTHER THAN PROCEDURAL IRREGULARITY[1]

General

49.13   If a hearing has taken account of irrelevant or improper considerations or if there is some relevant and material consideration of which it has failed to take account then this will prima facie constitute a ground of appeal.[2]

1 See ch 48 above for further discussion.
2 *D v Sinclair* 1973 SLT (Sh Ct) 47; cf *R v Kennedy* 1995 GWD 7-354.

Change in circumstances

49.14   The case of *D v Sinclair*[1] makes it clear that 'all the circumstances of the case', in the context of appeals, includes events after the date of the decision appealed against, with the result that such events can be invoked by an appellant to justify his argument that the hearing's decision should not be allowed to stand.

1 1973 SLT (Sh Ct) 47.

Appeal raising question as to justification of original ground of referral?

49.15   The Children (Scotland) Act 1995, s 51 (notably subsections (2) and (3)) appears to envisage that the principal content of appeals will be the examination of reports or their compilers by the sheriff. The implication is that appeals will be mainly against disposals by hearings, and in practice this is so.[1] Yet the direction of the appellate court's attention by s 51(5) to 'all the circumstances of the case', coupled with the consideration that the sheriff may discharge the child from any further hearing or other proceedings in relation to the grounds for the referral of the case or substitute his or her own disposal,[2] may suggest that in an appropriate case an appeal may be used as a means of setting aside the initial grounds of referral. It is submitted, whatever the position may have been under the earlier legislation, that the presence in the 1995 Act of provisions[3] for review of the establishment of grounds of referral suggest that it would not be appropriate to try to use a s 51 appeal to re-open the question of whether or not the grounds of referral had been properly established. It may, however, be possible to engage a s 51 appeal to argue that the grounds for referral were not properly accepted at a children's hearing.

1 Cf *H and H v McGregor* 1973 SC 95.
2 Children (Scotland) Act 1995, s 51(5)(c)(ii) and (iii).
3 C(S)A 1995, s 85 – discussed in ch 57 below.

APPEAL AGAINST GRANTING OF WARRANT

Whether warrant justified or not

49.16   In considering the merits of an appeal against a warrant the sheriff will require to have regard to whether the warrant is justified in terms of the statutory provision enabling the warrant to be granted in the first place and, where appropriate, whether or not the relevant principles of the Children (Scotland) Act 1995, s 16 have been observed. For example, in an appeal against the granting or continuing of a warrant under s 66(1) or s 69(4) or (7) of the 1995 Act the sheriff will require to be satisfied that all three of the s 16 principles have been duly regarded by the hearing – subject always to the derogation from these principles enacted by s 16(5)[1] and to the possibility that there may be circumstances where the continued detention of a child may be in that child's own interest.[2]

1 '... protecting members of the public from serious harm (whether or not physical harm)'.
2 Cf *Humphries v S* 1986 SLT 683 at 684L.

Irrelevantly pleaded grounds of referral as possible ground of appeal against warrant

49.17   In *McGregor v K*[1] the sheriff was regarded as having sustained an appeal against the granting of a warrant on the ground, inter alia, that he regarded the grounds of referral on the basis of a Schedule 1 offence against the child as irrelevantly pleaded because the attacker of the child was not named. On appeal to the Court of Session it was held that the grounds of referral were not irrelevant since there is no need, in averring a Schedule 1 offence, to name the alleged offender: but it seemed to be accepted that an irrelevantly averred statement of grounds of referral might form a prima facie ground of appeal. It was not argued in *McGregor v K* that the concept of a preliminary challenge to the relevancy of grounds of referral had been negatived in *McGregor v D*.[2] It is tentatively submitted that a warrant granted on the basis of grounds which are clearly irrelevant may be open to successful appeal. The incorporation into our law of the European Convention on Human Rights, art 7(1) may fortify such an appeal.[3]

1 1982 SLT 293.
2 1977 SC 330 at 336, 337 and 339.
3 Cf *Welch v United Kingdom* (1995) 20 EHRR 247.

Warrants authorising secure accommodation

49.18   In appeals against 'secure accommodation' warrants granted under the Children (Scotland) Act 1995, s 66(6) the sheriff will have to consider if certain matters other than the interests of the child have been duly regarded, i e the presence or otherwise of the 'secure accommodation' criteria set out in s 70(9) and (10) of the Act.

CHAPTER 50

Preliminary procedure in appeals to the sheriff

Territorial jurisdiction in appeals

50.01   The right of appeal is 'to the sheriff '[1] and in practice this means to the sheriff within whose jurisdiction the hearing took place. This has been recognised as being the correct approach to proceedings in relation to applications[2] and it is thought that jurisdiction in appeals would be regarded as being governed by analogy thereto. There is, in relation to appeals, no provision parallel to the rule in relation to applications that when the ground of referral is an offence by the child the sheriff having jurisdiction is the sheriff who could try the child.[3] The result would appear to be that a case which had been heard in one sheriff court under the Children (Scotland) Act 1995, s 68 provision might, in the event of the sheriff's having held the grounds established and directed the reporter to arrange a hearing, fall to be dealt with in a different sheriff court in the event of an appeal from the disposal by such hearing.

1 Children (Scotland) Act 1995, s 51(1).
2 *Sloan, Petr* 1991 SLT 527 at 529D.
3 C(S)A 1995, s 68(3)(a).

Who may appeal

50.02   A 'child or a relevant person (or relevant persons) or both (or all)'[1] may appeal against a hearing's decision. The reporter has no right of appeal from a hearing's decision – thus the reporter, however disappointed by a hearing's decision, whether because he considers it to be unwise, unreasonable or contrary to law, has no right of appeal to any tribunal. Whether or not, on averment of a seriously irregular practice on the part of the hearing, an application to the *nobile officium* of the Court of Session[2] or for judicial review[3] would be entertained is a matter for conjecture: so far, the occasion for testing this does not appear to have arisen.

1 Children (Scotland) Act 1995, s 51(1).
2 For discussion of the *nobile officium* of the Court of Session see ch 57 below.
3 See ch 61 below.

Position of any safeguarder appointed by children's hearing

50.03   A safeguarder appointed by the chairman at a children's hearing may sign an appeal on behalf of a child to the sheriff.[1] It has been decided in the sheriff court that a safeguarder has a right of appeal independent of the child, but this decision has been criticised.[2] This matter has been fully discussed already.[3]

1 Act of Sederunt (Child Care and Maintenance Rules) 1997, SI 1997/291, r 3.53(3).

2 By Sheriff David Kelbie in his commentary to *Ross v Kennedy* 1995 SCLR (Sh Ct) (Notes) 1160 at 1162.
3 See 17.14 above.

Form of appeal – r 3.53(1), Forms 61-63; framing the note of appeal

Importance of stating reasons for appeal – appeal by a child – obtaining copy reports

50.04   The forms are self-explanatory. The person preparing the note of appeal should have available to him or her, if grounds of referral have been served, all the papers sent to the client, including the service copy of the statement of grounds for the referral, the notice of decision and copy of any supervision requirement, copy reasons for decision and any notice served under the Children's Hearings (Scotland) Rules, r 21(1)(c). Where the appeal is at the instance of a relevant person that person should have received the reports which were considered by the hearing.[1] If any papers are not available the reporter should be asked to provide copies. On the basis of the information thus obtained, together with whatever the client can recall, the note of appeal, in as specific terms as possible, should be prepared. A child has no entitlement to receive the papers which were before a hearing. In practice the reporter may be prepared to supply copies to the child's solicitor on a written request. Once in possession of relevant information it is the prima facie duty of any solicitor to make this known to the client in order to obtain full instructions (although solicitors may be cautious of giving out copies of documents containing sensitive information concerning children). Solicitors acting for children may sometimes fear that conveying sensitive information to a child may seriously harm the child. Should this arise the solicitor may wish to discuss the matter with the Professional Practice Committee of the Law Society of Scotland.

1 Children's Hearings (Scotland) Rules 1996, SI 1996/3261, r 5(3).

Who may sign an appeal

50.05   An appeal may be signed by the appellant or his or her representative.[1] An appeal by a child may be signed on the child's behalf by any safeguarder appointed by the children's hearing.[2]

1 Act of Sederunt (Child Care and Maintenance Rules) 1997, SI 1997/291, r 3.53(2).
2 SI 1997/291, r 3.53(3) – discussed at 17.14 and 50.03 above.

Lodgement of answers

50.06   In any appeal except an appeal against the granting of a warrant granted by a hearing, any party on whom the appeal has been served[1] may, if they so wish, lodge answers not later than seven days before the appeal diet and any answers should be intimated to any other person upon whom the appeal has been served.[2] It is suggested that the answers should, as far as possible, follow the form of the note of appeal, i e if the appeal has been set out in numbered paragraphs, the answers should deal with each point in the same order.

1 See 50.12 below.
2 Act of Sederunt (Child Care and Maintenance Rules) 1997, SI 1997/291, r 3.55,

Possible challenge to competency of appeal

50.07 If any party intends to challenge the competency of an appeal it is suggested, if written answers are to be lodged, that the legal submission on competency should be set out at the beginning of the answers. Unless the only opposition to the appeal is on a point of law, any answers should also address the merits of the appeal.

Debate on competency of appeal

50.08 There is no formally enacted procedure for the sheriff to hear in advance a debate as to the competency of an appeal but when the appeal may be contrary to law (e g through being out of time – see 50.09 below) the appellant may ask the sheriff to hear preliminary debate on this matter and the sheriff may be prepared to hear such debate and rule accordingly. In some instances where matters of competency are raised it may be prudent for the court to hear the merits argued under reservation of the point of competency.[1]

1 Cf the position in questions as to the competency of applications under the Children (Scotland) Act 1995, s 68, discussed at 29.06 above.

Time limits in relation to appeals

Appeals against disposals by hearings

50.09 Any appeal must be taken 'within a period of three weeks beginning with the date' of the decision appealed against.[1] It has been held in the sheriff court (in *S, Appellants*[2]) that the date of the hearing itself is to be taken as the first day of this three-week period, so that an appeal against a hearing's decision issued on Wednesday, 18 February 1976 which was lodged on Wednesday, 10 March 1976 was held to be too late by a day and therefore incompetent. In the present writer's view the decision in *S, Appellants*, which was decided on the basis of English legal authorities and without citation of the relevant Scottish principles and cases, is open to question and it may be that the first day of the 21 days is the day after the day on which the hearing's decision was taken.[3] The decision, however, stands in the law reports and has been followed by other sheriffs. Accordingly, to be on the safe side, prospective appellants should not knowingly adopt the more liberal interpretation. The sheriff no longer has a discretion to allow an appeal which is out of time since the Act of Sederunt (Statutory Appeals) 1981, SI 1981/1591, para 2(2) has been repealed.[4] The Court of Session may be prepared to consider extending the time limit by the exercise of the *nobile officium*: in the one case where this was attempted the Inner House declined to exercise the *nobile officium* on the basis that the appeal was inappropriate but appeared to leave open the possibility that in an appropriate case such an application might be countenanced.[5]

1 Children (Scotland) Act 1995, s 51(1).
2 1979 SLT (Sh Ct) 37 (Sheriff Kermack).
3 See the discussion of time limitations in *Tudhope v Lawson* 1983 SCCR 435, *McCormick v Martin* 1985 SLT (Sh Ct) 57 and *B v Kennedy* 1992 SLT 870.
4 Sheriff Court Summary Application Rules 1993, SI 1993/3240, Sch 2.
5 *Thompson v Principal Reporter* 1998 SCLR 898.

Sundays and public holidays

50.10   It has been held authoritatively that in computing time limits under the Children (Scotland) Act 1995, Sundays and public holidays must be included when counting the days.[1] However, in the event of the three-week period ending on a *dies non* such as a Sunday or other day on which the court is closed for ordinary business, the practice of allowing lodgment of a court paper the first court day after the last day would presumably apply.[2]

1 *S v McGregor* (8 July 1980, unreported) Court of Session: 'His [counsel for the appellant] final argument was that in counting time limits there should be disregarded *dies non*, Sundays and, perhaps, holidays. He was unable to cite any Act or any authority for that proposition, which has perhaps the superficial glamour of latinity ... where s 42(4) of the [1968] Act states that the sheriff shall hear an application "within twenty-eight days of the lodging of the application" it means exactly what it says. An initial hearing outwith twenty-eight days is incompetent.' See also *B v Kennedy* 1992 SLT 870.
2 *B v Kennedy* 1992 SLT 870 at 872K; cf *Lanark County Council v Docherty* 1959 SLT (Sh Ct) 12.

Appeals against warrants granted by hearings

50.11   In appeals against the issue of any warrant by a children's hearing the appeal must be disposed of 'within three days of the lodging of the appeal': and failing such disposal the warrant shall cease to have effect at the end of that period.[1] This means three calendar days, not working or court days,[2] i e with Sundays and holidays not excluded from the computation of this period. It is accordingly an imperative duty on the sheriff clerk and all responsible for the administration of the sheriff courts to ensure that a sheriff can be made available even on a *dies non* in order to deal, at very short notice, with appeals of this type.

1 Children (Scotland) Act 1995, s 51(8).
2 *B v Kennedy* 1992 SLT 870.

Procedure in court when appeal lodged

Fixing diet and notifying parties

50.12   On receiving the appeal document the sheriff clerk must immediately assign a date (no later than 28 days after the lodging of the appeal) for the hearing and at the same time intimate it to the appellant or his representative and then notify, and send a copy of the note of appeal to, the child (if not the appellant) (unless the sheriff dispenses with intimation to the child), the reporter, the relevant person (if not the appellant), any safeguarder appointed by the sheriff for the purpose of the appeal or appointed by the hearing and 'any other person the sheriff thinks necessary'. The sheriff clerk should endorse a certificate of execution of intimation on the appeal.[1]

1 Act of Sederunt (Child Care and Maintenance Rules) 1997, SI 1997/291, r 3.54.

Dispensing or not with notification of the child

50.13 *The views of the child – the rules.* Notification of the child is by Form 64.[1] This contains the injunction 'YOU MUST ATTEND ON THE FOLLOWING DATE'. The sheriff may dispense with the attendance of the child. The disposal of an appeal is one of the determinations of the court to which the principle in the Children (Scotland) Act 1995, s 16 of giving the child an opportunity to express a view has application. Accordingly, if the sheriff decides to dispense with the attendance of a child who may be mature enough to express a view then the sheriff must find a way of ascertaining if the child wishes to express a view and, if so, how that view is to be conveyed. The modes of ascertaining the views of the child have already been noticed.[2] In practice the sheriff may wish to appoint a safeguarder or curator *ad litem*.[3]

1 SI 1997/291, r 3.54(3).
2 At 4.10 ff above – SI 1997/291, r 3.5(2).
3 Cf SI 1997/291, r 3.5(2)(c).

50.14 *The practicalities – appointment or not of a safeguarder.* It follows from the foregoing that on receipt of the note of appeal the sheriff clerk should without delay put the papers before the sheriff who must decide whether or not to dispense with notification on the child and whether or not to appoint a safeguarder (or, in practice, a curator *ad litem*) and, if so, where a safeguarder has been appointed by the hearing or by the sheriff in related proceedings, to appoint that person or someone else.[1] Parties may show cause why a safeguarder other than the person appointed by the hearing should be appointed. No formal procedure has been laid down in relation to the appointment of a safeguarder at this stage. If a party wishes to show cause why a different safeguarder should be appointed he or she may do so by motion, preferably written, to the sheriff. In that event it is suggested that the sheriff clerk should advise the other parties of the motion so that they may have the opportunity of being heard. On the other hand there is no practice, where the sheriff is considering the appointment of a safeguarder on his or her own motion, of consulting parties. In practice the reporter may suggest that the appointment of a safeguarder be considered in a particular case and there seems no reason why another party should not so suggest.

1 SI 1997/291, r 3.7.

Competency of calling witnesses in all appeals – citation of witnesses and parties

50.15 It is now clear that the sheriff is entitled to hear evidence in appeals alleging irregularity in the conduct of the hearing and in any other circumstances as the sheriff may consider appropriate – though it should be noted that the use of the term 'may'[1] (in contrast with the rules in relation to the hearing of applications under the Children (Scotland) Act 1995, s 68[2]) suggests that the sheriff has a discretion. In any court proceedings wherein parties are entitled to lead verbal testimony it is necessary to provide the parties with authority to cite witnesses to court. Act of Sederunt (Child Care and Maintenance Rules) 1997, r 3.11 refers to applications and does not refer specifically to appeals, nor do the forms referred to in it apply to appeals, but Form 64[3] refers to an appeal as an 'application' and therefore it may be inferred that the provisions of r 3.11 are intended to apply to appeals. Accordingly the assigning by the sheriff clerk of the diet for the appeal entitles the sheriff clerk to issue a first order or warrant to cite in relation to an appeal.[4] The sheriff may at this stage wish to consider whether or not to use his powers to call for additional reports by virtue of s 51(3)(c) of the 1995 Act.[5] In the writer's experience the sheriff is inclined not to take this unusual step this early in the proceedings.

1 SI 1997/291, r 3.56(3).
2 SI 1997/291, r 3.47(1): '… the sheriff shall, in relation to any ground of referral which is in dispute, hear evidence tendered by or on behalf of the Principal Reporter'.
3 'Intimation to child in application under section 51 of the Children (Scotland) Act 1995.'
4 SI 1992/291, r 34(1)(c) and (2); the style for citation of witnesses and havers is given in Form 41.
5 Discussed below at 52.09.

Securing the presence of parties and witnesses

Mode, medium and time of citation

50.16   *Ordinary appeals*   The procedures for citation of and intimation to parties and witnesses, already noticed,[1] may be carried out in the same way and by the same persons as in s 68 application procedure. In all appeals except those against the issuing of warrants citation or intimation shall be made not later than 48 hours, or in the case of postal citation 72 hours, before the diet.[2]

1 See 30.10 ff above.
2 SI 1997/291, r 3.13(1).

50.17   *Appeals against warrant.*   These time limits have no application to the intimation of an appeal against a decision to issue a warrant for the detention of a child, where the period of notice and mode of giving notice is 'as directed by the sheriff'.[1] In practice the sheriff clerk will generally notify parties in the first instance by telephone or even in person and then confirm postally or by personal delivery.

1 SI 1997/291, r 3.13(2).

Proof of citation and intimation

50.18   Should proof of citation or intimation be required then an execution of service in the style of Form 43 with any postal receipt will suffice.[1]

The rules provide that the execution may be lodged at the hearing unless the sheriff otherwise directs.[2] The rules do not make mandatory the lodging of such execution but it would appear to be good practice to do so.

1 SI 1997/291, r 3.17(1).
2 SI 1997/291, r 3.17(2).

Witness may be examined without being formally cited

50.19 In general the only effect of citation is to 'compel a person's attendance within the precincts of the court',[1] and a person who is otherwise entitled to give evidence must not be excluded from giving evidence because he has not been cited;[2] and in practice the reporter will usually ensure that the reporter who was present at the hearing is present at the appeal and that the authors and compilers of reports are also present at the appeal so that they may be examined by the sheriff if the sheriff decides that this is appropriate. If the reporter wishes to have a witness on 'standby' this should be checked in advance with the sheriff clerk. There would seem to be no good reason why parties' representatives, preferably after consultation amongst themselves, should not ask the sheriff clerk to ask the sheriff if the sheriff wishes to examine the authors of reports.

1 *McDonnell v McShane* 1967 SLT (Sh Ct) 61 at 63, per Sheriff Principal Sir Allan G Walker QC.
2 Evidence (Scotland) Act 1852, s 1; cf *Watson v Livingstone* (1902) 5 F 171 and *Parker v North British Rly Co* (1900) 8 SLT 18.

Legal aid

Appeal to the sheriff against warrant granted by hearing

50.20 Legal aid shall be available to a child or relevant person for an appeal against a decision of a hearing to grant a warrant for the detention of the child, without any inquiry being made into the resources of the child or relevant person.[1] (There does not appear to be any necessity to satisfy the sheriff that legal aid for the purpose of appealing against a warrant is in the interests of the child.)

1 Legal Aid (Scotland) Act 1986, s 29(2)(b)(i) and s 29(3), as substituted by Children (Scotland) Act 1995, s 92.

Appeal to the sheriff against any other decision of a hearing

50.21 Legal aid shall be available to a child or relevant person for an appeal against any other decision of a children's hearing by application to the sheriff who must be satisfied:

(a) that it is in the interests of the child that legal aid be made available; and
(b) after consideration of the financial circumstances of the child and any relevant person that the expenses of the case cannot be met without undue hardship to the child or to any relevant person or to the dependants of any of them.[1]

1 Legal Aid (Scotland) Act 1986, ss 29(2)(b)(ii) and 29(4).

Access to papers by parties and their legal advisers

Report of proceedings

50.22   The reporter is bound to keep a report of the proceedings before the hearing.[1] While there may be no exact analogy between such a report and the records of a public court which are, in principle, open to inspection, in practice the reporter will allow a potential appellant or his legal representative reasonable facilities to examine the report.

1 Children's Hearings (Scotland) Rules 1996, SI 1996/3261, r 31.

Social inquiry, and other reports in hands of relevant persons and reporters

50.23   Relevant persons, but not children, receive copies of all reports laid before hearings.[1] The incorporation of the European Convention on Human Rights may require that consideration be given to introductory *machinery* procedures whereby, subject to appropriate safeguards in relation to sensitive information, papes are made available to children of appropriate maturity.

1 Children's Hearings (Scotland) Rules 1996, SI 1996/3261, r 5(3).

Safeguarder entitled to receive copies of all papers

50.24   Any safeguarder appointed by the sheriff (whether or not he or she elects to become a party to the proceedings) is entitled to receive from the reporter 'copies of the application, all of the productions in the proceedings and any papers which were before the children's hearing'.[1]

1 SI 1997/291, rr 3.6 and 3.8(b).

Papers and records in hands of third party

50.25   Records in the hands of third parties may presumably be recovered by commission and diligence procedures already discussed,[1] but recourse to these procedures is rare in appeals.

1 At 30.38 above; as noticed already, at 50.04 above, the reporter may make copy reports available to a child's solicitor.

Precognition of reporter's witnesses by appellant's solicitor or appellant in person

50.26   In appeals, as in applications, witnesses should be aware of a general duty to be reasonably available for precognition on relevant matters by the appellant's lawyer.[1] The observations[2] in relation to precognition of children in relation to s 68 applications apply equally here. Problems could arise in the rare instances of unrepresented appellants.

1 See 30.28 ff above.
2 At 30.30 above.

CHAPTER 51

The safeguarder or curator *ad litem* at the stage of appeal to the sheriff

General

Considering the appointment

51.01   In appeals, as in applications, the sheriff must, as soon as reasonably practicable, consider if it is necessary to appoint a safeguarder, and, if he or she does so decide, to appoint one on such terms and conditions as appear appropriate.[1] As in s 68 application procedure, the sheriff should name any safeguarder appointed by the hearing unless he or she decides otherwise *ex proprio motu* or on the motion of a party on cause shown.[2] The former provision requiring the sheriff, where an appeal had been signed by a safeguarder appointed by the hearing, to appoint that person as safeguarder in the appeal[3] has not been re-enacted.

1 Children (Scotland) Act 1995, s 41(1); Act of Sederunt (Child Care and Maintenance Rules) 1997, SI 1997/291, r 3.7(1)(a).
2 1997 Rules, r 3.7(2).
3 Act of Sederunt (Social Work) (Sheriff Court Procedure) Rules 1971, SI 1971/92, as amended, r 12A(2).

Safeguarder and curator ad litem

51.02   As in s 68 application procedure, the court may appoint a curator *ad litem* rather than a safeguarder and a curator *ad litem* so appointed will in practice be regarded as having the same role, rights and powers as a safeguarder.

Definition, function and duration

51.03   The definition and function of the safeguarder, the criteria for his or her appointment, the provisions in relation to the panels of person entitled to become safeguarders, the provisions as to the powers and duties of the safeguarder (including the right to receive the papers), the specialities connected with solicitors and advocates acting as safeguarders, the provisions entitling a safeguarder to decide whether or not to enter the proceedings, and the provisions entitling even a safeguarder who has not entered the proceedings to obtain subsequent interlocutors in relation to the proceedings[1] apply to the stage of an appeal to the sheriff as they do at the application stage – see discussion in ch 34. It is submitted that the observations in ch 34[2] regarding appeal by the safeguarder to the sheriff principal and/or the Court of Session, the duty of a non-legally qualified safeguarder to take legal advice, the duration and termination of office of safeguarder appointed by the sheriff and as to confidentiality of documents provided to the safeguarder apply *mutatis mutandis* to the safeguarder in an appeal to the sheriff. It is thought that, as in s 68 procedure, the appointment of a safeguarder endures throughout 'the proceedings' and that therefore the appointment of a safeguarder for an appeal would last until the conclusion of the appeal, including any appeal or appeals to the sheriff principal and/or the Court of Session arising out of such appeal, and terminating when the sheriff finally disposes of the appeal by one of the modes specified in the Children (Scotland) Act 1995, s 51(5)(c). In *R v Grant*[3] it was held that there was no incompetency in a safeguarder appearing as respondent in an appeal to the Court of Session which had been taken by children who had instructed independent legal representation.

1 Act of Sederunt (Child Care and Maintenance Rules) 1997, SI 1997/291, rr 3.8-3.10.
2 At 34.17 ff above.
3 2000 SLT 372 at 373L-374D.

Safeguarder receives copies of all relevant papers

51.04   The safeguarder at the appeal stage is entitled on being appointed (i e before he or she decides on whether or not to become a party to the proceedings) to receive from the reporter copies of the application and of all the productions in the proceedings and any papers which were before the children's hearing.[1]

1 SI 1997/291, r 3.8(b).

51.05   The foregoing has noted those aspects of the safeguarder's role in appeals which are in common with the role in applications. It is the purpose of the rest of this chapter to mention those aspects of the safeguarder's role which are of particular relevance in appeals.

Safeguarder becoming or not a party to proceedings

Grounds for safeguarder deciding whether or not to become party to the appeal

51.06   The regulations give no guidance as to the criteria to be adopted by a safeguarder appointed by the sheriff in relation to an appeal as to whether or not he or she should become a party to the appeal. Appeals to the sheriff are comparatively few and appeals wherein a safeguarder is appointed by the sheriff are fewer still. Most are in 'care and protection' cases raising problems of peculiar delicacy and difficulty. That being so, it is suggested that the appointed safeguarder should be inclined to elect to become rather than not to become a party to the proceedings.

Decision not to become a party

51.07   The safeguarder nominated by the sheriff in connection with an appeal, like a safeguarder nominated in connection with an application, must decide whether or not he or she intends to become a party to the proceedings. If the decision is not to become a party he or she must, like the safeguarder at the application stage, intimate 'that he does not intend to become a party to the proceedings . . . [and] . . . at the same time report in writing to the sheriff on the extent of his enquiries and his conclusion as to the interests of the child in the proceedings'.[1] A safeguarder who has not become a party receives intimation of all interlocutors subsequent to his appointment and may subsequently seek leave (of the sheriff) to become a party.[2]

1 SI 1997/291, r 3.10(1).
2 SI 1997/291, r 3.10(2) and (3).

Safeguarder becoming party to the proceedings

51.08 The safeguarder in an appeal acquires *mutatis mutandis* the same rights as the safeguarder in an application:[1] notably, where he becomes a party, he acquires the same rights as any other party to cite witnesses[2] and, when the appeal hearing takes place, to adduce his witnesses and cross-examine the witnesses of others.[3] A safeguarder who elects not to become a party must nevertheless make his or her enquiries and report on the extent of these enquiries and his or her conclusion as to the interests of the children in the proceedings.[4]

1 See 34.12 ff above.
2 See 50.15 ff above.
3 See 52.11 below for discussion of the extent of such rights.
4 Act of Sederunt (Child Care and Maintenance Rules) 1997, SI 1997/291, r 3.10(1).

CHAPTER 52

Conduct of appeal to the sheriff

THE OUTSET OF THE APPEAL

Primary onus on appellant

52.01 The wording of the Children (Scotland) Act 1995, s 51(5), 'Where the sheriff is satisfied that the decision of the children's hearing is not justified in all the circumstances of the case he shall allow the appeal . . .', may be regarded as placing the primary onus on the appellant to 'satisfy' the sheriff that the hearing was wrong. As will be discussed more fully presently,[1] the sheriff has unusually extensive powers to call for additional information.[2] This may be interpreted as suggesting a more 'inquisitorial' approach by the sheriff than is usual in our adversarial tradition.[3]

1 At 52.09 below.
2 Children (Scotland) Act 1995, s 51(3)(c).
3 Cf ch 35 above for discussion of the inquisitorial and adversarial approaches.

Possibility of withdrawal of certain grounds of appeal

52.02 The opening address will be the appropriate time to intimate if any ground of appeal is not to be insisted upon. Appeals often require to be drafted quickly and on incomplete information and abandonment of certain lines of argument at this stage is common and proper practice. It is submitted, although there is no provision to this effect in the rules, that it is good practice for the sheriff clerk to record formally in the record of proceedings any departure from a ground of appeal made at this stage.

Amplification of grounds of appeal

52.03 The written note of appeal should have been set out in accordance with the appropriate form.[1] There is no provision for adding supplementary grounds of appeal at a later stage and the argument could no doubt be mounted that any such addition would constitute a fresh appeal which would, by the time the appeal diet had arrived, almost certainly be time-barred. There is, in contrast with the provisions governing appeals from the sheriff to the sheriff principal,[2] no express rule limiting the arguments at the appeal hearing to the matters raised in the note of appeal, subject to the power of the sheriff principal to allow such arguments on cause shown and on such conditions as the sheriff principal may consider appropriate. In *G v Templeton*[3] Sheriff Principal Risk, applying these provisions, did not regard last-minute thoughts by the appellant's agent as 'cause shown' and commented: 'I was particularly reluctant to entertain such arguments since, even if successful, they would not have altered the overall result of the case.' It is submitted that the absence, in the rules governing appeals to the sheriff, of any limitation on the scope of the arguments in such an appeal, and in the light of the presence of such limitation in appeals to the sheriff principal, lends force, on the principle *expressio unius, exclusio alterius*, to the view[4] that:

(a) the paramountcy of the interests of the child under the Children (Scotland) Act 1995, s 16(1),
(b) the short time limits within which papers have to be lodged,
(c) the difficulty which must sometimes be encountered in obtaining reliable information and clear instructions,
(d) the much-emphasised informality of the proceedings, and
(e) the wide powers of the court to adjourn the appeal,[5]

are all matters which could be urged in favour of the sheriff having the power to allow amplification of existing grounds of appeal, and even addition of fresh grounds of appeal, if satisfied that there would be a real risk of injustice if such a course were not allowed.[6] In the event of amplification being permitted, the sheriff would require to give sympathetic consideration to any motion for adjournment made by any other party to the appeal. Any appellant's solicitor intending to attempt to amplify his grounds of appeal ought to inform the other parties of his intention at the earliest possible time so that the necessity for an adjournment might possibly be avoided. Where an appellant is arguing his case in person the court may be ready to allow latitude and to allow a new ground of appeal to be presented.[7]

1 Act of Sederunt (Child Care and Maintenance Rules) 1997, SI 1997/291, r 3.53 and Forms 61, 62 or 63.
2 SI 1997/291, r 3.59(9).
3 1998 SCLR 180 at 182C.
4 Cf the 1st edn of this book at p 329.
5 1997 Rules, r 3.57.
6 For discussion of 'cause shown' and the principles which should govern the late allowance of additional arguments in the context of the procedure relating to a devolution issue under the Scotland Act 1998, s 98 and Sch 6 see *HM Advocate v Montgomery* 1999 SCCR 959 at 968E.
7 Cf the attitude of the Court of Session in *C v Kennedy* (4 July 1986, unreported).

COURSE OF APPEAL HEARING

Flexible nature of procedure

52.04   As noticed already,[1] the sheriff has extensive powers in appeals and appears to be expected to be ready if appropriate to exercise them on his or her own initiative. Moreover, since the relevant rules of procedure[2] are not highly prescriptive as to procedure it is therefore submitted that the discretion accorded to the court, always wide in matters under the

Children (Scotland) Act 1995, Pt II, chs 2 and 3, is particularly wide in relation to appeals. It follows that, subject to the rules and to basic principles of fairness, the sheriff has considerable latitude in deciding how best to order the proceedings in the light of the facts and circumstances of the individual appeal. What follows, in relation to the ordering of procedure, is accordingly only a general guide.

1 At 47.03 ff above.
2 SI 1997/291, r 3.56.

Opening statement by or on behalf of appellant and parties – who may be a 'party'

52.05 Common to all appeals is the provision for the court to 'hear the appellant or his representative and any party to the appeal'.[1] Generally the sheriff will wish to hear at the outset from the principal parties, i e the appellant and the respondent, but it is submitted that for the purpose of these proceedings any person who has received notification of the appeal under Act of Sederunt (Child Care and Maintenance Rules) 1997 r 3.54(1) should be regarded as a 'party' and as such entitled to be heard if desired.[2] Sometimes, as when the appellant is legally represented and when the matters which are to be argued in the appeal are fully set out in the note of appeal, this introductory address may be very brief and formal and will comprise little more than an introduction to the court of the parties, the persons appearing, and perhaps a formal reference to the note of appeal for the issues to be argued. In a more complex appeal the preliminary address may be used to bring to the attention of the court particular aspects of the case and, when the appellant is conducting his or her own case, it will give the sheriff the opportunity of raising with the party litigant any problems which the court foresees. Any safeguarder or curator *ad litem* should be heard on behalf of the child. If a party has in mind a particular point on which he or she wishes a ruling it would be proper and sensible to ask leave of the court to mention the point at the outset so that the sheriff is alerted to the point as soon as possible. In *H and H v McGregor* this was the course apparently adopted by Sheriff J C M Jardine whose judgment was described by Lord Justice-Clerk Wheatley as 'detailed and careful'.[3]

1 SI 1997/291, r 3.56(1).
2 It is understood that this approach has sometimes not found favour with the courts: it is nonetheless submitted that it is implicit in the 1997 Rules that persons who have received notification of the appeal should be allowed to be heard. It is submitted that the European Convention on Human Rights, art 6(1) supports this – cf *Kraska v Switzerland* (1993) 18 EHRR 188.
3 1973 SC 95 at 114.

Agreed matters

52.06 In some appeals there will be points which can be agreed between the parties. Sometimes the reporter's agreement will have been signified by an admission in written answers. In that event the opening speech should refer the court to such admissions. Alternatively, agreement may have been reached by discussion between the parties, and in this event the exact area of agreement should be specified in the opening speech.

Procedure where no evidence led or authors or compilers of reports examined

52.07   Most appeals raise issues affecting the merits of the disposal by the hearing and are conducted on the basis of the reports which were available to the hearing. The sheriff will frequently have familiarised him or herself with the reports and any other productions before the hearing of the appeal.[1] After hearing initially from the appellant and the respondent the sheriff may wish to hear additionally from one or more of the other parties. The sheriff may adjourn for a period or periods in order to consider further the reports and the submissions.

1 Cf *Sloan v B* 1991 SLT 530 at 551K. The reporter will of course have lodged the relevant papers in compliance with the Children (Scotland) Act 1995, s 51(2).

Examination of reporter and of authors or compilers of reports

52.08   Unless there have been preliminary discussions between the parties and the sheriff clerk and the agreement of the sheriff has been obtained towards limiting the evidence,[1] the reporter should have available to the court the authors or compilers of reports and the sheriff may examine them. Where the reporter conducting the appeal is not the reporter who conducted the case before the hearing whose decision is under appeal then the latter reporter should be available for examination at the appeal and the sheriff 'examine' him or her. Sheriffs generally administer the oath or affirmation.

1 See discussion above at end of 50.19.

Further report or reports called for by the sheriff

52.09   The sheriff may 'call for any further report which he considers may assist him in deciding the appeal'.[1] It is submitted that further reports may be commissioned not only from persons who have already submitted reports but also from other persons selected by the sheriff and this has occasionally been done, for example where the sheriff wished to have a psychiatrist's opinion. This appears to be the only instance in the civil practice of the sheriff court wherein the sheriff may, as it were, call the court's own witness. This power is not often used. When it is used it is thought that the sheriff should arrange through the sheriff clerk for the author(s) to appear as witness(es) and speak to the report(s).[2] The rules provide: 'on receipt of a further report, the sheriff shall direct the principal reporter to send a copy of the report to every party to the appeal'.[3] The additional report may contain matter which would be harmful to the child. In this event it is submitted that the sheriff may be entitled, having regard to the letter and spirit of s 16(1) of the Children (Scotland) Act 1995 and to r 3.56(4) of the Act of Sederunt (Care and Maintenance) Rules 1997, to direct that such matter should not be disclosed to the child.

1 Children (Scotland) Act 1995, s 51(3)(c).
2 Cf Children's Hearings (Scotland) Rules 1996, SI 1996/3261, r 5(1) and *McMichael v United Kingdom* (1995) 20 EHRR 205.
3 Act of Sederunt (Care and Maintenance Rules) 1997, SI 1997/291, r 3.56(2).

Leading evidence – order of witnesses

52.10 In any appeal the sheriff may hear evidence.[1] The order of witnesses is a matter for the discretion of the sheriff but the sheriff will generally allow the appellant the opportunity of leading evidence first if desired. Witnesses may be cross-examined by the other parties or their representatives and re-examined by the party leading the witness. As in s 68 application procedure, the sheriff should, as far as possible, not allow narrow technical considerations to impede the thorough investigation of the issues.[2]

1 Children (Scotland) Act 1995, s 51(3); Act of Sederunt (Child Care and Maintenance Rules) 1997, SI 1997/291, r 3.56(3).
2 Cf *W v Kennedy* 1988 SCLR 236, 1988 SLT 583; the case of *W* was of course held to have been superseded in its main point (the admissibility of hearsay in order to prove the content of the hearsay) in *F v Kennedy (No 1)* 1992 SC 28, 1992 SCLR 139, 1993 SLT 1277 but the observations of Lord Sutherland in favour of flexibility of procedure are, it is thought, still applicable where flexibility does not conflict with express law.

Standard of proof

52.11 The standard of proof indicated by the Children (Scotland) Act 1995 is that the sheriff is to be 'satisfied'.[1] It is submitted that in all appeals the standard of proof for any matter of fact is the balance of probabilities.[2] In cases based upon an alleged irregularity those acting for the appellant should (unless a narrative of the proceedings before the hearing can be agreed) call as witnesses all whom they have reason to believe have relevant information on the proceedings.

1 Children (Scotland) Act 1995, s 51(5).
2 See discussion at 42.08 ff above; even in appeals against disposals in cases under C(S)A 1995, s 52(2)(i) it is submitted that there is no question of the standard of beyond reasonable doubt since this only has application in proofs in s 52(2)(i) cases – C(S)A 1995, s 68(3)(b).

Competency of members of hearing as witnesses at appeal?

Appeals on the merits

52.12 Panel members, like sheriffs, are not exempt from being cited as witnesses to proceedings which have taken place before them. Sheriffs are often enough cited to give evidence in relation to charges of alleged perjury in cases over which they have presided. However in relation to the merits of a decision a sheriff or judge is only answerable to a superior court on appeal or judicial review.[1] A children's hearing is a judicial or at least a quasi-judicial body: it operates under statutory procedures, admits of legal representation before it, must act judicially in the sense of allowing and considering representations made to it by those appearing, must give reasons for its decision, and is subject to appeal. It is submitted that if Parliament had intended to introduce the unusual procedure of having members of the tribunal of first instance give evidence justifying their decision before the appellate court it would have said so in clear terms. The consideration that Parliament did make explicit provision by way of statutory amendment[2] for the reporter to give evidence at the appeal and refrained from making any such provision in relation to hearing members affords confirmation that such an extraordinary course was not in contemplation. It is also submitted that although a hearing member is the 'author' of a hearing's reasons for its decision, he or she does not thereby become the 'author' or 'compiler' of a 'report' or 'statement' in the sense intended in the Children (Scotland) Act 1995, s 51(3): it is accordingly submitted that a hearing member would not be an appropriate person for the sheriff to examine in terms of s 51(3).

1 Cf Human Rights Act 1988, s 9(1) and (2).
2 Children Act 1975, Sch 3, para 57, amending the Social Work (Scotland) Act 1968, s 49(3).

Appeals on irregularity

52.13 It may be thought that hearing members may be competent witnesses in appeals based on irregularity for the limited purpose of speaking to what happened at the hearing. It is submitted that generally the reporter should give such evidence and that hearing members should not be cited for this purpose. If for some reason, for example the illness of the reporter at the time of the appeal, it was thought necessary to cite a hearing member then it is submitted that it may be appropriate for the sheriff to limit the evidence taken from the hearing member to narration of the proceedings of the children's hearing but not to allow the hearing member to be asked to justify procedural decisions since it would be difficult to do so without investigating the hearing's view of the merits of the case.

Position if hearing member adduced as witness

52.14 The subject matter of the opinions expressed in the foregoing paragraphs has not as yet been considered in the Court of Session. Where a hearing member is cited as a witness he or she should attend the court in accordance with the citation. Should the hearing member be asked a question which appears to bear upon the merits of the decision of the hearing, or a question the answer to which might be confidential, the hearing member should ask for directions from the presiding sheriff under reference to the Children (Scotland) Act 1995, s 43 and the Children's Hearings (Scotland) Rules 1996, notably r 5(4). The panel member should, of course, comply with the direction of the sheriff. The sheriff may properly refuse to allow plainly incompetent evidence[1] but in the present state of the law the prudent course for the sheriff,[2] subject of course to the arguments presented to him or her at the time, may be to follow the normal practice and listen to the testimony of hearing members 'under reservation'.[3]

1 Cf *Merrin v S* 1987 SLT 193.
2 Cf *Sloan v B* 1991 SLT 530 at 546F–K, discussed at 29.06 ff above.
3 It may not follow, however, even in the state of the law as at present understood, that members of hearings fall within the category of ordinary or expert witnesses having the general civic duty to make themselves reasonably available for precognition (see 30.28 above). Until and unless the law is authoritatively stated to be that a hearing member is a competent witness, it may be thought that they are under no obligation to make themselves available for precognition except possibly where it is clear that the only matter about which he or she is to be asked is purely procedural.

SPECIALITIES OF APPEALS PROCEDURE

Position of reporter

52.15 The general duties of the reporter to the court have already been discussed in the context of the application stage.[1] It is submitted that similar considerations are relevant at the appeal stage. The reporter has a duty to try to make sure, as far as possible that no matter, whether of fact or of law, is overlooked or unfairly presented. He or she will have his or her own view as to the correct disposal of the appeal, in both its factual and legal aspects, and should accordingly focus such facts and be ready to marshal such legal argument as is necessary to support this view. The reporter is also a particularly valuable source of information as to what happened at the hearing. Moreover the reporter must always – and this will apply particularly (but not only) when the child or parent at the appeal is not professionally represented – try to make sure that the attention of the court is directed to any legal or factual matter which will assist the sheriff, including information tending to *support* the appeal.

1 In ch 30 above, notably at 30.03.

Possible exclusion of child from part of proceedings

52.16 Where the nature of the appeal or any evidence involved is such that the sheriff is satisfied that it is in the interests of the child that he or she should not be present at any stage of the appeal the sheriff may exclude the child during that stage and any relevant person, safeguarder or curator *ad litem* or other representative may remain.[1]

1 Act of Sederunt (Child Care and Maintenance Rules) 1997, SI 1997/291, r 3.56(4).

Possible exclusion of relevant persons and their representatives from part of proceedings

52.17 Where the sheriff is satisfied that it is necessary in order to obtain the views of the child or that the presence of a relevant person or representative(s) is or are causing or likely to cause significant distress to the child the sheriff may exclude such person(s).[1]

1 SI 1997/291, r 3.56(5).

Position where relevant person has been excluded from part of appeal

52.18   The Act of Sederunt (Child Care and Maintenance Rules) 1997, r 3.56(6) provides that where exclusion of a relevant person or representative has been ordered the sheriff shall, after the exclusion has ended, explain to the person(s) the substance of what has taken place during the period of the exclusion and allow them an opportunity to respond by leading evidence or otherwise. On the other hand, r 3.5, which allows for the views of the child to be conveyed orally to the sheriff,[1] permits the sheriff to direct that the views of the child are noted and sealed up in an envelope, marked 'confidential' and not made available to others.[2] Rule 3.56(6) is not said to be 'subject to' the provisions of r 3.5, but it is submitted that the paramountcy principle of the Children (Scotland) Act 1995, s 16(1) would require the sheriff to apply r 3.5(4) in preference to r 3.56(6) where the safety or welfare of the child so demanded. It is also submitted that it would be appropriate for the sheriff to advise the child of the possibility (subject to the sheriff's taking this course) that the child's views, or part of them, may be so kept confidential if the child requested.

1 SI 1997/291, r 3.5(2)(a).
2 SI 1997/291, r 3.5(4).

Confidential views of the child

52.19   The foregoing confidentiality provisions are remarkable and may give rise to great difficulty, involving as they do the possibility of keeping the child's views from parties. This matter has already been discussed.[1]

1 At 4.10 ff above.

CONCLUSION OF APPEAL

Concluding speeches

52.20   Although nothing is said in the Rules on this point, it will generally be desirable for the sheriff to allow parties to sum up their respective cases if they so desire.

Motion for additional fee for solicitor, safeguarder or curator ad litem

52.21   Any motion for an additional fee for solicitor or safeguarder should be made at the conclusion of the appeal. The competency of

such a motion and the relative procedures have already been discussed.[1]

1 See 39.10 ff above.

Proceedings summary in nature

52.22 Like application proceedings, the proceedings in appeals are
'summary'.[1] It follows that what was said in relation to the summary
nature of s 68 applications also applies to appeals.[2] In particular, parties
should take and keep as accurate notes as possible of what happens at the
appeal hearing in case an appeal should be taken against the decision of
the sheriff to the sheriff principal or the Court of Session.

1 SI 1997/291, r 3.20.
2 See 36.02 ff above.

CHAPTER 53

Disposing of the appeal

APPEAL AGAINST WARRANT

General

53.01 In these appeals only two disposals are open to the sheriff, namely to 'confirm the decision of the children's hearing'[1] and allow the warrant to stand, or to allow the appeal and 'recall the warrant'.[2]

1 Children (Scotland) Act 1995, s 51(4).
2 C(S)A 1995, s 51(5)(a).

Position pending appeal

53.02 When a hearing grants warrant for the apprehension and detention of a child (to find and keep a child in a place of safety) any appeal by the child or relevant person shall, as already noticed,[1] be disposed of within three days of the lodging of the appeal and if it is not disposed of within this time limit 'the warrant shall cease to have effect'.[2] It is a clear implication of this provision that the marking of an appeal does not of itself put the warrant, or any action which has been taken on it, into suspension.[3] There is no provision for 'interim liberation' pending consideration of the appeal by the sheriff.

1 At 50.11 above.
2 Children (Scotland) Act 1995, s 51(8).
3 Cf the position in a pending appeal in relation to a condition in a supervision requirement: see *Kennedy v M* 1995 SCLR 88 at 94D, E, 1995 SLT 717 at 717J–721B; *Stirling v D* 1995 SCLR 460, 1995 SLT 1089.

APPEAL AGAINST SUPERVISION REQUIREMENT WITH CONDITION AUTHORISING SECURE ACCOMMODATION

53.03 In any appeal wherein there is in force a supervision requirement containing a condition that the child shall be liable to be placed and kept in secure accommodation under the Children (Scotland) Act 1995, s 70(9) the sheriff, if satisfied that the decision to impose or continue that condition is not justified in all the circumstances of the case, shall direct that the condition shall cease to have effect.[1] It therefore appears that in an appeal against a disposal which included an authorisation in a supervision requirement of secure accommodation the sheriff would be entitled, even if otherwise refusing the appeal, or if allowing the appeal but only to the extent of remitting back to the hearing, to direct that the secure accommodation condition should cease to have effect.

1 Children (Scotland) Act 1995, s 51(5)(b).

OTHER DISPOSALS ON APPEAL

The statutory provisions

53.04   Where the sheriff decides that an appeal has failed he or she shall confirm the decision of the hearing.[1] Section 51(5)(c) of the Act provides that where the sheriff is satisfied that the decision of the children's hearing is not justified in all the circumstances of the case the sheriff shall allow the appeal and:

> '(c) in any case, he may, as he thinks fit—
>> (i)   remit the case with reasons for his decision to the children's hearing for reconsideration of their decision; or
>> (ii) discharge the child from any further hearing or other proceedings in relation to the grounds for the referral of the case; or
>> (iii) substitute for the disposal by the children's hearing any requirement which could be imposed by them under section 70 of this Act.'

1 Children (Scotland) Act 1995, s 51(4).

The application of the s 16 principles in considering disposal of appeals

53.05   Where the sheriff is considering disposing of the appeal other than under the Children (Scotland) Act 1995, s 51(5)(c)(iii)[1] only the paramountcy of welfare and the 'consulting the views of the child' principles are imported by s 16.[2] If the sheriff is minded to substitute his, or her own disposal then the 'no non-beneficial order' principle also applies. The reasoning behind these provisions would seem to be (a) that if the sheriff sustains the appeal by remitting back, he or she is not making any order with immediate effect but is simply asking the hearing to reconsider; and (b) that if the sheriff is discharging the child from any further hearing or other proceedings in relation to the grounds for the referral he or she must, *ex hypothesi*, have considered that the best interests of the child are served by so doing or that the proceedings are so seriously flawed as to require the referral to be discharged in any event: it is submitted that if the sheriff sees good reason in fact or in law to sustain an appeal by discharging the referral then none of the s 16 principles should operate so as to prevent such a disposal. See the discussion of the s 16 principles at 2.14ff above. It is submitted, moreover, that the paramountcy principle has no direct application to the deliberations of the sheriff in weighing the merits of the appeal. Of course the sheriff may require to consider if the hearing has applied this principle, or applied it appropriately, but if, for example, the sheriff's opinion was that the appeal ought to succeed and the referral be discharged then, it is submitted, the sheriff would not be entitled, as it were, to say to him or herself 'This appeal should succeed in law, but since the welfare of the child would not be served by so doing I will refuse it'. By contrast, where the sheriff is substituting his or her own disposal under s 51(5)(c)(iii), then the sheriff should operate under the same principles which apply where a hearing is deciding on the disposal of a child's case.

1 Sheriff substituting his or her own disposal.
2 Children (Scotland) Act 1995, s 16(1)–(4).

Sustaining an appeal to the extent of remitting back for reconsideration

53.06 Most successful appeals take the form of a remit back. The Children (Scotland) Act 1995 simply enjoins the sheriff to remit 'with reasons for his decision'. Interpreting the parallel provisions of the Social Work (Scotland) Act 1968, the Court of Session held in *Kennedy v A*[1] that the sheriff was not entitled, when sustaining an appeal and remitting for reconsideration, to give directions to a hearing. Lord Justice-Clerk Ross, delivering the opinion of the Second Division, stated:

> 'This was an appeal under s 49 of the Act of 1968, and if the sheriff is satisfied that the decision of the children's hearing is not justified in all the circumstances of the case, he may then, as he thinks fit, remit the case with reasons for his decision to the children's hearing for reconsideration of their decision. It is thus clear that the sheriff is required to give reasons for his decision, but it is one thing to give reasons for his decision and quite another thing to make observations or give directions. In our opinion, the sheriff clearly exceeded his powers in making these observations and giving these directions. He is not in the same position as this court which is expressly empowered under s 50(3) of the Act of 1968 to remit the case back to the sheriff for disposal "in accordance with such directions as the court may give".'

The operative words of s 51(5)(c)(i) of the 1995 Act exactly replicate those of s 49(5)(b) of the 1968 Act. The competence now given to the sheriff under s 51(5)(c)(iii) to substitute his or her own disposal for that of the hearing may raise a question as to whether the ratio of the decision in *Kennedy v A* remains in force. It may be, however, that the question will be an academic one since if the sheriff is minded to change the disposal he or she may employ the power under s 51(5)(c)(iii) rather than remit back with suggestions.

1 1986 SLT 358.

Sustaining an appeal by substituting a disposal

53.07 When considering sustaining an appeal by substituting her own disposal the sheriff must apply all three of the s 16 principles.[1] There was some opposition to this form of disposal while the Children (Scotland) Bill was going through Parliament. It was feared that sheriffs would be inclined to take over the work of the children's hearings. So far as the writer is aware there has been no sign of this as yet. There may however be cases where it will be appropriate for the sheriff to take this course. There may be cases where parties agree that a remit for reconsideration would waste time. Even without such agreement there may be cases where the sheriff is satisfied that it is essential in the interests of the welfare of the child that a clear course of action be followed without delay. It is submitted that such disposal should only be contemplated where the sheriff has considered the case very fully, possibly by commissioning a fresh report or reports. It is suggested that the sheriff should generally appoint a safeguarder or curator *ad litem* in such cases. It is submitted that the sheriff should make clear his or her intention to consider substituting a disposal and indicate what that disposal may be, including the conditions which she or he is considering imposing in the disposal.[2] The sheriff should hear parties' submissions on the disposal being contemplated, including the proposed conditions. If imposing a condition under s 70(7) of the Children (Scotland) Act 1995 (determining that there shall be a review at a time during the supervision requirement) the review will, it is submitted be a review by the children's hearing and not by the sheriff.

1 See discussions above at 47.05 and 53.05.
2 Children (Scotland) Act 1995, s 70(2)-(6), (8) and (9).

Sustaining by discharge an appeal on a ground other than procedural irregularity

53.08 The possibility of there being in existence admitted or proved grounds of referral and yet its being appropriate for the child to be discharged and no further action taken has already been encountered – it is one of the options open to a hearing in the course of its consideration of a case.[1] In appeals on the merits of the disposal by the hearing it would seem to be appropriate for the sheriff to discharge the referral if satisfied (a) that the appeal ought to succeed *and* (b) that on no reasonable view was the child in need of compulsory measures of supervision.

1 Children (Scotland) Act 1995, ss 65(7) and 69(1)(b).

Sustaining by discharge an appeal on a ground of procedural irregularity

53.09 In a case in 1986[1] a children's hearing which had already renewed a warrant for the detention of a child under the Social Work (Scotland) Act 1968, s 37(5) continued a hearing in order to consider the terms of a social work report which it had not had time to consider. The notification of the continued hearing to the appellant stated that this hearing was 'to consider the renewal of warrant in terms of s 37(5)'. This was an inaccurate notification and formed a ground of appeal by a parent. In rejecting this ground the Court of Session observed that the appellant parent had been present when the hearing had been continued and knew of the true (and lawful) purpose of the continuation. The court concluded:

'In the circumstances the error in the notice ... is not material, and in any event, it could not vitiate the later decision which is now appealed against.'

In the Orkney case[2] the sheriff had taken notice of the fact that the hearing had proceeded in the absence of the children and had dismissed the application as incompetent on that basis. In the course of holding that the sheriff had erred in so doing Lord President Hope, delivering the opinion of the First Division, stated:[3]

'A sheriff is not bound to hear evidence in an application made to him under s 42 where he is satisfied that under no circumstances whatsoever, whatever the evidence might be, could he hold the grounds for the referral established. But there is a sharp distinction between cases of that type and the present case where the alleged incompetency arose because of a defect in the procedure which could be put right.'

Putting the foregoing observations together, it is submitted that it would only be appropriate to sustain an appeal by discharging the child on the ground of a procedural error where such error was (a) not only material but so fundamental as to vitiate irreparably the subsequent decisions of the hearing; *and* (b) was incapable of rectification at a further hearing or otherwise. It may be that a gross procedural irregularity, such as convening a hearing on a day which was not the lawfully appointed day, might constitute such an example.[4] By contrast it may be thought appropriate to dispose of breaches even of certain of the principles of natural justice[5] – for example, if a hearing had failed to give parent or child their say at the hearing[6] by sustaining the appeal by a remit back so as to allow the hearing to repair the defect. In an unreported case the writer, in the special circumstances of the case, sustained an appeal by remitting back where a safeguarder's report commissioned by an earlier hearing had been rendered irrelevant by subsequent events and the safeguarder had not been able to investigate and advise on the interests of the child in the changed situation.

1 *C v Kennedy* (4 July 1986, unreported) Court of Session.
2 *Sloan v B* 1991 SLT 530.
3 At 546F.
4 Cf the early case of *H v Mearns* 1974 SC 152; see also *S v McGregor* (8 July 1980, unreported) Court of Session wherein the court stated: 'Once a timetable set out in an Act is disregarded to any extent the possibilities are endless and one could have case after case depending not on the Act but on the circumstances attendant on each individual case. It was not suggested that there was any discretionary power given to the sheriff which might have allowed him to extend the effect of the prescribed timetable'; see discussion of scope of appeal in chs 47 and 49 above.
5 '... the principles of natural justice must yield to the best interests of the child ...' – *Kennedy v A* 1986 SLT 358 at 362.
6 Children's Hearings (Scotland) Rules 1996, SI 1996/3261, r 20(3)(c).

Effect of sustaining appeal by discharging referral

53.10 The primary effect of sustaining an appeal by discharging the referral is to terminate the referral of the child's case to the hearing and to cause to cease to have effect any steps taken or ancillary orders made as a consequence of the referral. In an 'offence by the child' referral of any rehabilitation period under the Rehabilitation of Offenders Act 1974 would cease to have effect. The Children (Scotland) Act 1995 makes clear that the effect of discharge is to 'discharge the child from any further hearing or other proceedings in relation to the grounds for the referral of the case'.[1] It seems clear that this would exclude, for example, the subsequent referral of the child on different grounds which reflected the same facts. In practice it is thought that it would also exclude any prosecution of the child (but not parents or third parties) from criminal (but not presumably civil) proceedings founded upon these facts.

1 Children (Scotland) Act 1995, s 51(5)(c)(ii).

APPEAL AGAINST DECISION ON A REVIEW

Restriction on frivolous appeals

53.11   If, on an unsuccessful appeal against a supervision requirement which has been imposed at a hearing convened to review the requirement, the sheriff is satisfied that the appeal was frivolous he may order that no appeal against a decision to continue the same requirement made on a subsequent review shall be permitted until the expiration of 12 further months.[1] This provision is, of course, discretionary and, while a valuable safeguard against the upset to the child consequent upon repeated visits to the court on appeal, is not to be used oppressively.

1 Children (Scotland) Act 1995, s 51(7).

DECISION OF THE COURT

Oral decision: written note – when obligatory, when desirable

53.12   The decision of the court on an appeal is given orally at the conclusion of the appeal or at a diet fixed for this purpose.[1] Where the sheriff remits for reconsideration or substitutes his or her own decision for the decision of the hearing he or she must issue a written note of reasons within seven days.[2] In any other case there is no obligation to deliver a detailed opinion, written or oral. Generally, a brief oral explanation is given but in a particular case the sheriff may wish to issue a written note in order to make clear his or her attitude to some matter of fact or law. The sheriff clerk sends a copy of the decision to the reporter, the appellant (and to the child or relevant person, if not the appellant) and any safeguarder and also returns to the reporter any documents lodged in connection with the appeal.[3]

1 Act of Sederunt (Child Care and Maintenance Rules) 1997, SI 1997/291, r 3.58(1).
2 SI 1997/291, r 3.58(2), (4).
3 SI 1997/291, r 3.58(4).

Final procedure

53.13 Once the sheriff has given his or her decision the sheriff clerk will prepare and have signed an interlocutor and a copy of this, with any note appended by the sheriff, is sent by the sheriff clerk to the reporter, the appellant and any safeguarder appointed by the sheriff.[1] There are now no forms of interlocutor prescribed in the rules but the forms enacted in the Act of Sederunt (Social Work) (Sheriff Court Procedure) Rules 1971[2] may be employed, with appropriate adaptations.[3] The sheriff clerk will then return to the reporter any reports which he has lodged, including any additional reports lodged in response to a call by the court.[4] The rules do not provide specifically for return of any reports lodged by the appellant or by any safeguarder but it may be presumed that any such reports should also be returned at this stage.

1 SI 1997/291, r 3.58(4).
2 SI 1971/92.
3 SI 1971/92, Forms 9A, 9B and 9C.
4 SI 1997/291, r 3.58(4) – in practice it may be sensible for the sheriff clerk to refrain from returning the reports until the days of appeal have passed.

POSITION PENDING APPEAL

Suspension of supervision requirement pending appeal

53.14 When the imposition or continuation of a supervision requirement is appealed against, the child or relevant person may apply *to a hearing* for suspension of the requirement pending the appeal and the reporter must arrange a hearing forthwith.[1] Such applications are rare and it is thought that some practitioners are not aware of this provision. The position of the child pending appeal to the sheriff principal or the Court of Session is discussed later.[2]

1 Children (Scotland) Act 1995, s 51(9).
2 At 54.33 below.

Procedure – status of decision of hearing to suspend supervision requirement

53.15 When an application is made to suspend a supervision requirement pending appeal the reporter must forthwith convene a hearing to consider this application.[1] The hearing may then 'grant or refuse the application'[2] and the hearing's decision to grant or refuse will generally stand until the substantive appeal to the sheriff, a diet for which has to be assigned within 28 days of the lodging of the appeal.[3] It has been said that the decision of the hearing as to whether or not to suspend a supervision requirement pending appeal is itself appealable.[4] While this may be theoretically correct it is submitted that it would be unsatisfactory for the sheriff to be asked to consider on an interim basis an issue which would be due for full decision soon thereafter. It is suggested that a party strongly aggrieved by the imposition of a supervision requirement should, as well as applying to a children's hearing for suspension of the requirement, also ask the sheriff clerk to fix as early a diet as possible for the substantive appeal, thus securing as early a disposal of the appeal as would be achievable by attempting to appeal against a hearing's refusal to suspend a supervision requirement.

1 Children (Scotland) Act 1995, s 51(9) and (10).
2 C(S)A 1995, s 51(10).
3 SI 1997/291, r 3.54(5).
4 Wilkinson and Norrie *Parent and Child* (2nd edn, 1999) 19.102.

Position if sheriff sustains appeal and discharges referral

53.16   A supervision requirement persists when the sheriff's decision to discharge the referral has been made the subject of an appeal.[1] Accordingly, discharge of a referral by a sheriff 'cannot be operative until expiry of the 28 appeal days under s 50(2) [of the Social Work (Scotland) Act 1968]'.[2] If, however, the appeal is not heard before the date when the supervision requirement would expire,[3] then, unless the reporter arranges a review,[4] or unless application is made to the Court of Session to make an interim order pending appeal,[5] the supervision requirement will lapse by effluxion of time.[6] As far as the writer is aware, there has been no application to the Court of Session in a hearings case for an interim order pending appeal.

1 *Stirling v D* 1995 SCLR 460.
2 *Stirling v D* 1995 SCLR 460 at 464C.
3 Children (Scotland) Act 1995, s 73(2).
4 C(S)A 1995, s 73(8)(a).
5 Court of Session Act 1988, s 47(2); cf *Stirling v D* 1995 SCLR 460 at 465A and *Kennedy v M* 1995 SCLR 88 at 92D, F; discussed below at 54.33.
6 *Stirling v D* 1995 SCLR 460 at 463C–464C.

Position if sheriff sustains appeal and remits to the hearing for reconsideration

53.17   In general the sheriff has no power to order interim removal of a supervision requirement when he or she sustains the appeal but remits for reconsideration. It would appear that when a 'secure accommodation' authorisation has been made the sheriff has, in addition to his or her ordinary appellate powers, the power to direct that it shall cease to have effect.[1]

1 Children (Scotland) Act 1995, s 51(5)(b).

Part VII
Appeals from the sheriff

CHAPTER 54

Appeals generally: appeals to the sheriff principal

GENERAL

Appeals with and appeals without leave – election as to appeal to the sheriff principal or to the Court of Session

54.01   In principle, substantive decisions of sheriffs are subject to appeal by any party without leave (permission) of the sheriff who has made the decision. The aggrieved party may appeal to the sheriff principal or to the Court of Session. If the aggrieved party elects to appeal to the sheriff principal then the decision of the sheriff principal is final unless the sheriff principal grants leave to appeal to the Court of Session.[1] Any appeal to the Court of Session is final.[2] It may be, however, that an application to the Court of Session to exercise the *nobile officium* or for judicial review would be subject to appeal to the House of Lords.

1 Children (Scotland) Act 1995, s 51(11)(b).
2 C(S)A 1995, s 51(11)(b).

Appealable decisions

54.02   It is competent to appeal from the sheriff by way of stated case *on a point of law or in respect of any irregularity in the conduct of the case*.[1] A formal procedural decision, such as adjourning a hearing, would not normally be appealed[2] but no rigid rule can be laid down. In *G v Scanlon*[3] the decision of a sheriff not to allow the adjournment of a proof hearing was appealed. In *F v Constanda*[4] the decision of a sheriff to decline jurisdiction in the midst of a s 68 proof was appealed. A decision of the sheriff on an application under the Children (Scotland) Act 1995, s 57 (the provisions anent granting and continuing child protection orders) may not be made the subject of an appeal to the sheriff principal or the Court of Session.[5]

1 Children (Scotland) Act 1995, s 51(11)
2 Cf *H & H v McGregor* 1973 SC 95.
3 1999 SC 226, 1999 SLT 707, Extra Div.
4 1999 SLT 421, Extra Div, discussed at 54.07 below.
5 C(S)A 1995, s 51(15)(a) and (b).

Appeals on point of law and irregularity only – but appeals may raise factual issues

54.03   The grounds of appeal are: 'on a point of law'; or 'in respect of any irregularity in the conduct of the case'.[1] The distinction between a point of law and an irregularity in the conduct of the case may be a fine one since an error as to procedural law may be thought of as an irregularity in the conduct of the case. For example, in *Kennedy v M*[2] the sheriff held that the hearing erred in law in declining to make a specific ruling as to access to a child under supervision when a ruling had been specifically asked for. This was argued as a matter of law but could equally be regarded as a procedural irregularity. There is no provision for appeal on ground of fact, i e one cannot relevantly argue on appeal that, although the sheriff was entitled to come to the decision he did on the evidence before him, the appellate court ought to draw another conclusion which is equally open. The appellate court is limited by having available to it only the written record (if any) of the evidence. In a case wherein the whole verbal testimony had been officially noted and was consequently available in written form it was said in the House of Lords by Lord Macmillan:

> 'The appellate Court has before it only the printed record of the evidence. Were that the whole evidence, it might be said that the appellate Judges were entitled and qualified to reach their own conclusion upon the case. But it is only part of the evidence. What is lacking is evidence of the demeanour of the witnesses, their candour or their partisanship, and all the incidental elements so difficult to describe which make up the atmosphere of an actual trial. This assistance the trial Judge possesses in reaching his conclusion, but it is not available to the appellate Court. So far as the case stands on paper it not infrequently happens that a decision either way may seem equally open. When this is so, and it may be said of the present case, then the decision of the trial Judge, who has enjoyed the advantages not available to the appellate Court, becomes of paramount importance and ought not to be disturbed.'[3]

But this is not to say that the appellate court may not reverse the sheriff on a matter of fact. Certain decisions on matters of fact may be appealed as wrongous exercise of judgment or discretion[4] if it can be shown from such written record as is available in the form of the sheriff's stated case and any reports or documents referred to or incorporated therein, that the sheriff has made an error in stating or applying the law, taken account of irrelevant or improper considerations, failed to give adequate reasons for his factual conclusions, or otherwise gone 'plainly wrong'. Lord Macmillan, concluding his discussion of the powers of the appellate court in relation to factual findings, said:

> 'This is not an abrogation of the powers of a Court of Appeal on questions of fact. The judgment of the trial Judge on the facts may be demonstrated on the printed evidence to be affected by material inconsistencies and inaccuracies, or he may be shown to have failed to appreciate the weight or bearing of circumstances admitted or proved, or otherwise to have gone plainly wrong.'[5]

Of course a transcript of the evidence will not generally be available in cases in the children's hearing system, but the representative of the appellant seeking to displace a finding in fact should be ready to say whether the reasons given by the sheriff are unsatisfactory or that it unmistakably appears that the sheriff has not taken proper advantage of having seen and heard the witnesses.

1 Children (Scotland) Act 1995, s 51(11).
2 1995 SCLR 88, 1995 SLT 717, 1st Div.
3 *Thomas v Thomas* 1947 SC (HL) 45 at 59 per Lord Macmillan; see also *Morrison v J Kelly & Sons Ltd* 1970 SC 65 at 90 per Lord Cameron; and *Wordie Property Co Ltd v Secretary of State for Scotland* 1984 SLT 345 per LP Emslie at 347–348.
4 In *Osborne v Matthan (No 2)* 1998 SC 682 at 688I–699A a decision about welfare was described as an exercise of judgment rather than discretion.
5 *Thomas v Thomas* 1947 SC (HL) 45 at 59; see also per Lord Thankerton at 54ff.

Appeals raising factual issues and matters of mixed fact and law

54.04 Appeals based upon a challenge to the factual conclusions of the sheriff have succeeded where the sheriff was held to have misdirected himself as to the application of the law of corroboration,[1] where the sheriff was held to have misdirected himself on the application of the principle of the *mens rea* of assault,[2] where the sheriff was 'plainly wrong' in interpreting evidence designed to prove that lack of parental care was likely,[3] where and when the sheriff was held to have attached too much importance to one aspect and not enough importance to other aspects of the reports and other evidence before him.[4] The latter case is an interesting example of how the appellate court may, even in an appeal under summary procedure, scrutinise closely the written evidence (in the form of a medical report) before it and, in consequence of such scrutiny, quash the sheriff's findings-in-fact and consider the matter *de novo*.[5] The limitations of an appeal raising matters of fact is illustrated by the finding in *M v Ferguson*[6] that the sheriff had been entitled to infer assault from the medical evidence alone.[7] In *D v Kelly*[8] and *H v Harkness*[9] the respective sheriffs were held to have reached the wrong conclusion on the evidence in that they had failed to apply the relevant statutory test.

1 *D v Kennedy* 1974 SLT 168; *F v Kennedy* 1988 SLT 404.
2 *Kennedy v A* 1993 SLT 1134.
3 *McGregor v L* 1981 SLT 194.
4 *M v McGregor* 1982 SLT 41.
5 *M v McGregor* 1982 SLT 41 at 44.
6 1994 SCLR 487.
7 Cf also: *R v Kennedy* [1996] 20 Fam LB 7 (2 February 1996, 2nd Div); 1996 GWD 11-604; and *B v Harris* 1990 SLT 208, *sub nom C v Harris* 1989 SCLR 644.
8 1995 SC 414.
9 1998 SC 288, 1998 SLT 1431.

Appeal on ground of 'any irregularity in the conduct of the case'

54.05 Since the appeal is from 'any decision of the sheriff' and as the mode of appeal is by a case stated by the sheriff it might be thought reasonable to construe the reference to irregularity as a ground of appeal as referring primarily to an irregularity associated with the procedure in the sheriff court.[1] Alleged irregularities at the hearing stage may be made the subject of appeal to the sheriff, and any party wishing to contend that the appeal sheriff came to the wrong conclusion on the procedural issue may then raise the matter on further appeal.[2]

1 E g *H v Mearns* 1974 SC 152.
2 E g *Kennedy v M* 1995 SCLR 88 where the sheriff held inter alia that the hearing had given an inadequate statement of reasons and the sheriff's decision was challenged in the appeal to the Court of Session.

54.06 *Examples of appeals on points of procedure.* Procedural matters settled on appeal have included whether the ordinary civil procedures of dismissal and amendment have no place in Social Work (Scotland) Act 1968, s 42[1] applications;[2] which is the appropriate court for such applications when a child resides in one sheriffdom and is accused of an offence in another;[3] whether the offender against the child has to be named for grounds of referral to be relevantly stated;[4] the definition of 'guardian' in the context of Part III of the 1968 Act;[5] the circumstances in which was it competent for a hearing to have regard, when deciding on disposal, to material circumstances not contained within the grounds of referral;[6] that it was not appropriate for the sheriff to delay hearing evidence in a referral proof pending the holding of a criminal trial;[7] that a hearing was not bound to make a specific ruling as to access to a child simply because it had been asked to do so;[8] and that the sheriff had not exceeded the discretion vested in him to refuse to adjourn a referral proof.[9] The case of *Sloan v B*[10] raised a wide range of legal and procedural issues, including the power of the hearing to dispense with the presence of the child, the propriety or otherwise of preliminary 'business' meetings of hearings, the propriety or otherwise of the sheriff's having dismissed the referral as incompetent without hearing evidence, the competency of the sheriff admitting the press to a referral proof, the proper form and content of a stated case and the propriety or otherwise of the sheriff's having had regard to the contents of productions which had not yet been spoken to in evidence.

1 Now s 68 applications under the Children (Scotland) Act 1995.
2 *McGregor v D* 1977 SC 330, 1977 SLT 182.
3 *L v McGregor* 1980 SLT 17.
4 *McGregor v AB* 1981 SC 328.
5 *Kennedy v H* 1988 SLT 586; *C v Kennedy* 1991 SCLR 166; *S v Lynch* 1997 SCLR 971.
6 *M v Kennedy* 1991 SCLR 898, 1993 SLT 431; *O v Rae* 1992 SCLR 318.
7 *Ferguson v MP* 1989 SCLR 525.
8 *Kennedy v M* 1995 SCLR 88, 1st Div.
9 *G v Scanlon* 1999 SLT 707.
10 1991 SLT 530.

54.07 *Appeal on procedural point in the course of a s 68 proof.* In *F v Constanda*,[1] the sheriff, after having heard some three days' proof, granted an opposed motion on behalf of the reporter to decline to continue to exercise jurisdiction on the ground that he (the sheriff) had given the impression of possible bias in relation to one female child witness and possibly in relation to other female witnesses. The sheriff granted leave to appeal and appeal by stated case was proceeded with. Questions as to the competency of an appeal at this stage were not argued but the appeal was heard apparently on the basis that if the appeal were not competent under the Children (Scotland) Act 1995, s 51 then it could be heard under the *nobile officium*. The Extra Division which heard the appeal commented that the sheriff should have taken into account wider considerations, such as the interest of the child in a speedy disposal, and the undesirability of producing a situation wherein evidence would require to be heard twice, but rejected the argument that the objection should not have been stated and dealt with at the time when the alleged reason for declinature emerged. The Division made no comment on the competency issue but it is submitted that the appeal was competent: the sheriff's decision was in effect to refuse (admittedly on the motion of the reporter) to hear the evidence tendered by the reporter, contrary to the Act of Sederunt (Social Work) (Sheriff Court Procedure) Rules 1971, r 3.47(1) and it was such a refusal (in the context of the Act of Sederunt (Social work) (Sheriff Court Procedure) Rules 1971, r 8(1)) which led to the appeal by stated case in *McGregor v D*.[2] It seems clear, however, that this case is exceptional – the procedural point resulted in the case being aborted and such a decision must be susceptible of appeal. In general, as already noted,[3] incidental objections should be reserved and, if necessary, made the subject of appeal after the determination by the sheriff. It is submitted that the application for leave to appeal, although understandable, was unnecessary and incompetent – there is no provision about leave to appeal in the 1995 Act or the 1997 Rules. It is suggested that application should simply have been made to the sheriff to state a case and, unless the sheriff was minded to refuse to state a case,[4] the case would be stated.

1 1999 SLT 421.
2 1977 SC 330, 1977 SLT 182.
3 At 37.20 above; cf ch 29, notably at 29.06.
4 For discussion of refusal to state a case see 54.21 below.

Examples of appeals on points of substantive and evidential law

54.08 Substantive legal concepts considered on appeal have included the evidence required to establish the existence of such concepts as 'the same household',[1] lack of parental care,[2] wilful neglect,[3] failure to attend school without reasonable excuse[4] and assault.[5] In recent years important decisions have been handed down, fundamentally affecting the law of evidence. Some have decided matters of interest peculiar to hearings law, such as: the decision that in applications under the Social Work (Scotland) Act 1968, s 42[6] involving allegations of serious offences by named persons against children the standard of proof is the balance of probabilities;[7] the decision that the sheriff, in remitting a disposal back to the hearing for reconsideration, had given too much attention to the verdict of a jury acquitting a Schedule 1 offender;[8] the decision that where offences by the child alone constituted the facts of a case then the 'offence by the child' ground of referral, with its attendant criminal standard of proof, and not the 'moral danger' ground, should be founded upon;[9] and the decision that it was not open to the sheriff to hold grounds established on the basis of certified copy interlocutors in cases referring to another child where the sheriff in the earlier cases had not heard evidence.[10] Some cases have decided matters with potential implications far beyond the scope of the hearings system, such as the decision that the effect of the Civil Evidence (Scotland) Act 1988, s 2 was to override the best evidence rule so as to render admissible evidence of what a witness said previously, even although the witness had not been asked about the point at the proof.[11]

1 *A v Kennedy* 1993 SCLR 107, IH, 1993 SC 131, 1993 SLT 1188; *McGregor v H* 1983 SLT 626; *Templeton v E* 1998 SCLR 672, Sheriff Principal DJ Risk QC.
2 *M v McGregor* 1982 SLT 41; *McGregor v L* 1981 SLT 194.
3 *Kennedy v S* 1986 SLT 679.
4 *D v Kennedy* 1988 SLT 55.
5 *C v Harris* 1989 SCLR 644, sub nom *B v Harris* 1990 SLT 208.
6 Now s 68 applications under the Children (Scotland) Act 1995.
7 *Harris v F* 1991 SCLR 124.
8 *Kennedy v B* 1992 SCLR 55, 2nd Div.
9 *Constanda v M* 1997 SCLR 510.
10 *M v Constanda* 1999 SCLR 108.
11 *F v Kennedy (No 2)* 1992 SCLR 750.

WHO MAY APPEAL

54.09   The child, the relevant person, or the child and the relevant person, either alone or together, and the reporter may appeal from the sheriff to the sheriff principal or the Court of Session.[1] An authoritative decision on the powers of the safeguarder in this regard has yet to be made. In *R v Grant*[2] the sheriff had dispensed with service on the children in respect of a s 68 proof and they were described as not being 'parties' to the proof (although both were called as witnesses by the reporter). The sheriff had appointed a safeguarder. After proof the sheriff sustained the grounds of referral but on appeal to the sheriff principal the sheriff's decision was reversed. Thereafter the two referred children appealed independently to the Court of Session. It was not disputed that, despite not having been parties to the proceedings before the sheriff and the sheriff principal, the children were entitled to appeal to the Court of Session. The safeguarder appeared in the Court of Session through counsel. The sheriff principal had observed in his opinion that the position of a safeguarder 'may be rendered untenable by the independent opinions and decisions of the children he is supposed to protect'. Lord Prosser, delivering the opinion of an Extra Division, disapproved this observation, stating:

> 'However, it does not appear that the children's entering proceedings and being represented in any way "overturns" the safeguarder's opinions and decisions: so long as he remains the safeguarder, his responsibilities remain the same, whether or not the position adopted by the children is different. In the present case, although the safeguarder has not appealed, his counsel intimated that he now supported the children's appeal. Procedurally, section 51(12) does not provide for the safeguarder himself appealing under subsection (11), although in terms of Rule 3.9 of the Child Care and Maintenance Rules 1997 he may appear personally in proceedings or instruct legal representation, and is elsewhere regarded as a party to the proceedings. Our attention was drawn to a number of provisions in relation to safeguarders, and it was suggested by counsel for Mr and Mrs N that the appearance of the safeguarder in this appeal involved possible anomalies or even incompetency. It may be that there are situations in

which problems would arise, but it appears to us that the safeguarder is still safeguarder by virtue of his appointment by the Sheriff, and that there is no incompetency in his appearing, through counsel, not as an appellant but as a respondent.'[3]

It is submitted that the safeguarder's powers as curator *ad litem*[4] would entitle a safeguarder who has become a party to the proceedings to appeal to the sheriff principal or the Court of Session on behalf of the child and that the approach of the Court of Session in the case of *R v Grant* gives some support for the view. The observation by the sheriff principal about the instructing by the children of independent representation seems to misconstrue the position of the safeguarder vis-à-vis the child: the safeguarder's duty is to protect the interests of the child and while this may generally include reporting the views of the child, it is not confined to so doing, and the interests of the child may run counter to the wishes or instructions of the child. As already noticed, it has been decided in the sheriff court that the safeguarder appointed by a hearing (who does not enjoy the powers of a curator *ad litem*) has a right of appeal to the sheriff independent of that of the child, but this decision has been doubted.[5]

1 Children (Scotland) Act 1995, s 51(12).
2 2000 SLT 372.
3 2000 SLT 372 at 373L–374C.
4 SI 1997/291, r 3.8(a).
5 *Ross v Kennedy* 1995 SCLR (Notes) 1160, commentary by Sheriff David Kelbie, discussed at 17.14 above.

APPEAL BY STATED CASE – GENERAL PRINCIPLES

Responsibility on appellant to focus the issues

54.10 The rules and practices governing appeal by stated case in referrals cases will be noticed presently but it may be said at the outset that the purpose of the procedure is to enable the presiding judge to state the facts which formed the basis of his or her decision and the reasoning which led to the conclusions in fact and law with particular reference to the issue or issues, whether of law, fact, mixed fact and law or any permutation of these aspects, which the appellant wishes to be put into dispute. The practice of appellate courts is clear:

'... it was distinctly intimated that in future we should hold the appellant responsible for the sufficiency of the case ...;'[1]

'It has long been the practice of the Courts in Scotland to require the Commissioners [of Inland Revenue] to state at the end of the case the questions of law on which the opinion of the Court is desired, so framed as to focus the points of law at issue, the facts relevant to their decision being stated in the body of the case, along with their determination thereon. It is the practice for the parties to have an opportunity on the draft case of suggesting the inclusion of further facts and further questions';[2]

'I deplore the increasing tendency in stated cases to propound the general question in the form of the first question in this case ["Whether on the foregoing facts the Court were entitled to convict the appellant of the offence charged?"] and to attempt under it to raise all sorts of legal issues. If a legal issue is to be raised, it ought to be properly raised by a question defining the issue precisely. Unless this rule is followed, there is no real guarantee that a point taken in this Court was a live point in the lower Court, nor is there any guarantee that, when the case was being stated, the Judge stating it had in view the point sought to be argued here. If we allow undue latitude to parties under this popular general question it simply means that the ingenuity of counsel can, by searching for gaps and discrepancies in the stated case, raise arguments which were not live issues either at the trial or at the adjustment of the case.'[3]

The foregoing quotations derive respectively from valuation, revenue and criminal appeals. Procedures under the Children (Scotland) Act 1995, Pt II are of course *sui generis*[4] and civil as opposed to criminal and analogies with other procedures must be treated with caution,[5] but it is thought that the foregoing dicta accurately reflect what was the general practice of the Court of Session in dealing with appeals under the Social Work (Scotland) Act 1968, s 50, at least when parties have been legally represented throughout.[6] It is submitted that it is clear that they should inform the stance of sheriffs principal to appeals under the 1995 Act.

1 *Stirling Gaslight Co v Assessor for Stirling* (1899) 1 F 583 per Lord Kyllachy at 584.
2 *Ross & Coulter v Inland Revenue Comrs* 1948 SC (HL) 1 at 14 per Lord Thankerton.
3 *Drummond v Hunter* 1948 JC 109 at 113 per LJ-C Thomson, quoted with approval and applied to appeals under the Children (Scotland) Act 1995, s 51 by Lord Prosser, delivering the opinion of the court in *R v Grant* 2000 SLT 372 at 374 K–375D.
4 *McGregor v D* 1977 SC 330 at 336.
5 *McGregor v D* 1977 SC 330 at 336; *Kennedy v O* 1975 SC 308 at 315.
6 For further discussion of practice in relation to stated cases see the English revenue cases *Ransom v Higgs* [1973] 2 All ER 657 per Roskill LJ at 681–682 and *Johnson v Scott* [1978] STC 48 at 55. Some latitude may be allowed to a party conducting his own case: *C v Kennedy* (4 July 1986, unreported) Court of Session.

Importance of scrutinising and considering adjustments of the draft stated case

54.11 All parties should be astute to try to ensure that the necessary elements of a ground of referral have been dealt with in the findings and that the issues which they desire to be addressed by the appellate court are adequately identified. Of course the Court of Session may remit to the sheriff for clarification[1] but this should not be counted upon. In January 2000 the Court of Session, in an appeal from a sheriff principal who had reversed the sheriff, emphasised the importance of parties' identifying the issues in an appeal from the sheriff.[2] In this case the sole question stated was: 'On the whole facts of the case was the sheriff entitled to find the grounds of referral established?' Lord Prosser, delivering the opinion of an Extra Division, referred to the words of Lord Justice-Clerk Thomson quoted above[3] and stated:

'In the present case, the Sheriff says he found great difficulty in understanding what is meant by "on the whole facts of the case". His attention was not drawn to any specific area of alleged insufficiency of evidence. There was no suggestion that in holding the grounds established he either had, or must have, applied the wrong test or adopted a wrong approach ... Unsurprisingly with a case stated in such a way, it seems to us that the criticisms of what the Sheriff did take very much the form suggested by the Lord Justice-Clerk in *Drummond v Hunter*, with arguments being advanced before the Sheriff Principal or in this court, and alleged gaps and discrepancies being relied upon now, which the Sheriff has not been asked to consider, and which the stated case might well have dealt with more specifically and more amply if there had been any indication that this was required. Even once the stated case was available, no attempt seems to have been made to have additional questions included, at a stage when the Sheriff could still relate his findings and observations to those questions.'[4]

1 Cf *H v Harkness* 1988 SC 287; *M v Kennedy* 1991 SCLR 898, 1993 SLT 431, 2nd Div.
2 *R v Grant* 2000 SLT 374.
3 At 54.10.
4 2000 SLT 375B–D.

PROCEDURAL STEPS BEFORE THE HEARING OF THE APPEAL BY THE SHERIFF PRINCIPAL

Note of appeal – importance of giving notice of ground of appeal

54.12   Appeal to the sheriff principal is by application under the Children (Scotland) Act 1995, s 51(11)(a) requesting a stated case and specifying the point of law upon which the appeal is to proceed or the irregularity in the conduct of the case upon which the appellant proposes to rely.[1] It is important to identify in the application the issue or issues which the appellant wishes to argue in the appellate court. The sheriff principal may not entertain appeal points raising issues of law or irregularities in the conduct of the case unless notice has been given except where cause has been shown and in the event of cause being shown to the satisfaction of the sheriff principal then he or she may allow the arguments to be addressed, but only subject to such conditions as to the sheriff principal may seem appropriate.[2] While some latitude may be allowed to an unrepresented party[3] the appellate court will not readily allow argument on a matter not raised and, in the event of its being persuaded so to do in the interests of a child, unnecessary delay may be caused. In 1996 the Second Division had to consider a question framed so as to ask whether the sheriff had been entitled on the facts stated to hold that grounds under the Social Work (Scotland) Act 1968, s 32(2)(g) had been proved. The Division held that such a broad question did not permit the appellant to argue that there was no corroborated evidence that the appellant had been implicated in the offence.[4] In 1998 Sheriff Principal D J Risk QC held that the consideration that the solicitor for the appellant had not thought of a line of argument until preparing for the appeal hearing was not 'cause shown' under the 1997 Rules, r 3.59(9).[5] In 1996 an Extra Division refused to allow the respondent parent to lodge reports which had not been before the court below.[6] It is thought that an appeal based on a defect which was said to be 'patent, and disclosed on the face of the proceedings' and which could make 'the proceedings fundamentally null' would be entertained even if the point had not been taken in the court below.[7]

1 SI 1997/291, as amended by Act of Sederunt (Child Care and Maintenance Rules) (Amendment No 2) 1998, SI 1998/2130, r 3.59(1)(a), (b).
2 SI 1997/291, r 3.59(9).
3 *C v Kennedy* (4 July 1986, unreported) Court of Session.
4 *R v Kennedy* [1996] 20 Fam LB; 1996 GWD 11-604; 2 February 1996, 2nd Div.
5 *DG v Templeton* 1988 SCLR 180.
6 *Stirling v R* 1996 SCLR 191, 1996 GWD 1-4.
7 *Cf O'Malley v Strathern* 1920 JC 74 at 79 per LJ-G Clyde.

Form of application

54.13   An application might take this form:

Under the Children (Scotland) Act 1995, s 51(11)(a)
Act of Sederunt (Child Care and Maintenance Rules)
1997, rr 3.59–3.61
Sheriffdom of North Strathclyde at Dunoon

APPLICATION FOR A STATED CASE

by

Mary Smith, residing at … (mother of the child James Smith, born …)

Appellant

Dunoon, 10 May 1999.

The appellant respectfully requests the sheriff, in respect of her interlocutor of 3 May 1999, to state a case for the opinion of the sheriff principal on the following questions, namely:

1. Was the sheriff entitled to admit in evidence the statement of the child witness AB, aged five, to social worker CD, considering that the said child AB was not tendered as a witness and that her competency as a witness was only spoken to by the said social worker CD?

2. Did the sheriff act properly and regularly by adjourning the court to the playroom within the Royal Hospital for Sick Children, Yorkhill, Glasgow in order to take the evidence of the child EF, aged six?

3. If the answer to the foregoing question is in the negative, was the evidence of the said child EF admissible?

4. If the answer to either or both of the questions 1 and 3 is in the negative, was the sheriff entitled to hold as established the ground of

referral alleging the Schedule 1 offence of an assault involving bodily injury? and

5. On the whole facts of the case was the sheriff entitled to hold the grounds of referral established?

IN RESPECT WHEREOF

(signed) *Fiona Wynford*

Solicitor,
16 John Street, Dunoon

Agent for Appellant.

Timescales and obligations to intimate

Appeals against sheriff's decision on an appeal from the hearing and sheriff's decision in a s 68 application

54.14   The appeal must be lodged with the sheriff clerk within a period of 28 days 'beginning with the date of the decision appealed against'.[1] The alternative possible interpretations of the foregoing phrase have already been discussed[2] – to be on the safe side, the date of the decision appealed against should be regarded as 'day one'. There is no discretion in the sheriff or the sheriff principal to extend the time for appeal. In an application to the *nobile officium* the Court of Session refused the application on the basis that the appeal was without merit but refrained from ruling on the appropriateness of employing the *nobile officium* to allow a late appeal.[3] On lodging the note of appeal the appellant must at the same time intimate to the persons specified in Act of Sederunt (Child Care and Maintenance Rules) 1997, r 3.59. Accordingly; in the case of an appeal against a sheriff's decision in an appeal against the decision of a hearing, intimation must be made to the following (except, of course, where one of the following is the appellant):

- the reporter; the child (presumably unless service on the child has been dispensed with under r 3.3); the relevant person and any safe-guarder appointed by the sheriff.[4]

In the case of an appeal against a sheriff's decision in a s 68 application, intimation must be made to the following (again, except when the appellant):

- the child (unless service on the child has been dispensed with under r 3.3); any relevant person whose whereabouts are known; any safe-guarder appointed by the sheriff; and the reporter.[5]

1 Children (Scotland) Act 1995, s 51(13).
2 At 50.09 above.
3 *Thomson v Principal Reporter* 1998 SCLR 89, 1st Div.
4 SI 1997/291, r 3.59(2)(a), read with r 3.58(4).
5 SI 1997/291, r 3.59(2)(b) read with r 3.51(2).

Appeals in relation to applications under the Children (Scotland) Act 1995, s 85(1)

54.15 In the case of an appeal in relation to such applications (review of establishment of ground of referral), Act of Sederunt (Child Care and Maintenance Rules) 1997, r 3.59(2)(c) requires intimation to be made to 'the parties referred to in rule 3.62'. Rule 3.62, as well as making other requirements, lists the persons whose names, or names and addresses, are to be included in the s 85 application and specifies:

- 'the applicant and his representative (if any)'; the reporter; 'the safe-guarder (if any), and 'any other party to the application'. The said rule also specifies 'the name of the sheriff who made the finding'. Although the sheriff cannot be said to be a 'party' it would seem to be the intention of the rule that the sheriff who made the original finding should be among those notified of any appeal.

Lodgement of reports and statements

54.16 Where in an appeal the sheriff considers it necessary, he or she may require the reporter to lodge same with the sheriff clerk.[1]

1 SI 1997/291, r 3.60.

The draft stated case – timescales

54.17 Within *14 days* of the lodging of the application for a stated case the sheriff issues the draft stated case, containing a narrative of the proceedings, findings-in-fact, findings-in-law, 'appropriate questions of law or setting out any irregularity concerned' and a note of the reasons for his or her decision, and the sheriff clerk sends a copy to parties.[1] Parties then have *seven days* to propose adjustments and to state any point of law which they wish to raise in the appeal.[2] Such adjustments etc should be intimated to the other parties.[3] The sheriff may, of his or her own accord or on the motion of party, allow a hearing on adjustments and must so do if minded to reject any proposed adjustment; the sheriff may also 'allow such further procedure under this rule prior to the hearing of the appeal[4] as he thinks fit'.[5] Within *14 days* of the latest date on which adjustments could have been lodged or of the hearing, if any, on adjustments, the sheriff issues the stated case.[6] The sheriff may, *ex proprio motu* or on the motion of any party, reduce the periods prescribed in paragraphs (3), (4) or (6) of r 3.59 (set out in bold type in the foregoing) to such period or periods as he or she considers reasonable.[7] After the stated case has been issued the sheriff clerk places the papers before the sheriff principal and sends the case to parties with notification of the appeal diet.[8]

1 SI 1997/291, r 3.59(3).
2 SI 1997/291, r 3.59(4)(a) and (b).
3 SI 1997/291, r 3.59(4)(c).
4 One wonders if this is a mistake and if the reference should be to the hearing on the adjustments.
5 SI 1997/291, r 3.59(5).

6 SI 1997/291, r 3.59(6).
7 SI 1997/291, r 3.59(10).
8 SI 1997/291, r 3.59(8).

Form and content of stated case

54.18 The stated case, as well as stating the facts held by the sheriff to have been established, should also include the questions of law framed by the sheriff arising from the points of law stated by the parties 'and such other questions of law as he may consider appropriate', any adjustments proposed by a party and rejected by the sheriff (together with, if good practice is observed, a note of why the sheriff has rejected them) and a 'note of the irregularity in the conduct of the case averred by the parties and any questions of law or other issue which he considers arise therefrom'.[1] The Court of Session has emphasised the importance of setting out numbered findings-in-fact even in relation to facts which have been garnered from proceedings, such as the determination in a fatal accident inquiry, extrinsic to the testimony heard by the sheriff.[2] The sheriff's findings-in-fact should be stated simply as facts and not as probabilities.[3] The sheriff should not intersperse his or her findings-in-fact with comments.[4] The sheriff's note should summarise the principal arguments, including justification for any ruling on the admissibility of evidence, reasons for factual findings (including assessment of the credibility and reliability of witnesses) and an explanation of his or her conclusions in fact and in law.

1 SI 1997/291, r 3.57(7).
2 *Kennedy v A* 1986 SLT 358.
3 *S v Kennedy* 1987 SLT 667.
4 *Sloan v B* 1991 SLT 530 at 544.

Form of stated case in relation to sheriff's ruling on a motion of 'No case to answer'

54.19 No special provision is made in the rules for an appeal against a decision of the sheriff under Act of Sederunt (Child Care and Maintenance Rules) 1997, r 3.47(2) and (3) holding that there is insufficient evidence to establish a condition mentioned in the Children (Scotland) Act 1995, s 52(2)(i) (offence by the child). In such a position the sheriff has not proceeded to make any factual findings and therefore there could scarcely be findings-in-fact. It is submitted that the correct course for the sheriff to take in these circumstances is to set out the evidence adduced by the reporter and any inference drawn therefrom by the sheriff.[1]

1 Cf *Wingate v McGlennan* 1991 SCCR 133.

Provision for extension of time where sheriff temporarily absent

54.20 Where a sheriff is temporarily absent from duty for any reason the sheriff principal may extend the period within which the sheriff is to issue the draft stated case under the 1997 Rules, r 3.59(3) and the final stated case under r 3.59(6).[1]

1 Act of Sederunt (Child Care and Maintenance Rules) 1997, SI 1997/291, r 3.59(11).

Refusal or failure by sheriff to state a case

54.21 In contrast with the provisions governing appeal to the Court of Session, there is no provision for the refusal by the sheriff to state a case[1] or to defer consideration until the facts have been ascertained.[2] It is thought, however, that the sheriff may refuse to state a case where he or she considers the application for the appeal to be incompetent. An example would be where the sheriff considered that the person applying for the appeal had no right to appeal, such as an unmarried father who was not a relevant person. The sheriff might consider refusing to state a case if the application were not in proper form. An example would be if the application did not specify the point of law on which the appeal was to proceed.[3] It is thought that, on the analogy of criminal procedure,[4] the appellant, or would-be appellant, would have the right to apply to the *nobile officium* of the Court of Session to ordain the sheriff to state a case. It is suggested that sheriffs should not readily refuse to state a case if the person applying for the case has a colourable title to appeal. The course of refusing to state a case on the ground that no matter of law has been specified may be taken where no point of law has been properly specified and where the sheriff can identify no stateable ground of appeal. An example would be where the decision of the sheriff turned entirely on credibility of witnesses. In considering whether or not to refuse to state a case the sheriff should have regard to the interest of the child in achieving as early as possible a resolution of the case, and should be slow to refuse on the ground of a remediable defect in the application.[5] In the event of the sheriff failing or delaying to state a case then application may be made to the *nobile officium* of the Court of Session. It is thought that the sheriff principal has not the competence to ordain a sheriff to state a case.

1 Rules of the Court of Session 1994 ('RCS'), r 41.7(1)(b).
2 RCS, r 41.7(1)(c).
3 Cf SI 1997/291, r 3.59(1).
4 *McTaggart, Petr* 1987 SCCR 638; *Crowe, Petr* 1994 SCCR 784; *Leonard, Petr* 1995 SCCR 39; *Reid, Petr* 1996 SCCR 830.
5 Cf *Sloan v B* 1991 SLT 530 at 546G–K; *F v Constanda* 1999 SLT 421.

THE CONDUCT OF THE APPEAL HEARING

Note of authorities

54.22 It is good practice for all sides to notify in good time the sheriff clerk and the other parties of any legal authorities on which they propose to found.

Representation

54.23 In practice parties will generally be represented by solicitors or counsel, although parties may of course appear in person. Act of Sederunt (Child Care and Maintenance Rules) 1997, r 3.21(2) provides that a party may be represented by an authorised representative whom the sheriff considers to be suitable.[1] It has been doubted if a reporter who is not a solicitor or advocate can rely on the Reporters (Conduct of Proceedings before the Sheriff) (Scotland) Regulations 1997, regs 3 and 4 to entitle him or her to appear before the sheriff principal in appeal proceedings.[2] It may be, however, that such a reporter would be entitled to invoke r 3.21, although the enactment of the said regulations suggests that the legislature did not envisage that the Principal Reporter would rely on r 3.21. If relying on r 3.21 the reporter would, of course, have to satisfy the sheriff principal that he or she was a 'suitable person' to represent the Principal Reporter, and, having regard to the observations of Sheriff Principal Risk, it seems unlikely that a non-legally qualified reporter would be so regarded in Sheriff Risk's court.[3] The writer is inclined to the view that Sheriff Principal Risk takes an unduly narrow view of the ambit of regs 3 and 4 of the said Regulations, that it is the manifest purpose of these Regulations to accord to appropriately qualified reporters a right of audience in the sheriff court generally, and that a full consideration of all the relevant principles of statutory interpretation would support this view. It seems likely, however, that the Scottish Executive will clarify the matter by issuing amending regulations, and accordingly the matter need not be examined more extensively here.

1 SI 1997/291, r 3.21(2).
2 *Templeton v E* 1998 SCLR 672 at 679B; *N v Children's Hearing Reporter* (5 November 1998, unreported) Fort William Sheriff Court, Sheriff Principal D J Risk QC, both discussed but not ruled upon in *Miller v Council of the Law Society of Scotland* 2000 SLT 513.
3 *N v Children's Hearing Reporter* (5 November 1998, unreported) Fort William Sheriff Court.

Scope of appeal

54.24 As already noticed,[1] parties may not raise questions of law or irregularities in the conduct of the case of which notice has not been given.[2] The sheriff principal may, however, on cause shown, allow such questions to be raised on such conditions as he or she considers appropriate.[3] In what is thought to have been the first appeal to a sheriff principal under the Children (Scotland) Act 1995[4] Sheriff Principal D J Risk QC refused to entertain arguments which he was 'far from suggesting' were without merit, on the basis that the only cause which had been shown was that they had only occurred to the appellant's agent in the course of preparing his speech immediately before the diet of appeal. Sheriff Risk was particularly reluctant to entertain such arguments since he considered that, even if successful, they would not have altered the overall result of the case. In the event of a 'new point' being raised on appeal it may be possible for the sheriff principal, as a condition of allowing such point to be argued, to remit to the sheriff in order to allow the sheriff to report and comment.

1 At 54.10 above.
2 SI 1997/291, r 3.59(9).
3 SI 1997/291, r 3.59(9).
4 *G v Templeton* 1998 SCLR 180.

Course of appeal hearing

54.25   The appeal, like any other appeal to a sheriff principal, begins with the appellant outlining and justifying his or her stance under reference to the note of appeal. The other parties participating in the appeal, including any safeguarder, will then be given their opportunities to make submissions. All relevant case and statutory law should of course be cited.

Consideration of appeal

The s 16 principles

54.26   Where an appeal raises a question of pure law these principles, it is submitted, can have no direct application.[1] In matters, however, wherein the ground of appeal raises questions as to whether the court below has made a judgment relative to the welfare of the child then it is thought that the paramountcy principle, which applies to the determinations of a court on any matter with respect to a child, may be applicable. Similarly, in considering whether a sheriff has correctly interpreted an ambiguous statutory provision it is submitted that the appellate court would be entitled to have regard to the principle of the paramountcy of the welfare of the child imported by s 16(1).[2]

1 Cf discussion at 2.17 above; of course the issue may be whether the court below has misinterpreted or misapplied these principles.
2 This was the approach which commended itself to Lord Browne-Wilkinson when considering, in the context of the parallel (but significantly differently worded) provision in the Children and Young Persons Act 1933, the discretionary powers of the Secretary of State in relation to the James Bulger case – see *R v Secretary of State, ex p Bulger* [1997] 3 All ER 97 at 120.

Remitting to the sheriff for clarification

54.27   The Court of Session has the power – frequently enough used[1] – to remit to the sheriff for clarification. There is no provision conferring such power on the sheriff principal but it may be that a sheriff principal might be prepared to assume such power in an appropriate case with a view to the expeditious disposal of a case in the interests of a child.[2] A remit to the sheriff in *R v Grant*[3] might have reduced the delay in disposing of the case.

1 E g *Kennedy v A* 1986 SLT 358; *M v Kennedy* 1993 SLT 431.
2 Cf the oft-quoted words of Lord Sutherland in *W v Kennedy* 1988 SCLR 236, 1988 SLT 583.
3 2000 SLT 372, 2000 GWD 4-118, discussed at 54.11 above.

DISPOSAL OF THE APPEAL

The powers of the sheriff principal – the statutory provisions

54.28   The Children (Scotland) Act 1995, s 51(14) provides:

> 'On deciding an appeal under subsection (11) above the Sheriff Principal or as the case may be the Court of Session shall remit the case to the Sheriff for disposal in accordance with such directions as the court may give.'

These words substantially replicate the words of the Social Work (Scotland) Act 1968, s 50(3), defining the appellate powers of the Court of Session under that Act.[1] In *Kennedy v A*[2] the Court of Session pointedly contrasted these powers with the more limited powers conferred upon the sheriff in an appeal to the sheriff under s 49 of the 1968 Act. It would appear that s 51(14) of the 1995 Act equates the powers of the sheriff principal under the new legislation with the powers of the Court of Session under the 1968 Act. Of course the Court of Session has always jurisdiction to oversee the actings of any inferior tribunal and has the power *ex nobile officio* to correct any injustice, but so far as their statutory appellate jurisdictions are concerned, the powers of the sheriff principal and the Court of Session would seem to be identical. Examples of the exercise of the powers of the Court of Session on appeal will be given at 55.05ff below. Appellate courts generally regard it as being within their competence, where the court below has in their view erred, to re-examine the issues *de novo* and give their own decision as to what the court below should have done. The powers conferred by s 51(14), quoted above, would appear to be consistent with this approach.

1 'On deciding the appeal the Court of Session shall remit the case to the Sheriff for disposal in accordance with such directions as the Court may give.'
2 1986 SLT 358 at 362I, 2nd Div.

Power of appellate court to give directions as to disposal

54.29   Amongst the powers now conferred on the sheriff in appeals from disposals by children's hearings is the power, when upholding an appeal, to substitute the sheriff's preferred disposal.[1] No explicit power in these terms is expressly conferred on the appellate court but it is submitted that the unambiguous words of the Children (Scotland) Act 1995, s 51(14) convey such power to the appellate court. In his commentary on the 1995 Act Professor Norrie states:

> 'The appeal court is only entitled to give procedural directions and cannot give any indication as to how the case should be finally disposed of. The sheriff may decide under subs 5(c)(iii) above to substitute for the hearing's disposal his own disposal, but the appeal court cannot give any directions that this should be done, nor which disposal would be appropriate. The wording of this subsection is the same as that in s 50(3) of the 1968 Act, and in the context of the earlier statute the Court of Session has held that no such directions can be given: *Kennedy v A* 1986 SLT 358. That case cannot be taken to have been overruled by the new, anomalous, power of the sheriff in subs (5)(c)(iii).'[2].

Norrie expresses a similar view in his textbook.[3] It is respectfully submitted that this view may be incorrect. As already noted, the Court of Session in *Kennedy v A* was contrasting its own powers on appeal under the Social Work (Scotland) Act 1968, s 50(3) with the more limited powers of the sheriff under s 49 of that Act. Both the sheriff principal and the Court of Session now enjoy the powers conferred by s 51(14) of the 1995 Act and it is submitted that on a plain reading of this subsection these powers include the power in an appropriate case to give directions as to disposal. Norrie suggests that s 51(5)(c)(iii) of the 1995 Act is 'anomalous': it is not clear exactly what this means. If it means that the sheriff has been given additional powers then this is no doubt true but Acts of Parliament frequently change the powers of judges and others and in so doing may change the scheme of the legislation. Much of the thrust of the 1995 Act is to give more power to the sheriff, and this is consistent with many of the recommendations in the Clyde Report and perhaps with the European Convention, art 6. In any event, even under the 1968 Act the sheriff had the power to substitute his or her own view as to disposal by discharging the referral – what is so anomalous in conferring upon the sheriff the less drastic power of substituting his or her own disposal in some other way? When the Bill which became the Children (Scotland) Act 1995 was going through Parliament some of those consulted by the House of Commons, including the writer, expressed concern about the new provision, on the basis that the power of the children's hearings was liable to be subverted. As matters have turned out there has so far been no indication that the sheriffs are inclined to use this power so as to assume to themselves the jurisdiction of the hearings.[4]

1　Children (Scotland) Act 1995, s 51(5)(c)(iii).
2　*Children (Scotland) Act 1995* (W Green, 1998), commentary on s 51(14) at p 90.
3　*Children's Hearings in Scotland* (W Green, 1997) p 194.
4　See discussion above at 53.07.

Issuing judgment

54.30　The sheriff principal may pronounce his decision immediately or reserve judgment. In the latter event the sheriff principal must give a written judgment in 28 days and the sheriff clerk is to intimate it to parties.[1]

1　SI 1997/291, r 3.61.

Leave to appeal from the sheriff principal to the Court of Session

54.31　A decision of a sheriff principal in relation to an appeal from the sheriff may be appealed to the Court of Session on a point of law or in respect of any irregularity in the conduct of the case, but only with leave of the sheriff principal[1] On the face of it the decision as to whether or not to grant leave might be regarded as the court determining a matter 'with respect to a child', thereby bringing it within the ambit of the principle of the paramountcy of the welfare of the child.[2] In *G v Scanlon*[3] Lord Prosser, upholding the decision of a sheriff who had refused to adjourn a s 68 proof, stated:

'But the sheriff saw it as in K's [the child's] interests to proceed that day, and put that interest above any interest there might be in a deferment, without in any way suggesting that this would involve unfairness to anyone. We see no misapprehension on his part.'

This gives support to the view that certain procedural decisions may be subject to the paramountcy principle. It is nevertheless submitted that in relation to the granting of leave to appeal, the considerations which should affect the sheriff principal are those which have influenced courts in other fields of law and will be relevant where the sheriff principal is considering the issue of leave to appeal,[4] and that considerations as to the welfare of the child cannot of themselves provide sufficient reasons for granting or refusing leave. It may be, however, that where the question of whether or not to grant leave is delicately balanced, the decision may properly be influenced by the sheriff principal's impression of where the interests of the child lie. It is thought that favourable consideration should be given to granting leave when an important legal matter has to be resolved, for example where there is disagreement amongst sheriffs principal as to some matter of law or practice.

1 Children (Scotland) Act 1995, s 51(11)(b).
2 C(S)A 1995, s 16(1).
3 1999 SC 226, 1999 SLT 707 (Extra Div).
4 See discussion in Macphail *Sheriff Court Practice* (2nd edn) paras 18-48 to 18.50.

Time for applying for leave to appeal

54.32   Neither the Children (Scotland) Act 1995 nor the Act of Sederunt (Child Care and Maintenance Rules) 1997 prescribe a time limit for applying for leave. It is tentatively suggested that leave may be sought at any time within the 28 days allowed for the lodgement of the application for an appeal.[1] It is suggested that care must be taken to obtain leave well within this period. Leave can only be granted by the sheriff principal personally, whereas once obtained the appeal can be lodged within the 28 days. A difficulty might arise if obtaining leave were left till near the expiry of this period and it was then discovered that the sheriff principal was for some reason unavailable.[2]

1 Children (Scotland) Act 1995, s 51(13).
2 Cf *Kearney's Exrx v John Finlay MacLeod and Parker* 1965 SC 450.

POSITION PENDING APPEAL TO THE SHERIFF PRINCIPAL OR THE COURT OF SESSION

54.33   'The general rule is that the effect of an appeal is that the interlocutor appealed against need not be implemented until the appeal has been disposed of.'[1] Thus where a reporter had marked an appeal against an order of the sheriff the reporter did not require to comply with it.[2] If the reporter considers that the position of the child requires urgently to be reconsidered pending appeal, he or she should arrange a hearing.[3] By the same token, a supervision requirement persists (until expiry by effluxion of time) when the sheriff's decision to discharge the referral has been made the subject of an appeal.[4] Accordingly discharge of a referral by a sheriff 'cannot be operative until expiry of the 28 appeal days under s 50(2) [of the 1968 Act]'.[5] The Court of Session (but not the sheriff principal) has powers to make interim orders which are necessary for the proper disposal of appeals pending before it.[6] If the sheriff principal discharges the child from any further hearing or other proceedings in relation to the grounds of referral,[7] an appeal to the Court of Session will have the effect of keeping the referral in place and the reporter may require to arrange reviews.

1 Per LP Hope in *Kennedy v M* 1995 SCLR 88 at 94D, citing *Macleay v Macdonald* 1928 SC 776 per Lord Anderson at 782.
2 *Kennedy v M* 1995 SCLR 88.
3 *Kennedy v M* 1995 SCLR 88 at 94F; cf *Kennedy, Petr* 1988 SCLR 149 at 151.
4 *Stirling v D* 1995 SCLR 460.
5 *Stirling v D* 1995 SCLR 460 at 464C.
6 Court of Session Act 1988, s 47(2); cf *Stirling v D* 1995 SCLR 460 at 465.
7 Children (Scotland) Act 1995, s 51(5)(c)(ii).

CHAPTER 55

Appeals and applications to the Court of Session – and beyond

GENERAL

55.01   A party aggrieved by a decision of a sheriff in a referrals case may appeal without leave to the Court of Session on a point of law or irregularity in the conduct of the case.[1] A party aggrieved by a decision of a sheriff principal on appeal from a sheriff may, with the leave of that sheriff principal, appeal on the same grounds to the Court of Session.[2] Recourse may also be had to the *nobile officium* of the Court of Session. It is not part of the purpose of this book to advise in detail on Court of Session practice but the following is intended as a general guide.

1 Children (Scotland) Act 1995, s 51(11)(b)
2 C(S)A 1995, s 51(11)(b).

APPEAL FROM SHERIFF OR SHERIFF PRINCIPAL TO THE COURT OF SESSION

Application for stated case

55.02   The detailed rules for procedure in the Court of Session are set out in the Act of Sederunt (Rules of the Court of Session 1994) 1994, SI 1994/1443 (hereinafter 'RCS 1994'), in particular in rr 41.4–41.17 and rr 41.28–41.33 (as substituted by SI 1998/2637). Appeal is by stated case.[1] Application to the sheriff or the sheriff principal (hereinafter in this chapter referred to as 'the sheriff') to state a case must be made 'within a period of 28 days beginning with the date of the decision appealed against'.[2] The meaning of this provision has been discussed already.[3] Application is to be made by minute setting out the question on which the case is applied for. On receipt of the application the sheriff may require the reporter to return any statements which the reporter had lodged and which had been returned to the reporter.[4] Additional questions may be posed by other parties.[5] The sheriff must consider the application, together with any additional questions proposed by other parties in terms of RCS 1994, r 41.7, and decide whether or not to refuse to state a case in terms of r 41.7(1)(b)[6] or, if the application is made before the facts have been ascertained, to defer consideration until the facts have been ascertained, in terms of r 41.7(1)(c), and then intimate the decision to parties. If the decision is to state a case the sheriff must issue a draft in the form of Form 41.19 within 14 days of such intimation to parties.[7] The stated case should include a recital of the history of the referral so far as relevant, and a properly numbered list of findings in fact.[8] The principles of and good practice in the framing and adjusting of a stated case have been discussed already.[9]

1 Children (Scotland) Act 1995, s 51(11)(b).
2 C(S)A 1995, s 51(13).
3 At 50.09 above.
4 RCS 1994, r 41.30.
5 RCS 1994, r 41.6.
6 For discussion of some grounds of refusal see 54.21 above.
7 RCS 1994, r 41.9(1).
8 RCS 1994, r 41.9(2).
9 At 54.10 ff above.

Progress of stated case

55.03　Parties may propose amendments within 21 days of receiving the draft case, including the questions of law which they wish to pose to the appellate court.[1] In practice the sheriff will generally allow parties a hearing on their amendments. Within 28 days of the time allowed for proposing amendments the sheriff may add such additional questions as may seem necessary for the due disposal of the subject matter of the case.[2] Once the case has been signed the sheriff clerk is bound to deliver the stated case, duly signed, to the party who applied for it or, if more than one party has so applied, to the party who first applied.[3] At the same time the sheriff clerk returns to the reporter any reports or statements which the reporter has been required to lodge in connection with the appeal.[4] The party who receives the signed stated case has 28 days to intimate to the other parties that the appeal is proceeding.[5] The party who applied for the stated case must lodge the case in court with the productions and comply with the other provisions of RCS 1994, r 41.11(1). Further procedures are prescribed by the rules.[6] In one of the few examples so far of an appeal from the sheriff principal to the Court of Session, Lord Prosser, giving the opinion of an Extra Division, stated: 'the sheriff principal heard no evidence and made no findings in fact and having issued a full written judgement before stating the case, added no further comments in the case. We are thus concerned with the written judgement, and the questions posed by him for this court, together with the cases stated for his opinion by the sheriff'.[7]

1 RCS 1994, r 41.9(3).
2 RCS 1994, r 41.9(4).
3 RCS 1994, r 41.9(6).
4 RCS 1994, r 41.30(b).
5 RCS 1994, r 41.11(1).
6 RCS 1994, r 41.10 (2) and (3).
7 *R v Grant* 2000 SLT 372, Extra Div, 2000 GWD 4-118.

Abandonment of appeal

55.04　Failure to comply with RCS 1994, r 41.11(1) will result in the party being deemed to have abandoned the appeal, subject to the right to apply to be reponed.[1] Where a party has been held to have abandoned the appeal under these provisions, there are procedures aimed at securing that any other party who has applied for a stated case may be enabled to proceed with his appeal.[2]

1 RCS 1994, r 41.13.
2 RCS 1994, 4.12(2)and (3).

Determination of appeal

55.05 The Court of Session may direct that all or any part of the appeal is to be heard in private.[1] The Court of Session on deciding the appeal 'shall remit the case to the sheriff for disposal in accordance with such directions as the court may give'.[2] The writer's view as to the interpretation of this provision has already been stated.[3] The Court of Session may remit to the sheriff for clarification,[4] further procedure[5] or, in special circumstances, to hear further evidence[6] but a remit to hear further evidence may not be granted to make good an accidental omission by a party to lead essential evidence.[7] The court, although in principle refusing an appeal, may delete a particular finding.[8] The court may not award expenses against any party.[9] In one case[10] a child appealed against a decision of a sheriff to the effect that the offence of lewd and libidinous practices against her under the Sexual Offences (Scotland) Act 1976, s 5 had not been held as established by the sheriff in a referral and that the sheriff had not exercised his powers under the Sheriff Court Procedure Rules 1971, r 10 so as to hold established an offence under s 3 or s 4 of the 1976 Act.[11] (In this referral another ground of referral – being a member of the same household as a Schedule 1 offender – was undisputed.) The First Division refused the appeal and observed that it was of little importance whether the sheriff should have concluded that another offence had occurred, standing the acceptance of the other ground of referral and the consideration that the facts of the other offence would be open to investigation by the hearing on the principle laid down in *O v Rae*.[12]

1 RCS 1994, r 41.32.
2 Children (Scotland) Act 1995, s 51(14).
3 At 54.27 above.
4 RCS 1994, r 41.16(b); cf *D v Kennedy* 1974 SLT 168; *Kennedy v A* 1986 SLT 358; *M v Kennedy* 1991 SCLR 898, 1993 SLT 431.
5 *F v Kennedy (No 1)* 1992 SC 28 at 33, 1992 SCLR 138 at 143; and *M v Kennedy* 1993 GWD 34-2162.
6 *Kennedy v B* 1972 SC 128.
7 *Ferguson v S* 1992 SCLR 866.
8 *S v Kennedy* 1987 SLT 667.
9 RCS 1994, r 41(33).
10 *M v Kennedy* 1996 SLT 434.
11 The Sexual Offences (Scotland) Act 1976, ss 3–5 are now re-enacted in the Criminal Law (Consolidation) (Scotland) Act 1995, ss 5 and 6.
12 1992 SCLR 318.

Finality of determination by the Court of Session

55.06   The decision of the Court of Session is final and there is no appeal to the House of Lords.[1] The Secretary of State no longer has a reserve power to terminate a supervision requirement.[2]

1 Children (Scotland) Act 1995, s 51(11)(b).
2 Social Work (Scotland) Act 1968, s 52 (repealed by C(S)A 1995, Sch 5, extent of repeal – 'Part III, except section 31(1) and (3)').

Position pending appeal to the Court of Session

55.07   The position pending appeal has been noted already.[1]

1 At 54.33 above.

THE *NOBILE OFFICIUM* OF THE COURT OF SESSION

Definition

55.08   The Court of Session, as the supreme civil court in Scotland, has an 'extraordinary' equitable jurisdiction referred to as the '*nobile officium*'. By virtue of this jurisdiction the court may grant a remedy by making an order dealing with a situation which is not specifically regulated by existing, usually statutory, law.[1] In the first case[2] of the exercise of the *nobile officium* in relation to the children's hearings system Lord President Emslie summarised the nature of this jurisdiction thus:

> 'The power which we have is an extraordinary one and its limits are well understood and will not be extended. It may be exercised in highly special or unforeseen circumstances to prevent injustice or oppression. It cannot however be invoked in such a way as to defeat a statutory intention, express or implied, or to extend the scope of an Act of Parliament. When, on the other hand, the intention of a statute is clear but the necessary machinery for carrying out that intention in special circumstances is lacking, the power may be invoked to provide that machinery.'

1 For a survey of Court of Session practice in relation to the *nobile officium* see Maxwell, *The Practice of the Court of Session* (1980) p 12ff.
2 *Humphries v X & Y* 1982 SC 79.

Practice and procedure

55.09   The *nobile officium* is not an appellate jurisdiction. The process is initiated by petition to the Inner House. In vacation the *nobile officium* may be exercised by the Vacation Judge if the situation is urgent or if the Vacation Judge has been expressly authorised by the Inner House. The Court will scrutinise closely any petition for exercise of this remedy. The competency of the application may be challenged and the court may hear preliminary argument on competency[1] and, if not satisfied that the exercise of the *nobile officium* would be appropriate, dismiss the petition.[2] The power is exercised only if all other remedies have been exhausted.[3] The power is not exercised where an appeal to the sheriff would have been competent.[4]

1 *R v Kennedy* 1993 SCLR 623; *L v Kennedy* 1993 SCLR 693.
2 *R v Kennedy* 1993 SCLR 623.
3 Cf *L v Kennedy* 1993 SCLR 693 at 704 D–G.
4 *CM v Kennedy, BM v Kennedy* 1995 SCLR 15.

Some examples

55.10 The *nobile officium* has been exercised in order to extend the period during which a child was allowed to be detained by warrant granted under the Social Work (Scotland) Act 1968, s 37.[1] In view of the power now vested in the sheriff to grant warrant for the detention of a child without being subject to statutory time limitation,[2] it may be anticipated that the Court of Session may not now be prepared, or indeed be likely to be asked, to exercise its powers in this way. The power has also been exercised in order to allow the sheriff to hear part of the proof in an application to the court under s 42 of the 1968 Act in a court outwith the district in which the case was pending but within the same sheriffdom.[3] The power has been exercised to allow parties to apply out of time for an additional fee under the legal aid regulations in exceptional circumstances.[4] The *nobile officium* has also been exercised in order to allow the sheriff to hear further evidence,[5] but it has been emphasised that this course is permitted only when the circumstances are highly special and it appears that the existence of the new evidence was unforeseen and exceptional.[6] It is incompetent to attempt to lay additional evidence before the Court of Session on appeal by way of motion within the appeal process.[7] The retraction by a child of allegations of sexual abuse has been held not to be so unforeseen and exceptional as to warrant exercise of the *nobile officium*.[8] In a case wherein children had been received into care under a supervision requirement after proof of grounds of referral certain new evidence was held to be sufficiently unforeseen and exceptional and the First Division ordered the hearing of fresh evidence and directed the sheriff to report to the court after hearing the evidence.[9] The sheriff reported that the whole evidence had not persuaded him that the original grounds of referral were established and the First Division ruled that contact between the children and their families was to be re-established. The court reserved to itself the power to terminate the supervision requirement whenever it would be appropriate to do so. Later the Court of Session approved a staged return of the children and ordered that after return had been effected the sheriff would be directed to discharge the referral.[10] Standing the powers now conferred upon the sheriff to review a finding establishing grounds of referral,[11] it may be anticipated that the Court of Session may be unwilling to exercise the *nobile officium* for the purpose of admitting additional evidence. In *Thomson, Petitioner*[12] the First Division, refusing a petition to the *nobile officium* on its merits, refrained from expressing an opinion on whether or not the *nobile officium* might properly be invoked to allow an appeal out of time. In *F v Constanda*[13] an Extra

Division, considering an appeal the competency of which was in doubt, proceeded to deal with the appeal, apparently on the basis that if the appeal were incompetent the Court would have power to dispose of it under the *nobile officium*.

1 *Humphries v X & Y* 1982 SC 79.
2 Children (Scotland) Act 1995, s 67.
3 *Sloan, Petr* 1991 SLT 527.
4 *L, Petrs (No 5)* 1995 GWD 34-1747.
5 *H v Reporter for Strathclyde Region* (6 December 1989, unreported) Court of Session; referred to in *L v Kennedy (No 2)* (15 July 1993, unreported) Court of Session.
6 *L, Petrs (No 1)* 1993 SLT 1310 at 1317–1318; *L, Petrs (No 2)* 1993 SLT 1342.
7 *Stirling v R* 1996 SCLR 623.
8 *R v Kennedy* 1993 SCLR 623, *sub nom R Petrs* 1993 SLT 910.
9 *L v Kennedy (No 2)* (15 July 1993, unreported) Court of Session.
10 *L, Petrs (No 4)* 1995 GWD 16-879.
11 Children (Scotland) Act 1995, s 85.
12 1998 GWD 26-1283.
13 1999 SLT 421.

JUDICIAL REVIEW

Definition

55.11 Judicial review is a common law remedy by which the Court of Session, by virtue of its supervisory jurisdiction over inferior tribunals and public authorities, may review decisions of inferior tribunals and administrative bodies where the urgent interests of justice require intervention. It is generally invoked where the tribunal or body concerned is said to have exceeded its powers. Where there is a statutory remedy the person aggrieved will normally be expected to use it but there may be special circumstances where the court will entertain an application for judicial review where the statutory remedy has not been exhausted and a decision is required urgently.[1] Judicial review has been used with increasing frequency in recent years.

1 *British Railways Board v Glasgow Corporation* 1976 SC 224 at 237 and 239; *Nahar v Strathclyde RC* 1986 SLT 570 at 574.

An example

55.12 In 1987 a sheriff, sustaining an appeal against a decision by a children's hearing by remitting for reconsideration, had included in his interlocutor a direction that the hearing which was to reconsider should comprise a different chairman and different members from the hearing which had made the original decision. The reporter appealed against this by applying for a stated case but owing to illness on the part of the sheriff the preparation of the stated case was delayed. In the meantime a review was applied for by one of the parties and the reporter considered that he required guidance as to whether the order by the sheriff required to be obtempered and sought judicial review of the sheriff's interlocutor. Lord

Jauncey held that the review hearing now sought by the party was not the hearing following on the interlocutor of the sheriff, which was the only hearing which could be affected by the purported direction in that interlocutor, and consequently dismissed the petition for judicial review. However, in giving his opinion Lord Jauncey stated:

> 'If a body or an inferior court having pronounced a once-and-for-all order was then unable for a protracted period to implement the necessary machinery for review of that order there might be circumstances in which the appellant could have recourse to the Court of Session for a common law remedy.'[1]

1 *Kennedy, Petr* 1988 SCLR 149 at 151.

APPEAL TO THE HOUSE OF LORDS – *NOBILE OFFICIUM* AND JUDICIAL REVIEW

55.13 Since such procedures are not strictly procedures under the Children (Scotland) Act 1995 it is thought that the provision of the Act[1] providing for the finality of a decision of the Court of Session would not have application to them and that therefore appeal to the House of Lords may be competent.

1 Children (Scotland) Act 1995, s 51(11)(b).

APPEAL TO THE EUROPEAN COURT OF HUMAN RIGHTS

55.14 In certain circumstances appeal may be taken to the European Court of Human Rights. The only reported decision of the European Court dealing with hearings law at time of writing is *McMichael v UK*.[1] Since 2 October 2000, matters under the European Convention of Human Rights may be canvassed in the Scottish courts.

1 (1995) 20 EHRR 205: noticed and discussed at 1.08 above and elsewhere.

CHAPTER 56

The supervision requirement in relation to orders of courts

SUPERVISION REQUIREMENTS AND ORDERS OF CRIMINAL COURTS

Court ordering detention of child

56.01 As already noticed,[1] a child may be prosecuted in the ordinary criminal courts with the consent of the Lord Advocate. The continuing interest of the hearings system in a child who is under supervision is secured by the obligation imposed on the sheriff court and the power conferred on the High Court to obtain the advice of a children's hearing in relation to such a child before passing sentence.[2] A sentence of detention of a child who is under supervision of a children's hearing may result in the local authority recommending a review of the requirement.[3]

1 At 1.24 above.
2 Criminal Procedure (Scotland) Act 1995, s 49(3), discussed at 3.20 and 19.26 above.
3 Children (Scotland) Act 1995, s 73(4)(a) and (b) and (8).

Children's hearing abridging liberty of child

56.02 It would appear that a disposal by a children's hearing which would restrict the liberty of a child, for example a supervision requirement with a condition that a child reside in a named residential establishment under the Children (Scotland) Act 1995, s 70(3)(a) would put into abeyance an earlier order of court such as a probation order requiring the child to live at home: but the matter has not, so far as the writer is aware, been formally decided.

Condition of a supervision requirement may inhibit range of probation orders

56.03 It would also appear that once a hearing has imposed a requirement for compulsory measures of supervision it would not be competent for a judge sentencing subsequently to propose to impose as a condition of probation any condition inconsistent with that requirement, since the child would presumably not be regarded as free to agree to such a condition.[1]

1 Cf the remarks of Lord Cameron of Lochbroom in *P v P* 2000 SLT 781, 2000 SCLR 477, Extra Div, quoted at 56.06 below.

SUPERVISION REQUIREMENTS AND ORDERS OF THE CIVIL COURTS

The law before 1 November 1996

56.04   Until this date, when the Children (Scotland) Act 1995, s 11 came into force, the civil courts were regularly asked to make orders regulating 'custody' of and 'access' to children, usually as ancillary orders to matrimonial causes. The question arose whether an award of custody could lawfully be made while a supervision order by a children's hearing was in force in relation to the child. To this question Lord President Emslie gave an unequivocal answer in the case of *Aitken v Aitken*:[1]

> 'The existence of parental rights in relation to a child or of rights to his custody do not and cannot disable a children's hearing from making a supervision requirement in respect of a child who for any of the grounds specified in section 32(2) is in need of compulsory measures of care. The making of a supervision requirement does not deprive parents or a person to whom custody of a child has been awarded, of their rights in relation to the child. It is properly to be regarded as just another of those lawful orders which may temporarily prevent the exercise of those rights.'

The question then arose as to whether the civil court in a family action could make an order regulating access to a child who was subject to a supervision requirement. The answer to this question was supplied, equally unequivocally, by the Second Division *in D v Strathclyde Regional Council*:[2]

> 'Access is a modification of a party's legal right to have care and control of a child. While a child is under a supervision requirement that child is held to be in need of compulsory measures of care. This may involve the local authority keeping the child away from the factors or influences which led to the supervision requirement being made. This appears to involve a discretionary power being vested in the local authority in relation to a variety of matters including the persons who should be in contact with the child and under what conditions. If persons have aliunde a legal right to have contact with or access to the child that legal right is inhibited by and during the currency of the supervision requirement in that the local authority can decide that it is not in the child's interest that the legal right should be exercised. Access is something which is physically operable at the instant in time, whereas custody is a legal right which can be held even if it is not being physically exercised. Thus, as explained in *Aitken*, a court can grant a decree of custody while a child is in care under a supervision requirement, subject to the legal proviso that the right to exercise that custody is inhibited during the currency of the requirement.'

In a case in 1996, decided under the pre-1995 Act law, the effort was made to argue that the 'principle of access' to a child subject to a supervision requirement could be considered and ruled upon in a family action – on the analogy of the concept of custody as expounded in *Aitken*. The sheriff principal, reversing the sheriff, rejected this argument and held that the rule in *D v Strathclyde Regional Council* had to be applied. The sheriff principal stated:[3]

'It is clear that the exercise of custody does not necessarily involve contact whereas the exercise of the right of access necessarily does.'

1 1978 SC at 302, 1978 SLT 183 at 185.
2 1984 SLT 114 at 116, *sub nom Dewar v Strathclyde Regional Council* 1984 SC 102.
3 *A v G & Strathclyde Regional Council* 1997 SCLR 186 at 188F.

The present law

56.05 The Children (Scotland) Act 1995 has defined the relationship of parent and child in terms which expressly provide that parental rights are only enjoyed in order to enable the person having such rights to carry out the parental responsibilities, such as safeguarding and promoting the child's health, development and welfare and providing appropriate direction and guidance to the child.[1] It is a parental responsibility, if the child is not living with the parent, to maintain personal relations and direct contact with the child on a regular basis. The Act also replaced the old concepts of custody and access with residence and contact orders[2] and empowered the court inter alia to impose such rights and responsibilities on persons seeking them.[3] Section 3(4) of the Act provides:

'The fact that a person has parental responsibilities or parental rights in relation to a child shall not entitle that person to act in any way which would be incompatible with any court order relating to the child or the child's property, or with any supervision requirement made under s 70 of this Act.'

1 Children (Scotland) Act 1995, s 2(1) as read with s 1(1).
2 C(S)A 1995, s 11(2) (c) and (d).
3 C(S)A 1995, s 11(2).

P v P[1]

56.06 In this case a grandmother raised an action in the sheriff court seeking a declarator that she was entitled to make application for a parental responsibilities order under the Children (Scotland) Act 1995, s 11(2)(b) and in particular seeking a residence order. The genetic father lodged defences and applied for parental rights and responsibilities under s 11(2)(b) of the Act and a contact order. The child was under the supervision of a children's hearing. The pursuer, recognising the difficulties presented by the cases cited above,[2] submitted that a residence order should not be regarded as a specific order but rather as part of a more general order in relation to parental rights and responsibilities. The sheriff, after discussing the authorities and noting that s 1(4) of the Act provided that the parental responsibilities provided for superseded any analogous duties imposed on parents at common law, held in substance that as residence and contact orders were orders which involved immediate implementation, it was incompetent for the sheriff in a family action to make such orders while a child was subject to a supervision requirement.[3] On appeal an Extra Division, after hearing arguments more broadly based than those addressed to the sheriff, held, in relation to the pursuer's claim for a residence order, that the discretion conferred on the sheriff by s 11(7) of the Act was wide enough to enable him to take into account matters other than the existence of a supervision requirement. Lord Cameron of Lochbroom, delivering the opinion of the court, stated that the sheriff 'was bound to consider whether the making of the order was appropriate or not in the whole circumstances which he held to be relevant, and looking to the provisions of section 11(7) in particular, whether to make the order sought or not'. In dealing with the defender's claim for contact, the court, disapproving the decision of the sheriff principal in *A v G and Strathclyde Regional Council*, held in substance that an application for contact was not rendered incompetent by reason only of a child's being subject to a supervision requirement, but added that 'we would regard it as inappropriate, unless the circumstances were exceptional and justified the court in doing so on a proper application of the "three overarching principles", to grant such an order which would at the time of its making be inconsistent with a condition attached to a supervision requirement'.

1 1999 SCLR 679, Sh Ct; on appeal 2000 SCLR 477, IH.
2 At 56.04.
3 1999 SCLR 690A.

Arranging a hearing – relevant person; genetic father not having parental rights

56.07   The issue of residence and contact may be raised at a disposal hearing under the Children (Scotland) Act 1995, s 70(1) or at a review hearing under s 73(6) or (8) of the Act. An unmarried father who has not acquired any parental right or responsibility is not a relevant person.[1] It has been held by the Inner House in *L v H* that an unmarried father cannot invoke the provisions of the Law Reform (Parent and Child) (Scotland) Act 1986, s 3(1) in order to obtain the parental right of guardianship to enable him to appear and present his own case (as opposed to the child's case) before a children's hearing.[2] In *P v P*[3] the sheriff held that a specific issue order under the Children (Scotland) Act 1995, s 11(2)(c) cannot be used for this purpose.[4] In *L v H* the court suggested that such a father might make application to the chairman of the hearing to exercise his discretion under the Children's Hearings (Scotland) Rules 1986, r 14(d) to allow his presence as 'any other person whose presence at the sitting may in the opinion of the chairman be justified by special circumstances'. In *P v P*[5] it was observed that such a father may make application for parental responsibilities and rights under s 11 of the 1995 Act, and this would appear to supply the answer to the problem.

1 See the Children (Scotland) Act 1995, s 93(2) for the definition of 'relevant person'; a father with a responsibility or right in relation to, for example, contact would be a relevant person.
2 *L v H* 1996 SLT 612 at 616A,B.
3 1999 SCLR 679 at 691G ff – this part of the sheriff's judgment was not dealt with in the appeal to the Court of Session and is, it is respectfully submitted, correct.
4 Although Professor Norrie advances this as a possibility in his commentary to the decision of the Sheriff in *A v G and Strathclyde Regional Council* 1996 SCLR 787 at 800.
5 2000 SCLR 477 at 488F and 489D, 2000 SLT 781.

Powers of hearing

56.08 The hearing has a wide discretion in regulating contact. Even if expressly asked to rule on specific contact it may leave this matter to the discretion of the local authority.[1]

1 *Kennedy v M* 1995 SCLR 88 per LP Hope at 96E ff; but see dissenting opinion of Lord Marnoch at 100A ff– *quaere* if this approach may be affected by the European Convention on Human Rights, art 6(1).

Practice Guidance regarding contact

56.09 The former Scottish Office has issued guidance.[1]

1 *Scotland's Children – The Children (Scotland) Act 1995 – Regulations and Guidance – Volume 2, Children Looked After by Local Authorities* (The Stationery Office, Edinburgh, 1997), paras 29–49.

Hearings' law and adoption

Rights under the 1995 Act of potential adopter

56.10 Once an adoption order is made (but not before) the full parental rights and duties in relation to the child rest in the adopter.[1] Even before the adoption order is made the potential adopter could in appropriate circumstances be regarded as a relevant person[2] and as such acquire rights and duties under the Children (Scotland) Act 1995, Pt II. An adoption agency which has had a freeing for adoption order granted to it in respect of a child acquires the rights and duties of a parent in respect of that child.[3]

1 Adoption (Scotland) Act 1978, s 12(1), (2) and (3).
2 Children (Scotland) Act 1995, s 93(2) definition of 'relevant person'.
3 A(S)A 1978, s 18(5).

Report and advice hearings in relation to adoption

56.11 As already noticed,[1] the local authority must refer to the hearing for a report when applying for an adoption order or an order freeing for adoption and an approved adoption society is under obligation to refer the case of a child under supervision whom it considers would benefit from adoption to the reporter who must arrange an advice hearing. Here is an example of advice based on advice given in a particular case which it is suggested may be followed or adapted:

FORM OF REPORT BY CHILDREN'S HEARING OF ADVICE UNDER
SECTION 73(13) OF THE ACT PROVIDING FOR CONSIDERATION BY
SHERIFF IN HIS DETERMINATION OF DECISION OF ADOPTION
AGENCY

At: Lenton House, Laverock Square, Kirklenton   Date: 27 April 2000

To: The Sheriff Court, Kirklenton

On 27 April 2000 a children's hearing for Lentonshire Council, after
considering the case of

Name: Hilary ~ , a female child born 21.12.99.

Address: 4 Strathlachie Quadrant, Kirklenton.

and the [proposed application under section 86 of the Act]* [proposed
application under [section 12]* [section 18]* of the Adoption (Scotland)
Act 1978]* [proposed freeing for adoption]* provide the advice set out
below to assist the sheriff in his/her determination of the application.

ADVICE REFERRED TO IN THE FOREGOING ADVICE STATEMENT

1. There is an extensive history (11 years at least) of poor child care, inadequate parenting, alcohol abuse by the parents, offending behaviour on
the part of the parents, and violence amongst family members.

2. Older children have had to be removed from their parents' care. In the
case of one of these children secure accommodation had to be authorised
and used.

3. The parents do not accept the extent of these difficulties and continue to
minimise the difficulties which will be posed in bringing up Hilary, e g the
developmental delay which is likely owing to the effect of foetal alcohol
syndrome.

4. There is extreme antagonism on the part of the parents towards the
Social Work Department and the Department's advice is only accepted
when the parents choose to accept it. This would make monitoring of the
child's development difficult if not impossible and, without such
prolonged monitoring, the child's best interests would not be served.

5. The child's parents have not shown a consistent commitment to the
current contact arrangements.

6. The child's future has to be secured in a way which will promote her
well-being throughout her childhood and beyond. The parents have more
than once shown their inability to do this.

7. The child is still comparatively young and the hearing considers, for the
foregoing reasons, that her best interests will be served by being adopted
at the earliest possible time and that the freeing order should be granted
with the minimum delay consistent with due procedure.

8. The child is at present with short-term foster carers. There may have to
be a change of carers soon. The hearing considers that the child's best
interests will be served by her continuing for the present to be subject to

compulsory measures of supervision and therefore advises the sheriff, if minded to grant the freeing order, not to terminate the supervision requirement meantime.

(Sgd) *AB*

Chairman of the Children's Hearing

Certified a true copy

(Sgd) *CD* Reporter

1 At 19.24 above.

Advice hearings in relation to applications for parental responsibilities orders

56.12 As already noticed, a local authority which has satisfied itself that applying for a parental responsibilities order under the Children (Scotland) Act 1995, s 86 in the best interests of the child who is subject to a supervision requirement must refer the case to the reporter who must fix a review hearing.[1]

1 Children (Scotland) Act 1995, s 73(4)(c)(i) and (8)(a)(i).

CHAPTER 57

Review of establishment of grounds of referral

GROUNDS OF APPLICATION – COMPETENT APPLICANTS

Criteria for application

57.01 Section 85 of the Children (Scotland) Act 1995 contains entirely new provisions to allow application to be made to the sheriff for a review of a finding by a sheriff after a s 68 proof that one or more grounds of referral had been established. Hitherto this could only be done in the Court of Session by virtue of the *nobile officium*[1]. In order to make application for a s 85 review the applicant must claim:

'(a) to have evidence which was not considered by the sheriff on the original application, being evidence the existence or significance of which might materially have affected the determination of the original application;

(b) that such evidence –
　(i) is likely to be credible and reliable; and
　(ii) would have been admissible in relation to the ground of referral which was found to be established on the original application; and

(c) that there is a reasonable explanation for the failure to lead such evidence on the original application.'[2]

The latter is a less demanding test than that for the exercise of the *nobile officium* where the circumstances have to be 'exceptional and unforeseen'.[3]

1 *L v Kennedy* 1993 SCLR 693, *sub nom L, Petrs (No 1)* 1993 SLT 1310 and *L, Petrs (No 2)* 1993 SLT 1342; *R Petr* 1993 SLT 910.
2 Children (Scotland) Act 1995, s 85 (3)(a) and (b).
3 *R, Petr* 1993 SLT 910 at 914K.

Remedy only available where original sheriff has made a finding – including a finding after dispensing with evidence

57.02 Section 85 of the Children (Scotland) Act 1995 is only available where there has been 'a finding of the sheriff such as is mentioned in section 68(10) of this Act', i e a finding after evidence has been led *or following a deeming of grounds established pursuant upon an acceptance of grounds and consequent dispensing with evidence by virtue of s 68(8)*. The legislation provides no remedy to a child or relevant person who wishes to bring under review a supervision requirement of a hearing following upon an acceptance of the grounds of referral in the forum of the hearing. It may be thought strange that the remedy is afforded in cases which have been subjected to judicial scrutiny, with the parties probably legally advised, and not to cases where there has been no judicial scrutiny, with parties probably not legally advised. The rationale of this distinction is not easy to discern. If it be argued that the justification is that cases where the grounds of referral have been admitted should not be re-opened, where is the justification for allowing the remedy in respect of cases which have been admitted before the sheriff, with legal advice usually available, but not in respect of cases where the admission has been in the forum of the hearing, with legal advice not usually available? There seems no good reason to suppose that fresh evidence might not come to light in relation to a case wherein a person, in ignorance of that evidence, had admitted grounds at the sitting of the children's hearing. In this event it may yet be that the Court of Session might still have to be invited to exercise the *nobile officium*, although that court might take the view that it could not intervene since the legislature had made it clear that no remedy was intended in such a situation. In that event it may be that application to the European Court of Human Rights[1] might have to be considered.

1 Or, after 2 October 2000, by invocation of the Human Rights Act 1998 in the Scottish courts.

Who may apply

57.03   Only the referred child or any person who is a relevant person may apply for this remedy.[1] The reporter has no power to apply. It is submitted that this is an unfortunate omission. The reporter might well come into possession of information undermining an earlier finding. This omission is however, consistent with the scheme of the Act in so far as it has refrained from giving the reporter comprehensive responsibilities in the field of child protection. Other examples are the conferring upon the local authority the main responsibility for applying for Child Assessment Orders and Exclusion Orders. With the development of the hearings system the reporter has become increasingly identified as the advocate of the interests of children. The local authority has many other responsibilities in relation to caring for the vulnerable. It is submitted that there would be merit in moving towards recognising an officer such as the reporter as the public custodian of the interests of children. One facet of this recognition might be to confer on the reporter the right in an appropriate case to make application under s 85 of the Children (Scotland) Act 1995. It is notable that there is no provision for an application at the instance of a person named as an offender against the child as such person and therefore such a person, except where he happens to be a relevant person in relation to the child, is without remedy under this section.

1 Children (Scotland) Act 1995, s 85(4).

INITIAL PROCEDURE

Form of application

57.04   Rule 3.62 of the Act of Sederunt (Child Care and Maintenance Rules) 1997[1] prescribes the content of the application. No form of application is prescribed in the Rules. It is suggested that this style may be adopted:

SHERIFFDOM OF GLASGOW AND STRATHKELVIN AT GLASGOW

APPLICATION

under
Section 85 of the Children (Scotland) Act 1995
Act of Sederunt (Child Care and Maintenance
Rules) 1997, rr 3.62–3.64

by

AB, date of birth 4.11.1974, residing at 10 Turquoise Street, Glasgow, father of, and relevant person in relation to, the child CD, date of birth 15.03.1994, residing at 26 Aquamarine Avenue, Glasgow.

<u>Applicant</u>

against

ALAN   D   MILLER,   Principal   Reporter, Scottish Children's Reporter Administration, Ochil House, Springkerse Business Park, Stirling FK7 7XE.

<u>Respondent</u>

The applicant[2] respectfully craves the court:

to review the findings of Sheriff EF sitting in Glasgow Sheriff Court on 16 April 1998 namely that an offence specified in Schedule 1 of the Criminal Procedure (Scotland) Act 1995 was committed against the said child by the applicant all in terms of the court's interlocutor of 16 April 1998 aforesaid;
to discharge the referral to the children's hearing in respect of the said ground;
to order immediate termination of the supervision requirement in respect of said child following thereon;
and to make such other order or orders as to the court shall seem appropriate;
all in terms of the section 85 of the Children (Scotland) Act 1995.

CONDESCENDENCE

1. The applicant is the father of, and married to the mother of, the child CD, whose date if birth is 15 March 1994, and is as such a relevant person in relation to said child. The respondent is the principal reporter. The said child at present resides with her said mother Mrs AB at 26 Aquamarine Avenue, Glasgow. At the hearing before the sheriff hereinafter condescended upon the respondent was represented by XY, then an authority reporter at 10/20 Bell Street, Candleriggs, Glasgow G1 1LG.

2. The respondent, per the said XY, referred the said child to a hearing on 9 February 1998 on the ground that on 1 January 1998 she had been the victim of an offence mentioned in Schedule 1 of the Criminal Procedure (Scotland) Act 1995 and averred in the statement of facts that the applicant had committed the said offence. The grounds of referral are produced herewith and here held as repeated brevitatis causa. At the said hearing the said grounds were admitted by the child's mother but denied by the applicant and the hearing was satisfied that, owing to her young age, the child CD was not capable of understanding the explanation of the grounds of referral. The hearing, not being minded to discharge the referral, directed the respondent under s 65(7) and s 65(9) of the Children (Scotland) Act 1995 to make application to the sheriff for a finding.

3. The sheriff, on his own motion, appointed KL, solicitor, carrying on business at ——, as curator ad litem to the said child.

4. After sundry procedure Sheriff EF, sitting in the Sheriff Court of Glasgow and Strathkelvin at Glasgow, heard proof under s 68 of the Children (Scotland) Act 1995 from 13 to 16 April 1998 inclusive.

5. The evidence led by the reporter before the learned sheriff comprised principally: (a) verbal testimony by social worker MN of the —— office of the Social Work Department of Glasgow City Council that the child had said to said social worker that the applicant had committed the offence; (b) evidence by OP, a child psychologist of the —— Hospital, Glasgow that the said child, then aged 4 years and one month, was capable of giving trustworthy evidence; and (c) evidence of QR, consultant orthopaedic paediatrician at the same hospital, to the effect that the condition of the bones of the said child indicated 'an assault on the child'. The said child was called but, when examined by the sheriff as to whether she was a competent witness, did not say anything. The evidence of the social worker MN was objected to on the ground that the evidence of the child psychologist that the child was capable of giving trustworthy evidence was insufficient in law to enable the court to conclude that the child was a competent witness. The evidence was admitted under reservation of all questions of competency and relevancy. The present applicant gave evidence and admitted that the child had been under his sole care and control at the material time but denied the allegation of assault and said that the injuries to the child had been caused by a fall.

6. The learned sheriff, after hearing the evidence, repelled the objection which had been taken to the evidence of MN, held the grounds of referral to be established and remitted the case to the reporter to make

arrangements for a children's hearing to consider and determine the case, all in terms of s 68(10)(a) of the Children (Scotland) Act 1995.

7. Pursuant to said remit, a children's hearing was held on 24 April 1998 and a supervision requirement was made requiring the said child to reside with her mother the said Mrs AB but not as part of the same household as the applicant. Said requirement was continued on 16 April 1999 and again on 11 April 2000. It is still in force.

8. The applicant wishes the court to re-consider the decision of the learned sheriff on the following ground: the learned sheriff was wrong to conclude that an assault on the child had taken place, and the applicant refers to the new evidence hereinafter referred to.

9. The new evidence on which the applicant relies is: (i) evidence from ST, consultant orthopaedic paediatrician, —— Hospital, London that the medical records of the —— Hospital Glasgow are consistent with the conclusion that the said injuries were caused by a fall as testified by the applicant before the sheriff: (ii) evidence from Mrs AB, mother of the said child, confirmed by affidavit dated 18 July 2000, that the said child has retracted the statement given to the social worker MN to the effect that the applicant assaulted her; and the applicant believes that the said child, now aged 6 years and 4 months, will testify to this or at least be able to satisfy the court that she is a competent witness.

10. The evidence from ST was not available to the applicant at the time of the proof before the sheriff because at the time the applicant was unable to afford to commission such a report and his then solicitor advised that the Scottish Legal Aid Board would be unlikely to sanction the obtaining of such a report on the ground that the child had identified the applicant as having assaulted her and that it was therefore unlikely that the evidence of the Glasgow paediatrician would be capable of being displaced. The applicant was only able to commission the report from the London paediatrician after a public appeal in his neighbourhood had raised the funds which enabled him to obtain the records of the —— Hospital, Glasgow by application to the court under s 1 of the Administration of Justice (Scotland) Act 1972 and thereafter to commission and pay for a report by the said ST. The applicant was advised by his then solicitor not to appeal against the decision of the learned sheriff on the question of the admissibility of the evidence of MN on the ground that the medical evidence was so strong that an appeal would be unlikely to succeed.

11. The evidence of the said ST is likely to be credible and reliable. It would have been admissible at the proof on 13 to 16 April 1998. The explanation given above as to the failure to lead this evidence at the said proof is reasonable.

12. The evidence of the child's mother is likely to be credible and reliable. It would have been admissible at the proof on 13 to 16 April 1998. By virtue of its date it would have been impossible to lead it at the said proof.

13. The evidence of the child is likely to be credible and reliable. It would have been admissible at the proof if the child had been as mature as she is now, but as at the date of the proof it was not available owing to the child's immaturity.

14. The applicant produces and founds upon: (a) the Report dated 3 July 2000 by the said ST, consultant orthopaedic paediatrician, —— Hospital, London; and (b) affidavit of the said Mrs AB, mother of said child CD, dated 18 July 2000.

The applicant accordingly respectfully requests the court:

1) To assign a diet for the hearing of this application.
2) To grant warrant to cite the principal reporter and to appoint the principal reporter to lodge answers, if so advised, within twenty-one days or such other period as to the court shall appear just;
3) To appoint the applicant forthwith to intimate the application to: (i) Mrs AB, residing at ——, mother of and relevant person to the said child; (ii) Miss KL, solicitor, carrying on business at ——, curator ad litem to said child; and (iii) Sheriff EF, Sheriff Court of Glasgow and Strathkelvin at Glasgow, 1 Carlton Place, Glasgow, the presiding sheriff in the original application;
4) To grant warrant to cite witnesses and havers; and
5) To dispense with service on the said child CD for the following reasons: the said child is, by reason of age, too immature to receive and understand written documents from the court; and, in any event, the curator ad litem will be able to attend to the interests of the child.

IN RESPECT WHEREOF

(sgd) Fiona Crawford

FIONA CRAWFORD
Solicitor
16 Indigo Street
Glasgow.

Agent for applicant.

Some comments on the above proposed style

Comment 1. It is thought that the foregoing style contains averments in relation to all the issues identified by rule 3.62 of the Act of Sederunt (Child Care and Maintenance Rules) 1997. This style presupposes an original application containing only one ground of referral. In the event of there having been more that one ground of referral the applicant should narrate all the grounds of referral and identify which grounds s/he proposes to challenge.

Comment 2. The applicant has not founded on the sheriff's decision to admit the evidence of the social worker as to the hearsay evidence of the child. It is submitted that it would be incompetent to rely on this since the argument would be that that was an error of law by the sheriff and error of law is not a ground for review under s 85 of the Children (Scotland) Act 1995. It is thought however, that it was correct to include reference to this decision of the sheriff since it is submitted, when the matter comes to be argued it will be prudent to refer to any alleged error of law in case the sheriff who hears the application takes the view that he has a discretion under s 85(7) and that the exercise of such discretion in favour of the applicant would be more readily exercised if an error of law were identified – but the sheriff hearing an application under s 85 should not regard the application as an appeal against the original finding.

Comment 3. The applicant has founded on the mother's statement and the child's evidence. While a question may be raised as to whether, on a narrow reading of the statute, the evidence of the child could have been admissible in 1998 by virtue of the child's having (allegedly) acquired sufficient maturity in 2000, it is thought that it was the intention of the legislature to allow for the admission of such evidence in s 85 applications.[3]

1 SI 1997/291.
2 The 'FORM OF WARRANT TO CITE PRINCIPAL REPORTER' (Act of Sederunt (Child Care and Maintenance Rules) 1997, SI 1997/291, r 3.63(1), Form 65) which the sheriff clerk shall issue on receipt of an application such as this uses the term 'Appellant'. This is a misnomer since the procedure is a review and not an appeal and the applicant is not an appellant.
3 Cf *R v Kennedy* 1993 SLT 910; *L Petrs (No 1)* 1993 SLT 1310 and *L Petrs (No 2)* 1993 SLT 1342 cf also *T v T* (10 November 2000, unreported) Court of Five Judges, Court of Session.

Service of application

57.05   On receipt of the application the sheriff clerk assigns a diet for the hearing of the application and issues a warrant in the style of Form 65 of the Act of Sederunt (Child Care and Maintenance) Rules 1997. The warrant inter alia appoints the reporter, if so advised, to lodge answers, if so advised, within such period as the sheriff shall set. The sheriff clerk should consult the sheriff as to the contents of orders sought in the warrant, including as to whether or not service on the child or any other person should be dispensed with. Regard must be paid to Rule 3.4(2), which empowers the sheriff, on the application of the applicant or *ex proprio motu*, to order that a specified part of the application shall not be served on the child.[1] As in all procedures under this part of the Act except an application for a Child Protection Order the sheriff must consider if it is necessary to appoint a safeguarder and, if he thinks it necessary, appoint one.[2]

1 SI 1997/291, r 3.63(2).
2 Children (Scotland) Act 1995, s 41(1).

POSSIBLE PROCEDURE BEFORE FINAL HEARING OF APPLICATION

First hearing of the application – the rules

57.06   Rule 3.63 of the Act of Sederunt (Child Care and Maintenance Rules) 1997 provides, in relation to the proceedings at the diet so fixed: 'After hearing parties and allowing such further procedure as he thinks fit, the sheriff shall, if satisfied in terms of s 85(6) of the Children (Scotland) Act 1995, consider the evidence and may fix a further hearing for that purpose'.[1] Section 85(6) of the Act provides: 'Where the sheriff is satisfied on an application under subsection (1) above that the claims made in the application are established, he shall consider the evidence ...'. The 'claims' are those referred to in s 85(3) – the 'criteria' set out in the first paragraph of this chapter (applicant possesses new evidence, such evidence likely to be credible and reliable, and such evidence would have been admissible at the proof on the original application). Only if the sheriff is satisfied that these criteria exist shall he proceed to consider evidence. Since the warrant fixing the first hearing contains warrant to cite witnesses and havers it is competent to hear evidence in the course of the first hearing. It is accordingly submitted that the sheriff has been given a wide discretion entitling him to dispose of the application on the basis of the existing information and the evidence presented at the first hearing.

1 SI 1997/291, r 3.63(3).

The practicalities – possibility of dismissal of application without hearing evidence

57.07   Applications under s 85 of the Children (Scotland) Act 1995 are rare and a general practice has not yet developed. It is thought that such applications will always be unusual and it is suggested that parties should, through the sheriff clerk, liaise with the sheriff as to the appropriate form of procedure. In a seriously contested case there may be submissions by the reporter or other parties that the averments of the applicant do not 'establish' the claims which the applicant requires to make in terms of s 85(3). In this event the sheriff may, if persuaded by these submissions dismiss the application in terms of s 85(5). In *Y v Authority Reporter (Highland)*[1] the sheriff heard the applicant's solicitor, the reporter and the curator *ad litem* for the child on the application and the answers lodged for the reporter and, without issuing an opinion, dismissed the application.

1 24 April 1998, Wick Sheriff Court, Sheriff I A Cameron, unreported.

No obligation to hear evidence

57.08   There is no obligation placed on the sheriff to hear evidence (contrast the position at a hearing in an application under the Children (Scotland) Act 1995, s 68 where the sheriff must under r 3.47 'hear evidence tendered by or on behalf of the Principal Reporter ...').[1]

1 SI 1997/291, r 3.47.

Hearing of the application – the practicalities – should the sheriff considering the application be the same or a different sheriff from the sheriff who heard to original application?

57.09   There is no rule or statutory enactment governing this issue. An application under s 85 of the Children (Scotland) Act 1995 is not an appeal against the original decision. Accordingly, and since the sheriff who heard the original application will usually be better placed than any other sheriff to assess the merits of the s 85 application there would seem to be no good reason why, where practicable, that sheriff should not hear the new application. In *Y v Authority Reporter (Highland)*[1] the sheriff who dealt with the application and dismissed it at the initial stage was not the sheriff who had heard proof in the original application, but parties requested that, if the s 85 application were to proceed to proof, then the evidence should be heard by the sheriff who had heard the original proof. It is possible, however, to figure situations in which it would be preferable for a new sheriff to hear a s 85 proof – for example where the sheriff at the original proof had expressed such strong views as to the credibility of one of the principal parties as to appear to rule out in advance any re-consideration, or where the s 85 application may give rise to re-consideration of the original sheriff's decision to dispense with the hearing of evidence under s 68(8) of the Act.[2]

1 24 April 1998, unreported.
2 But sheriffs should take account of the wider interests of the child before deciding not to take a case, cf *F v Constanda* 1999 SLT 421 (Extra Div).

First hearing and further hearings – possibility of amendment of application and answers

57.10 It may be that applications under this section will only be raised where serious issues have arisen. It is submitted that in such event the first hearing may, after informal consultation with the sheriff via the sheriff clerk as suggested above, be used by parties as an opportunity to be heard on any legal issues arising and generally on the best way to proceed with the application. The complete discretion conveyed to the sheriff by rule 3.63 of the Act of Sederunt (Child Care and Maintenance) Rules 1997 to allow 'such procedure as he thinks fit' will, it is submitted, allow the sheriff to allow any party who wishes to lodge answers, to extend any time-limit in relation to the lodgement of answers and to allow such adjustment or amendment of the written pleadings as he deems appropriate, subject only to allowing the other side the opportunity to respond.

The effect of s 85(7)(b) of the Children (Scotland) Act 1995

57.11 This section empowers the sheriff, if satisfied on the evidence that a ground of referral which was not stated in the original application is established, to direct the reporter to fix a disposal hearing in accordance with s 68(10) of the Act. The sheriff may make such a decision *ex proprio motu* or on the motion of a party. It is submitted that if it is the intention of the reporter or other party (e g a safeguarder) to move the sheriff to use this power then such party should give notice to the other parties of this intention by averment in the written pleadings or otherwise. Any party so moving would in the first instance have the onus of proof. It is suggested that where the sheriff is considering making such a decision *ex proprio motu* he should give an indication of this and allow parties to make submissions.

FINAL HEARING OF APPLICATION

Hearing of the evidence

57.12　The sheriff should hear the evidence as in a proof under s 68 of the Children (Scotland) Act 1995. The onus of proof is, it is submitted, with the applicant and it is thought that the sheriff will normally direct the applicant to lead, although, under r 3.63 as already noted, the procedure is within the discretion of the sheriff. The proceedings are summary and no official record is kept apart from the formal interlocutors and the hand-written notes of the sheriff. Parties may instruct shorthand writers.[1]

1 See 36.03 above.

Hearing to consider the evidence

Principles to be applied by the sheriff

57.13　The sheriff may fix a hearing to hear parties' submissions on the evidence[1] but is not bound to do so and may, as in ordinary civil procedure, hear parties on the evidence at the conclusion of the proof. It is submitted that in considering the merits of an application under s 85 of the Children (Scotland) Act 1995 the sheriff is deciding a matter of mixed fact and law and is not bound directly by any of the s 16 principles.

1 SI 1997/291, r 3.63 read with r 3.64.

POWERS OF THE SHERIFF ON DISPOSAL

Application successful

Powers of the sheriff to appoint date on which supervision requirement is to terminate – parties to be ready to advise sheriff

57.14　Where the sheriff is satisfied that none of the grounds in the original application to which the application relates is established (and is not minded to exercise the power under s 85(7)(b) dicussed above at 57.11) he shall allow the application, discharge the referral to the children's hearing in respect of those grounds, and proceed in accordance with s 85(7) of the Children (Scotland) Act 1995 in relation to any supervision requirement (whether or not varied under s 73 of the Act) in relation to that ground. It is thought that the reference here is to s 85(7)(a) of the Act which empowers the sheriff, on sustaining an application, to order that the supervision requirement shall terminate immediately or 'on such date as he may specify'. It is thought that the s 16 principle of the paramountcy of the welfare of the child will apply at this stage and parties should be ready to make submissions to the sheriff as to which date should be selected. The sheriff will pay particular regard to the submissions of any safe-guarder or curator *ad litem* at this stage. It is submitted that the use of the word 'may' in the introductory words to s 85(7) does not, standing the use of the word 'shall' in s 85(6)(a), confer a discretion on the sheriff except in relation to selection of the said date.[1] It may however be prudent for the pleader to be ready for the possibility that the sheriff may take a different view and be ready with any argument which might persuade the sheriff to exercise any discretion in favour of the applicant.[2]

1 This is also Professor Norrie's view, see *Children (Scotland) Act 1995* (1998) p 172.
2 See 57.04 above Comment 2.

Obligation of sheriff to consider directing local authority to provide supervision or guidance for the child

57.15 Where the application has been successful the sheriff shall consider directing the local authority to provide supervision and guidance for the child[1] and the local authority shall provide this but their obligation shall be regarded as discharged where a child of sufficient age and maturity is unwilling to accept it.[2] The deliberations of the sheriff on this point should, it is submitted, be informed by the paramountcy principle in s 16(1) of the Children (Scotland) Act 1995. In practice the sheriff may also take into account any views of the child which are known.

1 Children (Scotland) Act 1995, s 85(9).
2 C(S)A 1995, s 85(10).

Application unsuccessful

57.16 Where the sheriff is satisfied that *any* ground in the original application is established the sheriff is to[1] proceed under s 68(10) of the 1995 Act and direct the reporter to fix a hearing for consideration and disposal of the case. In the event of the sheriff finding one or more grounds established and one or more not established it would seem to be proper practice for the sheriff so to state in his final interlocutor.

1 C(S)A 1995, s 85(6)(b) – the Act says 'may' but it is submitted that this must be for reasons of good grammar – the sheriff can have no discretion at this stage.

Section 85(7)(b)

57.17 As already noticed,[1] the sheriff may, on the evidence led, hold as established any ground of referral not stated in the original application.

1 Above at 57.11.

THE JUDGMENT OF THE COURT – THE FORMALITIES

57.18 The same provisions in relation to announcement of the decision of the sheriff apply here as in a decision after a hearing under s 68 of the Children (Scotland) Act 1995.[1]

1 Act of Sederunt (Child Care and Maintenance Rules) 1997, SI 1997/291, r 3.64(2), incorporating by reference r 3.51 – see above 40.01 ff.

APPEAL

57.19   Decisions under procedures under the Children (Scotland) Act 1995, s 85 are subject to appeal without leave by way of stated case to the sheriff principal (and thereafter with leave of the sheriff principal to the Court of Session) or the Court of Session on point of law or in respect of any irregularity in the conduct of the case. It is thought that only a substantive decision, i e a decision to dismiss under s 85(5), a final disposal in terms of s 85(6) or a decision under s 85(7)(b), would be regarded as appealable: a decision not to dismiss a case under s 85(5) would not, it is thought, be regarded as appealable.[1] A person aggrieved by such a decision would have to wait until the final disposal and then appeal against that disposal if so minded.

1 Cf *H & H v McGregor* 1973 SC 95.

Children (Scotland) Act 1995

1995 CHAPTER 36

Arrangement of Sections

* * *

Exclusion orders

Offences in connection with orders etc for protection of children

Fugitive children and harbouring

Implementation of authorisations etc

New evidence: review of establishment of grounds of referral

Chapter 4
Parental Responsibilities Orders, etc

Parental responsibilities orders

Miscellaneous

*   *   *

Interpretation of Part II

*   *   *

An Act to reform the law of Scotland relating to children, to the adoption of children and to young persons who as children have been looked after by a local authority; to make new provision as respects the relationship between parent and child and guardian and child in the law of Scotland; to make provision as respects residential establishments for children and certain other residential establishments; and for connected purposes.

[19th July 1995]

BE IT ENACTED by the Queen's most Excellent Majesty, by and with the advice and consent of the Lords Spiritual and Temporal, and Commons, in this present Parliament assembled, and by the authority of the same, as follows:—

PART II
PROMOTION OF CHILDREN'S WELFARE BY LOCAL AUTHORITIES AND BY CHILDREN'S HEARINGS ETC

CHAPTER 1
SUPPORT FOR CHILDREN AND THEIR FAMILIES

Introductory

16 Welfare of child and consideration of his views

(1) Where under or by virtue of this Part of this Act, a children's hearing decide, or a court determines, any matter with respect to a child the welfare of that child throughout his childhood shall be their or its paramount consideration.

(2) In the circumstances mentioned in subsection (4) below, a children's hearing or as the case may be the sheriff, taking account of the age and maturity of the child concerned, shall so far as practicable—
(a) give him an opportunity to indicate whether he wishes to express his views;
(b) if he does so wish, give him an opportunity to express them; and
(c) have regard to such views as he may express;
and without prejudice to the generality of this subsection a child twelve years of age or more shall be presumed to be of sufficient age and maturity to form a view.

(3) In the circumstances mentioned in subsection (4)(a)(i) or (ii) or (b) of this section, no requirement or order so mentioned shall be made with respect to the child concerned unless the children's hearing consider, or as the case may be the sheriff considers, that it would be better for the child that the requirement or order be made than that none should be made at all.

(4) The circumstances to which subsection (2) above refers are that—
(a) the children's hearing—
    (i) are considering whether to make, or are reviewing, a supervision requirement;
    (ii) are considering whether to grant a warrant under subsection (1) of section 66, or subsection (4) or (7) of section 69, of this Act or to provide under subsection (5) of the said section 66 for the continuation of a warrant;
    (iii) are engaged in providing advice under section 60(10) of this Act; or
    (iv) are drawing up a report under section 73(13) of this Act;
(b) the sheriff is considering—
    (i) whether to make, vary or discharge a parental responsibilities order, a child assessment order or an exclusion order;
    (ii) whether to vary or discharge a child protection order;
    (iii) whether to grant a warrant under section 67 of this Act; or
    (iv) on appeal, whether to make such substitution as is mentioned in section 51(5)(c)(iii) of this Act; or
(c) the sheriff is otherwise disposing of an appeal against a decision of a children's hearing.

(5) If, for the purpose of protecting members of the public from serious harm (whether or not physical harm)—

(a) a children's hearing consider it necessary to make a decision under or by virtue of this Part of this Act which (but for this paragraph) would not be consistent with their affording paramountcy to the consideration mentioned in subsection (1) above, they may make that decision; or

(b) a court considers it necessary to make a determination under or by virtue of Chapters 1 to 3 of this Part of this Act which (but for this paragraph) would not be consistent with its affording such paramountcy, it may make that determination.

CHAPTER 2
CHILDREN'S HEARINGS

Constitution of children's hearings

39 Formation of children's panel and children's hearings

(1) For every local government area there shall be a children's panel for the purposes of this Act, and any other enactment conferring powers on a children's hearing (or on such a panel).

(2) Schedule 1 to this Act shall have effect with respect to the recruitment, appointment, training and expenses of members of a children's panel and the establishment of Children's Panel Advisory Committees and joint advisory committees.

(3) Sittings of members of the children's panel (to be known as "children's hearings") shall be constituted from the panel in accordance with subsection (5) below.

(4) A children's hearing shall be constituted for the performance of the functions given to such a hearing by or by virtue of—
(a) this Act; or
(b) any other enactment conferring powers on a children's hearing.

(5) A children's hearing shall consist of three members, one of whom shall act as chairman; and shall not consist solely of male, or solely of female, members.

Qualifications, employment and duties of reporters

40 Qualification and employment of reporters

(1) The qualifications of a reporter shall be such as the Secretary of State may prescribe.

(2) A reporter shall not, without the consent of the Scottish Children's Reporter Administration, be employed by a local authority.

(3) The Secretary of State may make regulations in relation to the functions of any reporter under this Act and the Criminal Procedure (Scotland) Act 1975.

(4) The Secretary of State . . . may—
(a) by regulations empower a reporter, whether or not he is an advocate or solicitor, to conduct before a sheriff any proceedings which under this Chapter or Chapter 3 of this Part of this Act are heard by the sheriff;

(b) prescribe such requirements as they think fit as to qualifications, training or experience necessary for a reporter to be so empowered.

(5) In this section, "reporter" means—

(a) the Principal Reporter; or

(b) any officer of the Scottish Children's Reporter Administration to whom there is delegated, under section 131(1) of the Local Government etc (Scotland) Act 1994, any of the functions which the Principal Reporter has under this or any other enactment.

NOTES to s 40

Sub-s (4): words omitted repealed by the Scotland Act 1998 (Consequential Modifications) (No 1) Order 1999, SI 1999/1042, art 4, Sch 2, para 10.

Safeguards for children

41 Safeguarding child's interests in proceedings

(1) Subject to subsection (2) below, in any proceedings under this Chapter or Chapter 3 of this Part of this Act either at a children's hearing or before the sheriff, the hearing or, as the case may be, the sheriff—

(a) shall consider if it is necessary to appoint a person to safeguard the interests of the child in the proceedings; and

(b) if they, or he, so consider, shall make such an appointment, on such terms and conditions as appear appropriate.

(2) Subsection (1) above shall not apply in relation to proceedings under section 57 of this Act.

(3) Where a children's hearing make an appointment under subsection (1)(b) above, they shall state the reasons for their decision to make that appointment.

(4) The expenses of a person appointed under subsection (1) above shall—

(a) in so far as reasonably incurred by him in safeguarding the interests of the child in the proceedings, and

(b) except in so far as otherwise defrayed in terms of regulations made under section 101 of this Act,

be borne by the local authority—

    (i) for whose area the children's panel from which the relevant children's hearing has been constituted is formed;

    (ii) where there is no relevant children's hearing, within whose area the child resides.

(5) For the purposes of subsection (4) above, "relevant children's hearing" means, in the case of proceedings—

(a) at a children's hearing, that hearing;

(b) under section 68 of this Act, the children's hearing who have directed the application;

(c) on an appeal under section 51 of this Act, the children's hearing whose decision is being appealed against.

Conduct of proceedings at and in connection with children's hearing

42 Power of Secretary of State to make rules governing procedure at children's hearing etc

(1) Subject to the following provisions of this Act, the Secretary of State may make rules for constituting and arranging children's hearings and other meetings of members of the children's panel and for regulating their procedure.

(2) Without prejudice to the generality of subsection (1) above, rules under that subsection may make provision with respect to—

(a) the conduct of, and matters which shall or may be determined by, a business meeting arranged under section 64 of this Act;

(b) notification of the time and place of a children's hearing to the child and any relevant person in relation to the child and to such other persons as may be prescribed;

(c) how the grounds for referring the case to a children's hearing under section 65(1) of this Act are to be stated, and the right of the child and any such relevant person to dispute those grounds;

(d) the making available by the Principal Reporter, subject to such conditions as may be specified in the rules, of reports or information received by him to—

(i)   members of the children's hearing;

(ii) the child concerned;

(iii) any relevant person; and

(iv) any other person or class of persons so specified;

(e) the procedure in relation to the disposal of matters arising under section 41(1) of this Act;

(f) the functions of any person appointed by a children's hearing under section 41(1) of this Act and any right of that person to information relating to the proceedings in question;

(g) the recording in writing of any statement given under section 41(3) of this Act;

(h) the right to appeal to the sheriff under section 51(1)(a) of this Act against a decision of the children's hearing and notification to such persons as may be prescribed of the proceedings before him;

(i) the right of the child and of any such relevant person to be represented at a children's hearing;

(j) the entitlement of the child, of any such relevant person and of any person who acts as the representative of the child or of any such relevant person to the refund of such expenses, incurred by the child or as the case may be the person or representative, as may be prescribed in connection with a children's hearing and with any proceedings arising from the hearing;

(k) persons whose presence shall be permitted at a children's hearing.

43 Privacy of proceedings at and right to attend children's hearing

(1) Subject to subsection (3) below, a children's hearing shall be conducted in private, and, subject to any rules made under section 42 of this Act, no person other than a person whose presence is necessary for the proper consideration of the case which is being heard, or whose presence is permitted by the chairman, shall be present.

(2) The chairman shall take all reasonable steps to ensure that the number of persons present at a children's hearing at any one time is kept to a minimum.

(3) The following persons have the right to attend a children's hearing—
(a) a member of the Council on Tribunals, or of the Scottish Committee of that Council, in his capacity as such; and
(b) subject to subsection (4) below, a *bona fide* representative of a newspaper or news agency.

(4) A children's hearing may exclude a person described in subsection (3)(b) above from any part or parts of the hearing where, and for so long as, they are satisfied that—
(a) it is necessary to do so, in the interests of the child, in order to obtain the child's views in relation to the case before the hearing; or
(b) the presence of that person is causing, or is likely to cause, significant distress to the child.

(5) Where a children's hearing have exercised the power conferred by subsection (4) above to exclude a person, the chairman may, after that exclusion has ended, explain to the person the substance of what has taken place in his absence.

44   Prohibition of publication of proceedings at children's hearing

(1) No person shall publish any matter in respect of proceedings at a children's hearing, or before a sheriff on an application under section 57, section 60(7), section 65(7) or (9), section 76(1) or section 85(1) of this Act, or on any appeal under this Part of this Act, which is intended to, or is likely to, identify—
(a) any child concerned in the proceedings or appeal; or
(b) an address or school as being that of any such child.

(2) Any person who contravenes subsection (1) above shall be guilty of an offence and shall be liable on summary conviction to a fine not exceeding level 4 on the standard scale in respect of each such contravention.

(3) It shall be a defence in proceedings for an offence under this section for the accused to prove that he did not know, and had no reason to suspect, that the published matter was intended, or was likely, to identify the child or, as the case may be, the address or school.

(4) In this section "to publish" includes, without prejudice to the generality of that expression,—
(a) to publish matter in a programme service, as defined by section 201 of the Broadcasting Act 1990 (definition of programme service); and
(b) to cause matter to be published.

(5) The requirements of subsection (1) above may, in the interests of justice, be dispensed with by—
(a) the sheriff in any proceedings before him;
(b) the Court of Session in any appeal under section 51(11) of this Act; or
(c) the Secretary of State in relation to any proceedings at a children's hearing,
to such extent as the sheriff, the Court or the Secretary of State as the case may be considers appropriate.

NOTES to s 44
  Sub-s(2): As to Level 4, see the Criminal Procedure (Scotland) Act 1995 (c 46), s 225(2).

45 Attendance of child and relevant person at children's hearing

(1) Where a child has been notified in accordance with rules made under subsection (1) of section 42 of this Act by virtue of subsection (2)(b) of that section that his case has been referred to a children's hearing, he shall—
(a) have the right to attend at all stages of the hearing; and
(b) subject to subsection (2) below, be under an obligation to attend those stages in accordance with the notice.

(2) Without prejudice to subsection (1)(a) above and section 65(4) of this Act, where a children's hearing are satisfied—
(a) in a case concerned with an offence mentioned in [Schedule 1 to the Criminal Procedure (Scotland) Act 1995], that the attendance of the child is not necessary for the just hearing of that case; or
(b) in any case, that it would be detrimental to the interests of the child for him to be present at the hearing of his case,
they may release the child from the obligation imposed by subsection (1)(b) above.

(3) Subject to subsection (2) above, the Principal Reporter shall be responsible for securing the attendance of the child at the hearing of his case by a children's hearing (and at any subsequent hearing to which the case is continued under section 69(1)(a) of this Act).

(4) On the application of the Principal Reporter, a children's hearing, if satisfied on cause shown that it is necessary for them to do so, may issue, for the purposes of subsection (3) above, a warrant under this subsection to find the child, to keep him in a place of safety and to bring him before a children's hearing.

(5) Where a child has failed to attend a children's hearing in accordance with such notice as is mentioned in subsection (1) above, they may, either on the application of the Principal Reporter or of their own motion, issue a warrant under this subsection, which shall have the same effect as a warrant under subsection (4) above.

(6) A child who has been taken to a place of safety under a warrant granted under this section shall not be kept there after whichever is the earlier of—
(a) the expiry of seven days beginning on the day he was first so taken there; or
(b) the day on which a children's hearing first sit to consider his case in accordance with subsection (7) below.

(7) Where a child has been found in pursuance of a warrant under this section and he cannot immediately be brought before a children's hearing, the Principal Reporter shall, wherever practicable, arrange a children's hearing to sit on the first working day after the child was so found.

(8) Subject to section 46 of this Act, a person who is a relevant person as respects a child shall, where a children's hearing are considering the case of the child—
(a) have the right to attend at all stages of the hearing; and
(b) be obliged to attend at all stages of the hearing unless the hearing are satisfied that it would be unreasonable to require his attendance or that his attendance is unnecessary for the proper consideration of the case.

(9) Any person who fails to attend a hearing which, under subsection (8)(b) above, he is obliged to attend shall be guilty of an offence and shall be liable on summary conviction to a fine not exceeding level 3 on the standard scale.

    Sub-s (2): amended by the Criminal Procedure (Consequential Provisions) (Scotland) Act 1995 (c 40), s 5, Sch 4, para 97(2).

46 Power to exclude relevant person from children's hearing

(1) Where a children's hearing are considering the case of a child in respect of whom a person is a relevant person, they may exclude that person, or that person and any representative of his, or any such representative, from any part or parts of the hearing for so long as is necessary in the interests of the child, where they are satisfied that—
(a) they must do so in order to obtain the views of the child in relation to the case before the hearing; or
(b) the presence of the person or persons in question is causing, or is likely to cause, significant distress to the child.

(2) Where a children's hearing exercise the power conferred by subsection (1) above, the chairman of the hearing shall, after that exclusion has ended, explain to any person who was so excluded the substance of what has taken place in his absence.

47 Presumption and determination of age

(1) Where a children's hearing has been arranged in respect of any person, the hearing—
(a) shall, at the commencement of the proceedings, make inquiry as to his age and shall proceed with the hearing only if he declares that he is a child or they so determine; and
(b) may, at any time before the conclusion of the proceedings, accept a declaration by the child, or make a fresh determination, as to his age.

(2) The age declared to, or determined by, a children's hearing to be the age of a person brought before them shall, for the purposes of this Part of this Act, be deemed to be the true age of that person.

(3) No decision reached, order continued, warrant granted or requirement imposed by a children's hearing shall be invalidated by any subsequent proof that the age of a person brought before them had not been correctly declared to the hearing or determined by them.

Transfer etc of cases

48 Transfer of case to another children's hearing

(1) Where a children's hearing are satisfied, in relation to a case which they are hearing, that it could be better considered by a children's hearing constituted from a children's panel for a different local government area, they may at any time during the course of the hearing request the Principal Reporter to arrange for such other children's hearing to dispose of the case.

(2) Where a case has been transferred in pursuance of subsection (1) above, the grounds of referral accepted or established for the case shall not require to be further accepted or established for the purposes of the children's hearing to which the case has been transferred.

*   *   *

50 Treatment of child's case on remission by court

(1) Where a court has, under [section 49 of the Criminal Procedure (Scotland) Act 1995], remitted a case to a children's hearing for disposal, a certificate signed by the clerk of the court stating that the child or person concerned has pled guilty to, or has been found guilty of, the offence to which the remit relates shall be conclusive evidence for the purposes of the remit that the offence has been committed by the child or person.

(2) Where a court has under [subsection (7) of the said section 49] remitted a case to a children's hearing for disposal, the provisions of this Act shall apply to the person concerned as if he were a child.

NOTES to s 50

   Sub-s (1), (2): amended by the Criminal Procedure (Consequential Provisions) (Scotland) Act 1995 (c 40), s 5, Sch 4, para 97(3).

Appeals

51 Appeal against decision of children's hearing or sheriff

(1) Subject to subsection (15) below, a child or a relevant person (or relevant persons) or both (or all)—
(a) may, within a period of three weeks beginning with the date of any decision of a children's hearing, appeal to the sheriff against that decision; and
(b) where such an appeal is made, shall be heard by the sheriff.

(2) The Principal Reporter shall, in respect of any appeal under subsection (1) above, ensure that all reports and statements available to the hearing, along with the reports of their proceedings and the reasons for the decision, are lodged with the sheriff clerk.

(3) The sheriff may, on appeal under subsection (1) above, hear evidence from, or on behalf of, the parties in relation to the decision; and, without prejudice to that generality, the sheriff may—
(a) examine the Principal Reporter;
(b) examine the authors or compilers of any reports or statements; and
(c) call for any further report which he considers may assist him in deciding the appeal.

(4) Where the sheriff decides that an appeal under this section has failed, he shall confirm the decision of the children's hearing.

(5) Where the sheriff is satisfied that the decision of the children's hearing is not justified in all the circumstances of the case he shall allow the appeal, and—
(a) where the appeal is against a warrant to find and keep or, as the case may be, to keep a child in a place of safety, he shall recall the warrant;
(b) where the child is subject to a supervision requirement containing a condition imposed under section 70(9) of this Act, he shall direct that the condition shall cease to have effect; and
(c) in any case, he may, as he thinks fit—
   (i) remit the case with reasons for his decision to the children's hearing for reconsideration of their decision; or
   (ii) discharge the child from any further hearing or other proceedings in relation to the grounds for the referral of the case; or

(iii) substitute for the disposal by the children's hearing any requirement which could be imposed by them under section 70 of this Act.

(6) Where a sheriff imposes a requirement under subsection (5)(c)(iii) above, that requirement shall for the purposes of this Act, except of this section, be treated as a disposal by the children's hearing.

(7) Where the sheriff is satisfied that an appeal under subsection (1) above against the decision of a children's hearing arranged under section 73(8) of this Act is frivolous, he may order that no subsequent appeal against a decision to continue (whether with or without any variation) the supervision requirement in question shall lie until the expiration of twelve months beginning with the date of the order.

(8) An appeal under subsection (1) above in respect of the issue of a warrant by a children's hearing shall be disposed of within three days of the lodging of the appeal; and failing such disposal the warrant shall cease to have effect at the end of that period.

(9) Where a child or a relevant person appeals under subsection (1) above against a decision of a children's hearing in relation to a supervision requirement, the child or the relevant person may make application to a children's hearing for the suspension of the requirement appealed against.

(10) It shall be the duty of the Principal Reporter forthwith to arrange a children's hearing to consider the application under subsection (9) above, and that hearing may grant or refuse the application.

(11) Subject to subsections (13) and (15) below, an appeal shall lie by way of stated case either on a point of law or in respect of any irregularity in the conduct of the case—
(a) to the sheriff principal from any decision of the sheriff—
    (i)   on an appeal under subsection (1) of this section;
    (ii) on an application made under section 65(7) or (9) of this Act; or
    (iii) on an application made under section 85(1) of this Act; and
(b) to the Court of Session from any decision of the sheriff such as is mentioned in sub-paragraphs (i) to (iii) of paragraph (a) above and, with leave of the sheriff principal, from any decision of the sheriff principal on an appeal under that paragraph; and the decision of the Court of Session in the matter shall be final.

(12) An appeal under subsection (11) above may be made at the instance of—
(a) the child or any relevant person, either alone or together; or
(b) the Principal Reporter on behalf of the children's hearing.

(13) An application to the sheriff, or as the case may be the sheriff principal, to state a case for the purposes of an appeal under subsection (11)(a) or (b) above shall be made within a period of twenty-eight days beginning with the date of the decision appealed against.

(14) On deciding an appeal under subsection (11) above the sheriff principal or as the case may be the Court of Session shall remit the case to the sheriff for disposal in accordance with such directions as the court may give.

(15) No appeal shall lie under this section in respect of—
(a) a decision of the sheriff on an application under section 57 of this Act; or

(b) a decision of a children's hearing continuing a child protection order under section 59(4) of this Act.

CHAPTER 3
PROTECTION AND SUPERVISION OF CHILDREN

Children requiring compulsory measures of supervision

52   Children requiring compulsory measures of supervision

(1) The question of whether compulsory measures of supervision are necessary in respect of a child arises if at least one of the conditions mentioned in subsection (2) below is satisfied with respect to him.

(2) The conditions referred to in subsection (1) above are that the child—
(a) is beyond the control of any relevant person;
(b) is falling into bad associations or is exposed to moral danger;
(c) is likely—
   (i)   to suffer unnecessarily; or
   (ii) be impaired seriously in his health or development,
   due to a lack of parental care;
(d) is a child in respect of whom any of the offences mentioned in [Schedule 1 to the Criminal Procedure (Scotland) Act 1995] (offences against children to which special provisions apply) has been committed;
(e) is, or is likely to become, a member of the same household as a child in respect of whom any of the offences referred to in paragraph (d) above has been committed;
(f) is, or is likely to become, a member of the same household as a person who has committed any of the offences referred to in paragraph (d) above;
(g) is, or is likely to become, a member of the same household as a person in respect of whom an offence under [sections 1 to 3 of the Criminal Law (Consolidation) (Scotland) Act 1995] (incest and intercourse with a child by step-parent or person in position of trust) has been committed by a member of that household;
(h) has failed to attend school regularly without reasonable excuse;
(i) has committed an offence;
(j) has misused alcohol or any drug, whether or not a controlled drug within the meaning of the Misuse of Drugs Act 1971;
(k) has misused a volatile substance by deliberately inhaling its vapour, other than for medicinal purposes;
(l) is being provided with accommodation by a local authority under section 25, or is the subject of a parental responsibilities order obtained under section 86, of this Act and, in either case, his behaviour is such that special measures are necessary for his adequate supervision in his interest or the interest of others.

(3) In this Part of this Act, "supervision" in relation to compulsory measures of supervision may include measures taken for the protection, guidance, treatment or control of the child.

NOTES to s 52

In sub-s (2), paras (d), (g) amended by the Criminal Procedure (Consequential Provisions) (Scotland) Act 1995 (c 40), s 5, Sch 4, para 97(4).

Preliminary and investigatory measures

53 Provision of information to the Principal Reporter

(1) Where information is received by a local authority which suggests that compulsory measures of supervision may be necessary in respect of a child, they shall—
(a) cause inquiries to be made into the case unless they are satisfied that such inquiries are unnecessary; and
(b) if it appears to them after such inquiries, or after being satisfied that such inquiries are unnecessary, that such measures may be required in respect of the child, give to the Principal Reporter such information about the child as they have been able to discover.

(2) A person, other than a local authority, who has reasonable cause to believe that compulsory measures of supervision may be necessary in respect of a child—
(a) shall, if he is a constable, give to the Principal Reporter such information about the child as he has been able to discover;
(b) in any other case, may give the Principal Reporter that information.

(3) A constable shall make any report required to be made under paragraph (b) of section 17(1) of the Police (Scotland) Act 1967 (duty to make reports in relation to commission of offences) in relation to a child to the Principal Reporter as well as to the appropriate prosecutor.

(4) Where an application has been made to the sheriff—
(a) by the Principal Reporter in accordance with a direction given by a children's hearing under section 65(7) or (9) of this Act; or
(b) by any person entitled to make an application under section 85 of this Act,
the Principal Reporter may request any prosecutor to supply him with any evidence lawfully obtained in the course of, and held by the prosecutor in connection with, the investigation of a crime or suspected crime, being evidence which may assist the sheriff in determining the application; and, subject to subsection (5) below, it shall be the duty of the prosecutor to comply with such a request.

(5) A prosecutor may refuse to comply with a request issued under subsection (4) above where he reasonably believes that it is necessary to retain the evidence for the purposes of any proceedings in respect of a crime, whether the proceedings have been commenced or are to be commenced by him.

(6) The Lord Advocate may direct that in any specified case or class of cases any evidence lawfully obtained in the course of an investigation of a crime or suspected crime shall be supplied, without the need for a request under subsection (4) above, to the Principal Reporter.

(7) In subsections (3), (4) and (5) above "crime" and "prosecutor" have the same meanings respectively given by [section 307 of the Criminal Procedure (Scotland) Act 1995].

NOTES to s 53
   Sub-s (7): amended by the Criminal Procedure (Consequential Provisions) (Scotland) Act 1995 (c 40), s 5, Sch 4, para 97(5).

54 Reference to the Principal Reporter by court

(1) Where in any relevant proceedings it appears to the court that any of the conditions in section 52(2)(a) to (h), (j), (k) or (l) of this Act is satisfied with respect to a child, it may refer the matter to the Principal Reporter, specifying the condition.

(2) In this section "relevant proceedings" means—
(a) an action for divorce or judicial separation or for declarator of marriage, nullity of marriage, parentage or non-parentage;
(b) proceedings relating to parental responsibilities or parental rights within the meaning of Part I of this Act;
(c) proceedings for an adoption order under the Adoption (Scotland) Act 1978 or for an order under section 18 of that Act declaring a child free for adoption; and
(d) proceedings for an offence against section 35 (failure by parent to secure regular attendance by his child at a public school), 41 (failure to comply with attendance order) or 42(3) (failure to permit examination of child) of the Education (Scotland) Act 1980.

(3) Where the court has referred a matter to the Principal Reporter under subsection (1) above, he shall—
(a) make such investigation as he thinks appropriate; and
(b) if he considers that compulsory measures of supervision are necessary,
arrange a children's hearing to consider the case of the child under section 69 of this Act; and subsection (1) of that section shall apply as if the condition specified by the court under subsection (1) above were a ground of referral established in accordance with section 68 of this Act.

55 Child assessment orders

(1) A sheriff may grant an order under this section for an assessment of the state of a child's health or development, or of the way in which he has been treated (to be known as a "child assessment order"), on the application of a local authority if he is satisfied that—
(a) the local authority have reasonable cause to suspect that the child in respect of whom the order is sought is being so treated (or neglected) that he is suffering or is likely to suffer, significant harm;
(b) such assessment of the child is required in order to establish whether or not there is reasonable cause to believe that the child is so treated (or neglected); and
(c) such assessment is unlikely to be carried out, or be carried out satisfactorily, unless the order is granted.

(2) Where—
(a) an application has been made under subsection (1) above; and
(b) the sheriff considers that the conditions for making a child protection order under section 57 of this Act are satisfied,
he shall make such an order under that section as if the application had been duly made by the local authority under that section rather than this section.

(3) A child assessment order shall—
(a) specify the date on which the assessment is to begin;
(b) have effect for such period as is specified in the order, not exceeding seven days beginning with the date specified by virtue of paragraph (a) above;

(c) require any person in a position to produce the child to—
    (i)   produce him to any authorised person;
    (ii) permit that person or any other authorised person to carry out an assessment in accordance with the order; and
    (iii) comply with any other conditions of the order; and
(d) be carried out by an authorised person in accordance with the terms of the order.

(4) A child assessment order may—
(a) where necessary, permit the taking of the child concerned to any place for the purposes of the assessment; and
(b) authorise the child to be kept at that place, or any other place, for such period of time as may be specified in the order.

(5) Where a child assessment order makes provision under subsection (4) above, it shall contain such directions as the sheriff considers appropriate as to the contact which the child shall be allowed to have with any other person while the child is in any place to which he has been taken or in which he is being kept under a child assessment order.

(6) In this section "authorised person" means any officer of the local authority, and any person authorised by the local authority to perform the assessment, or perform any part of it.

56   Initial investigation by the Principal Reporter

(1) Where the Principal Reporter receives information from any source about a case which may require a children's hearing to be arranged he shall, after making such initial investigation as he thinks necessary, proceed with the case in accordance with subsection (4) or (6) below.

(2) For the purposes of making any initial investigation under subsection (1) above, the Principal Reporter may request from the local authority a report on the child and on such circumstances concerning the child as appear to him to be relevant; and the local authority shall supply the report which may contain such information, from any person whomsoever, as the Principal Reporter thinks, or the local authority think, fit.

(3) A report requested under subsection (2) above may contain information additional to that given by the local authority under section 53 of this Act.

(4) The Principal Reporter may decide, after an initial investigation under subsection (1) above, that a children's hearing does not require to be arranged; and where he so decides—
(a) he shall inform the child, any relevant person and the person who brought the case to his notice, or any of those persons, that he has so decided; and
(b) he may, if he considers it appropriate, refer the case to a local authority with a view to their making arrangements for the advice, guidance and assistance of the child and his family in accordance with Chapter 1 of this Part of this Act.

(5) Where the Principal Reporter has decided under subsection (4) above that a children's hearing does not require to be arranged, he shall not at any other time, on the basis solely of the information obtained during the initial investigation referred to in that subsection, arrange a children's hearing under subsection (6) below.

(6) Where it appears to the Principal Reporter that compulsory measures of supervision are necessary in respect of the child, he shall arrange a children's hearing to which he shall refer the case for consideration and determination.

(7) Where the Principal Reporter has arranged a children's hearing in accordance with subsection (6) above, he—
(a) shall, where he has not previously done so, request a report under subsection (2) above;
(b) may request from the local authority such information, supplementary or additional to a report requested under subsection (2) above, as he thinks fit;
and the local authority shall supply that report, or as the case may be information, and any other information which they consider to be relevant.

Measures for the emergency protection of children

57 Child protection orders

(1) Where the sheriff, on an application by any person, is satisfied that—
(a) there are reasonable grounds to believe that a child—
   (i)   is being so treated (or neglected) that he is suffering significant harm; or
   (ii) will suffer such harm if he is not removed to and kept in a place of safety, or if he does not remain in the place where he is then being accommodated (whether or not he is resident there); and
(b) an order under this section is necessary to protect that child from such harm (or such further harm),
he may make an order under this section (to be known as a "child protection order").

(2) Without prejudice to subsection (1) above, where the sheriff on an application by a local authority is satisfied—
(a) that they have reasonable grounds to suspect that a child is being or will be so treated (or neglected) that he is suffering or will suffer significant harm;
(b) that they are making or causing to be made enquiries to allow them to decide whether they should take any action to safeguard the welfare of the child; and
(c) that those enquiries are being frustrated by access to the child being unreasonably denied, the authority having reasonable cause to believe that such access is required as a matter of urgency,
he may make a child protection order.

(3) Without prejudice to any additional requirement imposed by rules made by virtue of section 91 of this Act, an application for a child protection order shall—
(a) identify—
   (i)   the applicant; and
   (ii) in so far as practicable, the child in respect of whom the order is sought;
(b) state the grounds on which the application is made; and
(c) be accompanied by such supporting evidence, whether in documentary form or otherwise, as will enable the sheriff to determine the application.

(4) A child protection order may, subject to such terms and conditions as the sheriff considers appropriate, do any one or more of the following—
(a) require any person in a position to do so to produce the child to the applicant;
(b) authorise the removal of the child by the applicant to a place of safety, and the keeping of the child at that place;
(c) authorise the prevention of the removal of the child from any place where he is being accommodated;

(d) provide that the location of any place of safety in which the child is being kept should not be disclosed to any person or class of person specified in the order.

(5) Notice of the making of a child protection order shall be given forthwith by the applicant to the local authority in whose area the child resides (where that authority is not the applicant) and to the Principal Reporter.

(6) In taking any action required or permitted by a child protection order or by a direction under section 58 of this Act the applicant shall only act where he reasonably believes that to do so is necessary to safeguard or promote the welfare of the child.

(7) Where by virtue of a child protection order a child is removed to a place of safety provided by a local authority, they shall, subject to the terms and conditions of that order and of any direction given under section 58 of this Act, have the like duties in respect of the child as they have under section 17 of this Act in respect of a child looked after by them.

58 Directions in relation to contact and exercise of parental responsibilities and parental rights

(1) When the sheriff makes a child protection order, he shall at that time consider whether it is necessary to give a direction to the applicant for the order as to contact with the child for—
(a) any parent of the child;
(b) any person with parental responsibilities in relation to the child; and
(c) any other specified person or class of persons;
and if he determines that there is such a necessity he may give such a direction.

(2) Without prejudice to the generality of subsection (1) above, a direction under that subsection may—
(a) prohibit contact with the child for any person mentioned in paragraphs (a) to (c) of that subsection;
(b) make contact with the child for any person subject to such conditions as the sheriff considers appropriate to safeguard and promote the welfare of the child.

(3) A direction under subsection (1) above may make different provision in relation to different persons or classes of person.

(4) A person applying for a child protection order under section 57(1) or (2) of this Act may at the same time apply to the sheriff for a direction in relation to the exercise or fulfilment of any parental responsibilities or parental rights in respect of the child concerned, if the person considers such a direction necessary to safeguard or promote the welfare of the child.

(5) Without prejudice to the generality of subsection (4) above, a direction under that subsection may be sought in relation to—
(a) any examination as to the physical or mental state of the child;
(b) any other assessment or interview of the child; or
(c) any treatment of the child arising out of such an examination or assessment,
which is to be carried out by any person.

(6) The sheriff may give a direction sought under subsection (4) above where he

considers there is a necessity such as is mentioned in that subsection; and such a direction may be granted subject to such conditions, if any, as the sheriff (having regard in particular to the duration of the child protection order to which it relates) considers appropriate.

(7) A direction under this section shall cease to have effect when—
(a) the sheriff, on an application under section 60(7) of this Act, directs that it is cancelled; or
(b) the child protection order to which it is related ceases to have effect.

59 Initial hearing of case of child subject to child protection order

(1) This section applies where—
(a) a child in respect of whom a child protection order has been made—
    (i) has been taken to a place of safety by virtue of section 57(4)(b) of this Act; or
    (ii) is prevented from being removed from any place by virtue of section 57(4)(c) of this Act;
(b) the Principal Reporter has not exercised his powers under section 60(3) of this Act to discharge the child from the place of safety; and
(c) the Principal Reporter has not received notice, in accordance with section 60(9) of this Act, of an application under subsection (7) of that section.

(2) Where this section applies, the Principal Reporter shall arrange a children's hearing to conduct an initial hearing of the child's case in order to determine whether they should, in the interests of the child, continue the child protection order under subsection (4) below.

(3) A children's hearing arranged under subsection (2) above shall take place on the second working day after that order is implemented.

(4) Where a children's hearing arranged under subsection (2) above are satisfied that the conditions for the making of a child protection order under section 57 of this Act are established, they may continue the child protection order and any direction given under section 58 of this Act (whether with or without variation of the order or, as the case may be, the direction) until the commencement of a children's hearing in relation to the child arranged in accordance with section 65(2) of this Act.

(5) In subsection (3) above, section 60 and section 65(2) of this Act any reference, in relation to the calculation of any period, to the time at which a child protection order is implemented shall be construed as a reference—
(a) in relation to such an order made under paragraph (b) of subsection (4) of section 57 of this Act, to the day on which the child was removed to a place of safety in accordance with the order; and
(b) in relation to such an order made under paragraph (c) of that subsection, to the day on which the order was made,
and "implement" shall be construed accordingly.

60 Duration, recall or variation of child protection order

(1) Where, by the end of twenty-four hours of a child protection order being made (other than by virtue of section 57(4)(c) of this Act), the applicant has made no attempt to implement the order it shall cease to have effect.

(2) Where an application made under subsection (7) below has not been determined timeously in accordance with subsection (8) below, the order to which the application relates shall cease to have effect.

(3) A child shall not be—
(a) kept in a place of safety under a child protection order;
(b) prevented from being removed from any place by such an order; or
(c) subject to any term or condition contained in such an order or a direction given under section 58 of this Act,
where the Principal Reporter, having regard to the welfare of the child, considers that, whether as a result of a change in the circumstances of the case or of further information relating to the case having been received by the Principal Reporter, the conditions for the making of a child protection order in respect of the child are no longer satisfied or that the term, condition or direction is no longer appropriate and notifies the person who implemented the order that he so considers.

(4) The Principal Reporter shall not give notice under subsection (3) above where—
(a) proceedings before a children's hearing arranged under section 59(2) of this Act in relation to the child who is subject to the child protection order have commenced; or
(b) the hearing of an application made under subsection (7) of this section has begun.

(5) Where the Principal Reporter has given notice under subsection (3) above, he shall also, in such manner as may be prescribed, notify the sheriff who made the order.

(6) A child protection order shall cease to have effect—
(a) where an initial hearing arranged under section 59(2) of this Act does not continue the order under subsection (4) of that section;
(b) where an application is made to the sheriff under subsection (7) below, on the sheriff recalling such order under subsection (13) below;
(c) on the person who implemented the order receiving notice from the Principal Reporter that he has decided not to refer the case of a child who is subject to the order to a children's hearing arranged in accordance with section 65(2) of this Act;
(d) on the Principal Reporter giving notice in accordance with subsection (3) above in relation to the order that he considers that the conditions for the making of it are no longer satisfied; or
(e) where such order is continued under section 59(4) of this Act or subsection (12)(d) below, on the commencement of a children's hearing arranged under section 65(2) of this Act.

(7) An application to the sheriff to set aside or vary a child protection order made under section 57 of this Act or a direction given under section 58 of this Act or such an order or direction continued (whether with or without variation) under section 59(4) of this Act, may be made by or on behalf of—
(a) the child to whom the order or direction relates;
(b) a person having parental rights over the child;
(c) a relevant person;
(d) any person to whom notice of the application for the order was given by virtue of rules; or
(e) the applicant for the order made under section 57 of this Act.

(8) An application under subsection (7) above shall be made—

(a) in relation to a child protection order made under section 57, or a direction given under section 58, of this Act, before the commencement of a children's hearing arranged in accordance with section 59(2) of this Act; and

(b) in relation to such an order or direction continued (whether with or without variation) by virtue of subsection (4) of the said section 59, within two working days of such continuation,

and any such application shall be determined within three working days of being made.

(9) Where an application has been made under subsection (7) above, the applicant shall forthwith give notice, in a manner and form prescribed by rules, to the Principal Reporter.

(10) At any time which is—

(a) after the giving of the notice required by subsection (9) above; but

(b) before the sheriff has determined the application in accordance with subsection (11) below,

the Principal Reporter may arrange a children's hearing the purpose of which shall be to provide any advice they consider appropriate to assist the sheriff in his determination of the application.

(11) The sheriff shall, after hearing the parties to the application and, if he wishes to make representations, the Principal Reporter, determine whether—

(a) the conditions for the making of a child protection order under section 57 of this Act are satisfied; or

(b) where the application relates only to a direction under section 58 of this Act, the direction should be varied or cancelled.

(12) Where the sheriff determines that the conditions referred to in subsection (11)(a) above are satisfied, he may—

(a) confirm or vary the order, or any term or condition on which it was granted;

(b) confirm or vary any direction given, in relation to the order, under section 58 of this Act;

(c) give a new direction under that section; or

(d) continue in force the order and any such direction until the commencement of a children's hearing arranged in accordance with section 65(2) of this Act.

(13) Where the sheriff determines that the conditions referred to in subsection (11)(a) above are not satisfied he shall recall the order and cancel any direction given under section 58 of this Act.

61 Emergency protection of children where child protection order not available

(1) Where, on the application of any person, a justice of the peace is satisfied—

(a) both that the conditions laid down for the making of a child protection order in section 57(1) of this Act are satisfied and that it is probable that any such order, if made, would contain an authorisation in terms of paragraph (b) or (c) of subsection (4) of that section; but

(b) that it is not practicable in the circumstances for an application for such an order to be made to the sheriff or for the sheriff to consider such an application,

he may grant to the applicant an authorisation under this section.

(2) Where on the application of a local authority a justice of the peace is satisfied—

(a) both that the conditions laid down for the making of a child protection order in section 57(2) of this Act are satisfied and that it is probable that any such order, if made, would contain an authorisation in terms of paragraph (b) or (c) of subsection (4) of that section; but

(b) that it is not practicable in the circumstances for an application for such an order to be made to the sheriff or for the sheriff to consider such an application,

he may grant an authorisation under this section.

(3) An authorisation under this section may—

(a) require any person in a position to do so to produce the child to the applicant;

(b) prevent any person from removing a child from a place where he is then being accommodated;

(c) authorise the applicant to remove the child to a place of safety and to keep him there until the expiration of the authorisation.

(4) An authorisation under this section shall cease to have effect—

(a) twelve hours after being made, if within that time—
   (i) arrangements have not been made to prevent the child's removal from any place specified in the authorisation; or
   (ii) he has not been, or is not being, taken to a place of safety; or

(b) where such arrangements have been made or he has been so taken when—
   (i) twenty-four hours have expired since it was so given; or
   (ii) an application for a child protection order in respect of the child is disposed of,
   whichever is the earlier.

(5) Where a constable has reasonable cause to believe that—

(a) the conditions for the making of a child protection order laid down in section 57(1) are satisfied;

(b) that it is not practicable in the circumstances for him to make an application for such an order to the sheriff or for the sheriff to consider such an application; and

(c) that, in order to protect the child from significant harm (or further such harm), it is necessary for him to remove the child to a place of safety,

he may remove the child to such a place and keep him there.

(6) The power conferred by subsection (5) above shall not authorise the keeping of a child in a place of safety for more than twenty-four hours from the time when the child is so removed.

(7) The authority to keep a child in a place of safety conferred by subsection (5) above shall cease on the disposal of an application in relation to the child for a child protection order.

(8) A child shall not be—

(a) kept in a place of safety; or

(b) prevented from being removed from any place,

under this section where the Principal Reporter considers that the conditions for the grant of an authorisation under subsection (1) or (2) above or the exercise of the power conferred by subsection (5) above are not satisfied, or that it is no longer in the best interests of the child that he should be so kept.

62 Regulations in respect of emergency child protection measures

(1) The Secretary of State may make regulations concerning the duties in respect of a child of any person removing him to, and keeping him in, a place of safety under section 61 above.

(2) Regulations under this section may make provision requiring—
(a) notification of the removal of a child to be given to a person specified in the regulations;
(b) intimation to be given to any person of the place of safety at which a child is being kept;
(c) notification to be given to any person of the ceasing to have effect, under section 61(4)(a) of this Act, of an authorisation.

Children arrested by the police

63 Review of case of child arrested by police

(1) Where the Principal Reporter has been informed by a constable, in accordance with [section 43(5) of the Criminal Procedure (Scotland) Act 1995], that charges are not to be proceeded with against a child who has been detained in a place of safety in accordance with that section, the Principal Reporter shall, unless he considers that compulsory measures of supervision are not required in relation to the child, arrange a children's hearing to which he shall refer the case.

(2) A children's hearing arranged under subsection (1) above shall begin not later than the third day after the Principal Reporter received the information mentioned in that subsection.

(3) Where the Principal Reporter considers that a child of whose detention he has been informed does not require compulsory measures of supervision, he shall direct that the child shall no longer be kept in the place of safety.

(4) Subject to subsection (3) above, a child who has been detained in a place of safety may continue to be kept at that place until the commencement of a children's hearing arranged under subsection (1) above.

(5) Subject to subsection (6) below, a children's hearing arranged under subsection (1) above may—
(a) if they are satisfied that the conditions mentioned in subsection (2) of section 66 of this Act are satisfied, grant a warrant to keep the child in a place of safety; and
(b) direct the Principal Reporter to arrange a children's hearing for the purposes of section 65(1) of this Act,
and subsections (3) to (8) of the said section 66 shall apply to a warrant granted under this subsection as they apply to a warrant granted under subsection (1) of the said section 66.

(6) A child shall not be kept in a place of safety in accordance with a warrant granted under subsection (5) above where the Principal Reporter, having regard to the welfare of the child, considers that, whether as a result of a change in the circumstances of the case or of further information relating to the case having been received by the Principal Reporter—
(a) the conditions mentioned in section 66(2) of this Act are no longer satisfied in relation to the child; or

(b) the child is not in need of compulsory measures of supervision,
and where he does so consider he shall give notice to that effect to the person who
is keeping the child in that place in accordance with the warrant.

NOTES to s 63
> **Sub-s (1):** amended by the Criminal Procedure (Consequential Provisions) (Scotland)
> Act 1995 (c 40), s 5, Sch 4, para 97(6).

Business meeting preparatory to children's hearing

64 Business meeting preparatory to children's hearing

(1) At any time prior to the commencement of proceedings at the children's
hearing, the Principal Reporter may arrange a meeting with members of the children's panel from which the children's hearing is to be constituted under section
39(4) of this Act for those proceedings (any such meeting being, in this Part of this
Act referred to as a "business meeting").

(2) Where a business meeting is arranged under subsection (1) above, the
Principal Reporter shall give notice to the child in respect of whom the proceedings are to be commenced and any relevant person in relation to the child—
(a) of the arrangement of the meeting and of the matters which may be consid-
     ered and determined by the meeting;
(b) of their right to make their views on those matters known to the Principal
     Reporter; and
(c) of the duty of the Principal Reporter to present those views to the meeting.

(3) A business meeting, subject to subsection (4) below—
(a) shall determine such procedural and other matters as may be prescribed by
     rules under subsection (1) of section 42 of this Act by virtue of subsection (2)(a)
     of that section; and
(b) may give such direction or guidance to the Principal Reporter in relation to the
     performance of his functions in relation to the proceedings as they think
     appropriate.

(4) Before a business meeting makes such a determination or gives such direction
or guidance to the Principal Reporter, the Principal Reporter shall present, and
they shall consider, any views expressed to him by virtue of subsection (2)(b)
above.

(5) Subject to any rules made under section 42(1) of this Act by virtue of subsection (2)(a) of that section and with the exception of sections 44 and, as regards any
determination made by the business meeting under subsection (3)(a) above, 51,
the provisions of this Act which relate to a children's hearing shall not apply to a
business meeting.

Referral to, and disposal of case by, children's hearing

65 Referral to, and proceedings at, children's hearing

(1) The Principal Reporter shall refer to the children's hearing, for consideration
and determination on the merits, the case of any child in respect of whom he is
satisfied that—
(a) compulsory measures of supervision are necessary, and

(b) at least one of the grounds specified in section 52(2) of this Act is established; and he shall state such grounds in accordance with rules made under section 42(1) of this Act by virtue of subsection (2)(c) of that section.

(2) Where a referral is made in respect of a child who is subject to a child protection order made under section 57, and that order is continued under section 59(4) or 60(12)(d), of this Act, the Principal Reporter shall arrange for the children's hearing under subsection (1) above to take place on the eighth working day after the order was implemented.

(3) Where a referral is made in respect of a child who is subject to a supervision requirement, the children's hearing shall, before disposing of the referral in accordance with section 69(1)(b) or (c) of this Act, review that requirement in accordance with subsections (9) to (12) of section 73 of this Act.

(4) Subject to subsections (9) and (10) below, it shall be the duty of the chairman of the children's hearing to whom a child's case has been referred under subsection (1) above to explain to the child and the relevant person, at the opening of proceedings on the referral, the grounds stated by the Principal Reporter for the referral in order to ascertain whether these grounds are accepted in whole or in part by them.

(5) Where the chairman has given the explanation required by subsection (4) above and the child and the relevant person accept the grounds for the referral, the children's hearing shall proceed in accordance with section 69 of this Act.

(6) Where the chairman has given the explanation required by subsection (4) above and the child and the relevant person accept the grounds in part, the children's hearing may, if they consider it appropriate to do so, proceed in accordance with section 69 of this Act with respect to those grounds which are accepted.

(7) Where the chairman has given the explanation required under subsection (4) above and either or both of the child and the relevant person—
(a) do not accept the grounds for the referral; or
(b) accept the grounds in part, but the children's hearing do not consider it appropriate to proceed with the case under subsection (6) above,
the hearing shall either direct the Principal Reporter to make an application to the sheriff for a finding as to whether such grounds for the referral as are not accepted by the child and the relevant person are established or shall discharge the referral.

(8) Subject to subsection (10) below, it shall be the duty of the chairman to explain to the child and to the relevant person the purpose for which the application to the sheriff is being made and to inform the child that he is under an obligation to attend the hearing before the sheriff.

(9) Where a children's hearing are satisfied that the child—
(a) for any reason will not be capable of understanding the explanation of the grounds for the referral required under subsection (4) above; or
(b) has not understood an explanation given under that subsection,
they shall either direct the Principal Reporter to make an application to the sheriff for a finding as to whether any of the grounds of the referral are established or discharge the referral.

(10) The acceptance by the relevant person of the grounds of the referral shall not be a requirement for a children's hearing proceeding under this section to consider a case where that person is not present.

66 Warrant to keep child where children's hearing unable to dispose of case

(1) Without prejudice to any other power enjoyed by them under this Part of this Act and subject to subsection (5) below, a children's hearing—
(a) arranged to consider a child's case under this Part of this Act; and
(b) unable to dispose of the case,
may, if they are satisfied that one of the conditions mentioned in subsection (2) below is met, grant a warrant under this subsection.

(2) The conditions referred to in subsection (1) above are—
(a) that there is reason to believe that the child may—
    (i)   not attend at any hearing of his case; or
    (ii) fail to comply with a requirement under section 69(3) of this Act; or
(b) that it is necessary that the child should be kept in a place of safety in order to safeguard or promote his welfare.

(3) A warrant under subsection (1) above may require any person named in the warrant—
(a) to find and to keep or, as the case may be, to keep the child in a place of safety for a period not exceeding twenty-two days after the warrant is granted;
(b) to bring the child before a children's hearing at such times as may be specified in the warrant.

(4) A warrant under subsection (1) above may contain such conditions as appear to the children's hearing to be necessary or expedient, and without prejudice to that generality may—
(a) subject to section 90 of this Act, require the child to submit to any medical or other examination or treatment; and
(b) regulate the contact with the child of any specified person or class of persons.

(5) Subject to subsection (8) below, at any time prior to its expiry, a warrant granted under this section may, on an application to the children's hearing, on cause shown by the Principal Reporter, be continued in force, whether with or without variation of any condition imposed by virtue of subsection (4) above, by the children's hearing for such further period, not exceeding twenty-two days, as appears to them to be necessary.

(6) Where a children's hearing are satisfied that either of the criteria specified in section 70(10) of this Act are satisfied, they may order that, pending the disposal of his case, the child shall be liable to be placed and kept in secure accommodation within a residential establishment at such times as the person in charge of that establishment, with the agreement of the chief social work officer of the relevant local authority, considers necessary.

(7) Where a children's hearing grant a warrant under subsection (1) above or continue such a warrant under subsection (5) above, they may order that the place of safety at which the child is to be kept shall not be disclosed to any person or class of persons specified in the order.

(8) A child shall not be kept in a place of safety or secure accommodation by virtue of this section for a period exceeding sixty-six days from the day when he was first taken to a place of safety under a warrant granted under subsection (1) above.

67 Warrant for further detention of child

(1) Where a child is being kept in a place of safety by virtue of a warrant granted under section 66 of this Act or under this subsection, the Principal Reporter at any time prior to the expiry of that warrant may apply to the sheriff for a warrant to keep the child in that place after the warrant granted under the said section 66 or, as the case may be, this subsection has expired.

(2) A warrant under subsection (1) above shall only be granted on cause shown and—
(a) shall specify the date on which it will expire; and
(b) may contain any such requirement or condition as may be contained in a warrant granted under the said section 66.

(3) Where the sheriff grants a warrant under subsection (1) above, he may also make an order under this subsection in such terms as are mentioned in subsection (6) or (7) of the said section 66; and any order under this subsection shall cease to have effect when the warrant expires.

(4) An application under subsection (1) above may be made at the same time as, or during the hearing of, an application which the Principal Reporter has been directed by a children's hearing to make under section 65(7) or (9) of this Act.

68 Application to sheriff to establish grounds of referral

(1) This section applies to applications under subsections (7) and (9) of section 65 of this Act and a reference in this section (except in subsection (8)) to "an application" is a reference to an application under either of those subsections.

(2) An application shall be heard by the sheriff within twenty-eight days of its being lodged.

(3) Where one of the grounds for the referral to which an application relates is the condition referred to in section 52(2)(i)—
(a) the application shall be made to the sheriff who would have jurisdiction if the child were being prosecuted for that offence; and
(b) in hearing the application in relation to that ground, the standard of proof required in criminal proceedings shall apply.

(4) A child shall—
(a) have the right to attend the hearing of an application; and
(b) subject to subsection (5) below, be under an obligation to attend such hearing; and without prejudice to the right of each of them to be legally represented, the child and the relevant person may be represented by a person other than a legally qualified person at any date fixed by the sheriff for the hearing of the application.

(5) Without prejudice to subsection (4)(a) above, the sheriff may dispense with the obligation imposed by subsection (4)(b) above where he is satisfied—
(a) in an application in which the ground of referral to be established is a condition mentioned in section 52(2)(d), (e), (f) or (g) of this Act, that the obligation to attend of the child is not necessary for the just hearing of that application; and
(b) in any application, that it would be detrimental to the interests of the child for him to be present at the hearing of the application.

(6) Where the child fails to attend the hearing of an application at which his attendance has not been dispensed with under subsection (5) above, the sheriff may grant an order to find and keep the child; and any order under this subsection shall be authority for bringing the child before the sheriff and, subject to subsection (7) below, for keeping him in a place of safety until the sheriff can hear the application.

(7) The child shall not be kept in a place of safety by virtue of subsection (6) above after whichever is the earlier of—
(a) the expiry of fourteen days beginning with the day on which the child is found; or
(b) the disposal of the application by the sheriff.

(8) Where in the course of the hearing of an application—
(a) under section 65(7) of this Act, the child and the relevant person accept any of the grounds for referral to which the application relates, the sheriff shall; or
(b) under section 65(9) of this Act, the relevant person accepts any of the grounds for referral to which the application relates, the sheriff may, if it appears to him reasonable to do so,
dispense with the hearing of evidence relating to that ground and deem the ground to be established for the purposes of the application, unless he is satisfied that, in all the circumstances of the case, the evidence should be heard.

(9) Where a sheriff decides that none of the grounds for referral in respect of which an application has been made are established, he shall dismiss the application, discharge the referral to the children's hearing in respect of those grounds and recall, discharge or cancel any order, warrant, or direction under this Chapter of this Act which relates to the child in respect of those grounds.

(10) Where the sheriff, after the hearing of any evidence or on acceptance in accordance with subsection (8) above, finds that any of the grounds for the referral to which the application relates is, or should be deemed to be, established—
(a) he shall remit the case to the Principal Reporter to make arrangements for a children's hearing to consider and determine the case; and
(b) he may if he is satisfied that—
    (i)   keeping the child in a place of safety is necessary in the child's best interests; or
    (ii) there is reason to believe that the child will run away before the children's hearing sit to consider the case,
    issue an order requiring, subject to subsection (12) below, that the child be kept in a place of safety until the children's hearing so sit.

(11) An order issued under subsection (10) above may, if the sheriff is satisfied that either of the criteria mentioned in section 70(10) of this Act is fulfilled, provide that the child shall be liable to be placed and kept in secure accommodation within a residential establishment at such times as the person in charge of the establishment, with the agreement of the chief social work officer of the relevant local authority, considers necessary.

(12) A child shall not be kept in a place of safety by virtue of subsection (10)(b) above after whichever is the earlier of the following—
(a) the expiry of three days beginning with the day on which he is first so kept; or
(b) the consideration of his case by the children's hearing arranged under subsection (10)(a) above.

69 Continuation or disposal of referral by children's hearing

(1) Where the grounds of referral of the child's case stated by the Principal Reporter are accepted or are established in accordance with section 68 or section 85 of this Act, the children's hearing shall consider those grounds, any report obtained under section 56(7) of this Act and any other relevant information available to them and shall—
(a) continue the case to a subsequent hearing in accordance with subsection (2) below;
(b) discharge the referral of the case in accordance with subsection (12) below; or
(c) make a supervision requirement under section 70 of this Act.

(2) The children's hearing may continue the case to a subsequent hearing under this subsection where they are satisfied that, in order to complete their consideration of the case, it is necessary to have a further investigation of the case.

(3) Where a children's hearing continue the case under subsection (2) above, they may, for the purposes of the investigation mentioned by that subsection, require the child to attend, or reside at, any clinic, hospital or other establishment during a period not exceeding twenty-two days.

(4) Where a child fails to fulfil a requirement made under subsection (3) above, the children's hearing may, either on an application by the Principal Reporter or of their own motion, grant a warrant under this subsection.

(5) A warrant under subsection (4) above shall be authority—
(a) to find the child;
(b) to remove the child to a place of safety and keep him there; and
(c) where the place of safety is not the clinic, hospital or other establishment referred to in the requirement made under subsection (3) above, to take the child from the place of safety to such clinic, hospital or other establishment for the purposes of the investigation mentioned in subsection (2) above.

(6) A warrant under subsection (4) above shall be granted for such period as appears to the children's hearing to be appropriate, provided that no warrant shall permit the keeping of a child in a place of safety after whichever is the earlier of—
(a) the expiry of twenty-two days after the warrant is granted; or
(b) the day on which the subsequent hearing of the child's case by a children's hearing begins.

(7) Where a child's case has been continued under subsection (2) above and the children's hearing are satisfied that—
(a) keeping the child in a place of safety is necessary in the interests of safeguarding or promoting the welfare of the child; or
(b) there is reason to believe that the child may not attend the subsequent hearing of his case,
they may grant a warrant requiring that the child be taken to and kept in a place of safety.

(8) A warrant under subsection (7) above shall cease to have effect on whichever is the earlier of—
(a) the expiry of twenty-two days after the warrant is granted; or
(b) the day on which the subsequent hearing of the child's case by a children's hearing begins.

(9) A warrant under subsection (4) or (7) above may contain such conditions as

appear to the children's hearing to be necessary or expedient, and without prejudice to that generality may—

(a) subject to section 90 of this Act, require the child to submit to any medical or other examination or treatment;

(b) regulate the contact with the child of any specified person or class of persons.

(10) Where a child is to be kept at a place of safety under a warrant granted under this section or is to attend, or reside at, any place in accordance with a requirement made under subsection (3) above, the children's hearing may order that such place shall not be disclosed to any person or class of persons specified in the order.

(11) Where a child is to reside in a residential establishment by virtue of a requirement made or warrant granted under this section, the children's hearing may, if satisfied that either of the criteria mentioned in section 70(10) of this Act is fulfilled, order that while the requirement or warrant remains in effect he shall be liable to be placed in secure accommodation within that establishment at such times as the person in charge of the establishment, with the agreement of the chief social work officer of the relevant local authority, considers necessary.

(12) Where a children's hearing decide not to make a supervision requirement under section 70 of this Act they shall discharge the referral.

(13) On the discharge of the referral of the child's case any order, direction, or warrant under Chapter 2, or this Chapter, of this Act in respect of the child's case shall cease to have effect.

70 Disposal of referral by children's hearing: supervision requirements, including residence in secure accommodation

(1) Where the children's hearing to whom a child's case has been referred under section 65(1) of this Act are satisfied that compulsory measures of supervision are necessary in respect of the child they may make a requirement under this section (to be known as a "supervision requirement").

(2) A children's hearing, where they decide to make such a requirement, shall consider whether to impose any condition such as is described in subsection (5)(b) below.

(3) A supervision requirement may require the child—
(a) to reside at any place or places specified in the requirement; and
(b) to comply with any condition contained in the requirement.

(4) The place or, as the case may be, places specified in a requirement under subsection (3)(a) above may, without prejudice to the generality of that subsection, be a place or places in England or Wales; and a supervision requirement shall be authority for the person in charge of such a place to restrict the child's liberty to such extent as that person may consider appropriate, having regard to the terms of the requirement.

(5) A condition imposed under subsection (3)(b) above may, without prejudice to the generality of that subsection—
(a) subject to section 90 of this Act, require the child to submit to any medical or other examination or treatment;
(b) regulate the contact with the child of any specified person or class of persons.

(6) A children's hearing may require, when making a supervision requirement, that any place where the child is to reside in accordance with the supervision requirement shall not be disclosed to any person specified in the requirement under this subsection or class of persons so specified.

(7) A children's hearing who make a supervision requirement may determine that the requirement shall be reviewed at such time during the duration of the requirement as they determine.

(8) A supervision requirement shall be in such form as the Secretary of State may prescribe by rules.

(9) Where a children's hearing are satisfied—
(a) that it is necessary to make a supervision requirement which includes a requirement under subsection (3)(a) above that the child reside in a named residential establishment; and
(b) that any of the criteria specified in subsection (10) below are satisfied,
they may specify in the requirement that the child shall be liable to be placed and kept in secure accommodation in that establishment during such period as the person in charge of that establishment, with the agreement of the chief social work officer of the relevant local authority, considers necessary.

(10) The criteria referred to in subsection (9) above are that the child—
(a) having previously absconded, is likely to abscond unless kept in secure accommodation, and, if he absconds, it is likely that his physical, mental or moral welfare will be at risk; or
(b) is likely to injure himself or some other person unless he is kept in such accommodation.

71 Duties of local authority with respect to supervision requirements

(1) The relevant local authority shall, as respects a child subject to a supervision requirement, give effect to the requirement.

(2) Where a supervision requirement provides that the child shall reside—
(a) in relevant accommodation; or
(b) in any other accommodation not provided by a local authority,
the relevant local authority shall from time to time investigate whether, while the child is so resident, any conditions imposed by the supervision requirement are being fulfilled; and may take such steps as they consider reasonable if they find that such conditions are not being fulfilled.

(3) In this section, "relevant accommodation" means accommodation provided by the parents or relatives of the child or by any person associated with them or with the child.

72 Transfer of child subject to supervision requirement in case of necessity

(1) In any case of urgent necessity, where it is in the interests of—
(a) a child who is required by a supervision requirement imposed under section 70(3)(a) of this Act to reside in a specific residential establishment or specific other accommodation; or
(b) other children in that establishment or accommodation,
the chief social work officer of the relevant local authority may direct that, notwithstanding that requirement, the child be transferred to another place.

(2) Any child transferred under subsection (1) above shall have his case reviewed, in accordance with section 73(8) of this Act, by a children's hearing within seven days of his transfer.

73 Duration and review of supervision requirement

(1) No child shall continue to be subject to a supervision requirement for any period longer than is necessary in the interests of promoting or safeguarding his welfare.

(2) Subject to any variation or continuation of a supervision requirement under subsection (9) below, no supervision requirement shall remain in force for a period longer than one year.

(3) A supervision requirement shall cease to have effect in respect of a child not later than on his attaining the age of eighteen years.

(4) A relevant local authority shall refer the case of a child who is subject to a supervision requirement to the Principal Reporter where they are satisfied that—
(a) the requirement in respect of the child ought to cease to have effect or be varied;
(b) a condition contained in the requirement is not being complied with; or
(c) the best interests of the child would be served by their—
   (i)   applying under section 86 of this Act for a parental responsibilities order;
   (ii) applying under section 18 of the Adoption (Scotland) Act 1978 for an order freeing the child for adoption; or
   (iii) placing the child for adoption,
   and they intend to apply for such an order or so place the child.

(5) Where the relevant local authority are aware that an application has been made and is pending, or is about to be made, under section 12 of the said Act of 1978 for an adoption order in respect of a child who is subject to a supervision requirement, they shall forthwith refer his case to the Principal Reporter.

(6) A child or any relevant person may require a review of a supervision requirement in respect of the child at any time at least three months after—
(a) the date on which the requirement is made; or
(b) the date of the most recent continuation, or variation, by virtue of this section of the requirement.

(7) Where a child is subject to a supervision requirement and, otherwise than in accordance with that requirement or with an order under section 11 of this Act, a relevant person proposes to take the child to live outwith Scotland, the person shall, not later than twenty-eight days before so taking the child, give notice of that proposal in writing to the Principal Reporter and to the relevant local authority.

(8) The Principal Reporter shall—
(a) arrange for a children's hearing to review any supervision requirement in respect of a child where—
   (i)   the case has been referred to him under subsection (4) or (5) above;
   (ii) the review has been required under subsection (6) above;
   (iii) the review is required by virtue of section 70(7) or section 72(2) of this Act;
   (iv) he has received in respect of the child such notice as is mentioned in subsection (7) above; or

(v) in any other case, the supervision requirement will expire within three months; and

(b) make any arrangements incidental to that review.

(9) Where a supervision requirement is reviewed by a children's hearing arranged under subsection (8) above, they may—
(a) where they are satisfied that in order to complete the review of the supervision requirement it is necessary to have a further investigation of the child's case, continue the review to a subsequent hearing;
(b) terminate the requirement;
(c) vary the requirement;
(d) insert in the requirement any requirement which could have been imposed by them under section 70(3) of this Act; or
(e) continue the requirement, with or without such variation or insertion.

(10) Subsections (3) to (10) of section 69 of this Act shall apply to a continuation under paragraph (a) of subsection (9) above of a review of a supervision requirement as they apply to the continuation of a case under subsection (1)(a) of that section.

(11) Where a children's hearing vary or impose a requirement under subsection (9) above which requires the child to reside in any specified place or places, they may order that such place or places shall not be disclosed to any person or class of persons specified in the requirement.

(12) Where a children's hearing is arranged under subsection (8)(a)(v) above, they shall consider whether, if the supervision requirement is not continued, the child still requires supervision or guidance; and where a children's hearing consider such supervision or guidance is necessary, it shall be the duty of the local authority to provide such supervision or guidance as the child is willing to accept.

(13) Where a children's hearing is arranged by virtue of subsection (4)(c) or (5) above, then irrespective of what the hearing do under subsection (9) above they shall draw up a report which shall provide advice in respect of, as the case may be, the proposed application under section 86 of this Act or under section 18 of the said Act of 1978, or the proposed placing for adoption or the application, or prospective application, under section 12 of that Act, for any court which may subsequently require to come to a decision, in relation to the child concerned, such as is mentioned in subsection (14) below.

(14) A court which is considering whether, in relation to a child, to grant an application under section 86 of this Act or under section 18 or 12 of the said Act of 1978 and which, by virtue of subsection (13) above, receives a report as respects that child, shall consider the report before coming to a decision in the matter.

74 Further provision as respects children subject to supervision requirements

The Secretary of State may by regulations provide—
(a) for the transmission of information regarding a child who is subject to a supervision requirement to any person who, by virtue of that requirement, has, or is to have, control over the child;
(b) for the temporary accommodation, where necessary, of a child so subject; and

(c) for the conveyance of a child so subject—
   (i) to any place in which, under the supervision requirement, he is to reside;
   (ii) to any place to which he falls to be taken under subsection (1) or (5) of section 82 of this Act; or
   (iii) to any person to whom he falls to be returned under subsection (3) of that section.

75 Powers of Secretary of State with respect to secure accommodation

(1) The Secretary of State may by regulations make provision with respect to the placing in secure accommodation of any child—
(a) who is subject to a requirement imposed under section 70(3)(a) of this Act but not subject to a requirement under subsection (9) of that section; or
(b) who is not subject to a supervision requirement but who is being looked after by a local authority in pursuance of such enactments as may be specified in the regulations.

(2) Regulations under subsection (1) above may—
(a) specify the circumstances in which a child may be so placed under the regulations;
(b) make provision to enable a child who has been so placed or any relevant person to require that the child's case be brought before a children's hearing within a shorter period than would apply under regulations made under subsection (3) below; and
(c) specify different circumstances for different cases or classes of case.

(3) Subject to subsection (4) below and without prejudice to subsection (2)(b) above, the Secretary of State may prescribe—
(a) the maximum period during which a child may be kept under this Act in secure accommodation without the authority of a children's hearing or of the sheriff;
(b) the period within which a children's hearing shall be arranged to consider the case of a child placed in secure accommodation by virtue of regulations made under this section (and different periods may be so prescribed in respect of different cases or classes of case).

(4) Subsection (8) of section 66 of this Act shall apply in respect of a child placed in secure accommodation under regulations made under this section as if such placing took place by virtue of that section.

(5) The Secretary of State may by regulations vary the period within which a review of a condition imposed under section 70(9) of this Act shall be reviewed under section 73 of this Act.

(6) The Secretary of State may by regulations make provision for the procedures to be applied in placing children in secure accommodation; and without prejudice to the generality of this subsection, such regulations may—
(a) specify the duties of the Principal Reporter in relation to the placing of children in secure accommodation;
(b) make provision for the referral of cases to a children's hearing for review; and
(c) make provision for any person with parental responsibilities in relation to the child to be informed of the placing of the child in secure accommodation.

Exclusion orders

76 Exclusion orders

(1) Subject to subsections (3) to (9) below, where on the application of a local authority the sheriff is satisfied, in relation to a child, that the conditions mentioned in subsection (2) below are met, he may grant an order under this section (to be known as "an exclusion order") excluding from the child's family home any person named in the order (in this Part of this Act referred to as the "named person").

(2) The conditions are—
(a) that the child has suffered, is suffering, or is likely to suffer, significant harm as a result of any conduct, or any threatened or reasonably apprehended conduct, of the named person;
(b) that the making of an exclusion order against the named person—
    (i) is necessary for the protection of the child, irrespective of whether the child is for the time being residing in the family home; and
    (ii) would better safeguard the child's welfare than the removal of the child from the family home; and
(c) that, if an order is made, there will be a person specified in the application who is capable of taking responsibility for the provision of appropriate care for the child and any other member of the family who requires such care and who is, or will be, residing in the family home (in this section, sections 77 to 79 and section 91(3)(f) of this Act referred to as an "appropriate person").

(3) No application under subsection (1) above for an exclusion order shall be finally determined under this section unless—
(a) the named person has been afforded an opportunity of being heard by, or represented before, the sheriff; and
(b) the sheriff has considered any views expressed by any person on whom notice of the application has been served in accordance with rules making such provision as is mentioned in section 91(3)(d) of this Act.

(4) Where, on an application under subsection (1) above, the sheriff—
(a) is satisfied as mentioned in that subsection; but
(b) the conditions mentioned in paragraphs (a) and (b) of subsection (3) above for the final determination of the application are not fulfilled,
he may grant an interim order, which shall have effect as an exclusion order pending a hearing by the sheriff under subsection (5) below held within such period as may be specified in rules made by virtue of section 91(3)(e) of this Act.

(5) The sheriff shall conduct a hearing under this subsection within such period as may be specified in rules made by virtue of section 91(3)(e) of this Act, and, if satisfied at that hearing as mentioned in subsection (1) above, he may, before finally determining the application, confirm or vary the interim order, or any term or condition on which it was granted, or may recall such order.

(6) Where the conditions mentioned in paragraphs (a) and (b) of subsection (3) above have been fulfilled, the sheriff may, at any point prior to the final determination of the application, grant an interim order.

(7) An order under subsection (5) or (6) above shall have effect as an exclusion order pending the final determination of the application.

(8) Where—
(a) an application is made under subsection (1) above; and
(b) the sheriff considers that the conditions for making a child protection order under section 57 of this Act are satisfied,
he may make an order under that section as if the application had been duly made by the local authority under that rather than under this section.

(9) The sheriff shall not make an exclusion order if it appears to him that to do so would be unjustifiable or unreasonable, having regard to—
(a) all the circumstances of the case, including without prejudice to the generality of this subsection the matters specified in subsection (10) below; and
(b) any requirement such as is specified in subsection (11) below and the likely consequences in the light of that requirement of the exclusion of the named person from the family home.

(10) The matters referred to in subsection (9)(a) above are—
(a) the conduct of the members of the child's family (whether in relation to each other or otherwise);
(b) the respective needs and financial resources of the members of that family;
(c) the extent (if any) to which—
    (i) the family home; and
    (ii) any relevant item in that home,
    is used in connection with a trade, business or profession by any member of the family.

(11) The requirement referred to in subsection (9)(b) above is a requirement that the named person (whether alone or with any other person) must reside in the family home, where that home—
(a) is or is part of an agricultural holding within the meaning of the Agricultural Holdings (Scotland) Act 1991; or
(b) is let, or is a home in respect of which possession is given, to the named person (whether alone or with any other person) by an employer as an incident of employment.

(12) In this Part of this Act—
"caravan" has the meaning given to it by section 29(1) of the Caravan Sites and Control of Development Act 1960;
"exclusion order", includes an interim order granted under subsection (4) above and such an order confirmed or varied under subsection (5) above and an interim order granted under subsection (6) above; except that in subsection (3) above and in section 79 of this Act, it does not include an interim order granted under subsection (4) above;
"family" has the meaning given in section 93(1) of this Act;
"family home" means any house, caravan, houseboat or other structure which is used as a family residence and in which the child ordinarily resides with any person described in subsection (13) below and the expression includes any garden or other ground or building attached to and usually occupied with, or otherwise required for the amenity or convenience of, the house, caravan, houseboat or other structure.

(13) The description of person referred to in the definition of "family home" in subsection (12) above, is a person who has parental responsibilities in relation to the child, or who ordinarily (and other than by reason only of his employment) has charge of, or control over him.

77 Effect of, and orders etc ancillary to, exclusion order

(1) An exclusion order shall, in respect of the home to which it relates, have the effect of suspending the named person's rights of occupancy (if any) and shall prevent him from entering the home, except with the express permission of the local authority which applied for the order.

(2) The sheriff, on the application of the local authority, may, if and in so far as he thinks fit, when making an exclusion order do any of the things mentioned in subsection (3) below.

(3) The things referred to in subsection (2) above are—
(a) grant a warrant for the summary ejection of the named person from the home;
(b) grant an interdict prohibiting the named person from entering the home without the express permission of the local authority;
(c) grant an interdict prohibiting the removal by the named person of any relevant item specified in the interdict from the home, except either—
    (i) with the written consent of the local authority, or of an appropriate person; or
    (ii) by virtue of a subsequent order of the sheriff;
(d) grant an interdict prohibiting the named person from entering or remaining in a specified area in the vicinity of the home;
(e) grant an interdict prohibiting the taking by the named person of any step of a kind specified in the interdict in relation to the child;
(f) make an order regulating the contact between the child and the named person, and the sheriff may make any other order which he considers is necessary for the proper enforcement of a remedy granted by virtue of paragraph (a), (b) or (c) of this subsection.

(4) No warrant, interdict or order (except an interdict granted by virtue of paragraph (b) of subsection (3) above) shall be granted or made under subsection (2) above if the named person satisfies the sheriff that it is unnecessary to do so.

(5) Where the sheriff grants a warrant of summary ejection under subsection (2) above in the absence of the named person, he may give directions as to the preservation of any of that person's goods and effects which remain in the family home.

(6) The sheriff may make an order of the kind specified in subsection (3)(f) above irrespective of whether there has been an application for such an order.

(7) On the application of either the named person or the local authority, the sheriff may make the exclusion order, or any remedy granted under subsection (2) above, subject to such terms and conditions as he considers appropriate.

(8) In this Part of this Act references to a "relevant item" are references to any item within the home which both—
(a) is owned or hired by any member of the family concerned or an appropriate person or is being acquired by any such member or person under a hire purchase agreement or conditional sale agreement; and
(b) is reasonably necessary to enable the home to be used as a family residence,
but does not include any such vehicle, caravan or houseboat or such other structure so used as is mentioned in the definition of "family home" in section 76(12) of this Act.

78 Powers of arrest etc in relation to exclusion order

(1) The sheriff may, whether or not on an application such as is mentioned in subsection (2) below, attach a power of arrest to any interdict granted under section 77(2) of this Act by virtue of subsection (3) of that section.

(2) A local authority may at any time while an exclusion order has effect apply for such attachment of a power of arrest as is mentioned in subsection (1) above.

(3) A power of arrest attached to an interdict by virtue of subsection (1) above shall not have effect until such interdict, together with the attached power of arrest, is served on the named person.

(4) If, by virtue of subsection (1) above, a power of arrest is attached to an interdict, the local authority shall, as soon as possible after the interdict, together with the attached power of arrest, is served on the named person, ensure that there is delivered—
(a) to the chief constable of the police area in which the family home is situated; and
(b) where the interdict was granted by virtue of section 77(3)(e) of this Act, to the chief constable of the area in which the step or conduct which is prevented by the interdict may take place,
a copy of the application for the interdict and of the interlocutor granting the interdict together with a certificate of service of the interdict and, where the application to attach the power of arrest was made after the interdict was granted, a copy of that application and of the interlocutor above granting it and a certificate of service of the interdict together with the attached power of arrest.

(5) Where any interdict to which a power of arrest is attached by virtue of subsection (1) above is varied or recalled, the person who applied for the variation or recall shall ensure that there is delivered to each chief constable specified in subsection (4) above a copy of the application for such variation or recall and of the interlocutor granting the variation or recall.

(6) A constable may arrest without warrant the named person if he has reasonable cause for suspecting that person to be in breach of an interdict to which a power of arrest has been attached by virtue of subsection (1) above.

(7) Where a person has been arrested under subsection (6) above, the constable in charge of a police station may—
(a) if satisfied there is no likelihood of that person further breaching the interdict to which the power of arrest was attached under subsection (1) above, liberate him unconditionally; or
(b) refuse to liberate that person.

(8) Such a refusal to liberate an arrested person as is mentioned in subsection (7)(b) above, and the detention of that person until his appearance in court by virtue of either subsection (11) below, or any provision of the [Criminal Procedure (Scotland) Act 1995], shall not subject that constable to any claim whatsoever.

(9) Where a person has been liberated under subsection (7)(a) above, the facts and circumstances which gave rise to the arrest shall be reported to the procurator fiscal forthwith.

(10) Subsections (11) to (13) below apply only where—
(a) the arrested person has not been released under subsection (7)(a) above; and
(b) the procurator fiscal decides that no criminal proceedings are to be taken in respect of the facts and circumstances which gave rise to the arrest.

(11) A person arrested under subsection (6) above shall, wherever practicable, be brought before the sheriff sitting as a court of summary criminal jurisdiction for the district in which he was arrested not later than in the course of the first day after the arrest, such day not being a Saturday, a Sunday or a court holiday prescribed for that court under [section 8 of the said Act of 1995], on which the sheriff is not sitting for the disposal of criminal business.

(12) [Subsections (1), (2) and (4) of section 15 of the said Act of 1995] (intimation to a person named by the person arrested) shall apply to a person arrested under subsection (6) above as they apply to a person who has been arrested in respect of an offence.

(13) Where a person is brought before the sheriff under subsection (11) above—
(a) the procurator fiscal shall present to the court a petition containing—
   (i) a statement of the particulars of the person arrested under subsection (6) above;
   (ii) a statement of the facts and circumstances which gave rise to that arrest; and
   (iii) a request that the person be detained for a further period not exceeding two days;
(b) the sheriff, if it appears to him that—
   (i) the statement referred to in paragraph (a)(ii) above discloses a *prima facie* breach of interdict by the arrested person;
   (ii) proceedings for breach of interdict will be taken; and
   (iii) there is a substantial risk of violence by the arrested person against any member of the family, or an appropriate person, resident in the family home,
   may order the arrested person to be detained for a period not exceeding two days; and
(c) the sheriff shall, in any case in which paragraph (b) above does not apply, order the release of the arrested person from custody (unless that person is in custody in respect of some other matter);
and in computing the period of two days referred to in paragraphs (a) and (b) above, no account shall be taken of a Saturday, a Sunday or any holiday in the court in which proceedings for breach of interdict will require to be raised.

(14) Where a person—
(a) is liberated under subsection (7)(a) above; or
(b) is to be brought before the sheriff under subsection (11) above,
the procurator fiscal shall at the earliest opportunity, and, in the case of a person to whom paragraph (b) above applies, before that person is brought before the sheriff, take all reasonable steps to intimate to—
(i) the local authority which made the application for the interdict;
(ii) an appropriate person who will reside in, or who remains in residence in, the family home mentioned in the order; and
(iii) any solicitor who acted for the appropriate person when the interdict was granted or to any other solicitor who the procurator fiscal has reason to believe acts for the time being for that person,
that he has decided that no criminal proceedings should be taken in respect of the facts and circumstances which gave rise to the arrest of the named person.

NOTES to s 78
Sub-s (8), (11), (12): amended by the Criminal Procedure (Consequential Provisions) (Scotland) Act 1995 (c 40), s 5, Sch 4, para 97(7).

79 Duration, variation and recall of exclusion order

(1) Subject to subsection (2) below, an exclusion order shall cease to have effect on a date six months after being made.

(2) An exclusion order shall cease to have effect on a date prior to the date mentioned in subsection (1) above where—
(a) the order contains a direction by the sheriff that it shall cease to have effect on that prior date;
(b) the sheriff, on an application under subsection (3) below, recalls the order before the date so mentioned; or
(c) any permission given by a third party to the spouse or partner of the named person, or to an appropriate person, to occupy the home to which the order relates is withdrawn.

(3) The sheriff may, on the application of the local authority, the named person, an appropriate person or the spouse or partner of the named person, if that spouse or partner is not excluded from the family home and is not an appropriate person, vary or recall an exclusion order and any warrant, interdict, order or direction granted or made under section 77 of this Act.

(4) For the purposes of this section, partners are persons who live together in a family home as if they were husband and wife.

80 Exclusion orders: supplementary provisions

(1) The Secretary of State may make regulations with respect to the powers, duties and functions of local authorities in relation to exclusion orders.

(2) An application for an exclusion order, or under section 79(3) of this Act for the variation or recall of such an order or of any thing done under section 77(2) of this Act, shall be made to the sheriff for the sheriffdom within which the family home is situated.

Offences in connection with orders etc for protection of children

81 Offences in connection with orders etc for protection of children

(1) A person who intentionally obstructs—
(a) any person acting under a child protection order;
(b) any person acting under an authorisation granted under section 61(1) or (2) of this Act; or
(c) a constable acting under section 61(5) of this Act,
shall, subject to section 38(3) and (4) of this Act, be guilty of an offence and shall be liable on summary conviction to a fine not exceeding level 3 on the standard scale.

Fugitive children and harbouring

82 Recovery of certain fugitive children

(1) A child who absconds—
(a) from a place of safety in which he is being kept under or by virtue of this Part of this Act;

(b) from a place (in this section referred to as a "relevant place") which, though not a place of safety such as is mentioned in paragraph (a) above, is a residential establishment in which he is required to reside by virtue of section 70(3)(a) of this Act or a hospital or other institution in which he is temporarily residing while subject to such a requirement; or
(c) from a person who, by virtue of a supervision requirement or of section 74 of this Act, has control over him while he is being taken to, is awaiting being taken to, or (whether or not by reason of being on leave) is temporarily away from, such place of safety or relevant place,

may be arrested without warrant in any part of the United Kingdom and taken to the place of safety or as the case may be the relevant place; and a court which is satisfied that there are reasonable grounds for believing that the child is within any premises may, where there is such power of arrest, grant a warrant authorising a constable to enter those premises and search for the child using reasonable force if necessary.

(2) Without prejudice to the generality of subsection (1) above, a child who at the end of a period of leave from a place of safety or relevant place fails to return there shall, for the purposes of this section, be taken to have absconded.

(3) A child who absconds from a person who, not being a person mentioned in paragraph (c) of subsection (1) above, is a person who has control over him by virtue of a supervision requirement may, subject to the same provisions as those to which an arrest under that subsection is subject, be arrested as is mentioned in that subsection and returned to that person; and the provision in that subsection for a warrant to be granted shall apply as respects such a child as it applies as respects a child mentioned in that subsection.

(4) If a child—
(a) is taken under subsection (1) above to a place of safety or relevant place; or
(b) is returned under subsection (3) above to a person,
but the occupier of that place of safety or of that relevant place, or as the case may be that person, is unwilling or unable to receive him, that circumstance shall be intimated forthwith to the Principal Reporter.

(5) Where intimation is required by subsection (4) above as respects a child, he shall be kept in a place of safety until—
(a) in a case where he is subject to a supervision requirement, he can be brought before a children's hearing for that requirement to be reviewed; or
(b) in any other case, the Principal Reporter has, in accordance with section 56(6) of this Act, considered whether compulsory measures of supervision are required in respect of him.

83 Harbouring

A person who—
(a) knowingly assists or induces a child to abscond in circumstances which render the child liable to arrest under subsection (1) or (3) of section 82 of this Act;
(b) knowingly and persistently attempts to induce a child so to abscond;
(c) knowingly harbours or conceals a child who has so absconded; or
(d) knowingly prevents a child from returning—
    (i) to a place mentioned in paragraph (a) or (b) of the said subsection (1);
    (ii) to a person mentioned in paragraph (c) of that subsection, or in the said subsection (3),
shall, subject to section 38(3) and (4) of this Act, to section 51(5) and (6) of

the Children Act 1989 and to Article 70(5) and (6) of the Children (Northern Ireland) Order 1995 (analogous provision for England and Wales and for Northern Ireland), be guilty of an offence and liable on summary conviction to a fine not exceeding level 5 on the standard scale or to imprisonment for a term not exceeding six months or to both such fine and such imprisonment.

Implementation of authorisations etc

84 Implementation of authorisations etc

Where an order, authorisation or warrant under this Chapter or Chapter 2 of this Part of this Act grants power to find a child and to keep him in a place of safety, such order, authorisation or warrant may be implemented as if it were a warrant for the apprehension of an accused person issued by a court of summary jurisdiction; and any enactment or rule of law applying to such a warrant shall, subject to the provisions of this Act, apply in like manner to the order, authorisation or warrant.

New evidence: review of establishment of grounds of referral

85 Application for review of establishment of grounds of referral

(1) Subject to subsections (3) and (4) below, where subsection (2) below applies an application may be made to the sheriff for a review of a finding such as is mentioned in section 68(10) of this Act.

(2) This subsection applies where the sheriff, on an application made by virtue of subsection (7) or (9) of section 65 of this Act (in this section referred to as the "original application"), finds that any of the grounds of referral is established.

(3) An application under subsection (1) above may only be made where the applicant claims—
(a) to have evidence which was not considered by the sheriff on the original application, being evidence the existence or significance of which might materially have affected the determination of the original application;
(b) that such evidence—
   (i)   is likely to be credible and reliable; and
   (ii) would have been admissible in relation to the ground of referral which was found to be established on the original application; and
(c) that there is a reasonable explanation for the failure to lead such evidence on the original application.

(4) An application under subsection (1) above may only be made by—
(a) the child in respect of whom the ground of referral was found to be established; or
(b) any person who is a relevant person in relation to that child.

(5) Where the sheriff on an application under subsection (1) above is not satisfied that any of the claims made in the application are established he shall dismiss the application.

(6) Where the sheriff is satisfied on an application under subsection (1) above that the claims made in the application are established, he shall consider the evidence and if, having considered it, he is satisfied that—

(a) none of the grounds of referral in the original application to which the application relates is established, he shall allow the application, discharge the referral to the children's hearing in respect of those grounds and proceed in accordance with subsection (7) below in relation to any supervision requirement made in respect of the child (whether or not varied under section 73 of this Act) in so far as it relates to any such ground; or

(b) any ground of referral in the original application to which the application relates is established, he may proceed in accordance with section 68(10) of this Act.

(7) Where the sheriff is satisfied as is mentioned in subsection (6)(a) above, he may—

(a) order that any supervision requirement so mentioned shall terminate—
    (i) immediately; or
    (ii) on such date as he may specify; or

(b) if he is satisfied that there is evidence sufficient to establish any ground of referral, being a ground which was not stated in the original application, find such ground established and proceed in accordance with section 68(10) of this Act in relation to that ground.

(8) Where the sheriff specifies a date for the termination of a supervision requirement in accordance with subsection (7)(a)(ii) above, he may, before such termination, order a variation of that requirement, of any requirement imposed under subsection (6) of section 70 of this Act, or of any determination made under subsection (7) of that section; and such variation may take effect—

(a) immediately; or

(b) on such date as he may specify.

(9) Where the sheriff orders the termination of a supervision requirement in accordance with subsection (7)(a) above, he shall consider whether, after such termination, the child concerned will still require supervision or guidance; and where he considers that such supervision or guidance will be necessary he shall direct a local authority to provide it in accordance with subsection (10) below.

(10) Where a sheriff has given a direction under subsection (9) above, it shall be the duty of the local authority to comply with that direction; but that duty shall be regarded as discharged where they offer such supervision or guidance to the child and he, being a child of sufficient age and maturity to understand what is being offered, is unwilling to accept it.

Interpretation of Part II

93 Interpretation of Part II

(1) In this Part of this Act, unless the context otherwise requires,—

"accommodation" shall be construed in accordance with section 25(8) of this Act;

"chief social work officer" means an officer appointed under section 3 of the Social Work (Scotland) Act 1968;

"child assessment order" has the meaning given by section 55(1) of this Act;

"child protection order" has the meaning given by section 57(1) of this Act;

"children's hearing" shall be construed in accordance with section 39(3), but does not include a business meeting arranged under section 64, of this Act;

"compulsory measures of supervision" means, in respect of a child, such measures of supervision as may be imposed upon him by a children's hearing;

"constable" means a constable of a police force within the meaning of the Police (Scotland) Act 1967;

"contact order" has the meaning given by section 11(2)(d) of this Act;

"disabled" has the meaning given by section 23(2) of this Act;

"exclusion order" has the meaning given by section 76(12) of this Act;

"family", in relation to a child, includes—

    (a) any person who has parental responsibility for the child; and

    (b) any other person with whom the child has been living;

"local authority" means a council constituted under section 2 of the Local Government etc (Scotland) Act 1994;

"local government area" shall be construed in accordance with section 1 of the said Act of 1994;

"parental responsibilities" has the meaning given by section 1(3) of this Act;

"parental responsibilities order" has the meaning given by section 86(1) of this Act;

"parental rights" has the meaning given by section 2(4) of this Act;

"place of safety", in relation to a child, means—

    (a) a residential or other establishment provided by a local authority;

    (b) a community home within the meaning of section 53 of the Children Act 1989;

    (c) a police station; or

    (d) a hospital, surgery or other suitable place, the occupier of which is willing temporarily to receive the child;

"the Principal Reporter" means the Principal Reporter appointed under section 127 of the said Act of 1994 or any officer of the Scottish Children's Reporter Administration to whom there is delegated, under section 131(1) of that Act, any function of the Principal Reporter under this Act;

"relevant local authority", in relation to a child who is subject to a warrant granted under this Part of this Act or to a supervision requirement, means the local authority for whose area the children's panel from which the children's hearing which granted the warrant or imposed the supervision requirement was formed;

"residence order" has the meaning given by section 11(2)(c) of this Act;

"residential establishment"—

    (a) in relation to a place in Scotland, means an establishment (whether managed by a local authority, by a voluntary organisation or by any other person) which provides residential accommodation for children for the purposes of this Act or the Social Work (Scotland) Act 1968;

    (b) in relation to a place in England and Wales, means a community home, voluntary home or registered children's home (within the meaning of the Children Act 1989); and

    (c) in relation to a place in Northern Ireland, means a home provided under Part VIII of the Children (Northern Ireland) Order 1995, or a voluntary home, or a registered children's home (which have respectively the meanings given by that Order);

"school age" shall be construed in accordance with section 31 of the Education (Scotland) Act 1980;

"secure accommodation" means accommodation provided in a residential establishment, approved by the Secretary of State in accordance with regulations made under section 60(1)(bb) of the Social Work (Scotland) Act 1968 or under paragraph 4(2)(i) of Schedule 4 to the Children Act 1989, for the purpose of restricting the liberty of children;

"supervision requirement" has the meaning given by section 70(1) of this Act, and includes any condition contained in such a requirement or related to it;

"voluntary organisation" means a body (other than a public or local authority) whose activities are not carried on for profit; and

"working day" means every day except—
- (a) Saturday and Sunday;
- (b) December 25th and 26th; and
- (c) January 1st and 2nd.

(2) For the purposes of—
(a) Chapter 1 and this Chapter (except this section) of this Part, "child" means a person under the age of eighteen years; and
(b) Chapters 2 and 3 of this Part—
"child" means—
   (i) a child who has not attained the age of sixteen years;
   (ii) a child over the age of sixteen years who has not attained the age of eighteen years and in respect of whom a supervision requirement is in force; or
   (iii) a child whose case has been referred to a children's hearing by virtue of section 33 of this Act;
and for the purposes of the application of those Chapters to a person who has failed to attend school regularly without reasonable excuse includes a person who is over sixteen years of age but is not over school age; and
"relevant person" in relation to a child means—
   (a) any parent enjoying parental responsibilities or parental rights under Part I of this Act;
   (b) any person in whom parental responsibilities or rights are vested by, under or by virtue of this Act; and
   (c) any person who appears to be a person who ordinarily (and other than by reason only of his employment) has charge of, or control over, the child.

(3) Where, in the course of any proceedings under Chapter 2 or 3 of this Part, a child ceases to be a child within the meaning of subsection (2) above, the provisions of those Chapters of this Part and of any statutory instrument made under those provisions shall continue to apply to him as if he had not so ceased to be a child.

(4) Any reference in this Part of this Act to a child—
(a) being "in need", is to his being in need of care and attention because—
   (i) he is unlikely to achieve or maintain, or to have the opportunity of achieving or maintaining, a reasonable standard of health or development unless there are provided for him, under or by virtue of this Part, services by a local authority;
   (ii) his health or development is likely significantly to be impaired, or further impaired, unless such services are so provided;
   (iii) he is disabled; or
   (iv) he is affected adversely by the disability of any other person in his family;
(b) who is "looked after" by a local authority, shall be construed in accordance with section 17(6) of this Act.

(5) Any reference to any proceedings under this Part of this Act, whether on an application or on appeal, being heard by the sheriff, shall be construed as a reference to such proceedings being heard by the sheriff in chambers.

NOTES to s 93

Sub-s (1): "constable": See the Police (Scotland) Act 1967 (c 77), s 51
"**local authority**": See the Local Government etc (Scotland) Act 1994 (c 39), s 2
"**local government area**": See the Local Government etc (Scotland) Act 1994, s 1
"**the Principal Reporter**": See the Local Government etc (Scotland) Act 1994, ss 127, 128, 131(1).

---

* * *

Criminal Procedure (Scotland) Act 1995

(c 46)

* * *

SCHEDULE 3
Indictments and Complaints

Sections 64(6) and 138(4)

1 An accused may be named and designed—
(a) according to the existing practice; or
(b) by the name given by him and designed as of the place given by him as his residence when he is examined or further examined; or
(c) by the name under which he is committed until liberated in due course of law.

2 It shall not be necessary to specify by any *nomen juris* the offence which is charged, but it shall be sufficient that the indictment or complaint sets forth facts relevant and sufficient to constitute an indictable offence or, as the case may be, an offence punishable on complaint.

3 It shall not be necessary to allege that any act or commission or omission charged was done or omitted to be done "wilfully" or "maliciously", or "wickedly and feloniously", or "falsely and fraudulently" or "knowingly", or "culpably and recklessly", or "negligently", or in "breach of duty", or to use such words as "knowing the same to be forged", or "having good reason to know", or "well knowing the same to have been stolen", or to use any similar words or expressions qualifying any act charged, but such qualifying allegation shall be implied in every case.

4 (1) The latitude formerly used in stating time shall be implied in all statements of time where an exact time is not of the essence of the charge.

(2) The latitude formerly used in stating any place by adding to the word "at", or to the word "in", the words "or near", or the words "or in the near neighbourhood thereof" or similar words, shall be implied in all statements of place where the actual place is not of the essence of the charge.

(3) Subject to sub-paragraph (4) below, where the circumstances of the offence charged make it necessary to take an exceptional latitude in regard to time or place it shall not be necessary to set forth the circumstances in the indictment, or to set forth that the particular time or the particular place is to the prosecutor unknown.

(4) Where exceptional latitude is taken as mentioned in sub-paragraph (3) above, the court shall, if satisfied that such exceptional latitude was not reasonable in the

circumstances of the case, give such remedy to the accused by adjournment of the trial or otherwise as shall seem just.

(5) Notwithstanding sub-paragraph (4) above, nothing in any rule of law shall prohibit the amendment of an indictment or, as the case may be, a complaint to include a time outwith the exceptional latitude if it appears to the court that the amendment would not prejudice the accused.

(6) The latitude formerly used in describing quantities by the words "or thereby", or the words "or part thereof", or the words "or some other quantity to the prosecutor unknown" or similar words, shall be implied in all statements of quantities.

(7) The latitude formerly used in stating details connected with the perpetration of any act regarding persons, things or modes by inserting general alternative statements followed by the words "to the prosecutor unknown" or similar words, shall be implied in every case.

(8) In this paragraph references to latitude formerly used are references to such use before the commencement of—
(a) in the case of proceedings on indictment, the Criminal Procedure (Scotland) Act 1887; and
(b) in the case of summary proceedings, the Summary Jurisdiction (Scotland) Act 1908.

5 The word "money" shall include cheques, banknotes, postal orders, money orders and foreign currency.

6 Any document referred to shall be referred to by a general description and, where it is to be produced in proceedings on indictment, by the number given to it in the list of productions for the prosecution.

7 In an indictment which charges a crime importing personal injury inflicted by the accused, resulting in death or serious injury to the person, the accused may be lawfully convicted of the aggravation that the assault or other injurious act was committed with intent to commit such crime.

8 (1) In an indictment or a complaint charging the resetting of property dishonestly appropriated—
(a) having been taken by theft or robbery; or
(b) by breach of trust, embezzlement or falsehood, fraud and wilful imposition,
it shall be sufficient to specify that the accused received the property, it having been dishonestly appropriated by theft or robbery, or by breach of trust and embezzlement, or by falsehood, fraud and wilful imposition, as the case may be.

(2) Under an indictment or a complaint for robbery, theft, breach of trust and embezzlement or falsehood, fraud and wilful imposition, an accused may be convicted of reset.

(3) Under an indictment or a complaint for robbery, breach of trust and embezzlement, or falsehood, fraud and wilful imposition, an accused may be convicted of theft.

(4) Under an indictment or a complaint for theft, an accused may be convicted of breach of trust and embezzlement, or of falsehood, fraud and wilful imposition, or may be convicted of theft, although the circumstances proved may in law amount to robbery.

(5) The power conferred by sub-paragraphs (2) to (4) above to convict a person of an offence other than that with which he is charged shall be exercisable by the sheriff court before which he is tried notwithstanding that the other offence was committed outside the jurisdiction of that sheriff court.

9 (1) Where two or more crimes or acts of crime are charged cumulatively, it shall be lawful to convict of any one or more of them.

(2) Any part of the charge in an indictment or complaint which itself constitutes an indictable offence or, as the case may be an offence punishable on complaint, shall be separable and it shall be lawful to convict the accused of that offence.

(3) Where any crime is charged as having been committed with a particular intent or with particular circumstances of aggravation, it shall be lawful to convict of the crime without such intent or aggravation.

10 (1) Under an indictment or, as the case may be, a complaint which charges a completed offence, the accused may be lawfully convicted of an attempt to commit the offence.

(2) Under an indictment or complaint charging an attempt, the accused may be convicted of such attempt although the evidence is sufficient to prove the completion of the offence said to have been attempted.

(3) Under an indictment or complaint which charges an offence involving personal injury inflicted by the accused, resulting in death or serious injury to the person, the accused may be lawfully convicted of the assault or other injurious act, and may also be lawfully convicted of the aggravation that the assault or other injurious act was committed with intent to commit such offence.

11 In an indictment or complaint charging a contravention of an enactment the description of the offence in the words of the enactment contravened, or in similar words, shall be sufficient.

12 In a complaint charging a contravention of an enactment—
(a) the statement that an act was done contrary to a enactment shall imply a statement—
   (i) that the enactment applied to the circumstances existing at the time and place of the offence;
   (ii) that the accused was a person bound to observe the enactment;
   (iii) that any necessary preliminary procedure had been duly gone through; and
   (iv) that all the circumstances necessary to a contravention existed,
   and, in the case of the contravention of a subordinate instrument, such statement shall imply a statement that the instrument was duly made, confirmed, published and generally made effectual according to the law applicable, and was in force at the time and place in question; and
(b) where the offence is created by more than one section of one or more statutes or subordinate instruments, it shall be necessary to specify only the leading section or one of the leading sections.

13 In the case of an offence punishable under any enactment, it shall be sufficient to allege that the offence was committed contrary to the enactment and to refer to the enactment founded on without setting out the words of the enactment at length.

14 Where—
(a) any act alleged in an indictment or complaint as contrary to any enactment is also criminal at common law; or
(b) where the facts proved under the indictment or complaint do not amount to a contravention of the enactment, but do amount to an offence at common law,
it shall be lawful to convict of the common law offence.

15 Where the evidence in a trial is sufficient to prove the identity of any person, corporation or company, or of any place, or of anything, it shall not be a valid objection to the sufficiency of the evidence that any particulars specified in the indictment or complaint relating to such identity have not been proved.

16 Where, in relation to an offence created by or under an enactment any exception, exemption, proviso, excuse, or qualification, is expressed to have effect whether by the same or any other enactment, the exception, exemption, proviso, excuse or qualification need not be specified or negatived in the indictment or complaint, and the prosecution is not required to prove it, but the accused may do so.

17 It shall be competent to include in one indictment or complaint both common law and statutory charges.

18 In any proceedings under the Merchant Shipping Acts it shall not be necessary to produce the official register of the ship referred to in the proceedings in order to prove the nationality of the ship, but the nationality of the ship as stated in the indictment or, as the case may be, complaint shall, in the absence of evidence to the contrary, be presumed.

19 In offences inferring dishonest appropriation of property brought before a court whose power to deal with such offences is limited to cases in which the value of such property does not exceed level 4 on the standard scale it shall be assumed, and it shall not be necessary to state in the charge, that the value of the property does not exceed that sum.

*   *   *

Children and Young Persons (Scotland) Act 1937

CHAPTER 37

An Act to consolidate in their application to Scotland certain enactments relating to persons under the age of eighteen years.

[1st July 1937]

BE it enacted by the King's most Excellent Majesty, by and with the advice and consent of the Lords Spiritual and Temporal, and Commons, in this present Parliament assembled, and by the authority of the same, as follows:—

* * *

PART II
PREVENTION OF CRUELTY AND EXPOSURE TO MORAL AND PHYSICAL DANGER

Offences

12 Cruelty to persons under sixteen

(1) If any person who has attained the age of sixteen years and [who has parental responsibilities in relation to a child or to a young person under that age or has charge or care of a child or such a young person], wilfully assaults, ill-treats, neglects, abandons, or exposes him, or causes or procures him to be assaulted, ill-treated, neglected, abandoned, or exposed, in a manner likely to cause him unnecessary suffering or injury to health (including injury to or loss of sight, or hearing, or limb, or organ of the body, and any mental derangement), that person shall be guilty of an offence, and shall be liable—

(a) on conviction on indictment, to a fine ..., or alternatively, or in default of payment of such a fine, or in addition thereto, to imprisonment for any term not exceeding [ten] years;

(b) on summary conviction, to a fine not exceeding [£400], or alternatively, or in default of payment of such a fine, or in addition thereto, to imprisonment for any term not exceeding six months.

(2) For the purposes of this section—

(a) a parent or other person legally liable to maintain a child or young person [or the legal guardian of a child or young person] shall be deemed to have neglected him in a manner likely to cause injury to his health if he has failed to provide adequate food, clothing, medical aid or lodging for him, or if, having been unable otherwise to provide such food, clothing, medical aid or lodging, he has failed to take steps to procure it to be provided under [the enactments applicable in that behalf];

(b) where it is proved that the death of a child under three years of age was caused by suffocation (not being suffocation caused by disease or the presence of any foreign body in the throat or air passages of the child) while the child was in bed with some other person who has attained the age of sixteen years, that other person shall, if he was, when he went to bed, under the influence of drink, be deemed to have neglected the child in a manner likely to cause injury to his health.

(3) A person may be convicted of an offence under this section—

(a) notwithstanding that actual suffering or injury to health, or the likelihood of actual suffering or injury to health, was obviated by the action of another person;

(b) notwithstanding the death of the child or young person in question.

(4) Where any person who has attained the age of sixteen years is tried on indictment for the culpable homicide of a child or young person under the age of sixteen years of [and he had parental responsibilities in relation to, or charge or care of, that child or young person], it shall be lawful for the jury, if they are satisfied that he is guilty of an offence under this section, to find him guilty of that offence.

(5) [Omitted]

(6) [Omitted]

(7) Nothing in this section shall be construed as affecting the right of any parent, teacher, or other person having the lawful control or charge of a child or young person to administer punishment to him.

NOTES to s 12

> **Sub-ss (1), (4):** words in square brackets substituted by the Children (Scotland) Act 1995 (c 36), s 105(4), Sch 4, para 7(2).
> **Sub-s (1)(a), (b):** words omitted repealed, words in square brackets substituted by the Children Act 1975 (c 72), Sch 3, para 2, Sch 4, pt III and the Criminal Justice Act 1988 (c 33), s 45.
> **Sub-s (2)(a):** first words in square brackets added by C(S)A 1995, Sch 4, para 7(2), second words in square brackets substituted by SI 1951/174, Schedule.

*   *   *

15 Causing or allowing persons under sixteen to be used for begging

(1) If any person causes or procures any child or young person under the age of sixteen years or, having [parental responsibilities in relation to, or having] charge, or care of such a child or young person, allows him, to be in any street, premises, or place for the purpose of begging or receiving alms, or of inducing the giving of alms (whether or not there is any pretence of singing, playing, performing, offering anything for sale, or otherwise) he shall, on summary conviction, be liable to a fine not exceeding [£50], or alternatively, or in default of payment of such a fine, or in addition thereto, to imprisonment for any term not exceeding three months.

(2) If a person having [parental responsibilities in relation to, or having], charge, or care of a child or young person is charged with an offence under this section, and it is proved that the child or young person was in any street, premises, or place for any such purpose as aforesaid, and that the person charged allowed the child or young person to be in the street, premises, or place, he shall be presumed to

have allowed him to be in the street, premises, or place for that purpose unless the contrary is proved.

(3) If any person while singing, playing, performing or offering anything for sale in a street or public place has with him a child who has been lent or hired out to him, the child shall, for the purposes of this section, be deemed to be in that street or place for the purpose of inducing the giving of alms.

NOTES to s 15

Sub-ss (1), (2): words 'parental responsibilities in relation to, or having' in square brackets substituted by the Children (Scotland) Act 1995 (c 36), s 105(4), Sch 4, para 7(3).

Sub-s (1): second words in square brackets substituted by virtue of the Criminal Procedure (Scotland) Act 1995 (c 46), s 225.

*   *   *

22 Exposing children under seven to risk of burning

If any person who has attained the age of sixteen years [and who has parental responsibilities in relation to a child under the age of seven years or charge or care of such a child], allows the child to be in any room containing an open fire grate not sufficiently protected to guard against the risk of his being burnt or scalded without taking reasonable precautions against that risk, and by reason thereof the child is killed or suffers serious injury, he shall on summary conviction be liable to a fine not exceeding [£25]:

Provided that neither this section, nor any proceedings taken thereunder, shall affect any liability of any such person to be proceeded against by indictment for any indictable offence.

NOTES to s 22

First words in square brackets substituted by the Children (Scotland) Act 1995 (c 36), Sch 4, para 7(4), second words in square brackets substituted by the Criminal Procedure (Scotland) Act 1995 (c 46), s 225.

*   *   *

33 Prohibition of persons under sixteen taking part in performances endangering life or limb

No [child] shall take part in any [performance to which [section 37(2)] of the Children and Young Persons Act 1963 applies, and] in which his life or limbs are endangered and every person who causes or procures [child], or, being his parent or guardian, allows him, to take part in such a performance, shall be liable on summary conviction to a fine not exceeding [£50] or, in the case of a second or subsequent offence, not exceeding [£100].

NOTES to s 33

The word 'child' where it twice occurs in square brackets substituted by the Employment Act 1989 (c 38), Sch 3, Pt III, para 11. Second words in square brackets substituted. Words therein in square brackets substituted by the Children and Young Persons Act 1963 (c 37), Sch 3, para 30 and the Children (Protection at Work) Regulations, SI 1998/267, reg 10. Third and fourth words in square brackets substituted by the Criminal Procedure (Scotland) Act 1995 (c 46), s 225.

*   *   *

Children's Hearings (Scotland) Rules 1996

SI 1996/3261

ARRANGEMENT OF RULES

Part V
Reference for Advice and Suspension of Supervision Requirements

Part VI
Forms, Miscellaneous and Supplemental

The Secretary of State, in exercise of the powers conferred on him by section 42(1) of the Children (Scotland) Act 1995, and of all other powers enabling him in that behalf, hereby makes the following Rules:

Part I
Interpretation, etc

1 Citation and commencement

These Rules may be cited as the Children's Hearings (Scotland) Rules 1996 and shall come into force on 1st April 1997.

2 Interpretation

(1) In these Rules, unless the context otherwise requires—
"the Act" means the Children (Scotland) Act 1995;
"the 1978 Act" means the Adoption (Scotland) Act 1978;
"the 1994 Act" means the Local Government etc (Scotland) Act 1994;
"the 1995 Act" means the Criminal Procedure (Scotland) Act 1995;
"the 1996 Regulations" means the Secure Accommodation (Scotland) Regulations 1996;
"chairman" means the chairman of a children's hearing;
"child" has the meaning given to that term by section 93(2)(b) of the Act;

"child protection order" has the meaning given to that term by section 57 of the Act;

"children's hearing" means a children's hearing as defined in section 39(3) of the Act;

"day" means a period of twenty-four hours commencing at midnight;

"enactment" includes any order, regulation or other instrument made under the Act;

"local authority" means the local authority for the area of the children's hearing;

"relevant person" has the meaning given to that term by section 93(2)(b) of the Act;

"Principal Reporter" has the meaning given to that term by section 93(1) of the Act;

"representative" has the meaning given to that term by rule 11(3) below;

"safeguarder" means a person appointed by a children's hearing under section 41(1) of the Act for the purpose of safeguarding the interests of the child in the proceedings;

"Scottish Children's Reporter Administration" has the meaning given to that term by section 128 of the 1994 Act;

"secure accommodation" means accommodation provided in a residential establishment in accordance with the 1996 regulations for the purpose of restricting the liberty of children.

(2) Unless the context otherwise requires, any reference in these Rules to:

(a) a numbered rule or Form shall be construed as a reference to the rule or Form bearing that number in these Rules; and any reference to a specified paragraph or sub-paragraph shall be construed as a reference to that paragraph or sub-paragraph in the rule in which that reference occurs; and

(b) a Form includes a Form substantially to the same effect as that set out in these Rules with such variation as circumstances may require.

PART II
CONSTITUTION AND ARRANGEMENTS OF CHILDREN'S HEARINGS

3 Recording and transmission of information at beginning of case

(1) Where the Principal Reporter receives information from any source of a case which may require a children's hearing to be arranged, he shall keep a record of the name and address where available of the person from whom the information was received.

(2) Where the Principal Reporter decides that no further action on the case is required as mentioned in subsection (4) of section 56 of the Act, or refers the case to the local authority under subsection (4)(b) of that section, or arranges a children's hearing under subsection (6) of that section, he shall—

(a) keep a record of that decision or, as the case may be, that course of action; and

(b) if the information was received from a local authority or an officer of a police force, give notice of that decision, or as the case may be, that course of action to that local authority or, the chief constable of that police force.

4 Business meeting preparatory to constitution of children's hearing

(1) Where the Principal Reporter arranges a children's hearing, he may, for the purpose of—

(a) determining any procedural matter specified in paragraph (2), and

(b) obtaining any direction or guidance in relation to the performance of his functions in relation to the proceedings,

arrange a meeting (in this rule referred to as a "business meeting") with members of the children's panel from which the children's hearing is to be constituted and with the provisions the same as in section 39(5) of the Act applying to the business meeting.

(2) A business meeting shall determine any of the following procedural matters as may be referred to the meeting by the Principal Reporter—

(a) whether notice of the children's hearing is to be given by the Principal Reporter under rule 7 to a person as a "relevant person" in terms of paragraph (c) of the definition of that term in section 93(2)(b) of the Act (person who appears to be a person who ordinarily (and other than by reason only of his employment) has charge of, or control over, the child);

(b) where notice of the children's hearing has been or is to be given by the Principal Reporter to the child under rule 6, whether notice is also to be given that the child is released under section 45(2) of the Act from the obligation to attend the hearing under subsection (1)(b) of that section; and

(c) where notice has been or is to be given by the Principal Reporter to a relevant person under rule 7, whether notice is also to be given that the hearing are satisfied under section 45(8)(b) of the Act that it would be unreasonable to require his attendance or that his attendance is unnecessary for the proper consideration of the case.

(3) Where the Principal Reporter arranges a business meeting under paragraph (1), he shall, not later than 4 working days before the date of the meeting—

(a) give notice in writing to the members of the panel who will attend the meeting of the date, time and place of the meeting;

(b) give notice in writing to the child, any relevant person and any safeguarder that the meeting has been arranged and of the date on which it is to be held;

(c) give to the members of the panel and to the child, any relevant person and any safeguarder—

   (i)   notice of the matters referred to the business meeting for determination or for direction and guidance;

   (ii) a copy of any documents or information relevant to these matters; and

   (iii) a copy of the grounds of referral of the case of the child prepared in terms of section 65 of the Act.

(4) The Principal Reporter shall, when giving notice under paragraph (3), advise the child, any relevant person and any safeguarder—

(a) of their entitlement to make their views on the matters to be considered by the business meeting known to the Principal Reporter, and

(b) that any such views shall be presented by him to the meeting.

(5) The Principal Reporter shall record in writing any views given to him other than in writing under paragraph (4), for the purpose of presenting these views to the business meeting for consideration.

(6) The Principal Reporter shall as soon as reasonably practicable after receiving any views give a copy of these views in writing to the members of the children's panel who will attend the business meeting and to the other persons who received notice of the meeting under paragraph (3).

(7) Before making a determination, or giving guidance or directions to the Principal Reporter, the business meeting shall consider any views given to them under paragraph (6).

(8) Where the business meeting has made a determination, or given guidance or directions to the Principal Reporter as to the exercise of his functions, the Principal Reporter shall as soon as reasonably practicable give notice in writing of the determination or, as the case may be, the guidance or direction, to the child, any relevant person and any safeguarder.

5 Notification of children's hearings and provision of documents to chairman and members, relevant persons etc

(1) Subject to the 1996 Regulations, where the Principal Reporter arranges any children's hearing, he shall wherever practicable at least seven days before the date of the hearing notify the chairman and members of the time and place of the hearing and, subject as aforesaid, as soon as reasonably practicable but not later than three days before the date of the hearing, he shall give to each of them a copy of any of the following documents as are relevant to the case of a child to be considered at the hearing:—

(a) a report of a local authority on the child and his social background;
(b) the statement of the grounds for the referral of the case to the children's hearing prepared under rule 18;
(c) any judicial remit or reference or any reference by a local authority;
(d) any supervision requirement to which the child is subject;
(e) any report prepared by any safeguarder appointed in the case;
(f) any views of the child given in writing to the Principal Reporter by virtue of rule 15(4).

(2) If the Principal Reporter has obtained any information (including any views of the child given orally to the Principal Reporter by virtue of rule 15) or any document, other than a document mentioned in paragraph (1) which is material to the consideration of the case of a child at any children's hearing, he shall make that information or copies of that document available to the chairman and members of the children's hearing before the hearing.

(3) Where the Principal Reporter gives a copy of any document to the chairman and members of the children's hearing under paragraph (1), or makes available to them information or any document or copy thereof under paragraph (2), he shall at the same time give a copy of the document or, as the case may be, make available the information or a copy of the document, to—

(a) each relevant person in relation to the child, whose case is to be considered at the children's hearing; and
(b) any father of the child whose case is to be considered at the children's hearing who is living with the mother of the child where both the father and the mother are parents of the child as defined in section 15(1) of the Act,

except that where a children's hearing is arranged to continue consideration of the case of the child by virtue of section 69(2) of the Act, this obligation of the Principal Reporter shall apply only in respect of any information or document which has not already been made available to the person concerned.

(4) The chairman and members of children's hearings shall keep securely in their custody any documents made available to them under this rule and, except as otherwise provided in rules 20(4) and 22(4), they shall not cause or permit any information contained in the documents or otherwise disclosed during the hearing to be made known to any person.

(5) Immediately after the conclusion of a children's hearing the chairman and members shall return to the Principal Reporter any documents which have been made available to them under this rule.

(6) Any information or document which the Principal Reporter makes available under this rule to the chairman and members of any children's hearing shall also be made available, if requested, to any member of the Scottish Committee of the Council on Tribunals who is attending that hearing and the Council on Tribunals shall be required to return all papers to the Principal Reporter at the end of the hearing.

(7) Any information or document which the Principal Reporter makes available under this rule to the chairman and members of any children's hearing shall also be made available, if requested, to any member of the Children's Panel Advisory Committee or to any member of a sub-committee of the Advisory Committee who has given notice of his intention to attend that hearing as an observer. Any person provided with papers under this rule shall not cause or permit any information contained in the said documents or otherwise disclosed during the hearing to be made known to any person and shall return to the Principal Reporter at the end of the hearing any document which has been made available to him.

6 Notification of children's hearings to children

(1) Subject to paragraphs (2) and (3), where the Principal Reporter arranges a children's hearing he shall not less than 7 days before the hearing give notice in writing to the child whose case has been referred to the hearing of his right and obligation to attend the hearing and of the date, time and place of the hearing.

(2) Where the Principal Reporter arranges a children's hearing—
(a) to consider under section 45(7), 59(2), 68(10) or by virtue of section 82(5) of the Act the case of a child kept in a place of safety;
(b) to consider under Chapters 2 or 3 of Part II of the Act the case of a child placed in secure accommodation under regulation 7 of the 1996 Regulations;
(c) to review an application under section 51(9) of the Act for the suspension of a supervision requirement; or
(d) to review the case of a child transferred under section 72 of the Act to a place of residence other than that named in the supervision requirement;
he shall as soon as reasonably practicable before the hearing give the notice required under paragraph (1) above in writing; provided that if such notice cannot be given in writing, the Principal Reporter may give notice to the child orally.

(3) Where under section 45(2) of the Act a children's hearing are satisfied either in a case as specified in 45(2) of the Act that the attendance of the child is not necessary or in any case that it would be detrimental to the interests of the child for him to be present at the hearing of his case, the Principal Reporter shall give him notice in writing of his right under section 45(1) of the Act to attend the hearing and of the date, time and place of the hearing.

(4) When giving to a child under this rule notice of a children's hearing to which rule 15 applies, the Principal Reporter shall inform the child—
(a) of the entitlement by virtue of section 16(2) of the Act and these rules to indicate whether he wishes to express his views;
(b) that if he does so wish, he will be given an opportunity to express them; and
(c) that any such views as may be given by the child to the Principal Reporter before the time at which the children's hearing is to be held will be conveyed by the Principal Reporter to the members of the children's hearing, to any relevant person and to any safeguarder, for the purpose of the hearing.

7 Notification of children's hearings to relevant persons and certain parents with right to attend

(1) Where a relevant person in relation to a child whose case is to be considered at a children's hearing, has a right to and is obliged under section 45(8) of the Act to attend at all stages of the hearing, the Principal Reporter shall give him notice in writing, if his whereabouts are known, of the right to and obligation to attend at all stages of the hearing and of the date, time and place of the hearing.

(2) Where under section 45(8) of the Act a children's hearing are satisfied either that it would be unreasonable to require the attendance of a relevant person at a children's hearing or that the attendance of that person would be unnecessary for the proper consideration of the case, the Principal Reporter shall give him notice in writing, if his whereabouts are known, of his right under section 45(8) of the Act to attend at all stages of the hearing and of the date, time and place of the hearing but that for the above reason or reasons he is not obliged to attend.

(3) Where a person has a right by virtue of rule 12(1) to attend at all stages of the children's hearing, the Principal Reporter shall give such notice in writing of his right, if his whereabouts are known.

(4) Any notice under this rule, except a notification to a relevant person of a children's hearing mentioned under rule 6(2), shall be given not later than seven days before the date of the children's hearing to which it relates.

(5) In the case of such a children's hearing mentioned in rule 6(2), the notice to the relevant person under paragraph (1) shall be given as soon as reasonably practicable in writing before the hearing, and if such notice cannot be given in writing the Principal Reporter may give notice to a relevant person orally.

8 Notification of children's hearing to chief social work officer

Where the Principal Reporter arranges any children's hearings he shall notify the chief social work officer of the local authority for the area in which the children's hearing is to sit of the date, time and place of the hearing, and of the name, date of birth and address, so far as is known of the child whose case is to be considered.

9 Withholding of address where disclosure may result in serious harm

Where in fulfilling his obligations under rules 5, 7 or 8 the Principal Reporter considers that the disclosure of the whereabouts of the child or any relevant person may place that person at risk of serious harm (whether or not physical harm) he may withhold such information as is necessary to prevent such disclosure and indicate the address of the person as that of the Principal Reporter.

10 Constitution of children's hearing and functions of chairman of children's hearing

(1) The selection of the chairman and the members of any children's hearing from among the members of the children's panel for a local authority area shall be made either directly by the chairman of the children's panel, or in his absence by the deputy chairman, or by the operation of standing arrangements in that behalf made by the chairman of the children's panel after such consulting the Principal Reporter and such members of the panel as he may think fit. Such standing arrangements may provide for the selection of the chairman and members of any

hearing to be made by members of the panel appointed for that purpose by the chairman of the panel.

(2) The chairman of the children's panel shall keep under review any standing arrangements which he has made under paragraph (1) and shall from time to time consult the Principal Reporter and such members of the panel as he thinks fit as to the operation of those arrangements.

(3) Except as otherwise provided by these Rules and any other enactment, the procedure at any children's hearing shall be such as the chairman shall in his discretion determine.

(4) Without prejudice to the generality of paragraph (3) and to the power of a children's hearing under the Act to continue a hearing for the further investigation of a case, the chairman of a children's hearing may at any time during the hearing adjourn the hearing provided that any adjournment under this rule shall be such as to enable the children's hearing to sit again on the same day as the adjournment was made.

(5) As soon as reasonably practicable after a children's hearing make—
(a) a decision disposing of the case of a child on a referral or at a review of a supervision requirement or a condition imposed under section 70(9) of the Act with respect to residence in secure accommodation;
(b) a decision to issue a warrant to find a child or for the keeping of a child in a place of safety or to continue a warrant for the keeping of such a child;
(c) a requirement or warrant, or continuation of a warrant, under section 69 of the Act,
the chairman shall make or cause to be made a report of the decision and a statement in writing of the reasons for the decision, and shall sign the report and statement.

PART III

GENERAL PROVISIONS AS TO CHILDREN'S HEARINGS

11 Representation for the purposes of assisting children and relevant persons at children's hearing

(1) Any child whose case comes before a children's hearing and any relevant person who attends that children's hearing may each be accompanied by one person for the purpose of assisting the child, or as the case may be, the relevant person at the hearing.

(2) Any representative attending any children's hearing may assist the person whom he represents in the discussion of the case of the child with the children's hearing.

(3) In these Rules any reference to a representative is a reference to a person who under this rule assists a child or a relevant person or both, and includes, unless the context otherwise requires, a reference both to any representative of a child and any representative of a relevant person.

12 General attendance at hearings of certain parents of the child (not relevant persons) and specific limited right of duly authorised officials etc

(1) A father of the child as described in rule 5(3)(b) shall be entitled to attend at all stages of the children's hearing while the hearing are considering the case of the

child but shall be subject to the same provisions as those contained in section 46 of the Act as if those provisions apply to him.

(2) A constable, prison officer or other person duly authorised who has in his lawful custody a person who has to attend a children's hearing shall be entitled to be present at the hearing for the purposes of escorting that person.

13 Persons who may attend children's hearings at chairman's discretion

Without prejudice to the right of a child and of a relevant person under rule 11 above to be accompanied at a children's hearing by a representative, and subject to subsections (1) to (3) of section 43 of the Act (provisions as to privacy of children's hearings), the persons whose presence at the children's hearing may be permitted by the chairman under the said subsection (1) shall be—
(a) the chairman and members of the Children's Panel Advisory Committee for the local authority area of the children's hearing and the clerk to the Children's Panel Advisory Committee of the local authority;
(b) any members or possible members of children's panels whose attendance is required at children's hearings for the purpose of their training as members of children's hearings, and their instructors;
(c) any student engaged in formal education or training in social work or any person engaged in research relating to children who may be in need of compulsory measures of supervision; and
(d) any other person whose presence at the hearing may in the opinion of the chairman be justified by special circumstances.

14 Safeguarders

(1) Where a children's hearing appoint a safeguarder under section 41(1) of the Act, the chairman shall state in writing the reasons for their decision to make that appointment.

(2) The Principal Reporter shall give the safeguarder a copy of such statement and also give notice of the date, time and place of the hearing at the same time and in the same manner as giving notice to a relevant person under rule 7.

(3) Any safeguarder appointed by a children's hearing shall be entitled to be present throughout the duration of any hearing of the case until the disposal of that case.

(4) Where a safeguarder is appointed by a children's hearing, he shall—
(a) prepare a report in writing on the case of the child; and
(b) prepare any further report in writing on the case as the hearing may require, and give the report or, as the case may be, the further report to the Principal Reporter.

(5) Any information or document which the Principal Reporter makes available in compliance with rule 5 (under exception of rule (5)(1)(e)) or otherwise to the chairman and members of any children's hearing shall also be made available to any safeguarder regardless of the date of his appointment in the proceedings.

(6) A safeguarder—
(a) shall keep securely in his custody any documents made available to him under paragraph (4);
(b) shall not cause or permit any information contained in the documents or otherwise disclosed during the hearing to be made known to any person, other than may be necessary for the performance of his own duties; and

(c) shall return to the Principal Reporter any document which has been made available to him under paragraph (4) above when he has completed the performance of all duties associated with his appointment.

15 Views of the Child

(1) The children's hearing, taking account of the age and maturity of the child whose case has been referred to the hearing for a purpose mentioned in paragraph (2) shall so far as practicable give the child an opportunity to indicate whether he wishes to express his views.

(2) This rule shall apply where the children's hearing—
(a) are considering whether to make, or are reviewing a supervision requirement;
(b) are considering whether to grant a warrant under subsections (4) or (5) of section 45, subsection (5) of section 63, subsection (1) of section 66, or subsection (4) or (7) of section 69, of the Act or to provide under subsection (5) of the said section 66 for the continuation of a warrant;
(c) are considering whether to continue a child protection order under section 59(4) of the Act;
(d) are engaged in providing advice under section 60(10) of the Act; or
(e) are considering whether to make a requirement under section 69(3) of the Act;
(f) are drawing up a report under section 73(13) of the Act; and
(g) are considering whether to issue a warrant under the 1996 Regulations.

(3) Where he has indicated his wish to express his views—
(a) the children's hearing and the chairman of the hearing may exercise any of their powers under the Act or these Rules as they or, as the case may be, he considers appropriate in order to ascertain the views of the child; and
(b) the children's hearing shall not make any decision or take any action mentioned in paragraph (2) unless an opportunity has been given for the views of the child to be obtained or heard and in terms of section 16(2)(c) of the Act they have had regard to such views as he may have expressed.

(4) Without prejudice to the generality of the powers mentioned in paragraph (3)(a), the views of the child may be conveyed to the children's hearing—
(a) by the child, or by his representative, individually or together in person;
(b) by the child in writing, on audio or video tape or through an interpreter; or
(c) by any safeguarder appointed by the hearing.

(5) For the purposes of this rule, a child of twelve years of age or more shall be presumed to be of sufficient age and maturity to form a view.

PART IV
CHILDREN'S HEARINGS ON REFERRAL AND AT REVIEW OF SUPERVISION REQUIREMENTS, ETC

16 Application of Part IV

This Part shall, subject to the provisions thereof, apply to (a) any children's hearing arranged under Part II of the Act or under the 1996 Regulations either for the purposes of considering and determining on referral the case of any child or for the review of a supervision requirement or a condition imposed by section 70(9) of the Act with respect to residence in secure accommodation; and (b) any children's hearing to which a case is stood referred under section 49(4) of the 1995 Act.

17 Statement of grounds of referral

(1) The statement of the grounds for the referral of a case to a children's hearing shall be signed by the Principal Reporter and shall specify which one or more of the conditions mentioned in section 52(2) of the Act is or are considered by the Principal Reporter to be satisfied with respect to the child, and the statement shall state the facts on the basis of which it is sought to show that any condition is satisfied.

(2) In the case of a condition mentioned in section 52(2)(i) of the Act, the statement of the facts constituting the offence shall have the same degree of specification as is required by section 138(4) of the 1995 Act in a charge in a complaint and the statement shall also specify the nature of the offence in question.

18 Notification of statement of grounds for referral

(1) Subject to paragraphs (2) and (3), where the Principal Reporter arranges a children's hearing under section 65(1) of the Act, he shall—
(a) prepare a statement of the grounds for the referral of the case to the children's hearing; and
(b) not less than seven days before the date of the hearing give a copy of the statement to the child and to each relevant person whose whereabouts are known.

(2) Notwithstanding paragraph (1), where before the children's hearing the child is kept in a safe place under the Act, or so kept by virtue of the 1996 Regulations, the provisions of paragraphs (1)(a) and (b) shall apply except that in paragraph (1)(b) the words "as soon as reasonably practicable" shall be substituted for the words "not less than seven days".

(3) Notwithstanding paragraph (1), where the Principal Reporter arranges a children's hearing under section 65(2) of the Act, the provisions of paragraphs (1)(a) and (b) shall apply except that in paragraph (1)(b) the words "not less than three days" shall be substituted for the words "not less than seven days".

(4) Notwithstanding that a children's hearing proceeds in accordance with section 65 of the Act to more than one hearing, nothing in this rule shall require a copy of the statement to be given to any person more than once.

19 Notification of application to sheriff for finding as to grounds if they consider it appropriate to do so for referral

Where a children's hearing have given a direction to the Principal Reporter under section 65 of the Act to apply to the sheriff for a finding as to whether or not any grounds for the referral of any case to them are satisfied, the Principal Reporter shall give notice of this in writing to the child and to any relevant person.

20 Conduct of children's hearing considering case on referral or at review of supervision requirement

(1) This rule applies to a children's hearing considering under section 65 of the Act a case on referral or at a review under section 73(8) of the Act of a supervision requirement.

(2) Unless a children's hearing consider the case of a child in the absence of the child, any relevant person and any representative, the chairman shall, before the

children's hearing proceeds to consider the case, explain the purpose of the hearing to such persons as are present.

(3) In proceeding with the case the children's hearing shall—
(a) consider a report of a local authority on the child and his social background, and any judicial remit or other relevant document and any relevant information available to them;
(b) consider any report submitted by the manager of any residential establishment in which the child is required to reside;
(c) discuss the case with the child, any relevant person, any safeguarder and representative if attending the hearing;
(d) take steps under rule 15 to obtain the views of the child, and endeavour to obtain the views of any relevant person and of any safeguarder, if attending the hearing, on what arrangements would be in the best interests of the child.

(4) The chairman shall inform the child and any relevant person of the substance of any reports, documents and information mentioned in paragraph (3)(a) and (b) if it appears to him that this is material to the manner in which the case of the child should be disposed of and that its disclosure would not be detrimental to the interests of the child.

(5) After the children's hearing have considered the case of the child and made a decision disposing of the case, but before the conclusion of the hearing at which the decision is made, the chairman shall inform the child, any relevant person, any safeguarder, and any representative, if attending the hearing, of—
(a) the decision of the hearing;
(b) the reasons for the decision;
(c) the right of the child and of the relevant person under section 51(1) of the Act to appeal to the sheriff against the decision and, where the appeal is against a decision relating to a supervision requirement, to apply to the children's hearing for suspension of the requirement appealed against.

(6) The children's hearing shall not dispose of the case by making a supervision requirement under section 70(1) of the Act requiring the child to reside at any place or places specified in the requirement (which for the purposes of this rule is a place or places where he is to be under the charge or control of a person who is not a relevant person) unless—
(a) they have received and considered a report from the local authority for the purposes of paragraph (3)(a), together with recommendations from that authority on—
   (i)   the needs of a child;
   (ii) the suitability to meet those needs of the place or places in which the child is to reside by virtue of the supervision requirement, and of the person or persons who is or are to have charge of or control over the child, and
(b) the local authority have confirmed to the hearing that in compiling the report they have carried out the procedures and gathered the information described in regulation 15 of the Fostering of Children (Scotland) Regulations 1996.

21 Notification of decisions, etc on referral or at review of supervision requirement

(1) Subject to sections 70(6) and 73(11) of the Act, as soon as reasonably practicable after a children's hearing have made a decision disposing of the case of a child under this Part of the Rules, the Principal Reporter shall send to the child, any relevant person, any safeguarder and the local authority—

(a) notice of the decision and a copy of any supervision requirement or, as the case may be, any continuation of a supervision requirement;
(b) a copy of the statement of reasons for the decision; and
(c) except in the case of a review which continues a supervision requirement, being a review in relation to which an order under section 51(7) of the Act is in force, notice of the right of the child or, as the case may be, a relevant person under section 51 of the Act to appeal to the sheriff against the decision,
and such notice shall be given in writing.

(2) Where a children's hearing have made a decision disposing of the case of a child, the Principal Reporter shall as soon as reasonably practicable give notice of the decision—
(a) to any person with whom the child is residing; and
(b) where the information leading to the investigation of the case of the child was given by an officer of a police force, to the chief constable of the police area.

(3) Where the decision was—
(a) to make a supervision requirement in relation to a child who has attained the age of 16 years; or
(b) to terminate a supervision requirement relating to such a child,
the Principal Reporter shall as soon as reasonably practicable give notice of the decision to the chief constable of the police area and if the child resides outwith the police area, to the chief constable of the police area in which the child resides.

PART V
REFERENCES FOR ADVICE AND SUSPENSION OF SUPERVISION REQUIREMENTS

22 Conduct of children's hearing on reference for advice by court, the local authority or approved adoption society

(1) This rule shall apply to any children's hearing arranged in order to consider the case of a child for the purpose of giving advice to the court, the local authority or the approved adoption society under any of the following provisions:—
section 73(13) of the Act (advice in relation to placing for adoption, application for adoption order, freeing for adoption order or parental responsibilities order);
subsection (1)(b) or (6) of section 49 of the 1995 Act (reference by court for advice in case of child not subject to supervision requirement);
section 49(3) of the 1995 Act (reference by court for advice in case of child subject to supervision requirement);
section 22A(2) of the 1978 Act (advice in relation to placing a child for adoption).

(2) Unless the children's hearing consider the case of a child in the absence of the child, a relevant person and any representative, the chairman shall, before the children's hearing proceed to consider the case, explain the purpose of the hearing to such persons as are present.

(3) The children's hearing shall proceed to consider the case of the child and during such consideration shall—
(a) consider the reference by the court, the local authority or the approved adoption society, any supervision requirement to which the child is subject, a report of a local authority on the child and his social background, and any other relevant document or any relevant information available to them;
(b) discuss the case of the child and afford to the child, any relevant person, any safeguarder and any representative, if attending the hearing, an opportunity of participating in the discussion and of being heard on the case;

(c) take steps on rule 15 to obtain the views of the child, and endeavour to obtain the views of any relevant person, and of any safeguarder if attending the hearing, on what arrangements with respect to the child would be in the best interests of the child; and

the children's hearing shall thereafter determine what advice they will give to the court, the local authority or, as the case may be, the approved adoption society.

(4) The chairman shall inform the child and each relevant person whose whereabouts are known of the substance of any reports, documents and information mentioned in paragraph (3)(a) if it appears to him that this is material to the advice that will be given and that its disclosure would not be detrimental to the interests of the child.

(5) After the children's hearing have considered the case of the child and determined the advice they shall provide, the hearing shall inform the child, any relevant person, any safeguarder and any representative, if attending the hearing of that advice.

(6) As soon as reasonably practicable after the children's hearing determine the advice they shall provide, the chairman shall make or cause to be made a report in writing providing that advice, including a statement of the reasons for that advice, and the chairman of the hearing shall sign the report and statement.

(7) Within 7 days following a determination by the children's hearing, the Principal Reporter shall send a copy of the report prepared under paragraph (6) to the court, the local authority or the approved adoption society, as the case may be, and the child, any relevant person and any safeguarder appointed in the proceedings.

(8) Where the Principal Reporter is obliged under section 73(8)(a)(iv) of the Act to arrange a children's hearing and he is advised by the adoption agency that it has determined that agreement to an application under section 16 or 18 of the 1978 Act is unlikely to be forthcoming, he shall be under an obligation to arrange a hearing to sit within 21 days of that notification from the local authority under section 73(4)(c) of the Act.

23 Application for suspension of supervision requirements pending hearing of appeals

(1) An application to a children's hearing by a child or relevant person under section 51(9) of the Act for the suspension of a supervision requirement pending an appeal under section 51(1) of the Act shall be made in writing to the Principal Reporter.

(2) The Principal Reporter shall give notice in writing separately to the child and relevant person of the date, time and place of the children's hearing at which the application will be considered.

(3) The children's hearing shall afford the applicant, and his representative, and any safeguarder if attending the hearing, an opportunity of being heard.

(4) The chairman of the children's hearing shall inform the applicant at the conclusion of the hearing of the decision of the hearing and the reasons for it.

(5) If the applicant fails to attend the hearing, the application shall be treated as abandoned.

(6) An application under this rule shall not be valid unless an appeal under section 51(1) of the Act has already been lodged.

PART VI

MISCELLANEOUS AND SUPPLEMENTAL

24 Social background report where child in a place of safety

Subject to the 1996 Regulations, where a children's hearing is arranged under section 65(2) of the Act, the children's hearing shall not proceed in relation to the case of the child in accordance with section 70(1) of the Act unless the Principal Reporter has made available to them a report of local authority on the child and his social background.

25 Form of supervision requirement

(1) Subject to paragraph (2) below, a supervision requirement under section 70(1) of the Act shall be in the form of Form 1.

(2) A supervision requirement under section 70(1) of the Act with a specification under section 70(9) of the Act (residence in secure accommodation) shall be in the form of Form 2.

(3) Subject to paragraph (4) below, a continuation under section 73(9)(e) of the Act of a supervision requirement (with any variation of the requirement or insertion in the requirement mentioned in paragraph (9)(c) and (d) of that subsection) shall be in the form of Form 3.

(4) A continuation under section 73(9)(e) of the Act of a supervision requirement (with a variation of the requirement or insertion in the requirement as mentioned in relation to a specification as to secure accommodation as described in section 70(9) of the Act) shall be in the form of Form 4.

26 Procedure relating to warrants, orders, and to requirements under section 69(3) of the Act

(1) Where a children's hearing consider in relation to a child the question whether they should—
(a) issue or continue a warrant or order under any of the following provisions of the Act:—

section 45(4) and (5) (warrants to find child, keep in a place of safety and bring before a hearing);

section 59(4) (continuation of child protection order);

section 63(5) (warrant to keep child in place of safety following arrest);

section 66(1) and (5) (warrants where children's hearing unable to dispose of case);

section 69(4) (warrant for fulfilment of requirement to attend or reside at clinic, hospital, etc); and

section 69(7) (warrant to take child to and keep in place of safety while case continued under section 59(4) of the Act);
(b) continue under section 59(4) of the Act any direction given under section 58 (direction as to parental responsibilities or parental rights when child protection order made); or
(c) issue a warrant under the 1996 Regulations;
(d) make a requirement under section 69(3) of the Act (requirement to reside at clinic, etc),

the children's hearing shall, before they make a decision to issue that warrant or as the case may be that requirement, take steps under rule 15 to obtain the views of the child, and endeavour to obtain the views of any relevant person and of any safeguarder, if attending the hearing, on what arrangements would be in the best interests of the child.

(2) Where a children's hearing have issued or, as the case may be, continued such a warrant, order, discretion or requirement as is mentioned in paragraph (1), the Principal Reporter shall send as soon as reasonably practicable to the child, any relevant person and any safeguarder appointed in the proceedings—

(a) a copy of the warrant, continuation of the warrant, continuation of the order, or requirement and a copy of the statement of the reasons for the decision; and

(b) notice of the right of the child, or, as the case may be, the relevant person under section 51 of the Act to appeal to the sheriff against the decision.

27 Forms of warrants and orders for finding and keeping a child in a place of safety

The orders or warrants listed and described in the left hand column of the chart below shall be in the form of the Forms (as defined in rule 2(2)(b)) opposite in the right hand column which are in the Schedule to these Rules and references to sections shall be to sections in the Act. The description in the left hand column is for ease of reference and does not reproduce the provisions of the Act in full.

	LEFT HAND COLUMN	*RIGHT HAND COLUMN*
S 45(4) & (5)	Warrant under section 45(4) or 45(5) to find a child, keep him in a place of safety and bring him before a children's hearing	Form 5
S 59(4)	Continuation under section 59(4) of a child protection order	Form 6
	Continuation under section 59(4) of a child protection order with first authorisation to remove child and to keep child in place of safety with/without order of non-disclosure of place of safety	Form 7
S 63(5)	Warrant under section 63(5) to keep a child in place of safety with/without order of non-disclosure of place of safety	Form 8
	Warrant under section 63(5) with order that child liable to be kept in secure accommodation with/without order of non-disclosure of place of safety	Form 9
	Continuation under section 63(5) of warrant to keep a child in place of safety	Form 10
	Continuation under section 63(5) of warrant to keep a child in a place of safety with first authorisation that child liable to be kept in secure accommodation with/without order of non-disclosure of place of safety	Form 11
S 66(1)	Warrant under section 66(1) to keep a child in a place of safety when hearing unable to dispose of case	Form 12
	Warrant under 66(1) to keep a child in a place of safety when hearing unable to dispose of case with order that child liable to be kept in secure accommodation with/without order of non-disclosure of place of safety	Form 13

S 66(5)	Continuation under section 66(5) of warrant granted under section 66(1) to keep a child in a place of safety	Form 14
	Continuation under section 66(5) of warrant granted under section 66(1) to keep a child in a place of safety with first order that child liable to be kept in secure accommodation with/without order of non-disclosure of place of safety	Form 15
S 69(4)	Warrant under section 69(4) to find a child and remove to a place of safety when requirement under section 69(3) not fulfilled (where continuation of case)	Form 16
	Warrant under section 69(4) to find child and remove to place of safety when requirement under section 69(3) not fulfilled with first order that child liable to be kept in secure accommodation with/without order of non-disclosure of place of safety (where continuation of case)	Form 17
S 69(7)	Warrant under section 69(7) to keep a child in a place of safety (where continuation of case)	Form 18
	Warrant under section 69(7) to keep a child in a place of safety when there is a continuation of the case by the children's hearing with order to keep child in secure accommodation with/without order of non-disclosure of place of safety (where continuation of case)	Form 19

28 Miscellaneous Forms

(1) A requirement under section 69(3) of the Act shall be in the form of Form 20.

(2) A notification by a Principal Reporter under section 60(3) of the Act shall be in the form of Form 21.

(3) A notification by a Principal Reporter under section 60(5) of the Act shall be in the form of Form 22.

(4) A report of a children's hearing of advice under section 60(10) of the Act shall be in the form of Form 23.

(5) A report of a children's hearing order under section 73(13) of the Act shall be in the form of Form 24.

29 Authentication of documents

(1) A report of any decision, a statement of reasons for a decision or of advice, a warrant or continuation of warrants for finding and keeping a child in a place of safety, or any other writing, authorised or required by Chapter 2 or 3 of the Act or these Rules to be made, given, issued or granted by a children's hearing or by the chairman of a children's hearing shall be sufficiently authenticated if it is signed by the chairman, or, if he is unavailable, by a member of that hearing.

(2) Any document authorised or required by these Rules to be made or executed

by the Principal Reporter shall be sufficiently authenticated if it is signed by the Principal Reporter or by a person duly authorised by him.

(3) Any copy of any document authorised or required by these Rules to be given or issued by the Principal Reporter may be certified as a true copy by the Principal Reporter or by a person duly authorised by him.

30 Service of notification and other documents

(1) Any notice in writing or other document and any oral notification authorised or required under these Rules to be given or issued by the Principal Reporter may be given or issued by the Principal Reporter or by a person duly authorised by him or by any constable.

(2) Any notice in writing or other document authorised or required by these Rules to be given or issued to a child or to a relevant person may be—
(a) delivered to him in person; or
(b) left for him at his dwellinghouse or place of business or where he has no known dwellinghouse or place of business, at any other place in which he may at the time be resident; or
(c) where he is the master of, or a seaman or other person employed in, a vessel, left with a person on board thereof and connected therewith; or
(d) sent by post in a registered or first class service recorded delivery letter to his dwellinghouse or place of business.

(3) Where the Principal Reporter or a person duly authorised by him gives to any relevant person a notification in writing under paragraph (1) of rule 7 above, or an oral notification under that paragraph as read with paragraph (4) of that rule, he shall execute a certificate of notification in the form of Form 25.

(4) Where a notice under rule 6 or 7 or a copy of such a statement as is mentioned in rule 18 is sent by post in accordance with paragraph (2)(d) of this rule, the notification or copy shall be deemed, for the purpose of rule 6, 7 or 18, as the case may be, to have been given the day following the date of posting.

31 Reports of proceedings of children's hearing

(1) In relation to the case of any child which comes before a children's hearing, it shall be the duty of the Principal Reporter to keep a report of the proceedings of that hearing and the report—
(a) shall include the information specified in paragraph (2) below; and
(b) may include such other information about the proceedings as the Principal Reporter thinks appropriate.

(2) The information referred to in paragraph (1)(a) above is as follows—
(a) particulars of the place and date of the hearing;
(b) the full name and address of the child and his sex and date of birth;
(c) the full name and address (so far as these can be obtained) of the father, the mother and any other relevant person in relation to the child;
(d) a record as to which (if any) of the persons mentioned in sub-paragraphs (b) and (c) above was present;
(e) the full name and address of any representative attending the hearing;
(f) the full name and address of any safeguarder;
(g) the terms of any decision disposing the case of the child, or of any decision to issue a warrant, made by the children's hearing or any other course of action taken by them with respect to the child; and

(h) in any case where the children's hearing proceed in accordance with section 65 of the Act—
  (i) particulars of the grounds of referral which are accepted or, as the case may be, not accepted, and by whom;
  (ii) a record of any direction under subsection (7) or (9) of section 65 to make application to the sheriff for a finding under that section; and
  (iii) a record of whether the children's hearing proceeded to consider that the case at a hearing.

32 Travelling and subsistence expenses

(1) Subject to paragraph (2), the local authority for the area of a children's hearing shall, if a claim is made to them, pay to or in respect of any child, or to any relevant person, or to any one representative of either attending any children's hearing, a sum equal to such travelling expenses and such expenses or subsistence as have, in the opinion of the local authority, been reasonably incurred by or in respect of the child or, as the case may be, by the relevant person or by any representative of either for the purpose of enabling the said child, relevant person or representative to attend that hearing.

(2) A claim under this rule shall be in writing and shall be made before the expiry of the period of one month commencing with the date of the children's hearing to which the claim relates.

33 Notification of 16th birthday of child subject to supervision requirement

When a child subject to a supervision requirement attains the age of 16 years, the Principal Reporter shall as soon as reasonably practicable give notice of that fact to the chief constable of the police area.

SCHEDULE

FORM 1
SUPERVISION REQUIREMENT

Rule 25(1)

(Place and Date)

  A children's hearing for (local authority area), having considered the case of (name and address of child) and in exercise of the powers conferred by section 70 of the Children (Scotland) Act 1995, being satisfied that he/she is in need of compulsory measures of supervision require him/her* [to be under the supervision of the chief social work officer of (name of local authority)]* [to reside in (name of place or places) [to comply with the conditions stated below.]

  [The children's hearing order that the place/places* where (name the child) is to reside in accordance with the requirement shall not be disclosed to (person or class of persons)]*

CONDITIONS REFERRED TO IN THE FOREGOING SUPERVISION REQUIREMENT

1 [   ]

. . . .

Chairman of the Children's Hearing

*Delete as appropriate

Form 2

SUPERVISION REQUIREMENT UNDER SECTION 70(1) OF THE ACT AUTHORISING PLACEMENT IN
SECURE ACCOMMODATION

Rule 25(2)

(Place and Date)

A children's hearing for (local authority area) having considered the case of (name and address of child) and in exercise of the powers conferred by sections 70(1), 70(3) and 70(9) of the Children (Scotland) Act 1995 being satisfied (firstly) that the child is in need of compulsory measures of supervision, and (secondly)

[that he/she* has previously absconded and is likely to abscond unless he/she* is kept in secure accommodation, and, that if he/she* absconds, it is likely that his/her* physical, mental or moral welfare will be at risk]*

[that he/she* is likely to injure himself/herself* or some other person unless he/she* is kept in secure accommodation]*,

require him/her* to be under the supervision of the chief social work officer for (name of local authority) and to reside in (name of residential establishment providing secure accommodation subject to the conditions noted below.

[name of the place or places]* (see Note below)

[The children's hearing order that the place where (name of child) is to reside shall not be disclosed to (person or class of person)]*

CONDITIONS REFERRED TO IN THE FOREGOING SUPERVISION REQUIREMENT

1 The child is liable to be placed and kept in secure accommodation in (name of residential establishment) at such times as the person in charge of the residential establishment, with the agreement of the chief social work officer of (name of local authority) considers it necessary that the child do so.

. . . .

Chairman of the Children's Hearing

*Delete as appropriate

Note: If the residential establishment providing secure accommodation does not have an open residential facility there will also need to be a reference to some such place.

Form 3

CONTINUATION UNDER SECTION 73(9)(e) OF THE ACT OF SUPERVISION REQUIREMENT

Rule 25(3)

(Place and date)

A children's hearing for (local authority area), considering the case of (name and address of child) and the supervision requirement (a copy of which is attached), and in exercise of its powers under section 73(9)(e) of the Act, continues the said requirement [in force]* [subject to the variations of that requirement noted below]* [with the insertions in the requirement noted below]*

[The children's hearing in [varying]* [imposing]* a requirement order that the place where (name of child) is to reside shall not be disclosed to (person or class of persons)]*

[VARIATION[S] REFERRED TO]*

[INSERTION[S] REFERRED TO]*

....

Chairman of the Children's Hearing

*Delete as appropriate

FORM 4

CONTINUATION UNDER SECTION 73(9)(E) OF THE ACT OF SUPERVISION REQUIREMENT WITH VARIATION AUTHORISING PLACEMENT IN SECURE ACCOMMODATION

Rule 25(4)

(Place and Date)

A children's hearing for (local authority area) having considered the case of (name and address of child) and in exercise of the powers conferred by sections 73(9)(e) of the Children (Scotland) Act 1995 being satisfied (firstly) that the child is in need of compulsory measures of supervision, and (secondly)

[that he/she* has previously absconded and is likely to abscond unless he/she* is kept in secure accommodation, and, that if he/she* absconds, it is likely that his/her* physical, mental or moral welfare will be at risk]*

[that he/she* is likely to injure himself/herself* or some other person unless he/she* is kept in secure accommodation]*,

grant continuation of the supervision requirement dated (ie sent date) a copy of which is attached, subject to the insertion of a requirement on him/her* to be under the supervision of the chief social work officer for (name of local authority) and to reside in (name of residential establishment providing secure accommodation. Subject to the conditions noted below and any other insertions in or variations of the supervision requirement noted below.

[name of place or places]* (see Note below)

[The children's hearing order that the place where (name of child) is to reside shall not be disclosed to (person or class of person)]*

CONDITIONS VARIATIONS AND INSERTIONS REFERRED TO IN THE SUPERVISION REQUIREMENT

1 The child is liable to be placed and kept in secure accommodation in (name of residential establishment) at such times as the person in charge of the residential establishment, with the agreement of the chief social work officer of (name of local authority) considers it necessary that the child do so.

....

Chairman of the Children's Hearing

*Delete as appropriate

Note: If the residential establishment providing secure accommodation does not have an open residential facility there will also need to be a reference to some such place.

Form 5

Warrant to Find a Child etc, under Section [45(4)]* [45(5)]* of the Act

Rule 27

(Place and date)

A children's hearing for (local authority area) in respect of the case of (name and address of child)* and exercise of the powers conferred on them by section [45(4)]* [45(5)]* of the Children (Scotland) Act 1995, being satisfied that it is necessary for them to do so, grant warrant to find the child, and keep him/her in a place of safety and to bring him/her before a children's hearing.

．．．．．．．．．．．．．．．．．．．．．．．．．．．．．．．．．．．

Chairman of the Children's Hearing

*Delete as appropriate

Form 6

Continuation under Section 59(4) of the Act of a Child Protection Order

Rule 27

(Place and date)

A children's hearing for (local authority area), in respect of the case of (name and address of child)* and exercise of the powers conferred on them by section 59(4) of the Children (Scotland) Act 1995, being satisfied that the conditions for the making of a child protection order under section 57 of the Act are established, continue the child protection order dated (insert date of CPO by sheriff, a copy of which is attached) [and the directions made under section 58 of the Act]* until (date) (insert date being date of hearing on eighth working day).

[For the duration of the Order the variation[s] of the [Order]* [and] [direction[s]]* as set out below shall have effect]*

[VARIATIONS OF [ORDER]* [AND]* [DIRECTIONS]*

1 (insert variations)]*

．．．．．．．．．．．．．．．．．．．．．．．．．．．．．．．．．．．

Chairman of the Children's Hearing

*Delete as appropriate

Form 7

Continuation under Section 59(4) of the Act of a Child Protection Order with First Authorisation of Removal of Child to Place of Safety

Rule 27

(Place and date)

A children's hearing for (local authority area), in respect of the case of (name and address of child)* and in exercise of the powers conferred on them by section 59(4) of the Children

(Scotland) Act 1995, being satisfied that the conditions for the making of a child protection order under section 57 of the Act are established, continue the child protection order dated (insert date of CPO by sheriff, a copy of which is attached) [and the directions made under section 58 of the Act]* until (date) (insert date being date of hearing on eighth working day).

[For the duration of the Order the variation[s] of the [Order]* [and] [direction[s]]* as set out below shall have effect]*

[VARIATIONS OF [ORDER]* [AND]* [DIRECTIONS]*

1 The applicant shall be authorised to remove the child to and keep it (name of place or places of safety) subject to the following conditions:

2 [The place or plans of safety shall not be disclosed to (person or class of persons)]*

3

. . . .

Chairman of the Children's Hearing

*Delete as appropriate

FORM 8
WARRANT UNDER SECTION 63(5) OF THE ACT FOR KEEPING A CHILD IN A PLACE OF SAFETY

Rule 27

(Place and date)

A children's hearing for (local authority area) in respect of the case of (name and address of child) and in exercise of the powers conferred on them by section 63(5) of the Act, being satisfied [that it is necessary that the child should be kept in a place of safety in order to safeguard or promote his/her welfare]* [there is reason to believe that the child may fail to comply with a requirement that under section 69(3) of the Act]* [there is reason to believe that the child may not attend at any hearing of his/her case]* grant warrant to (insert name and address and where appropriate full designation of applicant) to keep that child in (name of place or places) for a period from (date) to (date) both days inclusive (insert period not exceeding 22 days) [and for the bringing of that child, before a children's hearing at (insert time and/or date)].

[For the duration of this warrant the child should be subject to the conditions noted below]*

[The children's hearing in granting this warrant order that the place or places where the child is to reside in accordance with the warrant shall not be disclosed to (person or class of persons)]*

[CONDITIONS REFERRED TO IN THE FOREGOING WARRANT

1   (insert conditions)]*

. . . .

Chairman of the Children's Hearing

*Delete as appropriate

FORM 9

WARRANT UNDER SECTION 63(5) OF THE ACT FOR PLACING AND KEEPING A CHILD IN PLACE OF SAFETY WITH AUTHORISATION TO KEEP IN SECURE ACCOMMODATION

Rule 27

(Place and date)

A children's hearing for (local authority area), in respect of the case of (name and address of child) and in exercise of the powers conferred on them by section 63(5) of the Children (Scotland) Act 1995,

(firstly) being satisfied that [it is necessary that the child should be kept in a place of safety in order to safeguard or promote his/her* welfare]* [there is reason to believe that the child may not attend any hearing of his/her* case]* [there is reason to believe that the child may not comply with a requirement under section 69(3) of the Act]*

(secondly) being satisfied [that, having previously absconded, he/she* is likely to abscond unless kept in secure accommodation, and that if he/she* absconds it is likely that his/her* physical, mental or moral welfare will be at risk]* [that he/she* is likely to injure himself/herself* or some other person unless he/she* is kept in such accommodation]*,

grant warrant to (insert name and address and where appropriate full designation of applicant) to keep the child in (name of residential establishment providing the secure accommodation) for the period from (date) to (date) (insert period not exceeding 22 days) both days inclusive and order that during the duration of the warrant, pending the disposal of his/her case, the child shall be liable to be placed and kept in secure accommodation within the said residential establishment at such times as the person in charge of the residential establishment, with the agreement of the chief social work officer of (name of local authority), considers necessary.

[name of place or places]* (see Note below)

[For the duration of this warrant the child should be subject to the conditions noted below]* [The children's hearing in granting this warrant order that the place where the child is to reside in accordance with the warrant shall not be disclosed to (person or class of persons)]*

[CONDITIONS REFERRED TO IN THE FOREGOING WARRANT

1 (insert conditions)]*

. . . .

Chairman of the Children's Hearing

*Delete as appropriate

Note: If the residential establishment providing secure accommodation does not have an open residential facility, there will also need to be reference to some such place.

FORM 10

CONTINUATION UNDER SECTION 63(5) OF THE ACT OF A WARRANT FOR KEEPING A CHILD IN A PLACE OF SAFETY

Rule 27

(Place and date)

A children's hearing for (local authority area), in respect of the case of (name and address of child) and in exercise of the powers conferred on them by section 63(5) of the Children (Scotland) Act 1995, continues the warrant dated (insert date of warrant), a copy of which is attached, for the keeping of the child in a place of safety for a period from (date) to (date) both days inclusive (insert period not exceeding 22 days) [and for the bringing of that child before a children's hearing at (insert time and/or date)].

[The continuation of the warrant is subject to the variations]* noted below]*

[VARIATIONS REFERRED TO

1   (insert variations)]*

....

Chairman of the Children's Hearing

*Delete as appropriate

FORM 11

CONTINUATION UNDER SECTION 63(5) OF THE ACT OF A WARRANT FOR PLACING AND KEEPING A CHILD IN A PLACE OF SAFETY WITH FIRST AUTHORISATION TO KEEP THE CHILD IN SECURE ACCOMMODATION

Rule 27

(Place and date)

A children's hearing for (local authority area), in respect of the case of (name and address of child) and in exercise of the powers conferred on them by section 63(5) of the Children (Scotland) Act 1995.

(firstly) being satisfied that [it is necessary that the child shall be kept in a place of safety in order to safeguard or promote his/her* welfare]* [there is reason to believe that the child may not attend any hearing or his/her* case]* [there is reason to believe that the child may not comply with a requirement under section 69(3) of the Act]*

(secondly) being satisfied [that, having previously absconded he/she* is likely to abscond unless kept in secure accommodation, and that if he/she* absconds it is likely that his/her* physical, mental or moral welfare will be at risk]* [that he/she* is likely to injure himself/herself* or some other person unless he/she* is kept in such accommodation]*,

grant continuation, subject to the variations noted below of the warrant dated (insert date of warrant), a copy of which is attached,

Variations referred to above

1 The warrant is varied to read as a warrant to (name and address and where appropriate full designation of applicant) to keep the child in (name of residential establishment

providing secure accommodation) for the period from (date) to (date) (insert period not exceeding 22 days) both days inclusive and with an order that during the duration of the warrant pending the disposal of his/her case, the child shall be liable to be placed and kept in secure accommodation within the said residential establishment at such times as the person in charge of the residential establishment, with the agreement of the chief social work officer of (name of local authority), considers necessary.

[name of place or places]* (see Note below)

2 etc

....

Chairman of the Children's Hearing

*Delete as appropriate

Note: If the residential establishment providing secure accommodation does not have an open residential facility there will also need to be a reference to some such place.

FORM 12
WARRANT UNDER SECTION 66(1) OF THE ACT FOR KEEPING A CHILD IN A PLACE OF SAFETY

Rule 27

(Place and date)

A children's hearing for (local authority area) in respect of the case of (name and address of child), being unable to dispose of the case and in exercise of the powers conferred on them by section 63(5) of the Act, being satisfied [that it is necessary that the child should be kept in a place of safety in order to safeguard or promote his/her welfare]* [the child may not attend at any hearing of his/her case]* [there is reason to believe that the child may fail to comply with a requirement that under section 69(3) of the Act]* [there is reason to believe that the child may not attend at any hearing of his/here case]* grant warrant to (insert name and address and where appropriate full designation of applicant) to [find and keep the child in (name of place or places) for a period from (date) to (date) both days inclusive (insert period not exceeding 22 days) [and for the bringing of that child, before a children's hearing at (insert time and/or date)]*.

[For the duration of this warrant the child should be subject to the conditions noted below]*

[The children's hearing in granting this warrant order that the place or places where (the child) is to reside in accordance with the warrant shall not be disclosed to (person or class of persons)]*

[CONDITIONS REFERRED TO IN THE FOREGOING WARRANT

1 (insert conditions)]*

....

Chairman of the Children's Hearing

*Delete as appropriate

FORM 13

WARRANT UNDER SECTIONS 66(1) AND 66(6) OF THE ACT FOR PLACING AND KEEPING A CHILD IN PLACE OF SAFETY WITH AUTHORISATION TO KEEP IN SECURE ACCOMMODATION

Rule 27

(Place and date)

A children's hearing for (local authority area), in respect of the case of (name and address of child) being unable to dispose of the case and in exercise of the powers conferred on them by section 66(1) and 66(6) of the Children (Scotland) Act 1995,

(firstly) being satisfied that [it is necessary to keep the child in a place of safety in order to safeguard or promote his/her welfare]* [there is reason to believe that the child may not attend any hearing of his/her* case]* [there is reason to believe that the child may fail to comply with a requirement under section 69(3) of that Act]* and

(secondly) being satisfied [that, having previously absconded, he/she* is likely to abscond unless kept in secure accommodation, and that if he/she* absconds it is likely that his/her* physical, mental or moral welfare will be at risk]* [that he/she* is likely to injure himself/herself* or some other person unless he/she* is kept in such accommodation]*,

grant warrant to (insert name and address and where appropriate full designation of applicant) to [find and keep]* [keep]* the child in (name of residential establishment providing the secure accommodation) subject to the conditions noted below for the period from (date) to (date) both days inclusive (insert period not exceeding 22 days) and for the bringing of that child before a children's hearing at (insert time and date).

[name of place or places]* (see Note below)

[The children's hearing in granting this warrant order that the place where the child is to reside in accordance with the warrant shall not be disclosed to (person or class of person)]*

CONDITIONS REFERRED TO IN THE FOREGOING WARRANT

1 The child is liable to be placed and kept in secure accommodation in (name of residential establishment) at such times as the person in charge of the residential establishment, with the agreement of the chief social work officer of (name of local authority), considers it necessary that the child do so.

....

Chairman of the Children's Hearing

*Delete as appropriate

Note: If the residential establishment providing secure accommodation does not have an open residential facility there will also need to be a reference to some such place.

Form 14
Continuation under Section 66(5) of a Warrant of the Act for Keeping a Child in a Place of Safety

Rule 27

(Place and date)

A children's hearing for (local authority area), in respect of the case of (name and address of child), being unable to dispose of the case and in exercise of the powers conferred on them by section 66(5) of the Children (Scotland) Act 1995, being satisfied that (specify cause shown by the Principal Reporter) continue a warrant dated (insert date of warrant), a copy of which is attached, for a period from (date) to (date) both days inclusive (insert period not exceeding 22 days) and for the bringing of that child before a children's hearing at (insert time and date).

[The continuation of the warrant is subject to the variations of the warrant [as varied]* noted below]*

[VARIATIONS REFERRED TO IN THE FOREGOING WARRANT

1 (insert variations]*

....

Chairman of the Children's Hearing

*Delete as appropriate

Form 15
Continuation under Section 66(5) of the Act of a Warrant for Placing and Keeping a Child in a Place of Safety with First Authorisation to Keep in Secure Accommodation

Rule 27

(Place and date)

A children's hearing for (local authority area), in respect of the case of (name and address of child) being unable to dispose of the case, in exercise of the powers conferred on them by section 66(5) and 66(6) of the Children (Scotland) Act 1995

(firstly) being satisfied that (specify cause shown by the Principal Reporter,)

(secondly) being satisfied that the child having previously absconded, he/she* is likely to abscond unless kept in secure accommodation, and that if he/she* absconds it is likely that his/her* physical, mental or moral welfare will be at risk]* [that he/she* is likely to injure himself/herself* or some other person unless he/she* is kept in such accommodation]*,

grant continuation, subject to the variations noted below, of the warrant dated (insert date of warrant), a copy of which is attached.

[The children's hearing in granting this warrant order that the place where (name) is to reside in accordance with the warrant shall not be disclosed (person or class of persons)]*

[VARIATIONS REFERRED TO

1 The warrant is varied to read as a warrant to (name and address and where appropriate full designation of applicant) to keep the child in (name of residential establishment providing secure accommodation) for the period from (date) to (date) (insert period not exceeding 22 days) both days inclusive and with an order that during the duration of the warrant, pending disposal of his/her case, the child shall be liable to be placed and kept in secure accommodation within the said residential establishment at such times as the person in charge of the residential establishment with the agreement of the chief social work officer of (name of local authority), considers necessary.

[name of place or places]* (see Note below)

2

. . . .*

Chairman of the Children's Hearing

*Delete as appropriate

Note: If the residential establishment providing secure accommodation does not have an open residential facility there will also need to be a reference to some such place.

Form 16
Warrant under Section 69(4) of the Act for Apprehension of Child and Removal to Place of Safety

Rule 27

(Place and date)

A children's hearing for (local authority area) having considered the case of (name and address of child) continue the case and in exercise of the power conferred on them by section 69(4) of the Children (Scotland) Act 1995, being satisfied that (name of child) has failed to fulfil a requirement made under section 69(3) of the Act, grant warrant to (insert name and address and where appropriate full designation of person) to find the child for the purpose of removing him/her* (insert name of place or places of safety) and keeping the child there [and where that place or those places of safety is or are not (insert name of clinic, hospital or establishment named in section 69(3) requirement), to take him/her* from the place of safety to (insert name of clinic, hospital or other establishment) for the purpose of investigation]*

[For the duration of this warrant the child should be subject to the conditions noted below]*

[The place or places where the child is to reside shall not be disclosed to (person or class of persons)]*

[CONDITIONS REFERRED TO IN THE FOREGOING WARRANT

1 (insert conditions)]*

. . . .

Chairman of the Children's Hearing

*Delete as appropriate

Form 17

Warrant under Section 69(4) of the Act to Remove and Keep Child in Place of Safety with Authorisation to Keep in Secure Accommodation

Rule 27

(Place and date)

A children's hearing for (local authority area) having considered the case of (name and address of child) continue the case and in exercise of the power conferred on them by section 69(4) of the Children (Scotland) Act 1995, (firstly) being satisfied that the child has failed to fulfil a requirement made under section 69(3) of the Act, grant warrant to (insert name and address and where appropriate full designation of person) to find the child for the purpose of removing him/her* (insert name of place or places of safety) and keeping the child there [and where that place or those places of safety is or are not (insert name of clinic, hospital or establishment named in section 69(3) requirement), to take him/her* (insert name of clinic, hospital or other establishment) for the purpose of investigation]*

(secondly) being satisfied that, the child having previously absconded, he/she* is likely to abscond unless kept in secure accommodation, and that if he/she* absconds it is likely that his/her* physical, mental or moral welfare will be at risk]* [that he/she* is likely to injure himself/herself* or some other person unless he/she* is kept in such accommodation]*, orders that while the warrant or requirement under section 69(3) is in effect the child shall be liable to be placed in secure accommodation within (name of residential establishment providing secure accommodation)* (see Note below) at such times as the person in charge of the establishment, with the agreement of the chief social work officer of (name of local authority) considers necessary.

For the duration of this warrant the child should be subject to the conditions noted below]*

[The place or places where the child is to reside shall not be disclosed to (person or class of persons)]*

[CONDITIONS REFERRED TO IN THE FOREGOING WARRANT

1 (insert conditions)]*

. . . .

Chairman of the Children's Hearing

*Delete as appropriate

Note: If the place of safety does not provide secure accommodation there will also need to be a reference to some such secure accommodation.

Form 18

Warrant under Section 69(7) of the Act for Keeping a Child in a Place of Safety

Rule 27

(Place and date)

A children's hearing for (local authority area) having considered the case of (name and address of child) continue the case and in exercise of the powers conferred on them by section 69(7) of the Children (Scotland) Act 1995, being satisfied that [it is necessary that the child should be kept in a place of safety in the interests of safeguarding or promoting his/her* welfare]* [there is reason to believe that (name and address) may not attend the subsequent hearing of his/her* case]* grant warrant to (insert name and address and where appropriate full designation of person) for that child to be taken to and kept in (insert name of place or places of safety)]* [until the day on which the subsequent hearing of the child's case by a children's hearing begins]*

[For the duration of this warrant the child should be subject to the conditions noted below]* [The place or places of safety referred to if this warrant shall not be disclosed to (person or class of person)]*

[CONDITIONS REFERRED TO IN THE FOREGOING WARRANT

1 (insert conditions)]*

. . . .

Chairman of the Children's Hearings

*Delete as appropriate

FORM 19

WARRANT UNDER SECTION 69(7) OF THE ACT FOR PLACING AND KEEPING A CHILD IN PLACE OF SAFETY WITH AUTHORISATION TO KEEP IN SECURE ACCOMMODATION

Rule 27

(Place and date)

A children's hearing for (local authority area) having considered the case of (name and address of child) continue the case and in exercise of the powers conferred on them by section 69(4) of the Children (Scotland) Act 1995,

[being satisfied that it is necessary for the child to be kept in a place of safety in the interests of safeguarding or promoting his/her* welfare]* [there is reason to believe that the child may not attend the subsequent hearing of his/her* case]*

being satisfied [that, having previously absconded he/she* is likely to abscond unless kept in secure accommodation, and that if he/she* absconds it is likely that his/her* physical, mental or moral welfare will be at risk]* [that he/she* is likely to injure himself/herself* or some other person unless he/she* is kept in such accommodation]*

grant warrant to (insert name and address and where appropriate full designation of person) ordering the taking to and keeping of the said child in (name of residential establishment providing the secure accommodation) [for the period from (date) to (date) both days inclusive (insert period not exceeding 22 days)]* [until the day on which the subsequent hearing of the child's case by a children's hearing begins]* and order that while the warrant is in effect the child shall be liable to be placed in secure accommodation at such times as the person in charge of the residential establishment, with the agreement of the chief social work officer of (name of local authority), considers necessary.

[name of place or places]* (see Note below)

[For the duration of this warrant the child shall be subject to the conditions noted below]*

[The children's hearing in granting this warrant order that the place where (name) is to reside in accordance with the warrant shall not be disclosed to (person or class of person)]*

[CONDITIONS REFERRED TO IN THE FOREGOING WARRANT

1 (insert conditions)]*

. . . .

Chairman of the Children's Hearing

*Delete as appropriate

Note: If the residential establishment providing secure accommodation does not have an open residential facility there will also need to be a reference to some such place.

Form 20
Requirement under Section 69(3) of the Act

Rule 28

(Place and Date)

The children's hearing for (name of local authority) in respect of (name and address of child) having considered his/her case and being satisfied that, in order to complete their consideration of the case, it is necessary to have further investigation of the case, continue the case and for the purposes of the said investigation, in exercise of their powers under section 69(3) of the Act, require the child to [attend]* [reside at]* (insert name of clinic, hospital or establishment) during (insert time or period not exceeding twenty-two days).

. . . .

Chairman of the Children's Hearing

*Delete as appropriate

Form 21
Notification by Principal Reporter under Section 60(3) to Person who Implemented Child Protection Order that Conditions for the Making of the Order are No Longer Satisfied

Rule 28(2)

(Date and place)

To (name and address)

The Principal Reporter, hereby notifies you that having regard to the welfare of (name and address of child) he has decided that, [as a result of a change in the circumstances of his/her* case]* [in the light of further information relating to his/her* case having received by him]* that [the conditions of the making of a child protection order in respect of (name of child) are no longer satisfied]* or [the [term]* [condition]* [direction]* set out below is no longer appropriate]*.

[TERM, CONDITION OR DIRECTION REFERRED TO IN THE FOREGOING NOTIFI-CATION

1 (Insert term, condition or direction)]*

....

Principal Reporter
(on behalf of the Principal Reporter)

*Delete as appropriate

FORM 22
NOTIFICATION BY PRINCIPAL REPORTER UNDER SECTION 60(3) TO PERSON WHO IMPLEMENTED CHILD PROTECTION ORDER THAT CONDITIONS FOR THE MAKING OF THE ORDER ARE NO LONGER SATISFIED

Rule 28(3)

(Date and place)

To (name and address)

The Principal Reporter, hereby notifies you that having regard to the welfare of (name and address of child) has decided that, [as a result of a change in the circumstances of his/her* case]* [in the light of further information relating to his/her* case having received by him]* that [the conditions of the making of a child protection order in respect of (name of child) are no longer satisfied]* or [the [term]* [condition]* [direction]* set out below is no longer appropriate]*.

[TERM, CONDITION OR DIRECTION REFERRED TO IN THE FOREGOING NOTIFI-CATION

1 (Insert term, condition or direction)]*

....

Principal Reporter
(on behalf of the Principal Reporter)

*Delete as appropriate

FORM 23
FORM OF REPORT BY CHILDREN'S HEARING OF ADVICE UNDER SECTION 60(10) OF THE ACT FOR CONSIDERATION BY SHERIFF IN HIS DETERMINATION OF APPLICATION UNDER SECTION 60(7) OF THE ACT

Rule 28(4)

(Date and place)

To

On (date) a children's hearing for (local authority area), after considering the case of (name of child and address) and the application under section 60(7) to [set aside]* [vary]* [the child protection order]* [a direction under section 58 of the Act]* [the child protection order]* [direction]* continued under section 59(4)]* provide the advice set out below to assist the sheriff in his determination of the application.

ADVICE REFERRED TO IN THE FOREGOING ADVICE STATEMENT

1 (insert advice)

. . . .

Chairman of the Children's Hearing

*Delete as appropriate

Form 24
FORM OF REPORT BY CHILDREN'S HEARING OF ADVICE UNDER SECTION 73(13) OF THE ACT PROVIDING ADVICE FOR CONSIDERATION BY SHERIFF IN HIS DETERMINATION OF DECISION OF ADOPTION AGENCY

Rule 28(5)

(Date and place)

To

On (date) a children's hearing for (local authority area), after considering the case of (name of child and address) and the [proposed application under section 86 of the Act]* [proposed application under [section 12]* [section 18]* of the Adoption (Scotland) Act 1978]* [the proposed placing for adoption]* provide the advice set out below to assist the sheriff in his determination of the application.

ADVICE IN RELATION TO THE DECISION OF THE ADOPTION AGENCY

1 (insert advice)

. . . .

Chairman of the Children's Hearing

*Delete as appropriate

Form 25
CHILDREN (SCOTLAND) ACT 1995
CERTIFICATE OF NOTIFICATION OF CHILDREN'S HEARING TO RELEVANT PERSON

Rule 30

(to be subjoined to copy of notification)*

I,..[Principal Reporter/on behalf of Principal Reporter]* of (name of local authority) notified (name of relevant person) by

[speaking to him in person on (date), (time), (place)]*

[delivering a copy of the notification to him in person on (date), (time), (place)]* [leaving a copy of the notification for him at his [(address), (house), (business), (address of business) or (date)]

[leaving a copy of the notification for him on board (name of vessel) at (place) or (date)]*

[sending to him in [a recorded delivery/registered] letter and the post office receipt of said letter accompanies this certificate]*

....

Principal Reporter to the Children's Hearing

*Delete as appropriate

Act of Sederunt (Child Care and Maintenance Rules) 1997

SI 1997/291

*   *   *

CHAPTER 3
CHILDREN (SCOTLAND) ACT 1995

PART I
INTERPRETATION

3.1 Interpretation

(1) In this Chapter, unless the context otherwise requires—

"the Act" means the Children (Scotland) Act 1995 and expressions used in this Chapter which are also used in that Act shall have the meaning assigned to them for the purposes of Part II of the Act;

"service" includes citation, intimation or the giving of notice as required in terms of this Chapter.

(2) In this Chapter any reference, however expressed, to disputed grounds of referral shall be construed as a reference to grounds of referral which form the subject of an application under section 65(7) or (9) of the Act (application to sheriff).

PART II
GENERAL RULES

PROCEDURE IN RESPECT OF CHILDREN

3.2 Application

Rules 3.3 to 3.5 apply where by virtue of section 16(2) of the Act a child may be given an opportunity to indicate whether he wishes to express his views in relation to an application or proceedings in the circumstances stated in section 16(4)(b) and (c) of the Act.

3.3 Power to dispense with service on child

Where the sheriff is satisfied, taking account of the age and maturity of the child, that it would be inappropriate to order service on the child, he may dispense with—

(a) service on the child; and

(b) the attendance of the child at the hearing of the application.

3.4 Service on child

(1) Subject to rule 3.3 and to paragraph (2), after the issue of the first order or warrant to cite, as the case may be, the applicant shall forthwith serve a copy of the application and first order or warrant to cite on the child, together with a notice or citation in—

(a) Form 26 in respect of an application for a child assessment order under Part III of this Chapter;

(b) Form 27 in respect of an application to vary or set aside a child protection order in terms of rule 3.33;

(c) Form 28 in respect of an application for an exclusion order in terms of rules 3.34 to 3.39;

(d) Form 29 in respect of an application to vary or recall an exclusion order in terms of rule 3.40;

(e) Form 30 in respect of an application for a warrant to keep a child in a place of safety under Part VI of this Chapter; and

(f) Form 31 in respect of an application under section 65(7) or (9) of the Act made under Part VII of this Chapter.

(2) The sheriff may, on application by the applicant or of his own motion, order that a specified part of the application is not served on the child.

3.5 Procedure where child wishes to express a view

(1) Where a child has indicated his wish to express his views, the sheriff—

(a) may order such steps to be taken as he considers appropriate to ascertain the views of that child; and

(b) shall not make any order or disposal mentioned in paragraph (b) or (c) of section 16(4) of the Act unless an opportunity has been given for the views of that child to be obtained or heard.

(2) Subject to any order made by the sheriff under paragraph (1)(a) and to any other method as the sheriff in his discretion may permit, the views of the child may be conveyed—

(a) by the child orally or in writing;

(b) by an advocate or solicitor acting on behalf of the child;

(c) by any safeguarder or curator *ad litem* appointed by the court; or

(d) by any other person (either orally or in writing), provided that the sheriff is satisfied that that person is a suitable representative and is duly authorised to represent the child.

(3) Where the views of the child are conveyed orally to the sheriff, the sheriff shall record those views in writing.

(4) The sheriff may direct that any written views given by a child, or any written record of those views, shall—

(a) be sealed in an envelope marked "Views of the child - confidential";

(b) be kept in the court process without being recorded in the inventory of process;

(c) be available to a sheriff only;

(d) not be opened by any person other than a sheriff, and

(e) not form a borrowable part of the process.

3.6 Application

Rules 3.7 to 3.10 apply, as regards a safeguarder, to all applications and proceedings to which this Chapter applies except for proceedings under section 57 of the Act for a child protection order.

3.7 Appointment of safeguarder

(1) The sheriff—
(a) shall, as soon as reasonably practicable after the lodging of an application or the commencing of any proceedings, consider whether it is necessary to appoint a safeguarder in the application or proceedings; and
(b) may at that stage, or at any later stage of the application or proceedings, appoint a safeguarder.

(2) Where a safeguarder has been appointed in proceedings before the children's hearing or the sheriff in respect of related proceedings, the appointee shall, unless the sheriff on his own motion or on cause shown by a party directs otherwise, be the same person appointed as safeguarder by the children's hearing or the sheriff.

3.8 Rights, powers and duties of safeguarder on appointment

A safeguarder appointed in an application shall—
(a) have the powers and duties at common law of a curator *ad litem* in respect of the child;
(b) be entitled to receive from the Principal Reporter copies of the application, all of the productions in the proceedings and any papers which were before the children's hearing;
(c) subject to rule 3.5(1)(a), determine whether the child wishes to express his views in relation to the application and, if so, where the child so wishes transmit his views to the sheriff;
(d) make such enquiries so far as relevant to the application as he considers appropriate; and
(e) without delay, and in any event before the hearing on the application, intimate in writing to the sheriff clerk whether or not he intends to become a party to the proceedings.

3.9 Provision where safeguarder intimates his intention to become a party to the proceedings

(1) A safeguarder may appear personally in the proceedings or instruct an advocate or solicitor to appear on his behalf.

(2) Where an advocate or a solicitor is appointed to act as a safeguarder, he shall not act also as advocate or solicitor for the child in the proceedings.

3.10 Provision where safeguarder intimates his intention not to become a party to the proceedings

(1) Where a safeguarder intimates that he does not intend to become a party to the proceedings, he shall at the same time report in writing to the sheriff on the extent of his enquiries and his conclusion as to the interests of the child in the proceedings.

(2) The sheriff clerk shall intimate to a safeguarder who has not become a party to the proceedings all interlocutors subsequent to his appointment.

(3) A safeguarder who has intimated his intention not to become a party to the proceedings may subsequently seek leave so to become.

FIXING OF FIRST HEARING

3.11 Assigning of diet for hearing

Except where otherwise provided in these Rules, after the lodging of any application the sheriff clerk shall forthwith assign a diet for the hearing of the application and shall issue a first order or a warrant to cite in Form 32 or Form 33, as the case may be.

SERVICE, CITATION AND NOTICE

3.12 Service and notice to persons named in application

(1) Subject to the provisions of rule 3.4 (service on child), after the issue of the first order or warrant to cite, as the case may be, the applicant shall forthwith give notice of the application by serving a copy of the application and the first order or warrant to cite together with a notice or citation, as the case may be, on the persons named in the application or, as the case may be, a person who should receive notice of the application (subject to paragraph (2)) in—
   (a) Form 34 in respect of an application for a child assessment order under Part III of this Chapter;
   (b) Form 35 in respect of an application to vary or set aside a child protection order in terms of rule 3.33;
   (c) Form 36 in respect of an application for an exclusion order in terms of rules 3.34 to 3.39;
   (d) Form 37 in respect of an application to vary or recall an exclusion order in terms of rule 3.40;
   (e) Form 38 in respect of an application for a warrant to keep a child in a place of safety under Part VI of this Chapter; and
   (f) Form 39 in respect of an application under section 65(7) or (9) of the Act made under Part VII of this Chapter.

(2) Notice of the application shall be given in the case of a safeguarder by serving a copy of the application and the first order or warrant to cite together with notice in Form 40.

3.13 Period of notice

(1) Subject to paragraph (2), citation or notice authorised or required by this Chapter shall be made not later than forty-eight hours, or in the case of postal citation seventy-two hours, before the date of the diet to which the citation or notice relates.

(2) Paragraph (1) shall not apply in relation to citation or notice of the following applications or proceedings—
   (a) an appeal against a decision to issue a warrant for the detention of a child;
   (b) a hearing in respect of an exclusion order where an interim order has been granted in terms of rule 3.36;

(c) a hearing on an application to vary or set aside a child protection order or any direction given with the order; or
(d) an application for a child assessment order,
in which cases the period of notice and the method of giving notice shall be as directed by the sheriff.

3.14 Citation of witnesses, parties and persons having an interest

(1) The following shall be warrants for citation of witnesses, parties and havers:—
(a) the warrant for the first diet in an application;
(b) an interlocutor fixing a diet for the continued hearing of an application; and
(c) an interlocutor assigning a diet for a hearing of an appeal or application.

(2) In an application or an appeal, witnesses or havers may be cited in Form 41.

(3) The certificate of execution of citation of witnesses and havers shall be in Form 42.

3.15 Modes of service

(1) Service authorised or required by this Chapter shall be made by any mode specified in paragraphs (2) and (3).

(2) It shall be deemed legal service to or on any person if such service is—
(a) delivered to him personally;
(b) left for him at his dwelling-house or place of business with some person resident or employed therein;
(c) where it cannot be delivered to him personally and he has no known dwelling-house or place of business, left for him at any other place at which he may at the time be resident;
(d) where he is the master of, or a seaman or other person employed in, a vessel, left with a person on board or connected with the vessel;
(e) sent by first class recorded delivery post, or the nearest equivalent which the available postal service permits, to his dwelling-house or place of business, or if he has no known dwelling-house or place of business to any other place in which he may at the time be resident;
(f) where the person has the facility to receive facsimile or other electronic transmission, by such facsimile or other electronic transmission; or
(g) where the person has a numbered box at a document exchange, given by leaving at the document exchange.

(3) Where service requires to be made and there is not sufficient time to employ any of the methods specified in paragraph (2), service shall be effected orally or in such other manner as the sheriff directs.

3.16 Persons who may effect service

(1) Subject to paragraphs (2) and (3), service shall be effected—
(a) in the case of any of the modes specified in rule 3.15(2), by a sheriff officer;
(b) in the case of any of the modes specified in rule 3.15(2)(e) or (f), by a solicitor, the sheriff clerk, the Principal Reporter or an officer of the local authority; or
(c) in the case of any mode specified by the sheriff in terms of rule 3.15(3), by such person as the sheriff directs.

(2) In relation to the citation of witnesses, parties and havers in terms of rule 3.14 or service of any application, "officer of the local authority" in paragraph (1)(b)

includes any officer of a local authority authorised to conduct proceedings under these Rules in terms of rule 3.21 (representation).

(3) The sheriff clerk shall cite the Principal Reporter and the authors or compilers of any reports or statements whom the sheriff may wish to examine under section 51(3) of the Act (appeal against decision of children's hearing or sheriff).

3.17 Production of certificates of execution of service

(1) The production before the sheriff of—
(a) a certificate of execution of service in Form 43; and
(b) additionally in the case of postal service, the post office receipt of the registered or recorded delivery letter,
shall be sufficient evidence that service was duly made.

(2) It shall be sufficient to lodge the execution of service at the hearing, unless the sheriff otherwise directs or on cause shown.

3.18 Power to dispense with service

Subject to rule 3.3, the sheriff may, on cause shown, dispense with service on any person named.

MISCELLANEOUS

3.19 Expenses

No expenses shall be awarded in any proceedings to which this Chapter applies.

3.20 Record of proceedings

Proceedings under this Chapter shall be conducted summarily.

3.21 Representation

(1) In any proceedings any party may be represented by an advocate or a solicitor or, subject to paragraphs (2) and (3), other representative authorised by the party.

(2) Such other representative must throughout the proceedings satisfy the sheriff that he is a suitable person to represent the party and that he is authorised to do so.

(3) Such other representative may in representing a party do all such things for the preparation and conduct of the proceedings as may be done by an individual on his own behalf.

3.22 Applications for evidence of children by television link

(1) This rule and rule 3.23 shall apply to any proceedings in the sheriff court under Part II of the Act.

(2) An application to the court for the giving of evidence by a child by means of a live television link shall be made in Form 44.

(3) An application referred to in paragraph (2) shall be lodged with the sheriff clerk not later than 14 days before the hearing at which the child is to give evidence (except on special cause shown).

(4) The sheriff shall—
(a) order intimation of the application to be made to the other party or parties to the proceedings; and
(b) hear the application on the earliest practicable date.

3.23 Orders and transfer of cases

(1) The sheriff who hears an application under rule 3.22 shall, after hearing the parties and allowing such further procedure as the sheriff thinks fit, make an order granting or refusing the application.

(2) Where the sheriff grants the application, he may—
(a) transfer the case to be heard in whole; or
(b) hear the case himself or such part of it as he shall determine,
in another sheriff court in the same sheriffdom.

3.24 Exclusion of certain enactments

The enactments specified in column (1) of Schedule 3 to this Act of Sederunt (being enactments relating to matters with respect to which this Chapter is made) shall not, to the extent specified in column (3) of that Schedule, apply to an application or appeal.

Part III
Child Assessment Orders

3.25 Interpretation

In this Part, "application" means an application for a child assessment order in terms of section 55 of the Act.

3.26 Form of application

An application shall be made in Form 45.

3.27 Orders

(1) After hearing parties and allowing such further procedure as he thinks fit, the sheriff shall make an order granting or refusing the application.

(2) Where an order is made granting the application, that order shall be made in Form 46 and shall contain the information specified therein.

(3) Where the sheriff, in terms of section 55(2) of the Act, has decided to make a child protection order pursuant to an application, rules 3.31 to 3.33 shall apply.

3.28 Intimation

The local authority shall intimate the grant or refusal of an application to such persons, if any, as the sheriff directs.

PART IV

CHILD PROTECTION ORDERS

3.29 Interpretation

In this Part, "application" means, except in rule 3.33, an application for a child protection order in terms of section 57 of the Act.

3.30 Form of application

An application made by a local authority shall be in Form 47 and an application made by any other person shall be in Form 48.

3.31 Determination of application

(1) On receipt of an application, the sheriff, having considered the grounds of the application and the supporting evidence, shall forthwith grant or refuse it.

(2) Where an order is granted, it shall be in Form 49 and it shall contain any directions made under section 58 of the Act.

3.32 Intimation of making of order

Where an order is granted, the applicant shall forthwith serve a copy of the order on—
(a) the child, along with a notice in Form 50;
(b) any other person named in the application, along with a notice in Form 51.

3.33 Application to vary or set aside a child protection order

(1) An application under section 60(7) of the Act for the variation or setting aside of a child protection order or a direction given under section 58 of the Act or such an order or direction continued (whether with or without variation) under section 59(4) of the Act shall be made in Form 52.

(2) A person applying under section 60(7) of the Act for the variation or setting aside of a child protection order shall require to lodge with his application a copy of that order.

(3) Without prejudice to rule 3.5, any person on whom service is made may appear or be represented at the hearing of the application.

(4) Subject to section 60(11) of the Act, the sheriff, after hearing parties and allowing such further procedure as he thinks fit, shall grant or refuse the application.

(5) Where an order is made granting the application for variation, that order shall be in Form 53.

(6) Where the sheriff so directs, intimation of the granting or refusing of an application shall be given by the applicant to such person as the sheriff shall direct.

PART V
EXCLUSION ORDERS

3.34 Interpretation

In this Part, "application" means, except in rule 3.40, an application by a local authority for an exclusion order in terms of sections 76 to 80 of the Act; and "ancillary order" and "interim order" shall be construed accordingly.

3.35 Form of application

An application shall be made in Form 54.

3.36 Hearing following interim order

Where an interim order is granted under subsection (4) of section 76 of the Act, the hearing under subsection (5) of that section shall take place not later than 3 working days after the granting of the interim order.

3.37 Orders

(1) After hearing parties and allowing such further procedure as he thinks fit, the sheriff shall make an order granting or refusing the application.

(2) Where the sheriff grants an order in terms of paragraph (1), it shall be in Form 55 and shall be served forthwith by the local authority on—
(a) the named person;
(b) the appropriate person;
(c) the relevant child; and
(d) the Principal Reporter.

3.38 Certificates of delivery of documents to chief constable

(1) After the local authority have complied with section 78(4) of the Act, they shall forthwith lodge in process a certificate of delivery in Form 56.

(2) After a person has complied with section 78(5) of the Act, he shall lodge in process a certificate of delivery in Form 56.

3.39 Power to make child protection order in an application for an exclusion order

Where the sheriff, in terms of 76(8) of the Act, has decided to make a child protection order pursuant to an application, rules 3.31 to 3.33 shall apply.

3.40 Variation or recall of an exclusion order

(1) Any application for the variation or recall of an exclusion order and any warrant, interdict, order or direction granted or made under section 77 of the Act shall be in Form 57.

(2) After hearing parties and allowing such further procedure as he thinks fit, the sheriff shall make an order granting or refusing the application.

(3) Where an order is made granting the application for variation, that order shall be in Form 58.

(4) Intimation of the granting or refusing of an application shall be given by the applicant to such persons as the sheriff shall direct.

PART VI

WARRANT FOR FURTHER DETENTION OF A CHILD

3.41 Interpretation

In this Part, "application" means an application for a warrant to keep a child in a place of safety in terms of section 67 of the Act.

3.42 Form of application

An application shall be made in Form 59.

3.43 Orders

After hearing parties and allowing such further procedure as he thinks fit, the sheriff shall make an order granting or refusing the application.

PART VII

PROCEDURE IN APPLICATIONS UNDER SECTION 65(7) OR (9) OF THE ACT

3.44 Interpretation

In this Part, "application" means an application under section 65(7) or (9) of the Act (establishment of grounds for referral).

3.45 Lodging of application, etc

(1) Within a period of seven days beginning with the date on which the Principal Reporter was directed in terms of section 65 of the Act to make application to the sheriff, he shall lodge with the sheriff clerk an application in Form 60.

(2) Where a safeguarder has been appointed by the chairman at the children's hearing, the Principal Reporter shall intimate such appointment to the sheriff clerk and shall lodge along with the application any report made by the safeguarder.

3.46 Abandonment of application

(1) At any stage of the proceedings before the application is determined the Principal Reporter may abandon the application, either in whole or in part, by lodging a minute to that effect or by motion at the hearing.

(2) The Principal Reporter shall intimate such abandonment to—
(a) the child, except where service on the child has been dispensed with in terms of rule 3.3;
(b) any relevant person whose whereabouts are known to the Principal Reporter; and
(c) any safeguarder appointed by the sheriff.

(3) In the event of abandonment in whole in terms of paragraph (1), the sheriff shall dismiss the application and discharge the referral.

3.47 Hearing of evidence

(1) In the case of any condition mentioned in section 52(2) of the Act (conditions relative to compulsory measures of supervision), the sheriff shall, in relation to any ground of referral which is in dispute, hear evidence tendered by or on behalf of the Principal Reporter, including evidence given pursuant to an application granted under rule 3.23.

(2) At the close of the evidence led by the Principal Reporter in a case where it is disputed that the condition mentioned in paragraph (i) of section 52(2) of the Act is satisfied, the sheriff shall consider whether sufficient evidence has been led to establish that condition is satisfied and shall give all the parties an opportunity to be heard on the question of sufficiency of evidence.

(3) Where the sheriff is not satisfied that sufficient evidence has been led as mentioned in paragraph (2), he shall make a finding to that effect.

(4) Where the sheriff is satisfied that sufficient evidence has been led as mentioned in paragraph (2), the child, the relevant person and any safeguarder appointed may give evidence and call witnesses with regard to the condition in question.

(5) Where the nature of the case or of any evidence to be given is such that the sheriff is satisfied that it is in the interests of the child that he should not be present at any stage of the proceedings, the sheriff may exclude the child from the hearing during that stage and in that event any safeguarder appointed and the relevant person or representative of the child shall be permitted to remain during the absence of the child.

(6) Subject to paragraph (7), the sheriff may exclude any person, including the relevant person, while any child is giving evidence if the sheriff is satisfied that this is necessary in the interests of the child and that—
(a) he must do so in order to obtain the evidence of the child; or
(b) the presence of the person or persons in question is causing, or is likely to cause, significant distress to the child.

(7) Where the relevant person is not legally represented at the hearing and has been excluded under paragraph (6), the sheriff shall inform that relevant person of the substance of any evidence given by the child and shall give that relevant person an opportunity to respond by leading evidence or otherwise.

(8) Where evidence in a referral has been heard in part and a safeguarder thereafter becomes a party to proceedings, the sheriff may order the evidence to be reheard in whole or in part.

3.48 Amendment of grounds for referral

The sheriff may at any time, on the application of any party or of his own motion, allow amendment of any statement supporting the conditions of the grounds for referral.

3.49 Adjournment for inquiry, etc

Subject to the provisions of section 68(2) of the Act (applications to be heard within twenty-eight days of lodging), the sheriff on the motion of any party or on his own motion may continue the hearing in order to allow time for further inquiry into any application, in consequence of the amendment of any statement under rule 3.48, or for any other necessary cause, for such reasonable time as he may in the circumstances consider necessary.

3.50 Power of sheriff in making findings as to offences

Where in a ground of referral it is alleged that an offence has been committed by or against any child, the sheriff may find that any other offence established by the facts has been committed.

3.51 Decision of sheriff

(1) Subject to rule 3.47(3), the sheriff shall give his decision orally at the conclusion of the hearing.

(2) The sheriff clerk shall forthwith send a copy of the interlocutor containing that decision to—
(a) the child, except where service on the child has been dispensed with in terms of rule 3.3;
(b) any relevant person whose whereabouts are known;
(c) any safeguarder appointed by the sheriff; and
(d) the Principal Reporter.

(3) The sheriff may, when giving his decision in terms of paragraph (1) or within 7 days thereafter, issue a note of the reasons for his decision and the sheriff clerk shall forthwith send a copy of such a note to the persons referred to in paragraph (2).

3.52 Signature of warrants

Warrants, other than warrants granted by the sheriff under section 68(6) of the Act where the child has failed to attend a children's hearing, may be signed by the sheriff clerk but any warrant may, and a warrant under the said section 68(6) shall, be signed by the sheriff.

PART VIII
PROCEDURE IN APPEALS UNDER SECTION 51(1) OF THE ACT

3.53 Form of appeal

(1) An appeal to the sheriff under section 51(1) of the Act (appeal against decision of children's hearing) shall be in Form 61, 62 or 63 whichever is appropriate and shall be lodged with the sheriff clerk.

(2) Subject to paragraph (3), the appeal shall be signed by the appellant or his representative.

(3) An appeal by a child may be signed on his behalf by any safeguarder appointed by the children's hearing.

3.54 Appointment and intimation of first diet

(1) On the lodging of the appeal, the sheriff clerk shall forthwith assign a date for the hearing and shall at the same time intimate to the appellant or his representative and, together with a copy of the appeal, to—

(a) the Principal Reporter;

(b) subject to the provisions of paragraph (4), the child (if not the appellant);

(c) the relevant person (if not the appellant);

(d) any safeguarder appointed for the purposes of the appeal by the sheriff or appointed by the chairman of the children's hearing; and

(e) any other person the sheriff thinks necessary.

(2) The sheriff clerk shall endorse on the appeal a certificate of execution of intimation under paragraph (1).

(3) Intimation to a child in terms of paragraph (1)(b) shall be in Form 64.

(4) The sheriff may dispense with intimation to a child in terms of paragraph (1)(b) where he considers that such dispensation is appropriate.

(5) The date assigned for the hearing under paragraph (1) shall be no later than 28 days after the lodging of the appeal.

3.55 Answers

(1) Except in an appeal under section 51(8) of the Act (appeal against warrant by children's hearing), if any person on whom service of the appeal has been made wishes to lodge answers to the appeal he shall do so not later than 7 days before the diet fixed for the hearing of the appeal.

(2) Any person who has lodged answers shall forthwith intimate a copy thereof to any other person on whom service has been made under rule 3.54(1).

3.56 Procedure at hearing of appeal

(1) Before proceeding in accordance with section 51(3) of the Act to examine the Principal Reporter and the authors or compilers of any reports or statements, the sheriff shall hear the appellant or his representative and any party to the appeal.

(2) On receipt of a further report called for under section 51(3)(c) of the Act, the sheriff shall direct the Principal Reporter to send a copy of the report to every party the appeal.

(3) At any appeal the sheriff may hear evidence—

(a) where a ground of the appeal is an alleged irregularity in the conduct of a hearing, as to that irregularity;

(b) in any other circumstances where he considers it appropriate to do so.

(4) Where the nature of the appeal or of any evidence is such that the sheriff is satisfied that it is in the interests of the child that he should not be present at any stage of the appeal, the sheriff may exclude the child from the hearing during that stage and, in that event, any safeguarder appointed and the relevant person or representative of the child shall be permitted to remain during the absence of the child.

(5) Subject to paragraph (6), the sheriff may exclude the relevant person, or that person and any representative of his, or any such representative from any part or parts of the hearing for so long as he considers it is necessary in the interests of any child, where he is satisfied that—

(a) he must do so in order to obtain the views of the child in relation to the hearing; or

(b) the presence of the person or persons in question is causing, or is likely to cause, significant distress to the child.

(6) Where the relevant person has been excluded under paragraph (5) the sheriff shall, after that exclusion has ended, explain to him the substance of what has taken place in his absence and shall give him an opportunity to respond to any evidence given by the child by leading evidence or otherwise.

(7) Where an appeal has been heard in part and a safeguarder thereafter becomes a party to the appeal, the sheriff may order the hearing of the appeal to commence of new.

3.57 Adjournment of appeals

The sheriff may, on the motion of any party or on his own motion, adjourn the hearing of the appeal for such reasonable time and for such purpose as may in the circumstances be appropriate.

3.58 Decision of sheriff in appeals

(1) The sheriff shall give his decision orally either at the conclusion of the appeal or on such day as he shall appoint.

(2) The sheriff may issue a note of the reasons for his decision, and shall require to do so where he decides to follow the course of action provided for in sub-paragraph (i) or (iii) of section 51(5)(c) of the Act.

(3) Any note in terms of paragraph (2) shall be issued at the time the sheriff gives his decision or within 7 days thereafter.

(4) The sheriff clerk shall forthwith send a copy of the interlocutor containing the decision of the sheriff, and where appropriate of the note referred to in paragraph (2), to the Principal Reporter, to the appellant (and to the child or the relevant person, if not the appellant) and to any safeguarder appointed by the sheriff, and shall also return to the Principal Reporter any documents lodged by virtue of section 51(2) or (3) of the Act.

Part IX

Procedure in Appeals under Section 51(11) of the Act

3.59 Appeals

(1) [An application to the sheriff to state a case for the purposes of an appeal under section 51(11)(a) of the Act shall specify the point of law upon which the appeal is to proceed or the irregularity in the conduct of the case is concerned, as the case may be.]

(2) The appellant shall, at the same time as lodging a [the application for a stated case], intimate the lodging of an appeal from the decision of the sheriff—
(a) in the case of an appeal under section 51(1) of the Act, to the parties referred to in rule 3.58(4);
(b) in the case of an application made under section 65(7) or (9) of the Act, to the parties referred to in rule 3.51(2); and
(c) in the case of an application made under section 85(1) of the Act (review of establishment of grounds of referral), to the parties referred to in rule 3.62.

(3) The sheriff shall, within 14 days of the lodging of a [the application for a stated case], issue a draft stated case—
(a) containing findings in fact and law or, where appropriate, a narrative of the proceedings before him;
(b) containing appropriate questions of law or setting out the irregularity concerned; and
(c) containing a note stating the reasons for his decisions in law,
and the sheriff clerk shall send a copy of the draft stated case to the appellant and to parties referred to in paragraph (2).

(4) Within 7 days of the issue of the draft stated case—
(a) the appellant or a party referred to in paragraph (2) may lodge with the sheriff clerk a note of any adjustments which he seeks to make;
(b) the appellant or such a party may state any point of law which he wishes to raise in the appeal; and
(c) the note of adjustment and, where appropriate, point of law shall be intimated to the appellant and the other such parties.

(5) The sheriff may, on the motion of the appellant or a party referred to in paragraph (2) or of his own accord, and shall where he proposes to reject any proposed adjustment, allow a hearing on adjustments and may provide for such further procedure under this rule prior to the hearing of the appeal as he thinks fit.

(6) The sheriff shall, within 14 days after—
(a) the latest date on which a note of adjustments has been or may be lodged; or
(b) where there has been a hearing on adjustments, that hearing,
and after considering such note and any representations made to him at the hearing, state and sign the case.

(7) The stated case signed by the sheriff shall include—
(a) questions of law, framed by him, arising from the points of law stated by the parties and such other questions of law as he may consider appropriate;
(b) any adjustments, proposed under paragraph (4), which are rejected by him;
(c) a note of the irregularity in the conduct of the case averred by the parties and any questions of law or other issue which he considers arise therefrom,
as the case may be.

(8) After the sheriff has signed the stated case, the sheriff clerk shall—
(a) place before the sheriff principal all documents and productions in the appeal together with the stated case; and
(b) send to the appellant and the parties referred to in paragraph (2) a copy of the stated case together with a written note of the date, time and place of the hearing of the appeal.

(9) In the hearing of an appeal, a party referred to in paragraph (2) shall not be allowed to raise questions of law or irregularities in the conduct of the case of which notice has not been given except on cause shown and subject to such conditions as the sheriff principal may consider appropriate.

(10) The sheriff may, on an application by any party or of his own motion, reduce any of the periods mentioned in paragraph (3), (4) or (6) to such period or periods as he considers reasonable.

(11) Where the sheriff is temporarily absent from duty for any reason, the sheriff principal may extend any period specified in paragraph (3) or (6) for such period or periods as he considers reasonable.

Notes to r 3.59

Para (1): substituted by Act of Sederunt (Child Care and Maintenance Rules)(Amendment No 2) 1998, SI 1998/2130, para 2(a).

Paras (2), (3): words in brackets substituted by Act of Sederunt (Child Care and Maintenance Rules)(Amendment No 2) 1998, SI 1998/2130, para 2(b).

3.60 Lodging of reports and statements with sheriff

Where, in an appeal—

(a) it appears to the sheriff that any report or statement lodged under section 51(2) or (3) of the Act is relevant to any issue which is likely to arise in the stated case; and

(b) the report or statement has been returned to the Principal Reporter,

the sheriff may require the Principal Reporter to lodge the report or statement with the sheriff clerk.

3.61 Hearing

(1) The sheriff principal, on hearing the appeal, may either pronounce his decision or reserve judgement.

(2) Where judgement is so reserved, the sheriff principal shall within 28 days give his decision in writing which shall be intimated by the sheriff clerk to the parties.

PART X

APPLICATION FOR REVIEW OF ESTABLISHMENT OF GROUNDS OF REFERRAL—NEW EVIDENCE

3.62 Application

An application under section 85 of the Act for a review of a finding made in terms of section 68(10) of the Act (finding that grounds for referral established) shall contain—

(a) the name and address of the applicant and his representative (if any);

(b) the name and address of the Principal Reporter;

(c) the name and address of the safeguarder (if any);

(d) the name and address of any other party to the application;

(e) the date and finding made and the name of the sheriff who made the finding;

(f) the grounds for the making of the application;

(g) specification of the nature of evidence in terms of section 85(3) of the Act not considered by the sheriff who made the finding;

(h) the explanation for the failure to lead such evidence on the original application; and

(i) any reports, affidavits and productions upon which the applicant intends to rely.

3.63 Hearing on application

(1) After the lodging of the application in terms of rule 3.62, the sheriff clerk shall assign a diet for a hearing of the application and shall issue a warrant to cite in Form 65 which shall require the Principal Reporter to lodge answers if so advised within such time as the sheriff shall appoint.

(2) Subject to the provisions of rule 3.4 (service on child), after the issue of the warrant to cite, the applicant shall forthwith give notice of the application by serving a copy and the warrant on the persons named in rule 3.62.

(3) After hearing parties and allowing such further procedure as he thinks fits, the sheriff shall, if satisfied in terms of section 85(6) of the Act, consider the evidence and may fix a further hearing for that purpose.

3.64 Hearing to consider the evidence

(1) After hearing parties on the evidence and allowing such further procedure as the sheriff thinks fit, he shall make an order as appropriate in terms of section 85(6) and (7) of the Act.

(2) The provisions of rule 3.51 shall apply to any order made under paragraph (1).

*   *   *

Children's Hearings (Transmission of Information etc) (Scotland) Regulations 1996

SI 1996/3260

The Secretary of State, in exercise of the powers conferred on him by sections 17(1), 40(3), 42(1) and 74 of the Children (Scotland) Act 1995 and of all other powers enabling him in that behalf, and after consulting the Council on Tribunals, hereby makes the following Regulations:—

1 Citation and commencement

These Regulations may be cited as the Children's Hearings (Transmission of Information etc) (Scotland) Regulations 1996 and shall come into force on 1st April 1997.

2 Interpretation

In these Regulations unless the context otherwise requires—
"the Act" means the Children (Scotland) Act 1995;
"the Children's Hearings Rules" means the Children's Hearings (Scotland) Rules 1996;
"children's hearing" is a children's hearing as defined in section 39(3) of the Act;
"child" has the meaning given to that term by section 93(2)(b) of the Act;
"compulsory measures of supervision" has the meaning given to that term by section 93(1) of the Act;
"place of safety" has the meaning given to that term by section 93(1) of the Act;
"Principal Reporter" has the meaning given to that term by section 93(1) of the Act;
"relevant local authority" has the meaning given to that term by section 93(1) of the Act;
"relevant person" has the meaning given to that term by section 93(2)(b) of the Act;
"residential establishment" has the meaning given to that term by section 93(1) of the Act;
"responsible for" means any person who, by virtue of a supervision requirement, has or is to have control over the child;
"supervision requirement" has the meaning given to that term by section 70(1) of the Act.

3 Transmission by relevant local authority of information on child subject to supervision requirement

(1) Where—
(a) in any case a children's hearing have made, continued or varied or inserted a requirement in a supervision requirement in respect of a child; and

(b) a person other than the relevant local authority or a relevant person in relation to the child is responsible for a child under that requirement; and

(c) it appears to the relevant local authority that any report on the child and his social background put to the children's hearing for their consideration of the case would assist that person in the care and supervision of the child,

the relevant local authority shall, as soon as reasonably practicable after they receive notice under rule 21 of the Children's Hearings Rules of the making, continuation or variation or insertion of a requirement in the requirement, give a copy of that report to that person.

(2) Where at any time while a supervision requirement is in force in respect of a child it appears to the relevant local authority that any information they have about the child or his circumstances is relevant to the care of the child, they shall make that information available to any person who is responsible for the care of the child in terms of the supervision requirement.

4 Temporary accommodation of child subject to supervision requirement

(1) Where—

(a) a children's hearing have made, continued or varied or inserted a requirement in a supervision requirement; and

(b) a child is required to reside in a residential establishment or other place specified in the requirement; but

(c) the relevant local authority are unable to make immediate arrangements for his reception in that establishment or place,

the relevant local authority may arrange for the child to be temporarily accommodated in some suitable place, other than that specified in the requirement, for any period not exceeding 22 days commencing on the date of the making, continuation or variation or insertion of a requirement in the requirement.

(2) If it appears to the relevant local authority that they will be unable to make the arrangements mentioned in paragraph (1)(c) above before the expiry of the period of 22 days specified, the authority shall, before that period has expired, refer the case of the child to the Principal Reporter under section 73(4) of the Act on the ground that the supervision requirement ought to be reviewed.

(3) Where the relevant local authority refer the case of a child to the Principal Reporter under paragraph (2) above—

(a) the Principal Reporter shall under section 73(8) of the Act arrange for a children's hearing to review the supervision requirement as soon as is reasonably practicable and in any event within seven days of the date of receipt of the reference by the authority; and

(b) where the date of the sitting of the children's hearing arranged by virtue of sub-paragraph (a) above occurs after the expiry of the period of 22 days mentioned in paragraph (1) above, that period shall be deemed to extend to the date on which the children's hearing sits.

5 Conveyance by the relevant local authority of a child to a residential establishment etc

Whenever it is necessary to convey a child—

(a) to a residential establishment or other place in which he is required to reside by virtue of a supervision requirement;

(b) to any place to which he falls to be taken under subsection (1) or (5) of section 82 (recovery of certain fugitive children) of the Act; or

(c) to any person to whom he falls to be returned under subsection (3) of that
      section,
it shall be the duty of the relevant local authority to ensure that the child is
conveyed to that establishment or place or to that person.

The Emergency Child Protection Measures (Scotland) Regulations 1996

SI 1996/3258

The Secretary of State, in exercise of the powers conferred on him by section 62 of the Children (Scotland) Act 1995, and of all other powers enabling him in that behalf, hereby makes the following regulations:

1 Citation and commencement

These Regulations may be cited as the Emergency Child Protection Measures (Scotland) Regulations 1996 and shall come into force on 1st April 1997.

2 Interpretation

In these Regulations, unless the context otherwise requires—
"the Act" means the Children (Scotland) Act 1995;
"applicant" means the person or the local authority who applied to a justice of the peace for an authorisation under subsection (1) or, as the case may be, subsection (2), of section 61 of the Act;
"place of safety" has the meaning given to that term in section 93(1) of the Act;
"Principal Reporter" has the meaning given to that term in section 93(1) of the Act; and
"relevant person" in relation to a child has the meaning given to that term in section 93(2)(b) of the Act.

3 Duties of constable where child removed to place of safety

As soon as reasonably practicable after a child has been removed by a constable to a place of safety under section 61(5) of the Act, a constable shall, subject to regulation 5 below, take such steps as are reasonably practicable to inform the following persons of the matters specified in regulation 4 below:—
(a) any relevant person in relation to the child;
(b) any person, other than a relevant person, with whom the child was residing immediately before being removed to the place of safety;
(c) the local authority for the area in which the place of safety to which the child was removed is situated;
(d) where not falling within paragraph (c) above, the local authority for the area in which the child is ordinarily resident;
(e) the local authority for the area in which the child was residing immediately before being removed to a place of safety (where they are not the authority under (c) or (d) of this regulation); and
(f) the Principal Reporter.

4 The following matters are specified as matters on which the persons mentioned in regulation 3 above are to be informed:—
(a) the removal of the child by a constable to a place of safety;
(b) the place of safety at which the child is being, or is to be, kept;

(c) the reasons for the removal of the child to a place of safety; and

(d) any other steps which a constable has taken or is taking to safeguard the welfare of the child while in a place of safety.

5 Where a constable is informing the persons mentioned in paragraphs (a) and (b) of regulation 3 above, he may, where he considers it necessary to do so in order to safeguard the welfare of the child, withhold from those persons any of the information specified in regulation 4(b) and (d) above.

6 Where a child has been removed to a place of safety by a constable under section 61(5) of the Act, a constable keeping him in a place of safety shall, subject to subsections (6) to (8) of that section, continue to so keep him only so long as he has reasonable cause to believe that—

(a) the conditions for the making of a child protection order laid down in section 57(1) of the Act are satisfied; and

(b) it is necessary to keep the child in a place of safety in order to protect him from significant harm (or further such harm).

7 Duties where authorisation granted by justice of the peace to protect child

Where an authorisation is granted by a justice of the peace under subsection (1) or (2) of section 61 of the Act, the applicant shall implement the authorisation as soon as reasonably practicable.

8 Where an authorisation has been granted under section 61 of the Act, as soon as reasonably practicable after steps have been taken to prevent any person from removing the child from a place where he is then being accommodated, or the child has been removed to a place of safety, the applicant shall, subject to regulation 10 below, take such steps as are reasonably practicable to inform the following persons of the matters specified in regulation 9 below—

(a) any relevant person in relation to the child;

(b) any person, other than a relevant person, with whom the child was residing immediately before the grant of the authorisation;

(c) where not the applicant, the local authority for the area in which the place of safety to which the child was or is to be removed is situated;

(d) where not falling within paragraph (c) above and where not the applicant, the local authority for the area in which the child is ordinarily resident;

(e) where not the applicant, the local authority for the area in which the child was residing immediately before the grant of the authorisation (where they are not the authority under (c) or (d) of this regulation); and

(f) the Principal Reporter.

9 The following matters are specified as matters on which the persons mentioned in regulation 8 above are to be informed:—

(a) the grant of the authorisation and the steps taken to implement it;

(b) the place of safety at which the child is being or is to be kept or, as the case may be, the place at which the child is being accommodated;

(c) the reasons for the grant of the authorisation; and

(d) any other steps which the applicant has taken or is taking to safeguard the welfare of the child while in a place of safety.

10 Where an applicant is informing the persons specified in paragraphs (a) and (b) of regulation 8 above, he may, where he considers it necessary to do so in order to safeguard the welfare of the child, withhold from any of those persons any of the information specified in regulation 9(b) and (d) above.

11 Notice where authorisation ceases to have effect

Where an authorisation granted under subsection (1) or (2) of section 61 of the Act ceases to have effect by virtue of section 61(4)(a) of the Act (authorisation ceasing to have effect where not implemented within 12 hours of being made), the applicant shall immediately notify the justice of the peace who granted the authorisation and as soon as reasonably practicable give notice of this to the persons specified in regulation 8 above.

12 Duties where child subject to emergency protection measures

In regulations 13 to 16 below—
"emergency protection measures" in relation to a child means—
  (a) further to the grant of an authorisation by a justice of the peace under subsection (1) or (2) of section 61 of the Act, the prevention of the removal of the child by any person from a place where he is then being accommodated or, as the case may be, the removal of the child to a place of safety and keeping him there until the expiry of the authorisation; and
  (b) the removal of a child to a place of safety by a constable under section 61(5) of the Act, and keeping him there;
"specified person" means—
  (a) where an authorisation has been granted by a justice of the peace under subsection (1) or (2) of section 61 of the Act, the applicant for such authorisation; and
  (b) where a child has been removed to a place of safety by a constable under section 61(5) of the Act, a constable keeping him in such a place.

13 As early as is consistent with the protection and welfare of the child, the specified person, taking or having taken emergency protection measures, shall taking account of the age and maturity of the child—
(a) inform the child of the reasons for the emergency protection measures being taken or having been taken, and of any further steps which may be taken with respect to him under the Act or under these Regulations; and
(b) so far as practicable, give the child an opportunity to express his views, and have regard to any views as may be expressed before continuing with emergency protection measures or taking any such further steps.

14 Where emergency protection measures have been taken in relation to a child, the specified person shall do, what is reasonable in all the circumstances for the purpose of safeguarding the welfare of the child (having regard in particular to the length of the period during which the child will be subject to such measures).

15 Where further to emergency protection measures a child is taken to a police station as a place of safety, the specified person shall as soon as reasonably practicable take the child to another type of place of safety and keep the child in that other place.

16 Where a child is subject to emergency protection measures, the specified person in relation to—
(a) any relevant person in relation to the child; and
(b) any person with whom the child was living immediately before such measures were taken, shall allow, and
(c) any other person, may allow;
such contact (if any) with the child as, in the view of the specified person, is both reasonable and in accordance with the welfare of the child.

The Secure Accommodation (Scotland) Regulations 1996

SI 1996/3255

The Secretary of State, in exercise of the powers conferred on him by section 60(1) of the Social Work (Scotland) Act 1968, section 75 of the Children (Scotland) Act 1995, and section 44(5) of the Criminal Procedure (Scotland) Act 1995, and of all other powers enabling him in that behalf, and after consulting the Council on Tribunals, hereby makes the following Regulations:

1 Citation and commencement

These Regulations may be cited as the Secure Accommodation (Scotland) Regulations 1996 and shall come into force on 1st April 1997.

2 Interpretation

(1) In these Regulations, unless the context otherwise requires—
"the Act" means the Children (Scotland) Act 1995;
"the 1968 Act" means the Social Work (Scotland) Act 1968;
"the 1995 Act" means the Criminal Procedure (Scotland) Act 1995;
"the 1996 Regulations" means the Residential Establishments-Child Care (Scotland) Regulations 1996;
"the appropriate local authority" has the meaning given to that term in section 44(11) of the 1995 Act;
"children's hearing" has the meaning given to that term by section 93(1) of the Act;
"day" includes a part of a day;
"local authority" means a council constituted under section 2 of the Local Government etc (Scotland) Act 1994;
"managers" means—
    (a) in the case of a local authority, those officers having delegated powers under section 56 of the Local Government (Scotland) Act 1973 for the management of the residential establishment providing secure accommodation;
    (b) in any other case those who are responsible for management of the residential establishment providing secure accommodation;
"parent" has the meaning given to that term by section 15(1) of the Act and also includes any person who is not a parent of the child but who has parental responsibilities;
"person in charge" means the person in charge of a residential establishment providing secure accommodation who is responsible to the managers of that establishment;
"Principal Reporter" has the meaning given to that term by section 93(1) of the Act;
"relevant person" has the meaning given to that term by the meaning in section 93(2)(b) of the Act;
"residential establishment" has the meaning given to that term by section 93(1) of the Act;

"secure accommodation" means accommodation provided in a residential establishment for the purpose of restricting the liberty of children;
"supervision requirement" has the meaning given to that term by section 93(1) of the Act.

(2) In the calculation of the periods of 48 hours and 72 hours mentioned in these Regulations, Sundays and public holidays shall be excluded.

(3) In these Regulations any reference to a numbered regulation is to the regulation in these Regulations bearing that number and any reference in a regulation to a numbered paragraph is to the paragraph of that regulation bearing that number.

3 Approval by the Secretary of State of secure accommodation

Accommodation shall not be provided and used in residential establishments as secure accommodation unless it has been approved by the Secretary of State, on such terms and conditions as he thinks fit, for such provision and use.

4 Welfare of children in secure accommodation

(1) Subject to paragraph (2), the managers in consultation with the person in charge shall ensure that the welfare of a child placed and kept in such accommodation is safeguarded and promoted and that the child receives such provision for his education, development and control as is conducive to his best interests.

(2) For the purposes of paragraph (1) the managers and person in charge shall comply with such requirements of Part II of the 1996 Regulations as apply to them and the establishments for which they are responsible.

5 Maximum period in secure accommodation under the Act without authority

Subject to the provisions of regulation 8 the maximum period during which a child may be kept under the Act or the 1995 Act in secure accommodation without the authority of a children's hearing, or, as the case may be, of the sheriff, is an aggregate of 72 hours (whether or not consecutive) in any period of 28 consecutive days.

6 Children subject to certain supervision requirements — interim placement

(1) A child who is subject to a supervision requirement imposed under section 70 of the Act, but not subject to a condition imposed under subsection (9) of that section that he be liable to be placed and kept in secure accommodation, may not be placed in secure accommodation unless the chief social work officer of the local authority required to give effect to the supervision requirement and the person in charge are satisfied—
(a) that the criteria specified in paragraph (a) or (b) of section 70(10) of the Act are satisfied with respect to the child; and
(b) that it is in the child's best interests that he be placed and kept in secure accommodation,
and the chief social work officer shall, in addition, satisfy himself, in relation to the placing of the child in the residential establishment providing the secure accommodation, that the placement in that establishment is appropriate to the child's needs having regard to its statement of functions and objectives.

(2) On a child being placed in secure accommodation under paragraph (1), the chief social work officer of the local authority shall—

(a) forthwith in writing inform any relevant person in relation to the child and the Principal Reporter accordingly, and shall, in addition, so inform the child (in a manner appropriate to his age and understanding); and

(b) forthwith, and in any event not later than 24 hours from the time of that placement (whether or not the child is still held in secure accommodation) refer the case to the Principal Reporter and inform him in writing of—

(i) the details of that placement and any subsequent placement or release;

(ii) the reasons why at the time of placement the chief social work officer and the person in charge were satisfied with respect to the matters referred to and mentioned in paragraph (1) of this regulation and the reasons why at the time of writing they continue to be so satisfied or otherwise; and

(iii) the views of the chief social work officer and the person in charge as to the need or otherwise for the child's detention in secure accommodation;

(3) On receipt by the Principal Reporter of the referral and information under paragraph (2)(b), he shall arrange for a review of the child's case by a children's hearing under section 73(8) of the Act which shall apply as if the reference to a transfer under section 72(2) of the Act included a reference to a placement under this regulation.

(4) The review of the child's case referred to in paragraph (3) shall take place no later than 72 hours from the time of the placement of the child in secure accommodation.

7 Children looked after by local authority under Part II of the Act — interim placement

(1) A child who is being looked after by a local authority under chapters 1 or 4 of Part II of the Act may not be placed in secure accommodation unless the chief social work officer of the authority looking after the child and the person in charge are each satisfied with respect to the same matters as to which regulation 6(1) requires them to be satisfied and that the child may be in need of compulsory measures of supervision under Part II of the Act.

(2) On a child being placed in secure accommodation under paragraph (1), the chief social work officer of the local authority shall—

(a) forthwith, in writing, inform any relevant person in relation to the child and the Principal Reporter accordingly;

(b) forthwith and in any event not later than 24 hours from the time of that placement (whether or not the child is still held in secure accommodation) refer the child's case to the Principal Reporter and inform him in writing of—

(i) the details of that placement and any subsequent placement or release;

(ii) the reasons why at the time of placement the chief social work officer and the person in charge had cause to believe that the child may be in need of compulsory measures of supervision under Part II of the Act and the reasons why at the time of writing they still have such cause or otherwise;

(iii) the reasons why at the time of placement the chief social work officer and the person in charge were satisfied with respect to the matters referred to and mentioned in regulation 6(1) of these Regulations and the reasons why at the time of writing they continue to be so satisfied or otherwise; and

(iv) the views of the chief social work officer and the person in charge as to the need or otherwise for the child's detention in secure accommodation.

8 (1) On receipt by the Principal Reporter of the referral and information under regulation 7(2)(b) and within 72 hours of the time of the child's placement in

secure accommodation under regulation 7, the Principal Reporter shall consider and proceed, subject to paragraphs (2), (3) and (4), with the child's case in accordance with section 56 of the Act.

(2) Where the Principal Reporter decides under section 56(4) of the Act that a children's hearing does not require to be arranged—

(a) he shall, within those 72 hours, inform the local authority accordingly and that authority shall thereupon arrange for the child's discharge (if not already discharged) forthwith from secure accommodation and for any relevant person (not already informed) to be informed of his discharge; and

(b) if he considers that the proper course is to refer the child's case to the local authority with a view to arrangements for advice, guidance and assistance under Chapter 1 of Part II of the Act (support for children and their families), he shall, within these 72 hours, inform the authority accordingly.

(3) Subject to paragraph (4), where under section 56(6) of the Act, it appears to the Principal Reporter that the child is in need of compulsory measures of supervision the Principal Reporter shall arrange for a children's hearing to consider the child's case within 72 hours of the time of the child's placement in secure accommodation under regulation 7, and section 56(6) and (7) shall have effect accordingly.

(4) Notwithstanding the provisions of paragraph (3), the Principal Reporter shall have a further period of 24 hours in addition to the 72 hours referred to in paragraph (3), to fulfil his obligation thereunder if it is not reasonably practicable for him to arrange the hearing to convene within the 72 hours or for him within the 72 hours to state the grounds for referral.

9 Secure accommodation as a place of safety under the Act

(1) In cases (other than those in which a children's hearing or court has previously authorised detention in secure accommodation as a condition of a warrant or order) where—

(a) further to a warrant issued or continued by a children's hearing under section 45(4) or (5), 63(5), 66(1) or (5), 69(4) or (7) of the Act or an order or warrant issued by the sheriff under 67(1), 68(6) or 68(10) of the Act, a child is taken to and kept in a place of safety provided by a local authority; and

(b) subsequent to the issue of such a warrant or order the chief social work officer of the local authority and the person in charge are satisfied with respect to the same matters referred to in regulation 6(1),

the child may, subject to the following provisions of this regulation, be placed and kept in secure accommodation; and where the child is so placed, the Principal Reporter and any relevant person shall be informed in writing forthwith of this.

(2) Where a child has been placed in secure accommodation in accordance with paragraph (1), the Principal Reporter shall—

(a) where a warrant in respect of the child has been issued under sections 45(4) or 45(5) of the Act, arrange under section 65 of the Act a children's hearing to consider the child's case;

(b) where a warrant in respect of the child has been issued under sections 63(5) or 66(1) or 66(5) of the Act, arrange under section 66(5) of the Act a children's hearing to consider the child's case within 72 hours of the child being placed in secure accommodation;

(c) where a warrant in respect of the child has been issued under sections 69(4) or 69(7) of the Act, arrange under section 69(1) of the Act a children's hearing to consider the child's case within 72 hours of the child being placed in secure accommodation;

(d) where an order in respect of the child has been granted under sections 68(6) or 68(10) of the Act, arrange under sections 66(1) (notwithstanding a warrant under section 68(6) having been issued previously) or 69(1) respectively of the Act a children's hearing to consider the child's case within 72 hours of the child being placed in secure accommodation; and

(e) where a warrant has been issued in respect of the child under section 67(1) of the Act, apply within 72 hours of the child being placed in secure accommodation to the sheriff for a warrant under section 67(1) in respect of the child.

10 Information provided to a children's hearing by a local authority in relation to the use of secure accommodation

A local authority may submit a report in writing to the children's hearing recommending that a child be placed in a named residential establishment providing secure accommodation subject to a condition or order that he is liable to be kept in secure accommodation only if they are satisfied that the matters referred to in regulation 6(1)(a) and (b) are met.

11 Review of supervision requirement

(1) Where a children's hearing imposes or continues a condition under section 70(9) of the Act, either on the making of a supervision requirement under section 70(1) of the Act or the continuation of a supervision requirement under section 73(9)(e) of that Act, the Principal Reporter shall arrange a review of the supervision requirement under section 73(8) within 3 months of the condition under section 70(9) being made or continued.

(2) A review held under regulation 12(1) shall be considered a review held for the purposes of paragraph (1).

12 (1) A child subject to a supervision requirement with a condition imposed under section 70(9) of the Act or any relevant person may, in writing, require the Principal Reporter to make arrangements under section 73 of the Act to have the supervision requirement reviewed by a children's hearing if in the preceding 6 weeks the child has not been placed in secure accommodation by virtue of that condition.

(2) Where a notice is given to the Principal Reporter by a child or any relevant person under paragraph (1), the Principal Reporter shall arrange a children's hearing within 21 days of the receipt by him of the notice.

13 Child detained under section 44 of Criminal Procedure (Scotland) Act 1995: use of secure accommodation

(1) A child who is detained in residential accommodation provided by a local authority in accordance with an order under section 44 of the 1995 Act may be detained in secure accommodation only where the chief social work officer of the appropriate local authority and the person in charge of the residential establishment providing that secure accommodation are satisfied with respect to the same matters as to which regulation 6 requires them to be satisfied.

(2) Where paragraph (1) applies, the child shall be placed and subject to regulation 15 kept in secure accommodation only at such time and for so long as the person in charge with the agreement of the chief social work officer considers necessary.

14 Children otherwise dealt with under the Criminal Procedure (Scotland) Act 1995

(1) Where a child—
(a) is committed to a local authority under section 51(1)(a)(ii) or 51(4)(b) of the 1995 Act to be detained in a place of safety chosen by the authority, he may not, in pursuance thereof, be placed or detained in secure accommodation as a place of safety under the section;
(b) is to be kept in a place of safety under section 43 of the 1995 Act which is a residential establishment provided by a local authority, he may not, in pursuance thereof, be placed in secure accommodation provided in that establishment; or
(c) is to be detained under section 216(7) of the 1995 Act, in a place chosen by a local authority, he may not, in pursuance thereof, be placed in secure accommodation,
unless the chief social work officer of the authority and the person in charge are each satisfied with respect to the same matters as to which regulation 6 requires them to be satisfied in relation to the child.

(2) Where paragraph (1) applies, the child shall be placed and subject to regulation 15 kept in secure accommodation only at such time and for so long as the person in charge with the agreement of the chief social work officer considers necessary.

15 Review of the use of secure accommodation

(1) The chief social work officer of the appropriate local authority, in consultation with the person in charge, shall ensure that, where a child is detained in secure accommodation by virtue of regulations 13 or 14, arrangements are made by them to review the case of such a child—
(a) within 7 days of the child's placement in secure accommodation (whether or not the child is still held in secure accommodation);
(b) at such times as appear to them necessary or appropriate in the light of the child's progress; and
(c) in any event at intervals of not more than 3 months;
and the child shall be detained in secure accommodation only where, upon such review, the chief social work officer and the person in charge are satisfied that it is in the best interests of the child.

(2) In conducting such a review the chief social work officer and the person in charge shall have regard to all relevant circumstances including—
(a) the matters specified at regulation 6(1); and
(b) where practicable, the views of the child and the opinion of his parents.

(3) In conducting such a review the chief social work officer and the person in charge shall obtain the advice in relation to the detention of the child in secure accommodation of a secure placement review panel, which shall be set up by any local authority responsible for the management of a residential establishment providing secure accommodation (failing which the local authority in whose area the establishment is situated) and consist of at least 3 persons—
(a) none of whom may be the chief social work officer or the person in charge; and
(b) one of whom must be an independent person who is neither an office holder nor an employee of a local authority or the residential establishment.

(4) The chief social work officer and the person in charge shall provide the secure placement review panel with all the relevant facts of the child's case available to them in order that the secure placement review panel can give informed advice.

16 Records to be kept in respect of a child in secure accommodation

The managers, in consultation with the person in charge, shall ensure that a record is kept with respect to the child's placement in such accommodation, which shall include a record of—

(a) the child's full name, sex, and date of birth;

(b) the supervision requirement, order or other provision by reference to which the placement was made;

(c) the date and time of his placement in secure accommodation, the reasons for this, the names of the persons authorising the placement, and the address at which the child was living before the placement;

(d) the name and address of each person to whom notice was given by virtue of these Regulations of the child's placement;

(e) reviews undertaken with respect to the placement by virtue of section 73 of the Act;

(f) the date and time of his discharge, and his place of residence following discharge from secure accommodation, and the names of the persons authorising that discharge.

Memorandum by the Lord Justice-General on Child Witnesses

1 The following memorandum of guidance has been prepared at the suggestion of the Scottish Law Commission: see Report on the Evidence of Children and Other Potentially Vulnerable Witnesses (Scot Law Com No 125). Its purpose is to provide assistance to judges in the exercise of their discretionary powers, where a child is to give evidence by conventional means in open court, to put the child at ease while giving evidence and to clear the court of persons not having a direct involvement in the proceedings.

2 The general objective is to ensure, so far as is reasonably practicable, that the experience of giving evidence by all children under the age of 16 causes as little anxiety and distress to the child as possible in the circumstances.

3 The following are examples of the measures which may be taken, at the discretion of the presiding judge, with a view to achieving that objective—
(a) the removal of wigs and gowns by the judge, counsel and solicitors;
(b) the positioning of the child at a table in the well of the court along with the judge, counsel and solicitors, rather than requiring the child to give evidence from the witness box;
(c) permitting a relative or other supporting person to sit alongside the child while he or she is giving evidence;
(d) the clearing from the court room of all persons not having a direct involvement in the proceedings.

4 In deciding whether or not to take these or similar measures, or any of them, the presiding judge should have regard to the following factors—
(a) The age and maturity of the child.
     In general the younger the child the more desirable it is that steps should be taken to reduce formality and to put the child at ease while giving evidence.
(b) The nature of the charge or charges, and the nature of the evidence which the child is likely to be called upon to give.
     Particular care should be taken in cases with a sexual element or involving allegations of child abuse especially where the child is the complainer or an eye witness. Children directly involved in such cases are likely to be especially vulnerable to trauma when called upon to give evidence in the presence of the accused. The giving of evidence of a relatively formal nature, especially in the case of an

older child, is unlikely to cause anxiety or distress and in such cases it
will rarely be necessary to take special measures in the interests of the
child.
(c) The relationship, if any, between the child and the accused.
    A child who is giving evidence at the trial of a close relative may be
    especially exposed to apprehension or embarrassment, irrespective of
    the nature of the charge. The positioning of the child and the support
    of a person sitting alongside the child while giving evidence are likely
    to be of particular importance in these cases.
(d) Whether the trial is summary or on indictment.
    While informality may be easier to achieve in summary cases, the
    presence of a jury in cases taken on indictment is likely to present an
    anxious or distressed child with an additional cause for anxiety or
    distress. This makes it all the more necessary under solemn procedure
    that steps should be taken to put the child at ease.
(e) Any special factors placed before the court concerning the disposition,
    health or physique of the child.
    All children are different, and judges should take each child's partic-
    ular circumstances into account before deciding what steps, if any,
    should be taken to minimise anxiety or distress.
(f) The practicability of departing from normal procedure, including the
    size and layout of the court and the availability of amplification
    equipment.
    Whatever steps are taken, a child witness who gives evidence by
    conventional means must remain visible and audible to all those who
    have to hear and assess the evidence, including the jury and the
    accused.

5 In all cases before a witness under 16 years is led in evidence an opportunity should be given to those representing the Crown and the defence to
address the judge as to what special arrangements, if any, are appropriate.
Under solemn procedure such representations should be made outwith
the presence of the jury and preferably before the jury is empanelled or at
least before the commencement of the evidence.

6 If a relative or other supporting person is to sit alongside the child, that
person should not be a witness in the case and he or she should be warned
by the judge at the outset not to prompt or seek to influence the child in
any way in the course of the evidence.

7 The clearing of the court while a child is giving evidence will normally
be appropriate in all cases which involve an offence against, or conduct
contrary to, decency or morality: see section 166 and section 362 of the
Criminal Procedure (Scotland) Act 1975 [now section 50 of the Criminal
Procedure (Scotland) Act 1995]. In other cases this should only be done if
the judge is satisfied that this is necessary in order to avoid undue anxiety
or distress to the child. The statutory provisions that bona fide representatives of a newspaper or news agency should not be excluded should be
applied in all cases.

8 When taking any of the measures described above the judge should

have regard to the court's general duty to ensure that the accused receives a fair trial and is given a proper opportunity to present his defence.

J. A. D. Hope
Lord Justice-General

July 26 1990

Warrant for apprehension of a witness

Glasgow (date)

The sheriff, having seen the Execution of Citation dated (date) in Form 43 of the Act of Sederunt (Child Care and Maintenance Rules) 1997, and being satisfied that the witness has been funded to come to court [or adapt appropriately – eg 'being satisfied that the witness is able to come to court and refuses to do so'];

In terms of rule 29.10 of the Ordinary Cause Rules 1993, as applied to proceedings under the Children (Scotland) Act 1995 by rule 3.24 and Schedule 3 of the said Act of Sederunt, on the motion of (state party making the motion), GRANTS WARRANT FOR THE APPREHENSION OF:

(Full name and full address of the witness,
including date of birth if known)

for him/her to be brought to the Sheriff Court of Glasgow and Strathkelvin at Glasgow at 10 am on (date of continued hearing).

(Signature of sheriff)
(Name of sheriff in legible print)

Safeguarders – Fees as set by COSLA

	Recommended Fees 1999/2000 *(exclusive of VAT)* £
(a) fixed sum payable to safeguarders reporting to courts or hearings	96.00
(b) fixed sum payable to safeguarders submitting a supplementary report	48.00
(c) fixed sum payable to safeguarders attending court or hearing in relation to that specific appointment but not entering the proceedings as a party	38.00
(d) fixed sum payable to safeguarders entering court proceedings as a party (payable on a daily basis)	96.00
(e) a fixed sum payable to safeguarders where they have been appointed in relation to more than one child in a family and where the circumstances of each child are clearly different	£40 for each report for the other children

(f) travelling expenses as per Annexe 1

ANNEXE 1

Rates for travel and subsistence

Maximum rates for travel and subsistence allowances

Travel rates

Rates effective from 2 September 1997.

Motor mileage allowance

Engine capacity	*Rate per mile*
not exceeding 999ccc	31.7p
exceeding 999cc but not exceeding 1199cc	35.2p
exceeding 1199cc	43.5p
Flat rate over 100 miles	12.5p

Motorcycle allowance

Engine capacity	Rate per mile
up to 120cc	7.2p
120cc up to 150cc	7.3p
150cc up to 500cc	10.7p
over 500cc	14.5p

Subsistence allowance

Type of allowance	Rate
Breakfast	£4.48
Lunch	£6.17
Tea	£2.43
Dinner	£7.64
Standard overnight	£72.71
London overnight	£82.92

Selected forms for use in the sheriff court

Forms in the Act of Sederunt (Care and Maintenance Rules) 1997, SI 1997/291

The full set of forms is in Schedule 1 of the Act of Sederunt. The forms referred to in the text are reproduced here.

FORM 26

NOTICE TO CHILD OF APPLICATION FOR A CHILD ASSESSMENT ORDER

Rule 3.4(1)(a)

SECTION 55 OF THE CHILDREN (SCOTLAND) ACT 1995

CASE NUMBER

Dear [*insert name by which child is known*]

I am writing to tell you that because there are worries about the way you are being treated the sheriff [the person who has to decide is being asked to make a "Child Assessment Order" to make sure that you are being treated properly.

The application to the sheriff has been made by [*insert in simple language the person making the application, the reason for making it and the order(s)) sought*]. The sheriff would like to hear your views about what you would like to happen before making a decision.

You can tell the sheriff what you think by:

Going to see the Sheriff

The sheriff will consider what to do next on [*insert date, time and place of hearing*].

You can take someone like a friend, parent, teacher or a social worker with you to see the sheriff to support you; or

You can ask a lawyer to come with you and tell the sheriff your views.

If you think you would like to go to see the sheriff it is usually best to talk it over with a lawyer.

Not going to see the Sheriff

You can fill in the attached form or write down your views on a separate sheet of paper and send them back in the enclosed stamped addressed envelope **before** the date on which the sheriff is to hear the application, which is at the end of this letter.

REMEMBER

That someone like a friend or teacher can help you to fill in the form or write down your views.

- If you return the form it will be given to the sheriff and, if he needs more information, he will ask the Sheriff Clerk who works with him to contact you about this.

IMPORTANT NOTE—You do not have to do any of these things if you would prefer not to; however, it is very important for you to understand that, if you do not do anything, the sheriff might make an order without knowing what your views are:

> **If you are unsure about what to do you can get free legal advice from a Lawyer or Local Advice Agency or Law Centre about the application and about legal aid. The Scottish Child Law Centre can refer you to specially trained lawyers who can help you. They give advice on their free phone no (0800 317 500) any time between 9.00 am and 5.00 pm on Monday to Friday.**

The hearing to consider the application will be held on [insert date] at [insert time], in [insert name of court] SHERIFF COURT, [insert address of court].

You will see that, along with this letter, there is a copy of the application to the sheriff and the sheriff's order fixing the hearing. If you decide to get advice, or to be represented, make sure that you give your advisor a copy of the application, and the sheriff's order.

Signed . . . .   Date . . . .

To the Sheriff Clerk

I would like the Sheriff to know what I have to say before he or she makes a decision.

Write what you want to say here, or you can use a separate sheet of paper:

Name . . . .

Address . . . .

. . . .

. . . .

Court Reference Number . . . .
(if you know it)

FORM 27
NOTICE TO CHILD OF APPLICATION TO VARY OR SET ASIDE CHILD PROTECTION ORDER

Rule 3.4(1)(b)

SECTION 60 OF THE CHILDREN (SCOTLAND) ACT 1995

CASE NUMBER

KEEPING YOU SAFE

Dear *[insert name by which child is known]*

A Child Protection Order was made on....................................to keep you safe from harm. The sheriff [the person who has to decide] made the order, which says that you are to continue to live at *[insert address]* at present.

Now the sheriff has been asked to have another look at your situation, *[insert in simple language the person making the application, the reason for making it and the order(s) sought]*. The sheriff would like to hear your views about what you would like to happen before making a decision.

You can tell the sheriff what you think by:—

Going to see the Sheriff

—You can take someone like a friend, parent, a teacher or a social worker with you to see the sheriff to support you;
or

—You can ask a lawyer to come with you and tell the court your views.

Not going to see the Sheriff

—You can fill in the attached form and send it back in the enclosed stamped addressed envelope **before** the hearing date which is at the end of this letter.

REMEMBER

That someone can help you to fill in the form.

—If you return the form it will be given to the sheriff and, if he needs more information, he will ask the Sheriff Clerk who works with him to contact you about this.

IMPORTANT NOTE—You do not have to do any of these things if you would prefer not to; however, it is very important for you to understand that, if you do not do anything, the sheriff might make an order without knowing what your views are.

> **If you are unsure about what to do you can get free legal advice from a Lawyer or Local Advice Agency or Law Centre about the application and about legal aid. The Scottish Child Law Centre can refer you to specially trained lawyers who can help you. They give advice on their free phone no (0800 317 500) any time between 9.00 am and 5.00 pm Monday to Friday.**

The hearing to consider the application will be held on *[insert date]* **at** *[insert time]*, **in** *[insert name of court]* **SHERIFF COURT**, *[insert address of court]*.

You will see that, along with this letter, there is a copy of the application to the sheriff, and the sheriff's order fixing the hearing. If you decide to get advice, or to ask someone to go to see the sheriff for you, make sure that you give your advisor a copy of the application, and the sheriff's order.

Signed . . . .   Date . . . .

To the Sheriff Clerk

I would like the Sheriff to know what I have to say before he or she makes a decision.

Write what you want to say here, or you can use a separate sheet of paper:

Name . . . .

Address . . . .

. . . .

. . . .

Court Reference Number . . . .
(if you know it)

Form 28
Notice to Child of Application for an Exclusion Order

Rule 3.4(1)(c)

Section 76 of the Children (Scotland) Act 1995

┌─────────────────────┐
│ CASE NUMBER   │
│   │
└─────────────────────┘

KEEPING YOU SAFE

Dear *[insert name by which child is known]*

I am writing to tell you that because there are worries about your safety the sheriff [the person who has to decide] has been asked to sort out some practical arrangements to make sure you can be kept safe. The sheriff is being asked to make an "Exclusion Order" to make sure that *[insert name of person]* does not come into the family home at *[insert address]*. You are to stay [at home/where you are]* at present.

*delete as appropriate

The application to the sheriff has been made by *[insert in simple language the person making the application, the reason for making it and the order(s) sought]*. The sheriff would like to hear your views about what you would like to happen before making a decision.

You can tell the sheriff what you think by:—

Going to see the Sheriff

—You can take someone like a friend, parent, a teacher or a social worker with you to see the sheriff to support you;
or

—You can ask a lawyer to come with you and tell the court your views.

If you think you would like to go to see the sheriff it is usually best to talk it over with a lawyer.

Not going to see the Sheriff

—You can fill in the attached form or write down your views on a separate sheet of paper and send them back in the enclosed stamped addressed envelope **before** the date on which the court is to hear the application, which is at the end of this letter.

REMEMBER

That someone like a friend or teacher can help you to fill in the form or write down your views.

—If you return the form it will be given to the sheriff, and, if he needs more information, he will ask the Sheriff Clerk who works with him to contact you about this.

IMPORTANT NOTE—You do not have to do any of these things if you would prefer not to; however, it is very important for you to understand that, if you do not do anything, the sheriff might make an order without knowing what your views are.

If you are unsure about what to do you can get free legal advice from a Lawyer or Local Advice Agency or Law Centre about the application and about legal aid. The Scottish Child Law Centre can refer you to specially trained lawyers who can help you. They give advice on their free phone no (0800 317 500) any time between 9.00 am and 5.00 pm Monday to Friday.

The hearing to consider the application will be held on *[insert date]* at *[insert time]*, in *[insert name of court]* SHERIFF COURT, *[insert address of court]*.

You will see that, along with this letter, there is a copy of the application to the sheriff and the sheriff's order fixing the hearing. If you decide to get advice, or to ask someone to go to see the sheriff for you, make sure that you give your advisor a copy of the application, and the sheriff's order.

Signed . . . .   Date . . . .

To the Sheriff Clerk

I would like the Sheriff to know what I have to say before he or she makes a decision.

Write what you want to say here, or you can use a separate sheet of paper:

Name . . . .

Address . . . .

. . . .

. . . .

Court Reference Number . . . .
(if you know it)

Form 30
NOTICE TO CHILD OF APPLICATION FOR A FURTHER DETENTION WARRANT

Rule 3.4(1)(e)

SECTION 67 OF THE CHILDREN (SCOTLAND) ACT 1995

> CASE NUMBER

I am writing to tell you that as the childrens hearing has been unable to dispose of your case the sheriff has been asked to consider whether you should continue to stay at *[insert place of detention].*

The application to the sheriff has been made by the children's reporter who is looking into your circumstances. The sheriff would like to hear your views about continuing to stay at *[insert place of detention]* before making a decision.

You can tell the sheriff what you think by:—

Going to see the Sheriff

—The sheriff will consider what to do next on *[insert date, time and place of hearing]*

—You can take someone like a friend, parent, a teacher or a social worker with you to see the sheriff to support you;
or

—You can ask a lawyer to come with you and tell the sheriff your views.

If you think you would like to go to see the sheriff it is usually best to talk it over with a lawyer.

Not going to see the Sheriff

—You can fill in the attached form or write down your views on a separate sheet of paper and send them back in the enclosed stamped addressed envelope **before** the date on which the sheriff is to hear the application, which is at the end of this letter.

REMEMBER

That someone like a friend or teacher can help you to fill in the form or write down your views.

—If you return the form it will be given to the sheriff, who is the person who decides what will be done in your case, and, if he needs more information, he will ask the Sheriff Clerk who works with him to contact you about this.

IMPORTANT NOTE - You do not have to do any of these things if you would prefer not to; however, it is very important for you to understand that, if you do not do anything, the sheriff might make an order without knowing what your views are.

> **If you are unsure about what to do you can get free legal advice from a Lawyer or Local Advice Agency or Law Centre. The Scottish Child Law Centre can refer you to specially trained lawyers who can help you. They give advice on their free phone no (0800 317 500) any time between 9.00 am and 5.00 pm Monday to Friday.**

The hearing to consider the application will be held on *[insert place]* **at** *[insert time]*, **in** *[insert name]* **SHERIFF COURT,** *[insert address of Sheriff]*.

You will see that, along with this letter, there is a copy of the application to the sheriff, and the sheriff's order fixing the hearing. If you decide to get advice, or to ask someone to go to see the sheriff to for you, make sure that you give your advisor a copy of the application, and the sheriff's order.

Signed ....   Date ....

To the Sheriff Clerk

I would like the Sheriff to know what I have to say before he or she makes a decision.

Write what you want to say here, or you can use a separate sheet of paper:

Name ....

Address ....

....

....

Court Reference Number ....
(if you know it)

FORM 32
FORM OF FIRST ORDER UNDER THE CHILDREN (SCOTLAND) ACT 1995

Rule 3.11

SECTION 55 (Application for Child Assessment Order),

SECTION 60 (Application to vary or set aside Child Protection Order),

SECTION 76 (Application for Exclusion Order),

SECTION 79 (Application to vary or recall Exclusion Order) and

SECTION 67 (Application for warrant for further detention of child)

[Place and date]

The court assigns *[date]* at *[hour]* within the *[name court]* in chambers at *[place]*

for the hearing of the application;

appoints the applicant forthwith to give notice of the application and hearing to the persons listed in PART I of the application by serving a copy of the application and this order together with notices in *Forms [insert form Nos];*

*dispenses with notice and service on *[insert name]* for the following reason(s) *[insert reason(s)].*

[Note: *Insert details of any other order granted and in an application under section 76 for an exclusion order insert as appropriate.*

Meantime grants an interim exclusion order; *or* interim interdict; *or otherwise as the case may be.*]

. . . .

*Sheriff or sheriff clerk

*delete as appropriate

FORM 33

IN APPLICATION UNDER SECTION 65 OF THE CHILDREN (SCOTLAND) ACT 1995

Rule 3.11

FORM OF WARRANT TO CITE CHILD AND TO GIVE NOTICE/INTIMATE TO RELEVANT PERSON(S) AND SAFEGUARDER

[Place and date]

The court

1   Assigns *[date]* at *[hour]* within the *[name court]* in chambers at *[place]* for the hearing of the application;

2   Appoints the Principal Reporter forthwith

to cite AB *[name of child]*,
to give notice/intimate to BB *[insert name of relevant person or persons]* whose whereabouts are known and to [AB] (name and design) the safeguarder appointed by the sheriff,
by serving a copy of the application and relative statement of grounds of referral;

3   Grants warrant to cite witnesses and havers.

4   *Dispenses with notice and service on *[insert name]* for the following reason(s) *[insert reason(s)]*.

5   *Dispenses with the obligation to attend of *[insert name of child]* for the following reason(s) *[insert reason(s)]*.

....

*Sheriff or sheriff clerk

*delete as appropriate

Form 36

NOTICE OF APPLICATION FOR AN EXCLUSION ORDER TO PERSON NAMED IN APPLICATION OR ANY
OTHER PERSON

Rule 3.12(1)(c)

SECTION 76 OF THE CHILDREN (SCOTLAND) ACT 1995

Case No

Application to Sheriff Court at *[insert name]*
for an exclusion order under section 76 of the Children (Scotland) Act 1995 in
respect of
you/[insert name and address of named person]

To *[insert name and address of person to whom notice is given]*.

You are given notice that the court will hear this application—
[applicant to insert details of the date, time and place for hearing the application]

on . . . .

at . . . .

in . . . .

Along with this notice there is attached a copy of the application and the court's
order fixing this hearing *which includes details of any interim orders granted.

Signed . . . .   Date . . . .

*delete as appropriate

WHAT YOU SHOULD DO

YOU SHOULD ATTEND OR BE REPRESENTED AT THE HEARING.
**If you do not attend or are not represented at the hearing, the court may decide
the case in your absence**. If the order sought is to exclude you then the granting of
the order will have an effect on a number of your rights including the suspending
of any rights of occupancy you have. Details of the orders sought are contained in
the application form.

**YOU SHOULD OBTAIN ADVICE FROM A SOLICITOR OR LOCAL ADVICE
AGENCY OR LAW CENTRE.** You may be entitled to legal aid. Advice about
legal aid is available from any solicitor, advice agency or law centre.

*delete as appropriate

Form 37

Notice of Application to Vary or Recall an Exclusion Order to Person Named in
Application or any Other Person

Rule 3.12(1)(d)

Section 79 of the Children (Scotland) Act 1995

Case No

Application to Sheriff Court at *[insert name]*
to vary or recall* an exclusion order under section 79 of the Children (Scotland)
Act 1995 in respect of
you/[insert name and address of named person]*

*delete as appropriate

To *[insert name and address of person to whom notice is given]*.

You are given notice that the court will hear this application—
[applicant to insert details of the date, time and place for hearing the application]

on. . . . .

at . . . .

in . . . .

Along with this notice there is attached a copy of the application and the court's
order fixing this hearing.

Signed . . . .   Date . . . .

WHAT YOU SHOULD DO

YOU SHOULD ATTEND OR BE REPRESENTED AT THE HEARING.
If you do not attend or are not represented at the hearing, the court may decide
the case in your absence.
Details of the orders sought are contained in the application form.

**YOU SHOULD OBTAIN ADVICE FROM A SOLICITOR OR LOCAL ADVICE
AGENCY OR LAW CENTRE.** You may be entitled to legal aid. Advice about
legal aid is available from any solicitor, advice agency or law centre. If you
instructed any person to represent you at the original hearing which granted the
application you should consider bringing this application to their attention
without delay.

Form 39
Notice to Relevant Person in Application under Section 65 of the Children
(Scotland) Act 1995

Rule 3.12(1)(f)

1   *[Place and Date]*

To *[name and address of relevant person]*

TAKE NOTICE that the court has received the application which accompanies this intimation.

2   YOU MAY ATTEND COURT for the hearing of the application as shown below.

3   Place of hearing: Sheriff Court . . . .

Address . . . .

. . . .

. . . .

. . . .

. . . .

Date of hearing: . . . .

Time of hearing: . . . .

(signed)

Principal Reporter

WHAT YOU SHOULD DO

YOU SHOULD ATTEND OR BE REPRESENTED AT THE HEARING.
If you do not attend or are not represented at the hearing, **the court may decide
the case in your absence**. Details of the orders sought are contained in the application form.

**YOU SHOULD OBTAIN ADVICE FROM A SOLICITOR OR LOCAL ADVICE
AGENCY OR LAW CENTRE.** You may be entitled to legal aid. Advice about
legal aid is available from any solicitor, advice agency or law centre.

Form 41
Citation of Witness or Haver under the Children (Scotland) Act 1995

Rule 3.14(2)

KL [address], you are required to attend at   Sheriff Court on
at   to give evidence in the hearing of [an application by the Principal
Reporter] to the sheriff for a finding as to grounds for the referral of the case of
[name of child] to a children's hearing] OR
[an appeal to the sheriff against a decision of a children's hearing in a case of
[name of child]] OR
[an application by *[insert name and address]*] for [insert details of purpose of
hearing]]
[You are required to bring with you [specify documents]].

**If you fail to attend without reasonable excuse having demanded and been paid
your travelling expenses, warrant may be granted for your arrest.**

Signed PQ, Sheriff Officer;

or

XY Solicitor/Sheriff Clerk/

Principal Reporter/Officer of the Local Authority

[address]

Note:

Within certain specified limits claims for necessary outlays and loss of earnings
will be met. Claims should be made to the person who has cited you to attend and
proof of any loss of earnings should be given to that person. If you wish your travelling expenses to be paid prior to your attendance you should apply to the person
who has cited you.

FORM 42
*CERTIFICATE OF EXECUTION OF CITATION OF OR NOTICE TO CHILD
*CERTIFICATE OF EXECUTION OF NOTICE TO PERSON NAMED IN APPLICATION OR ANY OTHER
PERSON UNDER THE CHILDREN (SCOTLAND) ACT 1995

Rule 3.14(3)

1 [*Place, date*]

I [*Name and designation*] hereby certify that on the date shown above, I duly

*cited [*full name of child*]

*gave notice to [*full name of person*]

by

*posting, on [*date*] between the hours of [   ] and [   ] at the
   [*place*] Post Office, a copy of the foregoing application, warrant and *-
   citation/*intimation to *him/*her, in a *registered/*recorded delivery letter
   addressed as follows–[*full name and address*]

and the post office receipt for that letter accompanies this certificate.

*or by [set forth the mode of citation or intimation]
                          [signed]
                          *Principal Reporter
                          or solicitor for applicant
                          [/Officer of Local Authority/Sheriff clerk]
                          or Sheriff Officer
                          [*name and business address*]
                          and [*name and address of any witness*]

*Delete as appropriate

Form 43

Certificate of Citation of Witness or Haver under the Children (Scotland) Act 1995

Rule 3.17(1)

1 [Place and Date]

I [Name and designation] hereby certify that on the above date, I duly

cited [full name of witness]

by

*posting, on [date] between the hours of (   ) and (   ) at the [place] Post Office, a copy of [the foregoing application, warrant and] *citation/*intimation to *him/*her, in a *registered/*recorded delivery letter addressed as follows–[full name and address]

and the post office receipt for that letter accompanies this certificate.

*or by [set forth the mode of citation or intimation]

(signed, A B Principal Reporter)

C D Sheriff Officer

E F (Witness)

G H Solicitor

*delete as appropriate

Form 45

APPLICATION FOR A CHILD ASSESSMENT ORDER

Rule 3.26

SECTION 55 OF THE CHILDREN (SCOTLAND) ACT 1995

Case No

Date lodged

Application to Sheriff Court at

for a Child Assessment Order under section 55 of the Children (Scotland) Act 1995

Part 1 DETAILS OF APPLICANT AND OTHER PERSONS WHO THE APPLICANT BELIEVES SHOULD RECEIVE NOTICE OF THE APPLICATION

APPLICANT	*[insert name, address, telephone DX and fax numbers of local authority]*
CHILD	*[insert name, address, gender and date of birth]**
RELEVANT PERSON(S)	*[insert name, address and the basis for the person being a relevant person within the meaning of section 93(2)(b) of the Act]*
SAFEGUARDER	*[insert name, address, telephone, DX and fax numbers (if known) of any safeguarder appointed by a children's hearing or court in respect of the child]*
THE PRINCIPAL REPORTER	*[insert name, address, telephone, DX and fax numbers]*
ANY OTHER PERSON WHO SHOULD RECEIVE NOTICE OF THE APPLICATION	For example, any person who is caring for the child at the time of the application being made: *insert name, address and telephone number of person and provide details of their interest in the application and/or child*
	[The court may seek views from applicants in relation to other persons on whom service should be made.]

*Note: Information to be provided in Part 3 where applicant does not wish to disclose the address or whereabouts of the child or any other person to persons receiving notice of the application.

Part 2 INFORMATION ABOUT THE APPLICATION AND ORDERS SOUGHT

GROUNDS FOR MAKING APPLICATION
[applicant to provide details of grounds for making the application: including reasons why a Child Protection Order is not being sought.]

*OTHER APPLICATIONS AND ORDERS WHICH AFFECT THE CHILD

[insert details of any other applications or orders made which affect or are relevant to the child who is the subject of this application]

REPORTS/DOCUMENTARY EVIDENCE ETC
The following reports/documentary evidence is attached/will be produced*—
*delete as appropriate

[list any reports, statements or affidavits which are or will be produced at any subsequent hearing of the application]

Part 3 DETAILS OF THE ASSESSMENT AND ORDERS SOUGHT

ASSESSMENT

[in terms of section 55(3) insert the following details of the assessment sought]

a   The type of assessment is *[provide details of the type of assessment that is sought including information on health, development and/or the way the child has been treated.]*

b   The assessment would begin on *[insert date]*

c   The assessment will have effect for *[insert number of days]* from that date.

d   The person(s) to be authorised to carry out any assessment is/are *[insert name(s), designation and address]*

e   *[Insert name and address]* would be required to produce the child to the authorised person and permit that person or any other authorised person to carry out an assessment in accordance with the order.

OTHER ORDERS

[in terms of section 55(4) or (5) provide the following information about any other order sought]

*a   In terms of section 55(4) an order is sought to permit the child to be taken to

[insert details of the place] for the purpose of the assessment, and to authorise the child to be kept there for *[insert number of days]* days.

*b   In terms of section 55(5) the sheriff is requested to make the following directions as to contact with the child by *[insert name and address of person and his or her relationship with child]* while the child is in the aforementioned place

[insert details of any directions sought as to contact with the child]

*[Insert details and grounds for any order sought in relation
(a)   to non-disclosure of address or whereabouts of child; or
(b)   service of restricted documents on child.]*

*delete as appropriate

Part 4 DETAILS OF FIRST ORDER SOUGHT FROM THE SHERIFF

The applicant requests the sheriff to:

a Fix a hearing.

b Order service on the child, together with a notice in form 26 or order service of the following documents only *[insert details of documents to be served on child, e g notice inform 26 only]*

*c Order service of a copy of the application and the first order on the persons listed in Part I of this application, together with a notice in form 34.

*d Order that the address of *[insert name]* should not be disclosed in the application.

*e Dispense with service on the child or any other person for the following reasons *[insert details]*.

*delete as appropriate

Signed ....   Date ....
[name, designation and address
telephone, DX and fax numbers]

Form 47

Application for a Child Protection Order by Local Authority

Rule 3.30

Section 57 of the Children (Scotland) Act 1995

Case No

Date lodged

Application to Sheriff at

for a Child Protection Order under section 57(2) of the Children (Scotland) Act 1995

Part 1 DETAILS OF APPLICANT AND OTHER PERSONS WHO THE APPLICANT BELIEVES SHOULD RECEIVE NOTICE OF THE APPLICATION

APPLICANT	*[insert name, address, telephone DX and fax numbers of the local authority]*
CHILD	*[insert name, address, gender and date of birth]**
RELEVANT PERSON(S)	*[insert name, address and the basis for the person being a relevant person within the meaning of section 93(2)(b) of the Act]*
SAFEGUARDER	*[insert name, address, telephone DX and fax numbers (if known) of any safeguarder appointed by a children's hearing or court in respect of the child]*
THE PRINCIPAL REPORTER	*[insert name, address, telephone DX and fax numbers]*
ANY OTHER PERSON WHO SHOULD RECEIVE NOTICE OF THE APPLICATION	*[For example, any person who is caring for the child at the time of the application being made: insert name, address and telephone number of person and provide details of their interest in the application and/or child]*

*Note: Information to be provided in Part 3 where applicant does not wish to disclose the address or whereabouts of the child or any other person to persons receiving notice of the application.

Part 2 INFORMATION ABOUT THE APPLICATION AND ORDERS SOUGHT

GROUNDS FOR MAKING APPLICATION
[applicant to provide details of grounds for making the application:

see section 57(1) & (2) of the Act]

OTHER APPLICATIONS AND ORDERS WHICH AFFECT THE CHILD
[insert details of any other applications or orders made which affect or are relevant to the child who is the subject of this application]

SUPPORTING EVIDENCE
The following supporting evidence is produced—
[list reports, statements, affidavits or other evidence produced]

Part 3 DETAILS OF ORDER SOUGHT AND ANY TERMS, CONDITIONS OR DIRECTIONS

ORDER SOUGHT: The applicant requests the Sheriff to make a Child Protection Order in respect of the child *[insert name]*

*TERMS AND CONDITIONS TO BE ATTACHED TO ORDER

In terms of section 57(4) the applicant seeks an order to
[insert details of the order sought].

*DIRECTIONS IN RELATION TO THE EXERCISE OR FULFILMENT OF PARENTAL RESPONSIBILITIES OR PARENTAL RIGHTS

In terms of section 58(4) or (5) the applicant seeks the following direction(s)—
[insert details of the direction(s) sought].

*ANY OTHER ORDER(S)
(a) to non-disclosure of address or whereabouts of child; or
(b) service of restricted documents on child.]*

*delete as appropriate

Part 4 DETAILS OF FIRST ORDER SOUGHT FROM THE SHERIFF

The applicant requests the sheriff to:
a Make a child protection order in respect of the said child *[insert name of the child]* on the terms and conditions set out in Part 3 of the application, *and subject to the directions sought in Part 3 of the application.
*b Order the applicant to forthwith serve a copy of the Child Protection Order [and a copy of the application] on,
  i the child, together with a notice in form 50* or orders service of the following documents only *[insert details of documents to be served on child, e g notice inform 50 only]*; and
  ii the persons listed in Part 1 of this application, together with a notice in form 51.
*c Order that the address of *[insert name]* should not be disclosed in the application.
*d Dispense with service on the child or any other person for the following reasons *[insert details].*

*delete as appropriate

Signed . . . .   Date . . . .
[name, designation and address
telephone, DX and fax numbers]

FORM 48

APPLICATION FOR A CHILD PROTECTION ORDER BY ANY PERSON (OTHER THAN A LOCAL AUTHORITY)

Rule 3.30

SECTION 57 OF THE CHILDREN (SCOTLAND) ACT 1995

Case No

Date lodged

for a Child Protection Order under section 57(1) of the Children (Scotland) Act 1995

Part 1 DETAILS OF APPLICANT AND OTHER PERSONS WHO THE APPLICANT BELIEVES SHOULD RECEIVE NOTICE OF THE APPLICATION

APPLICANT	*[insert name and address, telephone DX and fax numbers and capacity in which application is made]*
CHILD	*[insert name, address, gender and date of birth]**
RELEVANT PERSON(S)	*[insert name, address and the basis for the person being a relevant person within the meaning of section 93(2)(b) of the Act]*
SAFEGUARDER	*[insert name, address, telephone DX and fax numbers (if known) of any safeguarder appointed by a children's hearing or court in respect of the child]*
LOCAL AUTHORITY	*[insert name and address, DX and telephone and fax numbers]*
THE PRINCIPAL REPORTER	*[insert name, address, telephone DX and fax numbers]*
ANY OTHER PERSON WHO SHOULD RECEIVE NOTICE OF THE APPLICATION	*[For example, any person who is caring for the child at the time of the application being made: insert name, address of person and provide details of their interest in the application and/or child]*

*** Note: Information to be provided in Part 3 where applicant does not wish to disclose the address or whereabouts of the child or any other person to persons receiving notice of the application.**

Part 2 INFORMATION ABOUT THE APPLICATION AND ORDERS SOUGHT

GROUNDS FOR MAKING APPLICATION
[applicant to provide details of grounds for making the application: see section 57(1) of the Act]

OTHER APPLICATIONS AND ORDERS WHICH AFFECT THE CHILD
[insert details of any other applications or orders made which affect or are relevant to the child who is the subject of this application]

SUPPORTING EVIDENCE
The following supporting evidence is produced—
[list reports, statements, affidavits or other evidence produced]

Part 3 DETAILS OF ORDER SOUGHT AND ANY TERMS, CONDITIONS OR DIRECTIONS

ORDER SOUGHT: The applicant requests the Sheriff to make a Child Protection Order in respect of the child *[insert name]*

*TERMS AND CONDITIONS TO BE ATTACHED TO ORDER

In terms of section 57(4) the applicant seeks an order to
[insert details of the order sought].

*DIRECTIONS IN RELATION TO THE EXERCISE OR FULFILMENT OF PARENTAL RESPONSIBILITIES OR PARENTAL RIGHTS

In terms of section 58(4) or (5) the applicant seeks the following direction(s)—
[insert details of the direction(s) sought].

*ANY OTHER ORDER(S)
[Insert here details and grounds for any order sought in relation
(a) to non-disclosure of address or whereabouts of child; or
(b) service of restricted documents on child.]

*delete as appropriate

Part 4 DETAILS OF FIRST ORDER SOUGHT FROM THE SHERIFF

The applicant requests the sheriff to:
a   Make a child protection order in respect of the said child *[insert name of the child]* on the terms and conditions set out in Part 3 of the application, * and subject to the directions sought in Part 3 of the application.
*b   Order the applicant to forthwith serve a copy of the Child Protection Order [and a copy of the application] on,
   i   the child, together with a notice in form 50* or orders service of the following documents only *[insert details of documents to be served on child, e g notice inform 50 only]*; and
   ii   the persons listed in Part 1 of this application, together with a notice in form 51.
*c   Order that the address of *[insert name]* should not be disclosed in the application.
*d   Dispense with service on the child or any other person for the following reasons *[insert details]*.

*delete as appropriate

Signed . . . .   Date . . . .
[name, designation and address
telephone, DX and fax numbers]

FORM 49
CHILD PROTECTION ORDER

Rule 3.31(2)

SECTION 57 OF THE CHILDREN (SCOTLAND) ACT 1995

IN THE SHERIFF COURT   Case No

at

on

In the application by *[Insert name and address]* for a Child Protection Order/Child Assessment Order* the sheriff makes a Child Protection Order in respect of the child *[insert name, address (unless order made re non disclosure), gender and date of birth of the child]*

TERMS AND CONDITIONS

*The sheriff orders that *[insert name and address of person]* is required to produce the child to the applicant *[insert name and address of the applicant]*.

*The sheriff authorises the removal of the child by the applicant to *[insert details of the place]* a place of safety and for the keeping of the child at that place.

*The sheriff authorises the prevention of the removal of the child from *[insert details of the place]*.

*The sheriff orders that the locality of the place of safety should not be disclosed to *[insert details of the person or class of persons]*.

DIRECTIONS

*In terms of section 58(1) and (2) the sheriff gives the following directions to the applicant as to contact with the child—
[insert details of any directions]

*In terms of section 58(4), (5) or (6) the sheriff gives the following directions as to the exercise or fulfilment of parental responsibilities or parental rights in respect of the   child—
[insert details of any directions]

*delete as appropriate

For the purpose of enforcing this order warrant is granted for all lawful execution, including warrant to open shut and lockfast places.

Signed . . . .

Sheriff at . . . .

Form 50
NOTICE OF CHILD PROTECTION ORDER TO CHILD IN TERMS OF SECTION 57 OF THE CHILDREN
(SCOTLAND) ACT 1995

Rule 3.32(A)

ARRANGEMENTS TO KEEP YOU SAFE

Dear *[insert name by which child is known]*

I am writing to tell you that because there were worries about your safety the court was asked to sort out some practical arrangements to make sure you are kept safe.

After hearing about your situation the court made an order, called a "Child Protection Order". That means that the court gave permission to *[insert in simple language the order(s) and any directions granted and their effect on the child]*

If you are unhappy with this order or any directions you can ask the court to change it. For example, you might want to ask the court to allow you *[insert an example e g to allow more contact with certain members of the family etc]*

Any change must be requested without delay

If you want to do this you can ask the court which made the order to listen to you. You will need a lawyer to help you.

Remember that if you do not agree with the order or any directions you must get advice **IMMEDIATELY.**

In the meantime you must do what the order says.

> **If you are unsure about what to do you can get free legal
> advice from a Lawyer or Local Advice Agency or Law
> Centre about the application and about legal aid. The
> Scottish Child Law Centre can refer you to specially trained
> lawyers who can help you. They give advice on their free
> phone no (0800 317 500) any time between 9.00 am and
> 5.00 pm Monday to Friday.**

You will see that, along with this letter, there is a copy of the application which was made to the court, and the order the court has made which affects you. If you decide to get advice, or to ask someone to go to court for you, make sure that you give your advisor a copy of the application, and the court's order.

Signed . . . .   Date . . . .

Form 51

NOTICE OF CHILD PROTECTION ORDER TO A NAMED PERSON

Rule 3.32(b)

SECTION 57 OF THE CHILDREN (SCOTLAND) ACT 1995

Case No

Notice of Child Protection Order made under section 57 of the Children (Scotland) Act 1995 in the Sheriff Court at

To *[insert name and address of person to whom notice is given]*.

You are given notice of the making of a Child Protection Order in respect of the child *[insert name, address, gender and date of birth of child]* by the sheriff at *[name of sheriff court]* on *[date of order]*.

Along with this notice there is attached a copy of the application and the order.

Signed .... Date ....

WHAT YOU SHOULD DO

*YOU MUST COMPLY WITH THE ORDER AND ANY DIRECTIONS CONTAINED WITHIN IT. FAILURE TO COMPLY IS AN OFFENCE UNDER SECTION 81 OF THE CHILDREN (SCOTLAND) ACT 1995 AND COULD LEAD TO YOU BEING FINED.

*YOU MAY WISH TO OBTAIN ADVICE FROM A SOLICITOR OR LOCAL ADVICE AGENCY OR LAW CENTRE. You may be entitled to legal aid. Advice about legal aid is available from any solicitor, advice agency or law centre.

*You may be able to contest or vary the order, and in such circumstances you should obtain legal advice without delay.

*delete as appropriate

FORM 52

APPLICATION TO VARY OR RECALL A CHILD PROTECTION ORDER

Rule 3.33(1)

SECTION 60 OF THE CHILDREN (SCOTLAND) ACT 1995

Case No

Date lodged

Application to Sheriff at

to vary or recall a Child Protection Order under section 60(7) of the Children (Scotland) Act 1995

Part 1 DETAILS OF APPLICANT AND OTHER PERSONS WHO THE APPLICANT BELIEVES SHOULD RECEIVE NOTICE OF THE APPLICATION

APPLICANT	*[insert name, address, telephone DX and fax numbers, and details of the capacity of the person making the application]*
CHILD	*[insert name, address, gender and date of birth]**
SAFEGUARDER	**If not applicant** *[insert name, address, telephone DX and fax numbers (if known) of any safeguarder appointed by a children's hearing or court in respect of the child]*
RELEVANT PERSON(S)	**If not applicant** *[insert name, address and telephone number (if known) and the basis for the person being a relevant person within the meaning of section 93(2)(b) of the Act]*
THE PRINCIPAL REPORTER	*[insert name, address, telephone DX and fax numbers]*
ANY OTHER PERSON WHO SHOULD RECEIVE NOTICE OF THE APPLICATION	*[For example, any person who is caring for the child at the time of the application being made: insert name, address and telephone number of person and provide details of their interest in the application and/or child]*

*Note: Information to be provided in Part 3 where applicant does not wish to disclose the address or whereabouts of the child or any other person to persons receiving notice of the application.

Part 2 INFORMATION ABOUT THE APPLICATION AND ORDERS SOUGHT

On *[date of order]* the Sheriff made a Child Protection Order in the following terms *[insert full details of order and conditions attaching to it] [Copy original order must be attached in terms of Rule 3.33].*

OTHER APPLICATIONS AND ORDERS WHICH AFFECT THE CHILD
[insert details of any other applications or orders made which affect or are relevant to the child who is the subject of this application]

ORDER(S) OR CONDITIONS THE VARIATION OR RECALL OF WHICH ARE SOUGHT
[applicant to insert details of order now sought]

GROUNDS FOR MAKING APPLICATION
[applicant to provide details of grounds for seeking the variation or setting aside]

SUPPORTING EVIDENCE
The following supporting evidence is produced—
[list reports, statements, affidavits or other evidence produced]

Part 3 DETAILS OF ORDER SOUGHT AND ANY TERMS, CONDITIONS OR DIRECTIONS

FIRST ORDER
The applicant requests the sheriff to:
a   Assign a hearing on the application.
*b   Order the applicant to forthwith serve a copy of the application together with the date of hearing on,
   i   The Principal Reporter
   ii   The Local Authority
   iii   The child, together with a notice in form 27; and
   iv   The persons listed in part 1 of this application, together with a notice in form 35.
*c   Dispense with service on the child or any other person for the following reasons *[insert details]*.

And thereafter to [enter details of what you want the Sheriff to vary or recall.]

*delete as appropriate

Signed . . . .   Date . . . .
[name, designation and address
telephone, DX and fax numbers]

Form 54
APPLICATION FOR EXCLUSION ORDER BY LOCAL AUTHORITY

Rule 3.35

SECTION 6 OF THE CHILDREN (SCOTLAND) ACT 1995

Case No

Date lodged

Application to Sheriff at

for an Exclusion Order under section 76(1) of the Children (Scotland) Act 1995

Part 1 DETAILS OF APPLICANT AND OTHER PERSONS WHO THE APPLICANT BELIEVES SHOULD RECEIVE NOTICE OF THE APPLICATION

APPLICANT	*[insert name and address, telephone DX and fax numbers]*
CHILD	*[insert name, address, gender and date of birth]**
THE NAMED PERSON	*[insert name and address of person to be excluded]*
SAFEGUARDER	*[insert name, address, telephone DX and fax numbers (if known) of any safeguarder appointed by a children's hearing or court in respect of the child]*
RELEVANT PERSON(S)	*[insert name, address and the basis for the person being a relevant person within the meaning of section 93(2)(b) of the Act]*
THE APPROPRIATE PERSON	*[insert name and address of person who is to have care of the child if the order is made]*
THE PRINCIPAL REPORTER	*[insert name and address, telephone DX and fax numbers]*
ANY OTHER PERSON WHO SHOULD RECEIVE NOTICE OF THE APPLICATION	*[insert name, address and telephone numbers of person and provide details of their interest in the application and/or child]*

*Note: Information to be provided in Part 3 where applicant does not wish to disclose the address or whereabouts of the child or any other person to persons receiving notice of the application.

Part 2 INFORMATION ABOUT THE APPLICANT AND ORDERS SOUGHT

CONDITIONS FOR MAKING APPLICATION
[applicant to provide details of grounds for making the application including the address of the family home and details of all persons resident there.]

ANY OTHER RELEVANT APPLICATION OR ORDER WHICH AFFECTS THE
CHILD
*[insert details of any other applications or orders made which affect or are relevant to the
child who is the subject of this application]*

SUPPORTING EVIDENCE
The following supporting evidence is produced—
[list reports, statements, affidavits or other evidence produced]

PROPOSALS BY THE LOCAL AUTHORITY FOR FINANCIAL OR OTHER
SUPPORT FOR THE NAMED PERSON
[Insert details; Section 76(9) + (10) of the Act refer]

**Part 3 DETAILS OF ORDER SOUGHT AND ANY TERMS, CONDITIONS
OR DIRECTIONS**

ORDER SOUGHT: The applicant requests the Sheriff to *[insert details of the order
sought and any terms and conditions to be attached to the order]* in respect of the child
[insert name]

ANCILLARY OR INTERIM ORDERS SOUGHT

In terms of section 77(3) the following orders or interim orders are sought:
[specify orders sought and provide information about the reasons for seeking order]

TERMS AND CONDITIONS TO BE ATTACHED TO ORDER

In terms of section 77(7) the applicant seeks an order to:
[insert details of the order sought].

DIRECTIONS AS TO PRESERVATION OF NAMED PERSON'S PROPERTY

In terms of section 77(5) the applicant seeks the following direction:
[insert details of the direction sought].

In terms of section 78(1) a power of arrest is sought in relation to:
*[insert details of interdict and provide information about the reasons for seeking power of
arrest]*

Part 4 DETAILS OF FIRST ORDER SOUGHT FROM THE SHERIFF

The applicant requests the sheriff to:
a   Fix a hearing.
b   Order the applicant to forthwith serve a copy of the application on,
    i   the child, together with a notice in form 28;
    ii   The named person, together with a notice in Form 36 and
    iii   The persons listed in paragraph 1 of this application, together with a
      notice in form 36.
*c   Dispense with service on the child or any other person for the following
    reasons *[insert details]*
*d   Make an interim exclusion order excluding the named person from the child's
    family home in terms of part 2* on the terms and conditions set out in part 3
    above, and subject to the directions sought.

*e   Grant the following ancillary order. *[specify order sought]*
*f   Grant a power of arrest.

*delete as appropriate

Signed ....   Date ....
[name, designation and address
telephone, DX and fax numbers

Form 56
CERTIFICATE OF DELIVERY TO THE CHIEF CONSTABLE

Rule 3.38(1) and (2)

SECTION 78 OF THE CHILDREN (SCOTLAND) ACT 1995

[Insert place and date] I, hereby certify that upon the   day of   I duly delivered to *[insert name and address]* Chief Constable of *[insert name of constabulary] [insert details of the documents delivered].* This I did by *[state method of service].*

Signed ....
(name, designation and address)
(add designation and business address)

Form 60
FORM OF APPLICATION TO SHERIFF UNDER SECTION 65 OF THE ACT

Rule 3.45(1)

SHERIFF COURT AT *[insert place]*

APPLICANT:

[insert name, address and designation of applicant]

in the case of

[insert name and address of child]

1 On *[date]* a children's hearing for *[local authority]* gave a direction to the Principal Reporter under section *65(7) or 65(9) of the Children (Scotland) Act 1995 in respect of *[insert name of child]*. The hearing appointed *[insert name and designation]* as a safeguarder/no safeguarder was appointed.*

2 A copy of the statement by the Principal Reporter of the grounds for the referral of the case of the said *[insert name of child]* to the children's hearing is attached together with any report of the safeguarder appointed for the purpose of safeguarding the interests of the child in the proceedings.

*3 The said *[insert name of child]* or *[insert name and address and status of the relevant person or persons]* did not accept the grounds of referral so far as relating to conditions *[specify conditions/statements not accepted]* of the statement of the Principal Reporter.

OR

*4 The children's hearing were satisfied that the said *[insert name of child]* will not be capable of understanding or has not understood the explanation of the grounds of referral given under section 65(4) of the Act.

5 The Principal Reporter therefore makes application to the sheriff to find whether the grounds of referral not accepted by the said* *[insert name of child]* or *[insert name of relevant person or persons]** or not understood by the said child are established.

6 The Principal Reporter requests the sheriff to remove the obligation on the child to attend the hearing in view of *[insert reason(s)]*. And to dispense with service on *[insert name and give reasons]**

. . . .

[name, designation and address   Date . . . .
telephone, DX and fax numbers

[Place and Date]

The court assigns *[date]* at *[hour]* within the *[name court]* in chambers at *[place]* for the hearing of the application; appoints the Principal Reporter forthwith*
a   to serve a copy of the application and relative statement of grounds of referral and this warrant on,

i   the child, together with a notice in form 31 or orders service of the following documents only
[insert details of documents to be served on child, eg, notice inform 31 only]; and

ii   *[insert name of relevant person or persons]* together with a notice in form 39;

iii the safeguarder *[insert name and designation]* appointed by the sheriff,*

*b Orders that the address of *[insert name]* should not be disclosed in the application.

*c Dispense with service on the child or any other person for the following reasons *[insert details]*.

*d Dispenses with the obligation on the child to attend the hearing in view of *[insert details]*

and grants warrant to cite witnesses and havers.

. . . .

*Sheriff or Sheriff Clerk

*delete as appropriate

FORM 61

APPEAL TO SHERIFF UNDER SECTION 51(1) OF THE ACT AGAINST DECISION OF CHILDREN'S HEARING IN RELATION TO A SUPERVISION REQUIREMENT

Rule 3.53(1)

Sheriff Court at

Appeal

under

Section 51(1) of the Children
(Scotland) Act 1995

by

*[insert names and addresses of child
and/or relevant person as
appropriate]*

APPELLANT

against

a decision of the children's hearing for
[local authority area] at *[insert place]*

1 On *[date]* the said *[insert names of child and relevant person as appropriate]* appeared before the children's hearing of *[local authority area]* at *[insert place]*.

2 The children's hearing appointed *[insert name and address]* to act as safe-guarder* or No safeguarder was appointed.

3 The grounds for the referral of the case stated by the reporter* *[were accepted by the appellant(s)]** *[were established to the satisfaction of the sheriff]* at *[place]* on *[date]*. A copy of the statement of the grounds of referral is attached hereto,

*or [A supervision requirement, made on *[date]* in respect of the said child, was under review by the children's hearing. The supervision requirement was to the effect that *[state terms of requirement]*.]

4 The children's hearing decided that the said child was in *[continuing] need of compulsory measures of care and ordered *[state the terms of the decision in the report of the proceedings of the children's hearing]*.

5 The measures prescribed by the supervision requirement are not appropriate in all the circumstances in respect that *[state shortly the reasons for this view]* *[or if appeal is on a point of law or on grounds of irregularity state briefly that point or the facts which constitute the irregularity]*.

6 The said *[insert names of child and relevant person as appropriate]* appeals to the sheriff against the said decision.

. . . .
[signed]
appellant(s)
*or solicitor for appellants
*or safeguarder appointed by the
chairman of the children's hearing
[insert name and address]

*delete as appropriate

[Place and date]

The court assigns *[date]* at *[hour]* within the *[name court]* in chambers at *[place]* for the hearing of the application;

Appoints the Sheriff Clerk forthwith*
a   To intimate a copy of the application and this warrant on,
    i.   The Principal Reporter; and
    *ii   the child together with a notice in form 64
    *iii the *[insert name of relevant person or persons]*
    *iv   the safeguarder appointed by the sheriff or the children's hearing,
    *v   any other person having an interest in the original proceedings.
*b   Dispenses with service on the child for the following reasons *[insert details]*.
c   Appoints answers to be lodged, if so advised, not later than 7 days before the said diet.
and grants warrant to cite witnesses and havers.

....

*Sheriff or Sheriff Clerk

*delete as appropriate

Form 62

APPEAL TO SHERIFF AGAINST ISSUE OF WARRANT BY CHILDREN'S HEARING UNDER SECTION 51(1) AND (8) OF THE ACT

Rule 3.53(1)

Sheriff Court at

Appeal

under

Section 51(1) of the Children

(Scotland) Act 1995 by

[insert names and addresses of child and/or relevant person as appropriate]

APPELLANT

against

a decision of the children's hearing for *[local authority area]* at *[insert place]* to issue a warrant for the detention of the said AB.

1   On *[date]* the said *[insert name of child]* was apprehended and kept at *[place]* on a warrant issued by the children's hearing at *[place]* under section *[insert section]* of the Children (Scotland) Act 1995.

2   The children's hearing appointed *[insert name and address]* to act as safeguarder* or No safeguarder was appointed.

3   The said warrant is unnecessary because *[state reasons]*.

4   The said *[insert names of child and relevant person as appropriate]* appeals to the sheriff against the said decision.

. . . .
[signed]
appellant(s)
*or solicitor for appellants
*or safeguarder appointed by the
chairman of the children's hearing
[insert name and address]

*delete as appropriate
_____

[Place and date]

The court assigns *[date]* at *[hour]* within the *[name court]* in chambers at *[place]* for the hearing of the application;

Appoints the Sheriff Clerk forthwith*
a   To intimate a copy of the application and this warrant on,
   i   The Principal Reporter; and

*ii   the child together with a notice in form 64
*iii   the *[insert name of relevant person or persons]*
*iv   the safeguarder appointed by the sheriff or the children's hearing,
*v   any other person having an interest in the original proceedings
*b   Dispenses with service on the child for the following reasons *[insert details]*.
and grants warrant to cite witnesses and havers.

. . . .

*Sheriff or Sheriff Clerk

*delete as appropriate

FORM 63

APPEAL TO SHERIFF AGAINST A REQUIREMENT BY THE CHILDREN'S HEARING UNDER SECTION 51(1) OF THE ACT

Rule 3.53(1)

Sheriff Court at [   ]

Appeal

under

Section 51(1) of the Children (Scotland) Act 1995

by

[insert names and addresses of child and/or relevant person as appropriate]

APPELLANT

against

a decision of the children's hearing for *[local authority area]* at *[insert place]* to make a supervision requirement in respect of the said *[insert name of child]*.

1 On *[date]* a children's hearing for *[local authority area]* made a requirement under section *[insert section]* of the Children (Scotland) Act 1995. A copy of the said requirement is appended hereto.

2 The children's hearing appointed *[insert name and address]* to act as safeguarder* or No safeguarder was appointed.

3 The said requirement is unnecessary because *[state reasons]*.

4 The said *[insert names of child and relevant person as appropriate]* appeals to the sheriff to *[state remedy]*.

. . . .
[signed]
appellant(s)
*or solicitor for appellants
*or safeguarder appointed by the
chairman of the children's hearing
[insert name and address]

*delete as appropriate

[Place and date]

The court assigns *[date]* at *[hour]* within the *[name court]* in chambers at *[place]* for the hearing of the application;

Appoints the Sheriff Clerk forthwith*

a   To intimate a copy of the application and this warrant on,
    i   The Principal Reporter; and
    *ii   the child together with a notice in form 64
    *iii the *[insert name of relevant person or persons]*
    *iv the safeguarder appointed by the sheriff or the children's hearing,
    *v   any other person having an interest in the original proceedings
*b   Dispenses with service on the child for the following reasons *[insert details]*.
c   Appoints answers to be lodged, if so advised, not later than 7 days before the said diet.
and grants warrant to cite witnesses and havers.

*delete as appropriate

. . . .

*Sheriff or Sheriff Clerk

Form SCRA F

Scottish
Children's Reporter
Administration

The children's reporter has arranged for

to attend a children's hearing for South Lanarkshire Council.

The reason[s] for this [is] [are]:

Statement of Facts
In support of the above it is stated:

. . . .
Date: 10/11/00   *for Authority Reporter*
Form of statement by children's reporter   Children (Scotland) Act 1995
of reasons for the referral of a child to   Rule 17 & 18 Form SCRA F
a children's hearing

Notes

The children's hearing will ask the child and relevant persons if they accept the reasons for arranging the hearing. If the reasons are accepted the children's hearing will discuss with the child and relevant persons what is best for the child. If any of the reasons are not accepted, the hearing may either discharge them or tell the reporter to apply to the sheriff who will decide if any of the reasons are proved.

If the sheriff decides that any of the reasons are proved, the children's hearing will then discuss what is best for the child, as if these reasons had been accepted. If the sheriff decides that no reasons are proved the case will be discharged.

**SCRA, Dava House, 43 Brousterhill, East Kilbride, G74 1AG
Telephone: 01355 232145   Fax: 01355 264690**

Index